MW01069104

Character Sketches

From the Pages of Scripture

God's biographies reveal the secrets of warning and instruction for our daily lives. "For whatsoever things were written aforetime were written for our learning, that we through patience and comfort of the scriptures might have hope" (Romans 15:4).

Illustrated in the World of Nature

"But ask now the beasts, and they shall teach thee; and the fowls of the air, and they shall tell thee: Or speak to the earth, and it shall teach thee: and the fishes of the sea shall declare unto thee" (Job 12:7–8).

Severt Andrewson

Character Sketches

From the Pages of Scripture
Illustrated in the World of Nature

VOLUME III

INSTITUTE IN
BASIC LIFE PRINCIPLES

Bound by Rand McNally and Company

©1985 Institute in Basic Life Principles

All rights reserved.

Reproduction of this work in any form or language, or by any means, electronic or mechanical, including photocopying, recording, or by any retrieval system, is prohibited without express written permission from the publisher.

All Scripture references are from the King James Version of the Bible, unless otherwise noted.

Printed in The United States of America.

Third Printing, December 1991

ISBN 0-916888-10-X

Library of Congress
Catalog Card Number: 76-3050

Table of Contents

PART FOUR • PUNCTUALITY

PART FIVE • RESOURCEFULNESS

PART SIX • THRIFTINESS

THE SECRETS OF GIVING

In the twelfth chapter of the book of Romans, seven spiritual gifts are listed with the assurance that every Christian has one of them. As we understand each gift and integrate the strengths and perspectives of each one with our own motivational gift, we will experience true and lasting joy, achievement, and fulfillment.

In this volume we will explore character through the eyes of the one with the gift of giving. As we understand the perspective and motivation of mature givers, we will be able to enter into their joy and rewards.

"... God loveth a cheerful giver" (II Corinthians 9:7). "Give, and it shall be given unto you ..." (Luke 6:38). "But when thou doest alms ... and thy Father which seeth in secret himself shall reward thee openly" (Matthew 6:3–4). "... Lay up for yourselves treasures in heaven ..." (Matthew 6:20). "... I will ... pour you out a blessing, that there shall not be room enough to receive it" (Malachi 3:10).

". . . He saw a man, named Matthew, sitting at the receipt of custom: and he saith unto him, Follow me. And he arose, and followed him" (Matthew 9:9).

EIGHT CHARACTERISTICS OF THE GIFT OF GIVING

The life of the Apostle Matthew demonstrates the spiritual gift of Giving. In his Gospel he includes more insights on the principles of giving than any other Gospel writer.

1 THE ABILITY TO DISCERN WISE INVESTMENTS

By making wise investments, a Christian increases the resources which can be used in giving. Even if a giver does not have personal funds, he or she has an ability to locate resources which can be used to meet the needs of others.

Matthew recorded the wise counsel of Christ on investments. *"Lay not up for yourselves treasures upon earth, where moth and rust doth corrupt, and where thieves break through and steal: But lay up for yourselves treasures in heaven, where neither moth nor rust doth corrupt, and where thieves do not break through nor steal" (Matthew 6:19–20).*

2 THE DESIRE TO GIVE QUIETLY WITHOUT PUBLIC FANFARE

The joy of a giver is to direct the attention of the receiver to the Lord, not to himself. The giver also desires to gain eternal rewards for giving rather than the momentary and unpredictable praise of men. Matthew is the only Gospel writer who emphasizes this important principle in giving.

"Take heed that ye do not your alms before men, to be seen of them: otherwise ye have no reward of your Father which is in heaven. . . . But when thou doest alms, let not thy left hand know what thy right hand doeth: That thine alms may be in secret: and thy Father which seeth in secret himself shall reward thee openly" (Matthew 6:1, 3–4).

3 THE MOTIVATION TO GIVE BY GOD'S PROMPTING RATHER THAN MAN'S APPEALS

The joy of a giver is knowing that by meeting basic needs, he or she is ministering directly to Christ. Matthew is careful to record Christ's teaching on this perspective.

"For I was an hungered, and ye gave me meat: I was thirsty, and ye gave me drink: I was a stranger, and ye took me in: Naked, and ye clothed me: I was sick, and ye visited me: I was in prison, and ye came unto me. . . .

"Inasmuch as ye have done it unto one of the least of these my brethren, ye have done it unto me" (Matthew 25:35–36, 40).

4 THE CONCERN THAT GIFTS BE QUALITY WITHOUT EXTRAVAGANCE

Since the giver wants to make the best use of resources, he or she will avoid extravagance. On the other hand, since all giving is actually ministering directly to Christ, gifts must be practical and of high quality.

Matthew details these characteristics in the gold, frankincense, and myrrh given by the Magi (see Matthew 2:11); the precious ointment given by Mary of Bethany (see Matthew 26:6–13); and the new sepulchre given by Joseph of Arimathaea. (See Matthew 27:57–60.)

5 THE ABILITY TO TEST FAITHFULNESS BY THE USE OF FUNDS THAT ARE GIVEN

A basic purpose of the giver is to advance the kingdom of God. He or she will entrust assets to those who are doing this. Those who make the wisest use of funds will receive more. Matthew records Christ's teaching on this important point.

Five talents, two talents, and one talent were given to three servants of the Lord. The ones who received five and two talents doubled theirs. However, the servant who received one talent buried it in the ground.

Christ rebuked this slothful servant and gave his talent to the servant who had ten talents. (See Matthew 25:14–30.)

6 THE COMMITMENT TO PERSONAL FRUGALITY AND CONTENTMENT WITH BASICS

The giver may have abundant personal assets; however, his focus is not on heaping up treasures for himself but in wisely managing what God has entrusted to him.

The giver's emotional detachment from his resources is evidenced by his tendency to be personally frugal, to be content with basic necessities, and to take joy in freely giving to needs which God reveals to him. Matthew demonstrated these characteristics when Jesus called him to be a disciple. Another Gospel writer relates what happened. *"And he left all, rose up, and followed him" (Luke 5:28).*

7 THE JOY IN SEEING AND MEETING NEEDS WHICH OTHERS OVERLOOK

One reason that givers do not respond to pressure appeals for money is that they assume that others will meet those needs. They look for individuals who are quietly and effectively doing the work of God and trusting Him for their resources.

Givers are also sensitive to the fulfillment of financial responsibilities. Matthew records Christ's condemnation of the Pharisees for their traditions which exempted sons and daughters from supporting their aged parents. (See Matthew 15:1–7.)

Matthew also is the only Gospel writer who included Christ's parable of giving just wages to laborers. (See Matthew 20:1–16.)

8 THE GOAL OF MOTIVATING OTHERS TO GIVE

Givers understand what Scripture means, when it says *". . . It is more blessed to give than to receive" (Acts 20:35)*. They want others to experience this same joy and fulfillment.

When Matthew became a disciple, he used his funds to sponsor a large dinner in which he introduced Christ to all of his friends and associates. (See Luke 5:29.)

BEFORE GIVING, WE MUST RECEIVE

"Behold, I stand at the door, and knock: if any man hear my voice, and open the door, I will come in to him, and will sup with him, and he with me" (Revelation 3:20).

It is opposite to our nature to give our resources to others. True giving therefore requires a new nature within.

We receive a new nature when we recognize that Jesus is standing at the "door of our heart" knocking and asking us to let Him in.

We "let Him in" by sincerely asking Him to enter the center of our life and repent of our sin of violating His ways.

"For all have sinned, and come short of the glory of God" (Romans 3:23).

"But God commendeth his love toward us, in that, while we were yet sinners, Christ died for us" (Romans 5:8).

"That if thou shalt confess with thy mouth the Lord Jesus, and shalt believe in thine heart that God hath raised him from the dead, thou shalt be saved" (Romans 10:9).

A prayer to receive Christ:

"Lord Jesus, come into the center of my life. I confess that I am a sinner and right now I do receive You as my risen Lord and Savior. Thank You for hearing and answering my prayer according to the promises of Your Word. Amen."

TEN BASIC CONCEPTS ON GIVING

1 GIVING MUST GROW OUT OF THE MOTIVATION OF LOVE

God's chapter on love (I Corinthians 13) teaches us that a person can give without loving. *"And though I bestow all my goods to feed the poor . . . and have not charity [love], it profiteth me nothing" (I Corinthians 13:3).*

God's account of the crucifixion of Christ teaches us that a person cannot love without giving. *"For God so loved the world, that he gave his only begotten Son . . ." (John 3:16).*

Giving from the motivation of love means that we are not calculating our gifts in order to receive in return. Genuine love is giving to the basic needs of others without the motive of personal reward.

When giving is done out of love, it expresses the true heart of God and allows Christ to continue to accomplish His redemptive work through our lives and resources.

"But whoso hath this world's good, and seeth his brother have need, and shutteth up his bowels of compassion from him, how dwelleth the love of God in him?" (I John 3:17).

2 GIVING MUST HAVE THE GOAL OF BRINGING PLEASURE TO GOD

Since giving is the very nature of God, those who practice it with a pure heart enter into intimate fellowship with Him. This is one of the clear reasons why *". . . God loveth a cheerful giver" (II Corinthians 9:7).*

The Greek word for *cheerful* is ἱλαρός (hil-ar-**os**) from this word we get the term "hilarious." A "hilarious" giver is one who is eager to give God the firstfruits of all of his increase, one who is looking for opportunities to give to the needs of others.

The pleasure which God receives from giving is illustrated in the sacrifices which God's people consistently offered. The gifts were a sweet savor unto Him. (See Leviticus 1:9.)

God is pleased with our giving because He knows that it will fulfill important functions throughout the Body of Christ.

"God so loved that He gave."

"Hereby perceive we the love of God, because he laid down his life for us: and we ought to lay down our lives for the brethren" (I John 3:16).

3 GIVING IS A PRIMARY METHOD OF BRINGING ABOUT UNITY IN THE BODY OF CHRIST

In order for a body to function harmoniously, each part must both give and receive. A cell which only receives becomes a cancer. A cell which only gives becomes dissipated.

God's comparison of Christians to a body is extensive throughout the New Testament. His ultimate goal is that the generosity among Christians in giving

". . . Walk in love, as Christ also hath loved us, and hath given himself for us an offering and a sacrifice to God for a sweet-smelling savour" (Ephesians 5:2).

and the humility of Christians in receiving will cause every Christian to understand his and her interdependence. This will result in a harmonious strengthening of every believer, that the Body of Christ may edify itself in love. (See Ephesians 4:16.)

The function of giving is so important that God periodically brings Christians into times of need and times of plenty. During times of need, He wants us to look to Him for provision. In response to our prayers He will prompt various Christians with abundance to meet our need.

This is precisely the circumstance which God arranged in the early Church to bring about unity between the Jewish and Gentile believers. He allowed a famine in Jerusalem to bring the Jews to a deep sense of need. He also sent the Apostle Paul to collect funds among the Gentiles for this need. He told the Gentiles that, *". . . now at this time your abundance may be a supply for their want, that their abundance also may be a supply for your want: that there may be equality" (II Corinthians 8:14).*

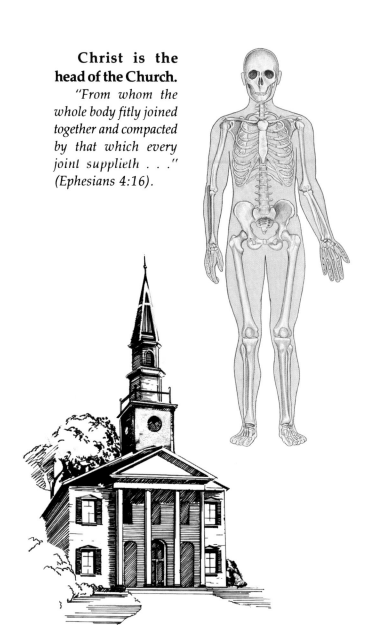

Christ is the head of the Church.
"From whom the whole body fitly joined together and compacted by that which every joint supplieth . . ." (Ephesians 4:16).

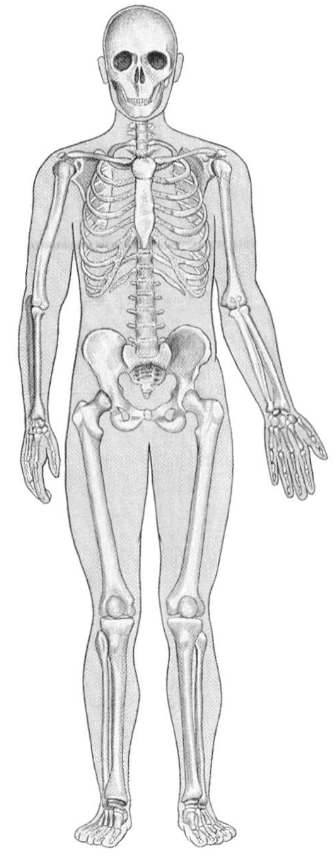

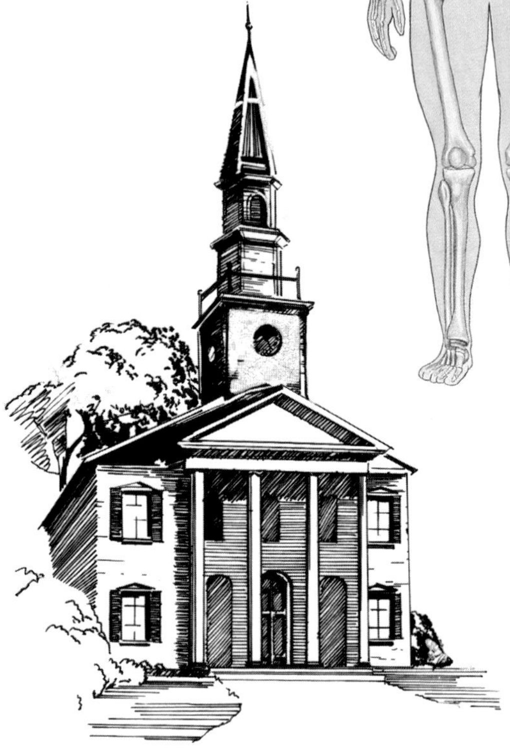

". . . According to the effectual working in the measure of every part, maketh increase of the body unto the edifying of itself in love" (Ephesians 4:16).

4 GIVING IS AN EFFECTIVE WAY OF DEALING WITH OUR ENEMIES

Love not only covers a multitude of sins, it also conquers our enemies. For this reason, God instructs us to feed our enemies if they are hungry and to give them drink when they are thirsty. For in so doing we will heap coals of fire upon their heads, and *". . . the Lord shall reward thee" (Proverbs 25:22).*

Hot coals were a welcomed blessing, not a means of retaliation. When someone traveled, he brought his fire with him in the form of hot coals in a tray upon his head. Often the coals would burn out, and it would be a gesture of kindness to add live coals to the tray.

The blessing that results from giving to our enemy is a greater love for him, since where our treasure is, there our heart will be also. (See Matthew 6:21.) This kind of love can win the heart of an enemy.

5 GIVING RESULTS IN OUR ESTABLISHING TREASURES IN HEAVEN

God wants us to set our affections on things above, not on the things of the earth. (See Colossians 3:2.) He knows that the things of this world capture our affection and decrease our love for Him.

For this reason the Lord warns us not to heap up treasures on earth, but rather to lay up treasures in heaven, *". . . Where neither moth nor rust doth corrupt, and where thieves do not break through nor steal: For where your treasure is, there will your heart be also" (Matthew 6:20–21).*

No gift given in the right way will lose its eternal reward—not even a cup of water. *"For whosoever shall*

Paul set the example for giving by *". . . labouring night and day, because we would not be chargeable unto any of you . . ." (I Thessalonians 2:9).*

The offering that he later gathered from the Gentile churches for the Jewish Christians provided a strong bond of fellowship between them.

give you a cup of water to drink in my name, because ye belong to Christ, verily I say unto you, he shall not lose his reward" (Mark 9:41).

The quality of what we give is important as well as the motive behind our giving. When Christ returns, that which we have done in His name will be tested. *". . . And the fire shall try every man's work of what sort it is. If any man's work abide which he hath built thereupon, he shall receive a reward. If any man's work shall be burned, he shall suffer loss: but he himself shall be saved; yet so as by fire" (I Corinthians 3:13–15).*

6 GIVING MUST BE BASED ON WHAT THE NAME OF JESUS REPRESENTS

Not only is it important to give with the right motive, but it is also important to use the right procedure. If we give a gift to another person in our own name, the receiver will glorify us. However, if we give that same gift in the name of Christ, then He receives the glory.

God wants others to see our good works and then glorify our Father Who is in heaven. By giving in the name of Jesus, we also have a built-in basis for evaluating the type of gifts we should give. They must be in harmony with the names of Christ. Thus, the following items would be proper gifts:

GIFT	NAME OF CHRIST
Bread	**He is the Bread of life.**
Water	**He is the Living Water.**
Wise counsel	**His name is Counselor.**
Peacemaking	**He is the Prince of Peace.**
Health care	**He is the Great Physician.**

7 GIVING MUST BE BASED ON FAITH

Faith is not a "blind leap in the dark." It is walking in the light of God's Word by obedience to the leading of the Holy Spirit.

By faith we discern what God wants us to give and when He wants us to give it. When our gifts meet precise needs at just the right time, the faith of both giver and receiver is increased.

Faith must be based on the fact that God is the provider of all of our resources. *". . . What hast thou that thou didst not receive? . . ." (I Corinthians 4:7).*

As we give by faith, we transfer our assets from temporal to eternal riches. *". . . For the things which are seen are temporal; but the things which are not seen are eternal" (II Corinthians 4:18).*

THE MIGHTY MESSAGE OF THE WIDOW'S MITES

One side of a mite shows the sun with eight rays. It represents the Sun of righteousness. (See Malachi 4:2.)

The other side of the mite has a ship's anchor, symbolizing the steadfastness of God's promises.

It seems fairly obvious that a larger gift of money would be more valuable to the work of the Lord than a smaller gift of money.

In the case of the widow in Christ's day, this was not true. When she gave two small bronze coins, Jesus remarked, *". . . Verily I say unto you, That this poor widow hath cast more in, than all they which have cast into the treasury" (Mark 12:43).*

By pointing out the value of her gift, Jesus identified a deeper principle in giving:

GOD MEASURES OUR GIVING NOT ON THE BASIS OF WHAT IS GIVEN BUT ON THE BASIS OF WHAT REMAINS AFTER WE HAVE GIVEN.

"For all they did cast in of their abundance; but she of her want did cast in all that she had, even all her living" (Mark 12:44).

Tiberius tribute denarius ca. A.D. 25 (enlarged twice)

The rich may well have thrown into the treasury silver denarii such as this. It was equal to a day's wages.

8 GIVING TEACHES THE FEAR OF GOD

The tremendous importance of having a proper awareness and reverence for God is explained in Scripture. *"By humility and the fear of the Lord are riches, and honour, and life" (Proverbs 22:4).*

The fear of the Lord in giving is the constant awareness that God is watching our motives and actions, and that He will reward us accordingly.

". . . He which soweth sparingly shall reap also sparingly; and he which soweth bountifully shall reap also bountifully" (II Corinthians 9:6).

Our sowing must begin with the firstfruits of all our increase. (See Proverbs 3:9.) It is significant that God has established the weekly giving of the tithe as a vital means whereby we learn to fear the Lord. *"Thou shalt truly tithe all the increase . . . that thou mayest learn to fear the Lord thy God always" (Deuteronomy 14:22–23).*

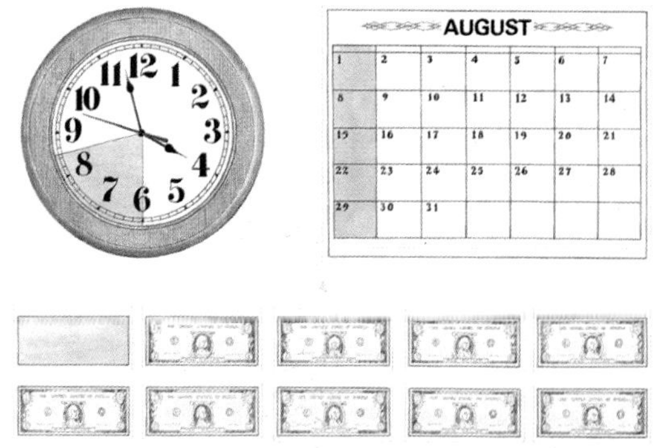

One of the primary purposes of tithing is to learn the fear of the Lord.

"And God is able to make all grace abound toward you; that ye, always having all sufficiency in all things, may abound to every good work" (II Corinthians 9:8).

9 GIVING IS LEARNING TO "PROVE GOD"

God has ordained that we acknowledge His reality by giving to Him. *". . . Prove me now herewith [tithes and offerings], saith the Lord . . ." (Malachi 3:10).*

By giving tithes and offerings to God, we prove that He can *". . . pour . . . out a blessing, that there shall not be room enough to receive it" (Malachi 3:10).*

If we do not give to God, He will not rebuke the devourer of our funds, and then we will experience unexpected and unnecessary losses. (See Malachi 3:11.)

When we prove God by honoring Him with our substance and the firstfruits of all of our increase, then our barns shall be filled with plenty. (See Proverbs 3:10.)

10 GIVING IS HAVING "A GOOD EYE"

A "good eye" is a generous eye and an "evil eye" is a stingy eye. Those who collected money for charitable purposes in the East used the expression, "Have a good eye." In other words, "Please be generous to this need."

This expression has sound Biblical basis. *"He that hath a bountiful eye shall be blessed; for he giveth of his bread to the poor" (Proverbs 22:9).*

An evil eye is one that is greedy. *"He that hasteth to be rich hath an evil eye, and considereth not that poverty shall come upon him" (Proverbs 28:22).*

". . . If therefore the light that is in thee be darkness, how great is that darkness!" (Matthew 6:23).

A "GOOD EYE"

AN "EVIL EYE"

". . . If thine eye be evil, thy whole body shall be full of darkness . . ." (Matthew 6:23).

HOW TO USE THIS BOOK

The *Character Sketches* series is designed to strengthen families and individuals in an exciting new approach to education. The goal is to encourage each family member to learn the facets of God's character, understand basic Biblical concepts, and by knowledge and application become mighty in God's Spirit.

One of the best times to go through this book as a family is after the evening meal. Whenever possible, the father should lead the discussion. Spending twenty to thirty minutes of preparation *beforehand* will greatly multiply the enjoyment and effectiveness of each session. Sessions should last between half an hour and one hour.

FIRST EVENING

1. Read the character definitions.

"Cautiousness is knowing the importance of right motives, timing, methods, and amounts in carrying out wise giving."

The first step in doing this is "Living within the protection of my God-given resources."

2. Give the quiz question on pages 24–27.

"Who can tell me what animal buries its enemies alive?" (Answer on page 32.)

3. Read the nature story caption.

"How is living within the protection of God-given resources illustrated in the world of nature?"

4. Read the nature story.

Practice beforehand adding feeling, emphasis, and curiosity. Adapt difficult words to the children's understanding.

5. Read the animal Scripture references.

Encourage further discussion.

6. Read the nature material.

Begin with the introductory paragraph. As you read, make as many analogies as you can to the Christian life and encourage your family to do the same.

7. Look for ways to apply the quality.

Consider family situations or decisions such as requests to borrow money or possessions, and ask "Will this help you to learn to live within the protection of your God-given resources?"

SECOND EVENING

1. Read the concept question for the chapter from pages 18–23.

"How would you respond to the following situation?" . . . After reading the situation, ask each person to give a response. Do not allow any answer to be criticized. Express appreciation for each answer without indicating if it is correct.

2. Read the Scripture story introduction.

"Can you tell from the following description who the person is who illustrates this aspect of the character quality?" Allow for responses; however, do not reveal whether their answer is correct or incorrect. The purpose is to build background and curiosity for the story.

3. Read the Scripture story title.

"How is the protection of living within God-given resources illustrated in Scripture?"

4. Read the story quiz question.

Allow for responses without indicating whether or not the answer is correct.

5. Read the Scripture story.

Before reading to your family, read the Scripture upon which the story is based and practice reading the story.

6. Allow for discussion.

"Do you see a further application of this story to our lives?" Be ready to give an illustration from your own experience.

7. Read the historical background and character sketch.

In your preparation write down points for discussion and application. Suggest a project that the family could work on which would reinforce the character quality: "Let us watch for God-given limitations such as time or money and discuss them."

CONCEPT QUESTIONS

WHAT WOULD YOU DO IN THESE SITUATIONS?

See page 31.

1 As a mother cleaned her home, the old vacuum cleaner finally quit. Amazingly, a few minutes later a salesman arrived at her front door with a special offer on vacuum cleaners. If you were visiting her when this happened, would you encourage her to buy one?

ANSWER: It is never wise for a husband or a wife to make a major appliance purchase without first discussing it with each other and doing further research on the product as well as the company which stands behind it. *". . . In the multitude of counsellors there is safety" (Proverbs 11:14). "Also, that the soul be without knowledge, it is not good; and he that hasteth with his feet sinneth" (Proverbs 19:2).* Living within the protection of her God-given resources would be to check with her husband and purchase only if the cash was available.

See page 43.

2 Two young men applied for a position as youth evangelist. The first constantly looked for new ways in which to win people to Christ; however, he was not a good public speaker. The second loved to read books and was an excellent public speaker. His school voted him most likely to succeed. Which one would you choose for the job and why?

ANSWER: Reading the right books and speaking effectively in public are commendable, but knowledge and praise tend to puff up a man with pride. A message prepared in the mind will only reach a mind, but a message prepared in a life will reach a life. The Apostle Paul did not come with words of man's knowledge, and his speech was considered contemptible. (See II Corinthians 10:10.) D. L. Moody had poor grammar, but he loved to win people to Christ. The best qualified is the one who loves people and who knows that his greatest ability can become the point of his greatest vulnerability.

See page 55.

3 A hard-working man built up his business so that it became very successful. One day he and his wife received an invitation that would open up many new business contacts. They would be the guests of a group of business leaders for a weekend at a resort. Should he and his wife go?

ANSWER: No. A wise businessman understands that nothing is free and by going to such an event he is becoming obligated to others who have their own motives for asking him. The dangers of temptation and compromise at a resort are not consistent with the hard work which has already made his business successful. A wise application of Proverbs 23:1–7 would be to decline the invitation and suggest another time to meet for discussion purposes only. He should remember that greed crouches at the door of every heart.

See page 67.

4 It is customary for a large company to have a hundred per cent employee participation in an annual charity drive. A Christian employee learns that part of the money will be used to fund abortions. However, his Christian friends urge him to give anyway. What should he do?

ANSWER: First, he should make a direct appeal to the head of the charity. If the charity refuses to stop funding abortions, he should appeal to the one in his company collecting the funds. He should explain his personal convictions, that he cannot voluntarily have any part in the murder of unborn children. If this fails, he could offer to give a donation to a Christian organization through his company, so that they could still reach their one hundred per cent giving goal. He must be gracious, keeping in mind that the majority is often wrong. (See Matthew 7:13.)

See page 81.

5 A Christian employee was rewarded for outstanding service by being offered an executive position. The new job would require extensive traveling. However, his salary would be doubled, and with the extra money he could buy a summer home which his wife and children want. Should he accept the position?

ANSWER: He should express appreciation for the offer, but explain that his commitments to the care and training of his family would not allow him to do extensive traveling. The greatest heritage and protection for a man's future is not a company position, wealth, or even a summer home, but Godly sons and daughters. (See Psalm 127:3–5.) No amount of money will regain lost opportunities to spend valuable teaching time with his children. By turning down continual traveling, he is emphasizing to his family that God-given relationships are more important than earthly possessions.

See page 93.

6 An older mother has sons and daughters who are grown and married. She prays for them daily, and whenever anyone takes a trip, she waits for a call to assure her of their safety. One son causes her to worry because he forgets to call. How would you counsel the mother?

ANSWER: It is right for a son to honor his mother with proper communication. (See Proverbs 23:22.) However, if she is really experiencing the potential of intercessory prayer, she will never need to worry, because the Holy Spirit will give her peaceful assurance when her prayer has been answered. The mother should learn to turn her fears of an accident into a Godly desire that, even if an accident occurs, spiritual growth will result from it. This is the confidence that Christians can have since we are indestructible until our work is done.

See page 105.

7 A very diligent father wanted to give beyond his tithe to Christian ministries. However, his job barely provided for the needs of his family. One day he was asked to join a lucrative business partnership. Would you encourage him to consider it?

ANSWER: No. Although his motive is good, the method of gaining additional funds through a business partnership would violate Scriptural principles. Eight reasons are listed in chapter seventeen of *Men's Manual*, Volume II, on why business partnerships should be avoided. Partnerships form entanglements which II Timothy 2:4 tells us to avoid. They also tend to cause bitterness by bringing about bondage to undefinable personal expectations.

See page 117.

8 A certain husband was always quick to volunteer himself or his money for church projects. Often his wife and family would have to go without. Other times he would not be able to keep his promises. His wife was frustrated. How would you counsel the man?

ANSWER: His impetuous giving may indicate a lack of self-acceptance. Thus, the first step is to have him thank God for his unchangeable features. Accepting God's design also includes God's priorities of seeing *". . . how he may please his wife" (I Corinthians 7:33).* Their marriage oneness requires that he gain the counsel of his wife before making a decision which affects her and the children. He may also be trying to compensate for the guilt of moral impurity. By resolving these, he can be free to fulfill God's purposes.

See page 131.

9 After going many months without a job, a family faced serious financial need. A job was accepted, which would begin the next month, and a friend offered to lend them money to help in the meantime. Would you encourage the family to accept the loan?

ANSWER: No. By accepting the loan they would lose their friend and become his servants. *"... The borrower is servant to the lender" (Proverbs 22:7)*. For this reason we are told to give to the poor rather than to lend to them. (See Proverbs 19:17.) If an emergency exists and no funds are given by family, friends, or church, funds should be sought by decreasing costs, selling items, doing odd jobs, or asking to start the new job earlier. In this way, the family would honor God's design for financial freedom.

See page 143.

10 A Christian contractor accepted stock in an old gold mine as payment for a $20,000 job. Shortly afterwards gold was discovered and the stock increased to $80,000. He sold the stock and was then offered a new investment for $80,000. This promised even greater returns which he could use to help in Christian work. How would you advise him?

ANSWER: The contractor should be urged to tithe on the sale of the stock. If this means that he lacks sufficient funds for a new investment, he should accept it as a protective signal from the Lord not to go ahead with the venture. The lure of quick profits for whatever purpose is warned about in Scripture. (See Proverbs 28:22.) One of the best ways to conquer greed and express gratefulness would be for him to pay his debt of love to the Lord out of the firstfruits of what he had already received.

See page 155.

11 A young man with a marvelous singing voice was given many career offers. One was with an opera company. It would provide world travel, recognition, opportunities to witness, and a large salary. The second was directing the music program of a local church. Which would you encourage him to accept?

ANSWER: The Scripture that may apply to this situation is found in Matthew 16:25, *"... Whosoever will save his life shall lose it: and whosoever will lose his life for my sake shall find it."* He may be able to use opportunities to witness with the opera company, but he would also be involved in operas which violate the principles of Scripture. His voice was given to him by the Lord. By using it to sing only God's praises and training others to do the same, he would be multiplying the gift that was given to him by the Lord.

See page 167.

12 The owner of a store was told that if he did not sell alcoholic beverages, he would go under financially. Then he heard a message which stated that Christians who were not experiencing financial blessing were living outside of God's will. How would you counsel this store owner?

ANSWER: Financial success is not a consistent measure of living in the will of God. Paul experienced financial needs, and he urged every Christian to learn how to do the same. (See Philippians 4:12.) Christ gave up His riches for us. A man's greatest treasure is a name that is not compromised. Gratefulness is accepting losses and difficulties as part of God's loving provision.

See page 181.

13 For many years a young man saved every dollar to buy a car. Finally he had the car picked out and sufficient funds to buy it. Then he learned of a special need in his church. Would you counsel him to buy the car to help him get to work or give the money to the church?

ANSWER: God honors faith, and faith is strengthened by sacrificial giving. God is debtor to no man. It is impossible to outgive Him. The more that we give to God, the more He is free to give to us. (See II Corinthians 9:6.) By giving the money to the Lord, the young man will not only lay up treasures in heaven, but he will also transfer his affections there. (See Matthew 19:21.) If the Lord has prompted him to give, he should obey God by immediately giving as God has directed.

See page 193.

14 Throughout high school a Christian girl admired a certain Christian fellow. Before graduation, he invited her to go with him to the school prom. He assured her that they would not participate in any drinking or dancing, but would use the event as an opportunity to witness for the Lord. Should she accept the date?

ANSWER: No. Both the girl and the fellow have had ample opportunity to witness to their classmates. By attending the prom, they would actually damage the witness they had, since many non-Christians would be surprised that they would attend such an event. Even if they avoided the drinking they would violate I Thessalonians 5:22, *"Abstain from all appearance of evil."* By rejecting this compromise, the girl would honor the ways of God and not violate His timing for a friendship.

See page 205.

15 The members of a church believed that their pastor was wrong in the way he handled a discipline problem. Several members carried out a secret plan which resulted in the dismissal of the pastor. One of the deacons, however, felt that he should personally give the pastor financial help until he got a new job. But he knew that this would cause reaction among the rest of the congregation. What should he do?

ANSWER: It is always Scripturally right to give to basic needs. Jesus taught that we should even give food and water to our enemies. (See Romans 12:20.) If he experiences rejection for doing what is good and does not take up an offense or become bitter, God will bless him for it. He is then meeting needs that others are unable or unwilling to meet.

See page 217.

16 A twenty-three-year-old young man recognized God's call to go into the ministry. His schooling was finished, but his parents wanted him to work in their family business for another six or seven years. How would you advise him?

ANSWER: When Christ was twelve, He was aware of God's calling on His life. In obedience to His parents He returned to Nazareth where He grew in wisdom and stature. He continued to work in the family business until He was thirty. (See Luke 2:42–52.) If God is clearly leading this young man into the ministry, the evidence of a respectful appeal should be obvious to his parents. However, the anniversaries of Christ's life reveal a calling at the age of twelve, then training, and finally sending at the age of thirty. By following his parent's wishes this young man would build character in his life that would enhance his ministry. It would also provide the opportunity for God to change the hearts of his parents.

See page 231.

17 A Christian rancher faithfully attended church. However, during sub-zero weather, his sheep were ready to give birth to their lambs. If he was away when a lamb was born, it would stick to the ground and die. Should he be faithful to his church and consider any frozen lamb as a sacrifice, or should he stay home with the sheep?

ANSWER: He should stay home with the sheep. This is clearly stated in the Law and confirmed by Christ. Care of endangered livestock takes precedence over observing the Sabbath. (See Luke 14:5.) By doing this he will be caring for God-given resources.

See page 243.

18 When a high school boy with exceptional running ability explained to his coach that his Christian activities must come before track events, the coach agreed to let him run whenever he could. He won every race. The state championship meet, however, conflicted with a speaking engagement that he had at a Christian camp. What should he do?

ANSWER: Since he had given his word to speak at the camp, and since his coach had already agreed that his Christian activities would take precedence over track events, he should speak at the camp. By sacrificing personal fame to fulfill this responsibility, he would increase the respect for his message by those at the camp, and respect for his Christianity by those at the school. By seeking first the kingdom of God and His righteousness (see Matthew 6:33), he would make the most of his limited time.

See page 255.

19 While playing an instrument at a nearby church service, a young man was very attracted to the young lady who accompanied him on the piano. He was given permission by her father to date her, and soon they were deeply in love. All parents were in favor of the marriage except the girl's father. How would you counsel them?

ANSWER: God has ordained that the girl's father has the primary responsibility for the final approval of his daughter's marriage. (See Exodus 22:16–17 and I Corinthians 7:38.) Based on this, the fellow and the girl should separate and grow in the Lord. As character is developed through obedience and patience, God may change the heart of the father, or let them see why he stopped the marriage. In later years they will recognize that valuable resources come out of right relationships.

See page 267.

20 While a man was waiting for a bus, a second man noticed an envelope laying on the ground. They picked it up and discovered $30,000. The second man was an attorney and explained how they could take steps to legally split the money between them. What would you do in this case?

ANSWER: This is the famous, effective, and well-worn swindle known as the pigeon drop. The "lawyer" plants the money and tries to convince the one who found it to put up several thousand dollars of his own money in "good faith." But God warns, *". . . If thou hast stricken thy hand with a stranger, Thou art snared with the words of thy mouth . . ." (Proverbs 6:1–2)*. After the "pigeon" puts up the money, both it and the lawyer disappear. The effectiveness of this swindle lies in the greed of human nature. However, by refusing such entrapments, we extend our ability to give as God directs.

See page 281.

21 A young Christian mother, trying to make ends meet, was given an opportunity to win $10,000. All she had to do was buy one chance for $5. The proceeds would be used to help starving people in other countries. Should she buy the chance?

ANSWER: No. God gives clear warnings in Scripture against gambling in all forms. This includes lotteries, raffles, bingo, and other types of chances. Gambling is based on a desire to gain without labor and to "get rich quick." *"He that hasteth to be rich hath an evil eye, and considereth not that poverty shall come upon him" (Proverbs 28:22)*. Buying a chance to earn $10,000 is not God's way of making the most of limited resources.

See page 293.

22 A young father decided that he would concentrate on his business until he was able to retire with a good income. Then he would take it easy and look for an opportunity to serve the Lord. By saving now and working hard for his retirement, he could be self-supporting. Would you encourage him to carry out these plans?

ANSWER: No. Retirement to a life of ease is contrary to the principles of Scripture. God's "retirement program" is heaven. When the rich farmer said to himself, *"Soul, thou hast much goods laid up for many years; take thine ease,"* God said, *"Thou fool!" (Luke 12:19–20)*. Paul illustrates how to combine employment and Christian service with his tentmaking. Retirement is not only damaging to spiritual fruitfulness and family strength, but also to physical life itself. The average life expectancy of a man who retires is only eighteen months. Saving for known needs during times of plenty does not include saving for retirement.

See page 305.

23 After agreeing to reach financial freedom, a husband and wife finally decided that the fastest way to reach their goal was for the husband to look for a job with higher pay. Does this sound like a wise conclusion?

ANSWER: Probably not. The fastest way to gain financial freedom is not to increase income but to decrease spending. Every dollar saved is equivalent to over a dollar and a half earned when costs and taxes are considered. Also, when riches increase, the desires of those who have them increase. (See Ecclesiastes 5:11.) Only by reducing expenses will we learn how to live with basic provisions.

See page 317.

24 The family car was already three years old and starting to need repair. The father wondered if it would not be a wiser use of money to get a new car than to pour a lot of money for repairs into the old car? How would you advise him?

ANSWER: Normal repairs on a three-year-old car would be far more economical than buying a new car. The idea that a new car will solve problems is a financial trap that many people willingly fall into. However, if they would stop to count the cost, as we are told to do in Luke 14:28, they would see that the higher depreciation, the lost interest on their money, and many other hidden costs put them into continual financial bondage. Cars are not made to last. Thieves and rust are witnesses against the one who says that they are a good investment. He would demonstrate better thriftiness by finding a good mechanic and taking care of the car he has to extend its usefulness.

See page 331.

25 The Christians in a high school were looked down on and mocked. For this reason one Christian avoided them so that he could be accepted by the non-Christian students and witness to them. What would you say to this Christian student?

ANSWER: He should begin witnessing to the non-Christian students by not only identifying with the Christians but helping them to mature in their attitudes and behavior. Moses chose to suffer affliction with God's people, and God rewarded him for it. (See Hebrews 11:24–27.) Paul instructs us to do good to all men, especially to Christians. (See Galatians 6:10.) By loving other Christians, we not only communicate an effective witness, but we strengthen those who are carrying out God's work.

See page 343.

26 After thirty years of happy marriage, a wife lost her husband. She sorrowed deeply over his death. A month later she was asked to teach a class of girls. However, she felt that she still needed more time to recover emotionally from the loss of her husband. How would you advise her?

ANSWER: Jesus wept over the death of Lazarus; however, prolonged sorrow would have destroyed the message of his death, that Christ is our resurrection and life. (See John 11:25.) We are not to sorrow as those who have no hope. (See I Thessalonians 4:13.) We are to turn tears into wells of water. (See Psalm 84:6.) God is the protector and the husband of the widow. He can use her sense of loss and inadequacy to strengthen the lives of the girls she teaches and thereby bring joy out of sorrow.

See page 355.

27 A fifteen-year-old girl wanted to become a Christian. However, her parents told her that if she did, she would disgrace them since they did not believe in God. She did not want to dishonor her parents. What would you tell her to do?

ANSWER: She should express sincere appreciation to her parents for the good influences that they have had upon her life, and explain that becoming a Christian is fulfilling the character goals that they have for her life. She should make a further appeal to her parents, clearly explaining what salvation is—praying that God would also prompt them to become Christians. Her ultimate decision, however, must be to accept Christ as her Savior based on Matthew 10:37. By appealing to her parents and becoming a Christian, she is giving honor to whom honor is due.

See page 367.

28 After a Christian businessman sold some valuable equipment, the Christian buyer decided not to pay the full price for it. The seller knew he could take their contract into court and easily force him to pay the remaining money. What would you tell the seller to do?

ANSWER: He should not go to court. I Corinthians 6:1–8 clearly teaches that it is better to be defrauded than to take a Christian brother to court before unbelievers. He should, however, present his case in writing to the buyer and ask for a written answer. Then he should follow the steps of Matthew 18:15–17. Any remaining debt should be committed to the Lord and opportunities should be looked for to benefit the life of the debtor. In this way God's higher principle will be fulfilled in returning good for evil.

HOW WELL DO YOU KNOW THE WAYS OF ANIMALS?

As part of Adam's character training for marriage and family responsibilities, God brought every animal and bird to him for naming. In order to give them accurate names, Adam had to understand their nature and ways. (See Genesis 2:18–20.)

A. Red Squirrel

B. Porcupine

C. Common Loon

D. Prairie Dog

E. Octopus

F. Pack Rat

MATCH THE FOLLOWING STATEMENTS WITH THE PROPER SPECIES ON THIS PAGE.

1. WHAT ANIMAL BURIES ITS ENEMIES ALIVE?

Answer: Page 32

2. WHAT SPECIES CAN SWIM FASTER THAN FISH?

Answer: Page 44

3. WHAT SPECIES USES COLOR TO ESCAPE FROM ITS ENEMIES?

Answer: Page 56

4. WHAT SPECIES DO OTHERS DEPEND UPON FOR THEIR SAFETY?

Answer: Page 68

5. WHAT SPECIES MAKES ITS HOME WITH RATTLESNAKES?

Answer: Page 82

6. WHAT SPECIES IS MOST LIKELY TO CHEW ON YOUR AX HANDLE?

Answer: Page 94

God assumes that we know or will find out the ways of sheep, foxes, lions, bears, eagles, and many other creatures so that when He uses them as illustrations, we can understand and apply what He is saying.

MATCH THE FOLLOWING STATEMENTS WITH THE PROPER SPECIES ON THIS PAGE.

7. WHAT SPECIES DEPENDS ON ITS ACCURACY FOR THE PRESERVATION OF ITS LIFE?
   Answer: Page 106

8. WHAT SPECIES HAS AN ABILITY THAT IS THE DREAM OF EVERY HOSPITAL?
   Answer: Page 118

9. WHAT SPECIES CAN BE CAPTURED BY PAINTING THE TRAP YELLOW?
   Answer: Page 132

10. WHAT SPECIES SIMULATES THE ACTION OF A CANNON?
    Answer: Page 144

11. WHAT SPECIES FUNCTIONS BEST DURING FREEZING NIGHTS AND WARM DAYS?
    Answer: Page 156

12. WHAT SPECIES BUILDS A HOME THAT CAN BE UP TO TWENTY FEET TALL AND NINE FEET WIDE?
    Answer: Page 168

13. WHAT SPECIES LAYS ITS EGGS BY THE PRECISE TIMING OF THE MOON?
    Answer: Page 182

14. WHAT SPECIES ALMOST BECAME EXTINCT BECAUSE OF ITS TEETH?
    Answer: Page 194

A. Grunion

B. Bald Eagle

C. Mistletoe

D. Elk

E. Oyster Catcher

F. Aphid

G. Maple Tree

H. Turkey Vulture

The wisdom which God gave to Solomon included a thorough understanding of the world of nature. *". . . He spake also of beasts, and of fowl, and of creeping things, and of fishes. And there came of all people to hear the wisdom of Solomon . . ." (I Kings 4:33–34).*

MATCH THE FOLLOWING STATEMENTS WITH THE PROPER SPECIES ON THIS PAGE.

A. Muskie

B. Moss

C. American Egret

D. Musk Ox

E. Skunk Cabbage

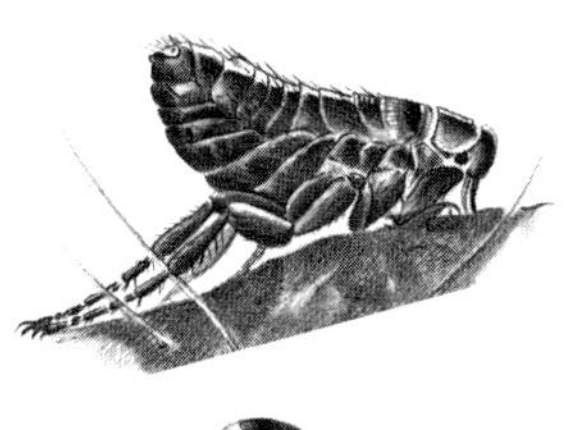

F. Common Flea

G. Cliff Swallow

15. WHAT SPECIES LIVES HUNDREDS OF YEARS AND HAS ITS OWN UNIQUE HEATING SYSTEM?

Answer: Page 206

16. WHAT SPECIES CAUSES A MAJOR CELEBRATION WHEN IT COMES INTO TOWN?

Answer: Page 218

17. WHAT SPECIES CAN ACCELERATE ITSELF TWENTY TIMES FASTER THAN THE APOLLO MOON ROCKET?

Answer: Page 232

18. WHAT SPECIES CAN WALK ON THE GROUND WITHOUT ITS FEET TOUCHING THE GROUND?

Answer: Page 244

19. WHAT SPECIES IS MORE AFRAID OF A MOSQUITO THAN OF A PACK OF WOLVES?

Answer: Page 256

20. WHAT SPECIES HAS 550 TEETH IN ITS MOUTH?

Answer: Page 268

21. WHAT SPECIES PRODUCES ITS OWN LIGHT IN A DARK AREA?

Answer: Page 282

Scripture gives direct instructions to learn from the creatures which God created: *"Go to the ant, thou sluggard; consider her ways . . ." (Proverbs 6:6); "Consider the ravens . . ." (Luke 12:24);* and *". . . Consider the lilies of the field . . ." (Matthew 6:28).*

MATCH THE FOLLOWING STATEMENTS WITH THE PROPER SPECIES ON THIS PAGE.

22. WHAT SPECIES PUTS UP TO 50,000 PIECES OF FOOD IN A SINGLE STORAGE SPACE?

Answer: Page 294

23. WHAT SPECIES CHEWS ITS FOOD WITH ITS FEET?

Answer: Page 306

24. WHAT SPECIES WAS ENDANGERED BY A SHAKESPEAREAN PLAY?

Answer: Page 318

25. WHAT SPECIES EATS ITS FOOD IN THREE STAGES LIKE A COW?

Answer: Page 332

26. WHAT SPECIES REQUIRES A 32° F TEMPERATURE FOR SURVIVAL THROUGHOUT THE WINTER?

Answer: Page 344

27. WHAT SPECIES DEPENDS ON A THICK SNOW COVER FOR ITS SURVIVAL?

Answer: Page 356

28. WHAT SPECIES USES A BUILT-IN LIFE JACKET?

Answer: Page 368

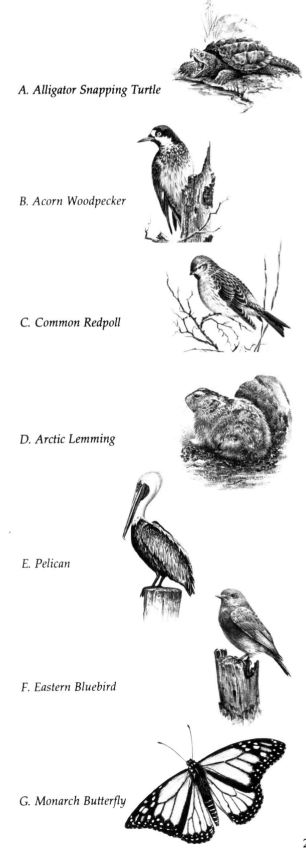

A. Alligator Snapping Turtle

B. Acorn Woodpecker

C. Common Redpoll

D. Arctic Lemming

E. Pelican

F. Eastern Bluebird

G. Monarch Butterfly

Cautiousness

. . . Is knowing the importance of right motives, timing, methods, and amounts in carrying out wise giving

"Also, that the soul be without knowledge, it is not good; and he that hasteth with his feet sinneth."

Proverbs 19:2

PART ONE

CAUTIOUSNESS IN GIVING . . .

Is remembering that wrong motives, timing, methods, or amounts can bring damage to the very ones that we desire to help.

1 ***Living within the protection of my God-given resources***

Illustrated in the World of Nature. . . . . Prairie Dog
From the Pages of Scripture. . . . . Barnabas

2 ***Realizing that my greatest ability is also the point of my greatest vulnerability***

Illustrated in the World of Nature . . . . Common Loon
From the Pages of Scripture . . . . Cyrus

3 ***Remembering that greed crouches at the door of every heart***

Illustrated in the World of Nature . . . . Octopus
From the Pages of Scripture. . . . . Uriah

4 ***Recognizing that the majority is often wrong***

Illustrated in the World of Nature . . . . Red Squirrel
From the Pages of Scripture . . . . Caleb

CHAPTER ONE

Cautiousness

. . . Is living within the protection of my God-given resources

"But we will not boast of things without our measure, but according to the measure of the rule which God hath distributed to us, a measure to reach even unto you."

II Corinthians 10:13

Living Lessons on Cautiousness . . .

FROM THE PAGES OF SCRIPTURE

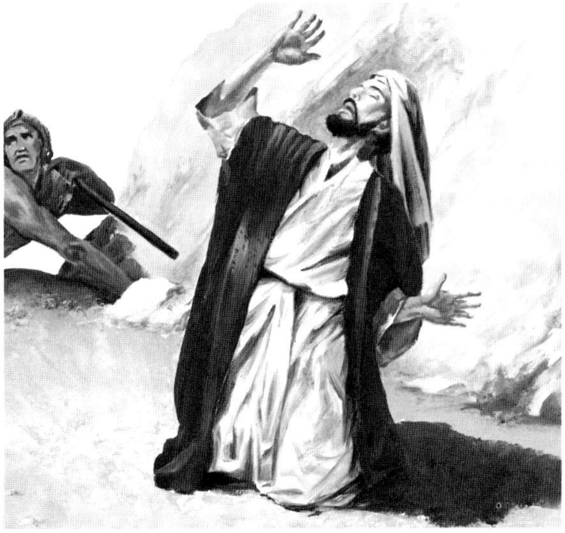

All of life is an exchange. We exchange our work time for wages. Then we exchange our wages for food, clothing, and other items.

Those who want to learn the important insights that are required for wise giving must enter into another level of trading. They must exchange temporal things for greater spiritual discernment.

The Apostle Paul testified that he willingly suffered the loss of all things that he might know more about Christ. (See Philippians 3:7–10.)

Years before Paul discovered this principle, it was demonstrated to him by one who had exchanged his possessions for spiritual discernment.

ILLUSTRATED IN THE WORLD OF NATURE

PRAIRIE DOG *Cynomys ludovicianus*

The prairie dog is a sociable rodent that digs extensive burrows underground. Together with the bison, the prairie dog is responsible for changing the character of the early prairie.

The prairie dog is only fourteen to seventeen inches long, but it consumes incredible amounts of food. To prepare for the hot, dry summer weather, the prairie dog has a unique water storage system.

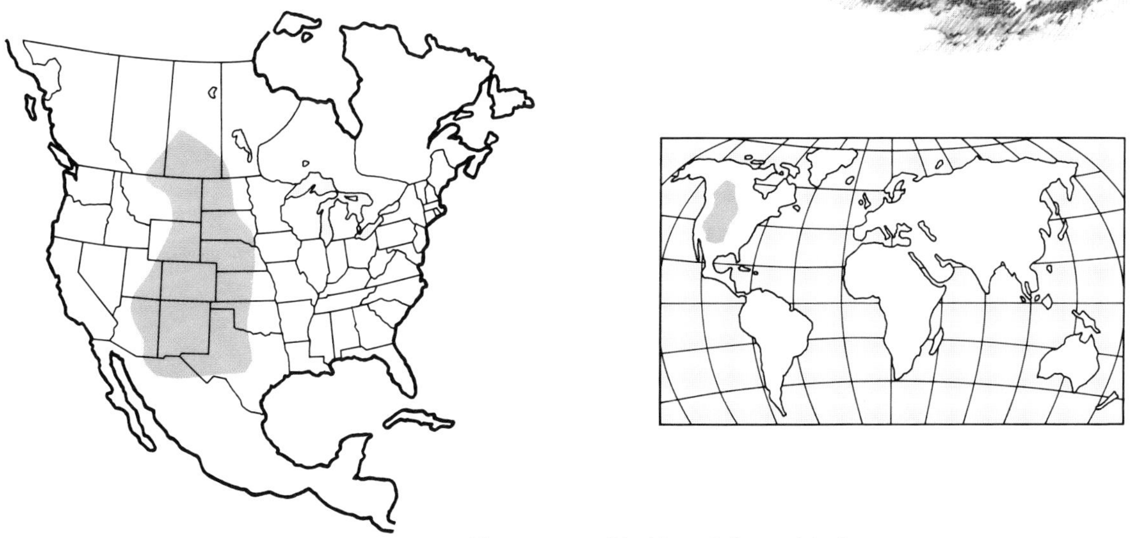

The range and habitat of the prairie dog

How is living within the protection of God-given resources illustrated in the world of nature?

A steep tunnel led to the entrance mound located ten feet above the home of four furry pups. Several hours earlier, their father had cautiously peeped through the narrow shaft, carefully scanning the surrounding habitat.

The experienced father knew that a hungry coyote could be lurking behind any nearby brush or rock. Confident that the area around the burrow was free from predators, the pups' father and mother scampered from the nest to search for food.

Lured from the safe proximity of their home by succulent vegetation, the pair failed to notice the quiet and calculated movements of their deadly enemy.

A clever coyote silently stalked them. Without warning, it suddenly sprang forward and raced toward the entrance mound. Cut off from the protection of their underground lair, the parents found themselves helpless.

They tried in vain to escape, but the coyote quickly cornered them and turned them into a tasty meal.

The four pups began to wonder why their parents had not returned. Finally, they realized that they were on their own. Survival would now depend on their ability to live within the protection of their God-given resources.

What seemed to be an unending and useless maze of tunnels crosscutting beneath the prairie floor would soon become a valuable provision left behind by their parents.

Early one morning the prairie sky turned an ominous gray. Large drops of rain began to pelt the young pups as they played.

Fearing the growing intensity of the thunder and lightning, they instinctively retreated to the shelter of their home. The well-constructed rim of the entrance mound that their parents had designed successfully protected the burrow from serious water damage.

While the pyramid-shaped entrance was able to protect the pups from rain, it could not keep a large rattlesnake from slithering into the main passageway.

Pursued by the deadly reptile, the pups scurried down the tunnel and huddled breathlessly in the dark. The rattlesnake slid past them into a side tunnel. Using loose soil, the pups hurriedly sealed the poisonous intruder within the dead-end chamber.

While this underground drama unfolded, the fury of the storm increased, sending floodwaters across the basin. The floodwaters overflowed the protective entrance mound and burst into the hollow chambers.

With their main escape route cut off and the burrow filling up with water, the pups followed a narrow shaft that led them to within a few inches of the surface.

The air trapped within the shaft lasted long enough for the pups to dig their way to freedom through the rain-softened sod.

By living within God-given resources, four furry prairie dogs escaped destruction.

THE CHARACTERISTICS OF

THE PRAIRIE DOG IN SCRIPTURE

The prairie dog is one of the species of burrowing rodents. Its Hebrew name is *chapharperah,* which means digging animal; a burrower; an inhabitant of secret places.

The prairie dog, like most burrowing rodents, is totally defenseless when confronted by one of its natural enemies. Its survival depends completely on its ability to reach the safety of its burrow.

Often in Israel's history, soldiers and civilians alike sought safety in the rocks and caves when superior armies invaded their land.

". . . And because of the Midianites the children of Israel made them the dens which are in the mountains, and caves, and strong holds" (Judges 6:2).

David himself demonstrated the wise caution of fleeing to the rocks when pursued by King Saul. His Psalms therefore became rich with the spiritual imagery of safety in the shelter of the rock.

"But the Lord is my defence; and my God is the rock of my refuge" (Psalm 94:22). "He only is my rock and my salvation: he is my defence; I shall not be moved" (Psalm 62:6).

As the prairie dog scurries to the safety of his den, he is an illustration of the need for Christians to enter into the safety of Christ and the victory that He has already won on Calvary.

CHARACTERISTICS AND PHYSICAL FEATURES OF THE PRAIRIE DOG

Preparation is serious business for the prairie dog. Without its intricate system of mounds and tunnels, it is defenseless against both predators and the extremes of the prairie environment. Much of the prairie dog's time is occupied by digging, building, repairing, or expanding its underground defense. Because an attack or storm may come without warning, the prairie dog must be in a constant state of readiness.

An adult prairie dog standing erect

HOW DOES THE LITTLE PRAIRIE DOG GET A BIGGER PERSPECTIVE?

The prairie dog's mounds are not simply piles of dirt excavated from underground burrows. These mounds have specific purposes, one of which is to serve as a lookout platform from which the prairie dog can stand watch. Since the height of a mound may approach three feet, a prairie dog standing on its hind legs can gain quite a height advantage when looking out over the flat prairie.

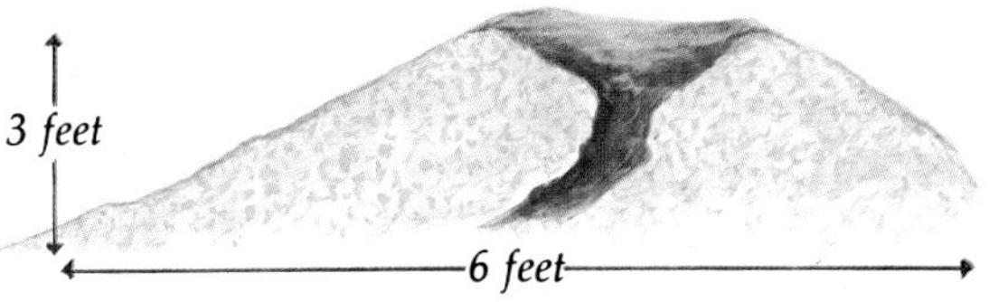

Soil washed away by rain is scraped to the center of the mound and packed.

HOW DOES THE PRAIRIE DOG DECORATE WITH ITS NOSE?

A prairie dog uses its nose to pack the inside walls of its burrow. After a rain, the walls become soft and may cave in unless repaired. By ramming its blunt nose into the clay walls of the tunnels, the walls become rock hard when dry. Prints of its nose can be found decorating each of the underground chambers.

The hot days of the prairie summer bake the prairie dog's mound to bricklike hardness.

WHY DOES THE LIFE OF THE PRAIRIE DOG DEPEND ON A WELL-TRIMMED LAWN?

The prairie dog eats all of the vegetation within a ten-foot circle around its burrow. It "mows" the grass as close to the ground as possible. This gives the prairie dog the visibility it needs to see predators. If a coyote can surprise the prairie dog above the ground, away from its burrow, the prairie dog is completely helpless; but a coyote has little chance of catching a prairie dog that is sitting in a ten-foot clearing.

HOW DO LITTLE INSECTS CAUSE PRAIRIE DOG HOMES TO BE DESTROYED?

Bison are attracted by the mounds of clay which the prairie dog builds. The bison love to break up the mounds and roll in the dust. Because bison are bothered by numerous insect pests in the summer, they seek comfort by coating their hides with a thick layer of dust. Unfortunately, this usually means the destruction of the prairie dog's mound.

Lightning reflexes and a clear field of vision allow the prairie dog to graze in the presence of a coyote.

An "all clear" is sounded both with a bark and with a flip in the air.

A strong sense of family holds the prairie dog community together.

A prairie dog kiss

Two prairie dogs approach each other suspiciously with their heads lowered.

WHAT DOES THE PRAIRIE DOG HAVE IN COMMON WITH NOAH?

Like Noah, the prairie dog prepares for floods. In the early spring, torrential rains can cause flash floods on the flat prairie. The raised mound surrounding the burrow serves as a dike to prevent floodwaters from entering the underground home. If the flooding is severe and water does enter the burrow's system of tunnels, a secondary defense has been prepared.

Each burrow has several tunnels which rise very close to the surface, thus creating airlocks that trap enough air to sustain a prairie dog up to an hour or more. This is usually enough time for the floodwaters to recede and allow the prairie dog to dig himself out.

HOW DO PRAIRIE DOG CITIES SURPASS OUR CITIES?

Prairie dogs live in their own large cities on the prairie. One prairie town was 240 miles long and eleven miles wide. It contained over 400,000,000 prairie dogs.

Each prairie dog city is divided into wards, and each ward is broken into family groups called coteries. A coterie usually consists of several males, one being dominant, several adult females, and the young from the past two years.

Most of the boundaries between wards are made by natural geographic features such as streams, woods, or hills. The boundaries between coteries, however, are imaginary and are a constant point of bickering within the prairie dog city.

HOW DOES THE PRAIRIE DOG WARN OF DANGER?

The prairie dog barks and flicks its tail in particular ways which have meaning to other prairie dogs. The bark is a two-syllable call which carries two degrees of danger, an alert and a warning.

The alert means to take notice of potential danger. The more emphatic and higher-pitched the warning, the more immediate the need is to take cover. In both cases the jerking tail serves as a visual cue. The position of the tail also indicates the degree of danger. An upright tail means that danger is imminent.

When an alert is sounded, each prairie dog in the area stands up to see what is going on. When a warning is given, each dog makes a mad scramble for his hole without looking back. They remain quietly in their burrows until the all clear is sounded.

The all clear signal is given with an apparent joyful leap into the air. Sometimes the prairie dog throws its front paws into the air with such force that it falls over backwards.

HOW DO PRAIRIE DOGS CHECK OUT FRIENDS WITH A KISS?

When two prairie dogs meet near a boundary, they greet each other by lowering their heads to the ground and gently rubbing lips, first on one side and then on the other. As they touch and smell each other, they can identify relatives. If they are not family, a squabble will break out until one retreats.

HOW DO YOUNG PRAIRIE DOGS LEARN TO STAY IN THEIR OWN BACKYARD?

Young prairie dogs are born in the spring and learn the family boundaries quickly because they are attacked aggressively by neighbors every time they cross the imaginary line which separates two coteries. However, the boundaries relax in the summer and interfamily contacts become more friendly. As mating season approaches in the fall, the boundaries become tight again.

HOW SOPHISTICATED ARE PRAIRIE DOG BURROWS?

Prairie dogs dig remarkable burrows. The entrance is a plunge hole which is perhaps ten feet deep. At the bottom of the plunge hole are several four- to ten-inch diameter passageways which turn slightly upward.

Along these tunnels may be numerous dead-end chambers, each with its own specific purpose. Food may be stored in one chamber. Another chamber may be a bedroom equipped with a mattress of soft grass.

Some burrows are large enough to house fifteen individuals and may have as many as seventeen lateral tunnels radiating from the central entrance.

Near the top of the plunge hole is a small ledge which is safe from most predators. This serves as a guard post from which the prairie dog can scold the intruder or wait quietly in silence until the all clear is sounded by a more adventuresome neighbor.

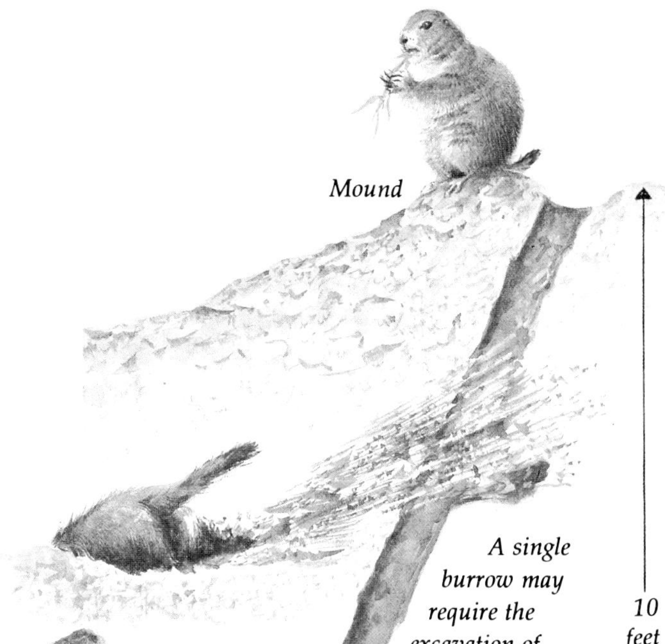

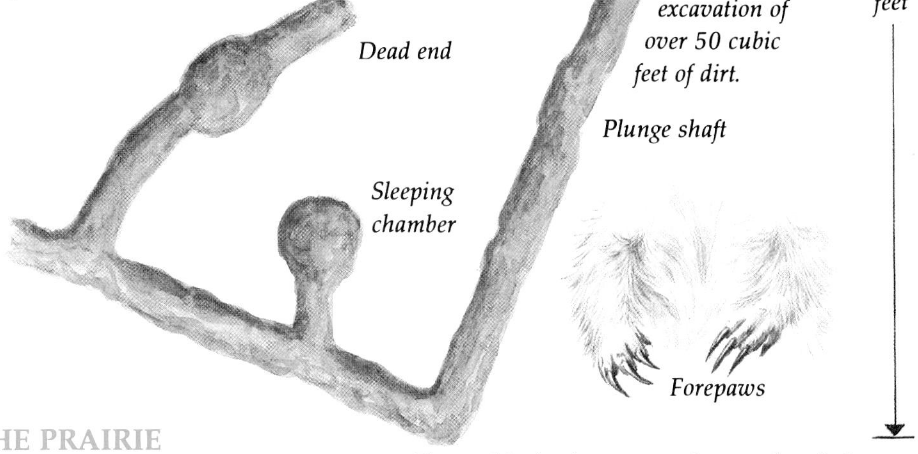

WHAT IS DIFFERENT ABOUT THE PRAIRIE DOG'S FOOT?

The prairie dog has five front toes, while most rodents have only four. Its long claws and extra toe are important as digging tools. The prairie dog digs with its front feet and in the same motion kicks the loosened dirt away with its back feet. When a prairie dog gets so deep that it cannot throw the dirt out of its hole in a single stroke, it starts over again at the entrance.

The prairie dog has a second stomach called a cecum for storing food. This allows the prairie dog to fill up quickly but digest his food slowly.

HOW DOES THE PRAIRIE DOG PROVIDE FOR WATER DURING DRY SEASONS?

The prairie is very dry during the summer. To collect drinking water, the prairie dog stores grass in an isolated chamber underground. The grass soaks up enough water from the humid subterranean air to provide a continual supply of pure water. The prairie dog simply eats the moist grass to quench its thirst.

Underground guard post

HOW ARE PRAIRIE DOG BURROWS "TEMPERATURE CONTROLLED"?

In the summer, the plunge hole serves as a chimney through which the warm air rises, creating a draft which draws fresh air into the burrow and circulates it throughout the system. In the winter, snow insulates the burrow and the prairie dog's own body heat serves as a furnace. With the entrance blocked by snow, heat is trapped inside the burrow.

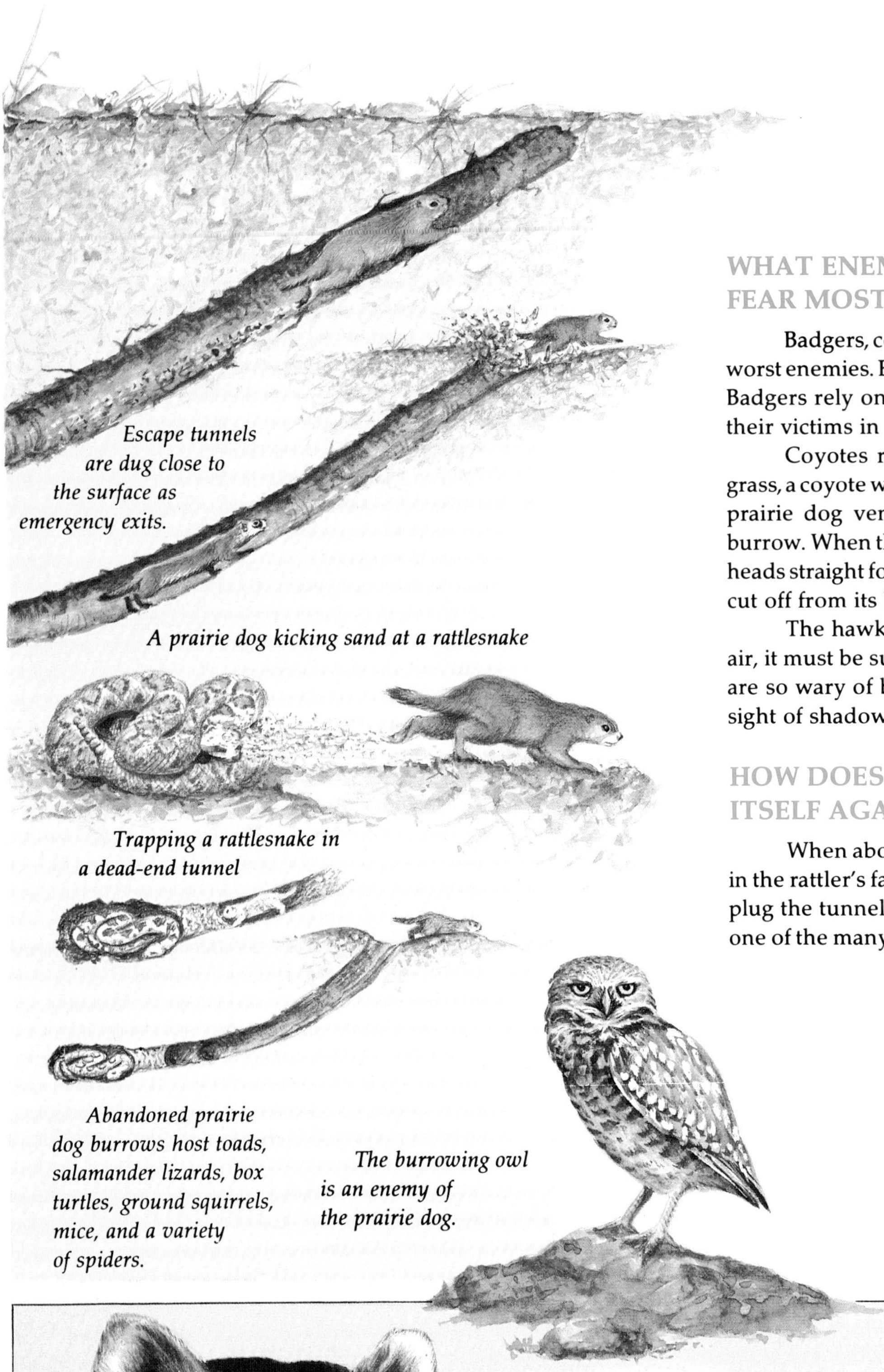

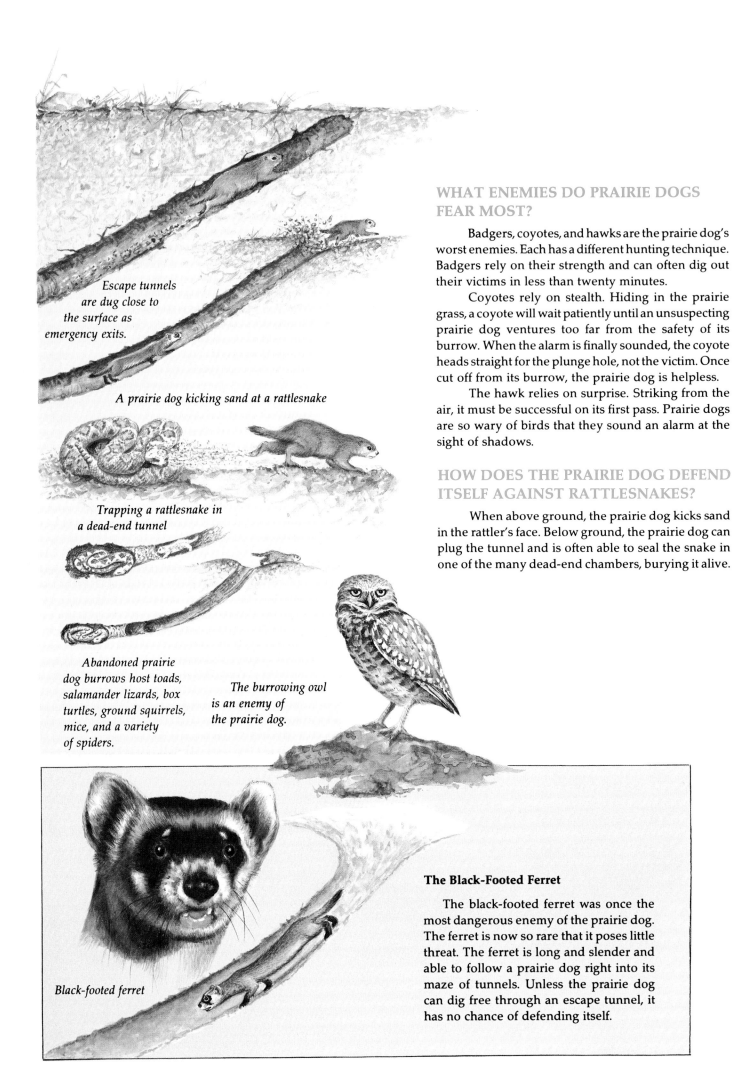

Escape tunnels are dug close to the surface as emergency exits.

A prairie dog kicking sand at a rattlesnake

Trapping a rattlesnake in a dead-end tunnel

Abandoned prairie dog burrows host toads, salamander lizards, box turtles, ground squirrels, mice, and a variety of spiders.

The burrowing owl is an enemy of the prairie dog.

WHAT ENEMIES DO PRAIRIE DOGS FEAR MOST?

Badgers, coyotes, and hawks are the prairie dog's worst enemies. Each has a different hunting technique. Badgers rely on their strength and can often dig out their victims in less than twenty minutes.

Coyotes rely on stealth. Hiding in the prairie grass, a coyote will wait patiently until an unsuspecting prairie dog ventures too far from the safety of its burrow. When the alarm is finally sounded, the coyote heads straight for the plunge hole, not the victim. Once cut off from its burrow, the prairie dog is helpless.

The hawk relies on surprise. Striking from the air, it must be successful on its first pass. Prairie dogs are so wary of birds that they sound an alarm at the sight of shadows.

HOW DOES THE PRAIRIE DOG DEFEND ITSELF AGAINST RATTLESNAKES?

When above ground, the prairie dog kicks sand in the rattler's face. Below ground, the prairie dog can plug the tunnel and is often able to seal the snake in one of the many dead-end chambers, burying it alive.

Black-footed ferret

The Black-Footed Ferret

The black-footed ferret was once the most dangerous enemy of the prairie dog. The ferret is now so rare that it poses little threat. The ferret is long and slender and able to follow a prairie dog right into its maze of tunnels. Unless the prairie dog can dig free through an escape tunnel, it has no chance of defending itself.

How is the protection of living within God-given resources illustrated in Scripture?

The difference between blind fear and wise caution is spiritual perception. Who increased his faith and spiritual perception and was able to make a bold decision while those around him hesitated in fear?

(Pause for a response—see page 17.)

William Tyndale, one of England's leading reformers, was approached one day by a sincere-looking young man who offered to help him. In reality, the young man was a spy employed by the Archbishop of Canterbury. Tyndale, one of the first men to translate the Bible into English, was arrested, tried for heresy, and on October 6, 1536, was strangled and burned at the stake.

In A.D. 37, one of the early Church leaders was approached by a sincere-looking man who offered to help him and the other Christians. Most of the Christians, however, were in hiding from this very man!

Burning with hatred, he had dedicated himself to one cause—the destruction of anyone who followed Christ. He regarded them as politically and spiritually dangerous. His unrelenting persecution had already resulted in the murder of one Christian and the imprisonment of many others.

Armed with new authority from the religious leaders of his day, he traveled from city to city to broaden his attack against the followers of Christ.

This was the background of the man who now offered to help the people he had so recently persecuted. Little wonder that all the Church leaders had fled from him. All, except for one man.

This leader was a man of Godly reputation. He had been a wealthy landowner on the island of Cyprus, who after believing had totally dedicated himself and all his possessions to the Lord. That complete dedication included selling his land and giving the money to the Apostles to sustain needy Christians. In return God gave him a greater faith which increased his ability to discern the motives of others.

The leader cautiously listened as the man who had so oppressed the believers told how God had struck him and his companions to the ground with a brilliant light. The man also revealed that he had heard the voice of Christ from heaven asking why he was persecuting Him. This experience, claimed the man, had brought him to repentance. He himself was now a follower of Christ.

As the respected leader listened, he perceived a spirit like his own, the spirit of one totally dedicated to the Lord. With confidence he brought the man to the Apostles and introduced him as a new brother in Christ.

Because God had provided Barnabas with special wisdom and insight, he was able to open the door of fellowship to a new convert. He later helped open the Mediterranean world to the Gospel during missionary journeys with this same man—the Apostle Paul.

When Barnabas kindly received Paul as a brother in the Lord, he demonstrated his confidence in the Lord to protect him from a possible trap. This spiritual discernment was a God-given resource that would continue to benefit him and Paul throughout their missionary journeys.

From Acts 4:36–37; 9:26–31

BARNABAS, ONE WHO GAVE MONEY, TIME, AND TALENT IN EXCHANGE FOR SPIRITUAL DISCERNMENT

One of the coins *at the time of Barnabas which could have been brought to the Apostles for an offering to the Lord*

The atmosphere in the early Church was one of excitement, joy, and anticipation. Jesus had been raised from the dead. Peter and the Apostles proclaimed the good news of salvation, and thousands of people received the message. Some who believed were very poor and needed food, clothing, and shelter. The wealthy were moved with compassion and sold possessions and land in order to meet these needs.

A WEALTHY LEVITE HELPS THE POOR

Barnabas was a Levite from the island of Cyprus. He is mentioned by name as one who *"having land, sold it, and brought the money, and laid it at the apostles' feet" (Acts 4:37)*. The property he sold was probably in Cyprus, as Levites did not receive an inheritance of land. The Lord Himself was to be their inheritance. (See Numbers 18:20.) It is likely that Barnabas was a wealthy man since land on Cyprus was valuable, producing wine, oils, figs, honey, and wheat. It took courage to part with his wealth, but it reflected a grateful heart, full of compassion and love.

Jupiter and Mercurius

In their later travels, *Barnabas' leadership and Paul's preaching were illustrated by the names given them by the Lycaonians of Lystra. They called Barnabas "Jupiter," who was their chief god, and Paul "Mercurius," who was the spokesman of the gods. Pictured above are sculptures of Jupiter and Mercurius. (See Acts 14:6–12.)*

PERSECUTION SCATTERS THE CHURCH

A young rabbi by the name of Saul, concerned that the believers in Jesus were threatening to split apart the nation's religious tradition, led the great persecution against the church which was in Jerusalem. After the stoning of Stephen, Saul arrested both men and women who professed that Jesus was the Son of God and the promised Messiah. He dragged them to prison where they were to await trial.

When some fled to nearby Damascus, he received permission from the high priests to pursue them and bring them back to Jerusalem for trial. They would be prosecuted for the crime of blasphemy, and if proven guilty, they would be liable for death by stoning. The Roman government allowed the cooperative Sadducean priests this privilege in cases strictly religious.

BARNABAS STANDS ALONE IN SUPPORT OF SAUL

While on his way to Damascus, Saul saw the risen Lord and became a believer. After spending three years in Arabia, he testified in Damascus and then returned to Jerusalem in order to meet Peter. (See Galatians 1:18.) But, the disciples were skeptical about Saul's professed conversion. He had created havoc among them. Would God reveal Himself to someone as cruel as Saul?

Barnabas no doubt had heard from the believers at Damascus. He discerned that Saul was a true believer and recognized God's working in his life. Barnabas saw in Saul the abundance of gifts which the Lord had given to be used for His purposes. He introduced Saul to Peter with whom Saul stayed for fifteen days. Saul also met James, the Lord's brother. (See Galatians 1:18–19.)

Having met Saul, these pillars of the Jerusalem church also discerned with Barnabas a genuine conversion to the Lord and fully endorsed him to the skeptical disciples. Skepticism was replaced with trust, and Saul was able to minister the Word with the support and encouragement so necessary for his effectiveness.

Early church building at Antioch

BARNABAS REMEMBERS SAUL

Because of the growth of the church at Antioch, the church in Jerusalem sent Barnabas to help with the work there. As a result of his ministry, many were added to the Church. (See Acts 11:24.) Barnabas remembered Saul's abilities and felt that they were needed in Antioch. He personally went to find Paul in Tarsus and convinced him to return with him to help with the work. For an entire year they ministered to the Christians and taught them the Word of God.

CHARACTER SKETCH OF BARNABAS

HOW DID BARNABAS' NAME INDICATE HIS CHARACTER?

The man's given name was Joseph, but he was surnamed "Barnabas" by the Apostles. In Aramaic, which the Apostles spoke, *Barnabas* means "son of prophecy," but the Greek translation given by Luke is "son of consolation." (See Acts 4:36.) This is the same word used by the Lord when referring to the Holy Spirit, whose ministry is to exhort, console, and encourage. (See John 14:26.)

In the city of Antioch, Barnabas, Simeon, and Lucius functioned as "prophets." Their task was to proclaim the good news of salvation in Christ Jesus. Manaen and Paul were the "teachers." Theirs was the task of instructing the believers in foundational doctrine.

Exhortation was an important aspect of prophecy as illustrated in Acts 15:32, *"And Judas and Silas, being prophets also themselves, exhorted the brethren with many words, and confirmed them."* Barnabas was engaged in this ministry at Antioch. He *". . . exhorted them all, that with purpose of heart they would cleave unto the Lord" (Acts 11:23).*

WHY WAS BARNABAS ABLE TO DISCERN SAUL'S MOTIVES?

There is a rare Biblical eulogy given to Barnabas, *"For he was a good man, and full of the Holy Ghost and of faith . . ." (Acts 11:24).* Three things characterized Barnabas. First, he was a good man. James described a good man as one who had compassion on the needy. (See James 1:27; 2:14–17.) Barnabas had pity for the poor. He removed any barrier between himself and the Lord. Proverbs 21:13 states, *"Whoso stoppeth his ears at the cry of the poor, he also shall cry himself, but shall not be heard."*

Second, he was filled with the Holy Spirit. He was obedient to the prompting of God's Spirit and did not grieve Him. (See Ephesians 4:30; 5:18.) Barnabas was in a position to receive spiritual discernment concerning Saul's character and motives.

Third, he was a man of faith. He was able to visualize the great work which God had planned for Saul. While others were dwelling on Saul's past, Barnabas was focusing on his future.

HOW DID BARNABAS' GENEROSITY ENCOURAGE OTHERS?

Barnabas' gift was held up as an example for others to follow. He is contrasted with Ananias and Sapphira, who also sold a possession but kept back some of the money for themselves, lying to the Apostles. (See Acts 5:1–10.)

Barnabas had been exhorting the disciples in Antioch for a year when a need was revealed concerning their fellow believers in Judea. *"Then the disciples, every man according to his ability, determined to send relief unto the brethren which dwelt in Judaea" (Acts 11:29).* Barnabas was able to teach about giving, because he practiced it himself.

He was an example to the Apostle Paul, who encouraged the Gentile churches throughout the Roman Empire to contribute to the needs of their poorer brothers in Christ. This was no doubt a major factor in the mutual love and cooperation which developed between the Gentile and Jewish Christians.

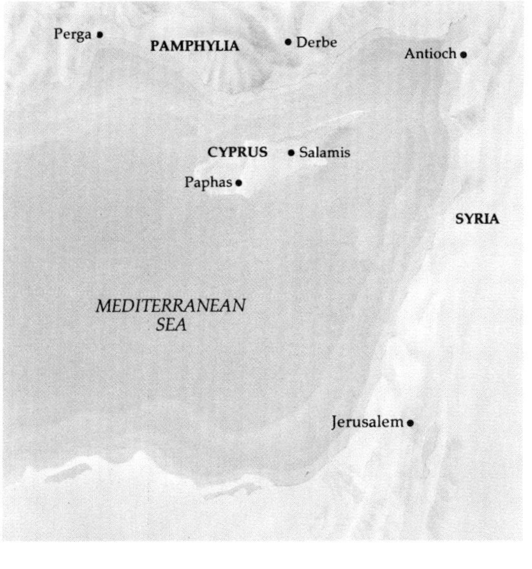

Barnabas owned land *on the island of Cyprus. He sold the land and gave the money to the disciples for the care of Christians in Jerusalem.*

BARNABAS
bar*-nə-bəs*

CHAPTER TWO

Cautiousness

. . . Is realizing that my greatest ability is also the point of my greatest vulnerability

"Wherefore let him that thinketh he standeth take heed lest he fall."

I Corinthians 10:12

". . . Therefore will I rather glory in my infirmities, that the power of Christ may rest upon me."

II Corinthians 12:9

Living Lessons on Cautiousness . . .

FROM THE PAGES OF SCRIPTURE

The true test of a man's character is not determined by his achievements, but by how he responds to the praise that accompanies his success.

Pride, overconfidence, and ingratitude will result in swift judgment and destruction. Success demands an acknowledgment that it is God who lifts up one and takes down another. (See Psalm 75:6–7.)

If a ruler ever had a right to be proud, one eastern sovereign could have legitimately claimed the honor. He had handily conquered the wealthiest and most powerful empire that the ancient world had ever seen.

However, unlike the emperor whom he replaced, he was acutely aware that his victory and future reign depended completely on God.

ILLUSTRATED IN THE WORLD OF NATURE

COMMON LOON *Gavia immer*

Loons are large black-and-white birds which live almost entirely in the water. They are excellent divers, surpassed in speed and agility only by the penguin. Loons are good fliers, but they have considerable trouble landing and taking off because of their heavy bodies and small wings. The voice of the loon has become a symbol of the northern wilderness of the United States.

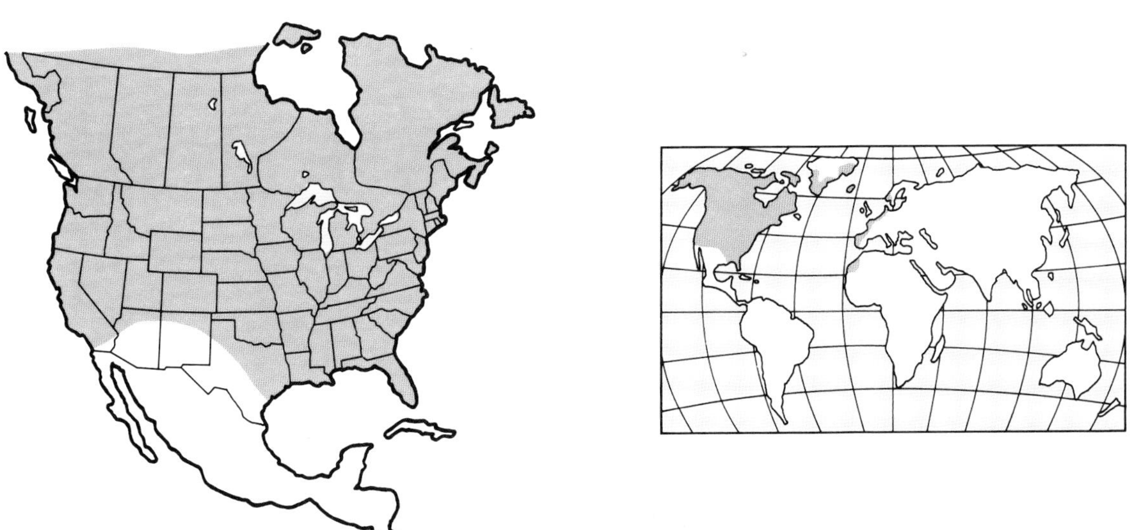

The range and habitat of the common loon

How is unexpected vulnerability illustrated in the world of nature?

The indignant native jealously glared at the large flock of migrants as they circled the mountain lake and shattered the mirrorlike surface of his private fishery with a less-than-polite landing.

Days had become noticeably shorter and the night air whispered subtle warnings of an approaching snowfall that would soon adorn the majestic pines.

A veteran of many migrations himself, he instinctively sensed that the long flight to the warm, southern marshlands would require an added reserve of energy.

The fish that inhabited the lake were no match for his agility and experience. His webbed feet generated powerful, dart-like movements that enabled him to chase down even the slipperiest catch.

With his ample supply of food now threatened by the noisy colony of intruders, the solitary bird retreated to a smaller nearby lake. There he found an abundant supply of savory perch and sunfish.

As night began to overshadow the forest, the faint calls of his uninvited neighbors echoed through the timbers.

Lured by migratory instincts, he decided to join the large flock. His determined wings beat against the water as he half flew and half ran across the shimmering pond. The tiny lake supplied a limited runway and nearly prevented him from clearing the treetops.

That night a heavy frost blanketed the woodland refuge. One by one the lake birds departed from the area.

Finally, the native bird began the difficult journey southward. However, as he gained altitude, he spotted the small lake where he had feasted the day before. Confidently, he swooped down on the well-stocked pond, ignoring the rim of ice that had reduced its dimensions.

He dove under the water and ate fish to his heart's content. After a short while he decided to rejoin the migrating flock.

Once again he flapped his wings and pushed his feet against the water as he ran down the lake for his takeoff. To his dismay he discovered that the lake was now smaller than the day before. Ice jutted out from the shore in every direction.

He tried again and again to take off without success. The fish that he had just eaten laid heavily in his stomach. He decided to wait until evening; perhaps the stronger wind would give him the needed lift to clear the lake.

But even with the help of the stronger wind the large bird was unable to take off from the rapidly shrinking lake. He was helplessly trapped.

Soon the lake froze over, forcing him to go ashore. Ironically, the loon's great ability to dive, swim, and catch fish had produced a lack of cautiousness which exposed him to the frozen, snow-swept wilderness, where he would soon die.

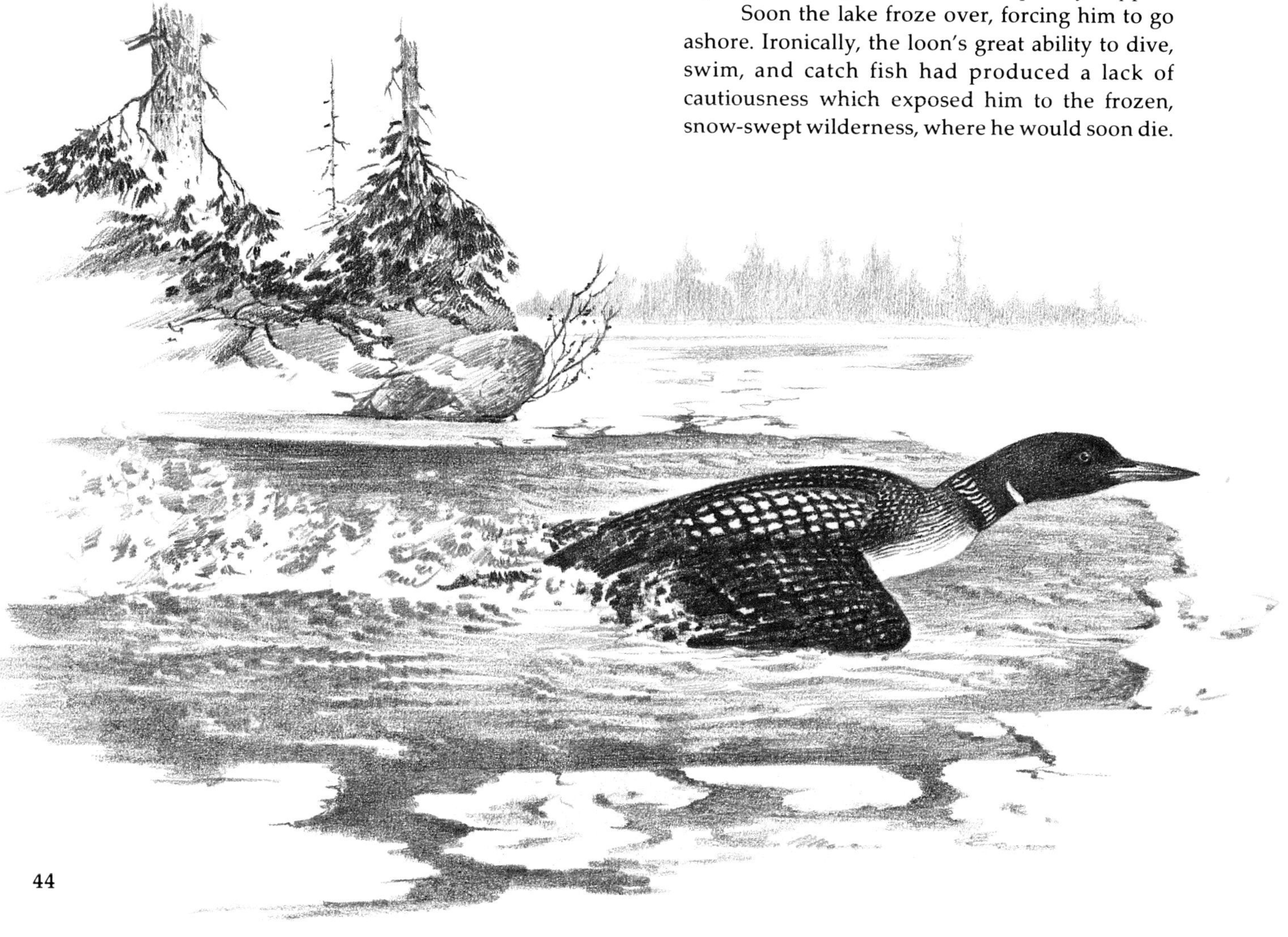

THE CHARACTERISTICS OF

THE LOON IN SCRIPTURE

The loon's vulnerability on land and on small lakes is a valuable illustration of a Christian's need to be committed to Christ and to wisely consider every venture before entering into it.

"And whosoever doth not bear his cross, and come after me, cannot be my disciple. For which of you, intending to build a tower, sitteth not down first, and counteth the cost, whether he have sufficient to finish it?" (Luke 14:27–28).

The abilities which make the loon successful in catching fish are limitations in living on land. In the same way, Christians have special abilities to be fishers of men. (See Matthew 4:19.) This limits our ability to be involved in worldly pursuits. (See II Timothy 2:4.)

We are to be in the world but not of the world. *"Dearly beloved, I beseech you as strangers and pilgrims, abstain from fleshly lusts, which war against the soul" (I Peter 2:11).*

Like the loon, God wants the Christian to *". . . mount up with wings . . ." (Isaiah 40:31)* and to *". . . ride upon the high places of the earth . . ." (Isaiah 58:14).*

Once a Christian comes down from his "spiritual soaring," it is very difficult to get back up again. (See Hebrews 12:15.) Just as the loons continually call to each other, we are to exhort one another daily. (See Hebrews 3:13.)

CHARACTERISTICS AND PHYSICAL FEATURES OF THE COMMON LOON

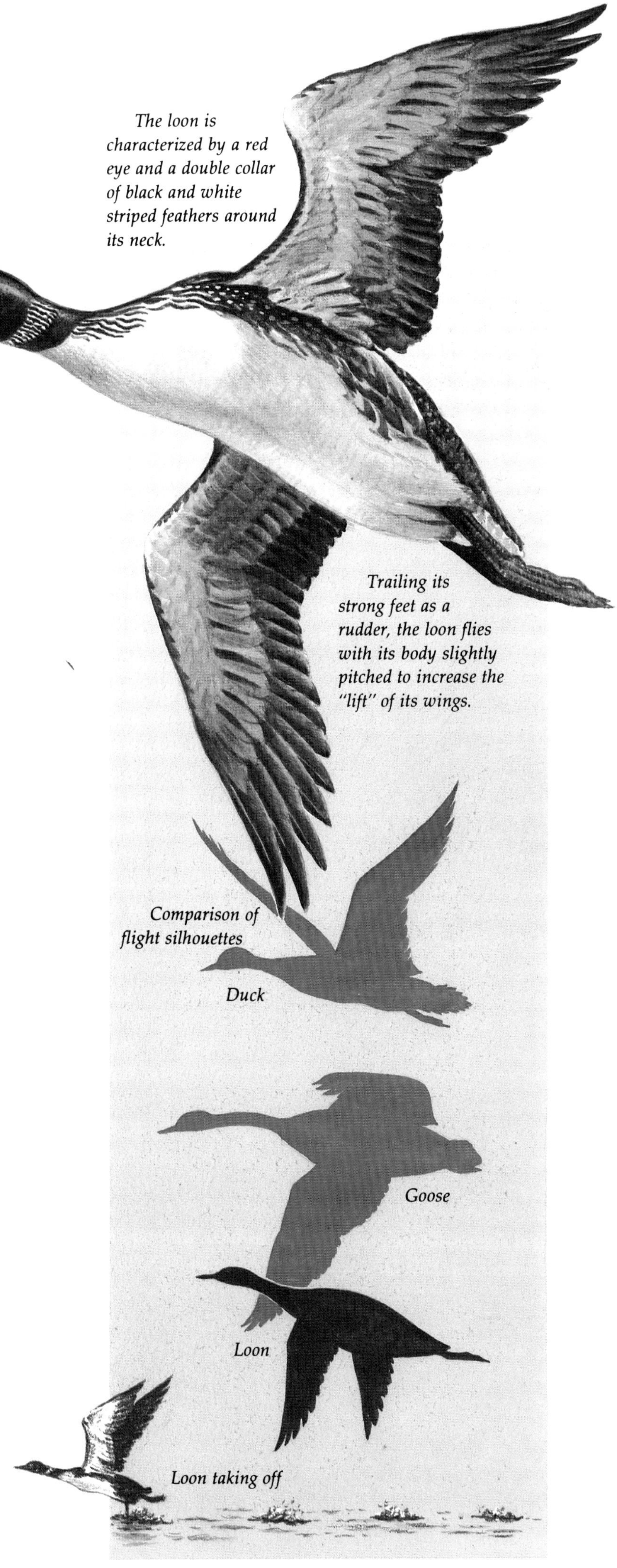

The loon is characterized by a red eye and a double collar of black and white striped feathers around its neck.

Trailing its strong feet as a rudder, the loon flies with its body slightly pitched to increase the "lift" of its wings.

Comparison of flight silhouettes

Duck

Goose

Loon

Loon taking off

The loon's limited ability on land and in the air requires it to be especially cautious. On land it is completely helpless and can be easily captured. While the loon is a good flier, it has considerable difficulty getting into the air. When landing in small lakes, an unwary loon can sometimes become trapped, being unable to take off again in the short distance it used for landing.

WHY DOES THE LOON APPEAR TO BE HUNCHBACKED?

Loons have very small wings, so small that they must flap them 260 times a minute (4.3 times a second!) just to stay airborne. Their wings are also located further back than those of most other birds, causing them to look slightly hunchbacked.

Even with these limitations, loons can fly more than 60 miles per hour in level flight and can reach 80 miles per hour in shallow dives. They have been observed flying as high as 29,000 feet, and can make a trip from Wisconsin to Florida in two days.

HOW DO THE BONES OF LOONS GIVE BOTH BENEFITS AND LIMITATIONS?

Most birds have pneumatic bones—bones that contain air cells which make them very light. Loons, however, have solid bones, making them much heavier than other birds of the same size. This extra weight is helpful in diving but not in flying.

WHY DO LOONS BECOME EASILY TRAPPED IN SMALL LAKES?

Loons have considerable trouble taking off because of their small wings and heavy bodies. They need up to a quarter mile of "runway" to become airborne. They half run and half fly, legs paddling rapidly and wings beating against the water until they can lift off. Even after takeoff, a loon leaving a small lake may have to circle several times before gaining enough speed and altitude to clear the surrounding trees.

HOW DOES THE "CRASH LANDING" OF LOONS DIFFER FROM OTHER WATERFOWL?

Unlike ducks which land on their feet and slide across the water as if on miniature water skis, loons crash chestfirst into the water and then skid across the water like feathered boats.

HOW DO THE COLORS OF LOONS' FEET HELP THEM TO FISH?

The loon's feet are black and white. When viewed from above, the black side of the feet appears dark against the water. When viewed from below, the white side appears light against the sky. Thus, the loon's prey are unlikely to see it and be alerted by its moving feet.

WHY IS A QUIET "HONEYMOON" ESSENTIAL FOR A LOON?

Loons seem to require greater solitude than other waterfowl as they go through their mating and nesting season. If they are disturbed during this time, loons may fail to mate or they may abandon their nest. For this reason they select isolated wilderness lakes wherever possible.

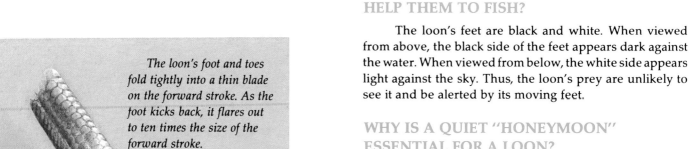

The loon's foot and toes fold tightly into a thin blade on the forward stroke. As the foot kicks back, it flares out to ten times the size of the forward stroke.

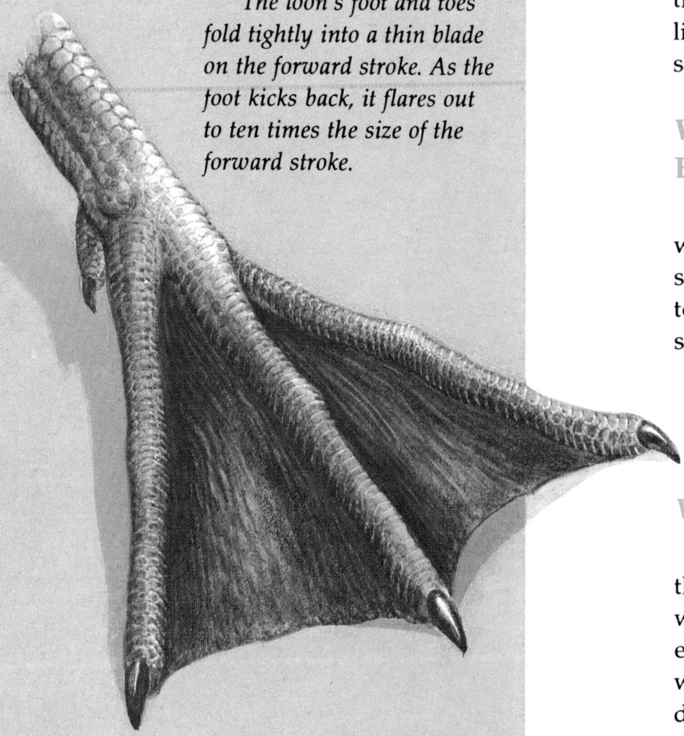

WHY DOES A LOON ONLY SHOW ITS FEET?

With most birds, the legs separate from the body at the hip. The leg bones of the loon, however, are enclosed within its body all the way to the ankle. Only the foot is exposed near the tail. The enclosed leg produces less drag when swimming, and maximum thrust is produced by the direct attachment of the wide foot to its body. This makes the loon a fast, powerful swimmer but a poor runner.

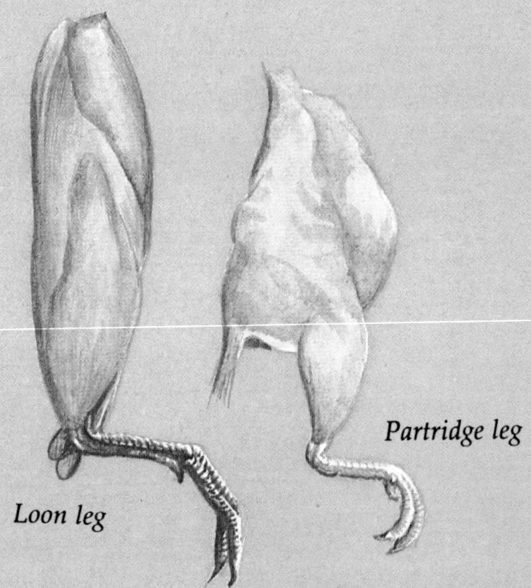

WHAT DOES A LOON HAVE IN COMMON WITH A LUMMOX?

The name loon comes from the English word "lumme," meaning an awkward person. The word "lummox" comes from the same root word. Because its legs are near the tail, the loon cannot stand. It "walks" by sliding forward on its chest, using its wings and bill as well as its feet to push itself along. The loon is so awkward on land that it is easily captured there.

HOW DOES A LOON CHANGE TACTICS IN CATCHING BIG AND LITTLE FISH?

When fishing, the loon trolls slowly through the water with its head just below the surface. When it sees a fish, it upends itself and the chase is on. The loon catches its prey in its sharp-edged bill, swallowing smaller fish without even rising to the surface. If the fish is large, it is brought to the surface where the loon tosses it into the air and swallows it headfirst in a single gulp.

***Loons are compelled** to come ashore only to raise their young. However, when on land, they are like prisoners in shackles. Because their feet are attached at the ankle for a more powerful swimming stroke, loons are unable to run or even walk without great difficulty.*

Erupting from the surface *after a long dive, a loon often raises itself out of the water, stretching its neck and shaking the water from its feathers much like a dog shaking water from its fur.*

Like a periscope, the head of a loon rises and then submerges.

The loon is a marathon diver capable of traveling hundreds of yards before surfacing.

Dives to depths of 200 feet occasionally entangle loons in commercial fishing nets.

HOW DOES A LOON USE AIR SACS TO OPERATE LIKE A SUBMARINE?

The loon's heavy body allows it to sink until only its head is above water. Just as a submarine expels air from its ballast tanks to dive, the loon controls its buoyancy by inflating or deflating tiny air sacs under its skin. It can sink rapidly and swim away to avoid even the quickest predator.

HOW CAN A LOON SWIM FASTER THAN ANY FISH?

The loon is a superb diver, spending perhaps ninety-nine per cent of its time in the water. Powerful strokes from its webbed feet produce a burst of tremendous speed that can catch even the quickest fish. Underwater, the streamlined body looks like a high-performance torpedo with wings. It can make sharp turns and sudden stops using the tips of its feathers as rudders.

HOW DOES "ZONE CONTROL" OF BLOOD CIRCULATION INCREASE THE LOON'S ENDURANCE?

Like the dolphin, the loon has a diving reflex which can restrict the flow of blood to portions of its body for a short period of time. When flying at high altitudes where the air is thin, the loon restricts the flow of blood to its massive leg muscles, thus conserving precious oxygen. When diving, it can restrict the flow to its digestive system and wings and is thus able to hold its breath longer.

WHAT IS THE RECORD FOR THE LOON'S LONGEST DIVE?

An average dive lasts approximately forty seconds; however, three-minute dives that cover three hundred to four hundred yards are not uncommon. One record dive lasted almost fifteen minutes and extended over two and a quarter miles.

WHY WOULD A LOON STARVE TO DEATH IF IT DID NOT EAT STONES?

Loons have no teeth and yet they are able to grind up and digest large fish bones. The loon fills its gizzard with small stones that pulverize the bones on the way to the bird's stomach. The gizzard is a strong muscular pocket located between the loon's mouth and stomach.

Because the gizzard must be replenished daily, the loon spends many hours snatching small stones and pebbles from the bottom of a lake. Without an ample supply of stones, the loon would eventually starve.

Winter
Summer
The checked pattern of the loon is created by individual feathers.
Preening
Chicks can fly and become independent by the eleventh week.
Loon chick
Nesting
Adult carrying chick
Loon calling for company before a storm

HOW DO WHITE SQUARES, STRIPES, AND SPOTS SHOW THE MATURITY OF A LOON?

Adults molt twice a year, each time changing their plumage dramatically. During the spring migration, loons wear their breeding plumage, a contrasting black and white. This lasts until late summer, when it is replaced by dull gray. Perfect adult plumage of white squares, stripes, and spots is not attained until three and a half to four years of age.

WHY DOES THE LOON WAVE ITS FEET IN THE AIR?

Loons preen themselves continually so that their feathers are literally sparkling clean. On sunny days, the white breast of the loon is so smooth and clean that it reflects light like a mirror. To preen hard-to-reach feathers, the loon often rolls over on its side with one or both feet waving in the air.

HOW DO LOONS PROVIDE A PORTABLE CRADLE FOR THEIR YOUNG?

Loon chicks take to the water as soon as their down is dry. Parents often carry them on their backs during the first few weeks. The adult submerges and gently rises from underneath the chick with its wings slightly spread to form a cradle. When the "ride" is over, the adult merely dives or tumbles the chick off like a bucking bronco. As the chicks grow, they become more independent and are seldom seen riding after three weeks of age.

HOW DOES A LOON PROTECT ITS YOUNG BY OFFERING TO LAY DOWN ITS OWN LIFE?

Loons abandon their nest with little provocation in the early stages of nesting. However, after the twenty-eight to thirty day incubation period, the parents become very protective. If surprised on the nest, one of the parents will act as a decoy, calling loudly and offering itself as a sacrifice to lure the predator away from the nest.

HOW IS "THE CALL OF THE NORTH" ACTUALLY MADE UP OF FOUR DIFFERENT CALLS?

Loons have four basic calls, each with its own meaning. The powerful wail is a greeting and indicates that a loon wants to meet another loon. It may be calling a mate or a lost chick. The tremolo is a signal of alarm. It is the only call made in flight.

The yodel is made only by the male and is a sign of aggression usually given at the boundaries of a loon's territory. Because no two loons have exactly the same yodel, the yodel gives a particular loon a distinct identity. It becomes his "name." The hoot, or talking call, is a series of one-syllable notes which allows the loon to maintain contact with other members of the small family group.

To the tenderfoot, the tremolo or "laugh" can strike terror in the heart, as it resembles the call of a wolf. However, to a seasoned camper, the call is a reassuring sound of the wilderness.

How is the danger of a person's ability illustrated in Scripture?

When one ruler conquered the world, he praised the gods of gold and silver. The man who conquered this foolish king displayed much greater wisdom. He praised the God of heaven and earth who had predicted his rise to power one hundred and fifty years earlier.

Who was this discerning conqueror who understood that a person's greatest ability is also the point of his greatest vulnerability?

(Pause for a response—see page 17.)

The prudent king pondered over the wrinkled military plans with great interest. The secret blueprints revealed the impregnable design of the mightiest city in the ancient world.

Massive stone walls rose up behind a broad moat that encircled the entire city. The towering parapets that overlooked the fertile valley were able to support patrols of chariots drawn by four horses. Surprisingly, this seemingly impenetrable stone barrier was not the city's greatest strength.

The king's clever general carefully traced the key to his invasion plans with the finger of his war-calloused hand. A victorious smile lit up the confident countenance of the old soldier as he pointed to the river that ran beneath the city gates.

He carefully explained to his sovereign that the city's greatest strength, an unlimited source of water, would provide the necessary point of vulnerability for his invading forces.

As the general's well-disciplined troops neared the ancient stronghold, entire divisions of enemy soldiers surrendered without a fight.

While plans of conquest slowly unfolded outside the walls, the arrogant ruler of the city sponsored a lavish feast to honor his own glorious achievements.

As the drunken king raised a golden goblet to wish himself long life and continued success, foreign soldiers were cleverly diverting the river and providing an underground access for their assault force.

That very night the city fell. The foreign monarch received a liberator's welcome. His spirit of understanding and generous treatment of his new subjects strengthened and unified the kingdom.

Unlike the emperor he had defeated, the wise new ruler recognized that God had given him the victory. With a spirit of gratefulness, he allowed Jewish exiles to return to Jerusalem and rebuild their temple. In return, he requested daily prayer for himself and his sons.

One hundred and fifty years earlier Isaiah had prophesied that this conqueror would one day rule the world and rebuild God's temple.

Thus, with God's help, King Cyrus perceived that Babylon's greatest vulnerability could be found within its greatest strength. With this important insight, he conquered the city without a battle.

From Daniel 5, Isaiah 44:28, Ezra 1:1–2, and the historical accounts of Herodotus and Xenophon.

CYRUS THE GREAT, A CAUTIOUS RULER WHO ASSISTED IN THE REBUILDING OF JERUSALEM

The riches and wealth *of Jerusalem were transported to Babylon when Nebuchadnezzar captured Jerusalem.*

The life and history of Cyrus the Great, founder of the Persian Empire, illustrate the words, "*. . . Promotion cometh neither from the east, nor from the west, nor from the south. But God is the judge: he putteth down one, and setteth up another" (Psalm 75:6–7).*

GOD PREDICTS JUDGMENT THROUGH THE PROPHET ISAIAH

Even before Cyrus' birth, Isaiah prophesied to King Hezekiah that the riches of Judea, which he displayed to a group of Babylonian ambassadors, would someday be carried off to Babylon. (See Isaiah 39.) This was an amazing prophecy, since at that time Babylon was dominated by the Assyrians. But over a century later, Nebuchadnezzar sacked the city of Jerusalem and brought the spoil back to Babylon, as Isaiah foretold. Jerusalem and Judea were left in ruin.

The "Hanging Gardens of Babylon" *probably were built by King Nebuchadnezzar after he married a mountain princess. He apparently hoped the gardens would make her feel at home.*

THE SCENE IS SET FOR THE REIGN OF CYRUS

Isaiah's prophecy contained hope as well as judgment. He actually mentioned Cyrus by name, *"That saith of Cyrus, He is my shepherd . . . even saying to Jerusalem, Thou shalt be built; and to the temple, Thy foundation shall be laid" (Isaiah 44:28)*. Isaiah also predicted that Cyrus would come from the east and declared the fulfillment of this prophecy, proof of Jehovah's unique ability to predict future events. (See Isaiah 46:9–11.)

About eighty years later, the Medes and Babylonians converged on Nineveh, ending Assyria's world dominance. In 605 B.C. Nebuchadnezzar invaded Judea, seized valuables from the Jerusalem temple, and took token hostages. In 597 B.C. Nebuchadnezzar returned to Jerusalem, taking captive the royal family and ten thousand of the leading citizens. Vast treasures were confiscated during this campaign.

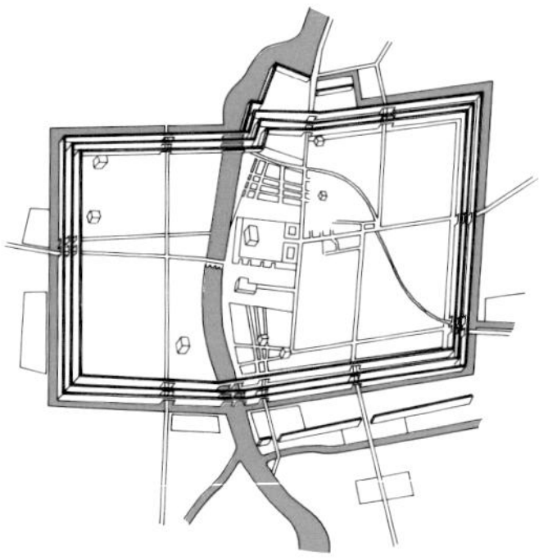

The 200 square mile area of ancient Babylon *was supplied by canals bringing water from the River Tigris, while the River Euphrates, which bisected the city was spanned with bridges.*

THE FALL OF BABYLON

Twenty-seven years after the final destruction of Jerusalem, Cyrus inherited the throne of his father. After unifying the Persian people, he attacked the weak and corrupt king of the Medes. The Median general in command deserted his king and turned his army over to Cyrus rather than fight. Cyrus took the Median capital, Ecbatana, without a battle.

Cyrus succeeded in welding the Medes and Persians into a unified kingdom and swiftly moved west, subduing territories all the way to Asia Minor. In 539 B.C. he turned toward Babylon, the most fortified city in the world. In September, the army attacked and defeated the Babylonians at Opes on the Tigris River.

On October 10, the city of Sippur, just north of Babylon, surrendered to Cyrus without a fight. Within two days Cyrus' troops occupied the impregnable city of Babylon. Ancient records mention that this feat was achieved by diverting the Euphrates River which flowed under the walls. The details, however, are not described. It is possible that Cyrus did not wish to record his strategies for others to imitate.

The famous Cyrus cylinder*, discovered by nineteenth-century archeologists, praises Cyrus for his benevolent treatment of captured people. Ezra 6:3–5 tells how Cyrus allowed captured vessels of gold and silver to be returned to Jerusalem.*

STRATEGY OF A GENEROUS CONQUEROR

Seventeen days after the occupation of the city, Cyrus personally entered Babylon and presented himself as a liberator and benefactor. He allowed transplanted nationalities to return to their homelands. Jews were encouraged to return to Judea and rebuild the temple the Babylonians had destroyed. Cyrus even returned some of the vessels plundered from the temple and provided financial assistance. (See Ezra 6:3–4.) About fifty thousand captives returned home. (See Ezra 2:64–65.)

Cyrus continued to strengthen his empire which survived for over two centuries. In 530 B.C. he was fatally wounded in battle and was buried in the Persian capital Pasargadae. His tomb can be seen today.

CHARACTER SKETCH OF CYRUS THE GREAT

WHY DID GENERALS SURRENDER TO CYRUS RATHER THAN FIGHT?

Cyrus had a reputation for being benevolent to his captives. When the Medes surrendered, he treated them with respect and dignity. They became allies who shared in his future success. He also allowed displaced captives from former administrations to return to their homelands. Cyrus was regarded as a liberator rather than a conqueror.

Cyrus also had a reputation for being a brilliant military strategist. One of his most spectacular victories was against Croesus, the wealthy king of Lydea. When their battle became deadlocked, Croesus retreated to Sardis for the winter. He expected Cyrus to wait until spring before attacking. In the meantime, he planned to add reinforcements from Babylon, Egypt, and Greece.

Instead, Cyrus attacked immediately. Although Croesus had a greatly superior cavalry, Cyrus had the larger army. Cyrus canceled Croesus' strength by placing camels at the head of his procession. When the horses caught scent of the camels, they panicked and became unmanageable. Cyrus routed his enemy and added Croesus' great wealth to his growing empire.

WAS CYRUS' TREATMENT OF CONQUERED NATIONS COMMON IN HIS DAY?

Cyrus reversed the policies of the Assyrian and Babylonian empires. Both of these former world powers had ruled by terror. They believed that by being cruel and even torturing their captives, other nations would not dare to rebel. Another tactic used was the displacing of captives from their homelands to break their national spirit. When Assyria conquered Samaria in 722 B.C., Sargon deported the leading citizens and replaced them with exiles from other territories.

A tactic used by Nebuchadnezzar was to change the names of the captives to encourage them to forget their past loyalties. Daniel's name was changed to Belteshazzar. Daniel must have winced every time someone referred to him as "Bel's Prince" instead of by his given name, "Jehovah's Prince." These policies were reversed when Cyrus came into power. (See Daniel 2:26; 6:20.) It is not surprising that Cyrus' reign was welcomed by many.

IN WHAT WAY DID CYRUS INFLUENCE WORLD HISTORY?

Cyrus' kindness toward conquered peoples was so politically successful that it has been followed by civilized countries up to the present day. Cyrus' Persian successors, the Greeks, and then the Romans, allowed smaller countries under their rule to maintain as much autonomy as was considered to be safe.

Cyrus' pro-Jewish policies were especially helpful to the struggling remnant that returned to Judea. When the temple reconstruction was challenged by local politicians, a decision was requested of Darius the Great. Darius found Cyrus' proclamation concerning the rebuilding of the temple. As a result, he allowed the construction to continue and even commanded the Jews' enemies to provide financial assistance. (See Ezra 6:1–12.)

Continuing this policy, in 458 B.C. Artaxerxes I allowed Ezra to return to Jerusalem with a contingent of fellow Jews to help rebuild the temple. In 445 B.C. he allowed Nehemiah to return and fortify the defenses of the city. (See Nehemiah 2:1–8.)

A reconstruction of *the Ishtar Gate of Babylon is adorned with enameled brickwork depicting 575 dragons and bulls. The double tower was forty feet high.*

CYRUS
sī-rəs

CHAPTER THREE

Cautiousness

. . . Is remembering that greed crouches at the door of every heart

"And he said unto them, Take heed, and beware of covetousness: for a man's life consisteth not in the abundance of the things which he possesseth."

Luke 12:15

Living Lessons on Cautiousness . . .

FROM THE PAGES OF SCRIPTURE

The Scriptures clearly warn that a person should be cautious when eating a meal at the table of a rich man. Ironically, the one who penned the words of this caution was the son of a prosperous ruler who sponsored such a dinner.

Because an unsuspecting guest failed to exercise cautiousness and recognize the warning signals of greed, he forfeited his life. His experience lives on as a vivid illustration of the fact that no heart is immune to the subtleties of greed.

ILLUSTRATED IN THE WORLD OF NATURE

OCTOPUS *Octopus vulgaris*

The 135 species of octopus that belong to the shellfish family vary greatly in size and habitat. Some octopods never grow any larger than a few inches. Other species grow to be more than twenty-five feet from arm tip to arm tip.

All octopods have eight arms radiating from a central body. Each arm is lined with two rows of suckers which can grip tightly to almost any surface.

The common octopus lives on the bottom of shallow coastal shores, but other species live in the ocean depths. Octopods sleep most of the day in small caves or under ledges and hunt at night.

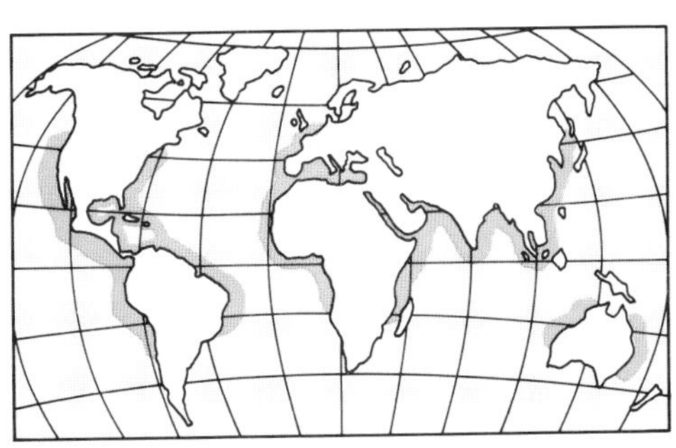

The range and habitat of the octopus

How is the insatiable appetite of greed illustrated in the world of nature?

It was a baffling mystery. How could a sixteen-inch long octopus escape from a tightly locked retaining tank?

The janitor watched through the glass as the slippery escape artist skimmed along the sandy bottom of its tank. He remembered the excitement that the strange-looking creature had caused when it first arrived at the metropolitan aquarium.

He recalled the children's beaming faces as they anxiously pressed their noses against the fogged-over glass to get the first look at the new resident. After what seemed like an endless wait, one of the marine biologists deposited the slimy mass of squirming tentacles into the display tank.

Once inside its new glass home, the octopus began to flex its powerful tentacles. The boys and girls giggled with delight as they stood on tiptoe and carefully followed every movement of the amazing animal.

That night, under the cover of darkness, the octopus pulled itself up over the edge of its tank and slid into the adjacent tank filled with a rare species of lobster. Dozens of tiny suction cups soon began to pull one of the unsuspecting victims toward the octopus' venomous beak. Even before paralyzing its helpless prey, the slimy intruder had already begun to enjoy its meal through tiny taste buds located along the rims of its tentacles.

The next morning the janitor decided to check on the octopus. "After all, he is a new tenant," he whispered to himself in an attempt to justify his boyish curiosity.

As he entered the saltwater display area, he suddenly realized that the octopus was gone! Hurrying off to notify the curator, he caught a glimpse of a vague form out of the corner of his eye. There was the octopus, greedily hovering over three dead lobsters.

Greatly disturbed by the loss of their valuable specimens, aquarium officials decided to place the octopus into a smaller, metal retaining cage. The stainless steel cage was designed to allow the oxygen-rich water to flow freely through the enclosure. With the eight-legged poacher securely locked away, the janitor confidently went home for the evening.

Early the next morning, he rose and hurried off to work. He could not believe his eyes! The octopus had escaped again. To make matters worse, he noticed another dead lobster partially concealed in the corner of the tank.

After carefully checking every hinge and seam, the frustrated curator coaxed the octopus back into its cell and firmly locked the lid.

That night the mystery was solved. Determined to unravel the underwater puzzle, the janitor decided to spend the night at the aquarium. In the shadows of a dimly-lit exit sign the amateur detective witnessed an amazing escape. Slowly, the octopus threaded itself through one of the half-inch holes in the metal cage.

Like a greedy man, the octopus had taken advantage of even the smallest opportunity to satisfy its insatiable appetite.

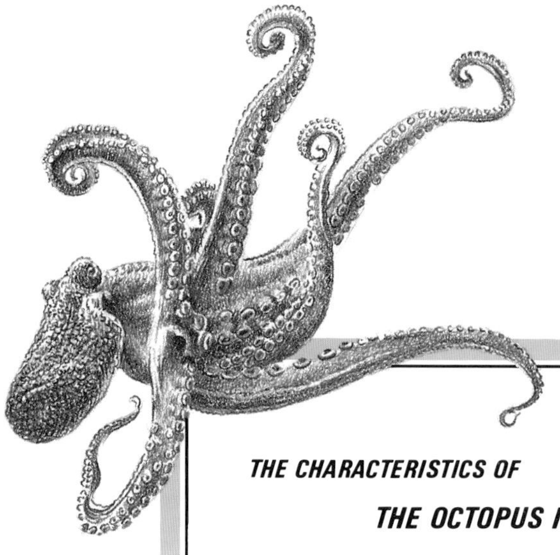

THE CHARACTERISTICS OF

THE OCTOPUS IN SCRIPTURE

The unusual ability of the octopus to thread itself through a small opening to satisfy its own appetite bears a striking resemblance to evil men who can slip into families and capture the affections of immature or guilt-ridden young women.

"For of this sort are they which creep into houses, and lead captive silly women laden with sins, led away with divers lusts" (II Timothy 3:6).

The octopus is one of the "creeping" things of the sea listed in Psalm 104:25. *"So is this great and wide sea, wherein are things creeping innumerable, both small and great beasts."*

Some of the strongest warnings in the Levitical law were against "creeping things". *"Whatsoever goeth upon the belly . . . or whatsoever hath more feet among all creeping things that creep upon the earth, them ye shall not eat; for they are an abomination" (Leviticus 11:42).*

Creeping things are consistently associated with that which is evil. (See Ezekiel 8:10; Acts 10:12.) The quiet stealth of the octopus is therefore also a picture of how wicked men creep into churches for evil purposes.

"For there are certain men crept in unawares, who were before of old ordained to this condemnation, ungodly men, turning the grace of our God into lasciviousness . . ." (Jude 4).

The life-sapping tentacles of the octopus are also a picture of the entanglements of life which Christians are to avoid. (See II Timothy 2:4.)

CHARACTERISTICS AND PHYSICAL FEATURES OF THE OCTOPUS

The constant vigilance of the female octopus results in the successful incubation of her young, but at the cost of her life. The price of her unrelenting concern for her eggs is the disregard for her own needs. By yielding her own rights to food and shelter, she is able to adequately care for and protect her young.

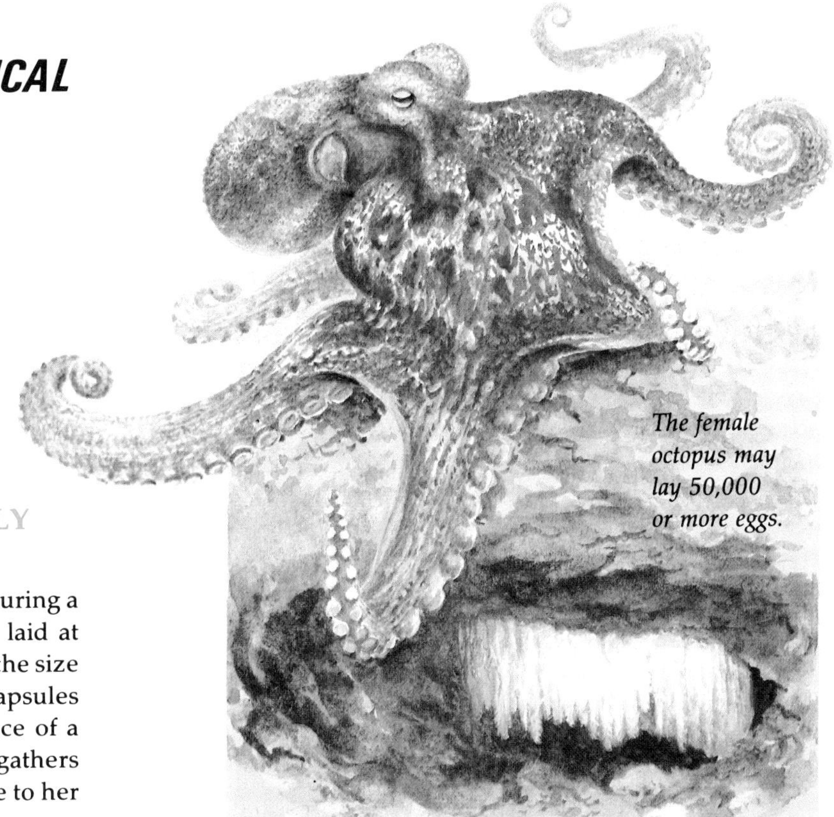

The female octopus may lay 50,000 or more eggs.

HOW COULD ONE OCTOPUS MULTIPLY TO 50,000 IN TEN DAYS?

A female octopus may lay up to 50,000 eggs during a period of seven to ten days. The eggs are always laid at night. Each one is encased in an oval capsule about the size of a piece of rice. As soon as the eggs are laid, the capsules are hung in grape-like clusters around the entrance of a cave or under a ledge. Occasionally, an octopus gathers rocks with which she can quickly block the entrance to her nest if threatened.

Single eggs are combined to form grapelike clusters, and the eggs are hung from the roof of a cave or under a ledge.

Erecting a stone wall defense

HOW DOES AN OCTOPUS VACUUM AND SPRAY-CLEAN ITS EGGS?

An incubating female octopus is very particular about keeping her eggs clean. By rubbing her sucker-covered arms over the eggs, she removes any dirt particles or small marine creatures that might settle on them. Each sucker acts as a tiny vacuum cleaner.

After vacuuming, the female octopus rinses off the eggs with a jet of water squirted through a funnel under her body. During incubation, she is very territorial and possessive of her nest, allowing no other octopus to approach without a challenge.

Female cleansing eggs

HOW IS THE BIRTH OF AN OCTOPUS LIKE THE FOURTH OF JULY?

Octopus eggs hatch eight to ten weeks after being fertilized, depending on the temperature of the water. As the tiny embryo begins the struggle to escape from its shell, it explodes with different colors. Color sacs in the skin flash from orange to red to yellow to blue and a dozen shades in between. The harder the tiny octopus struggles, the more it sparkles. Thus, the young octopod's colorful struggle for independence is like a Fourth of July celebration.

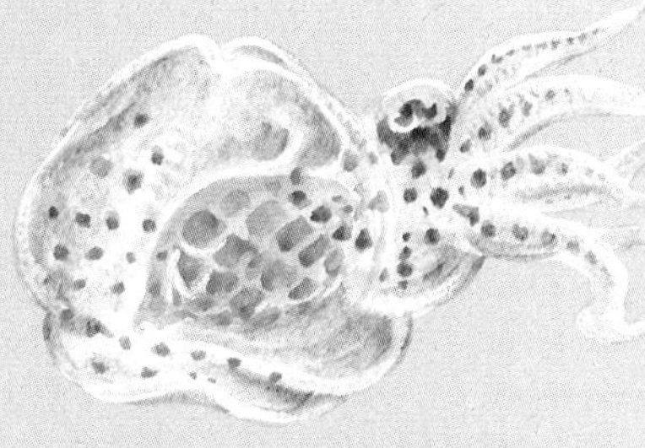

After six weeks of constant care, the young struggle free.

HOW DO WHISKERS BECOME WARTS ON THE OCTOPUS?

Young octopods are covered with small whiskers that are sensitive to touch and probably serve to tell the direction of water currents. As the octopus grows, a small wart develops at the base of each whisker. Eventually, a rough, pebbly skin covers the entire body of the mature octopus.

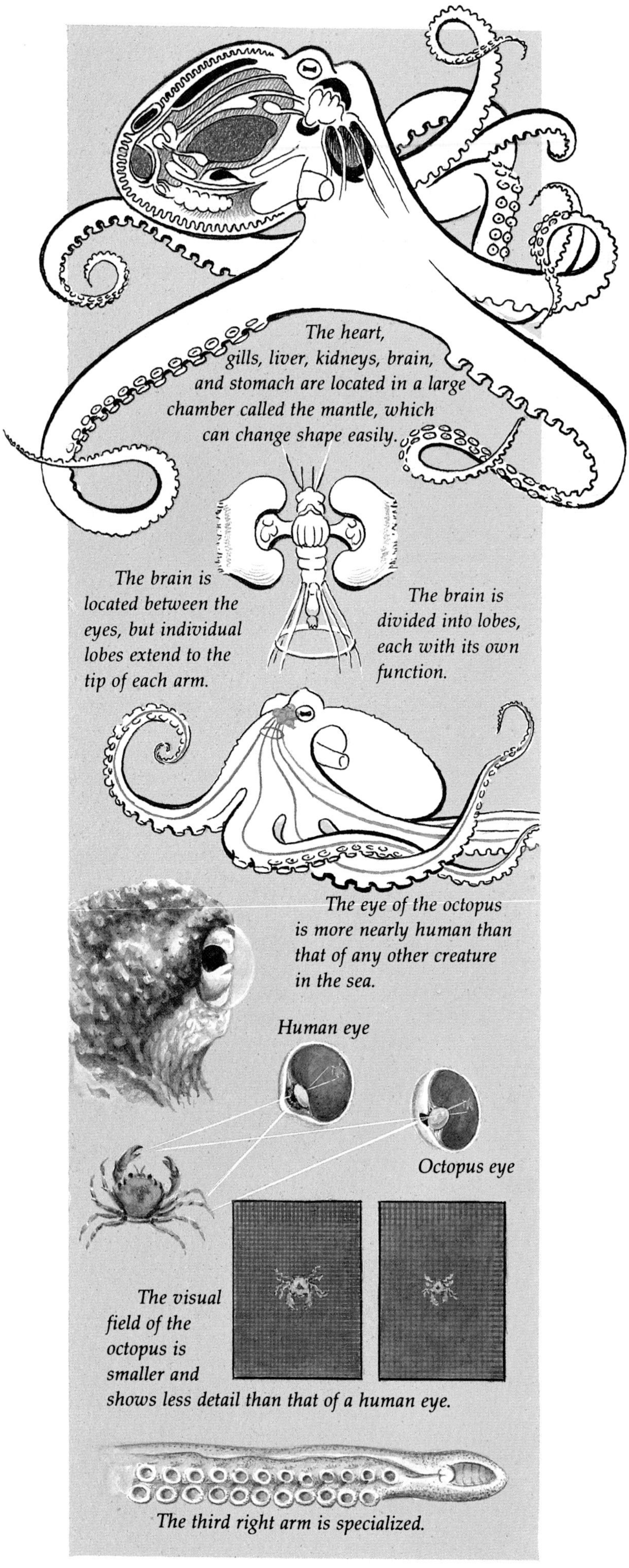

The heart, gills, liver, kidneys, brain, and stomach are located in a large chamber called the mantle, which can change shape easily.
The brain is located between the eyes, but individual lobes extend to the tip of each arm.
The brain is divided into lobes, each with its own function.
The eye of the octopus is more nearly human than that of any other creature in the sea.
Human eye
Octopus eye
The visual field of the octopus is smaller and shows less detail than that of a human eye.
The third right arm is specialized.

HOW CAN A SIXTY POUND OCTOPUS GO THROUGH A TWO INCH OPENING?

An octopus has no bones. Except for the hard beak at the mouth, its body is soft and baggy. All it needs for an escape is a crack large enough to let its beak slip through. The rest of the body, including the stomach and other organs that are contained in the dome-shaped head, is so soft that it can be flattened almost paper thin. A sixty-pound octopus can creep through a two-inch hole. An octopus was observed squeezing its sixteen-inch-long body through a half-inch hole in an aquarium.

HOW CAN AN OCTOPUS BE FRIGHTENED TO DEATH?

The octopus has been found to be one of the most sensitive of all invertebrates. It has a delicate nervous system that requires regular periods of sleep, such as our own human nervous system. Because this system is so sensitive, the octopus can actually be scared to death if treated roughly.

An octopus can be easily trained to discriminate between different shapes and colors, although it can only remember this information for a few days. Its brain is divided into fourteen distinct sections or lobes. There is one lobe for each of its eight arms, one lobe for sight, one lobe for touch, and one lobe each for the control of blood flow, color changes, escape mechanisms, and memory.

WHY WILL OCTOPODS ALWAYS HAVE EIGHT ARMS EVEN IF ONE IS CUT OFF?

The common octopus always has eight arms or tentacles. If one is injured or severed, it can be regrown in a short time. Since blood flow is controlled by the brain, an injury can be quickly sealed to limit bleeding. Because each arm has its own nervous system, a severed arm may move away from the body and still appear to be under the control of the octopus.

WHY DO THE EYES OF THE OCTOPUS STRIKE FEAR IN PEOPLE?

The octopus is sometimes called the devilfish because of its soulful eyes. These eyes appear more nearly human than those of any other creature in the sea in that they are capable of showing such emotions as gentleness, rage, and affection. A person's reaction to seeing such expressive eyes in such a grotesque body is usually one of fear.

HOW DOES THE OCTOPUS EYE DIFFER FROM THE HUMAN EYE?

The pupil of the octopus eye is rectangular rather than round. The eye itself has two protective coats, while the human eye has one. The image formed in the octopus eye is made by moving the entire lens instead of simply changing the shape of the lens, as is done in the human eye. Finally, because the octopus eye has fewer light receptors, it sees much less detail than can the human eye.

HOW DOES AN OCTOPUS TASTE ITS FOOD?

An octopus actually tastes its food with its arms. Both the smell and taste organs are located around the lips of the suckers on the arms. An octopus can actually seize a lobster and taste it before eating it.

HOW MANY SUCKERS ARE ON EACH ARM?

Each arm, or tentacle, contains a double row of up to 240 suckers. The suckers range in size from mere pinheads to ones that are two and one-half inches in diameter. The larger ones can exert a pull of up to twenty pounds each. Because the suckers can lose their gripping strength when the linings become rough or worn, octopods regularly rub their arms together by coiling and uncoiling them rapidly. This removes the old skin and allows it to be replaced with a new smooth lining.

DO OCTOPODS ATTACK PEOPLE?

While octopods are formidable hunters with the combined grip of their arms exceeding 2,000 pounds, they are quite shy and retiring around humans. However, when frightened without a means of escape, they will attach themselves to the closest solid object. If that object happens to be a diver, the diver may find himself in a terrifying grip. Experienced divers do not panic when surprised by an octopus, but simply hug, stroke, and pat the creature until, assured that it is not being threatened, it releases its grip.

CAN OCTOPODS POISON PEOPLE?

Octopods produce a very potent venom in their salivary glands. The poison is literally spit into a wound made by the powerful beak and paralyzes the victim within a minute or two. While the venom is lethal to crabs, lobsters, and eels, it has little effect other than a slight burning sensation on humans. Because an octopus must bring its prey up against its body in order to bite, bites against humans are extremely rare.

HOW DOES THE OCTOPUS EMPLOY JET PROPULSION?

The octopus propels itself in three distinct ways:

Crawling: The octopus seems to flow over rocks like a thick syrup. One arm after another glides forward to take a firm hold on a rock. As the octopus pulls its large body forward, rear legs release their grips and begin to search for other holds. It is amazing that an octopus never trips over itself. All eight arms work in coordination with each other, thereby giving the octopus a very graceful appearance.

Swimming: The octopus swims with a pulsating wave motion of all eight arms together. The arms are drawn up beside the body and then thrust out and down like whips.

Jet Propulsion: This method is by far the most spectacular method of transportation for the octopus. Behind the head, the octopus has a collar of skin and muscle called a mantle. Between this mantle and the body is a cavity into which the octopus can draw water and then lock it in. When the octopus needs to move quickly, it can shoot out a jet of water through a small funnel under its body. The reaction of the jet of water against the ocean forces the octopus backwards with its arms trailing.

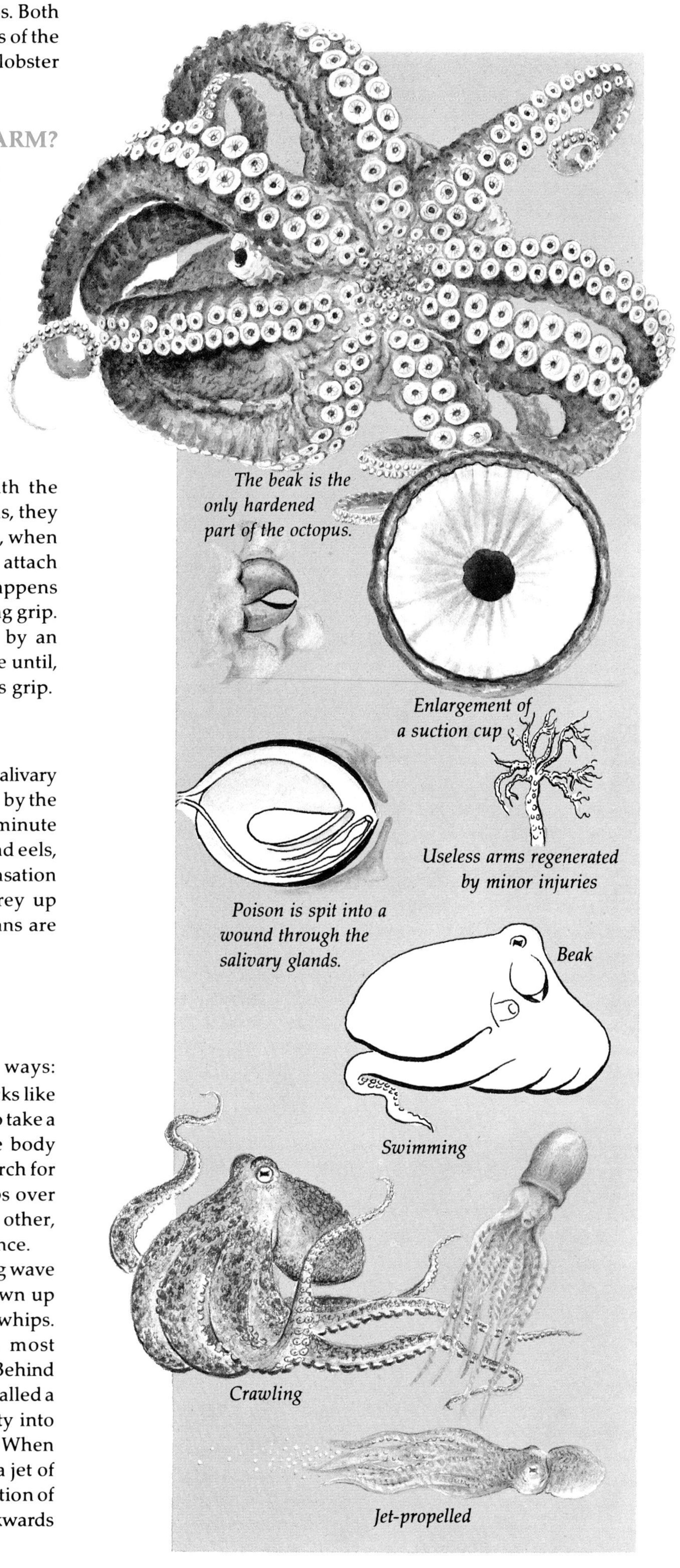

The beak is the only hardened part of the octopus.
Enlargement of a suction cup
Useless arms regenerated by minor injuries
Poison is spit into a wound through the salivary glands.
Beak
Swimming
Crawling
Jet-propelled

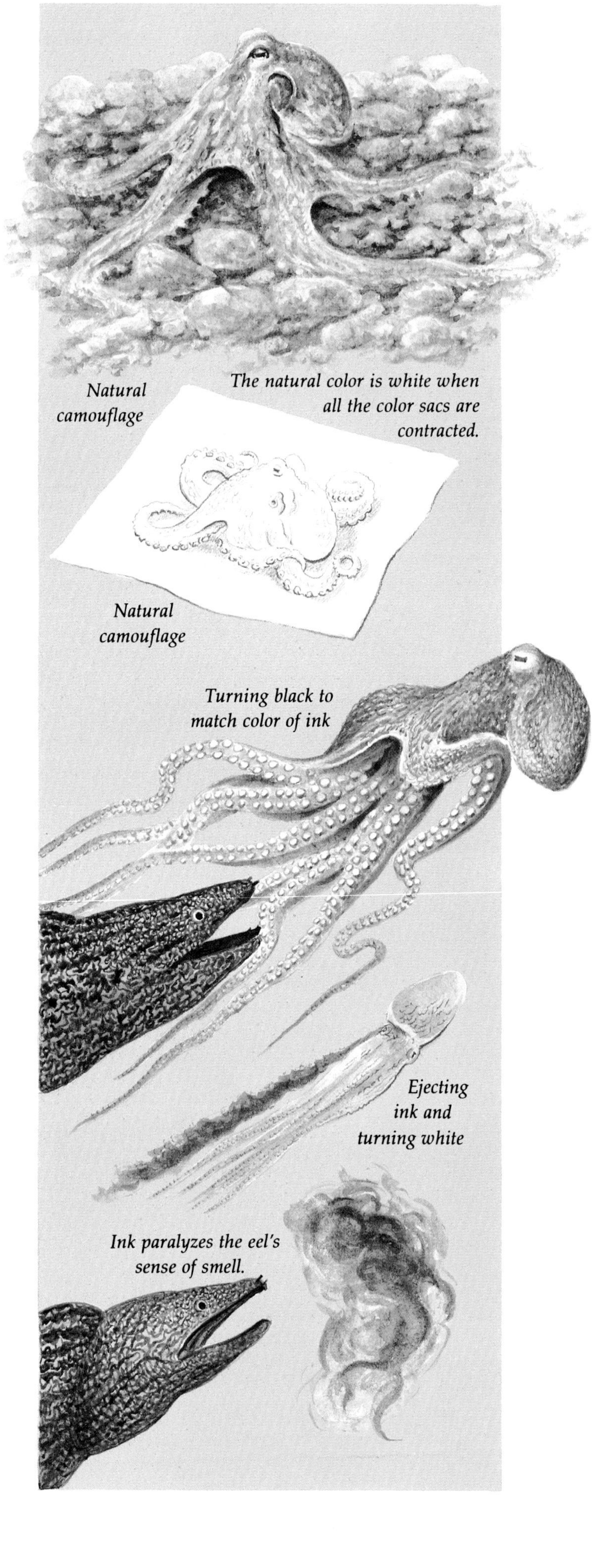
Natural camouflage
The natural color is white when all the color sacs are contracted.
Natural camouflage
Turning black to match color of ink
Ejecting ink and turning white
Ink paralyzes the eel's sense of smell.

HOW CAN OCTOPODS TURN RED, GREEN, OR WHITE WITH STRIPES OR POLKA DOTS?

Contained in three distinct layers in the skin are remarkable elastic sacs of red, yellow, and blue coloring. The octopus can enlarge each sac to sixty times its original size. An adult octopus may have as many as 2,000,000 of these tiny spots of color spread over its entire body. By shrinking some sacs and stretching others, an octopus can change color almost instantly.

When frightened, all the sacs shrink and the octopus pales to white. When enraged or excited, the octopus opens only the red sacs and turns its whole body red. When hiding among seaweed, it can turn green by mixing blue and yellow. When crawling on a gravel-bottom ocean floor, it turns to a salt and pepper color.

Octopods have even created stripes and polka dots when tested on experimental backgrounds. This ability to camouflage itself aids the octopus in hunting for food and hiding from enemies.

HOW DOES AN OCTOPUS USE AN ILLUSION TO ESCAPE FROM ITS ENEMIES?

The greatest enemy of the octopus is the moray eel. The eel can poke its snakelike head into the tiny cave where the octopus sleeps during the day. If the octopus is too big to be swallowed whole, a moray will wrap itself around and around a single arm until it is severed.

To defend itself against the eel and other enemies, the octopus uses an inky black fluid which it stores in its body. When attacked, the octopus uses its color sacs to turn black to match the color of the ink. He then ejects the right amount of ink to match the size and shape of his own body. With the eel's attention diverted by the black fluid, the octopus turns to white and jets away to safety.

The ink also temporarily paralyzes the eel's sense of smell. A sprayed eel may grope around for hours and may even harmlessly bump into the same octopus that sprayed it.

HOW DO MALE OCTOPODS FLEX THEIR MUSCLES FOR FEMALES?

The male octopus has especially large suckers on its second pair of arms. To gain the attention of females, the male flexes these large suckers in a display of masculinity.

The third right arm of the male is equipped with a groove that runs from the body to the end of the arm where it culminates in a spade-like tip. With this arm the male is able to transfer its seed to the female during the mating process. If the tip is accidentally severed during this time, it continues to live inside the female for several days, thus ensuring the fertilization of the eggs.

How is the need to be cautious about greed illustrated in Scripture?

A banquet was once prepared by a ruler who had fallen into the bondage of greed. By failing to detect the warning signals of that greed, his unsuspecting guest left the feast carrying his own death warrant. Who was the guest?

(Pause for a response—see page 17.)

Somewhat confused, the courageous captain pondered his unusual orders. According to the urgent message, officially stamped with the royal seal, he was to withdraw from the battle front and immediately report to the king.

After arriving at the palace, he received a royal welcome and praise for his valor in battle. In return for his faithful service and loyalty, the king insisted that he enjoy a well-deserved leave with his wife.

Momentarily tempted by the pleasant thoughts of his home, he quickly concluded how inappropriate it would be to remain at home while his men suffered the hardships of war. The king was an experienced warrior and surely would understand the polite refusal of his gracious offer.

The next evening the king sponsored a lavish banquet to honor the presence of the devoted officer. The courageous captain was ceremoniously escorted to a place of prominence at the king's table. His considerate host showered him with attention and encouraged him to eat and drink to his heart's content.

Once again the captain failed to properly evaluate the unusual amount of regal recognition.

The following morning, the king instructed the anxious soldier to return to the battle and deliver an important communication to his general. Thus, with his own death warrant, he began his final journey back to the battlefield.

A few days later, the faithful captain was ordered to lead his men to the front of the battle. His squadron fought valiantly and soon approached the gates of the city. High above the battlefield, an enemy archer took careful aim and fatally pierced the captain's heart. The general quickly dispatched a messenger to inform the greedy king that his instructions had been faithfully fulfilled.

Years later the king's son penned these words. *"Eat thou not the bread of him that hath an evil eye. . . . Eat and drink, saith he to thee; but his heart is not with thee" (Proverbs 23:6–7).*

These words could have very well referred to King David and the fateful meal that spring evening. Solomon observed what captain Uriah had failed to realize. The sinful nature of man necessitates a constant caution to the signs of greed.

From II Samuel 11

URIAH, A SOLDIER WHO HELPED DAVID BECOME A KING

***A Hittite warrior** typically wore a curled beard, coiled hair, a peaked cap, a tight-fitting coat with half-length sleeves, braided kilt, and pointed shoes.*

David was a fugitive in Israel, slandered and persecuted by King Saul as a usurper to the throne. He took refuge in a cave where his family joined him. *"And every one that was in distress, and every one that was in debt, and every one that was discontented, gathered themselves unto him; and he became a captain over them: and there were with him about four hundred men" (I Samuel 22:2).*

The "distressed" were persecuted by Saul because of their loyalty to David. The "debtors" were oppressed by creditors allowed to violate the laws of loan and interest under Saul's misrule. The "discontent" were those who perceived the steady decline of Saul's and the nation's spiritual condition. They recognized in David their hope for better things. The band of four hundred soon grew to about six hundred and remained with David throughout his career. (See I Samuel 23:13; 25:13; 27:2; 30:9–24; II Samuel 15:18.)

A DISTINGUISHED SOLDIER AND ONE OF "THE THIRTY"

Among the elite members of this group was Uriah, a Hittite. He is listed as one of "The Thirty," who were renowned throughout Israel for their courage, military skill, and leadership ability. It was not common for a foreigner to marry an Israelite, but Eliam, another member of "The Thirty," considered Uriah worthy of his beautiful daughter, Bathsheba. (See II Samuel 11:3; 23:34, 39.)

The events which led to Uriah's tragic death began after David was securely established on the throne. The Ammonites had interrupted a time of peace by rebelling against David. In response, he sent his general, Joab, and the army to squelch the revolt.

Joab routed the Syrian allies of the Ammonites, causing the Ammonites to retreat to their fortified capital, Rabbah. He then ordered the army home to wait out the winter rains. The following spring, David sent Joab and the army back to battle.

***While Uriah was fighting David's battle**, David stayed home to enjoy personal ease. There, he faced an unexpected battle with temptation and suffered a tragic defeat.*

A TRAGIC SIN, A MISCALCULATION, AND A DESPERATE PLOT

While Uriah participated in the siege of Rabbah, David committed adultery with Uriah's wife in Jerusalem. In an attempt to conceal his sin, David asked Joab to send Uriah to him with a field report. After hearing the report, David urged Uriah to spend the night with his wife. Instead, Uriah spent the night with the palace guard. After Uriah spent the following night in the same manner, David changed his plan of deception to a plot of murder. Uriah was ordered back to Joab carrying his own death warrant.

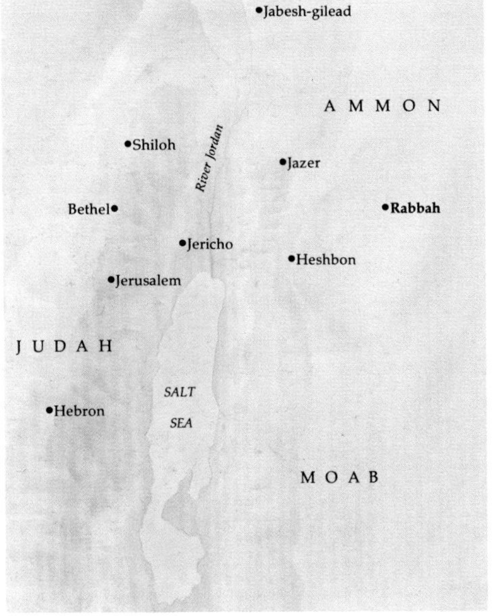

***Uriah was sent from the battle at Rabbah** to meet with King David at Jerusalem.*

MURDER AT THE KING'S COMMAND

According to David's instructions, Joab positioned Uriah and his command at a location where opposition would be the strongest. While the bulk of the Israeli army fought some distance away, the mighty men of Rabbah answered the challenge of Uriah and his men. Engaged in hand-to-hand combat, Uriah and his men almost succeeded in pushing the Ammonites back through their own gate. Joab had given orders to all but Uriah to retreat if they got too close to the city wall. With their enemy now within bowshot of the wall, archers struck and killed Uriah and some of his men.

David's devious scheme was a costly one. He murdered a skillful soldier and valuable leader. Innocent companions of Uriah were needlessly sacrificed. Joab's credibility and respect as a field general were compromised. The morale of the entire army was weakened, and the Ammonites were given occasion to mock the God of Israel.

CHARACTER SKETCH OF URIAH THE HITTITE

WHY WOULD A HITTITE SERVE IN THE ARMY OF JEHOVAH?

Nothing in the Hittite culture would encourage its sons or daughters to worship the true God of Israel. Esau's Hittite wives were a source of grief to his parents. (See Genesis 27:46.) In the time of Moses and Joshua, the Hittites had become so perverse that the Lord wanted them completely removed from the face of the earth. (See Deuteronomy 7:1–5; Judges 3:5–7.) The culture was spiritually blind, having rejected the light previously given to them.

Uriah was one of those outstanding Gentiles in the Old Testament who recognized the God of Israel as the only true God. Along with Rahab of Jericho and Ruth of Moab, Uriah the Hittite was one of the first fruits of the promise given to Abraham, *". . . and in thee shall all families of the earth be blessed" (Genesis 12:3).*

The prophet Isaiah proclaimed that one of Israel's purposes was to be *". . . a light to the Gentiles, that thou mayest be my salvation unto the end of the earth" (Isaiah 49:6).* Uriah saw the light and received it. His Hebrew name *Uriah* means literally, "Jehovah is my light."

WHY DID URIAH NOT GO HOME TO HIS WIFE?

Uriah was not just a common soldier—he was one of "The Thirty." Military service was his life, and he knew the importance of remaining available for duty. As the commanding officer of other soldiers, it was vital for him to be ready at a moment's notice. The situation at Rabbah, where civilian forces supplemented the professional forces, gave Uriah an even greater responsibility. How could he, a captain and a professional, spend an evening at home when the entire army was at war?

Uriah was also aware of specific laws concerning military camps. Because the Lord Himself was fighting in behalf of Israel, He had established laws to remind the men of His presence. Spending the evening with Bathsheba would have made him ritually unclean and ineligible for service until the following evening. (See Deuteronomy 23:9–14; Leviticus 15:16; I Samuel 21:5.)

As a cautious and vigilant soldier, Uriah sacrificed his own personal pleasure in order to be available to his commanding officer during a time of war.

WAS URIAH'S SACRIFICE IN VAIN?

The life and death of Uriah did further the spiritual safety and welfare of his country. After Uriah's death, David married Bathsheba. He thought he had concealed his sin; but the Lord, who alone knew all that had happened, sent the prophet Nathan to rebuke David. Nathan likened the faithful Uriah to a poor man who owned one beloved lamb. He likened David to a cruel, rich man who butchered the poor man's lamb to feed a mere stranger.

When David reflected on Uriah's life and character, his conscience was stricken and he came to his senses. He cried out to the Lord for forgiveness and begged for restoration. David's intimate prayer for cleansing is recorded in Psalm 51.

Uriah lost his life but not his good name, a most valuable possession which no one can ever take away. (See Proverbs 22:1.) He is even mentioned in connection with the listing of Christ's ancestors, along with the two other Gentiles in the geneology—Rahab and Ruth. (See Matthew 1:5–6.)

***David was brought to conviction and repentance** when the prophet Nathan compared Uriah and his wife to a shepherd and his pet lamb.*

URIAH
u-rī-ə

CHAPTER FOUR

Cautiousness

. . . Is recognizing that the majority is often wrong

"Enter ye in at the strait gate: for wide is the gate, and broad is the way, that leadeth to destruction, and many there be which go in thereat: Because strait is the gate, and narrow is the way, which leadeth unto life, and few there be that find it."

Matthew 7:13–14

Living Lessons on Cautiousness . . .

FROM THE PAGES OF SCRIPTURE

The fact that the majority is usually wrong was painfully clear to a courageous leader in the nation of Israel. He boldly spoke out for the minority at a crucial time in the history of the chosen people. The majority ignored his counsel and rejected his warnings. Too late to escape the judgment of God, they realized that their cautious leader had been correct.

Because he had acknowledged wise counsel and carefully examined every warning, God granted him added years. He also received exceptional strength and an unusual vitality that enabled him to conquer a foreign kingdom and establish a lasting heritage for his descendants.

ILLUSTRATED IN THE WORLD OF NATURE

RED SQUIRREL *Tamiasciurus hudsonicus*

The red squirrel is known by a number of other common names: chickaree, boomer, barking squirrel, pine squirrel, rusty squirrel, red robber, egg-eater, chatterbox, and adjudaumo, an Indian name meaning "tail-in-the-air."

The red squirrel lives a solitary life. Seven years is old for him, although some red squirrels have lived up to ten years in captivity. Litters of three to eight are born after a brief gestation period of thirty-eight days. The young are born blind, pink, and hairless. They leave the nest for the first time during their seventh week. The red squirrel does not hibernate but remains active in even the coldest weather.

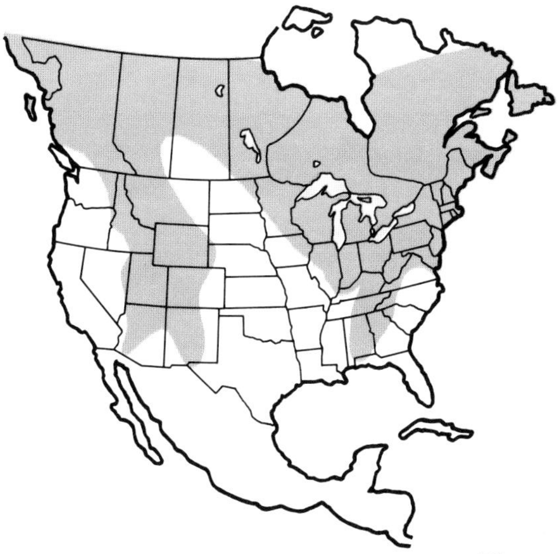

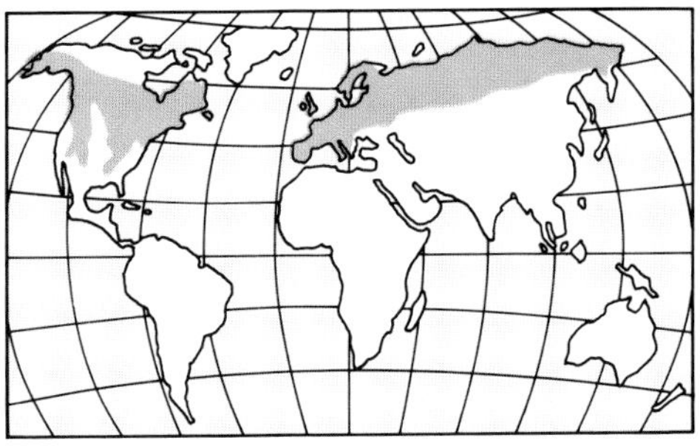

The range and habitat of the red squirrel

How is a mistaken majority illustrated in the world of nature?

With a single springlike vault a tiny red blur catapulted out of the fluffy white snow drift. Securing its sharp claws in the rugged pine bark, the vigilant sentry quickly scampered upward to his treetop outpost.

From his favorite branch, the furry watchman scanned the forest below. Always prepared to scold an unwelcome intruder, the energetic sentinel often shattered the wilderness with warnings of danger.

Far below the majestic pines, a large family of porcupines clumsily plodded through the freshly fallen snow. As they slowly passed through the forest, the red squirrel's tail suddenly stiffened with apprehension.

The squirrel had spotted the sleek brown fur of a hungry fisher as it glistened in the winter sun. The ability to digest the razorlike quills made porcupine meat a popular delicacy on the fisher's forest menu.

As the clever fisher neared the unsuspecting porcupines, it vanished into the snow. The fisher had marked their position and quietly began to tunnel toward the porcupines. In an attempt to warn the other animals, the red squirrel erupted into a frenzy of foot stomping and tail jerking accompanied by a shrill series of vocal alarms.

Ignoring the frantic warnings, the porcupines confidently continued their unhurried journey. They could have easily climbed the tree and avoided danger. However, they were confident that no predator would attack their well-protected hides.

As the fisher approached its unsuspecting victims, the warnings of the red squirrel intensified. The porcupines paused momentarily and glanced at the noisy chatterbox with an air of indignation.

With blinding speed, the fisher lunged from its snow tunnel, viciously tearing into the underbelly of one of the porcupines.

The red squirrel watched the fisher as he licked his paws in a moment of satisfied contentment. The blood-stained snow bank provided a sober reminder to other creatures of the fate of one that had chosen to listen to a wrong majority instead of the solitary voice of caution and warning.

THE CHARACTERISTICS OF

THE RED SQUIRREL IN SCRIPTURE

The red squirrel vividly illustrates alertness to danger in the world of nature. He faithfully fulfills his duties as the "watchman of the woods." Names like boomer, barking squirrel, and chatterbox accurately describe this furry little sentry.

The silent dogs mentioned in Isaiah 56:9–11 provide a sharp contrast to the red squirrel.

"All ye beasts of the field, come to devour, yea, all ye beasts in the forest. His watchmen are blind: they are all ignorant, they are all dumb dogs, they cannot bark; sleeping, lying down, loving to slumber. . . . They all look to their own way, every one for his gain. . . ."

The alertness of the red squirrel and its ability to sound a noisy alarm fulfill the requirements God had established for the watchmen of Jerusalem.

"I have set watchmen upon thy walls, O Jerusalem, which shall never hold their peace day nor night . . ." (Isaiah 62:6).

The need to warn non-Christians is the responsibility of every Christian.

"When I say unto the wicked, O wicked man, thou shalt surely die; if thou dost not speak to warn the wicked from his way, that wicked man shall die in his iniquity; but his blood will I require at thine hand" (Ezekiel 33:8). (See also Ezekiel 3:18.)

CHARACTERISTICS AND PHYSICAL FEATURES OF THE RED SQUIRREL

The red squirrel has many enemies. It is pursued by the bobcat, lynx, mink, weasel, hawk, owl, and even by large fish, such as the muskie and pike. With so many enemies, it must be cautious and ever alert to the presence of danger.

Because its reaction to any possible intruder is so vocal, the squirrel serves as an alarm for many other forest creatures. At the sound of the red squirrel's signal, every ear within a quarter of a mile is alerted to the presence of danger.

HOW DO SUGAR AND CONES GET INTO THE RED SQUIRREL'S DIET?

The red squirrel eats almost every kind of food, although it is mostly an eater of pine cones. A single squirrel may consume over one hundred pounds of nearly all kinds of seeds, fruits, berries, cones, nuts, and insects each year. Even mushrooms, including varieties that are poisonous to man, are a part of the red squirrel's diet. In spring, the red squirrel may become carnivorous and feed on bird eggs and the newly hatched young.

The red squirrel's favorite snack is the sap that flows in maple and birch trees in early spring. If there is no natural source of this sugary liquid through a break in the tree bark, the squirrel chews a small, saucerlike hole in the top of a branch. As the hole fills with the sweet sap, the squirrel gently laps it up.

WHY IS THE RED SQUIRREL CALLED THE JOHNNY APPLESEED OF PINE TREES?

The red squirrel's habit of burying seeds in the ground as a method of storage results in the planting of many pine trees. The red squirrel classifies the things that it stores into two categories: hard and soft. The hard items, such as nuts and seeds, are either buried or carried away to a storage hoard. Soft items such as fruits, berries, and mushrooms are arranged in a tree fork or on a hollow limb to dry.

Each fall, the red squirrel stores more food than it will need. Thus, each spring the excess seeds and nuts germinate in the warm soil and provide a new crop of trees.

ARE RED SQUIRRELS RIGHT-HANDED OR LEFT-HANDED?

Red squirrels use both forepaws equally well to hold nuts and acorns while they eat. However, they do not use either paw to carry objects. Everything is picked up with the teeth and carried in the mouth.

Mushrooms are often stored in the forks of trees to dry.

Strawberries are only a small part of the 100 pounds of food that a red squirrel consumes in a year.

Licking maple sap from a broken branch

An average squirrel will collect ten bushels of nuts and pine cones.

***Middens are food stockpiles** which the red squirrel builds during times when food is plentiful.*

__The summer coat of both__ the male and female red squirrel is characterized by a black line about three inches long which separates the body's snuff brown upper half from the white underparts. The winter coat is much brighter in color, and the black lateral line is hardly visible.

The squirrel's tail provides shade and insulation, and serves as a signal flag, parachute, balance pole, and a rudder.

HOW CAN A RED SQUIRREL FALL WITHOUT INJURY?

A fall usually does not even knock the wind out of a red squirrel. When falling, the squirrel twists like a cat until it is horizontal. The tail and all four legs are spread to catch as much air as possible. This slows the fall and distributes the impact evenly over the squirrel's body. Falls of over 100 feet have been survived without injury.

WHY DO THE TEETH OF RED SQUIRRELS WIGGLE?

Red squirrels can wiggle their noses, their ears, and even their teeth. A peculiar characteristic of the red squirrel's lower jaw is the ability of the bottom front incisors to move sideways. The teeth can separate and close much like a pair of tweezers. This is helpful when picking seeds from pine cones or pieces of nuts from shells.

WHAT WILL HAPPEN TO A RED SQUIRREL IF IT LOSES ITS TAIL?

The tail is very tender. If a squirrel is caught by its tail, the skin is apt to strip off, leaving only the bony stub. This is a common occurrence among squirrels, with as many as half of the population having some injury to the tail. It is a serious handicap, for the loss of the tail limits a squirrel's jumping power. Without the tail as a balance or parachute, a squirrel is also more likely to be injured in a fall.

ARE ALL RED SQUIRRELS RED?

Red squirrels are not always red. Occasionally they are white, and sometimes they are black. Black squirrels are called melanistic and are very rare. White squirrels are called albinos and are a bit more common.

WHY WAS IT DANGEROUS FOR PIONEERS TO DECORATE THEIR HATS WITH SQUIRREL TAILS?

The early colonists organized game drives that would result in the killing of hundreds of deer and other big game animals. This infuriated the Indians, who killed only what they needed for food. The Indians passed a sentence of death on white hunters. The white hunter often wore a coonskin cap trimmed with squirrel tails while going into the woods. Wearing such a cap was a way for an early settler to lose his scalp.

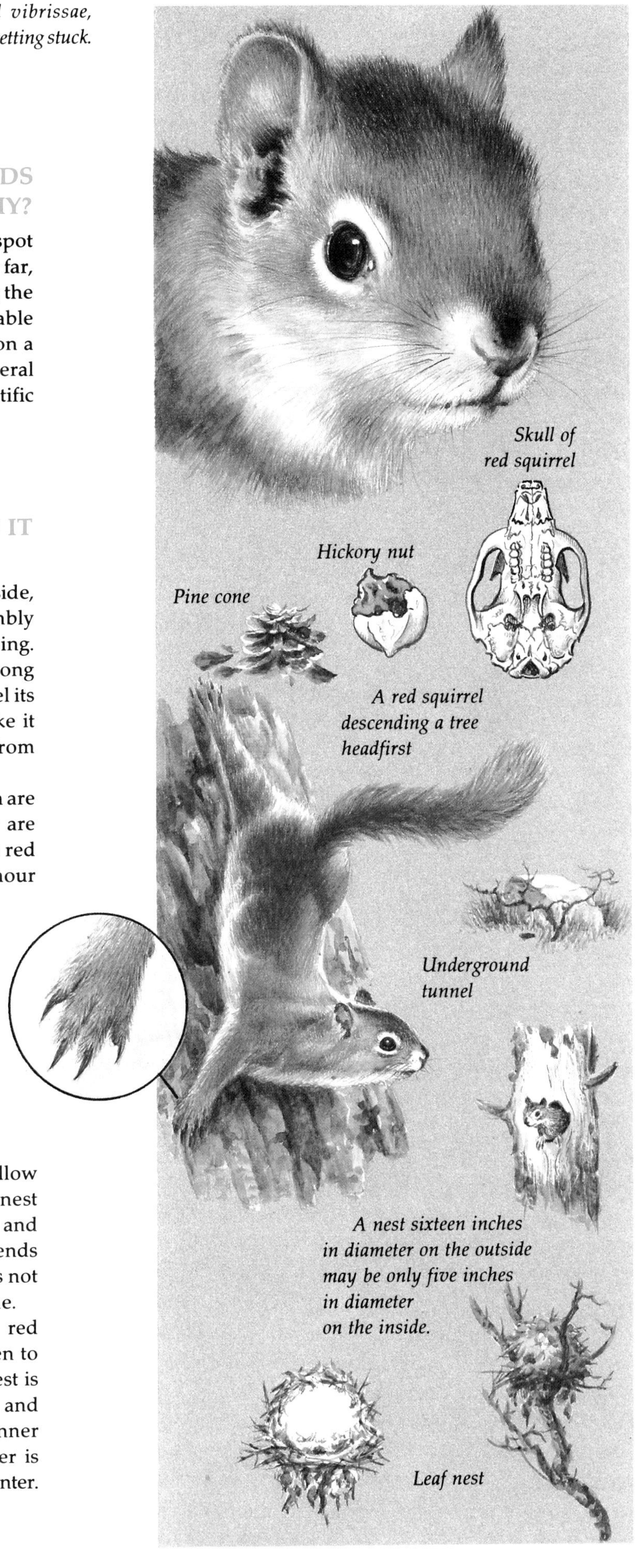

***The red squirrel's whiskers,** called vibrissae, measure the size of a hole it can enter without getting stuck.*

WHY DO RED SQUIRRELS NOD THEIR HEADS "YES" WHEN THEY SPOT A DISTANT ENEMY?

Red squirrels have very keen eyesight and can spot enemies while they are still far off. To determine how far, the squirrel nods its head up and down. By comparing the angle of sight from the two positions, the red squirrel is able to pinpoint the exact distance. As a squirrel balances on a flimsy branch preparing to leap, it will lift its head several times to estimate the distance before jumping. The scientific name for this technique is "parallax."

HOW CAN THE RED SQUIRREL RUN ON BRANCHES WITHOUT LOOKING WHERE IT IS GOING?

Sensory hairs located on the feet, forelegs, underside, and the base of the tail allow the squirrel to run nimbly along branches without needing to watch where it is going. Because these hairs sense the difference between a strong branch and a weak twig, the red squirrel can literally feel its way along without missing a step. The hairs also make it possible for the animal to keep the right distance away from other objects.

The foot itself is equipped with sharp claws which are hooked slightly. In the winter the soles of the feet are covered with hair to prevent slipping on icy limbs. The red squirrel can hold on so tightly that a forty-mile-per-hour wind cannot shake it loose.

As a safety precaution, the red squirrel also limits its range to a rather small area of perhaps only 200 to 250 yards in diameter. It memorizes the paths through the trees and branches as well as on the forest floor as a means for a quick escape.

WHY DOES THE RED SQUIRREL HAVE MORE THAN ONE NEST?

Red squirrels build nests in several locations: hollow stumps, the forks of trees, and even underground. One nest may be used as a nursery, another for a bedroom, and others for storage purposes. Since the red squirrel spends much of its time running from one nest to another, it is not likely to be found at any particular nest at a given time.

The most noticeable nest is the one that the red squirrel builds in a tree near the main trunk, about ten to twenty feet from the ground. This globular-shaped nest is made up of three layers: an outer layer of sticks and hardwood leaves; a waterproof middle layer; and an inner lining of grass, moss, or feathers. The inside chamber is about six inches across and about four inches high in the center.

__When carrying her young,__ a mother red squirrel usually picks it up by a flap of skin on the belly. The young one wraps its legs securely around its mother's neck and curls its tail over her back. The attachment is so tight that the mother can run, leap, and climb without hesitation.

A sentinel of the forest, the red squirrel alerts others of danger.

Red squirrels instinctively hide on the opposite side of a tree or flatten themselves on the top of a limb.

HOW FAR CAN THE RED SQUIRREL'S ALARM BE HEARD?

Red squirrels can be heard for over a quarter of a mile. They guard their territories jealously and are acutely aware of everything that goes on within their boundaries. Any intruder is scolded mercilessly with angry "tcherrrs" and explosive "chucks." Many other animals, including moose, elk, and deer, monitor the red squirrel's chatter for signals of danger.

Each of the red squirrel's vocal outbursts is accompanied by a stamping of the feet and a jerk of the tail. A red squirrel may become so agitated that it occasionally rushes head-first down a tree, threatening to attack an intruder that is many times its own size. However, it does not attack but merely races back up the tree, still scolding loudly. Sometimes it will even follow a foe for the fun of harassing him at a safe distance.

CAN RED SQUIRRELS SWIM?

Yes. Red squirrels are good swimmers and can escape predators by diving into a lake and swimming away. While in the water, however, they become easy prey for snapping turtles and large fish, such as pike and muskie.

WHAT IS THE RED SQUIRREL'S GREATEST ENEMY?

Perhaps the greatest enemy of the squirrel is fear. When surprised, it may actually become paralyzed and fall easy victim to even the slowest enemy. Red squirrels are so fearful of skunks that they flee at the sight of a black-and-white stuffed animal.

HOW DO RED SQUIRRELS TAKE A BATH?

Red squirrels bathe by rolling in damp moss. They scrub their faces after a meal by rubbing against rough tree bark. Unlike most other rodents, they do not scratch themselves with their hind legs but prefer to scratch against tree limbs.

WHY DO RED SQUIRRELS OFTEN ABANDON THEIR NESTS?

While the red squirrel is very meticulous about its personal appearance, it is very careless about its home. Nests are usually filthy and full of such parasites as ticks and botflies. When a nest becomes too dirty for habitation or too filled with insects, the red squirrel simply abandons the nest.

How is the fact that the majority is often wrong illustrated in Scripture?

Who gave a special inheritance to his descendants by following the Lord with his whole heart and refusing to accept the wrong conclusion of the majority?

(Pause for a response—see page 17.)

Under cover of darkness, a group of scouts quietly scrambled up a mountainside. These men had been handpicked by their leaders. The report that they were to bring back would determine the course of their whole nation.

The men found a place of hiding from which they could view the countryside and then waited. Soon the morning light filled the sky and the men looked out over the breathtaking landscape.

One of the men silently resolved that this mountain would become the heritage for his children and their children.

Meanwhile, the other scouts stared in disbelief at the massive walls of a nearby city and the colossal size of the giants who guarded it. "How could we possibly conquer such a stronghold?" murmured most of the men.

But two of the twelve reminded the rest, "Did not God promise to give us this land? Has he not already destroyed great armies and nations who opposed us?"

The scouts, divided in opinion, returned to their camp. The majority quickly spread their discouraging report. When the two courageous scouts gave their report and challenged the nation to trust God and obey Him, many of the people picked up stones to kill them. Minds were already made up. The people would listen to the majority opinion.

The decision to not go in and conquer the land cost the nation forty years of wandering in the wilderness. During all those years, the commitment made by that faithful scout was never forgotten. It gave him strength, vigor, and purpose in life.

At the age of eighty-five, he again climbed that mountainside; this time with a group of mighty men who shared his vision and his faith.

This courageous man and his soldiers conquered the walled cities and the giants who lived in them. He was then given that mountain with all of its special significance.

It was on this very mountain that Abraham, Isaac, and Jacob were buried. They had received God's promise of this land, and Caleb, by refusing to agree with a mistaken majority, helped to fulfill that promise.

From Numbers 14 and Joshua 14

***Caleb was a slave in Egypt** during the first forty years of his life. He was well acquainted with hard labor.*

CALEB, A MAN WHO KNEW THE DANGER OF DISOBEYING GOD'S COMMANDS

Caleb was born a slave in the hot plains of Egypt. His youth was spent serving the whims of a capricious tyrant. He was thirty-eight years old when the Lord miraculously delivered His people out of the hands of the Egyptians.

Caleb saw the power of God in opening up the sea and then closing it back over the enemy army. He observed the holiness of God at Sinai when the Law was given. He also observed the reluctance of his kinsmen to obey the Lord. He was embarrassed by their petty complaints, grieved with their rebellion against Moses, and dismayed at their desire to return to Egypt.

Caleb knew that the greatest danger he faced was within his own people's unbelieving hearts. God had already demonstrated His ability to defeat the powerful Egyptians. He could certainly defeat the Canaanites.

DISBELIEF DELAYS ENTRY INTO THE LAND

The people, however, were reluctant to occupy the Promised Land. They insisted on sending out spies to determine the feasibility of war. One man from each of Israel's twelve tribes was chosen to be a spy. Caleb represented the tribe of Judah, and Joshua was chosen to represent Ephraim. (See Deuteronomy 1:21–23; Numbers 13:6, 8.)

Their reconnaissance report was mixed. Before Joshua and Caleb could speak, the other spies said the mission was impossible. Caleb exhorted the people to take possession of the land, but they refused to listen and would have stoned both Joshua and Caleb had not the Lord Himself intervened. (See Numbers 14:6–10.)

ORIENTAL WASP *Vespa orientalis*

***One of God's secret weapons was the hornet,** a member of the wasp family. There was no need for Israel to fear the giants. God would have put them to flight with the hornet as he did later. (See Exodus 23:28.) "And I sent the hornet before you, which drave them out from before you . . ." (Joshua 24:12).*

CALEB CLAIMS HIS INHERITANCE AT LAST

Forty years later the Lord permitted the nation of Israel to enter the land. A new generation had replaced their faithless fathers. Under Joshua's command the land was conquered in seven years. It was now time to divide the land among the tribes and root out the remaining Canaanites who had retreated into their walled cities.

Before the first lot was drawn, Caleb asked Joshua for the hill country surrounding the city of Hebron. The area contained great fortified cities occupied by the most formidable opponents in the land. Caleb, now eighty-five, was confident that the Lord would enable him to conquer this area. (See Joshua 14:6–15.)

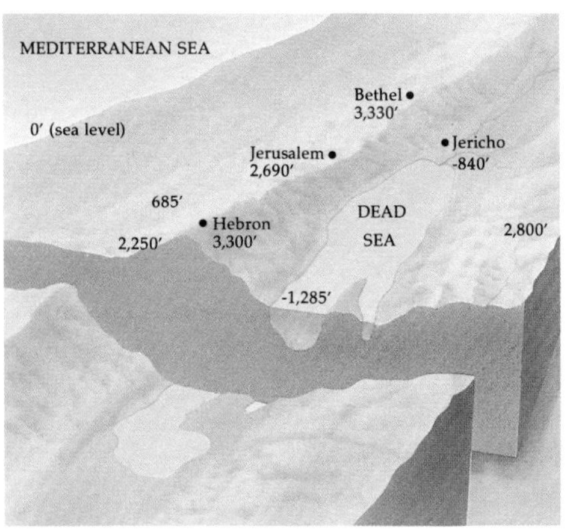

***Hebron, located in the hill country** of Judea, was the highest city in Palestine.*

THE WAR-WISE VETERAN WARNS AGAINST APATHY

Caleb, wise in experience and strong in faith, knew that the real danger to the younger generation was complacency regarding the remaining Canaanites. It would be easy to reason that there was enough land for both them and the Canaanites. They had been at war for seven years and were eager for rest. Why risk their lives with further fighting?

Caleb recalled the Lord's words, *"And thou shalt consume all the people which the Lord thy God shall deliver thee; thine eye shall have no pity upon them: neither shalt thou serve their gods; for that will be a snare unto thee" (Deuteronomy 7:16).*

Caleb motivated the younger men by conquering the powerful city of Hebron himself. Then he offered his daughter in marriage to the man who would conquer the walled city of Debir. Othniel took the challenge and won his bride. (See Joshua 15:14–17.) The area surrounding Hebron was now secure and became a stronghold of Israel throughout the history of the nation.

CHARACTER SKETCH OF CALEB

WHY WAS THE HILL COUNTRY OF HEBRON SO SIGNIFICANT TO CALEB?

Caleb had first seen Hebron when Moses had sent him and the other spies into the land. The sons of Anak, men of unusual strength and stature, lived there. When the spies saw them, their hearts melted with fear. They felt like grasshoppers next to these giants. (See Numbers 13:22, 33.)

But, Caleb focused his attention on the grapes, pomegranates, figs, and clear mountain springs. Here, at the highest elevation in the entire land, he had a breathtaking view of the inheritance that the Lord had promised to give to His people.

It was at Hebron that Abraham built an altar immediately after the promise was given. (See Genesis 13:14–18.) Hebron was the burial site of Abraham, Isaac, and Jacob in the cave of Machpelah. (See Genesis 49:30–33; 50:13.)

As a man of faith, this mountain had special significance to Caleb. It reminded him of the faith of his fathers who feared the Lord and were buried there. This was to be his home, and he wanted to demonstrate the power of God to his family by possessing it.

WHAT WAS THE SECRET OF CALEB'S SUCCESS?

Caleb was successful in conquering the most feared men in the land, the Anakim of Hebron. He was an example to the leaders of the other tribes to do the same. But even though they tried to occupy their territories, many were unable to penetrate the stronger cities. A lengthy list of cities which the Israelites failed to occupy is given in Judges 1:19–36.

Caleb's secret is given as follows, *"Hebron therefore became the inheritance of Caleb the son of Jephunneh the Kenezite unto this day, because that he wholly followed the Lord God of Israel" (Joshua 14:14).* Caleb himself asserted with clear conscience, *"... I wholly followed the Lord my God" (Joshua 14:8).*

Moses also said of Caleb, *"... Thou hast wholly followed the Lord my God" (Joshua 14:9).* And God Himself, the perfect discerner of hearts, said, *"But my servant Caleb, because he had another spirit with him, and hath followed me fully, him will I bring into the land whereinto he went; and his seed shall possess it" (Numbers 14:24).*

WHAT WERE CALEB'S LASTING CONTRIBUTIONS?

Caleb gave to his family some of the best land in the country. More importantly, he gave a land free of the wicked Canaanites, who later became such a snare to many of the Israelites.

Joshua sadly declared before his death, *"Know for a certainty that the Lord your God will no more drive out any of these nations from before you; but they shall be snares and traps unto you, and scourges in your sides, and thorns in your eyes, until ye perish from off this good land which the Lord your God hath given you" (Joshua 23:13).*

Another contribution was Caleb's being an example to follow. Because Caleb both challenged his family to obedience and demonstrated obedience himself, Othniel, Caleb's nephew, conquered the fortified city of Debir near Hebron.

Later, when the Israelites cried to the Lord for help, it was Othniel whom the Lord used to deliver the nation from the Mesopotamians. Othniel became the first judge after Joshua, and the nation had forty years of peace. (See Judges 3:8–11.)

Caleb refused to be discouraged *by the report that "... the cities are great and walled up to heaven; and moreover we have seen the sons of the Anakims there" (Deuteronomy 1:28).*

CALEB
***cā**-leb*

Contentment

. . . Is realizing that God has already provided everything that I need for my present happiness

"And having food and raiment let us be therewith content."
I Timothy 6:8

CONTENTMENT IN GIVING . . .

Is being free from personal wants, comparisons, and expectations so that my alertness and ability to give to others will not be diminished.

PART TWO

CHAPTER FIVE

Contentment

. . . Is valuing God-given relationships more than earthly possessions

"While we look not at the things which are seen, but at the things which are not seen: for the things which are seen are temporal; but the things which are not seen are eternal."

II Corinthians 4:18

Living Lessons on Contentment . . .

FROM THE PAGES OF SCRIPTURE

The axiom "Familiarity breeds contempt" is all too often true. We tend to take for granted those who are closest to us.

Only when loved ones are gone is their importance to our lives recognized. It is then that we wish we could turn the clock back and reclaim lost opportunities to express appreciation and deepen fellowship.

Scripture reveals how one wise and perceptive person was able to avoid such regrets in a very important relationship.

ILLUSTRATED IN THE WORLD OF NATURE

PACK RAT *Neotoma albigula*

The pack rat is a member of the wood rat family of which there are about twenty different species. The young, born in litters of two to six, weigh about one-half ounce. They are usually weaned by the third week and by the third month are ten times their birth weight. Adults are about eighteen inches long, half of that length belonging to the tail.

Pack rats are amazingly well adapted to desert conditions. They are swift runners along logs, rocks, and rafters and are excellent climbers. In addition to the ground nest, they often build secondary nests in nearby trees.

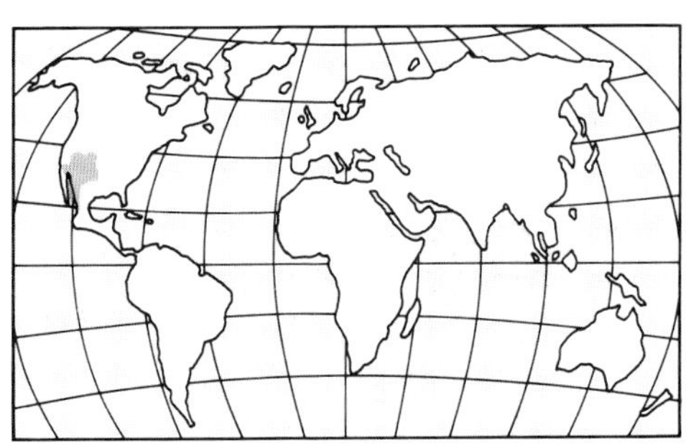

The range and habitat of the pack rat

How is the unimportance of possessions illustrated in the world of nature?

Balancing himself on his long tail, the pack rat violently lashed out at his mate. The female rat successfully repulsed the attack with sharp claws and a nasty bite. With his left ear severely damaged, the humiliated male darted from his nest to search for more solitary surroundings.

Exploring for a more suitable home, the wounded rat discovered a vacant cactus and quickly began to establish his territorial presence. Satisfied with the progress on his new nest, the pack rat anxiously scouted out the desert environment.

A search for shiny trinkets and sparkling baubles to furnish his dwelling brought him to the broken-down porch of an old abandoned shack. When his twitching nose and whiskers sensed that no danger was present, the curious rat scampered across the rough pine floor. Behind a dusty pile of logs near the crumbling fireplace, a small string caught the pack rat's inquisitive eye.

Nosing his way into an old leather pouch, the pack rat uncovered three gold nuggets. Delighted with his newfound treasure, the excited rat scurried back toward his nest, protectively carrying one of the nuggets between his teeth.

Suddenly, a glimmer in the desert sand distracted the impulsive pack rat. The midday sun had brilliantly lit up a discarded gum wrapper. Fascinated by the silvery reflection, the pack rat gladly abandoned his gold in exchange for the shiny but worthless paper.

His second trip from the shack was similarly sidetracked by the captivating movements of a colorful feather animated by the desert breeze. Once again the foolish pack rat swapped his nugget for a prize of lesser value.

For the third time he entered the shack, scooped up the remaining nugget, and ran toward his nest. As he bounded along, his eyes constantly searched the horizon for other things more attractive than what he was carrying.

Suddenly, he saw the most interesting object yet, a shiny key chain at the base of a large cactus. The pack rat was so absorbed in making his new exchange that he failed to notice a coyote crouching nearby.

With the heavy key chain in his mouth he again started out for his nest. Seconds later he felt himself being thrown into the air. He lost the keys and came down into the jaws of the hungry coyote.

His discontent caused him to lose his life in exchange for shiny trinkets.

Severt Anderson

THE CHARACTERISTICS OF

THE PACK RAT IN SCRIPTURE

The persistent obsession of the pack rat to collect bright, shiny things is an apt illustration of the nature of man. *"Surely every man walketh in a vain shew . . . he heapeth up riches, and knoweth not who shall gather them" (Psalm 39:6).*

The pack rat's practice of exchanging one thing for another is exemplary of human conduct. We exchange time for money, and money for food, etc. Paul wisely exchanged temporal things in order to experience more of Christ. (See Philippians 3:8.)

The pack rat's inability to live in harmony and its ultimate resorting to a solitary existence is an accurate commentary on anyone who would seek after wealth. *"He that is greedy of gain troubleth his own house; but he that hateth gifts shall live" (Proverbs 15:27).*

The destructive end of the featured pack rat is also predictive of the person who makes wealth his goal. *"But they that will be rich fall into . . . many foolish and hurtful lusts. . . . For the love of money is the root of all evil: which while some coveted after, they have erred from the faith, and pierced themselves through with many sorrows" (I Timothy 6:9–10).*

The pack rat's lack of contentment with possessions illustrates Ecclesiastes 5:10, *"He that loveth silver shall not be satisfied with silver; nor he that loveth abundance with increase. . . ."*

YSICAL

T

fill its nest with objects compels it to seek more and more, and to be increasingly discontented with what it already possesses.

WHERE DO PACK RATS FIND WATER IN THE DESERT?

Since water is scarce in the desert, pack rats obtain water by eating the juicy pulp of such desert cacti as the prickly pear and the cholla (**choy**-yah). These are almost ninety per cent water.

The cactus, however, is covered with long sharp spines, barbed like the quills of a porcupine. If touched, the spines break off easily and can work their way deep into the skin. A pack rat gently bites off each spine at its base, creating a safe work area in which to "eat" a drink of water.

Cholla cactus

Ninety per cent water

A thirsty pack rat gets a "drink" by biting off a piece of cactus.

HOW DOES THE PACK RAT USE THE CHOLLA CACTUS TO PROTECT ITSELF?

The small limbs of the cholla cactus break off at the lightest touch and fall to the ground. A pack rat gathers these limbs to build a "barbed wire" fence around its nest. It plants the limbs near the entrances and down the runways that lead away from its nest. Since a pack rat rarely travels farther than 100 yards from its nest, it is never more than a quick dash from the protection of its prickly fortress.

CAN OTHER ANIMALS GET WATER FROM THE CHOLLA CACTUS?

In laboratory experiments, other rats have died on a diet of cactus. The pack rat has a remarkable ability to tolerate the concentrations of oxalic acid which are found in the plant without suffering any ill effects.

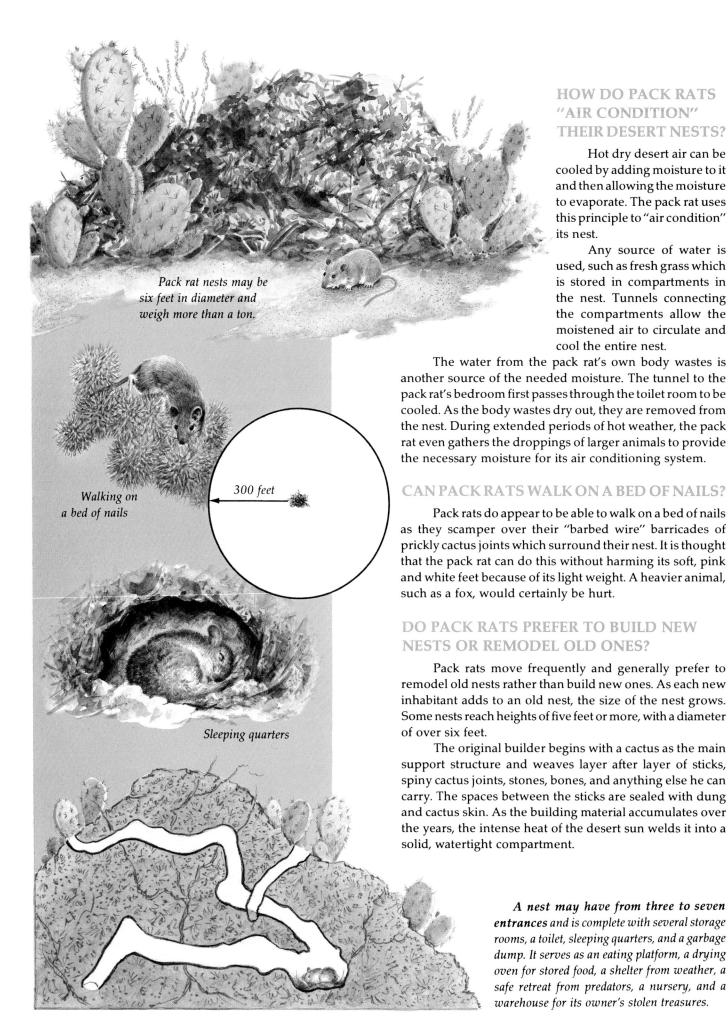

Pack rat nests may be six feet in diameter and weigh more than a ton.

HOW DO PACK RATS "AIR CONDITION" THEIR DESERT NESTS?

Hot dry desert air can be cooled by adding moisture to it and then allowing the moisture to evaporate. The pack rat uses this principle to "air condition" its nest.

Any source of water is used, such as fresh grass which is stored in compartments in the nest. Tunnels connecting the compartments allow the moistened air to circulate and cool the entire nest.

The water from the pack rat's own body wastes is another source of the needed moisture. The tunnel to the pack rat's bedroom first passes through the toilet room to be cooled. As the body wastes dry out, they are removed from the nest. During extended periods of hot weather, the pack rat even gathers the droppings of larger animals to provide the necessary moisture for its air conditioning system.

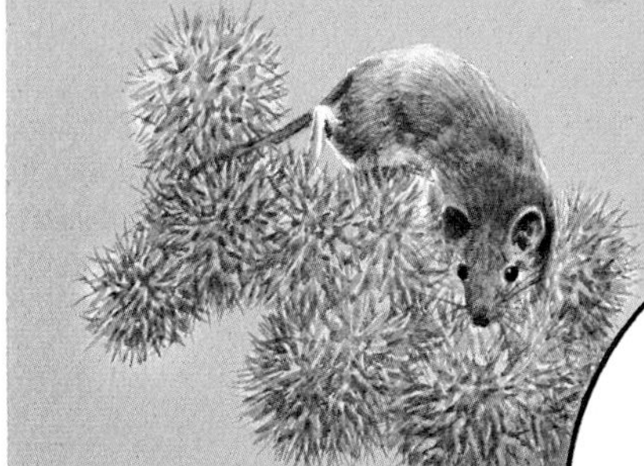

Walking on a bed of nails

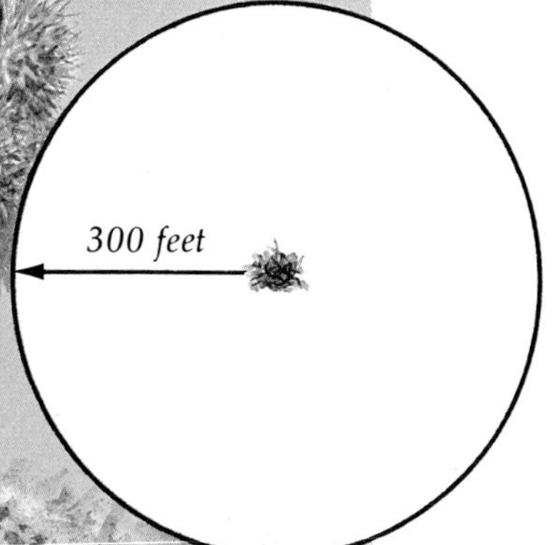

CAN PACK RATS WALK ON A BED OF NAILS?

Pack rats do appear to be able to walk on a bed of nails as they scamper over their "barbed wire" barricades of prickly cactus joints which surround their nest. It is thought that the pack rat can do this without harming its soft, pink and white feet because of its light weight. A heavier animal, such as a fox, would certainly be hurt.

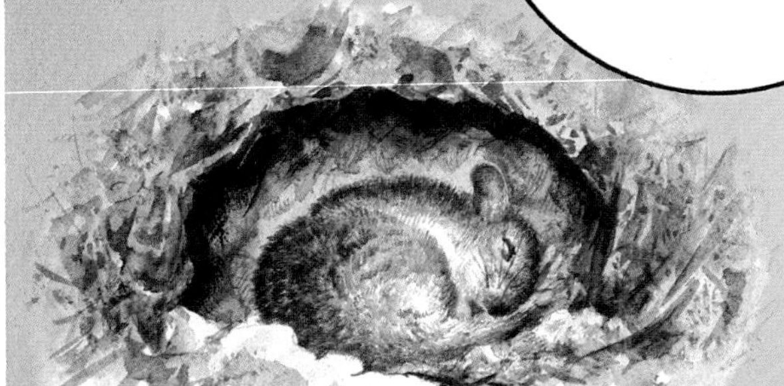

Sleeping quarters

DO PACK RATS PREFER TO BUILD NEW NESTS OR REMODEL OLD ONES?

Pack rats move frequently and generally prefer to remodel old nests rather than build new ones. As each new inhabitant adds to an old nest, the size of the nest grows. Some nests reach heights of five feet or more, with a diameter of over six feet.

The original builder begins with a cactus as the main support structure and weaves layer after layer of sticks, spiny cactus joints, stones, bones, and anything else he can carry. The spaces between the sticks are sealed with dung and cactus skin. As the building material accumulates over the years, the intense heat of the desert sun welds it into a solid, watertight compartment.

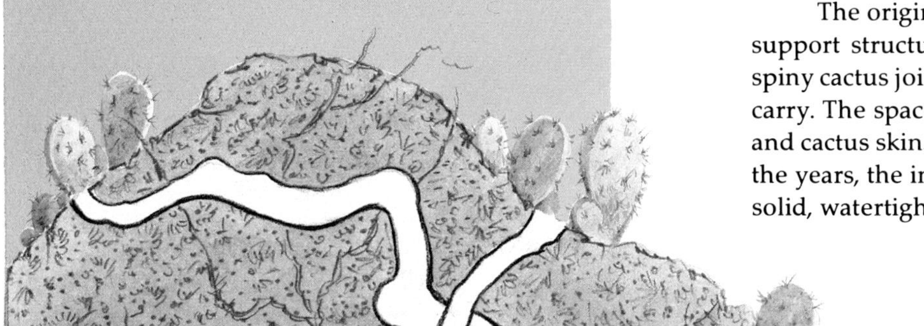

***A nest may have from three to seven entrances** and is complete with several storage rooms, a toilet, sleeping quarters, and a garbage dump. It serves as an eating platform, a drying oven for stored food, a shelter from weather, a safe retreat from predators, a nursery, and a warehouse for its owner's stolen treasures.*

new rooms to the nest. Where a pack rat has abandoned his home, the other inhabitants soon leave also because of the deterioration of the nest.

HOW ALERT ARE NEWBORN PACK RATS?

After a gestation period of four to five weeks, the female pack rat usually gives birth to three young. The newborn pack rats are blind, deaf, and practically hairless. The teeth of the young are so shaped that, even when the jaw is closed, a diamond-shaped opening is left. This allows the mother to feed the young without being bitten. With the help of their feet, the young are able to hang onto the mother continuously for the first three weeks of their lives.

HOW DOES A PACK RAT LOSE ITS EARS?

The ears of the adult pack rat are typically ragged and deeply notched. Some older pack rats may have only stubs. These wounds are not from cactus spines or predators, but from fights with other pack rats.

Fights are the most vicious between the male and the female following mating season. A female seeks to drive her mate from her nest before the young are born. The pair rear up on their back legs, balance with their tails, and strike at each other with their front claws. The female usually wins.

If two pack rats, regardless of sex, are placed in the same cage, they will fight to the death. In the wild, each individual requires approximately twenty acres of privacy to avoid fighting with his neighbor.

WHAT IS THE HISTORICAL VALUE OF THE PACK RAT'S NEST?

Archeologists examining one pack rat nest estimated that it had been in continual use for several thousand years. Inside the nest was found a well-kept museum of artifacts that had been gathered by countless generations of pack rats. The amazing collection included silverware, nails, animal bones, false teeth, gold nuggets, arrowheads, coins, knives, and pieces of brightly colored cloth that had been preserved by the dry desert conditions.

Mother carrying young

The rock wren may take shelter in the warmth of the pack rat's nest.

Battle scars

HOW MUCH RATTLESNAKE VENOM DOES IT TAKE TO KILL A PACK RAT?

Rattlesnakes often inhabit the pack rat's nest. Experiments have shown that it takes 130 times as much rattlesnake venom to kill a pack rat as it takes to kill other rats of similar size. Since only the very largest of rattlers can deliver enough venom to harm a pack rat, the two co-exist peacefully. If a fight does break out between the two, it is usually the pack rat who takes the offensive and seeks to drive the snake out of the nest.

HOW DO PACK RATS TALK WITH THEIR TAILS?

Pack rats respond to disturbances by thumping their rear feet on the ground and by vibrating their tails against branches or twigs. By varying the speed and volume of the sounds, they are able to communicate with one another over considerable distances. When angry, the pack rat clicks his teeth together and squeals shrilly.

Both rattlesnakes and pack rats vibrate their tails when alarmed.

The tail acts like a turn signal by pointing in the direction the pack rat will turn.

HOW CAN A SMALL PIECE OF GLASS DESTROY THE CACTUS CASTLE OF THE PACK RAT?

The pack rat has many enemies. Wildcats, lynx, coyotes, foxes, wolves, badgers, bears, hawks, owls, and even skunks take their turn preying on the pack rat while it is in the open. Only the badger and the bear are powerful enough to tear down the pack rat's cactus castle.

The pack rat's greatest menace comes from fire. During seasons of drought, the nest becomes a tinderbox of kindling which can be reduced to a pile of glowing coals in only a few minutes. Indians used the nests as ready-made signal fires. The nest is so combustible that even a curved piece of glass can ignite the heap with concentrated sunlight.

Indians used pack rat nests for signal fires.

HOW DO PACK RATS USE A SECOND HOME FOR PEST CONTROL?

Many insect pests trouble the pack rat. To relieve himself, at least temporarily, the pack rat simply moves. He may move to an unoccupied nest or may build a second set of living quarters in the same nest. Two sets of living quarters, both in good condition, are often found in a single nest. The more recently occupied chamber always has fewer insects than the older one.

The most common insects which plague the pack rat are fleas, ticks, mites, lice, botflies, and kissing bugs. The larva of the botfly burrows under the skin of the throat in the pack rat and forms a lump the size of a marble. Although ugly to look at, the lump does little harm.

The bloodsucking kissing bug hides all day and ventures out at night to gorge itself on the blood of the pack rat. Apparently the pack rat is able to tolerate these bites without any discomfort. Many humans, however, are allergic to the kissing bug and have very painful reactions to the welts it leaves behind.

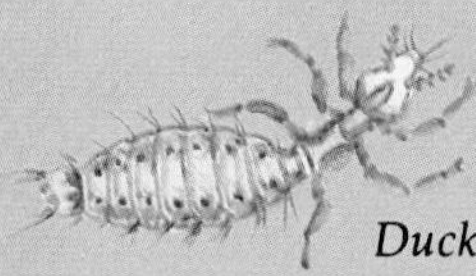

Duck louse

Dog flea

Sheep tick

Insect pests often force the pack rat to "pack up" and leave its nest.

How is the importance of God-given relationships illustrated in Scripture?

Who sacrificed a valuable possession for an important relationship, but was severely criticized for doing it by a greedy observer?

(Pause for a response—see page 17.)

The tension of an impending crisis filled the room as guests ate a meal. A few miles away, jealous rulers plotted the death of the group's leader.

During the meal, one of the hosts did something very unexpected. Everyone at the table was amazed. Finally, one of the most respected dinner guests openly condemned the action as useless and out of place.

The leader of the group quickly defended the host and tried to reason with the angry guest, whose warped mind failed to grasp the significance of the action.

After the meal, the critic slipped away from that group and met with the hostile officials in the nearby city. He asked what they would pay him if he cooperated with their plan. They agreed on a price.

As the disgruntled member of the group returned from that secret meeting, he might have congratulated himself for the shrewdness of his plan. He would do his part in the plot, collect the money, and then his leader could miraculously escape as he had done on previous occasions, or he would set up his kingdom as he had promised.

Several days later, the conspiracy was carried out. The greedy critic did his part and collected his reward. But events did not turn out as he had planned. His leader was captured and condemned to die. It was then that the horror of what this angry man had just done penetrated his twisted mind.

He grabbed the money which he had received and met again with the jealous leaders. He tried to explain that he was wrong and that he wanted to return the money in exchange for the life of his leader. They laughed at him and refused to talk any further about it. He flung the money to the floor and walked out into the darkness.

Instead of perceiving in a new light the act which he had so severely criticized just six days earlier, he prepared a noose for his own neck.

The action he condemned was the anointing of Jesus with very expensive ointment. The action demonstrated to everyone that the one who did it treasured the fellowship of Christ more than earthly possessions. What he had done demonstrated just the opposite.

He traded fellowship with Christ for thirty pieces of silver and caused the name Judas to be despised forever. She exchanged her treasure for deeper fellowship with Christ and caused the name Mary of Bethany to be honored forever.

From John 12:1–8 and Matthew 26:3–16; 27:3–5

The reputed site of Mary's home in Bethany. *It is here that Jesus enjoyed the rich fellowship of Mary, Martha, and Lazarus.*

MARY OF BETHANY, A PERCEPTIVE FRIEND

Everything that we know about the life and character of Mary of Bethany is revealed from just three events recorded in the Gospels. Each incident focuses on a different aspect of her person, revealing a perceptive woman who knew and appreciated the mission of Christ more than the religious leaders of her time, and perhaps more than the Lord's handpicked disciples.

ENJOYING THE PRESENCE OF CHRIST

Our first glimpse of Mary takes place during one of the Lord's frequent visits to her home. Mary lived with her sister, Martha, and brother, Lazarus. One day as Mary listened to Jesus' teaching, Martha felt the pressure of preparing dinner for many guests. Martha criticized her sister for not helping and even criticized the Lord for being insensitive to the situation.

The Lord did not condemn Martha's industriousness, but neither would He condemn Mary. He praised Mary for choosing the "better part." This involved enjoying Christ's presence rather than simply doing things for Him. Mary recognized that Christ's teaching provided a spiritual meal that would satisfy more than a physical meal. (See Luke 10:38–42.)

The tomb *from which Lazarus was raised*

CONFIDENT OF CHRIST'S POWER OVER DEATH

The second view of Mary occurs after the death of her brother, Lazarus. He had become sick while Jesus was ministering elsewhere. The sisters sent for Jesus, hoping He could return before their beloved brother died. Since it would have taken the messenger at least a day to reach Jesus on the east side of the Jordan River, and since Lazarus had been dead four days when He arrived, we can conclude that Lazarus died before their message reached Jesus. The Lord's intentional delay of two days was not to wait for Lazarus to die, but that the full impact of the death and resurrection would be felt by all present.

When Jesus arrived, Mary was in her home with the other mourners. Jesus called for her. She quickly responded and fell at His feet saying, *"... Lord, if thou hadst been here, my brother had not died" (John 11:32)*. Jesus went to the tomb of Lazarus and commanded His friend to come forth. From that day forward, the religious leaders of the nation agreed among themselves that they must put Jesus to death lest the entire nation should believe in Him. (See John 11:53.)

A jar made of alabaster, *the same type of container which held the "precious ointment" poured out on Jesus by Mary*

EAGER TO SHARE A COSTLY GIFT

The final scene of Mary occurs several days after Lazarus' resurrection. A feast, probably to express gratitude to Jesus, was held at the home of Simon the Leper. Martha was serving, and Mary was again recalling and meditating on the miraculous events of the last few days. In an act of deep emotion and devotion, she anointed the Lord's head and feet with a costly perfume.

The guests felt that Mary's actions were entirely inappropriate. Judas was especially critical. Again the Lord defended Mary. *". . . Let her alone: against the day of my burying hath she kept this. For the poor always ye have with you; but me ye have not always" (John 12:7–8)*. He praised her gift, saying, *"... Wheresoever this gospel shall be preached in the whole world, there shall also this, that this woman hath done, be told for a memorial of her" (Matthew 26:13)*.

Mary had listened to the words of Christ, believed His teaching, and acted upon it. She was one of the first persons to begin to understand the real significance of the Lord's life, death, and resurrection.

CHARACTER SKETCH OF MARY OF BETHANY

WHY WOULD THE LORD WANT US TO REMEMBER MARY'S GIFT?

Mary of Bethany reminds us to guard our priorities. It is true that the Lord wants us to minister to those in need. He Himself set the example in compassion for the poor, the sick, the helpless, the widow, and the orphan. But Mary reminds us not to replace worship with works. There are times when it is appropriate to "waste" our abilities and possessions in grateful devotion to our Lord. (See Matthew 26:8.)

Mary also teaches us to look beyond physical needs to man's spiritual needs. Food, clothes, and shelter are important, but a man's soul is more important. Mary recognized that the Lord's life, death, and resurrection was the real purpose of His earthly mission. He came to provide eternal life by dying for our sins. (See I Corinthians 15:1–4.) This is the message that should accompany our acts of compassion.

WHAT DID MARY'S ACTION COST HER?

Judas estimated the value of Mary's perfume at three hundred denarii, about a year's wage for a common laborer. (See John 12:5.) It was probably imported from India in a sealed alabaster jar to conserve the perfume. Wealthy people broke the seal only for very special guests. Inexpensive olive oil mixed with fragrant spices was more commonly used.

In that day the economic situation of an unmarried woman such as Mary was precarious. A woman depended on the financial support and physical protection of either her father or husband. It appears that Mary had neither. It is possible that this perfume was part of her bridal gift, or dowry, for some future husband. In any case, Mary demonstrated that her contentment and security were found in Christ.

WHY WAS MARY MORE SPIRITUALLY PERCEPTIVE THAN OTHERS?

Spiritual perception is a by-product of faith which *". . . cometh by hearing, and hearing by the word of God" (Romans 10:17)*. Mary listened to the words of Christ. (See Luke 10:39.) Jesus had said, *"Therefore doth my Father love me, because I lay down my life, that I might take it again. No man taketh it from me, but I lay it down of myself. I have power to lay it down, and I have power to take it again . . ." (John 10:17–18)*.

Mary pondered these teachings and was beginning to understand that Jesus needed to die and rise again to atone for her sin. Jesus had just demonstrated His power over death in the miraculous resurrection of her brother.

Mary recognized that He indeed had the power to take His life back from the dead. She understood more fully the meaning of the Lord's statement to Martha, *". . . I am the resurrection, and the life: he that believeth in me, though he were dead, yet shall he live: And whosoever liveth and believeth in me shall never die . . ." (John 11:25–26)*.

Mary was the first to understand the significance of Christ's words and, knowing that His death was imminent, anointed His body for burial with the most precious substance that she possessed.

The home of Mary, Martha, and Lazarus *was an oasis of fellowship and refreshment for Christ in the town of Bethany.*

MARY OF BETHANY
me(ə)r-ē of **beth**-e-nē

CHAPTER SIX

Contentment

. . . Is realizing that I am indestructible until my work is done

"But I trusted in thee, O Lord: I said, Thou art my God. My times are in thy hand. . . ."

Psalm 31:14–15

Living Lessons on Contentment . . .

FROM THE PAGES OF SCRIPTURE

Every major accomplishment for God will stir up two types of enemies: those on the outside and those on the inside. Outside enemies mock, criticize, and hinder. They are easier to detect and repel. Those on the inside are like parasites that sap the strength and courage of the workers.

Both types of enemies rose up to stop the work of a great man of God. His inward character was the crucial determining factor in the final outcome.

ILLUSTRATED IN THE WORLD OF NATURE

PORCUPINE *Erethizon dorsatum*

The porcupine is a large, prickly rodent, which weighs up to twenty pounds and is approximately thirty inches long. It spends half of its solitary life in trees. During the winter it does not hibernate, but chooses rather to remain in the tops of trees for several weeks, eating all the bark it can reach.

Although fully protected by its quills, the porcupine will not provoke an attack. It will rather retreat to safety. Indians and early settlers valued the porcupine for saving the lives of many lost forest travelers since even a weak and hungry man could catch it for a meal.

The range and habitat of the porcupine

How is the contentment of indestructibility illustrated in the world of nature?

Moments after his birth, an amazing little animal instinctively stood up, arched his back, and energetically swung his well-equipped tail.

Minutes later, thirty-three thousand razorlike quills hardened and became a formidable defense against any potential attacker.

Under the careful guidance of his parents, the young arrival to the forest developed skill in using his God-given arsenal. One day as he was slowly moving through the forest, the young explorer started up a large pine tree and found an exposed layer of sugar-covered bark.

He had no sooner begun enjoying the sticky sweetness when he heard a thunderous roar behind him. Suddenly, a short-tempered black bear stormed through the underbrush, enraged by the invasion of its territory.

As the angry bear approached, the feasting porcupine clutched the tree with his long, curved claws. The bear stood up to its full height and, with one swipe of its powerful paw, sent the porcupine catapulting through the air into a nearby thicket.

The loose skin of the porcupine absorbed much of the shock; thus, he quickly recovered. Immediately he went into a defensive posture and waited for the next attack.

But another attack would not be coming. The bear had suddenly lost all interest in the porcupine, the pine tree, and its territory. Sitting on its haunches, the injured bear frantically tried to remove a dozen painful quills from the soft pad of its paw. Soon the distracted bear limped away into the woods.

The porcupine continued his journey through the forest. As he climbed up on a fallen log, he heard the rustle of leaves and the snarl of a hungry coyote. The porcupine immediately saw the coyote's prey—a helpless fawn paralyzed with fear.

In no mood to be disturbed by an intruder, the coyote lunged at the porcupine. With a swift flick of his tail, the well-armed defender sent scores of barbed quills into the coyote's jaw and forehead. The attacker yelped with pain as it tried to rub the quills out with both front paws. It was a futile attempt.

The fawn and the porcupine quietly watched as the howling coyote retreated into the forest. The fawn's life was preserved because of the contentment of indestructibility which had given special courage to her protector.

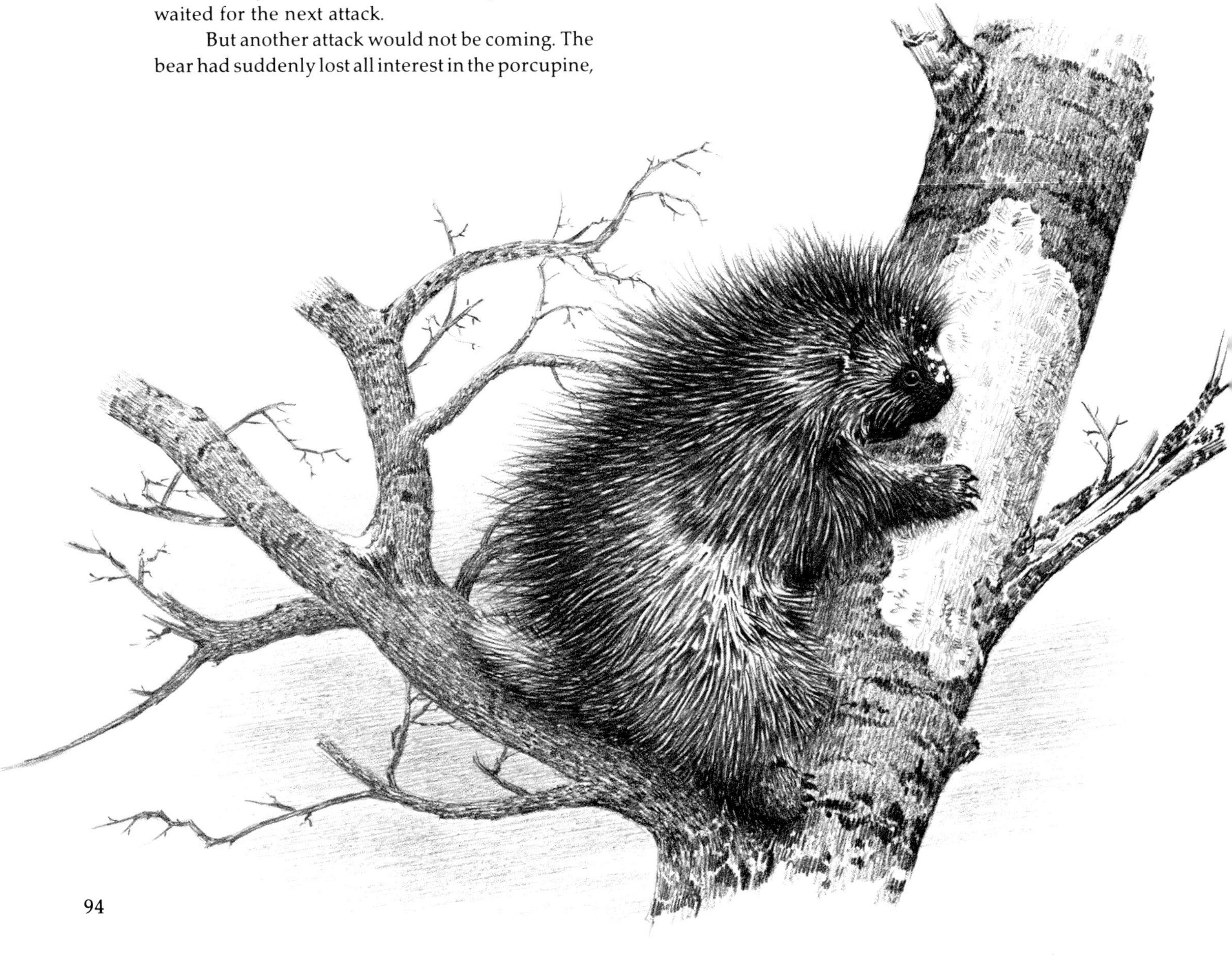

THE CHARACTERISTICS OF

THE PORCUPINE IN SCRIPTURE

The protection which gives the porcupine its confidence is an illustration of the security that every Christian can have when surrounded by spiritual enemies. (See Ephesians 6:13–17.)

Just as the armor of the porcupine is designed primarily for defense, so our armor is designed that we *"... may be able to withstand in the evil day, and having done all, to stand" (Ephesians 6:13).*

The porcupine's only offensive weapon is its sharp quill. Similarly the only weapon which God has provided for the Christian is the sword of the Spirit, which is the Word of God. (See Ephesians 6:17.) This sharp weapon, like the quill, continues to do its work once it enters the person.

The porcupine has two vulnerable areas: its "glass jaw," and its underside. The Christian also has vulnerable areas which need to have constant protection: his mouth and his heart.

"Keep thy tongue from evil, and thy lips from speaking guile" (Psalm 34:13). "Keep thy heart with all diligence; for out of it are the issues of life" (Proverbs 4:23).

The porcupine spends great amounts of time in the tree turning the bark into sweet nourishment, just as we are to meditate day and night upon God's Word. Scripture is *"... sweeter also than honey and the honeycomb" (Psalm 19:10).*

CHARACTERISTICS AND PHYSICAL FEATURES OF THE PORCUPINE

The porcupine is confident in the protection provided by its layer of quills. It has no need to run from an attacker. Unlike the deer and rabbit that flee in the face of possible danger, the porcupine is content to stand firm, so secure is it in its safekeeping.

WHY IS THE PORCUPINE SMARTER THAN HE ACTS?

Porcupines are generally considered the stupidest animal in the woods. They have been mocked and laughed at for doing such foolish things as walking right up to an armed hunter and chewing on his boot! However, recent observations show that the porcupine is really quite bright. It is able to learn complex mazes and recognize shapes. It even has a well-developed memory.

It is its very poor eyesight that has given the porcupine its undeserved reputation. The porcupine is so nearsighted that it cannot distinguish shapes beyond a few yards. To find its way in the woods, it must rely on its memory and follow the strong smell of its own urine, with which it carefully marks its trails.

HOW DOES A PORCUPINE LEAVE A TRAIL IN THE SKY?

In the summer, porcupines eat a variety of leafy plants. Lily roots are their favorite. However, in the winter their diet is limited to the bark and twigs of hemlocks, aspens, and pines. Beginning at the top of the tree, a porcupine will clip away the small twigs that grow on the outermost branches, sometimes spending months in the same tree.

HOW DOES A PORCUPINE SWEETEN A TREE?

Porcupines also feed on the inner layer of bark called the *cambium.* This layer carries the food which the leaves produce in the summer. If the bark is eaten completely around the tree, the tree will die. This is called *girdling.*

Porcupines usually do not completely girdle a tree. Rather, they eat only a portion of the bark and return year after year to feed on the sugar which builds up above the partially girdled section. In some instances the sugar content above an old eaten area may be 300 times the amount found below. One porcupine returned to the same tree for eleven consecutive years as if the tree were part of a preplanned menu.

WHY ARE PORCUPINES ATTRACTED TO PEOPLE?

Porcupines crave salt and eat anything which has been saturated with salty perspiration or the salt used to melt snow and ice. Ax handles, shovels, railings, and porch steps are all eaten. A porcupine will return to a cabin night after night to satisfy its need for salt.

Porcupines also like to chew on animal bones and discarded deer antlers. These appear to have a nutritional value for the porcupine because of their high mineral content.

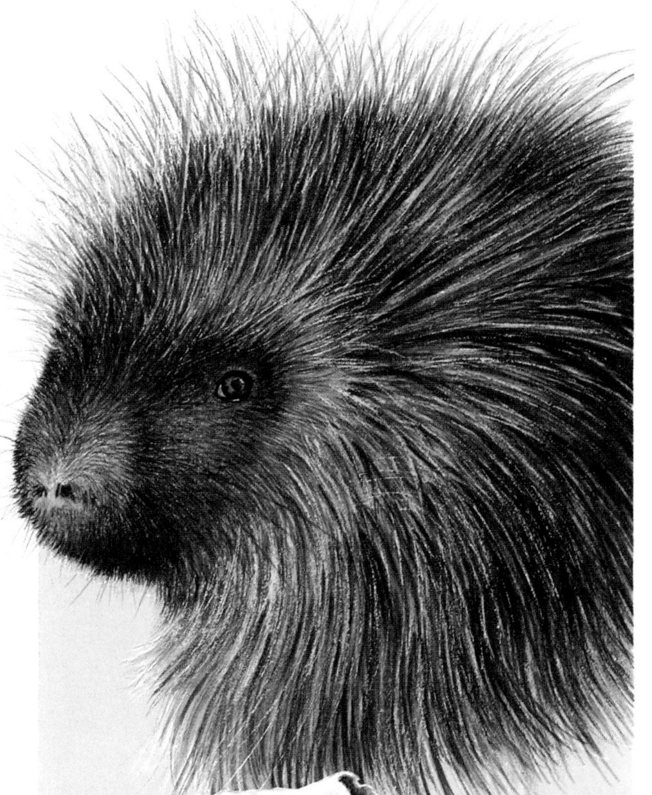

Of all the rodents in North America, the porcupine's skull is exceeded in size only by the beaver's.

Partially girdled tree

Pine tree stripped

Broad tooth marks record the presence of a porcupine. As bark re-covers the damaged area, the marks are preserved for the life of the tree.

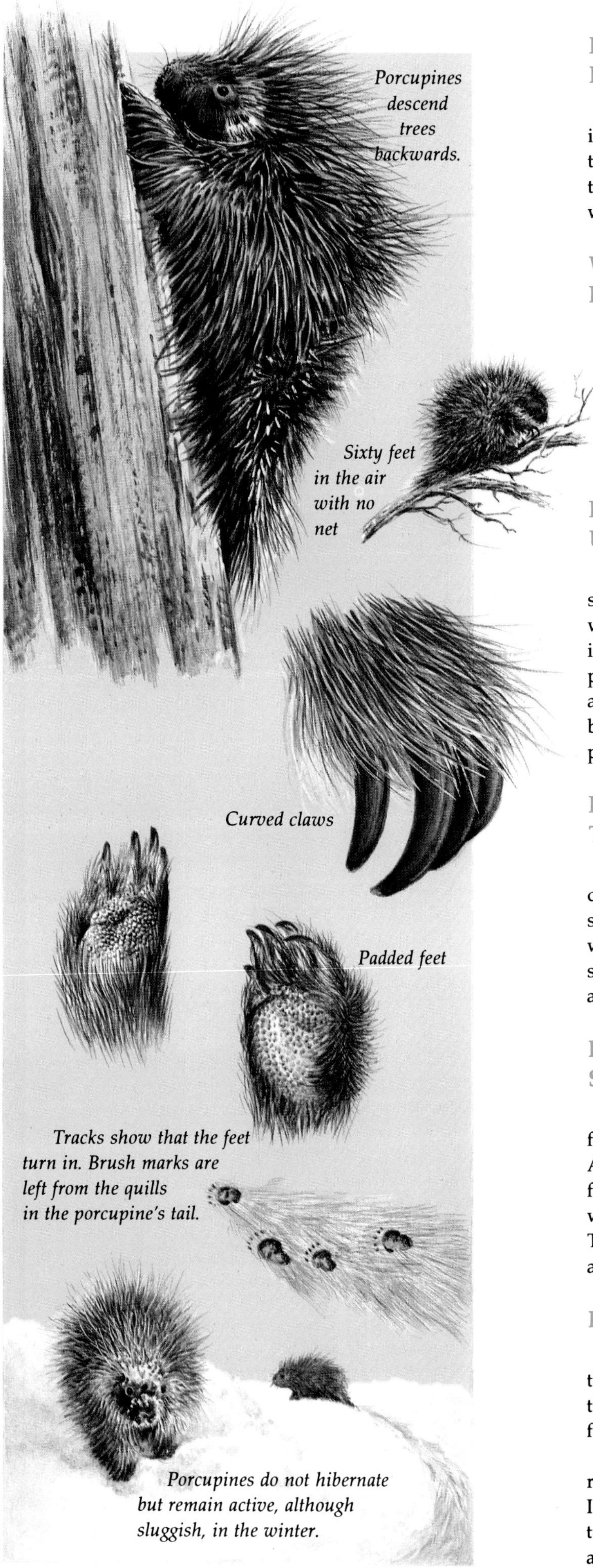
Porcupines descend trees backwards.
Sixty feet in the air with no net
Curved claws
Padded feet
Tracks show that the feet turn in. Brush marks are left from the quills in the porcupine's tail.
Porcupines do not hibernate but remain active, although sluggish, in the winter.

HOW DOES THE PORCUPINE SHARPEN ITS TEETH?

Porcupines have twenty teeth, but only the four front incisors need sharpening. Because the enamel is softer on the back side of these teeth, it wears away more quickly than the front side. This creates a sharp, chisel-like edge with which the porcupine chips and peels away bark from trees.

WHAT DO LUMBERJACKS AND PORCUPINES HAVE IN COMMON?

A porcupine uses the bristles located under its tail just as a lumberjack uses the spikes strapped to his boots. Wrapping its forelegs around a tree, a porcupine hitches itself up like an inchworm and then digs the sharp bristles under its tail into the tree. It then can lift itself up and repeat the process again.

HOW CAN A PORCUPINE WALK UPSIDE DOWN?

A porcupine can sleep comfortably in the top of a sixty-foot tree. It can stand erect on the outermost limbs which may be less than half an inch in diameter. To do this, its feet are equipped with long, curved claws and broad, padded soles. The porcupine's grip is so sure that it can walk along a branch as it hangs upside down. Its tail is used for balancing and serves as a third leg to form a tripod when the porcupine stands erect.

HOW DOES A PORCUPINE "SWIM" IN THE SNOW?

A porcupine has muscle control for each one of its quills. By spreading the quills, it can actually float on the surface of deep snow. It literally swims along by paddling with its short legs. In the same way, the porcupine is a good swimmer in water. Its dense inner coat holds much air, allowing the animal to float easily.

HOW DOES A PRICKLY PORCUPINE SHOW AFFECTION?

During courtship, the male porcupine serenades the female with a low humming sound punctuated with grunts. As he sings, he may stand up and begin to sway back and forth, keeping time to the music. Occasionally, the female will also stand up and place her forepaws on his shoulders. They gently hit each other on the head and push one another over.

HOW IS THE PORCUPINE ITS OWN ENEMY?

Internal parasites are perhaps the greatest enemy of the porcupine. Because porcupines do not clean their dens, the filth sometimes becomes so deep that there is little room for the animals themselves.

Living under such conditions, the porcupine continually reinfects itself with both roundworms and tapeworms. Incredible numbers of both have been found in its intestinal tract. One eleven-pound porcupine had 1,528 tapeworms and 5,184 roundworms. In comparison, an average-size dog may show symptoms of illness with only two or three tapeworms or 150 roundworms.

DOES A PORCUPINE SHOOT ITS QUILLS?

A porcupine lumbers about the forest with a complete disregard for danger. When threatened, it has an automatic defense no less effective than a swarm of 10,000 hornets. It turns its face away from its enemy, arches its back, and raises its tail slightly. When its opponent gets close, it flicks its tail and drives home the loosely held quills. While it cannot shoot its quills, the porcupine strikes like lightning with its tail. Even a black bear can be driven away with a single, well-directed slap.

HOW MANY QUILLS DOES A PORCUPINE HAVE?

Counting one quill a second, it would take almost ten hours to count a porcupine's quills. The head is covered with approximately 1,250. The tail alone may have over 1,600. Over 33,000 quills cover the body. Considering that thirty quills would drive away a dog, the porcupine is more than equipped to drive off a great number of attackers at a single time without running out of quills.

Quills are made of the same material that forms claws, hoofs, scales, and feathers.

A walking pincushion

Covered by several layers of hair, porcupines are more vulnerable to heat than to cold.

CAN YOU GET WOOL FROM A PORCUPINE?

Quills are only one of the five different types of hairs found on a porcupine. Near the skin, porcupines are covered with a short, fine wool for warmth. A second coat of guard hairs protects the soft inner fur from dirt and moisture. Under the tail are found strong bristles used in climbing. Finally, there are long individual hairs which may be six to eight inches long. These form an outer coat, covering even the quills themselves.

Porcupine quills are not poisonous, but are covered with swarms of infectious germs.

CAN A PORCUPINE QUILL CUT THROUGH A MAN?

The dark tips of a porcupine's quills are covered with tiny scales which unfurl when embedded in warm flesh. These barbs make the quills very hard to pull out. They also cause the quills to gradually work their way more deeply into the flesh. Normal contractions of muscles literally pull the quills deeper and deeper at a rate of twenty-five millimeters a day. Quills have been known to work their way through a finger or leg, emerging on the other side after several weeks.

One man, who was struck on the back by a falling porcupine, discovered a needlelike object coming through the skin of his abdomen six months after the encounter. A quill had been overlooked and had traveled through the man's muscles without piercing any vital organs. Mountain lions have been found with quills buried in their brains. Coyotes have starved to death because a mouth full of quills made it impossible for them to eat.

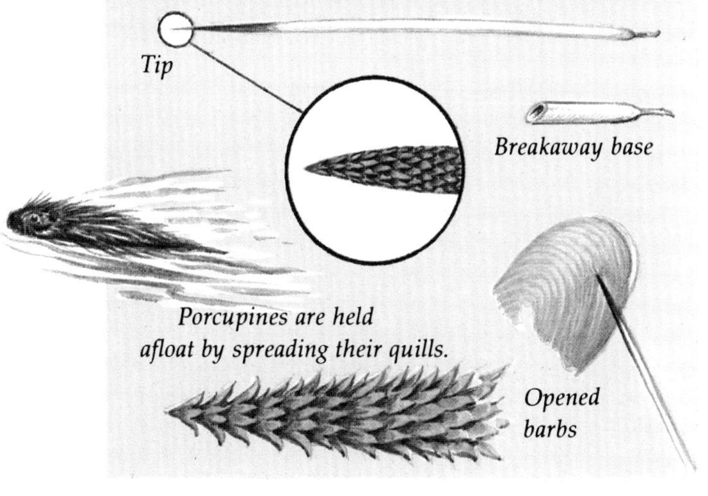

Porcupines are held afloat by spreading their quills.

Mother and daughter only minutes after birth

HOW CAN MOTHER PORCUPINES GIVE BIRTH WITHOUT GETTING HURT?

Newborn porcupines, called *porcupettes,* are born with a fully developed set of quills. The quills are limp and pliable at birth, but harden within minutes. To insure safety to both mother and young, the baby is born in a tough, round membranous sac. Thus, the porcupette can be born headfirst, backwards, or sideways.

Proportionately, porcupines have the largest offspring of any mammal. If human babies were proportionately as large, they would weigh nearly eighty pounds at birth. Instinctively, a porcupette will hide its head, arch its back, and twitch its tail within minutes after birth. It is also born with its eyes open, eats solid food within days, and is completely weaned within three weeks.

Fisher

Twenty per cent of a fisher's diet is porcupine. It eats everything but the quills.

WHAT ANIMAL CAN EFFECTIVELY ATTACK A PORCUPINE?

Occasionally, the pelt of a porcupine, quill side down, is found on the ground. This is the work of a fisher, a large member of the weasel family. He is perhaps the only predator to pose any real threat to the porcupine.

About one-fifth of the fisher diet is porcupine. The lightning fast animal attacks from the side to avoid the porcupine's thrashing tail. Flipping the porcupine over on its back, the fisher grabs the unprotected belly or neck.

In deep snow, a fisher may tunnel under the porcupine to reach its vulnerable underside. When a fisher misjudges his attack, he winds up with a face full of quills. However, the fisher's skin is apparently able to dissolve the quills before they can do much harm.

The unprotected nose and belly are points of vulnerability.

WHAT IS THE MOST VULNERABLE SPOT OF A PORCUPINE?

A porcupine has a "glass jaw." The skull is shaped in such a way that major nerves and blood vessels can be damaged by a sharp blow to the head, just above the nose.

Porcupine Quill Artistry

Porcupine quills have long been used by Indians to decorate garments, pouches, baskets, canoes, and quivers. They were sewn, woven, and even strung like beads. Red, yellow, and blue colors were added from the juices of wild roots and berries.

Indian traders selling colored "cure-all" elixirs found that their products were more often used as dyes for porcupine quills than for medicine.

How is the contentment of indestructibility illustrated in Scripture?

By every human standard he should have quit and gone back to the comforts and prestige of his former occupation. But, his awareness of God's hand upon his life gave him the sense of indestructibility that he needed until his work was done. Who was he?

(Pause for a response—see page 17.)

In 445 B.C. captains and soldiers, mounted on well-trained horses, left the splendor of the capital city of Persia and headed west. In this official delegation was a high-ranking adviser of the most powerful ruler in the world.

The adviser was on a mission that would go down in history as the most important event of his day. He knew that the task that lay before him was urgent, but he did not know the danger that he was to encounter in attempting to carry it out.

When the delegation passed over the Jordan River and entered into a provincial city, a meeting was held with several governors. The adviser gave each one an official letter. The governors were startled by the contents. They were surprised to learn that such a high-ranking official would want to help the despised remnant in the city of Jerusalem.

Two evil men learned about the adviser's plans and purposed to do all they could to stop him. As soon as the delegation left town, these evil men held an emergency meeting and laid out their strategy.

Meanwhile, the official and his party traveled on to Jerusalem. Several days later, a special meeting was held in Jerusalem with all the rulers, priests, and nobles. The king's adviser reminded his listeners that the rubble and ashes of the once towering city walls were a stark testimony to the judgment of former days. Then he told them about the king's desire to have the walls rebuilt.

The people were excited to begin the task. No sooner had they begun, however, than the opposition unleashed its continuous attacks. They began with mocking and then made false accusations and requests for meaningless conferences. When these failed, they prepared to come upon the builders with armed force, but the builders anticipated their move and doubled their protection.

One evening the king's adviser was informed that a man by the name of Shemaiah had a special revelation to give him. The adviser went to Shemaiah's house and listened to the message. "God has warned me that there is a special plot against your life. Your enemies will come in by night and will slay you. Come, let us flee to the temple and lock ourselves inside. That is the only way to save your life."

The adviser studied the fearful eyes of the "prophet," and without hesitation responded, "Who am I, that I should flee to the temple to save my life. No, I will not do it."

That prophet had been hired by those two wicked men to trick the king's adviser into violating God's Law by going into the temple. What those wicked men did not realize was that a death threat would have little effect.

The adviser was accustomed to death threats. One of his duties had been to drink of the king's cup in order to test it for poison. In addition to this, he knew that his present work was ordained by God, and that meant that he was indestructible until his work was done. Under Nehemiah's leadership, the walls were rebuilt in the remarkably short time of fifty-two days!

From Nehemiah 1–6

***Esther was queen to Ahasuerus,** also known as Xerxes (486–465 B.C.). Xerxes was the father of Artaxerxes. Thus, Esther's influence was significant to the work of Nehemiah.*

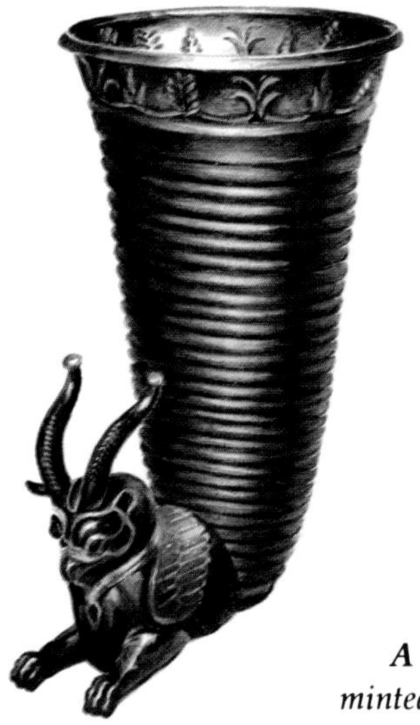

***A Persian coin** minted in ca. 400 B.C.*

***A silver drinking cup** used by a Persian king or nobleman during Nehemiah's day*

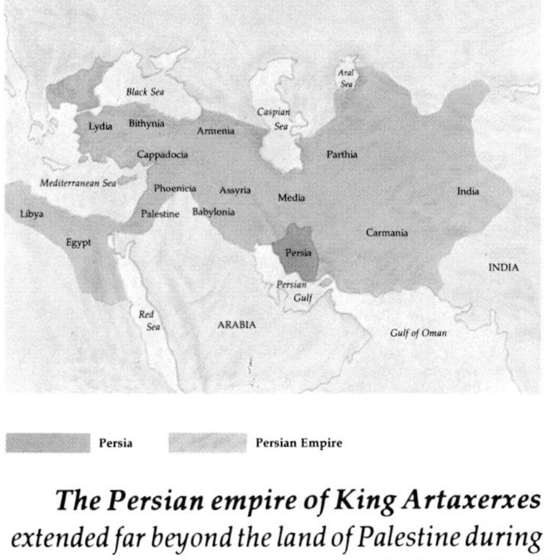

***The Persian empire of King Artaxerxes** extended far beyond the land of Palestine during the time when Nehemiah rebuilt the walls of Jerusalem.*

NEHEMIAH, ONE WHO ACHIEVED BECAUSE OF HIS CONFIDENCE IN GOD'S PROTECTION UNTIL HIS WORK WAS DONE

As the cupbearer to King Artaxerxes, Nehemiah was a high court official of the Persian government. When he heard that Jerusalem was in ruins and her inhabitants were discouraged, Nehemiah purposed to help. However, receiving the approval and support of the king was only one of many obstacles to be overcome.

NEHEMIAH'S RESPONSE TO RIDICULE, ANGER, AND THREATS

The first challenge that Nehemiah faced in Jerusalem was the ridicule of three local politicians—Sanballat, Tobiah, and Geshem. They hated the Jews, and *". . . it grieved them exceedingly that there was come a man to seek the welfare of the children of Israel" (Nehemiah 2:10)*. They insinuated that Nehemiah was rebelling against Artaxerxes by rebuilding the city's defenses. Nehemiah asserted his assurance of God's help and reminded the petty politicians that he was the duly appointed leader of Jerusalem. (See Nehemiah 2:19–20.)

When the rebuilding began, Sanballat *". . . was wroth, and took great indignation, and mocked the Jews" (Nehemiah 4:1)*. Tobiah mocked the project, *". . . Even that which they build, if a fox go up, he shall even break down their stone wall" (Nehemiah 4:3)*. Nehemiah's response to their anger was prayer followed by persistence. (See Nehemiah 4:4–6.)

Once the lower half of the wall was completed, Nehemiah's enemies *". . . conspired all of them together to come and to fight against Jerusalem, and to hinder it" (Nehemiah 4:8)*. He responded to this threat with prayer and the establishment of a round-the-clock watch to monitor the enemy. (See Nehemiah 4:9.)

NEHEMIAH'S RESPONSE TO DEFECTION AND EXPLOITATION

The next two obstacles came from within the community. The men of Judean descent threatened to defect, complaining about overwork in an impossible and dangerous task. Nehemiah exhorted them to focus on God, reorganized the work to reflect the reality of an imminent attack, and required the other men to remain in the city at night. (See Nehemiah 4:10–23.)

The second internal problem arose between the rich and the poor. The rich were lending money to the poor at interest. This violated the Law (see Leviticus 25:35–37), demoralized the poor, and jeopardized the entire project. Nehemiah rebuked the rich, pleading with them to make restitution. Their response was positive, and the work was resumed. (See Nehemiah 5.)

NEHEMIAH'S RESPONSE TO SLANDER AND TEMPTATION

The attack now shifted back to the outside. Just before Jerusalem's gates were installed, Sanballat and Geshem attempted to lure Nehemiah to a meeting thirty miles away. Nehemiah refused their written offer four times. A fifth letter was an open accusation of treason against Nehemiah. A rumor, likely to reach Artaxerxes, was circulated which predicted that Nehemiah would declare himself king and rebel against the empire as soon as the defenses were complete. Nehemiah denied the rumor, accused his foes of slander, and predicted that this scheme would fail. He then cried out to the Lord for strength. (See Nehemiah 6:1–9.)

The final attack was a warning of assassination delivered to Nehemiah by a false prophet. Nehemiah was advised to seek refuge in the holy place of the temple to save his life. He refused the temptation to go into this prohibited area and responded by crying out to the Lord. (See Nehemiah 6:14.) The wall was rebuilt after fifty-two days of hard effort. Jerusalem was now a safe place in which to live, and the city could resume its task of revealing Jehovah to the world around.

CHARACTER SKETCH OF NEHEMIAH

WHAT DID IT COST NEHEMIAH TO LEAVE PERSIA?

The historian Herodotus, Nehemiah's contemporary, wrote that the office of cupbearer was "one of no trifling honor." Among Nehemiah's responsibilities was the job of protecting the king from assassination.

Since Artaxerxes' own father had been killed by the head of the palace guard, Nehemiah must have proven himself to be a man of outstanding character and trustworthiness. Nehemiah enjoyed the friendship of the world's most powerful ruler and had access to the riches and pleasures of the fabulously wealthy empire.

But like Moses, who refused to identify with the powerful and wealthy Egyptians, *"Choosing rather to suffer affliction with the people of God, than to enjoy the pleasures of sin for a season; Esteeming the reproach of Christ greater riches than the treasures in Egypt: for he had respect unto the recompence of the reward" (Hebrews 11:25–26)*, so Nehemiah chose to leave Persia and suffer with his people in Jerusalem. In terms of Nehemiah's personal safety, comfort, and position, the cost was great.

WHY WAS NEHEMIAH ABLE TO LEAD SO EFFECTIVELY?

Nehemiah accomplished in fifty-two days what good men before him had not been able to accomplish in almost a century. One aspect of Nehemiah's character undergirded his many abilities. Nehemiah never asked others to make a sacrifice that he himself was not willing to make.

For example, he asked his countrymen to move into and help rebuild a ruined, unwalled city. But he set the example by leaving the capital of the empire, the palace itself. He asked men to participate in hard labor and set the example by not even removing his own work clothes at night. (See Nehemiah 4:23; 5:16.)

He asked the rich to forgive the poor of their interest-bearing loans. He set the example by refusing the customary food allowance which would have burdened the poor. In addition, he fed a large number of people at his own expense. (See Nehemiah 5.)

He called for courage and then modeled courage by refusing to cower at an alleged assassination attempt. Nehemiah earned the respect and allegiance of all the people.

WHAT KEPT NEHEMIAH FROM BECOMING DISABLED BY FEAR?

Most men fear what they can see or hear and react accordingly. Nehemiah saw rubble, backbreaking labor, and powerful enemies. He heard ridicule, threats, and slander. Most men would have given up. But Nehemiah saw and heard what most men do not perceive—the God of Israel, Whom he feared more than men or things.

His initial prayer for the project began, *". . . I beseech thee, O Lord God of heaven, the great and terrible God . . ." (Nehemiah 1:5)*. Later, he admonished the greedy nobles and rulers of Jerusalem *". . . to walk in the fear of our God . . ." (Nehemiah 5:9)*. He refused to accept certain rights *". . . because of the fear of God" (Nehemiah 5:15)*. He appointed his brother, Hananiah, as his successor because *". . . he was a faithful man, and feared God above many" (Nehemiah 7:2)*.

The fear of God in Nehemiah's heart gave him contentment in knowing that he was indestructible until his God-given task was completed.

Nehemiah was free from personal ambition *and confident of God's call and protection. These were essential qualities in rebuilding the walls.*

NEHEMIAH
nē-(h)ə-mī-ə

CHAPTER SEVEN

Contentment

. . . Is avoiding the bondage of personal expectations

"My soul, wait thou only upon God; for my expectation is from him."

Psalm 62:5

Living Lessons on Contentment . . .

FROM THE PAGES OF SCRIPTURE

Expectations destroy relationships. They compete with the principles of contentment. When God commanded the armies of Israel to conquer an evil and wicked city, He warned the soldiers not to expect personal gain from the battle. They would get their reward at a later time.

One man listened to these warnings, but became the willing prisoner of his own expectations. In the course of fulfilling his selfish desires, he brought tragedy to his nation, his family, and himself.

ILLUSTRATED IN THE WORLD OF NATURE

OYSTER CATCHER *Haematopus palliatus*

In the United States, the oyster catcher resides on the east and west coast beaches. The western species is completely black. The eastern species is black with a white breast. Both species are easily identified by a bright red bill which is twice as long as the head. Oyster catchers are large birds, fifteen to twenty inches tall. Flocks of these birds contain a large majority of older birds—some as old as twenty-three years.

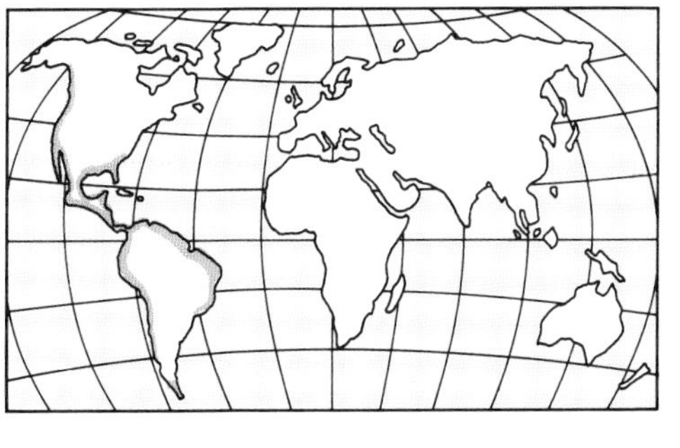

The range and habitat of the oyster catcher

How is the bondage of expectations illustrated in the world of nature?

Thunderclouds overshadowed the silent bird as he pointed his scarlet bill into the salty ocean breeze. The tide had just receded, exposing a vast array of shoreline delicacies.

Wading into the shallows, the hungry shorebird feasted on oysters, crabs, and mussels while other shorebirds probed the wet sand for worms and cockles. But with the delicacies there were hidden dangers.

After devouring all of the available oysters, the bird turned his attention to an abundant supply of limpets. These one-shelled creatures had attached themselves tightly to rocks with a single padlike foot. The confident bird expected each limpet to be relaxed and easy to pry loose with one quick flip of his beak.

This was the case well into the afternoon. Gradually, the foamy advances of the tide began to infringe on the busy shoreline. As the swelling surf warned the feeding bird to retreat from the shore, he decided that there was time to enjoy one more meal.

The agile hunter spotted a delicious-looking limpet fastened to a saw-toothed rock. Assuming that the shellfish would be an easy prey, he jabbed his pointed bill between the limpet and the rock. Aroused by the incoming tide, the limpet had already tightened its grip on the reef. The bird tried in vain to pry the limpet loose, and when he attempted to withdraw his bill, he discovered that he was trapped!

The frightened bird frantically attempted to free himself from the limpet's viselike grip. Meanwhile, the surging tide began to lap against the rock where the bird was hopelessly caught. The struggles of the bird only caused the limpet to increase its hold.

Soon, powerful waves broke in along the shore and splashed over the bird. Suddenly, the pinned bird stopped struggling. He folded his wings and just stood still. The limpet responded by loosening its grip for a moment. In that instant, the oyster catcher yanked his bill free and flew to safety. Only by surrendering his struggle for freedom was he able to experience it.

Nevert Andrewson

THE CHARACTERISTICS OF

THE OYSTER CATCHER IN SCRIPTURE

The oyster catcher ceases to struggle if initial attempts to free itself are unsuccessful. Similarly, Christians are to stop striving or contending with others who reject the truth which they give. *"And the servant of the Lord must not strive; but be gentle unto all men . . ." (II Timothy 2:24).*

Further counsel is given by God for this important point in Scripture. *"Cease from anger, and forsake wrath: fret not thyself in any wise to do evil" (Psalm 37:8). "A soft answer turneth away wrath: but grievous words stir up anger" (Proverbs 15:1).*

When an oyster catcher finds itself in a territorial confrontation with another oyster catcher, it will end the battle by yielding its rights and becoming vulnerable.

As Christians, we are told to submit ourselves to the older. *"Likewise, ye younger, submit yourselves unto the elder. Yea, all of you be subject one to another, and be clothed with humility: for God resisteth the proud, and giveth grace to the humble" (I Peter 5:5).*

Haematopus palliatus is the scientific classification assigned to the oyster catcher. The Greek root words mean "blood" and "taking that which is hidden." Christians identify with God by the blood of Christ and grow by daily feeding on the hidden truths of the Word of God.

CHARACTERISTICS AND PHYSICAL FEATURES OF THE OYSTER CATCHER

The oyster catcher exhibits the unique characteristic of becoming motionless when a confrontation gets out of hand. During territorial fights between two males, one will suddenly freeze, fold its head under its wing, and stop struggling. By making itself completely vulnerable to its adversary, the battle is ended.

In spite of their ability to open tightly closed seashells, oyster catchers occasionally get their beaks caught. They will starve or drown unless the shell can be removed. If initial attempts to free themselves fail, they simply cease the struggle.

WHAT DOES AN OYSTER CATCHER'S BILL AND A RIFLE SIGHT HAVE IN COMMON?

The eyes of the oyster catcher are located almost directly behind its straight bill. This gives the bird a unique advantage in being able to sight down its bill and aim directly at its intended target.

Accuracy is extremely important for the oyster catcher as it often gets only one shot at an open shell. If it misses, the shell will close and the bird must continue to hunt. When hammering at a closed shell, the oyster catcher is so accurate that it can continue to pound even as the closed shell is still bouncing from a previous strike.

The oyster catcher is easily identified by its long, red bill.

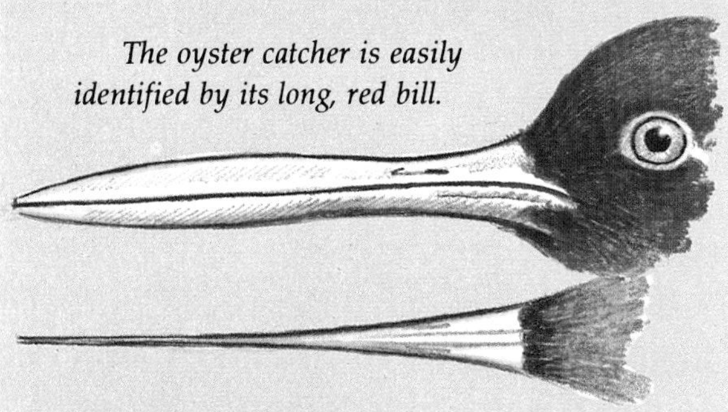

The thin, blunt bill is perfect for chiseling and prying.

HOW IS AN OYSTER CATCHER'S BILL LIKE A SIX-IN-ONE TOOL?

The oyster catcher's bill is an incredible combination of tools. It is flattened vertically and blunt on the end. It can hammer, pry, snip, slice, poke, and probe. It can reach into long cracks or holes and tweeze out even the smallest of edibles.

The dimensions of the bill make it a perfect pry bar. It is twice the length of its own head which gives it a decided leverage advantage. The thin screwdriver-type end allows the oyster catcher's bill to be used like a power chisel for hammering through shells or slipping between the partially closed halves of mussel shells.

Many other birds have a fourth toe. The oyster catcher has only three.

WHAT KEEPS THE OYSTER CATCHER FROM SLIPPING ON WET ROCKS?

The feet of the oyster catcher are covered with tiny grippers called *pectinations* which serve much like those on the boots of rock climbers. These pectinations cover the entire foot, giving the oyster catcher a good grip in every direction. The toes are also slightly webbed at the base. This helps prevent the feet from sinking into wet sand.

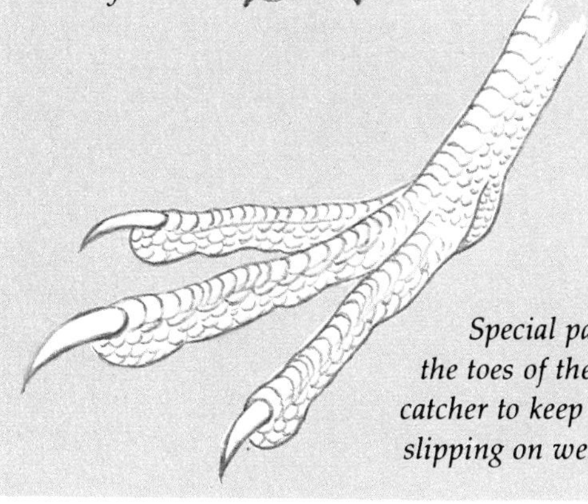

Special pads line the toes of the oyster catcher to keep it from slipping on wet rocks.

Beach-
combing
oyster
catcher
Beachcombing
oyster catchers
feed only on shells
that are closed.
Each type
of shell has
points of
weakness.
Cockle shell
Crab
Animals beneath
the sand are located
by touch.

WHY DOES THE OYSTER CATCHER'S HEAD BULGE ON THE LEFT SIDE?

Because the head and bill of the oyster catcher are all one structure, the constant prying open of shells actually begins to deform the shape of the head. With very few exceptions, oyster catchers pry open shells in a clockwise direction. This exerts tremendous pressure on the skull, causing the left side to bulge.

HOW DOES THE METHOD OF FEEDING DIVIDE OYSTER CATCHERS INTO TWO GROUPS?

Oyster catchers can be divided into two groups of feeders, beachcombers and waders. Beachcombers hammer closed shells on the beach, while waders pry apart partially opened shells in the water. Both the beachcombers and the waders teach their young their respective ways of feeding.

Both groups appear to share the common practice of probing the sand for small worms. On any given beach, all three techniques can be observed. However, on closer observation it becomes apparent that the techniques of feeding are quite segregated.

HOW LONG WILL IT TAKE AN OYSTER CATCHER TO CATCH AND EAT 200 OYSTERS?

Beachcombers feed on mussels, cockles, and limpets that have been left exposed by a receding tide. The oyster catcher carries the mussel to a firm patch of sand, flips the shell onto its back and begins to chisel away at the shell's weakest point.

Only a small hole is required for the oyster catcher to insert its bill and pry open the shell. The bird then quickly scissors out the flesh of the mussel and begins to look for another. The entire operation may take less than twenty seconds. It is not uncommon for a single bird to eat up to 200 mussels in one hour.

WHAT WILL HAPPEN TO AN OYSTER CATCHER IF IT BREAKS ITS BILL ON AN OYSTER?

Oysters, mussels, and cockles all have a "soft spot." The flat ventral surface on the underside of these shells has only a fraction of the strength of the dorsal or upper half. If the oyster catcher were to attack the dorsal side it would be apt to break its bill, which would result in certain death from starvation.

HOW DO OYSTER CATCHERS "FEEL" WITH THEIR BILLS?

While oyster catchers have keen eyesight, they rely on their sense of touch to find food under the sand. They repeatedly probe the sand every few inches until their bills hit something. The oyster catcher immediately digs up the spot to locate the rock, stick, crab, cockle, or worm.

HOW DOES THE OYSTER CATCHER RESEMBLE A SEWING MACHINE?

An oyster catcher runs back and forth along the beach, constantly probing the sand with its long bill. This up and down motion resembles the action of a sewing machine needle.

Crabs are stunned with a quick blow to the brain center.
Waders feed only on shells that are already slightly open.
The empty shells are simply discarded on the beach.
The adductor muscle holds the halves together.

HOW MANY COCKLES CAN AN OYSTER CATCHER EAT IN ONE DAY?

One oyster catcher was observed to eat 336 large cockles during a single tide. On the average, each oyster catcher will consume one-half of its body weight each day. Flocks numbering in the thousands may eat a million cockles in a single day.

HOW DO OYSTER CATCHERS CATCH CRABS?

Waders feed by surprising their victims and stunning them with a quick blow to the adductor muscle before the victims can defend themselves. When underwater, mussels and cockles open their shells in order to feed. A wading oyster catcher will stalk the open mollusk and strike quickly and accurately to stun the adductor muscle which the animal uses to close its shell. Temporarily paralyzed, the mollusk is easy prey for the oyster catcher, who effortlessly cuts out the exposed flesh and feeds.

Waders also feed on crabs. Crabs have a weak spot at their mouth which the oyster catcher capitalizes on. The oyster catcher will surprise the crab, flip it over onto its back, and stab into its brain in almost the same motion. The shell is then pried off and the flesh scissored out.

HOW IS AN OYSTER CATCHER'S BILL MORE POWERFUL THAN A MAN'S HAND?

So strong is the adductor muscle that holds the two halves of the oyster together that a man cannot pull the two shell halves apart with his bare hands. Humans require the use of a strong oyster knife to cut the muscle before the shell can be opened. An oyster catcher accomplishes this easily with its strong bill.

WHAT IS THE MESSAGE OF AN OYSTER CATCHER'S TRACKS IN THE SAND?

The three toes of the oyster catcher make a clear set of arrowlike tracks in the sand. The arrows point to where the oyster catcher has been. To follow an oyster catcher, one goes opposite to the direction the arrows are pointing.

Gulls often steal food from the oyster catcher.

To remove a stubborn mussel, the oyster catcher will swing its bill like a baseball bat.

Incubating an "adopted" egg

Faking injury

WHY DOES A SEA GULL WAIT FOR AN OYSTER CATCHER TO BEGIN ITS MEAL?

A gull's bill is not designed like an oyster catcher's and cannot open shells. A gull will often wait until an oyster catcher is half finished with a meal and then chase it away and finish the meal itself. The gull will always wait until the meal has begun. If the gull should chase the oyster catcher away too soon and the shell closes, the gull has no way of reopening it.

WHY MUST AN OYSTER CATCHER BE ACCURATE ON ITS FIRST STRIKE?

If an oyster catcher is not accurate in its first strike, or does not move quickly enough to sever the adductor muscle, the mussel can clamp tightly around the oyster catcher's bill. This can create quite a problem. If the shell cannot be disengaged, the situation can be fatal for the oyster catcher. Often the oyster catcher will use its bill like a baseball bat, pounding the shell to bits on a rock.

HOW CAN AN OYSTER CATCHER'S DISCONTENT AFFECT ITS YOUNG?

Oyster catchers usually lay two to three eggs in their nest. However, they will quickly desert their own nests for another nest of four eggs. Fortunately, nesting parents vigorously protect their nests from neighboring parents who may have fewer eggs, thus forcing the greedy neighbors to return to their own nests.

Oyster catchers are also attracted to larger eggs. Upon occasion, oyster catchers have been known to desert their own eggs for the larger eggs of the herring gull. Observers have presented increasingly larger eggs to nesting oyster catchers with amazing results. One bird tried to incubate an egg which it could not straddle.

WHY DO OYSTER CATCHERS OFTEN FAKE INJURY?

When disturbed by man or other potential predators, oyster catchers fake injury by flapping their wings and running erratically away from the nest. Leaving their young hidden by their protective coloration, every attempt is made to lure the intruder away.

When confronted by an intruder away from the nest, oyster catchers may immediately rise to the attack with their powerful bills. But if the adversary does not flee, it may just as quickly tuck its beak under its back feathers and pretend nothing has happened. This alternating behavior is often very confusing to would be trespassers.

How is the bondage of wrong expectations illustrated in Scripture?

Giving up expectations is not easy. That is why God invites us to transfer them to Him. The Lord assures us that He will fulfill every expectation that will benefit our lives if we are faithful to learn the discipline of contentment.

Which man in Scripture lost his life because he decided to disobey God's command so that he could fulfill his own expectations?

(Pause for a response—see page 17.)

Hundreds of supernatural lessons should have prepared him for this crucial test. Previous tests involved the multitudes, but this test he faced alone. Little did he know that the lives of his wife, his children, and all his future generations hung in the balance during this crucial time.

As a boy, he had witnessed the moving of the mighty hand of God. He knew how the Lord had provided not only for his needs, but for the needs of the whole nation.

There were times when finding sufficient supplies of food and water was humanly impossible. In each instance, God graciously assured the people that He would fulfill their basic needs. Times of waiting taught them important lessons in contentment.

How could he have forgotten the day when he and the people had asked God for food? The Lord answered by showering them with bread from heaven that day and for the next forty years!

Had he also forgotten how he and the people had cried out to God with parched throats for water? There in the barren desert their leader struck a rock according to God's command causing fresh, cool fountains to miraculously flow forth.

And when they had grown tired of bread, had not God filled their camp with flocks of tender quail? Could this man also have lost sight of the fact that the leather soles of his sandals had lasted for over forty years of wandering?

These and many other powerful lessons should have caused him to quickly turn away from the objects that now tempted him, but he kept staring at them. The longer he looked, the more he became attached to the forbidden articles. Finally, he scooped them up, nervously hurried off to his tent, and buried them.

Several days later he quietly stood before the entire nation. At his leader's urging, he confessed how he had violated the command of the Lord. *"When I saw among the spoils a goodly Babylonish garment, and two hundred shekels of silver, and a wedge of gold of fifty shekels weight, then I coveted them, and took them . . ." (Joshua 7:21).*

In one foolish act, he had forsaken the provision of the Lord and relied on himself. By doing so, he entered into the bondage of wrong expectations. He and his family were led into the valley. There Achan, his wife, and his children were stoned to death.

From Joshua 7

Jericho was the "firstfruits of Canaan." *To plunder from it or to rebuild it was forbidden by God. (See Leviticus 27:28–29.)*

Joshua brought Achan to confession *and judgment just as Peter did with Ananias and Sapphira in the New Testament. Their sins were identical—stealing what belongs to God.*

Achan was stoned in the valley of Achor, *the "valley of trouble." It became a reminder of the past, but also a "door of hope" for the future if the nation would heed the lesson it taught. (See Hosea 2:15.)*

ACHAN, A TRAGIC EXAMPLE OF DISCONTENTMENT

The Lord wanted to do great things for the nation of Israel. He wanted to give them a rich land flowing with milk and honey. But He also wanted them to remember that He was the source and sustainer of their prosperity.

To help remind His people that all of their possessions were gifts from Him, He asked them to give back the firstfruits. The first production of an orchard (see Leviticus 19:23–25); the first of the annual production of grain, wine, olive oil, and sheared wool (see Exodus 23:16; Deuteronomy 18:4); coarse meal (see Numbers 15:20–21); honey, and of all the produce of the land (see II Chronicles 31:5) were the Lord's.

THE FIRSTFRUITS OF THE CONQUEST

Now that the Lord was about to give His people the promised land of Canaan, He claimed for Himself the firstfruits of the conquest—namely, the city of Jericho. This first city was to be an offering to the Lord. It was to be devoted to Him as a sign that He had given them the whole land. Joshua commanded the people not to take any spoil from Jericho except precious metals which were to be deposited into the tabernacle treasury. Everything else was to be destroyed and burned. (See Joshua 6:17–19.)

The Lord made it clear even to those of little faith that He was their strength. He miraculously opened up the Jordan River to provide access to the land, and now He would miraculously topple the massive wall barrier around the first city. On the seventh day and on the thirteenth trip around the city, the priests blew their horns, the people shouted, and the walls fell.

THE COST OF DISOBEDIENCE

Now that He had removed the obstacles, the Lord expected His people to finish the work by destroying the wicked inhabitants along with their possessions. In willful disobedience to the express command (see Joshua 6:18), Achan saw, coveted, took, and hid a garment which should have been burned and gold and silver which should have been turned over to the priests. He buried them beneath his tent, saving them for a future day when he could claim that they came from the spoil of another conquest.

The Lord would not overlook this treacherous act. The young nation needed to learn that God would not continue to pour out His blessing if they violated His clear commands. In the next battle, He allowed thirty-six men to be killed in defeat against the small town of Ai. The Israelites' hearts melted with fear, and Joshua interceded for them before the Lord. The Lord stated that the nation had sinned and was in need of cleansing before the campaign could be successfully resumed. He declared that the thief, his stolen spoil, and all his other possessions were to be burned.

SWIFT PUNISHMENT AND A LESSON FOR THE NATION

The next morning Achan was discovered. Before his execution, he confessed in front of the entire assembly what he had done and why he had done it. *". . . And all Israel stoned him with stones, and burned them with fire, after they had stoned them with stones. And they raised over him a great heap of stones unto this day. So the Lord turned from the fierceness of his anger . . ." (Joshua 7:25–26).*

Israel learned a costly lesson. They learned that they must not strive after possessions in their own human efforts. God would give them all that they needed if they honored Him with the firstfruits and acknowledged Him as the giver of every good and perfect gift.

CHARACTER SKETCH OF ACHAN

WHAT CAUSED ACHAN TO COMMIT SUCH A FOOLISH SIN?

Achan gives the answer in his confession before the assembly. *"When I saw among the spoils a goodly Babylonish garment, and two hundred shekels of silver, and a wedge of gold of fifty shekels weight, then I coveted them, and took them; and, behold, they are hid in the earth in the midst of my tent, and the silver under it" (Joshua 7:21).*

Achan's downfall began with a deliberate decision to continue to look at the beautiful garment and the money. He became distracted from his assigned duties as a soldier and soon coveted the forbidden spoil.

A battle began in his mind. He was deciding whether or not to yield the members of his body as instruments of unrighteousness unto sin or as instruments of righteousness unto God. (See Romans 6:13.) He chose the former and took the prohibited items. The evil look and the evil thought led to the evil deed.

Now Achan had to deal with his conscience. He ignored its prompting to repentance. In spite of thirty-six deaths, Achan refused to confess his sin until the lot finally fell at his feet. The "innocent" look had started a process of sin which destroyed him.

WHY DID OTHERS HAVE TO SUFFER FOR ACHAN'S SIN?

Because of Achan's private sin, thirty-six men were killed attempting to capture the city of Ai. Parents lost sons, wives lost husbands, and children lost fathers. The Lord declared to Joshua, *"Israel hath sinned, and they have also transgressed my covenant which I commanded them: for they have even taken of the accursed thing, and have also stolen . . ." (Joshua 7:11).* The Lord held the entire assembly responsible for the secret sin of one of its members. This is a principle stated throughout Scripture.

The Apostle Paul compared God's people to the members of a body. *"And whether one member suffer, all the members suffer with it; or one member be honoured, all the members rejoice with it" (I Corinthians 12:26).*

For this reason we are to *". . . consider one another to provoke unto love and to good works: Not forsaking the assembling of ourselves together . . . but exhorting one another . . ." (Hebrews 10:24–25).* We are not individual islands unto ourselves; we are a corporate body. We stand or fall together.

WHY WAS ACHAN'S PUNISHMENT SO SEVERE?

Achan was stoned, burned, and buried under a pile of rocks for stealing. God made Achan an example to the nation. The Lord was teaching His people that an act of direct disobedience to His revealed will is worthy of death. (See Numbers 15:30–31.)

The first man to break the fourth commandment by gathering sticks on the sabbath day was stoned as an example to the others. (See Numbers 15:32–36.) The first professing Christians who lied to the Holy Spirit were struck dead as a sobering example to the early Church. (See Acts 5:1–11.)

Achan's punishment demonstrated the exacting nature of God's law. But the story of Achan is also a reminder of God's forbearance and mercy toward us who deserve the same when we violate God's commands. (See Lamentations 3:22.)

***Achan illustrated the corporate nature** of one person's willful disobedience. When he sinned, God said, "Israel hath sinned . . ." (Joshua 7:11).*

The same principle is emphasized in the New Testament Church. "And whether one member suffer, all the members suffer with it . . ." (I Corinthians 12:26).

The monument of stones from the judgment of Achan stood as a stark reminder to all Israel of the consequences of discontentment and disobedience.

ACHAN
ā-kan

CHAPTER EIGHT

Contentment

. . . Is rejoicing in the way that God designed me

"I will praise thee; for I am fearfully and wonderfully made: marvellous are thy works; and that my soul knoweth right well."
Psalm 139:14

Living Lessons on Contentment . . .

FROM THE PAGES OF SCRIPTURE

Comparison breeds discontent. For this reason God warns us that we are not wise if we try to compare ourselves among ourselves. (See II Corinthians 10:12.) Instead, God wants us to thank Him for the way that He designed our unchangeable characteristics, such as appearance, family background, or basic mental abilities.

If we fail to be thankful, we will develop attitudes of inferiority or superiority. In either case, we will become self-centered and will not be able to freely give to others. Instead, we will develop wrong motivations to gain wealth and influence. This is the destructive pattern that developed in the life of a man who had a visible reason to compare himself with others.

ILLUSTRATED IN THE WORLD OF NATURE

TURKEY VULTURE *Cathartes aura*

The turkey vulture is not particularly attractive, swift, or powerful. It is voiceless, except for a few angry grunts and hisses that it makes as it fights with others for a share of a meal. Its scientific name comes from a Greek word meaning "cleanser." It is a bird that greatly benefits man in spite of its appearance and smell.

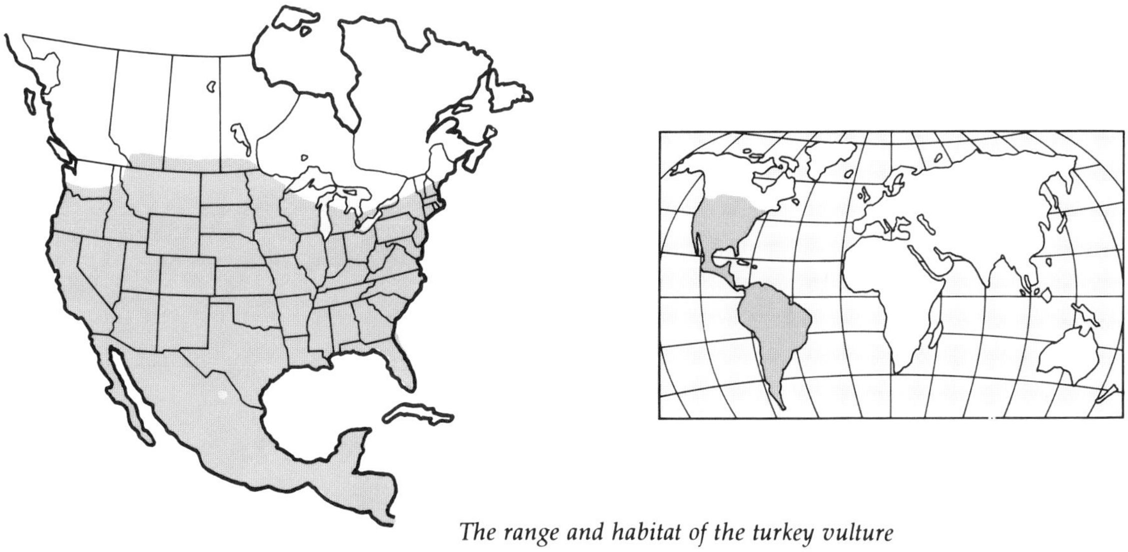

The range and habitat of the turkey vulture

How is the importance of contentment with God's design illustrated in the world of nature?

Leaning against the dried out slats of an old chuckwagon, two trail hands paused for a cool drink of water. As they climbed back into their saddles, they noticed some strange movements in the distance.

Just beyond a giant cactus, they caught sight of two turkey vultures fighting over the remains of a jackrabbit.

"Aren't they the ugliest birds you ever did see!" laughed one of the cowboys.

"Yep," answered the old drover. "Look at that puny bald head on that big clumsy body." One of the cowboys got off his horse and with a few well-aimed rocks easily scared off the scavengers.

That evening, the tired cowboys huddled around the campfire to escape the chill of the cool desert night. One by one they curled up in their bedrolls and dozed off to sleep.

That night, one of the longhorns broke away from the main herd. Shaken with fever and convulsions, it finally collapsed onto a patch of buffalo grass.

Two days later, as the noonday sun began to blister the arid landscape, circling turkey vultures descended and began to devour the decaying carcass.

Preoccupied with their meal, the busy vultures failed to sense the presence of another scavenger. Without warning, a hungry coyote lunged at the birds from a nearby ridge. The vultures escaped, leaving only bare bones for the disappointed coyote.

Aroused by the commotion, the two trail hands approached the skeleton. The coyote swiftly fled into the desert.

The cowboys dismounted and examined the scene. As they stood over the pile of bones, they did not realize that the ugly birds that they had mocked and driven away were now responsible for helping to protect them from certain death.

By so completely consuming the carcass of the steer they had removed the threat of the highly contagious disease anthrax from the cowboys and the herd. As the turkey vultures fulfilled God's design of feeding on death, others were given protection in life.

THE CHARACTERISTICS OF

THE TURKEY VULTURE IN SCRIPTURE

". . . There shall the vultures also be gathered, every one with her mate" (Isaiah 34:15).

Most people are repulsed by the physical appearance and the basic function of the vulture. Despite its reputation, the vulture has been specifically designed and equipped to fulfill God's purposes.

The Hebrew word for *vulture* is *'ayah* (ah-**yaw**) which means "the screamer." Its root meaning may stem from *'iy* (ee) and *'owy* (**o**-ee) which mean "one crying woe."

The vulture thrives on death, preventing the spread of disease by feeding on the carcasses of the dead. Scripture makes special mention of the vulture's keen eyesight, equipping the bird with an alertness for death. *"There is a path which no fowl knoweth, and which the vulture's eye hath not seen" (Job 28:7).*

The vulture is also a symbol of God's judgment. The wages of sin is death. When a dead body of a person becomes a meal for the vulture, it means that a proper burial has not been provided due to disaster, vengeance, or judgment.

When David stood against Goliath, he declared that God would give the giant's body over to the fowls of the air to punish his defiance. (See I Samuel 17:46.)

The vulture is specifically identified as unclean meat. *"But these are they of which ye shall not eat . . . the glede, and the kite, and the vulture after his kind" (Deuteronomy 14:12–13).*

CHARACTERISTICS AND PHYSICAL FEATURES OF THE TURKEY VULTURE

Because the turkey vulture never kills its own food, it must rely on finding animals that have been killed by others or have died from natural causes. It is always the last to eat and must be content to wait.

It can go for extended periods of time without food. Yet, it has also been known to so gorge itself at a meal that it cannot lift itself off the ground after eating. Regardless of the supply of food, the turkey vulture must be content to accept whatever is provided.

HOW DO THREE WEAKNESSES OF THE TURKEY VULTURE INSURE THAT IT WILL FULFILL GOD'S PURPOSES?

The turkey vulture has dull claws, weak talons, and a thin beak. Thus, it is not able to attack or tear apart a live animal. The turkey vulture must wait for its prey to die of other causes. In fact, the turkey vulture must often wait until the carcass is softened by decay or ripped open by another predator before consuming it.

HOW DOES A TURKEY VULTURE STAY HEALTHY ON A STEADY DIET OF DECAYED AND DISEASED MEAT?

The turkey vulture eats only rotting carcasses, which are often infested with maggots and bacteria. Frequently, it will eat the remains of animals that have died of a disease. Once inside the turkey vulture's digestive tract, however, the deadly bacteria are destroyed.

Even bacteria from the dreaded diseases of hog cholera and anthrax cannot survive in a turkey vulture's digestive tract.

WHAT DISINFECTING ABILITY DOES THE TURKEY VULTURE HAVE THAT IS THE DREAM OF EVERY HOSPITAL?

Infectious germs are an ever present danger where diseases are treated. Disinfectants are sometimes ineffective in killing the bacteria.

God has equipped the turkey vulture with an unusual method and an amazing ability to disinfect itself and its surroundings after being exposed to deadly germs. It uses the product of its own excrement. The same chemicals which killed the bacteria in its stomach continue to kill the germs outside of its body.

HOW DOES THE TURKEY VULTURE SAVE LIFE BY FEEDING ON THE DEAD?

By removing the carcasses of discarded animals, the turkey vulture has limited the spread of disease and prevented potential epidemics among both man and beast. In fact, the turkey vulture is widely respected and protected for sanitary reasons.

Turkey vulture claiming a fish

Feeding

The yellow-lined eyes of the turkey vulture are eight times sharper than man's.

Dull claws, weak talons, and a thin beak pose little threat to living prey.

Taking a "sun" shower
Solar-powered turkey vultures are lifted by rising air masses.
Turkey vultures average over 1,000 square centimeters of wing area for each pound of weight.
Wing tip feathers control flight.
Folded wings extend beyond the body and tail.
Early straight wing designs were not as stable as later V-shaped models.

HOW DOES A TURKEY VULTURE BATHE WITHOUT ANY WATER?

In spite of its messy meals, a turkey vulture is surprisingly clean. This fact is even more remarkable since it does not bathe with water. Instead it literally eats itself clean.

During meals, the turkey vulture's feathers become matted with dried blood, pieces of rotting flesh, and bacteria. To clean itself, the vulture uses its beak to meticulously scrape and straighten every feather. Thus, eating the refuse on its body is the final part of its meal.

HOW IS THE HEALTH OF THE TURKEY VULTURE BENEFITED BY A BALD HEAD?

Since the turkey vulture cannot reach its own head, it was created without feathers from the neck up. To clean its head, the turkey vulture stands in the sun, thereby allowing the ultraviolet radiation to kill any remaining bacteria.

HOW DOES THE TURKEY VULTURE KNOW IT IS TIME TO BEGIN ITS DAILY WORK?

Turkey vultures usually roost until late morning. They are not lazy, but are waiting for thermal air currents to develop. As the ground absorbs heat from the sun, the air above the ground is also warmed and begins to rise.

By late morning the air in these thermal currents is rising so rapidly that turkey vultures actually can glide downward within a column of rising air and still gain altitude. It is like walking slowly down an escalator that is going up. By waiting for the "thermals" to develop, turkey vultures can soar to great heights with a minimum of effort.

WHY IS THE TURKEY VULTURE USUALLY THE FIRST ONE TO SPOT A MEAL AND ALWAYS THE LAST ONE TO EAT IT?

The turkey vulture is extremely farsighted. It can see small objects from the sky several miles beyond what a person can see. By soaring high above the ground, a group of turkey vultures can effectively scan a ground area of a hundred miles.

When the turkey vulture arrives for its meal, it will often be met by other animals, even other types of vultures such as the black vulture. The turkey vulture will patiently wait until all the others are finished before it begins to eat. However, by the time it is finished eating, the carcass is thoroughly cleaned of meat.

HOW DID THE TURKEY VULTURE HELP TWO PILOTS TO BECOME FAMOUS?

Wilbur and Orville Wright began their study of flight around 1900 and made their first successful flight on December 7, 1903. During those three years, they spent much of their time watching the natural flight of birds and, in particular, the soaring ability and balance of the turkey vulture.

They noticed how the heavier parts of the turkey vulture were grouped below the horizontal line of its wings. Its body seemed to swing like a pendulum from its V-shaped wings. The Wrights realized later that the "dihedral angle" of the turkey vulture's wings greatly increased its stability.

DOES THE TURKEY VULTURE HAVE A POOR SENSE OF SMELL SINCE IT EATS ROTTEN MEAT?

No. It has a keen sense of smell. The area of the brain that controls the sense of smell in a turkey vulture is three times larger than that of a black vulture. It is known that a turkey vulture will not try to eat a meal before it first smells it and decides that it is ready to be eaten.

WHY DOES THE TURKEY VULTURE BEGIN ITS MEAL WITH THE EYE OF THE ANIMAL?

When the turkey vulture arrives at the site of a potential meal, it will always go to the eye first. Since the eye is an involuntary muscle, it responds even when an animal is unconscious. The turkey vulture knows that if the eye blinks, the animal is not yet dead. In such a case, the turkey vulture will back off and wait until death comes.

The talons of the turkey vulture are too weak to tear apart fresh meat. It must wait until the flesh decomposes enough to tenderize the meat. Sometimes this may take several days, unless another animal begins to feed on it first.

HOW DO TURKEY VULTURES DEMONSTRATE COOPERATION?

Turkey vultures operate in groups rather than individually. In the sky they scatter evenly over a large area. With their keen eyes they watch not only for carcasses on the ground, but also for movements from each other.

When any turkey vulture descends to the ground, neighboring vultures immediately note this as a signal that food has been found. Soon a flock of turkey vultures will have descended from a sky that had appeared empty.

DO TURKEY VULTURES EAT ANYTHING BESIDES ROTTING MEAT?

Sometimes turkey vultures will supplement their diet with rotten pumpkins or other softened vegetables. Eating decaying flesh and vegetables is necessary because the vulture's beak is weak and flimsy. It looks more like a big, hooked nose rather than a sleek instrument of death.

Turkey vultures lack quick-focusing eyes needed to pursue and catch moving prey.

Together a group of vultures can search over 100 square miles at a time.

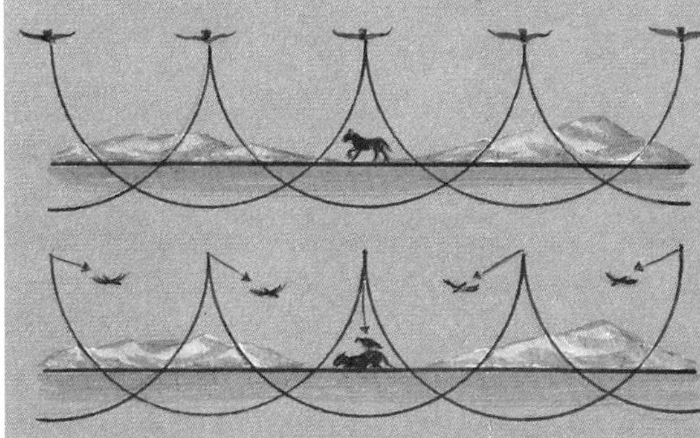

Pumpkin patch

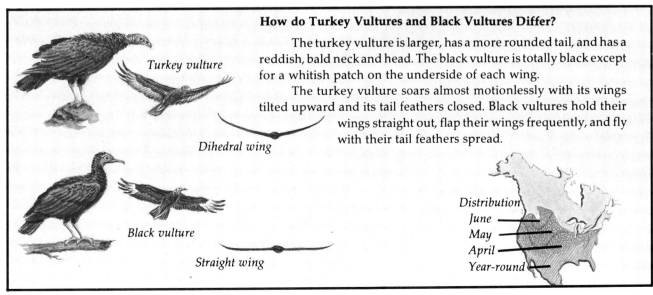

How do Turkey Vultures and Black Vultures Differ?

The turkey vulture is larger, has a more rounded tail, and has a reddish, bald neck and head. The black vulture is totally black except for a whitish patch on the underside of each wing.

The turkey vulture soars almost motionlessly with its wings tilted upward and its tail feathers closed. Black vultures hold their wings straight out, flap their wings frequently, and fly with their tail feathers spread.

Turkey vulture

Dihedral wing

Black vulture

Straight wing

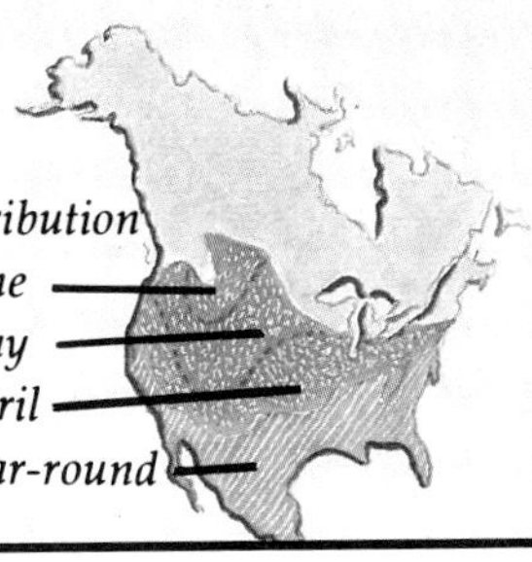

GROWTH AND DEVELOPMENT OF THE TURKEY VULTURE

Eggs

Turkey vultures lay one to three eggs with dull white, chocolate, and lavender markings.

Nests

The eggs are layed in almost any sheltered depression available. Parents make little or no attempt to prepare a nest, although they often return to the same location, preferring the same hollow log or stump for several years in a row.

Brooding females are very docile and can be carefully approached and even handled without apparent fear. However, if surprised or irritated, they defend themselves by disgorging food in the direction of the intruder.

Chicks

Chicks hatch after about thirty days and make their first flights after eight to nine weeks. Their coloring is almost completely opposite that of the adult. They are covered with a pure white down and have dark black heads. In time, their feathers begin to moult and are replaced with the darker plumage of the adult. The head gradually fades to gray, then pink, and finally red. Nestlings are often seen spreading their wings in the sun in imitation of their parents. They fold their wings again every time a cloud passes over.

Adult

The rusty black adults have a purple sheen on the lower neck and back. Their wings grow to perhaps three times the length of their body. Adult turkey vultures average more than nine hours per day in the air searching for food. When mature, their eyes are lined with a yellow ring which causes the eye to stand out against the dark red head.

Feeding

Like many birds of prey, turkey vultures feed their young by regurgitating pieces of partially digested food. The strong disease-killing enzymes of the parent's stomach protect the young from infection.

HOW DOES THE TURKEY VULTURE DEFEND ITSELF?

A turkey vulture is not swift enough to escape from an enemy nor is it strong enough to fight. Instead, it defends itself by blowing through its nostrils and making low, hissing sounds.

If this does not frighten an intruder or an attacker away, its only other defense is to throw up the foul contents of its stomach. Surprisingly, the turkey vulture is quite accurate and can hit a target as far away as ten feet.

WHY DOES THE TURKEY VULTURE SUFFER WITH COMPARISON?

If compared to the eagle, hawk, or osprey, the turkey vulture would be an apparent loser. It is not equipped for speed, strength, or beauty. Its feet are more like a chicken's feet than those of other majestic birds of prey. It does not have the viselike grip of the eagle nor the quickness of the hawk. Its wings are far out of proportion to the rest of its body and its head is wrinkled, red, and featherless. Its face also lacks attractive qualities. Nevertheless, the job it performs is vital for the health of mankind.

How is contentment with God's design illustrated in Scripture?

When a man rejects God's design for his life, he can easily develop an attitude of inferiority. This response often drives a man to concentrate on symbols of status such as wealth, position, and reputation.

Who in Scripture learned that personal wealth and physical stature are not important to God?

(Pause for a response—see page 17.)

The bidding became furious as scores of wealthy businessmen shouted out their lucrative offers. Driven by the desire for power and status, a small man in the crowd stepped forward and ultimately submitted the highest bid.

After signing the official documents, he triumphantly strutted from the auction hall and began to prepare for this long-awaited opportunity to gain great wealth and power.

With his newly acquired authority, the new official began to oppress his own countrymen. He soon became the most hated individual in the entire region. People frowned at the mention of his name and fled when they caught a glimpse of him walking down the narrow streets.

As the head of the tax and customs bureau, he quickly accumulated an impressive fortune. However, the material wealth he acquired failed to satisfy the longing in his soul. His Hebrew name, meaning "the just one" or "benevolent one," mocked him because of his dishonest way of life.

Overwhelmed with guilt and bitterness, he desperately sought a solution. One day he did a curious thing for a man in his position. After he did it, he heard someone call out his name. He was surprised, for the voice was filled with understanding, love, and acceptance.

The official's heart responded to the gentle words. Many in the crowd began to grumble when their teacher announced that He would be the guest of such a wicked man.

The official then amazed his enemies with the statement, "Behold, Lord, I will give half of my goods to the poor; and if I have taken anything by false accusation, I will restore him fourfold."

With that humble confession the crooked tax collector trusted the Lord Jesus and became content with God's design for his life. By realizing that his physical stature and material wealth were unimportant to God, he began to fulfill the true meaning of his name, Zacchaeus.

From Luke 19:1–10

ZACCHAEUS, A MAN WHO MADE RESTITUTION AFTER HIS CONVERSION

Jericho's fresh water spring *produces 1,000 gallons of water a minute. The water, combined with the mild climate, makes it possible to grow fruits and vegetables year around. In Scripture Jericho is called "... the city of palm trees ..." (Deuteronomy 34:3).*

Shortly before Jesus met Zacchaeus, He had met another wealthy man. The man was respected among the Jews, but his encounter with Jesus left him "very sorrowful." Jesus observed, *"... How hardly shall they that have riches enter into the kingdom of God! For it is easier for a camel to go through a needle's eye, than for a rich man to enter into the kingdom of God."* But He added, *"... The things which are impossible with men are possible with God" (Luke 18:24–25, 27).* The life of Zacchaeus illustrates this last statement.

TAXATION—A CORRUPT SYSTEM THAT APPEALED TO CORRUPT MEN

Zacchaeus lived in the city of Jericho. He was rich because of his job as chief tax collector. In those days the Roman government sold tax districts to the highest bidder. Zacchaeus bought the Jericho district and in turn distributed his district to subordinates who did the actual collecting. Zacchaeus was given a tax quota by the Romans, and everything collected above that quota was his profit. He could ensure himself a good return by offering his subordinates the same system of incentives.

The taxes to collect were many and varied. There were land taxes, a head tax, export and import taxes collected at the city gates, a crop tax, income taxes, road taxes, a tax to enter the city, animal and vehicle taxes, a salt tax, sales tax, tax on the transfer of property, and emergency taxes. The system was oppressive and led to widespread abuse. Both the government and the taxpayer were regularly cheated.

The tax collectors were known to take bribes from the rich for underassessing their goods and to extort more taxes from others by overassessment. It is not surprising that the Jews hated the tax collectors, who were called "publicans." As the "chief publican," Zacchaeus was possibly the most avoided man in Jericho, regarded as a traitor who sold his services to a foreign oppressor to make money for himself by exploiting his countrymen.

Zacchaeus was a chief tax collector. *His residence in Jericho was logical since the city was located on the main trade route from east of the Jordan into Judea.*

The dress *of a wealthy merchant*

A SEARCHING HEART

When Jesus passed through Jericho that day, Zacchaeus' curiosity was stirred. He had heard of the famous Galilean who had healed the sick, raised the dead, and challenged the teaching of the religious leaders. In Jericho, Jesus had just restored the sight of blind Bartimaeus whom Zacchaeus had seen many times begging at the city gate. He wanted to see Jesus for himself. Because of his short stature, he could not see over the crowd which had gathered and risked embarrassment by climbing into a tree.

A man of Zacchaeus' fame would not remain unnoticed. The spectacle of this wealthy but despised little man up in the tree drew not only the attention of the crowd but the attention of Jesus as well. However, Jesus saw something in Zacchaeus that the others did not. He saw more than a curious bystander. He perceived a heart receptive to the good news of salvation.

The sycamore fig tree *that Zacchaeus climbed has strong lateral branches that make it easy to climb.*

THE ENCOUNTER THAT CHANGED A LIFE

Jesus then said, *"... Zacchaeus, make haste, and come down; for to-day I must abide at thy house" (Luke 19:5).* The request was modest, but Zacchaeus' response was generous. *"And he made haste, and came down, and received him joyfully" (Luke 19:6).* He later promised to give half of his possessions to the poor and to restore what he had wrongfully taken. What a contrast is Zacchaeus to the rich young ruler who would not obey Jesus' request and left His presence full of sorrow. Zacchaeus obeyed Jesus and received the joy of salvation.

CHARACTER SKETCH OF ZACCHAEUS

WHAT ATTRACTED ZACCHAEUS TO JESUS?

The record simply states, *"And he sought to see Jesus who he was . . ." (Luke 19:3).* He was curious like others in the crowd who pressed in to get a glimpse of the famous Galilean, but his enthusiastic and joyful response to the Lord indicates that more than mere curiosity was at work in the heart of Zacchaeus.

He knew he was guilty of cheating his own countrymen. John the Baptist had clearly commanded the tax collectors, *". . . Exact no more than that which is appointed you" (Luke 3:13).* Zacchaeus may have heard about the conversion of Jesus' disciple, Matthew, who had been a tax collector. If those in his own lucrative profession were willing to follow this man, perhaps he should pursue the matter further.

At the same time, Jesus was looking for Zacchaeus. *"For the Son of man is come to seek and to save that which was lost" (Luke 19:10).* The Father was revealing Himself to Zacchaeus who had a receptive heart. (See Matthew 16:17.) The Father in turn revealed Zacchaeus to His Son, and Zacchaeus was found and saved. (See John 6:35–40.)

WHY DID THE CROWD DISAPPROVE OF CHRIST'S VISIT WITH ZACCHAEUS?

In addition to the expected animosity that the people felt toward Zacchaeus, there was also a religious reason why they were offended by Jesus' association with him.

All tax collectors were considered ceremonially unclean because of their continual contact with Gentiles and their custom of working on the Sabbath. Jewish people were taught by the scribes not to eat with anyone who was ritually unclean. Eating with a tax collector was a violation of scribal law. That is why tax collectors, or publicans, were closely associated with sinners and harlots. (See Matthew 9:10–11; 11:19; 21:31.)

The Lord's response to this criticism was, *". . . They that are whole have no need of the physician, but they that are sick: I came not to call the righteous, but sinners to repentance" (Mark 2:17).*

HOW DID ZACCHAEUS DEMONSTRATE HIS FAITH IN CHRIST?

Zacchaeus demonstrated his new faith by repenting of his former sins and making restitution. Jewish custom for those desirous of a reputation for piety was to give one-fifth of one's annual income to the poor. In fact, the Pharisees went to great lengths to publicize their giving. (See Matthew 6:1–4.)

Zacchaeus, however, desiring only the praise of God, decided to give half of his entire estate to the poor whom he had formerly exploited; and since Moses required a fourfold repayment in the case of theft, Zacchaeus used this figure to make restitution for everything he had obtained dishonestly. (See Exodus 22:1.)

His spontaneous generosity reflected a drastically changed value system. His treasure, now in heaven, was being stored *". . . where neither moth nor rust doth corrupt, and where thieves do not break through nor steal" (Matthew 6:20).*

The Lord did not ask Zacchaeus to give up all his wealth, as He had the rich young ruler, nor to leave his occupation and home, as He had Matthew. Zacchaeus was to continue his vocation as a new man. He was left to initiate local reform in a corrupt tax system and to be salt and light in Jericho.

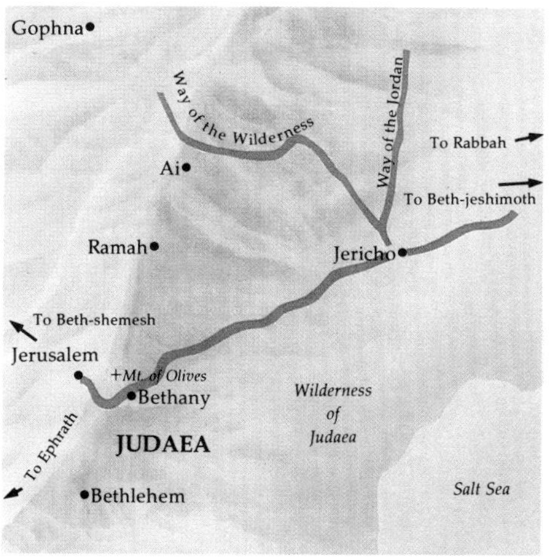

Highways running through Jericho

***The location of Jericho** and the events that occurred around there add additional significance to the account of Zacchaeus. The road between Jerusalem and Jericho descends 3,320 feet in fifteen miles. It was the setting of Jesus' parable of the Good Samaritan. It was also at Jericho that Jesus healed blind Bartimaeus.*

ZACCHAEUS
*zak-**kē**-us*

Gratefulness

. . . Is making known to God and others in what ways they have benefited my life

"For who maketh thee to differ from another? and what hast thou that thou didst not receive? now if thou didst receive it, why dost thou glory, as if thou hadst not received it?"

I Corinthians 4:7

PART THREE

GRATEFULNESS IN GIVING . . .

At the heart of all true giving there must be a spirit of genuine gratefulness. Only as we recognize the truth that we have "freely received" will we be able to obey the instruction to "freely give." (See Matthew 10:8.)

Our first recipient of gratefulness must be the Lord since *"every good gift and every perfect gift is from above . . ." (James 1:17)*. When God is given His proper praise, we then receive direction from Him on how to effectively express gratefulness to others.

CHAPTER NINE

Gratefulness

. . . Giving expressions of appreciation that will honor the design of God

"That I may publish with the voice of thanksgiving, and tell of all thy wondrous works."

Psalm 26:7

Living Lessons on Gratefulness . . .

FROM THE PAGES OF SCRIPTURE

People will often express their deepest gratefulness by giving you the very gift which they would like to receive. This is not only true among individuals, it is also true between God and people.

God's greatest gift to us was the sacrifice of His Son. Therefore, from the beginning of mankind God delighted in the sweet savor of a correctly offered sacrifice.

One man who gave such a gift was attacked by another who attempted to use his gift to exalt his own achievements rather than the redemptive work of Christ.

ILLUSTRATED IN THE WORLD OF NATURE

APHID *Aphis gossypii*

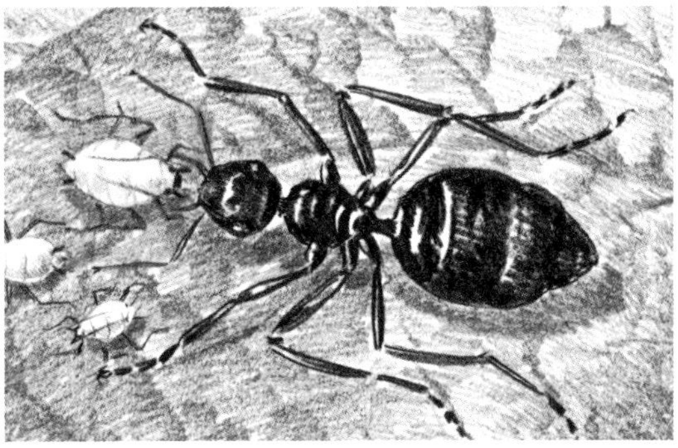

Aphids are small pear-shaped insects rarely more than one-eighth of an inch long. They come in a variety of colors including yellowish green, dark green, black, and brown. Because they pierce the moist tissues of plants and suck them dry, they do considerable damage to cultivated crops, particularly cotton and corn.

Amazingly, these feeble creatures migrate incredible distances, perhaps covering sixty miles in a single day. Fortunately, aphids have many enemies which help to keep their numbers in check.

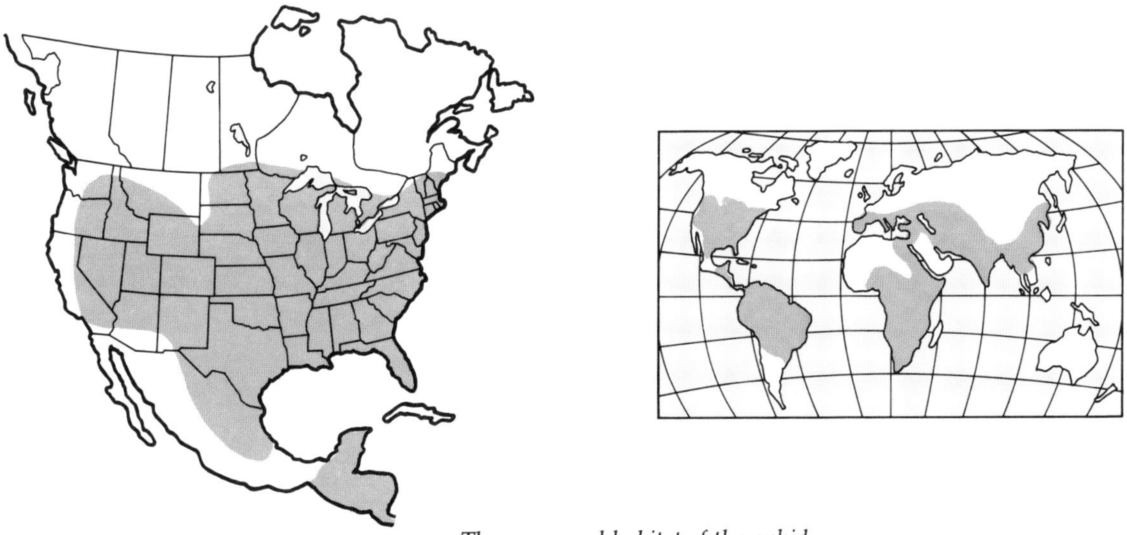

The range and habitat of the aphid

How is appreciation that honors the design of God illustrated in the world of nature?

The injured leopard stared nervously into the rain forest. Snarling and pawing at the ground, the restless cat frantically tried to escape the hunter's snare. The leopard instinctively sensed that it must flee from an unseen danger.

Slowly and methodically the deadly foe approached—a long column of migrating driver ants.

The determined attackers marched forward, devouring everything in their path. As they advanced, the terrified leopard yanked the steel cable in a final but fruitless effort to escape. Within several hours the once powerful cat had been turned into a pile of bones.

The driver ants relentlessly pushed on, not realizing that their next confrontation would be with a much more formidable adversary. Unlike the leopard, a colony of harvester ants had no intentions of fleeing. They would stand their ground and fight to the death.

As the aggressive driver ants entered the fields of the harvester ants, the battle began. Workers swiftly returned from their food trails to join in the defense of their colony.

With jaws open for action, the harvester ants reared up against the vicious invaders. While one harvester ant grabbed a charging enemy by a leg or an antenna, another defender would tear the intruder apart with its powerful jaws.

As the brave harvester ants fell, others rushed to take their places. The long column of ruthless aggressors seemed endless. Finally, with sheer numbers, the driver ants overran the community.

The courageous harvester ants had not only fought for their own survival. They had also provided protection for a group of fellow workers that had faithfully benefited their colony.

Throughout the summer these co-laborers had diligently worked to produce honeydew for the harvester ants. Several pounds of it had already been stored in the ants' nest in preparation for the coming winter.

These loyal friends of the harvester ants were aphids. The tiny workers enjoyed an unusual compatibility with the industrious ants.

The aphids were not strong in themselves. They depended on the ants for protection. In return, the aphids produced a continual source of sweet honeydew sugar to strengthen the ants for the work they were to accomplish.

The ants and the aphids displayed an extraordinary sense of service and appreciation for each other that honored the design of God.

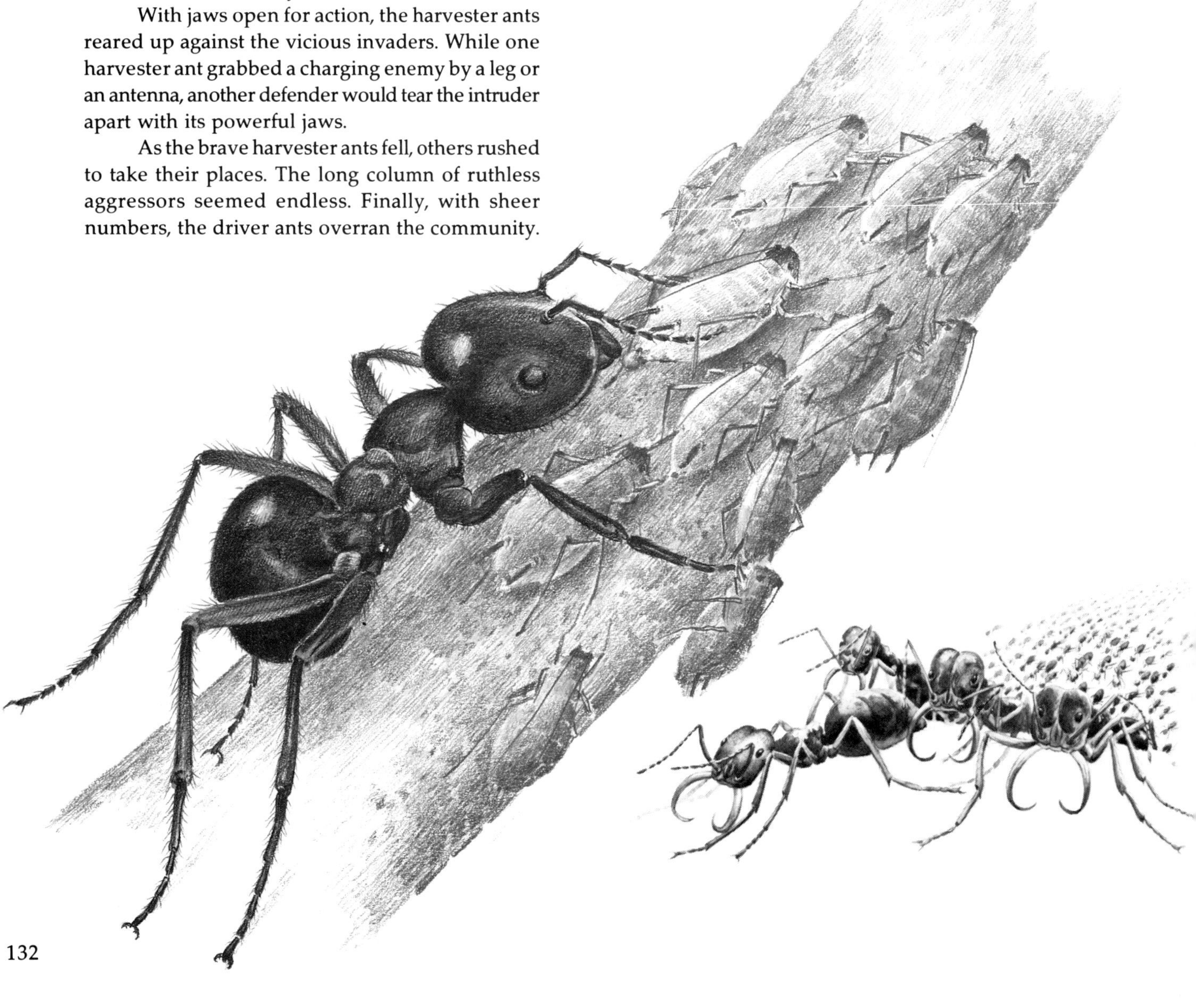

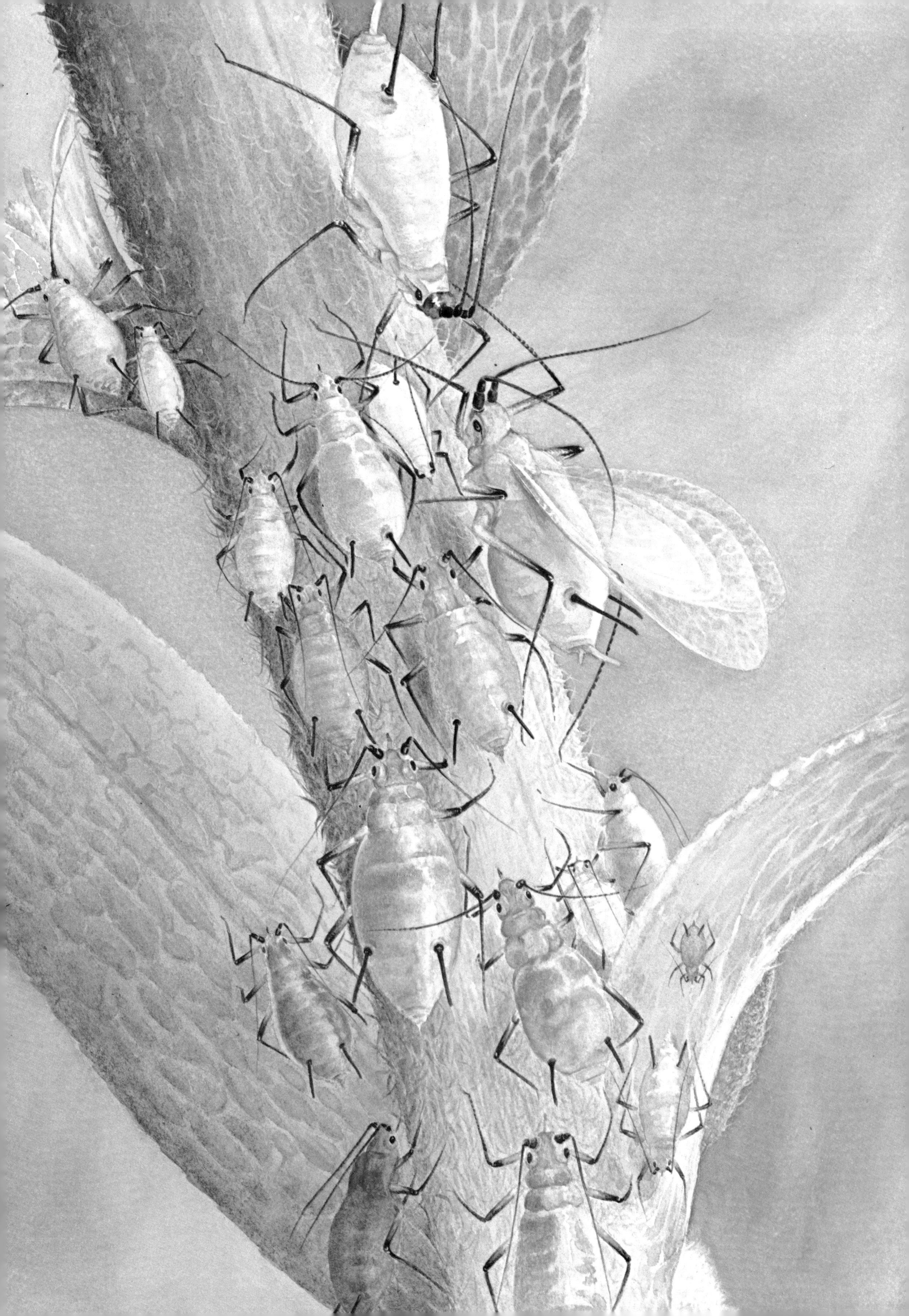

THE CHARACTERISTICS OF

THE APHID AND ANT IN SCRIPTURE

Scripture reveals that the ways of the ant contain valuable lessons for successful living.

"Go to the ant, thou sluggard; consider her ways, and be wise: Which having no guide, overseer, or ruler, Provideth her meat in the summer, and gathereth her food in the harvest" (Proverbs 6:6–8).

With no guide, overseer, or ruler to force or coerce, the ants' incredible diligence and achievement must come from another motivation—their mutual interdependence upon one another and upon those that become a part of their community.

This is precisely the type of edification that Christ called for in the local church. (See Ephesians 4:16.)

Although not related to the ant, the aphid becomes a part of the ant's community. The interaction between the ant and the aphid gives the clearest explanation of how the ant provides (sets aright, establishes) her meat (feed for the preparation of food) in the summer, and gathers (brings in) her food (edible products and food sources) in the harvest.

The aphid is able to multiply rapidly and destroy crops. Thus it is one of those "pestilences" which God uses to judge His people and the wicked when they violate His ways. (See I Kings 8:35–39.)

CHARACTERISTICS AND PHYSICAL FEATURES OF THE APHID AND ANT

Without the ants' care, aphids have difficulty surviving. On plants not tended by ants, the average number of aphids was observed to be less than seventy. On identical plants where aphids were tended by ants, the average number was 1057. Many species of aphids disappear completely when ants are prevented from caring for them.

In return for care and protection aphids provide the ant with sweet, nourishing food. A colony of a million ants will receive over half a ton of food in a single year from aphids. The aphids illustrate God's design for genuine appreciation—an awareness of interdependence.

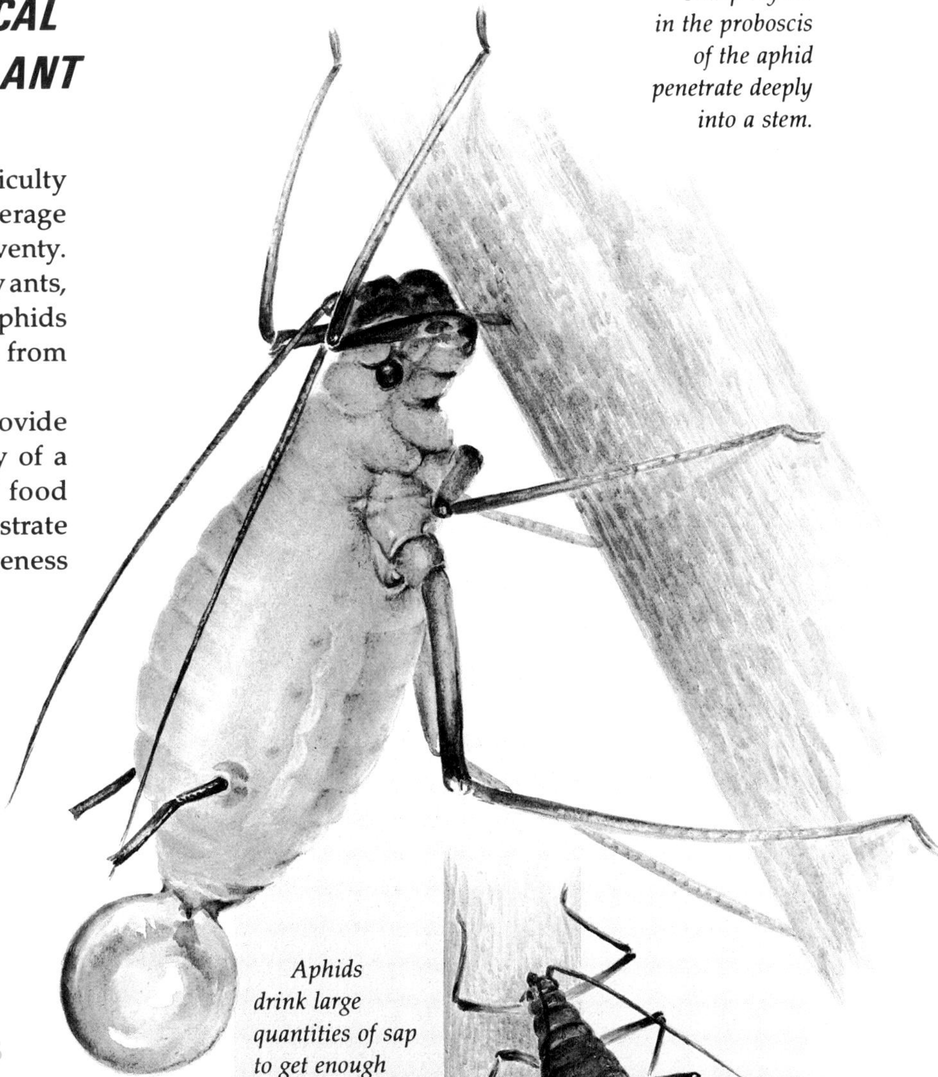

Sharp stylets in the proboscis of the aphid penetrate deeply into a stem.

WHY DO APHIDS HAVE SIX LEGS AND TWELVE FEET?

Aphids have six legs, but each leg ends with a double foot. Thus aphids, unlike most other insects, have twelve feet. Each foot is tipped with a tiny claw. Because of this, aphids can attach themselves so tightly to a stem that their legs pull off before their hold can be broken.

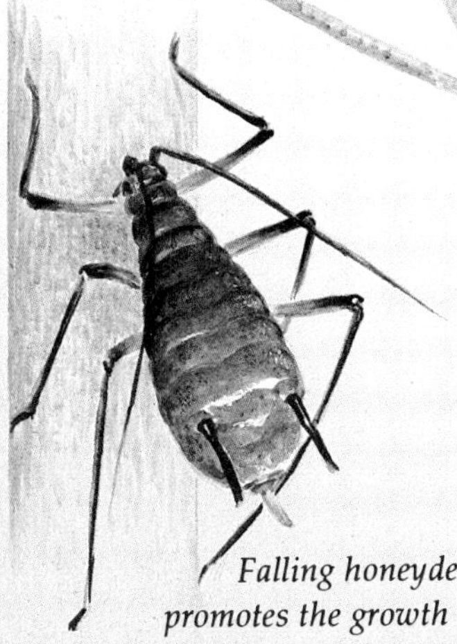

Aphids drink large quantities of sap to get enough protein to grow.

WHAT DO APHIDS AND MOSQUITOES HAVE IN COMMON?

Both the aphid and the mosquito have a tubular mouth called a *proboscis.* In the same way that a mosquito cuts through skin and inserts its proboscis to suck blood, the aphid cuts through the plant's surface and places its proboscis into the vessels of the plant to suck out liquid sugar.

The mosquito injects an irritating substance into the blood stream to prevent coagulation. Aphids also inject a salivary secretion into plant wounds to prevent the liquid sugar from solidifying.

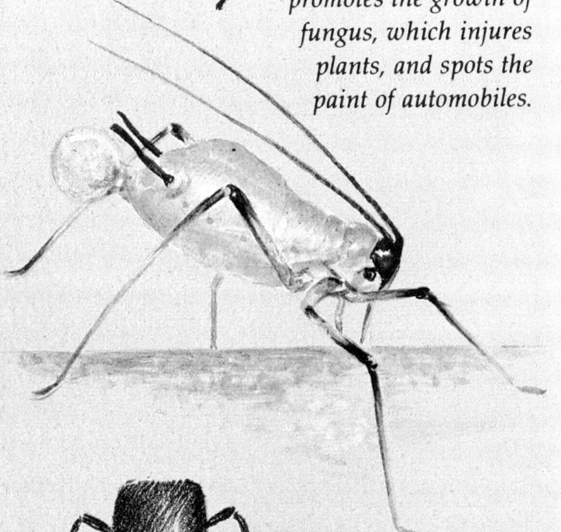

Falling honeydew promotes the growth of fungus, which injures plants, and spots the paint of automobiles.

HOW DOES THE APHID ILLUSTRATE THE FUNCTION OF FREELY RECEIVING AND FREELY GIVING?

When an aphid taps into a plant, the pressure in the plant's phloem system often pumps more liquid sugar into the aphid than it can assimilate or hold. The excess sap simply flows through the aphid's body and results in droplets of honeydew, which provides nourishing food for the ants.

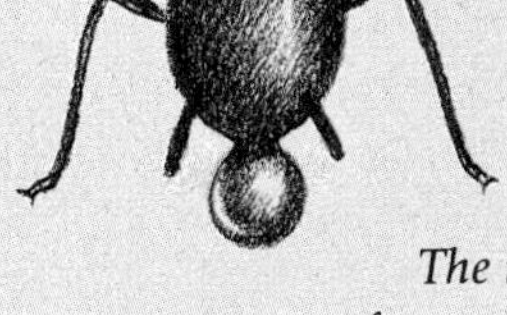

The tail end of an aphid

IN WHAT WAY DOES AN APHID OUTPRODUCE A COW?

When aphids tap into a healthy plant, they will secrete up to two drops of honeydew per hour. A single drop may equal one-fourth of the aphid's total weight. To match this output, a cow would have to give sixty gallons of milk an hour.

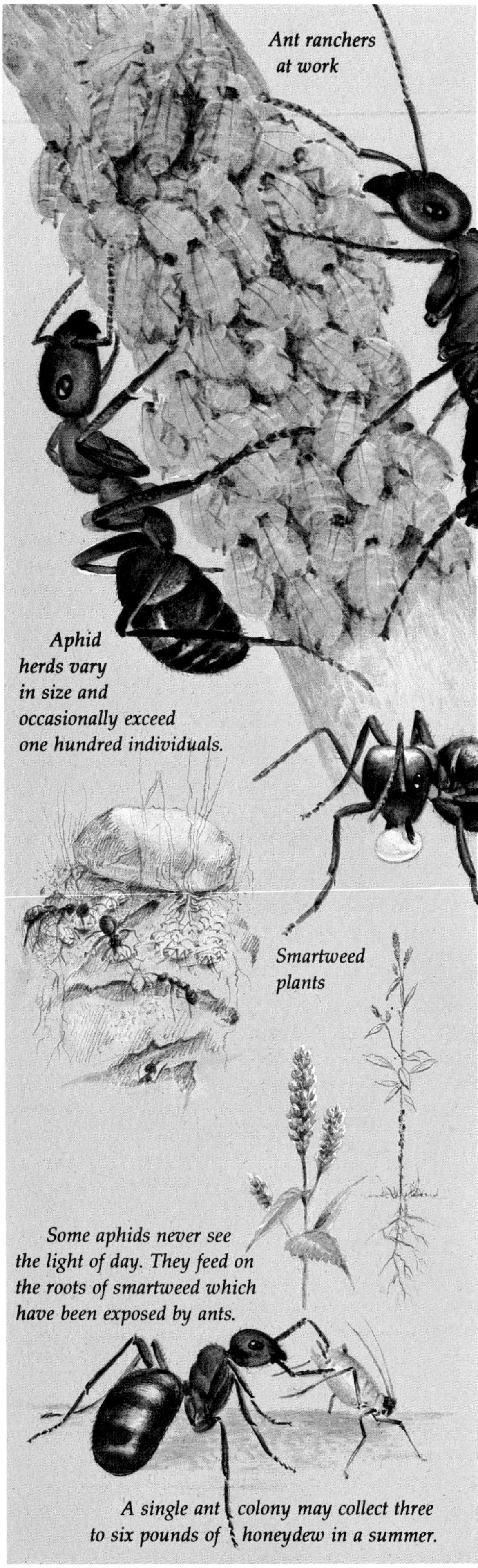

Ant ranchers at work

Aphid herds vary in size and occasionally exceed one hundred individuals.

Smartweed plants

Some aphids never see the light of day. They feed on the roots of smartweed which have been exposed by ants.

A single ant colony may collect three to six pounds of honeydew in a summer.

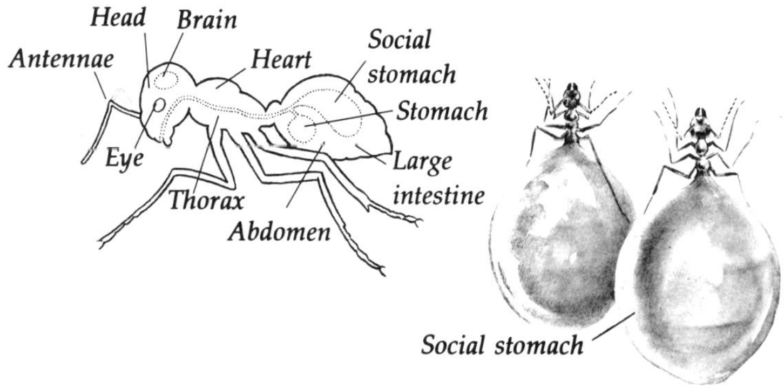

HOW DO ANTS AND APHIDS PROVIDE FOR THEIR "POOR"?

There are no "poor" ants or aphids in an ant colony. Both ants and aphids are diligent workers. Each one is like a self-employed farmer, producing food for itself and storing additional food for those it has chosen to serve.

The ant is able to store food in its "social stomach," or crop. When two ants meet, honeydew from the "social stomach" of one can be brought up and shared with the other. The social stomach can also be greatly enlarged to provide the equivalent of a storage tank of honeydew for the winter, thus making ample provision during times of need.

HOW DOES THE ANT WHO HAS NO GUIDE BECOME A GUIDE?

Ants are not only given to diligence among themselves, but they also assist the aphid to be fully productive in its work. If an ant observes that the plant upon which the aphids are feeding is losing its sap, the ant will guide the flock of aphids to a new plant, which may be as far as one hundred and fifty feet away. Ants have also been known to build fences around working aphids to protect them from intruders.

SINCE APHIDS GIVE BIRTH TO LIVE YOUNG, WHERE DO APHID EGGS COME FROM?

During the warm months of the year, aphids give birth to live young. However, as the cold air signals the approach of winter, aphids produce young by laying eggs. These eggs are carried by the ants to their underground nursery and cared for until they hatch. Then they are raised by the ant nurses in the warmth and protection of the subterranean nest. In the spring they are transported back to the surface where they are placed on healthy plants.

HOW CAN ONE WRONG STEP CAUSE AN ANT TO TRAVEL IN CIRCLES UNTIL IT DIES?

Ants have extremely poor eyesight but a keen sense of smell. As worker ants search for food, they leave a trail of tiny drops that contain a scent common to the whole colony. Other workers follow this trail to locate food and return to their nest.

It is important that a scout ant never mislead its fellow workers by stepping over its own trail. To do so would confuse the followers and cause them to travel in circles until they die from exhaustion.

CAN AN ANT OUTDISTANCE AN APHID?

Ants may make as many as four round trips a day to and from a food source which may be as far as four hundred feet from its nest. That is equivalent to a man walking sixty-eight miles.

An aphid, however, which is much smaller than the ant, is capable of going several hundred miles in a few hours, providing conditions are right.

HOW IS IT POSSIBLE FOR AN APHID TO FLY HUNDREDS OF MILES IN A FEW HOURS?

Most aphids do not have wings, but those that do are drawn upward by air warmed by the ultraviolet rays of the sun. An average flight may last one to three hours and may range from only a few hundred feet to several hundred miles, depending upon the wind conditions. Flight never begins if the temperature is less than sixty-two degrees Fahrenheit. This insures that there will be enough updrafts of warm air to lift the aphid into the sky.

WHY DOES AN APHID STOP ITS FLIGHT WHEN IT SEES YELLOW?

When a flying aphid reaches heights which may exceed 2,000 feet, its eyes develop a keener sensitivity to certain shades of yellow. They are attracted to this color because it is the color of young plants. With its sensitive eyes the aphid is able to avoid false landings.

HOW CAN APHIDS BE TRAPPED BY COLOR?

Because flying aphids look for the yellow color of young plant shoots, they can be easily trapped. Rose growers place yellow bowls of water among their roses as aphid traps. The aphids are attracted and drowned.

WHAT IS THE RELATIONSHIP BETWEEN THE FOOD SUPPLY AND THE WINGS ON AN APHID?

Aphids are made up of winged females, wingless females, winged males, and clones. Winged females appear when food becomes scarce or particular plants become overpopulated. Their ability to fly allows them to leave and begin new colonies under more favorable conditions.

Winged females are also produced in the fall during which time they mate and lay shiny black eggs. These eggs go through a complete insect metamorphosis and become adult aphids the following spring. At all other times, female aphids are born without wings. Winged males show up only in the fall during mating season. They die shortly afterward.

WHAT IS THE REPRODUCTIVE PROCESS OF PARTHENOGENESIS?

Parthenogenesis is a type of reproduction which allows a single female parent to bring about exact reproductions of itself without the male. These clones do not go through the normal stages of insect development and are more vulnerable to conditions that would destroy them.

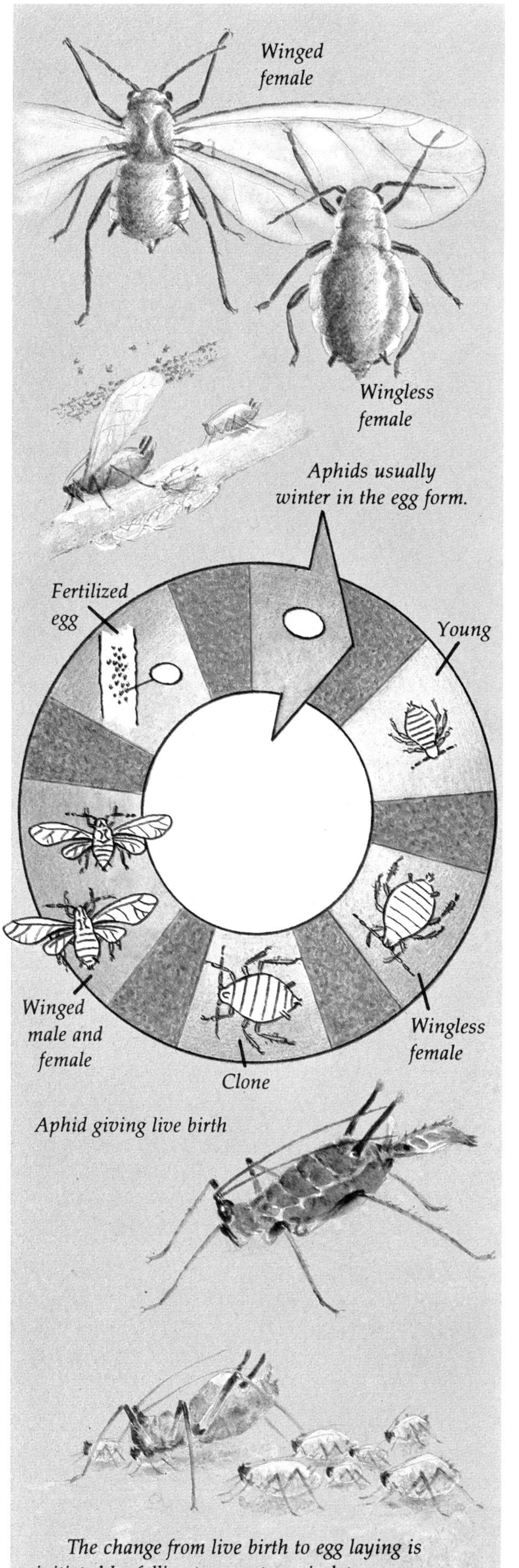

The change from live birth to egg laying is initiated by falling temperatures in late summer.

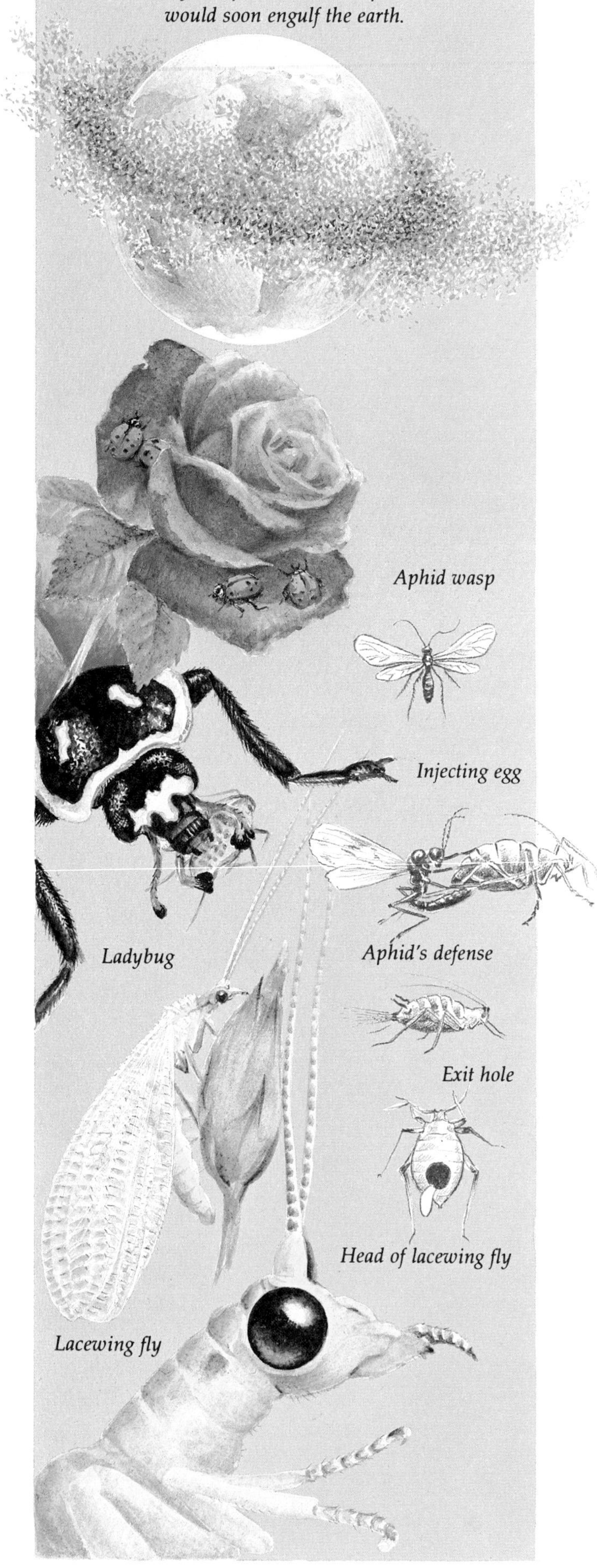

Aphids can produce fifty generations a year. If uncontrolled, aphids would soon engulf the earth.

HOW COULD JUST ONE APHID DESTROY ALL THE CROPS IN THE WORLD IN A SINGLE SUMMER?

In warm weather, a wingless female can bear as many as twenty-five daughters a day. All are born wingless and without fathers. The offspring mature in seven to ten days and can begin producing their own offspring without mating.

Theoretically, if the young are undisturbed, the number of offspring from a single parent can exceed 3,700,000 in less than a month. If all lived, aphids could easily cover the face of the earth in a single summer.

WHY IS THE APHID NECESSARY FOR THE MATURITY OF THE LADYBUG?

A young female ladybug must consume at least one hundred aphids before she can lay her first eggs. One generation of ladybugs could easily devour over 140,000 aphids.

HOW DOES AN APHID WASP ILLUSTRATE SATAN'S PROGRAM OF INFILTRATION?

The aphid wasp is small enough to crawl through the eye of a small needle, and yet it can kill thousands of aphids in its lifetime. The aphid wasp approaches the aphid from the rear and punctures the aphid's soft shell with its stinger.

There it deposits an egg inside the aphid's abdomen. Nothing happens until the egg hatches and the larva begins to consume the aphid from the inside out. After a short time, the aphid swells and turns brown, and the tiny aphid wasp larva emerges through a neatly cut circular door in the aphid's skin.

HOW IS AN APHID LION LIKE A "WOLF IN SHEEP'S CLOTHING"?

The lacewing fly is so ferocious that it must separate its young to prevent them from attacking one another. The female lays an individual egg on the end of a short thread of silk which is attached to a plant with aphids. There the egg waves in the breeze until it hatches.

The larva, called an aphid lion, then climbs to the plant where it feeds on all the aphids it can find. Piercing the aphid with its tubelike mouth, the larva sucks out the aphid's body fluids and then hangs the empty shell on one of the many bristles that cover its body. With each new trophy, the aphid lion more closely resembles a colony of aphids and is able to move freely among its prey.

HOW DOES THE APHID PROTECT ITSELF WITH CAPSULES AND "CANNONS"?

Blood cells in the aphid's body secrete capsules that envelope the eggs which the aphid wasp lays. When these capsules are successful, the wasp egg does not hatch.

The second means of self-defense comes from a pair of tubelike appendages called *cornicles*. These are mounted like cannons on the aphid's abdomen and secrete a waxlike substance into the eyes of a would-be attacker, causing temporary blindness.

How is appreciation that honors the design of God illustrated in Scripture?

The true worth of a gift can only be measured by the receiver. Therefore, two mites were worth more than costly treasures and obedience preferred over sacrifice. Who in Scripture gave a gift that was highly treasured by the receiver but ended in the death of the giver?

(Pause for a response—see page 17.)

An angry man burst into his home. His raging voice shattered the quietness of the dwelling. He had done his best, but had been humiliated.

His grieving parents tried to reason with him, but he glared at them with resentment. He refused to listen to their reasoning and stormed out of the house.

The parents sat in sorrow. Their son's irrational outburst served as a painful reminder of their past sin. They quietly recalled the day he had been born. He had been their joy and hope for the future.

They had given him special attention and instructed him in the ways of God. However, something had gone wrong in his heart. He had become proud and decided to do things in his own way. When his way was not acceptable, he reacted.

In the tension of the moment, another member of the household followed him into the fields and firmly but lovingly rebuked the angry young man for his actions and attitudes. His concern and reproof stung the heart of the listener as he recognized the truth contained in each statement. At that critical moment, he had a choice to make.

Hundreds of years later a similar scene took place. A Godly prophet stood before a crowd of frustrated people. They had tried to serve the Lord and prosper, but in their own way. God had turned His back on them.

The prophet solemnly proclaimed, "Thus says God, 'Why do you transgress the commandments of the Lord so that you do not prosper? Because you have forsaken the Lord, He has also forsaken you!' "

At that moment those who listened to the words of the prophet were confronted with the same choice as the young man in the field. Both made the same decision.

The crowd rejected the prophet's admonitions. Infuriated by his rebukes, they rose up and killed him. The young man in the field also rose up against his messenger of truth and slew him.

The young man was angry because he had given a gift to God and it was rejected. The one who rebuked him had also given a gift—a perfect lamb. The lamb foreshadowed the death of Christ and His payment for sin. This sacrifice was accepted by the Lord.

The message of that offering and reproof was later praised by Christ Himself as He rebuked the nation of Israel.

"Behold I send to you prophets so that upon you may come all the righteous blood shed upon the earth, from the blood of righteous Abel to the blood of Zacharias son of Barachias, whom you slew between the temple and the altar."

Cain presented the fruit of the ground as an offering to the Lord—it was rejected. Abel's offering of a lamb was an expression of gratefulness that honored the design of God's plan of redemption—it was accepted.

From Genesis 4, II Chronicles 24:20, and Matthew 23:34–35

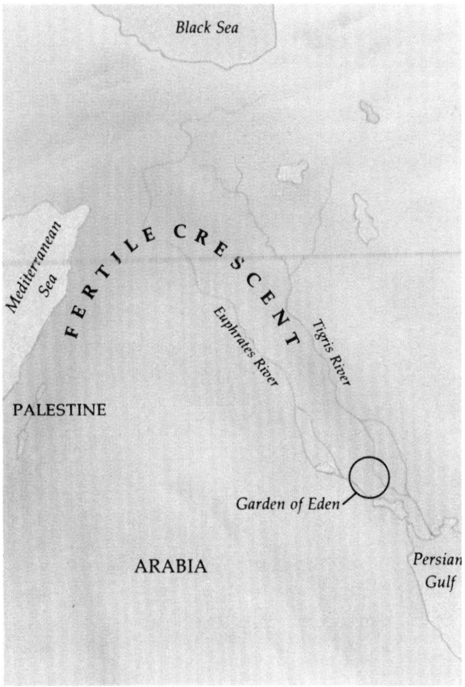

Abel lived just outside Eden. *The land surrounded by the two rivers is even now referred to as the "fertile crescent" of the East.*

As a shepherd, Abel *learned the qualities of patience, attentiveness, and gentle care of the flock. Through his Godly life, Abel became a clear Old Testament picture of Christ's sacrificial work in the New Testament.*

ABEL, A BROTHER WHO TEACHES US VALUABLE LESSONS IN GIVING

The account of Abel and his older brother Cain is a sobering illustration of the results of the Fall. Cain, the first man-child to be born and the first hope of Adam and Eve of a redeemer, turned out to be a murderer. The life of his younger brother, Abel, demonstrated the importance and potential of giving a gift which honors the designs of God.

GOD'S DESIGN FOR A REDEEMER

"I have gotten a man from the Lord!" Eve exclaimed as she viewed her firstborn son Cain. (See Genesis 4:1.) Hopefully, this son would be the redeemer which God promised to Adam and Eve after they had sinned in the Garden of Eden. (See Genesis 3:15.)

God pictured His redeemer to Adam and Eve by slaying animals and with their skins making a covering for them. This covering which required a sacrifice of blood became a rejection and replacement of their own efforts to provide a covering by the leaves produced from the ground.

The contrasting offerings of Cain and Abel bear a striking similarity to the offerings and lessons of the Garden. Abel slew a sacrificial lamb and presented it to the Lord as his offering. Cain's offering from his fields was rejected. His angry response indicated that this was no casual event, but a special attempt to gain God's redemption for their sin-cursed world. However, God had already established the truth He confirms in the New Testament. *". . . Without shedding of blood is no remission" (Hebrews 9:22).*

GOD'S DESIGN FOR A FIRSTBORN SON

During a terrifying night in Egypt every firstborn son died. The only survivors were those whose homes had the blood sprinkled on the top and the sides of the door posts. (See Exodus 12:12–13, 29.) It is significant that this requirement for redemption was applied to both Egypt and Israel. That night of death resulted in Israel's freedom from the bondage of Egypt.

When Israel left Egypt and came to Mount Sinai, God further clarified the need for every firstborn male to be redeemed. (See Exodus 13:12–13 and Numbers 18:15–16.) Thus it was a universal picture of the coming Redeemer who was the first begotten of the Father and perhaps a way of acknowledging the sin of the firstborn son of Adam and Eve.

A Hebrew firstborn could be redeemed with money; however, in reference to this Peter confirms the truth that for salvation we are *". . . not redeemed with corruptible things, as silver and gold . . . But with the precious blood of Christ, as of a lamb without blemish and without spot" (I Peter 1:18–19).*

GOD'S DESIGN FOR A LIVING WITNESS

"Jesus Christ the same yesterday, and to-day, and for ever" (Hebrews 13:8). God's basic principles do not change with time, customs, or culture. Christ's death, burial, and resurrection were *". . . foreordained before the foundation of the world . . ." (I Peter 1:20).* His death was pictured and proclaimed from Genesis to the cross. God sent the prophets to rebuke and remind the world of this eternal truth, and Abel is listed as the first prophet who sealed with his life the message of God's redemptive truth. Thus God states in Hebrews 11:4, that through Abel's gift, which honored God's design, *". . . he being dead yet speaketh."*

CHARACTER SKETCH OF ABEL

WHY DID EVE NAME HER SECOND SON ABEL?

The literal meaning of *Abel* is "breath, vanity, or vapor." Before Adam and Eve sinned, they and their descendants had the potential of living indefinitely. But God warned that on the very day that they sinned, that potential would end.

After the Fall God compares life to a vapor, *". . . For what is your life? It is even a vapour, that appeareth for a little time, and then vanisheth away" (James 4:14).*

Solomon summed up all of life in the word *vanity.* (See Ecclesiastes 1:2.) And Isaiah comments, *"Cease ye from man, whose breath is in his nostrils . . ." (Isaiah 2:22).*

Abel's name was thus a continual reminder of the brevity of life and the need to live each day in the fear of God.

HOW DID ABEL ACHIEVE THE STATUS OF A PROPHET?

Old Testament prophets proclaimed God's truth. They vigorously confronted God's people when they turned from God's ways. They were living epistles of God's message and usually suffered persecution and sometimes death.

Jesus acknowledged that Abel was such a prophet when He said, *"Woe unto you! . . . The blood of all the prophets, which was shed from the foundation of the world, may be required of this generation; From the blood of Abel unto the blood of Zacharias . . ." (Luke 11:47, 50–51).*

A further function of the prophet is to speak with authority about Christ's righteousness and redemptive work. The offering which Abel gave to the Lord so precisely fulfilled the picture of Christ's atonement for sin that his offering is listed with special distinction in Hebrews 11:4. *"By faith Abel offered unto God a more excellent sacrifice than Cain, by which he obtained witness that he was righteous, God testifying of his gifts: and by it he being dead yet speaketh."*

Abel fulfilled all the functions of a prophet when he sacrificed to the Lord and then talked with Cain in the field. Scripture clearly indicates that Cain's wrath was not toward Abel but to the truth that he lived and spoke.

WHAT DID ABEL HAVE IN COMMON WITH JACOB?

Both were secondborn. Both had older brothers who forsook the Lord. And both were recognized by God for their efforts to seek Him.

These similarities may also indicate that Abel demonstrated the characteristics of secondborn children which were so obvious in Jacob. A secondborn child tends to need greater approval and is often more competitive to get it. The secondborn tends to have a greater capacity for loyalty.

When Jacob saw that his older brother despised his birthright, he eagerly bought it up. It may be that Abel similarly snatched up the opportunity of the spiritual heritage which Cain despised.

Abel like Jacob developed the heart of a shepherd and, with the accompanying qualities, understood more clearly how to give a gift that honored the designs of the chief Shepherd.

JACOB

***Similarities between Abel and Jacob are significant:** both were secondborn, both were shepherds, both had older brothers who rejected the Lord, and both were loved by God for their faith in Him. (See Hebrews 11:4, 21.)*

ABEL
ā-bel

CHAPTER TEN

Gratefulness

. . . Is paying my debt of love out of the firstfruits of all my increase

"Honour the Lord with thy substance, and with the firstfruits of all thine increase: So shall thy barns be filled with plenty, and thy presses shall burst out with new wine."

Proverbs 3:9–10

Living Lessons on Gratefulness . . .

FROM THE PAGES OF SCRIPTURE

Grateful praise is a vital, energy-producing power in our lives. However, gratefulness is destroyed by the false assumption that what we have belongs to us, or by the wrong conclusion that God owes us a full, happy, and healthy life.

One day Christ performed a miracle, and out of the contrasting responses to it, we learn how the principle of tithing can protect us from the destruction of an ungrateful spirit.

ILLUSTRATED IN THE WORLD OF NATURE

CHRISTMAS MISTLETOE *Phoradendron flavescens*

While there are over 900 different varieties of mistletoe, only two are commonly found in the United States: the leafy, or Christmas mistletoe, which is popular as a Christmas decoration, and the lesser known dwarf mistletoe. Both kinds of mistletoe are parasites.

The mistletoe plant grows only in one place—high in the branches of trees. The most common variety, Christmas mistletoe, forms large clumps that average two to three feet in diameter.

Dwarf mistletoe is a serious problem in some areas of the southern United States because it grows on commercially produced trees such as fir and pine. Neither kind of mistletoe has roots of its own, and both are dependent on the water and minerals provided by the tree on which they live.

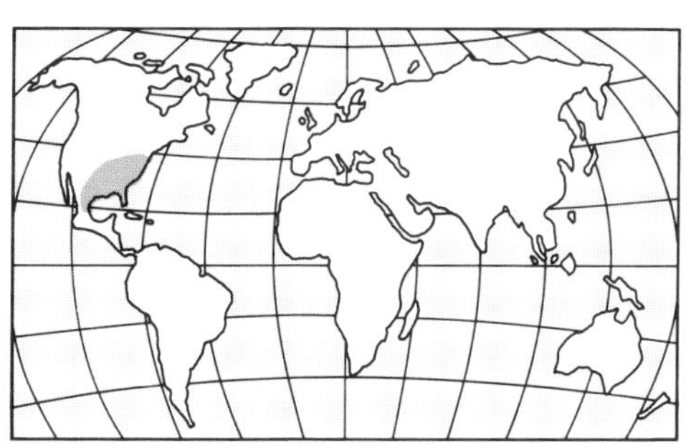

The range and habitat of the Christmas mistletoe

How is the need to avoid ungrateful people illustrated in the world of nature?

The story that we now have to tell is a lurid one, but it must be told.

A group of well-established residents of a forest community decided it was time to warn their young ones of a seductive stranger. She was very attractive in outward appearance, but her fruit was bitter and full of death.

The young ones looked up to their elders and listened intently as the older sages of the community drew upon many years of experience to vividly and effectively sound the alarm.

"Her pattern is to slip into our community undetected and take up residence as though she were one of us. She may wait several years before making her first move, but then she begins to deceptively work her way into the heart of an unsuspecting victim.

"She has no roots and is totally unpredictable. From outward appearance she would give no indication of being a threat. However, when the right conditions exist, she attaches herself to her victim and begins sapping him of life-giving strength and vitality.

"For many years this delusive stranger has been involved in the occult, taking on the characteristics of darkness. She avoids the light. She is like a cancer in the life of her unsuspecting host and slowly but surely breaks down his defenses with her subtle designs.

"Only too late will her host realize just how destructive she really is. When life is finally ebbing he will wonder why he did not listen to the warnings of those who have watched her work again and again.

"She avoids more mature residents and instead chooses to work her lustful wiles on tender youths. Wherever she goes, she encourages inappropriate conduct by promoting promiscuity.

"She is totally selfish, always stealing from her victim to satisfy her own desires. Others will admire her for her beauty and even take what she has to give them, but her fruit will soon poison them. She formerly worked in a hospital, but left only a trail of misery and woe."

The wise elders then pointed to a large scar on one of their members and explained to their wide-eyed listeners, "Do you see that horrible scar? It will disfigure him for the rest of his life. He is an example of what we are trying to warn you about. She was with him for many years and he could not get rid of her. It took a major catastrophe to free him from her destructive power, and now look at what is left."

They concluded their somber message by saying, "Your best hope of escape is to consistently look up to your Creator, to give Him continual praise from a grateful heart, and to pray that He will deliver you from this seductive stranger."

These long-standing residents are mighty oaks and tall cedars warning the younger trees about the deadly parasite known as mistletoe.

THE CHARACTERISTICS OF

THE MISTLETOE IN SCRIPTURE

Scripture abounds with references on the characteristics of the mistletoe. With its parasitic nature and slow destruction of its victim, the mistletoe presents a vivid illustration of the work of evil. This explains its wide use in occult circles.

Like the tree of the knowledge of good and evil described in Genesis 3:3–19, the color, shape, and texture of the mistletoe are very attractive, but its fruit is highly poisonous.

The seeds of the mistletoe, like temptations, spread to other trees by their own power and through the appetites of those that indulge in them. (See James 1:13–15 and I Corinthians 15:33.)

The infection and distorted growth which a mistletoe seed produces in a new victim depict the corrupting force of sin sown in a life. Once a tree is infected by a seed, it will take several years before the growth of the mistletoe plant begins, much like secret sin that its victim attempts to cover up. (See Galatians 6:7–8.)

The deceptive camouflage of some mistletoe is a picture of the envoys of Satan who appear as ministers of righteousness to deceive unsuspecting Christians. (See II Corinthians 11:13–15.)

CHARACTERISTICS AND PHYSICAL FEATURES OF THE MISTLETOE

Mistletoe characterizes a lack of gratefulness; it always asks for more. In extreme cases, the parasitic mistletoe draws off so much of a tree's rich sap that the host tree dies. When this happens, the mistletoe will also die, a victim of its own greed.

A truly grateful person enriches the life of the giver by returning benefit for what it has received.

The Christmas mistletoe pictured here grows mostly on broadleaf trees.

Cedar waxwings and many other winter birds eat the white, shiny berries of the mistletoe.

HOW DID THE MISTLETOE GET BRANDED AS A ROBBER AND A DUNG TREE?

The scientific name for the leafy mistletoe is *Phoradendron,* which comes from a Greek word meaning "tree thief." Although mistletoe plants contain chlorophyll and can make their own food, they prefer to steal water and minerals from the trees on which they live.

The Anglo-Saxon word *mistletan* meant "little dung tree." Although mistletoe is not a tree itself, its wood is as strong and hard as any tree. The reference to dung comes from the way its seeds are spread. Birds swallow the berries containing the mistletoe seeds. As the seeds pass through the birds' digestive tracts, they are spread to new trees.

HOW DID A DESTRUCTIVE ROBBER BECOME A STATE FLOWER?

Early settlers cherished the Christmas mistletoe as a decorative flower because it blooms in late November, stays green throughout the winter, and holds its attractive berries until spring. During the long winter months the mistletoe was the only available green plant that the early settlers could use to decorate the graves of loved ones. It was partly for this reason that the mistletoe became the state flower of Oklahoma.

The seed of the mistletoe is hidden in the berry's sticky interior.

HOW DOES THE FRUIT OF MISTLETOE FORCE ITS RECIPIENT TO MULTIPLY ITS DESTRUCTION?

Each berry contains a single seed surrounded by fleshy pulp. When this pulp ripens, it turns into a sticky liquid that oozes out whenever the skin of the berry is broken. Birds that eat mistletoe berries often have to scrape them off of their feathers by rubbing against the branches of a tree, thereby giving the seed a new place to grow.

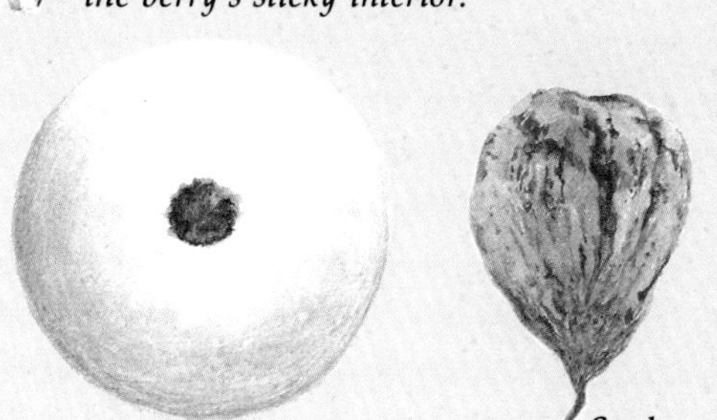

Berry *Seed*

HOW DID MISTLETOE ENTER HOSPITALS AND INFLICT ITS VICTIMS WITH FALSE HOPE AND PHYSICAL DESTRUCTION?

As late as the mid-1700's, doctors used mistletoe as a cure for epilepsy, toothaches, and snakebites. However, extracts of the mistletoe are poisonous and were often more harmful than the condition they were reported to cure.

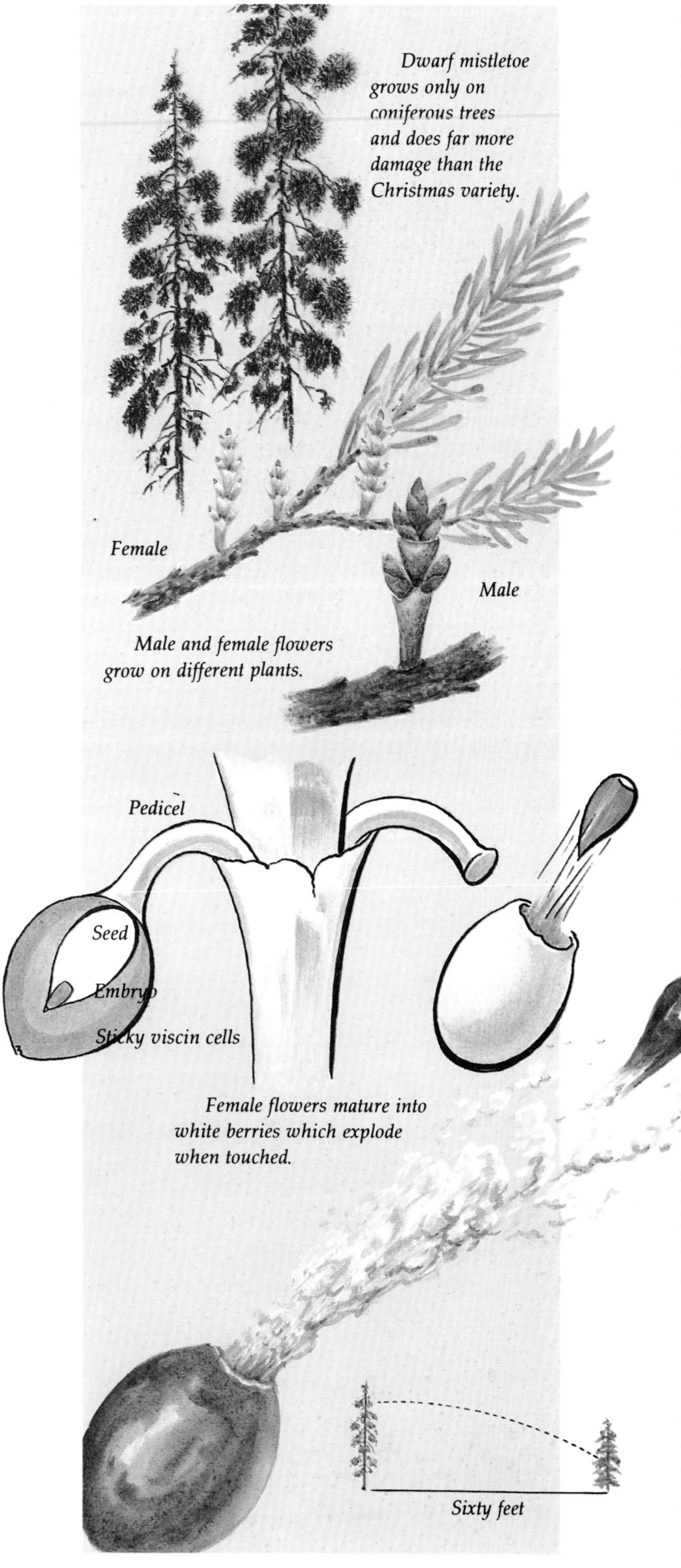

Dwarf mistletoe grows only on coniferous trees and does far more damage than the Christmas variety.

Male and female flowers grow on different plants.

Female flowers mature into white berries which explode when touched.

HOW DOES A WITCH'S BROOM INDICATE THE PRESENCE OF MISTLETOE?

A "witch's broom" is a snarl of small tree branches that is often caused by the presence of mistletoe. A tree's first reaction to the presence of mistletoe is a swelling or bump around the point of infection.

This knot enlarges and leads to the production of a tangle of branches that looks like the twisted straws of an old broom. Different species of mistletoe seem to cause their own characteristic type of "witch's broom" on different trees.

HOW DOES THE HEALTH OF THE MISTLETOE PRODUCE THE DEATH OF ITS HOST?

When mistletoe has grown to such an extent that it is stealing more moisture and minerals than its tree-host can afford to lose, the tree becomes weak and more susceptible to disease. Each spring the tree produces fewer leaves until the mistletoe is the only greenery on its bare limbs.

When the tree finally dies and no longer provides any nourishment, the mistletoe can continue to produce its own food by means of its own chlorophyll. Mistletoe cannot, however, produce its own food indefinitely. After the host dies, the mistletoe is also doomed to die.

HOW DOES SOME MISTLETOE PRACTICE DECEPTION TO ELUDE ITS ENEMIES?

Most species of mistletoe have thick, leathery leaves that do not appeal to insects. There are, however, several types of tender mistletoe found in Australia that copy the shape of their host's leaves. Hiding in the tree's foliage, these are relatively safe from chewing insects.

HOW DOES THE MISTLETOE DEFY THE POWER OF THE SUN?

Most other plants send their roots down and their stems upward in order to draw in the life-giving energy of the sun. The mistletoe, however, does not need sunlight for its growth, since it is stealing its primary nourishment from its host tree.

WHAT CAUSES THE MISTLETOE TO BE UNPREDICTABLE?

The mistletoe is completely unpredictable in the direction it grows. It has no true root but penetrates the bark of its host with a wedgelike spike. This action is similar to the bite of a mosquito in a person. Because the mistletoe does not depend upon sunlight, the plant simply grows opposite to the direction of its "wedge." The result is that the mistletoe often grows upside down.

HOW DOES THE MISTLETOE SIMULATE THE ACTION OF A CANNON?

As the berries of the dwarf mistletoe ripen, pressure builds up inside the fruit. At maturity, it only takes a slight bump to break the fruit loose from its stem. When this happens, the fruit explodes and the liquid inside the fruit shoots the seed out, just as if it were shot from a cannon. Occasionally, a seed may travel up to sixty feet and reach a traveling speed of sixty miles per hour.

THE LIFE CYCLE OF THE DWARF MISTLETOE

The dwarf mistletoe grows very slowly and takes about six years to complete its life cycle. Once it is established, it usually adds only one pair of leaves per branch each year.

Seeds

The seeds are either scattered by birds or shot from the berry. Either way, they land on the needles of evergreen trees where they remain until the first rain washes them down the needles and onto the stem.

Germination

Seeds can germinate almost anywhere but can cause infection only by penetrating young, thin tree bark. The seed sends out a wedge-shaped probe called a haustorium to cut through the bark. The number of annual tree rings that the haustorium crosses tells the age of the mistletoe plant.

First Shoots

Once the mistletoe establishes its infection, it usually incubates for two to five years before sending out any visible growths. These first shoots resemble tiny, closed pine cones. It is not until the following spring that these first shoots begin to grow branches.

Pollination

Flowering and pollination take place during the late spring of about the fifth year of the plant's life. Mistletoe is not self-pollinating and cannot produce seeds until a nearby plant has matured enough to produce pollen. For some isolated plants, this may be a wait of many years.

Seed Dispersal

The fruit ripens in early fall and contains only one seed in each berry. It ripens at a time that is perfect for attracting migrating birds that eat the fruit and that transport the seeds many miles. Seeds are also dispersed when the berries explode.

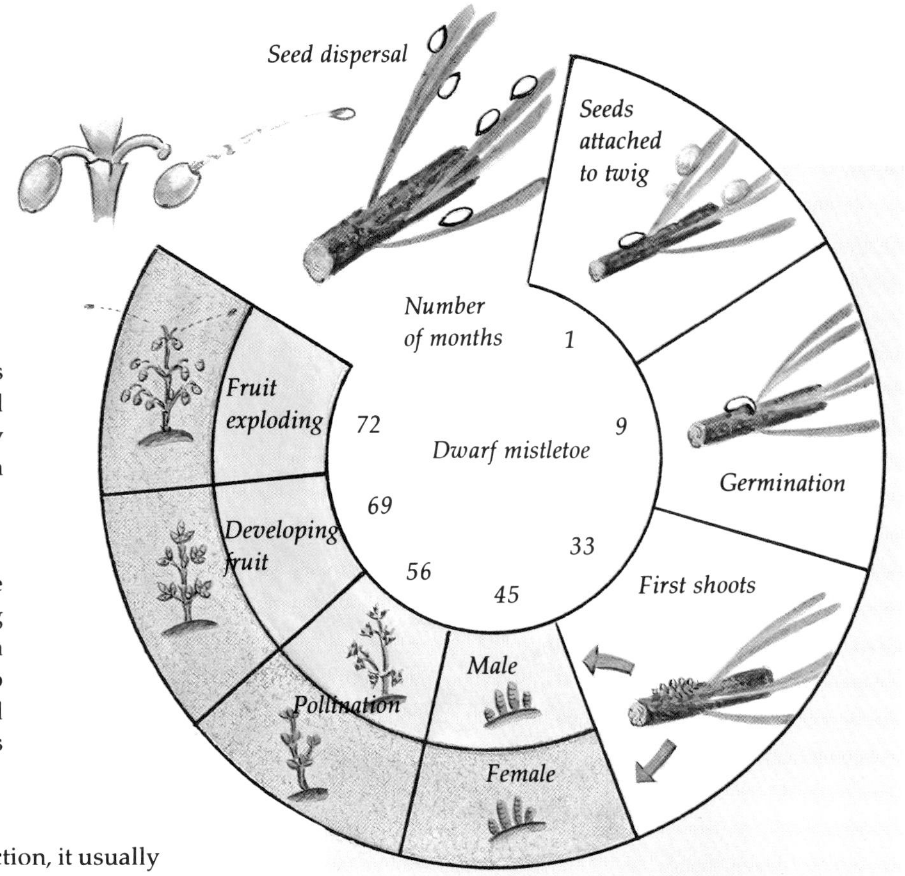

Mistletoe "root" penetrating the annual growth rings of its host, magnified forty times.

Clumps of Christmas mistletoe may grow to be five feet in diameter and weigh fifty pounds.

HOW ARE MISTLETOE SEEDS LIKE OPPORTUNISTIC GERMS?

Both the mistletoe seeds and opportunistic germs are extremely small but potentially destructive. They both wait for the right conditions and then begin to relentlessly feed on their hosts. Mistletoe seeds, like opportunistic germs, take from their hosts and never give in return. The feeding and reproduction of each one produce weakness and eventual death in their victims. Before the hosts die, the seeds and germs spread to new hosts to continue their destructive work.

WHAT TREE IS ABLE TO WITHSTAND THE MISTLETOE?

One of the few trees that is able to resist the destructive forces of the mistletoe is the incense cedar. One mistletoe plant that was observed growing on a 425-year-old cedar had 409 annual growth rings of its own.

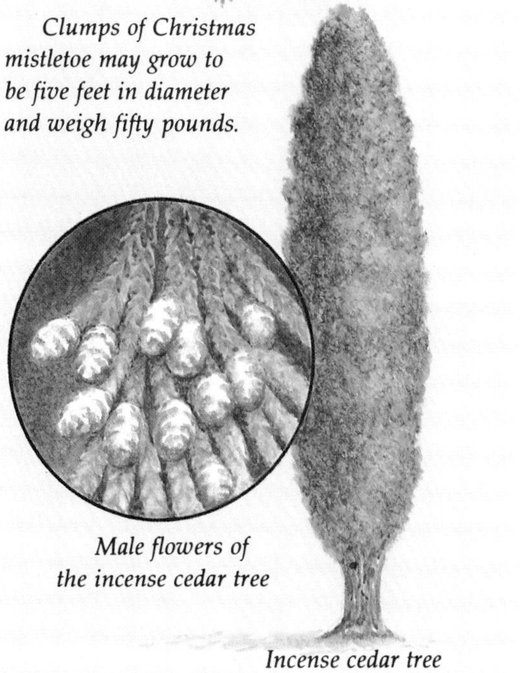

Male flowers of the incense cedar tree

Incense cedar tree

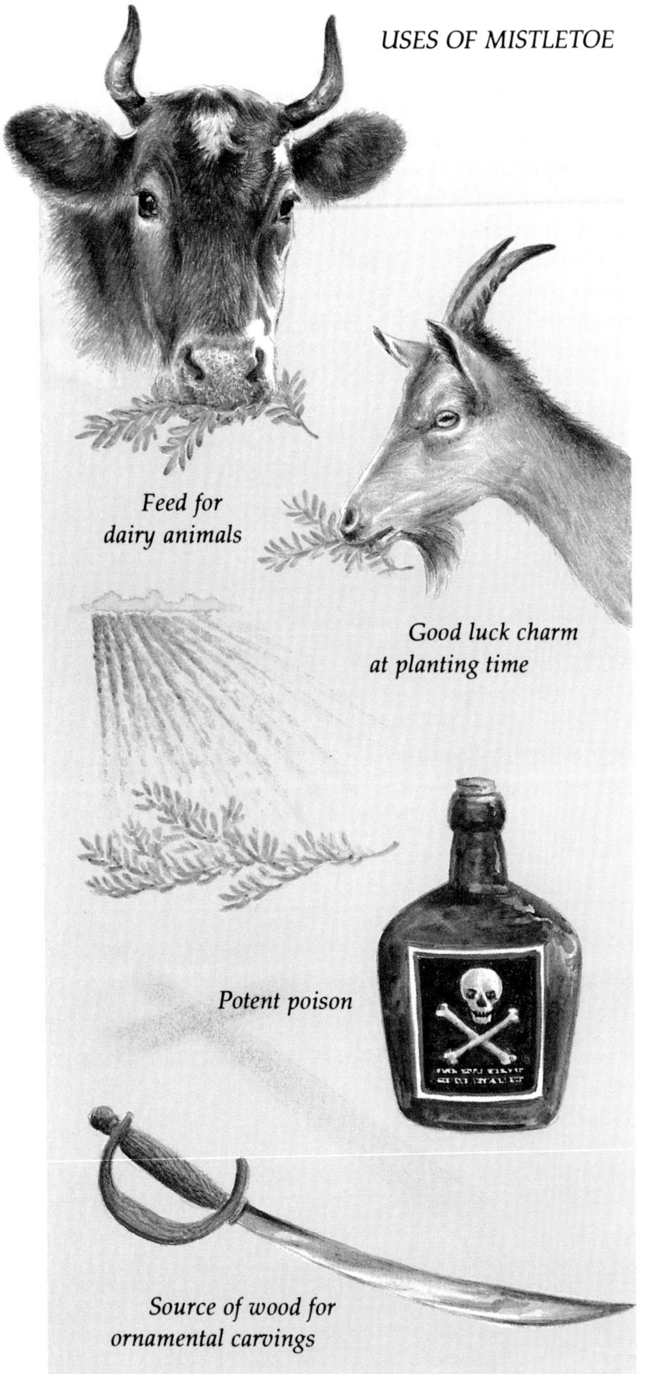

HOW DID THE MISTLETOE BECOME A PART OF OCCULT WORSHIP?

No plant is richer in heathen symbolism than the mistletoe. For this reason, early Christians would have nothing to do with it.

Druids were deceived into believing that it was supernatural because it grew without roots in the tops of trees. They would ceremoniously cut down clumps of Christmas mistletoe, not allowing them to touch the ground. Two white bulls would then be sacrificed at the base of the tree as payment for the mistletoe.

HOW HAS THE MISTLETOE BEEN USED AS A COUNTERFEIT TO THE PASSOVER?

In ancient Egypt when Pharaoh refused to free Israel from slavery, the Lord slew all the firstborn sons throughout the land. The only firstborn sons who were spared were those who lived in homes with door posts sprinkled by the blood of a sacrificial lamb. This protection at the door spoke of Christ's work in salvation.

After occult worshipers ceremoniously gathered mistletoe, they hung the boughs with the white berries over the door posts to protect those inside the house.

HOW HAS MISTLETOE BECOME A LICENSE FOR PROMISCUITY?

An accepted custom at Christmas time is engaging in indiscriminate hugging and kissing under the mistletoe. This promiscuous license may be a carry-over from the custom of centuries ago that required enemies who met under a clump of mistletoe to disarm themselves, embrace, and refrain from combat for the remainder of the day.

HOW DOES MISTLETOE GIVE LIFE AND DEATH AT THE SAME TIME?

In the southern United States truckloads of mistletoe are harvested as feed for goats and cows. The leaves are apparently high in protein and increase milk production. As a medicine, mistletoe has some therapeutic value, but its berries are highly poisonous and cause acute stomach pain and heart failure. As a parasite of trees, it damages over one billion board feet of lumber each year.

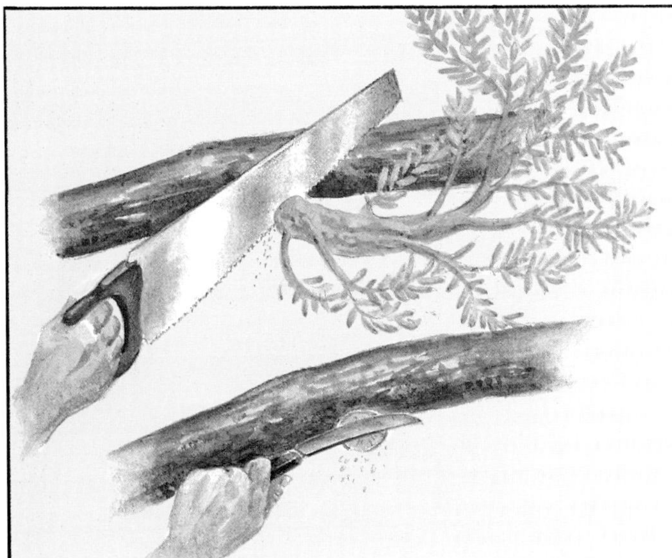

How to Remove Mistletoe

Removing mistletoe is very difficult. If any part of the mistletoe's "root" is left in the tree, it will regenerate and start a new growth.

It is best to eliminate mistletoe by cutting off the entire infected branch a foot or so behind the growth.

If a branch is too important to remove, the mistletoe must be sawed off and the infected area scraped as deeply as possible. Wrapping the branch with black plastic to exclude all light will also help to eventually kill whatever "root" remains.

How is the gratefulness of firstfruits illustrated in Scripture?

Ingratitude is like a disfiguring blight on the soul. An ungrateful person may be unconcerned because their attitude is often concealed. However, anyone who gives to that person will quickly detect the problem.

Who in Scripture demonstrated genuine gratefulness out of the firstfruits of what he received and in so doing gained an even greater gift?

(Pause for a response—see page 17.)

The kind teacher just stood there for several moments. He marveled at the gift he had just received. Finally, he spoke to the grateful man who had given it to him and asked him a very pointed question.

That question caused the man to reflect back over many years. He remembered the horrifying day when he had first noticed that something was wrong.

A tiny patch of skin on his cheek had become discolored and soon the pinkish blotch began to spread. Before long, he lost all feeling in his skin and his eyebrows began to disappear. Spongy tumor-like growths began to cover his face and body. Internal organs also suffered from the damaging disease.

Marked deformities occurred in his hands and feet as the tissues between his bones deteriorated. The sensory nerve endings in his hands and feet no longer responded to heat or pain. As a result, he became the victim of numerous accidental injuries.

As embarrassing and humiliating as all this was, it did not compare with the greater torture which he was forced to endure—rejection by his loved ones, friends, and neighbors.

People who had once filled his life with joy and fellowship now required him to call out the frightening words, "Unclean, unclean," whenever he approached. When they heard these words, they were filled with fear and pity and scattered.

His only companions were foreigners who were afflicted with the same condition. The discouraged invalid soon discovered that those around him were infected with an even greater affliction—deep-rooted bitterness.

Humanly speaking, they all had good reason to be bitter. There was no hope for a cure and their progressive deterioration left them vulnerable to many other ailments.

The man who now knelt before the teacher had received total healing of his leprosy. He had discovered the miracle on his way to see the priest. It seemed only proper to use the first portion of his newly acquired health and strength to return and give sincere thanks.

The gift of gratefulness deeply impressed the one who had healed him, but it also prompted him to ask an important question. "Were there not ten cleansed? Where are the other nine?"

Ten lepers were healed, but only this Samaritan returned to give thanks. His grateful heart earned him an even greater gift from the Lord Jesus—healing in his soul from the bitterness that would continue to consume his former companions.

From Luke 17:11–19

A SAMARITAN LEPER TEACHES ABOUT THE DANGER OF INGRATITUDE

Our Lord Jesus, the master teacher of spiritual truths, used different methods to teach His disciples. He used encounters with the combative and critical Pharisees. He also used situations from real life to illustrate spiritual principles.

During the Lord's final journey to Jerusalem, where He would be crucified, He began to prepare His disciples for the spiritual dangers that they would face without Him. Through two parables and an encounter with the Pharisees, He warned them about the danger of material riches. (See Luke 16.) Using questions and a parable, He warned them against bitterness and spiritual pride. (See Luke 17:1–10.) He then used a real life situation to teach the danger of ingratitude. (See Luke 17:11–19.)

OPPORTUNITY ON THE WAY TO JERUSALEM

The Lord and His disciples were passing near the border of Samaria and Galilee. They were close to the entrance of a certain village when they noticed ten lepers some distance away. There was no mistaking the fact that these men had leprosy. Not only was the disease disfiguring, but a leprous man was required by law to tear his clothing, dishevel his hair, and cry, "Unclean! Unclean!" with his mouth covered. (See Leviticus 13:45.) The reason for these seemingly unsympathetic regulations was that the disease in its worst form was contagious and fatal. The only defense against it in those days was quarantine.

A PLEA TO BE HEALED

Because lepers were forbidden to have contact with other people, they had no way to earn a living and were dependent on charity. The mental and emotional effects of leprosy were almost as serious as the physical effects. Some people believed that victims were being punished for being more sinful than those without the disease. Lepers were ritually unclean and were more accustomed to rejection than pity. Their only companions were other lepers. Few people lived in more miserable circumstances. It is no wonder that they cried out at the sight of One who had been known to cure their dreaded disease, *". . . Jesus, Master, have mercy on us" (Luke 17:13)*. (See Luke 5:12–13.)

TEN ARE HEALED, ONE IS MADE WHOLE

The Lord did have mercy on them and granted their request. He sent them to the priests who were responsible for diagnosing this disease, regulating the quarantines, and declaring a cured leper fit to rejoin the community. They were all cleansed, but only one returned *"... and with a loud voice glorified God, And fell down on his face at his feet, giving him thanks: and he was a Samaritan" (Luke 17:15–16)*.

Jesus was touched by the faith of the Samaritan, which was expressed by his gratitude; but He was greatly disappointed by the ingratitude of the other nine who were Israelites. All should have returned to give glory to God. (See Luke 17:18.) But the nine were so absorbed in their physical healing that they spared no thought of appreciation for the Healer. Only one considered the source of his healing.

Jesus warned His disciples of the danger of ingratitude. Even though all ten men were healed of their leprosy, only one received the healing of his soul. The Lord was able to say to the grateful leper, *"... Arise, go thy way: thy faith hath made thee whole" (Luke 17:19)*. The Samaritan leper was made whole in both body and soul.

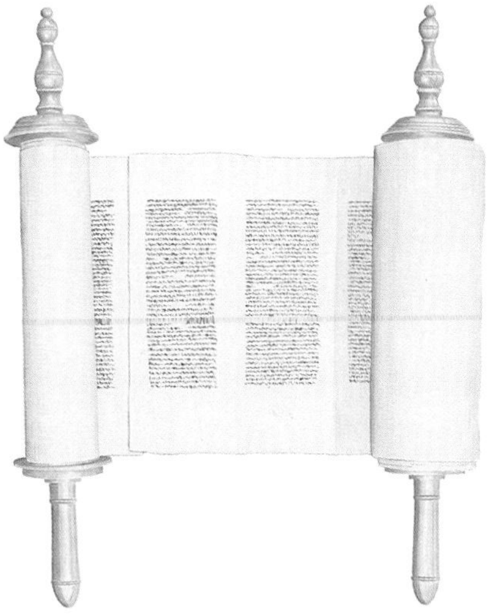

"Take heed in the plague of leprosy, *that thou observe diligently, and do according to all that the priests the Levites shall teach you: as I commanded them, so ye shall observe to do" (Deuteronomy 24:8).*

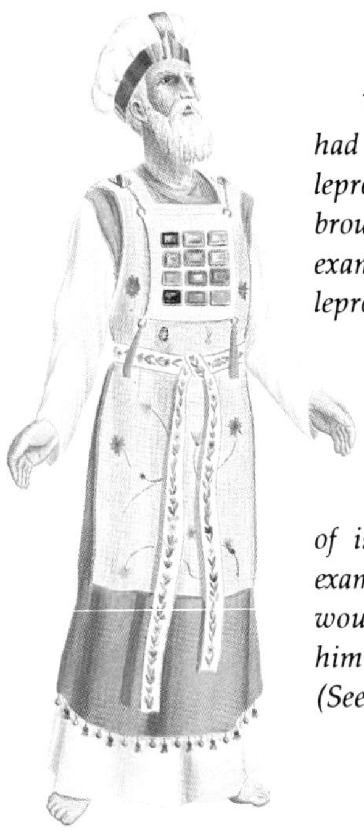

When a man's skin *had the symptoms of leprosy, he was to be brought to a priest and examined. If there was leprosy, the man would be pronounced unclean.*

If it was not certain, the man went through times of isolation and more examinations. The priest would then pronounce him clean or unclean. (See Leviticus 13:1–8.)

The High Priest

The law of the leper *in the day of his cleansing is recorded in Leviticus 14:4–7. "Then shall the priest command to take for him that is to be cleansed two birds alive [sparrows] ... one of the birds be killed in an earthen vessel ... and shall let the living bird loose into the open field."*

CHARACTER SKETCH OF THE GRATEFUL LEPER

WHY DID JESUS TELL THE LEPERS TO SEE THE PRIESTS?

When the Lord heard the lepers' pitiful cries, He neither touched them nor said, "You are cured!" Rather, He told them to go in their leprous condition and show themselves to the priests. According to Mosaic Law, priests were to inspect their skin to certify that they were fully healed. (See Leviticus 14:1–3.) The Lord put their faith to the test by asking them to act as though they had already been healed. As they obeyed His command, so it happened. *". . . And it came to pass, that, as they went, they were cleansed" (Luke 17:14).*

In addition to fulfilling the Law's command, it is likely that the Lord wanted these men to be a testimony to the priests that they might believe in Him as the Messiah. When He had healed a leper on a previous occasion, He charged him to *". . . tell no man: but go, and shew thyself to the priest, and offer for thy cleansing, according as Moses commanded, for a testimony unto them" (Luke 5:14).* After the Lord's resurrection, the priests remembered these things, *". . . and a great company of the priests were obedient to the faith" (Acts 6:7).*

WHY DID ONLY ONE LEPER RETURN TO THANK JESUS?

The text states, *". . . and he was a Samaritan" (Luke 17:16).* The Samaritans were a despised people. One Jewish author spoke of them as "no nation" and as "the foolish people that dwell in Shechem." When the Jews destroyed the Samaritans' temple on Mount Gerizim about 128 B.C., the breach between the two groups was final. It is an indication of the horror of leprosy that nine Jews would even consent to live with a Samaritan.

But Samaritans, like the publicans, harlots, and sinners, were in general more open to the Gospel. The New Testament almost always speaks favorably of them, and they are portrayed as people who responded enthusiastically to Jesus Himself and to the Apostles of the early Church. Apparently, they did not have as much difficulty recognizing their need of salvation.

The Samaritan woman of Sychar acknowledged her sin and accepted the Savior. (See John 4:3–42.) In one of Christ's parables, a generous Samaritan took pity on a fellow sinner. (See Luke 10:30–37.) The Samaritan leper also recognized his desperate need of spiritual restoration as well as of physical healing.

WHAT DOES THE GRATEFUL LEPER TEACH US ABOUT GOD'S KINGDOM?

The grateful leper teaches us that faith is the only basis for membership in God's kingdom. This Samaritan was brought into the kingdom because he believed. The nine Jews, who thought they were already in the kingdom, were excluded.

Many Jews felt that they deserved salvation because they were the descendants of righteous Abraham. They did not appreciate God's goodness and benefits because they expected them. Although the Jewish lepers recognized their need of healing, they felt no spiritual need.

When Jesus told some Jews that being natural descendants of Abraham was not sufficient to merit salvation, they became incensed and said He was born of fornication. They also accused Him of being a Samaritan and of having a devil. (See John 8:41, 48.) Their pride prevented them from entering into the kingdom. The Samaritan was not proud in spirit; but, rather, he was poor in spirit. To him belonged the promise, *"Blessed are the poor in spirit: for theirs is the kingdom of heaven" (Matthew 5:3).*

Leprosy is identified as a highly infectious disease. *Therefore, strict precautions were prescribed for it in the Law. ". . . His clothes shall be rent, and his head bare, and he shall put a covering upon his upper lip, and shall cry, Unclean, unclean. . . . He shall dwell alone; without the camp shall his habitation be" (Leviticus 13:45–46). Freedom from this daily ordeal makes the ungratefulness of the nine more astonishing.*

THE GRATEFUL LEPER

CHAPTER ELEVEN

Gratefulness

. . . Is multiplying the ministry of those who have given to me

"And God is able to make all grace abound toward you; that ye, always having all sufficiency in all things, may abound to every good work."

II Corinthians 9:8

". . . Freely ye have received, freely give."

Matthew 10:8

Living Lessons on Gratefulness . . .

FROM THE PAGES OF SCRIPTURE

God exhorts us to present ourselves as a living sacrifice to Him. (See Romans 12:1–2.) Only as we die to personal ambitions can we properly use the gifts that we have received from God and others. A great Christian in the early Church illustrated these truths.

He lived during the reign of Nero and was personally affected by the godlessness of that wicked emperor's life. As a courageous and tireless Christian, he demonstrates for us one of the most beautiful testimonies of true gratefulness by multiplying the ministry of the one who brought the Gospel to him.

ILLUSTRATED IN THE WORLD OF NATURE

MAPLE TREE *Acer saccharum*

There are at least thirteen species of maple trees in the United States. Of these, the sugar maple is the most important. Also called the rock or hard maple, it is an attractive tree that can grow to a height of 135 feet with a trunk five feet in diameter.

The production of maple syrup from maple sugar water is a major business in the northern United States. Each day during the spring, the sugar water is collected and taken to a sugar house. By flowing through a series of evaporation tanks, the liquid is condensed to produce maple syrup.

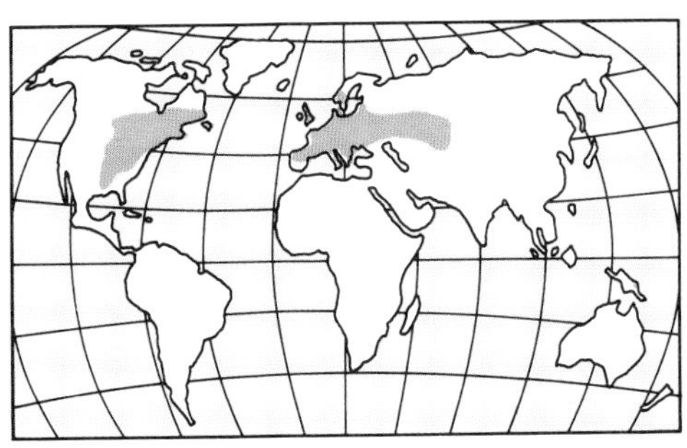

The range and habitat of the maple tree

How is the process of multiplying the ministry of those who give to us illustrated in the world of nature?

The footsteps of a solitary Indian crunching through the snow broke the stillness of the early morning. With great skill, the brave took one powerful swing with his tomahawk and then quietly watched for the results.

The one he had injured was revered by all the members of that early American settlement. They held him in high esteem for his impressive age and stately appearance. He had seen God work many times during his long life. He had passed the test of time and had weathered countless storms.

Because of his outstanding qualities, he was chosen to be the central figure of the struggling little colony. Often the Pilgrim families came to visit him. They included him in picnics and other outings and enjoyed the sense of security he provided.

Councils with the Indians were always held in his presence. He supervised their deliberations and gently nodded as both sides reached agreements. He warned the settlers of approaching danger from violent storms. When they saw him waving, the settlers would hurry to the shelter of their cabins.

As the seasons passed things began to change. The busy colonists had little time for him. During this period, he also experienced a barrenness in his own life. He became quiet and withdrawn, and now he was wounded.

The wound produced no ordinary results. He did not become bitter. Instead he demonstrated a new sweetness from his inner being.

His response caused the Pilgrims to once again gather around him. They received a new measure of strength and vitality from his life. He was able to draw upon all that God had given him over the years and share it with those around him in a remarkable way.

As he refreshed them, the thankful Pilgrims praised God for His marvelous provision through the life of this stalwart member of their community.

By inflicting the wound, the Indian had revealed something that the settlers had never seen or tasted before. Thereafter, they looked upon this dignified resident not only as the majestic maple tree in the center of their village, but as the giver of rich maple sugar water at the end of a long, cold winter.

The Pilgrims eagerly gathered the precious liquid from the maple tree. By investing their time and energy, they turned the sugar water into delicious syrup. The syrup became a highly sought-after product which they shared with others.

By sharing what they had received, both the maple tree and the settlers multiplied the provision that God had freely given to them.

THE CHARACTERISTICS OF

THE MAPLE TREE IN SCRIPTURE

The conditions that allow the maple tree to produce rich, sweet syrup are highly symbolic of a similar process in the Christian life which produces spiritual fruit.

The maple tree must be mature before it is able to produce the sought-after maple syrup. The older the tree, the more syrup it is able to produce. Older and more mature Christians are instructed by God to give spiritual food to the younger ones. *"The elders which are among you I exhort . . . Feed the flock of God . . ." (I Peter 5:1–2).*

The bountiful product of the maple tree must be harvested during a season that follows the harsh testings of winter cold and snow.

God reminds us that one who finds nourishment during barren seasons by putting his roots deep into the Word shall produce *". . . his fruit in his season . . ." (Psalm 1:3).*

Before the maple tree can benefit others, it must be wounded by cutting. The more cuts it receives, the greater the flow will be from its inner life. Paul explained that the troubles he experienced were directly related to the spiritual nourishment he was able to give to other Christians. (See II Corinthians 1:2–11.)

The maple syrup from the tree must be further purified just as our words and actions must be refined by the purifying fire of God's Word. (See I Peter 4:12–13.)

CHARACTERISTICS AND PHYSICAL FEATURES OF THE MAPLE TREE

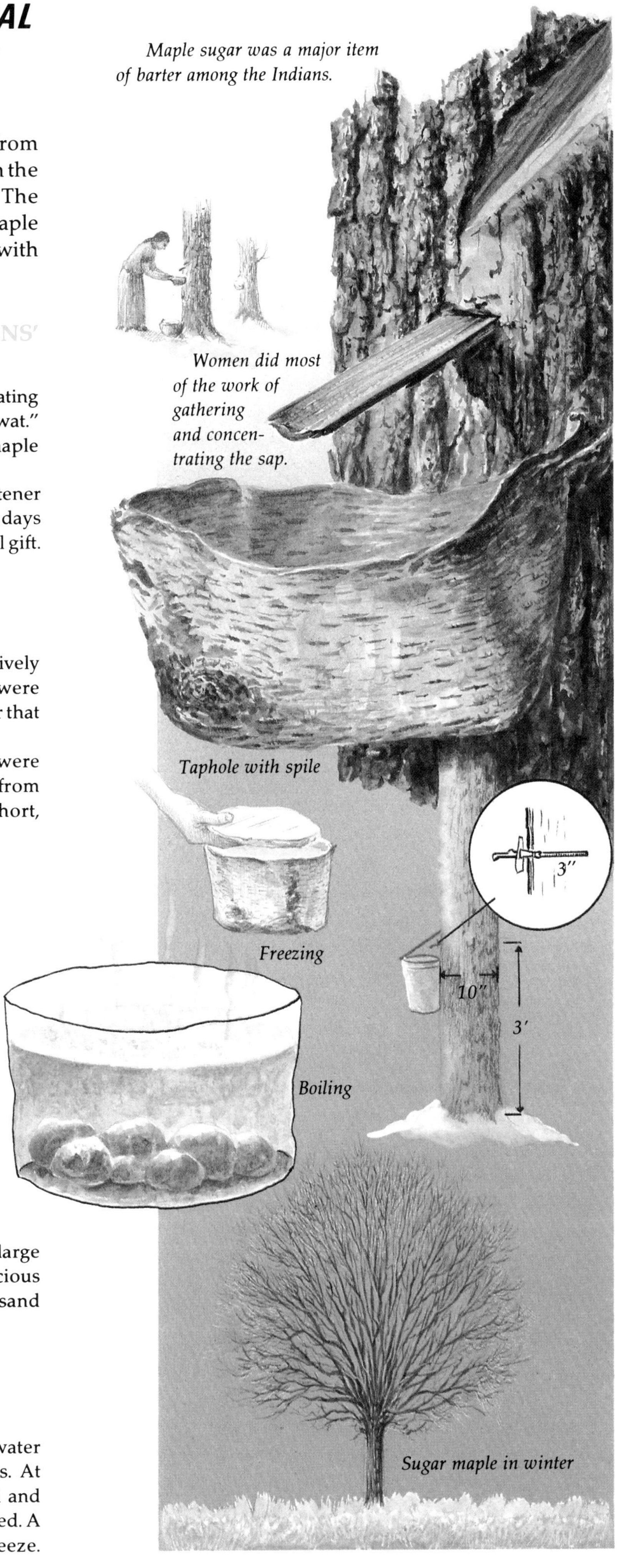

Maple sugar was a major item of barter among the Indians.
Women did most of the work of gathering and concentrating the sap.
Taphole with spile
3″
Freezing
10″
3′
Boiling
Sugar maple in winter

The maple tree receives needed nutrients from the soil and warm sunlight and seasonal rains from the heavens. It transforms these gifts into sugar water. The American Indians were the first recipients of the maple tree's sweet product; and they, in turn, shared it with the early American settlers.

WHAT WAS THE MEANING OF THE INDIANS' CELEBRATION OF "SEENSIBAUKWAT"?

Early settlers were surprised to find Indians celebrating spring in a carnival-like atmosphere called "seensibaukwat." This celebration centered around the production of maple syrup, about which the settlers knew nothing.

Because American Indians had no source of sweetener other than maple syrup and maple sugar, the first bright days of spring brought them the promise of this very special gift.

WHY DID EARLY AMERICAN SETTLERS NOT KNOW ABOUT MAPLE SYRUP?

Because European springs are short and comparatively mild without fluctuating temperatures, the settlers were unacquainted with the tremendous flow of sugar water that yielded maple syrup.

Years later, when thousands of sugar maples were planted in Europe, attempts to produce maple syrup from them were unsuccessful because of the region's short, mild spring.

WHAT SWEET SECRET DID THE EARLY COLONISTS GIVE TO THE INDIANS?

The early colonists discovered that the Indians did not know about honey from beehives. Records indicate that colonists brought honeybees with them from England to Virginia in 1622. They showed the Indians how to produce honey from the hives.

HOW MANY GALLONS OF SUGAR WATER DOES IT TAKE TO PRODUCE ONE GALLON OF SYRUP?

Between forty and fifty gallons of sugar water must be gathered from the maple tree to produce one gallon of maple syrup. The sugar water is boiled in large vats to evaporate the water and produce a rich and delicious syrup. The syrup is then strained to remove any sand and bark.

HOW DID THE INDIANS THICKEN THE SUGAR WATER?

The Indians used heated rocks to boil the sugar water in hollowed out gourds, skins, or birch-bark buckets. At night they would set their containers out in the cold and early the next morning remove any ice which had formed. A tasty concentration of syrup remained which did not freeze.

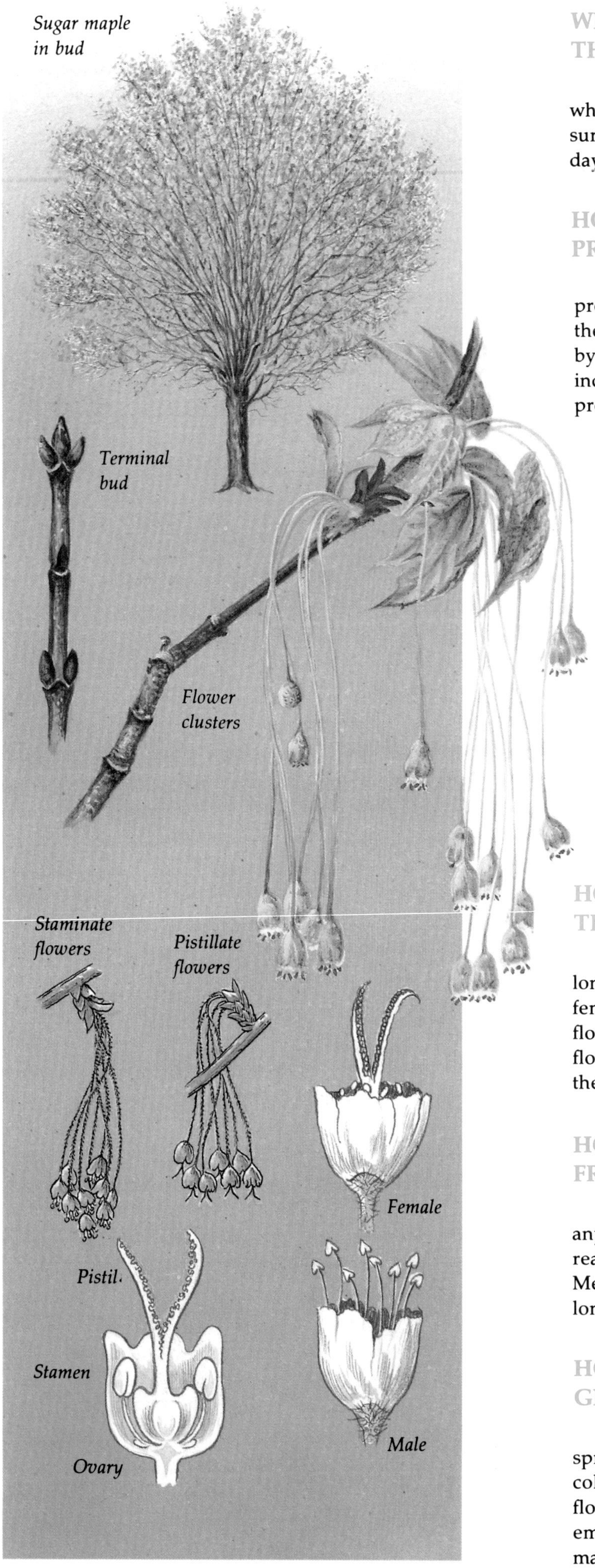

WHY DOES SUGAR WATER FLOW BEST ON THE SOUTH SIDE OF THE TREE?

The pumping action within the maple tree works best when there is a great contrast in temperatures. Because surfaces facing the south absorb the most heat during the day, they have the greatest pumping action.

HOW IS SUGAR WATER ABLE TO BUILD PRESSURE GOING AGAINST GRAVITY?

The hydraulics of the sugar sap continues to be a profound mystery to biologists; however, one view is that the fluid within the trunk of the tree expands when warmed by the sun. As it expands, the pressure inside the tree increases. This forces the sugar water to flow upward with a pressure reaching twenty pounds per square inch. When a tap is inserted between one and one and three-quarters of an inch into the trunk, it allows the sugar water to flow out of the tree.

HOW DO LEAVES IN THE SUMMER PRODUCE SUGAR IN THE SPRING?

Sugar is produced by the leaves in the summer and flows down the tree's trunk to be stored in the roots during the winter. The trunk, however, retains some of this sugar water in its sap wood. It remains there until spring. As the pumping action of the warming sun forces water up and down inside the trunk of the tree, the sugar is flushed out of the tree trunk. Some trees produce over eighty gallons of sugar water per season before the buds burst open and the trees begin to convert the sugar into food.

HOW DOES THE FEMALE FRUIT OF A MAPLE TREE DEVELOP WINGS?

The bell-shaped maple tree flowers that hang from long strings are called "pedicels." They are either male or female. Male flowers are called "staminate" and female flowers are called "pistillate." After blooming, the male flowers wither, but the female flowers develop slowly into the characteristic winged fruit of the maple.

HOW DOES MAN'S IMPATIENCE STOP HIM FROM PLANTING SUGAR MAPLE GROVES?

Unlike fruit and nut trees which produce crops anywhere from three to nine years, sugar maples do not reach tappable size until forty to fifty years after planting. Men who want quick results are not willing to invest the long years of waiting for the rewarding product.

HOW DOES THE MAPLE TREE ILLUSTRATE GIVING TO OTHERS BEFORE ONESELF?

The maple tree is usually the last tree to bloom each spring. This allows maximum time for sugar water to be collected. In late April or early May the tree bursts into flower. The next day the yellow blossoms are joined by the emerging leaves. This produces a dramatic change in the maple tree's production of sugar water in just a few short days.

HOW DOES GOD REWARD THE MAPLE TREE FOR GIVING ITS SYRUP TO OTHERS?

Maple trees which are tapped must work harder to make up for what is lost, but they produce larger quantities of sugar water and contain more nutritive material than trees that have not been tapped. Sugar groves that have been tapped for fifty and a hundred years contain trees with larger girths than trees of the same age which were not tapped.

HOW DOES THE MAPLE TREE WRAP ITS LEAVES IN BLANKETS FOR THE WINTER?

The next year's maple buds are produced before the summer is over. They are protected during the winter by bud scales, which are wrapped around the infant leaf like a baby blanket. Inside the blanket a tiny, perfectly developed maple leaf waits for the spring.

WHAT DO MAPLE LEAVES HAVE IN COMMON WITH BALLOONS?

When the sap rises from the roots in the spring, the infant leaf is inflated with sap just as a balloon would inflate if filled with water. As the leaf unfurls, it breaks open the bud scales that have protected it over the long winter months.

WHAT DO BUD SCALES REVEAL ABOUT MAPLE TWIGS?

When the bud scales are broken off by the emerging leaves, they leave a small scar at the base of the leaf stem. By counting the number of scars on a twig, the age of the twig can be determined.

HOW MANY MAPLE TREES WOULD IT TAKE TO PRODUCE A MILLION LEAVES?

One. A fifty foot maple with a trunk fifteen inches in diameter may have as many as 146,250 leaves. The same tree ten years later may have grown enough to produce 162,500 leaves. During those ten years the tree will have littered the forest floor with over a million and a half leaves. The leaves on a single acre of mature trees collect enough solar energy to supply fifty homes with electricity for one full year.

WHAT UNIQUE FEATURE ALLOWS THE MAPLE TREE TO BE EASILY RECOGNIZED?

Maples are easily identified by their leaves. They have four sharply pointed lobes which grow directly opposite each other, and a fifth lobe at the top. The bark of the young sugar maple is smooth and gray but becomes flaky and dark brown when mature.

DO THE MAPLE'S ROOTS GROW AS DEEP AS ITS BRANCHES ARE TALL?

No. The root system of the maple tree is very shallow. It seldom penetrates more than a few feet into the soil. However, it spreads out in all directions, at least as far as the canopy of leaves above. Because of its spreading root structure, the maple is very resistant to storm and wind damage.

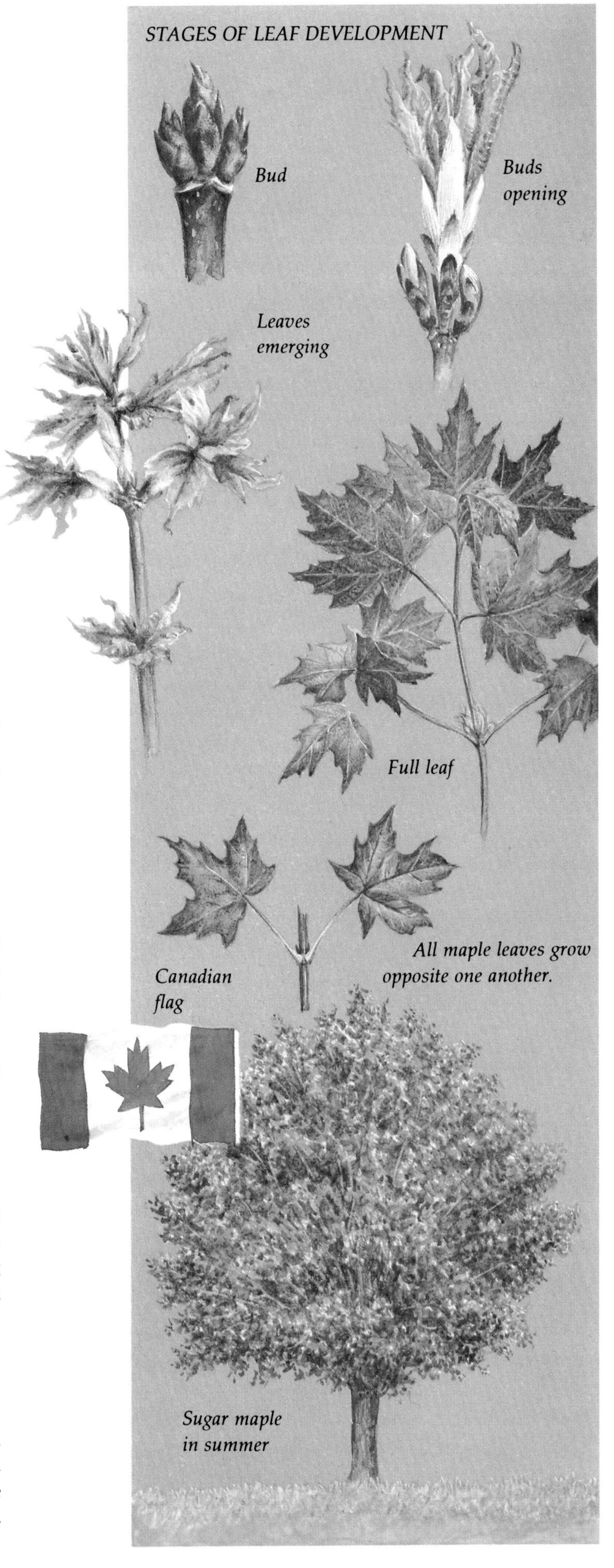

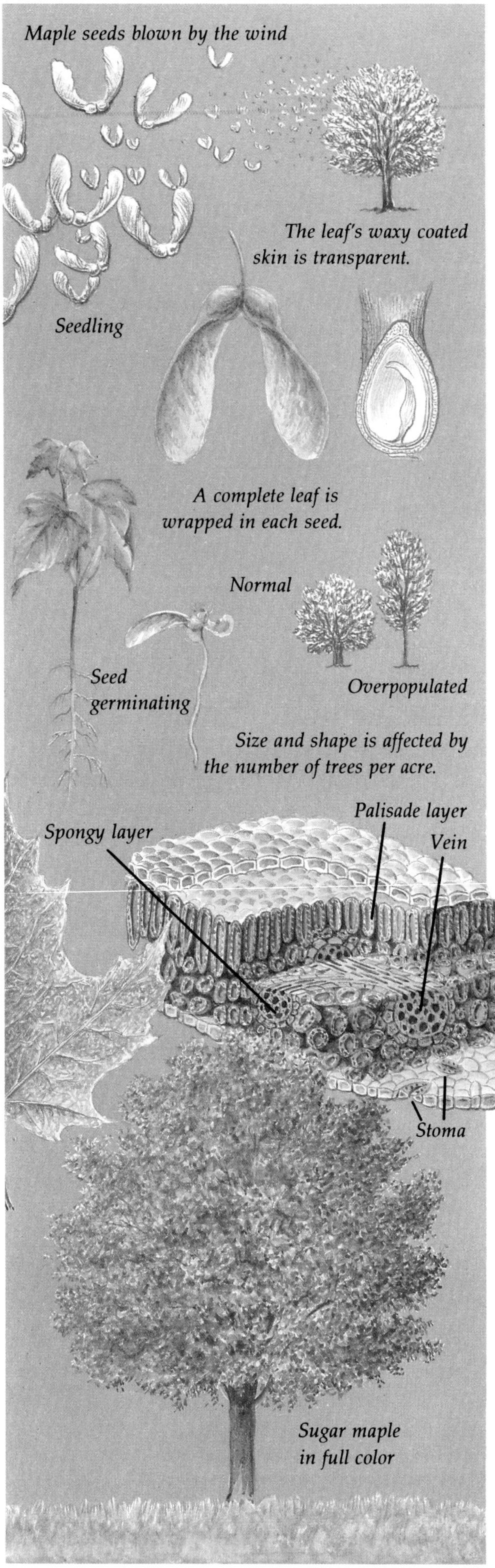
Maple seeds blown by the wind
The leaf's waxy coated skin is transparent.
Seedling
A complete leaf is wrapped in each seed.
Normal
Seed germinating
Overpopulated
Size and shape is affected by the number of trees per acre.
Palisade layer
Spongy layer
Vein
Stoma
Sugar maple in full color

WHAT IS THE NORMAL AGE OF A MAPLE TREE?

Most maple trees live to be about one hundred years old. However, some have attained the age of three hundred years. A maple tree must reach the age of thirty-five to forty years before it can produce seeds.

HOW DOES THE "PATIENCE" OF A MAPLE TREE ALLOW IT TO BECOME THE DOMINANT TREE IN THE FOREST?

Many trees require complete sunlight for their saplings to grow. But the maple can grow tall and spindly in the dense shade of older trees. It may wait in this condition for years until the older trees die.

When this happens and sunlight floods the forest floor, the maple sapling grows rapidly, occasionally doubling its size in the next year. Over the years the maple typically becomes the dominant tree in an area.

HOW DOES THE MAPLE TREE TURN SUNLIGHT INTO SUGAR WATER?

The leaf is the food factory of the tree. Within its thin structure, a process called photosynthesis uses chemical reactions to change simple compounds of water and carbon dioxide into complex molecules of sugar.

Energy from the sun is absorbed in the palisade layer of the leaf. Water and air are mixed together in the spongy layers. Then all three ingredients are brought together in just the right proportions by an agent known as chlorophyll. The sugar that is produced by this process flows to all the growing parts of the tree.

WHAT PRODUCES THE SPECTACULAR COLORS IN THE MAPLE LEAVES?

All during spring and summer there are many different chemicals present in each leaf. But, because of the dominance of chlorophyll, each leaf is green. In the fall, as certain chemicals in the leaf stem dry up, the chlorophyll disappears. It is then that the other chemicals become visible.

Carotene, which is found in daffodils, carrots, and corn, causes the brilliant yellow. Anthocyanin is multicolored, turning red if the soil is acidic and blue if it is alkaline. These two agents combine to form the fall rainbow of colors for which the maple tree is famous.

WHAT IS GOD'S TIME CLOCK FOR COLORS IN MAPLE TREES?

The angle of the sun may be the signal that causes trees to change color in the fall. Because the atmosphere acts like a prism, sunlight is broken into a spectrum of colors. When the sun is directly overhead, there is little separation. But when the sun drifts lower in the sky during early fall, there is less blue and more red sunlight.

This change in the color of sunlight may be the trigger that causes chlorophyll, which absorbs blue light, to fade away at about the same time each fall.

How is the generosity of gratitude illustrated in Scripture?

A grateful Christian in Thessalonica provides a striking contrast to a selfish emperor in Rome. This Christian enjoys today what the emperor lost his kingdom trying to obtain. Who is he?

(Pause for a response—see page 17.)

When Nero was a young man, his mother and stepfather determined that they would prepare him to become the next emperor of Rome. They hired the best available Greek tutors to school their son in science and the humanities. During these formative years, Nero's humanistic teachers instilled in him their ungodly philosophy.

In A.D. 54 Nero was officially crowned emperor. After taking power, he quickly poisoned his stepfather's son. Tiring of her continual interference, Nero murdered his own mother. He also killed his wife and married another woman. While Nero was establishing his evil reign and pursuing his study of music and Greek philosophy, a significant event took place in the eastern region of the empire.

A prominent citizen of Thessalonica cried out to the Lord to send someone to teach him the truth. God answered his prayer by giving Paul the "Macedonian call." After the man of Thessalonica heard the truth, he was so grateful that he dedicated his life to carry the Gospel to others.

He sailed with Paul to the seat of the proconsul from which the whole province of Asia could be influenced. Paul's preaching and the witness of this Godly Christian were extremely effective in this stronghold of paganism.

Condemning the idols that were fashioned to worship the sensual goddess Diana threatened the corrupt business of the local silversmiths. Led by the angry craftsmen, a mob seized the courageous witness from Thessalonica. For two hours his life hung in a delicate balance before he was finally freed.

Undaunted by this dangerous experience, the dedicated ambassador of God returned home to collect a generous offering. Along with the Apostle Paul, he transported the gift to suffering Christians in Jerusalem.

When Paul was captured in Jerusalem and appealed to Caesar, this courageous companion went with him to Rome. It was there that his life was directly affected by Nero.

Fire broke out in Rome and a significant part of the city was burned. Nero, who was suspected of setting the fire, seized upon the incident to blame the Christians. He put many to death, including Paul and his dedicated servant from Thessalonica. But God always writes the last chapter.

By multiplying the gift of salvation that he had received, Aristarchus along with Paul and others dealt a fatal blow to the ungodly philosophy of the day.

Nero later left Rome to sing in a music festival in Greece. When he returned, he found his kingdom in the midst of civil war. Aristarchus left Rome as a triumphant martyr and still sings the praises of Him whose kingdom is from everlasting to everlasting.

From Acts 19:21–20:38

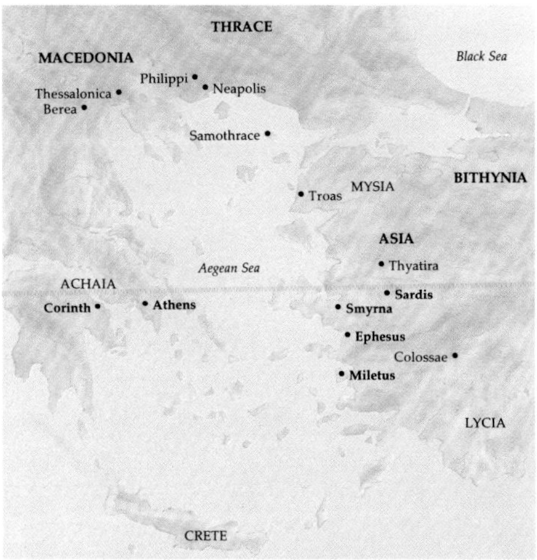

The Macedonian call *redirected Paul from Asia to the city of Thessalonica.*

ARISTARCHUS, DIRECTED BY THE SPIRIT TO MACEDONIA

The Apostle Paul was on his second missionary journey. With his companion, Silas, he visited the churches previously established in Syria and Cilicia. (See Acts 15:40–41.) Timothy joined them at Lystra, and Paul desired to break new ground with the Gospel. Paul's first thought was to visit the Roman province of Asia, but he was *". . . forbidden of the Holy Ghost to preach the word in Asia" (Acts 16:6)*. He then decided to reach the large Roman cities on the coast of the Black Sea in the province of Bithynia, but again *". . . the Spirit suffered them not" (Acts 16:7)*.

Not knowing exactly where to minister, the party headed west and reached the seaport of Troas on the east coast of the Aegean Sea. In a vision during the night, *". . . there stood a man of Macedonia, and prayed him, saying, Come over into Macedonia, and help us" (Acts 16:9)*. The man of this vision represented those who were to readily believe the Gospel in the Macedonian cities of Philippi, Thessalonica, and Berea. One of those Macedonians was Aristarchus of Thessalonica. He would accept the Good News with joy and spend the rest of his life in grateful service to the Lord and to Paul.

The Arcadian Way*—the main street of Ephesus on which the riot of the silversmiths probably occurred. It was in this riot that Aristarchus was seized.*

A GRATEFUL CONVERT—ARISTARCHUS OF THESSALONICA

Paul obeyed God's prompting immediately and crossed the Aegean Sea to the province of Macedonia. After an effective ministry in Philippi, Paul and Silas left the city at the request of the officials. (See Acts 16:16–40.) Their next destination was Thessalonica where for three weeks they preached in the Jewish synagogue. They explained to the Thessalonians how the Old Testament predicted that the Messiah was to suffer and rise from the dead. They identified Jesus as the Messiah.

"And some of them believed, and consorted with Paul and Silas; and of the devout Greeks a great multitude, and of the chief women not a few" (Acts 17:4). It is likely that one of these converts was Aristarchus. "Devout Greeks" possibly refers to God-fearing converts to Judaism who underwent circumcision as an initiation to the faith. This would explain Aristarchus' Greek name and his inclusion among the circumcision. (See Acts 27:2; Colossians 4:10–11.)

GRATITUDE EXPRESSED IN FRIENDSHIP AND SERVICE

Aristarchus became an intimate and valued companion of Paul. The first time he is mentioned by name in the New Testament is during the riot which occurred in Ephesus on Paul's third missionary journey. The preaching of the Gospel had been so well received in Ephesus that the silversmiths who made idols were suffering economic hardship. These silversmiths incited a riot, and Aristarchus was seized. He is referred to as one of Paul's "companions in travel." (See Acts 19:29.) The riot was stopped, and Aristarchus was apparently released without harm, but the dangerous situation prompted Paul to leave.

Aristarchus returned to his homeland where he helped raise a collection from the Macedonian churches for the persecuted and impoverished Jewish Christians in Judea. He accompanied Paul to Jerusalem with the collection as a representative of the church at Thessalonica.

The Arch of Galerius *in the heart of the city of Thessalonica*

When Paul was arrested in Jerusalem, he appealed his case to Caesar. After the request was granted, Aristarchus began the long journey with his friend. Whether he went all the way to the capital is not certain, but he did reappear as Paul's assistant in Rome, where Paul called him "my fellow prisoner." (See Colossians 4:10.) According to other historical records, Aristarchus was martyred during the persecution of Caesar Nero.

CHARACTER SKETCH OF ARISTARCHUS

HOW DID ARISTARCHUS RECOGNIZE THE VALUE OF THE GIFT OF SALVATION?

Each time Luke mentions Aristarchus, he is curiously identified with his home locale, something Luke seldom did when writing about others. Aristarchus is referred to as a Macedonian (see Acts 19:29), a Thessalonian (see Acts 20:4), or as both (see Acts 27:2). This suggests that he was a well known figure in that part of the world and also indicates that he may have been a man of means.

The city of Thessalonica enjoyed local autonomy and was the most prosperous of all the Macedonian cities. It was a major seaport located on the main Roman trade route.

When Aristarchus heard the good news of the gift of salvation, he recognized its value as exceeding any of his possessions. He was like the man in the parable *"who, when he had found one pearl of great price, went and sold all that he had, and bought it" (Matthew 13:46).*

Aristarchus exchanged prosperity for persecution. (See Acts 17:5.) He endured hardship with Paul as a good soldier of Jesus Christ. He did these things not to earn his salvation, but in appreciation for it.

HOW DID ARISTARCHUS EXPRESS HIS GRATITUDE TO THE APOSTLE PAUL?

Aristarchus expressed his gratitude in friendship, unswerving loyalty, and dedicated service. Paul was the human instrument used by the Lord to bring the Gospel to the Macedonians. He was a man of strong affections, whose epistles reveal a heart overflowing with love for many individuals mentioned by name.

Paul valued companionship and almost always traveled and labored with others. When Paul was left in Athens without co-workers, he sent for Silas and Timothy "to come to him with all speed." (See Acts 17:14–15.)

Aristarchus was privileged to become Paul's intimate and valued companion. He shared in Paul's labors, travels, and hardships, enduring through both good and bad times. When Paul was under house arrest in Rome, he was allowed a companion to share his confinement. Aristarchus and Epaphras probably alternated serving in this assignment. The Apostle gratefully acknowledged the restrictions Aristarchus endured when he warmly referred to him as "my fellow prisoner." (See Colossians 4:10.)

HOW DID THE MACEDONIAN CHURCHES EXPRESS THEIR GRATITUDE TO GOD?

Paul commended the Macedonians, *"For it hath pleased them of Macedonia and Achaia to make a certain contribution for the poor saints which are at Jerusalem. It hath pleased them verily; and their debtors they are. For if the Gentiles have been made partakers of their spiritual things, their duty is also to minister unto them in carnal things" (Romans 15:26–27).*

Paul cited the Macedonian churches at Philippi, Thessalonica, and Berea as examples of sacrificial giving when he wrote to the more prosperous and less persecuted Corinthians. In spite of their "deep poverty" which resulted from "a great trial of affliction," they gave to the poor of Jerusalem "to their power" and even "beyond their power." And they gave with an attitude of abounding joy. (See II Corinthians 8:1–5.)

The Macedonian churches had received spiritual treasure through the nation of Israel and were more than willing to share their earthly treasure by helping God's chosen people in their distress.

Aristarchus lived during the reign of Nero. *Nero was the fifth emperor of Rome. He ruled from A.D. 54 to 68. In July of A.D. 64, fire broke out near the Capena Gate and destroyed half of the city.*

Nero blamed Christians for the fire and used the cleared area for his notorious golden house. Nero committed suicide on June 9, A.D. 68.

ARISTARCHUS
*ar-əs-**tär**-kəs*

CHAPTER TWELVE

Gratefulness

. . .Is accepting difficulties as part of God's loving provision

". . . Despise not thou the chastening of the Lord, nor faint when thou art rebuked of him: For whom the Lord loveth he chasteneth, and scourgeth every son whom he receiveth."

Hebrews 12:5–6

Living Lessons on Gratefulness . . .

FROM THE PAGES OF SCRIPTURE

God led Abraham to the land of Canaan and promised to give it to him and all his descendants. Following this, a famine broke out in the land. Instead of staying in the land and digging deeper wells, Abraham went down to Egypt and sowed the seeds of future destruction.

Many years later, one of Abraham's descendants remained in the Promised Land during a time of severe famine. This adversity turned out to be God's means of giving him and his descendants a priceless heritage.

ILLUSTRATED IN THE WORLD OF NATURE

BALD EAGLE *Haliaeetus leucocephalus*

The bald eagle is one of the largest and most handsome members of the raptor family. The term "bald" has nothing to do with any lack of feathers on its head. It is called "bald" because of the sharp pattern of its white head, dark body, and white tail.

Its broad, strong wings enable the eagle to carry objects which approach its own weight of approximately twelve pounds. As a symbol of strength and freedom, the bald eagle appears on money, flags, stamps, and buildings; and it was even the ancient hieroglyphic symbol which led to the modern letter *a*.

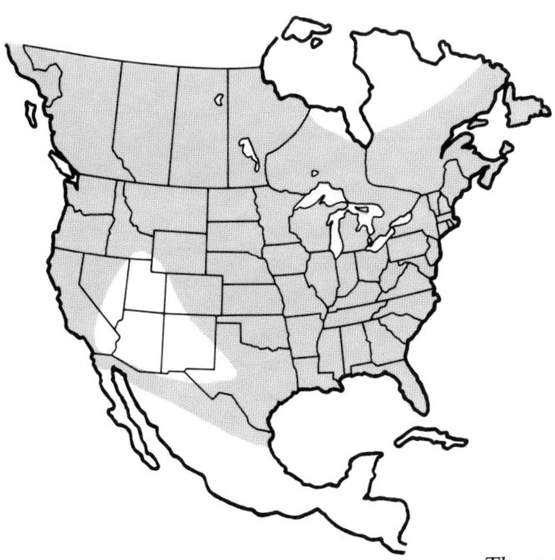

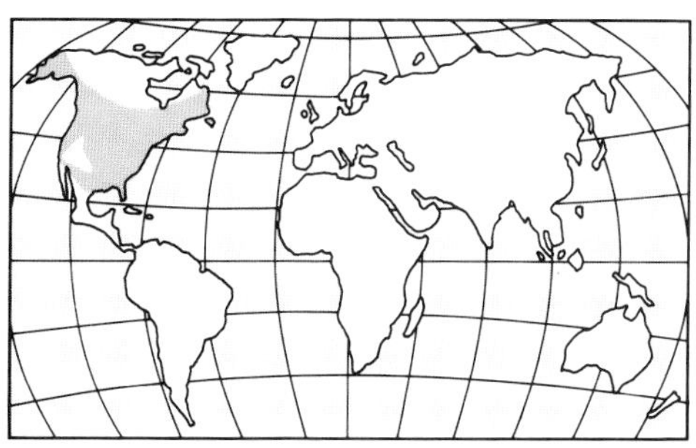

The range and habitat of the bald eagle

How is the need to thank God for the disciplines of adversity illustrated in the world of nature?

A magnificent eagle* soared to the heights of a rocky crag and calmly turned to witness a spectacular sight in the wilderness below. A vast multitude of men, women, and children had entered his desolate domain.

High atop the mountain, a little eaglet cried out for food, and seemingly out of nowhere a nutritious meal appeared. Far below a similar cry went up for food, and out of the heavens God provided delicious manna.

When the thirsty people pleaded for water, God fulfilled their need in a miraculous way. A rock was struck and water gushed forth. As if to amplify this spiritual picture, the eagle provided a drink for its young one—the blood of a slain lamb.

After the people grew weary of manna, God provided an abundance of quail. Similarly, the eagle supplied the eaglet with fresh meat. Many times the eaglet's cries seemed to go unheeded. But high above, the alert eyes of the soaring parent carefully watched. Vital skills were being taught through the motivation of hunger.

One day the powerful eagle fluttered over its nest. It was time for the eaglet to venture into the desert sky. God gave a comparable signal to His fledgling nation. The cloudy pillar that had hovered over their place of worship moved forward, indicating that it was time to advance.

The protective parent pushed the young bird out of the nest, forcing the eaglet to use its own wings. After a few desperate flaps, the eaglet faltered. Instantly the eagle swooped down alongside the young bird. The updraft, created by the eagle's wings, provided the necessary lift for the fledgling to maintain flight.

In the distance, the echoes of clashing swords and shouts of war could be heard as God led His nation through their first battle. Just as the eagle's wings aided its young, the uplifted hands of the nation's leader in a gesture of prayer turned the tide of battle and provided victory.

The harsh disciplines of wilderness training were as vital for the young nation of Israel as they were for the survival of the eaglet. Later God used the eagle to illustrate that important wilderness experience.

"As an eagle stirreth up her nest, fluttereth over her young, spreadeth abroad her wings, taketh them, beareth them on her wings: So the Lord alone did lead [His people through the wilderness] . . ." (Deuteronomy 32:11–12).

*The eagles in the near east provided rich imagery for Biblical truth; and although they were not of the bald eagle variety, they possess the same characteristics.

THE CHARACTERISTICS OF

THE BALD EAGLE IN SCRIPTURE

Often God uses the majestic appearance and awesome skills of the eagle to symbolize important truths for His people.

God warns that a rebellious youth attracts destructive companions like carrion draws hungry eagles.

"The eye that mocketh at his father, and despiseth to obey his mother, the ravens of the valley shall pick it out, and the young eagles shall eat it" (Proverbs 30:17).

God explains that a man who puts his trust in riches will see them *". . . fly away as an eagle toward heaven" (Proverbs 23:5).* The rich man's wealth will be dissipated when trouble comes just as the updrafts of a storm carry the eagle out of sight.

God warned His people on numerous occasions that if they persisted in evil, He would send armies against them that would be *". . . as swift as the eagle flieth . . ." (Deuteronomy 28:49).*

The eagle's ability to overcome the law of gravity by stretching out its wings in flight is an important analogy of the Christian's ability to rise above the law of sin by entering into Christ's victory and by engrafting God's Word into his soul.

"But they that wait upon the Lord shall renew their strength; they shall mount up with wings as eagles; they shall run, and not be weary; and they shall walk, and not faint" (Isaiah 40:31).

CHARACTERISTICS AND PHYSICAL FEATURES OF THE BALD EAGLE

The eagle is designed to achieve its full potential through the disciplines that are required of it in adversity. Violent storms allow it to reach its highest flights. Scarcity of food forces it to develop its sharp eyesight, amazing speed, and accurate diving. Its lonely environment allows it to care for its mate and to skillfully train its young.

HOW DOES A HIGHER NEST REQUIRE LESS EFFORT, RATHER THAN GREATER EFFORT?

The eagle usually chooses a high crevice or tree crotch on which to build its nest. This nest is no ordinary structure. Hundreds of sticks must be carried up to the nesting site.

Each year the nest is remodeled until it contains tens of thousands of sticks. Additional building material may include broom sticks, construction lumber, light bulbs, or pieces of cloth.

With a high nest the eagle gains greater protection for its young. A lofty nest also provides a better position from which to monitor its territory, and it is an energy-saving launching pad. By swooping down from a high nest the eagle attains speed and then climbs into the sky.

HOW DOES THE EAGLE'S DESIRE FOR A CLEAN NEST PROVIDE SHELTER FOR OTHERS?

When the eagle's nest becomes too dirty, new sticks and grass are carried to it and piled on top of the old floor. This continual enlarging of the nest may cause it to reach twenty feet in depth and nine and one-half feet across.

The result is that shelter is often provided for other birds such as the Baltimore oriole and the English sparrow. Occasionally a porcupine may also join the group by building a den in the lower part of the nest.

WHY DOES THE EAGLE COVER ITS YOUNG WITH ITS WINGS?

Because of the height of an eagle's nest there is usually no shade to protect the young from the intense heat of the sun. Therefore the parent spreads its huge wings over the young eaglets. It also spreads its wings over its young like an umbrella during a driving rainstorm.

Baltimore oriole
Choice branches are gathered from dead limbs on nearby trees.
English sparrow
Newly hatched eaglet
9½ feet
The male brings his mate a sprig of greenery to signify that the nest is complete.
Parent
The eagle hides its young in the shadow of its wings. (See Psalm 17:8.)
Three-month-old

Eaglet exercising before first flight

An eagle literally jumps into the air. Then, with a single down beat, it is airborne. Gliding speeds may exceed 100 miles per hour, and altitudes of 10,000 feet can be reached in minutes.

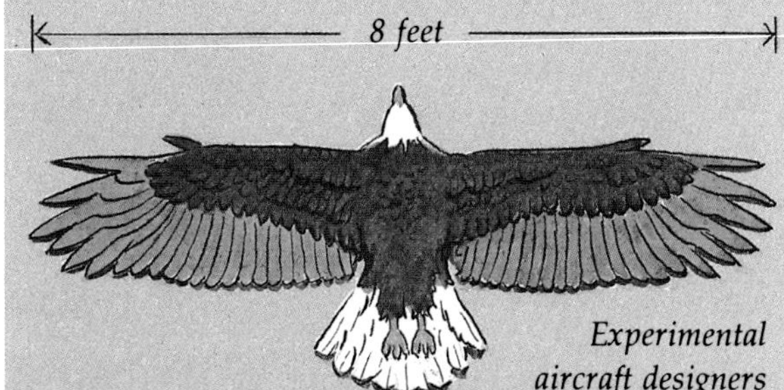

Experimental aircraft designers have unsuccessfully attempted to duplicate the eagle's slotted wing design.

Primary feathers may be twenty inches long.

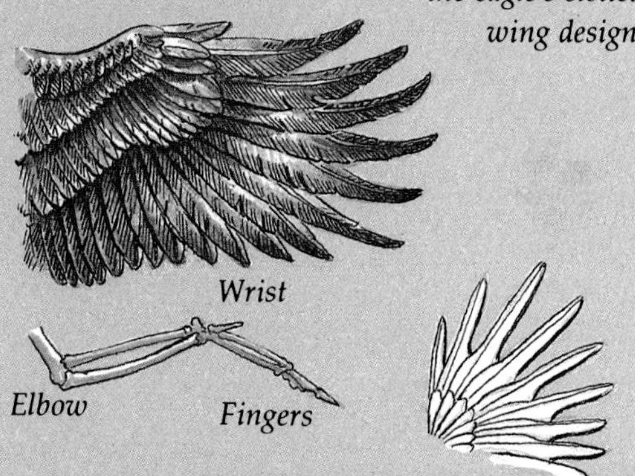

Over twelve hundred feathers were counted on one eagle wing.

HOW ARE NESTING RANGES DIFFERENT FROM HUNTING RANGES?

Eagles are very alert to the boundaries of their territories. A nesting range of fifty to one hundred acres will be vigorously defended against all who enter it. Aerial battles are common along these lines.

Hunting ranges, however, extend far beyond the nesting territory of the eagle. These hunting ranges are shared peacefully even though they overlap.

HOW DO DISCIPLINES IN THE NEST PREPARE THE EAGLET FOR SUCCESSFUL FLIGHT?

While the eaglet is still in the nest, it begins hopping from rim to rim. Later it stretches its wings and flaps them awkwardly. Finally the hopping turns to jumping. Some jumps are as high as fifteen feet above the nest. The result of all this preparation is that the eaglet's first flight is almost always successful and may extend for a mile or more.

HOW IS HUNGER USED TO MOTIVATE EAGLETS TO FLY?

Most eaglets voluntarily fly from the nest between their tenth and fifteenth week. However, if a reluctant eaglet decides to stay in the nest, its parents may withhold food. Rather than bringing dinner to the nest, the parents leave it on a nearby limb. Eventually hunger motivates the eaglet to take its first flight.

HOW DO STORMS BENEFIT THE EAGLE?

The eagle's main feathers, called primaries, are tapered at the ends, forming slots which serve as shock absorbers. The primaries also increase the wings' efficiency by reducing drag. When storms approach, strong thermal updrafts, together with this wing construction, allow the eagle to fly much higher than it would during normal weather conditions.

The eagle's deep yellow eyes *are set far apart on each side of its head, giving it 35 to 50 degrees of binocular vision. This gives the eagle the depth perception which it needs to judge distances. Diving at over 100 miles per hour, the eagle must know exactly when to pull out of a dive, or it would crash into the ground.*

HOW MUCH WEIGHT CAN AN EAGLE CARRY IN FLIGHT?

An eagle is able to carry objects which approch its own body weight. Since an eagle may weigh up to twelve pounds, it can pick up a wide variety of objects. Eagles have been known to transport small lambs several miles.

HOW CAN A FISH DROWN AN EAGLE?

Muscles in the eagle's legs are able to tighten the eagle's talons into a viselike grip. The three forward toes close against the fourth. At the end of each toe is a needle-sharp claw over an inch and a half long that can penetrate even the thickest hide.

Occasionally, the eagle's grip becomes so tight that it can only be released when upward pressure is applied to the legs. If an eagle attacks a fish which is too large for it to carry and it cannot release its grip, it must either drag the fish to shore or drown.

WHAT IS IMPLIED BY SAYING THAT A PERSON HAS "AN EAGLE EYE"?

An eagle has eyes that are larger and six times sharper than those of a person. While a person may have difficulty seeing a quarter at thirty-five yards, an eagle can spot one at over 200 yards.

Fish and rabbits can be seen from over a mile away. Since the eye is so large, its movement within the eagle's small skull is quite limited. To compensate for this, the eagle must constantly turn its head in order to see in different directions.

HOW DOES AN EAGLE KEEP AN ACCURATE RECORD OF WHAT IT HAS EATEN?

Indigestible material that does not pass through the eagle's digestive system is pressed into small pellets, called "castings," that are regurgitated every few days. Studies of these castings have given an accurate record of the eagle's diet.

Ninety per cent or more of its diet has been found to be fish. Only ten per cent included small mammals and birds. While reports of eagles killing geese, lambs, and even sea otters are true, they are exceptions unless food is scarce.

Eagles' primary diet consists of fish.
Nonskid pads and sharp claws create an effective hunting weapon.
Eagle tracks
A rabbit can be spotted from a distance of over a mile.
Eagle skull

HOW DOES HIGHER FLIGHT DECREASE IRRITATIONS FOR THE EAGLE?

In spite of an eagle's size and awesome strength it is often harassed by smaller birds, such as crows, hawks, king birds, and even gnat catchers. This harassment has been observed to drive the great eagle to the ground. However, by catching a thermal updraft and soaring to higher altitudes the eagle leaves behind all of these irritations.

HOW DO EAGLES LITERALLY FALL IN LOVE?

During the mating season a spectacular midair ceremony will take place. A female will carry a stick high up into the air and drop it near a prospective male. If interested, his response to her gesture will be to swoop down, catch the stick, and return it to her. This dropping and retrieving of the stick may be repeated many times.

To complete their mating ceremony, both eagles will soar to a great height, lock their talons together, draw in their wings, and begin tumbling to the earth together. Just before hitting the ground they unlock their talons, stretch out their wings, and return to the heights.

HOW DO EAGLETS ESTABLISH A PECKING ORDER IN THE NEST?

The first eaglet to hatch is given a head start in size and strength. By the time the second or third eaglet joins the feeding, a very clear and respected pecking order has been established.

HOW DO EAGLES "CARRY" THEIR YOUNG ON THEIR WINGS?

In speaking of His protective care over the nation of Israel God states, *". . . I bare you on eagles' wings . . ." (Exodus 19:4)*.

The Hebrew word for "bare" is *nacah,* and its primary root means "to lift." This is exactly what the parent eagle does to assist its young in flight. As it flies alongside the eaglet, whirlpools of air formed by its primary feathers provide the eaglet with additional lift.

Eagles rarely get wet. They dip only their feet into the water.

Eagle waiting for trout

Vultures are forced to the ground, where they regurgitate their food as a defense.

The eagle rolls over on its back and thrusts its talons into a Canada goose's breast.

Trapped by Deception

Eagle feathers were prized by Indians, but the capture of a live eagle was the ultimate hunting trophy. A pit, large enough for a sitting man, was dug and covered with sticks and grass. Food was offered daily until the normally cautious eagle would carelessly land on the trap.

When the eagle had become accustomed to his daily feeding, a brave would enter the pit during the night and wait for the eagle's return. Slipping his hands between the branches that covered the pit, the brave would grab the eagle's feet and tie them tightly with a leather thong.

How are the benefits of thanking God for the discipline of adversity illustrated in Scripture?

David testified that during all his years he had never seen the righteous forsaken or their children begging bread.

Which one of David's forefathers demonstrated this truth by remaining in the Promised Land during a famine while many of his relatives fled to a neighboring country?

(Pause for a response—see page 17.)

It was time for God's judgment to fall upon the nation. Prosperity had caused the people to become sensual and self-sufficient. Every man did what was right in his own eyes.

God's hand of discipline affected the crops, resulting in a severe famine. Soon family after family abandoned the homeland, failing to grasp the real meaning of the scorched soil and withered crops.

When the relatives of one Godly man decided to leave the country, he determined to remain in Israel and trust God for his needs.

During the next ten years, he diligently cared for his land. Each fall this hardworking farmer gathered in his precious crop and thanked God for it, whether it was sparse or abundant. He also allowed the poor to share in whatever yield his fields produced. God began to bless his spirit of generosity.

With the increased income from more successful harvests, he was able to purchase surrounding fields. Soon he had become greatly respected and admired as a prosperous, yet generous landowner.

One day he greeted the workers in one of his fields. They cheerfully replied, "The Lord bless you." It was then that this Godly man noticed a young woman gleaning barley. He was immediately attracted by special character qualities that he saw in her.

When he asked his foreman about the young woman, the foreman confirmed his impressions. After briefly talking with her, the wealthy landowner marveled at how she further demonstrated the qualities that had first drawn him to her. He realized that both of them had experienced adversity and had learned how to praise God through it.

She had been through deep sorrows. Her husband and several of her relatives had died. She was without financial resources, but had learned to trust God for her daily needs.

She responded with deep gratefulness to every kindness that was shown to her. When this generous landowner gave her the freedom to glean among the sheaves and quench her thirst with his water, she humbly knelt and sincerely thanked him.

Because they both thanked the Lord for the discipline of adversity, God brought Boaz and Ruth together in marriage, and a son was born named Obed. Obed later had a son named Jesse who grew up to have a son named David.

From Ruth 1–4

God's Law made provision for the poor. *Farmers could not pick up grain that fell from wagons. The poor could also glean in the fields during harvest.*

BOAZ, A MAN WHO LOVED THE LAW AND VIEWED ADVERSITY FROM A HIGHER PERSPECTIVE

Boaz lived in a period of the history of Israel which was characterized by anarchy and confusion. It was the time after Joshua and before Samuel, an era when *"... every man did that which was right in his own eyes" (Judges 21:25)*. (See also Ruth 1:1.) When famine struck and depleted the food supply, many of the people left for more fertile lands. Some may have gone to Egypt, where the Nile River irrigated the land except in the most extreme droughts. Others, like Boaz's near relative, Elimelech, went to the land of Moab. But Boaz chose to remain in Israel.

A HIGHER PERSPECTIVE ON THE FAMINE

Boaz was familiar with God's Word given to Moses. He did not regard this famine as an accident of nature. The Law listed famine as a punishment for disobedience to God's commands. (See Leviticus 26:19–20; Deuteronomy 28:23.) But the Godly knew that even in famine the Lord would preserve them. (See Job 5:20; Psalm 33:19; 37:19.) After the rains returned, Boaz is pictured as prospering. His relative, Elimelech, who had fled to Moab, lost his wealth, sons, and life. Only Elimelech's wife, Naomi, returned with her daughter-in-law, Ruth. They entered the land in abject poverty.

The bronze pillar *that Solomon placed in front of the temple, on the northside, was named after his great-great-grandfather, Boaz. The pillars were beautifully adorned with capitals and lily-work.*

A HIGHER PERSPECTIVE ON THE POOR

Boaz could have looked down on the poor family of his faithless relative. He could have scorned Ruth because of her Moabite ancestry. But Boaz viewed the adversity of this family from a perspective different than most. He saw the poverty of Naomi and Ruth as an opportunity to offer assistance, not as an excuse to justify neglect. When he noticed Ruth gathering leftover grain in his fields, he was kind to her, fed her, provided for her protection, and even supplied her with extra grain.

A HIGHER PERSPECTIVE ON THE LAW'S INTENT

Naomi was encouraged by Boaz's sensitivity to their situation and to the spirit of the Mosaic Law. The Law urged kindness to the stranger and the widow. (See Deuteronomy 24:19–21.) The same Law provided for the redemption of the dead man's house. The possessions of a deceased man were to be redeemed, or bought back, by a near relative. His posterity was to be redeemed by his brother. (See Deuteronomy 25:5–6.) Naomi believed that Boaz would respond to the spirit of these laws as well. She directed Ruth to ask Boaz to be her kinsman-redeemer.

Boaz could not grant Ruth's request immediately because there was a closer relative who had to be offered the right of first refusal. But Boaz was impressed with Ruth's fidelity to her mother-in-law and also to the God of Israel. He quickly approached the nearer relative and informed him of his right to redeem the land of Elimelech. The near relative agreed. But when Boaz stated that he would also have *"... to raise up the name of the dead upon his inheritance" (Ruth 4:5)*, he refused. The nearer relative gave his legal rights to Boaz.

Boaz married Ruth, and they had a son named Obed. All were blessed. Ruth entered the Godly house of Boaz, her redeemer. Naomi became part of the house of Obed, her redeemer. (See Ruth 4:14.) Boaz became the great-grandfather of David from whose seed came our Redeemer, Jesus Christ. (See Ruth 4:21–22; Matthew 1.)

Loosing the Shoe

Boaz had to loose the shoe of a near kinsman who refused to marry Ruth and raise up a name to her dead husband.

CHARACTER SKETCH OF BOAZ

WHAT WAS THE CAUSE OF BOAZ'S PROSPERITY?

Boaz was a beneficiary of the sure promise of God given to the nation of Israel. *"This book of the law shall not depart out of thy mouth; but thou shalt meditate therein day and night, that thou mayest observe to do according to all that is written therein: for then thou shalt make thy way prosperous, and then thou shalt have good success" (Joshua 1:8).*

A careful examination of Boaz's dealings with Naomi and Ruth reveals that he was very familiar with God's Law. But Boaz did not obey only the letter of the Law. He went beyond the letter and obeyed from his heart the spirit of the Law.

For example, the Law provided for the poor by commanding farmers not to harvest the corners of their fields clean and not to gather up grain dropped by the reapers. (See Leviticus 19:9.) Boaz went beyond this duty for Ruth and actually ordered his workers to leave whole handfuls of grain for her to find. (See Ruth 2:16.)

If a man died, the Law provided for the redemption of his property and posterity by urging his brother to marry the widow. Their firstborn son would then bear the name of the deceased. (See Deuteronomy 25:5–6.) Boaz could have refused to marry Ruth according to the letter of the Law because he was not Elimelech's brother. But the intention of the Law—to help a man's widow—was clear, and he consented to marry her.

Boaz knew the Law of God. He meditated on the meaning of that Law and sought to obey it according to its full intent. As a result, he prospered according to the promise.

HOW DID BOAZ VIEW NAOMI AND RUTH'S ADVERSITY?

Boaz viewed these pathetically poor women returning from Moab through eyes of mercy and love. Others viewed them with apathy, contempt, and superstition. For example, Naomi's family was indifferent to her need for food. (See Ruth 2:18.)

Superstition may have been a factor in the nearer relative's unwillingness to marry Ruth. He explained his refusal, *". . . Lest I mar mine own inheritance . . ." (Ruth 4:6).* Because the men in Elimelech's family had died, Ruth and Naomi were considered "bad luck." The nearer kinsman did not want his family to die as they had.

Another example of this occurred when Judah did not want his son, Shelah, to marry Tamar. (See Genesis 38.) Boaz, on the other hand, helped his family members, and treated them with dignity. He saw the hand of God in the lives of these women and sought to cooperate in God's perfect will for them.

IN WHAT WAYS DID GOD REWARD BOAZ FOR HIS KINDNESS?

The Lord rewarded him with a good name. He received the blessing of the city elders. (See Ruth 4:11–12.) He was blessed by finding and marrying a virtuous woman. *". . . For her price is far above rubies. The heart of her husband doth safely trust in her, so that he shall have no need of spoil" (Proverbs 31:10–11).* He also was blessed with a Godly seed. *". . . And Boaz begat Obed, And Obed begat Jesse, and Jesse begat David" (Ruth 4:21–22).* (See also Proverbs 17:6.)

RUTH
rüth

***The beautiful romance of Boaz and Ruth** is set against the background of apostacy in the nation and adversity in Ruth's family.*

The Meaning of Names:

Ruth, *"friend"*
Chilion *(Ruth's husband who died in Moab), "pining, sickly"*
Mahlon *(Ruth's brother-in-law who also died), "puny"*

BOAZ
***bō**-az*

Punctuality

. . . Is showing high esteem for other people and their time

"To every thing there is a season, and a time to every purpose under the heaven."

Ecclesiastes 3:1

PART FOUR

PUNCTUALITY IN GIVING . . .

Gifts that are given at the wrong time can actually damage the ones who receive them. For this reason, a wise giver will discern and obey the promptings of the Holy Spirit on when to give or to withhold a gift.

CHAPTER THIRTEEN

Punctuality

. . . Is responding immediately when God directs me to give a gift

"And they came, every one whose heart stirred him up, and every one whom his spirit made willing, and they brought the Lord's offering to the work of the tabernacle of the congregation, and for all his service, and for the holy garments."

Exodus 35:21

Living Lessons on Punctuality . . .

FROM THE PAGES OF SCRIPTURE

To be punctual in giving is to cooperate with the bigger schedule and purpose of God. The gifts which we give according to His timing are like precious jewels in the eyes of those who receive them and those who benefit from them. They reflect a multitude of spiritual truths.

One day a man was asked by his friend to give a very precious gift—the most precious that he possessed. The man recognized that this gift was in harmony with God's larger program and he quickly gave it. This gift took on greater significance than the giver ever imagined. It continues to communicate an important message for us today.

ILLUSTRATED IN THE WORLD OF NATURE

GRUNION *Leuresthes tenuis*

The grunion is a member of a family of fish called "silversides." They inhabit the coastal waters of southern California. Other silversides include swordtails, commonly found in tropical aquariums; shiners, often used as fishing bait; skipjacks, and jacksmelt. All are characterized by a silver band running along each side.

The grunion possesses the unique ability to spawn on land. Grunion fry can feed on small bits of plankton as soon as they hatch, and they actually begin to grow as they are washed off the beach. Maturing in less than a year, they grow to be five to seven inches long.

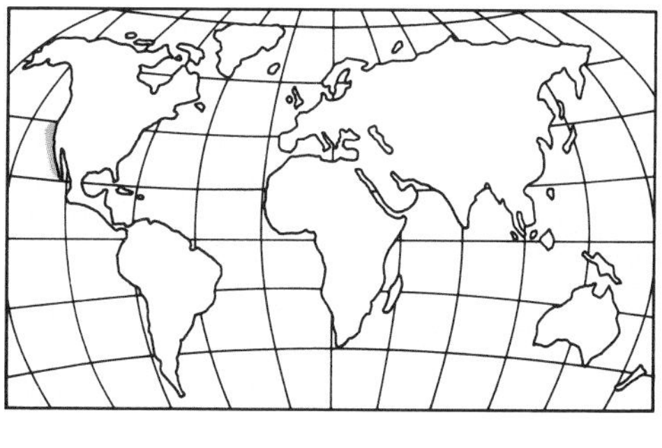

The range and habitat of the grunion

How is the need to obey God's timing for giving illustrated in the world of nature?

On a chilly evening in March, a crowd gathered on a southern California beach. They had come to see for themselves one of God's most spectacular demonstrations of precise timing.

They sat down and waited patiently as the rising tide broke higher and higher against the beach. The brilliant orange sun disappeared beneath the horizon of the ocean. The last shades of daylight soon vanished. A new moon began to reflect against the shimmering surface of the water.

The crowd waited quietly. They observed that a definite change in the tide had taken place. Each wave seemed to drain more water from the beach than it left behind. Soon, the ocean surf near the beach sparkled like a sea full of silver coins. Suddenly, several shiny objects tumbled onto the shore.

The moonlight lit up their bright bodies as they persistently fought the undertow of the receding waves. A hush came over the crowd as a group of male grunions investigated the conditions along the beach. More waves hit the beach and when they receded, only wet sand and foam remained.

Minutes passed and then it happened. The surf crashed against the shore covering the beach with a mass of squirming fish. Each wave added to their numbers.

The female grunions, swollen with eggs, flicked their tails into the wet sand and arched upward. They used their tails like a drill to bury themselves up to their gills. At that moment they deposited their fully developed eggs.

The males then flopped and twisted across the beach. They coiled around the females and fertilized the eggs. With their precious gift of new life placed in the proper depth and level of the beach, the grunions began to wriggle free from the sand and flop toward the receding waters.

A shout went up from the waiting crowd. They ran along the beach, scooping up the remaining fish and depositing them into plastic buckets. For every grunion they captured, ten other grunions slipped back into the ocean.

As those patient fishermen left for home with their catch, they marveled at what they had just witnessed. To insure the survival of their young, the grunions not only chose the right day but also the right wave before they came to spawn their young.

If the parent fish had come a day too soon, the freshly laid eggs would have been washed out to sea with the next night's higher tide. If they would have arrived a day too late, their young would have been stranded on the beach when they hatched. The punctuality of the grunion is a wonder of God's creation.

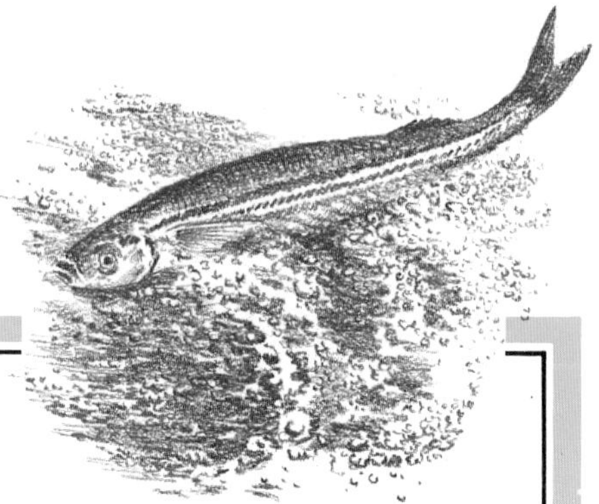

THE CHARACTERISTICS OF

THE GRUNION IN SCRIPTURE

Both fishing and precise timing figure prominently in the ministry and message of Christ. At least one-third of the twelve apostles were fishermen by trade, and much of Christ's ministry occurred along the seashore.

Christ used the precise timing and location of a school of fish to help Peter recognize His Lordship. (See John 21:6–8.) He used the exact timing of catching one particular fish to pay a tax. (See Matthew 17:27.)

He multiplied two fish to feed 5,000 (see Matthew 14:19) and prepared a fish breakfast for His discouraged disciples. (See John 21:9.)

In fact, the fish became the symbol of early Christians because its Greek letters, *ιχθύς*, formed an acrostic of the phrase, "Jesus Christ is God our Savior."

The patient fishermen who discerned the time of the grunions' appearing were in sharp contrast to the nation of Israel, who should have discerned the time of Christ's coming. *". . . Ye can discern the face of the sky; but can ye not discern the signs of the times?" (Matthew 16:3).*

Just as the tide reached its peak on the shore, so Christ will come again when *". . . the times of the Gentiles be fulfilled . . ." (Luke 21:24–28).* Meanwhile God tells us that it is *". . . high time to awake . . . for now is our salvation nearer than when we believed" (Romans 13:11).*

CHARACTERISTICS AND PHYSICAL FEATURES OF THE GRUNION

The grunion is capable of reproducing at any time. However, for any of its eggs to mature, hatch, and successfully return to the sea, they must be laid to coincide precisely with the peak of the tide.

The grunion must, therefore, be able to wait patiently for the right tide, recognize when it has reached its peak, and then act quickly to successfully spawn its young. Failure to meet any one of these three requirements will mean that the eggs that are laid will not survive.

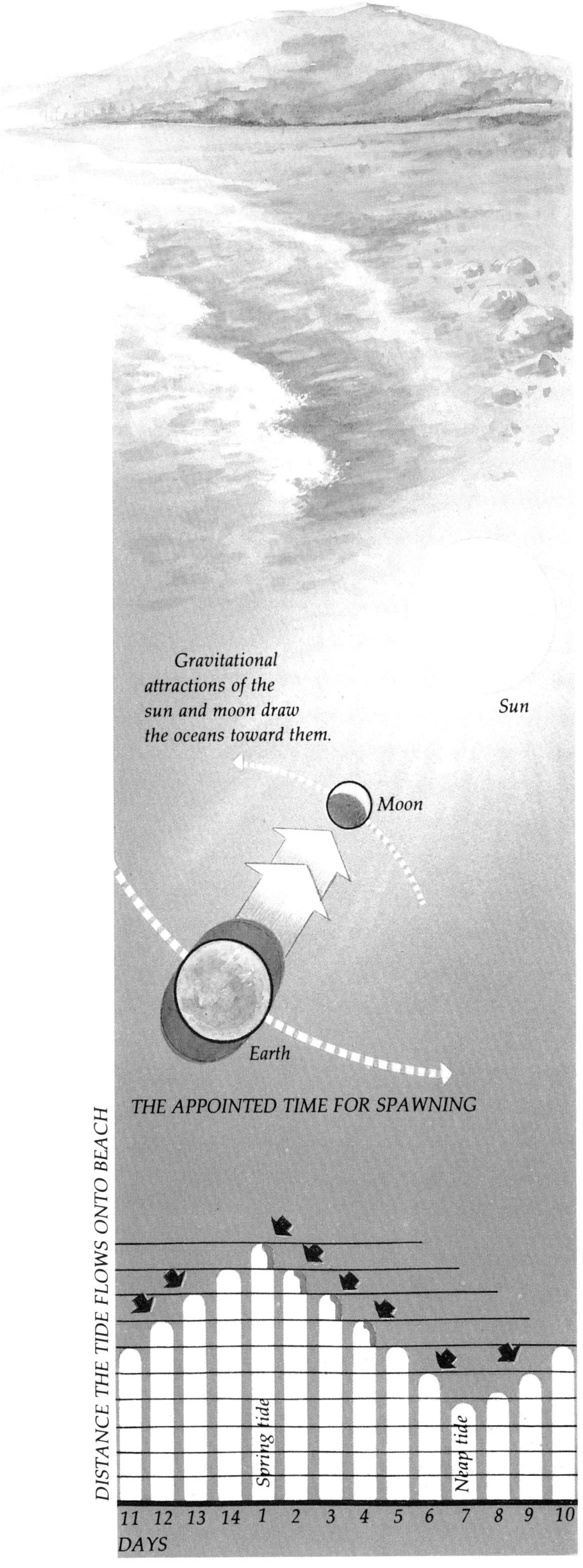

HOW ARE THE SUN AND MOON VITAL TO THE SURVIVAL OF THE GRUNION?

The sun and moon control the tides which allow the grunion to lay its eggs in the sand and the hatched grunions to return to the water. The gravitational attraction of the sun and moon actually lifts the oceans. Tidal bulges are formed on opposite sides of the earth. While the earth rotates, these tidal bulges move around the earth forming high and low tides.

In most places there are two high tides and two low tides each day. These are separated by a period of twelve hours and fifty minutes. Tides are high when the moon is directly overhead or below. At some places the water level at high tide may rise fifty feet above the low tide level.

WHAT CAUSES ONE HIGH TIDE TO DIFFER FROM ANOTHER HIGH TIDE?

The height of tides changes continuously. It fluctuates according to a predictable cycle of twenty-seven days, seven hours, forty-three minutes, and eleven seconds. When the sun and the moon are in a straight line with the earth, the tides are the highest and wash the farthest up on to the beach. These are called "spring tides."

As the sun and the moon move out of alignment, the tides become lower. Tides are the lowest when the sun and moon are at right angles to the earth. These tides are called "neap tides."

WHY IS THE FOURTEENTH DAY SIGNIFICANT ON A GRUNION'S "CALENDAR"?

Unlike most other fish, the grunion lays its eggs on land. This act of laying eggs, called *spawning,* must be carried out with precise timing if the eggs are to survive.

The eggs must be laid only after the highest spring tide has peaked and begun to recede. If the grunion's eggs are deposited on nights before the highest tide, which occurs on the fourteenth day, they will be washed out to sea the next night.

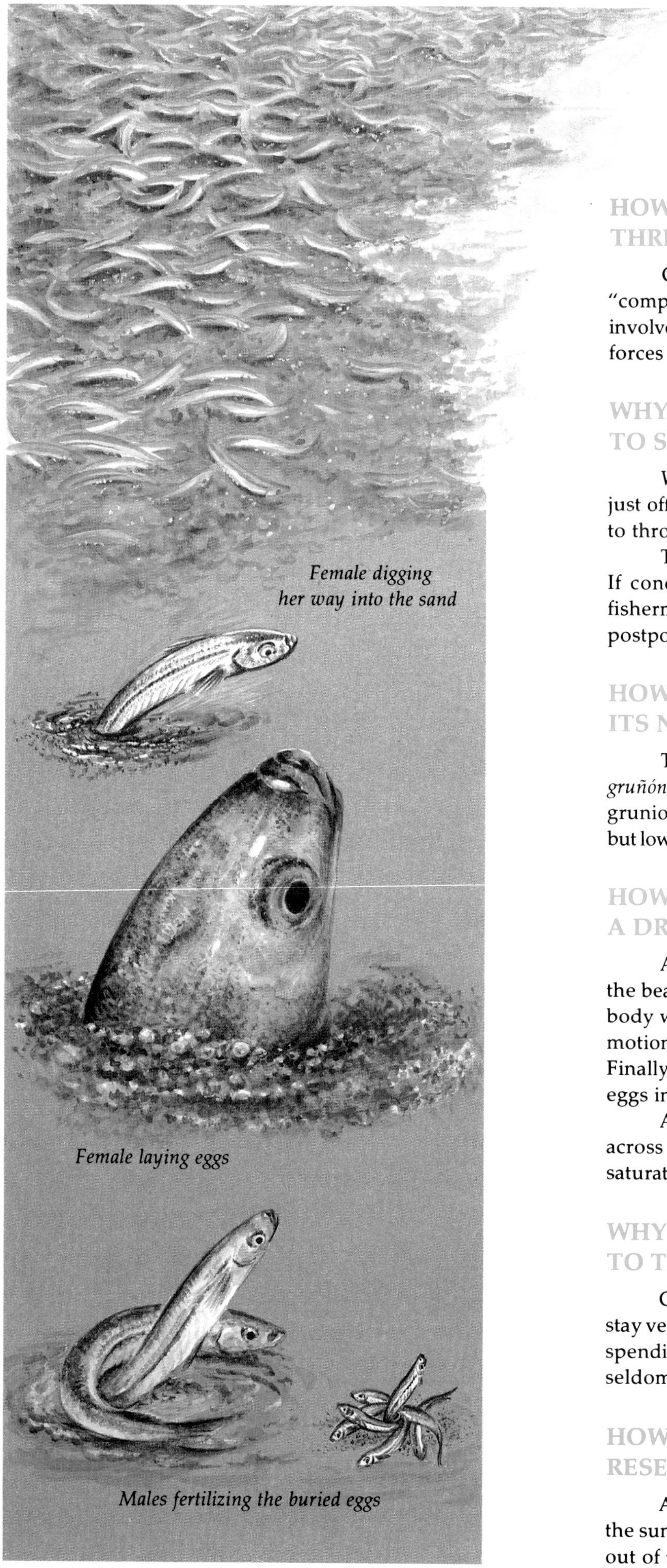

Female digging her way into the sand

Female laying eggs

Males fertilizing the buried eggs

HOW LONG CAN A GRUNION SURVIVE OUT OF WATER?

The grunion can survive out of water for up to twenty minutes. This is more than ample time for it to lay its eggs on the sandy beach and return to the water. The total spawning process usually takes less than three minutes. Sometimes it is accomplished in the time between two ocean waves.

HOW CAN GRUNIONS CHOOSE THE RIGHT THREE MINUTES IN WHICH TO SPAWN?

God has designed the grunion with a unique ability to "compute" the timetables for the tides. This ability probably involves sensitivity to the minute changes in the gravitational forces which are created by the moon.

WHY DOES THE MALE GRUNION COME TO SHORE FIRST?

When grunions begin to spawn, the shallow waters just off shore become crowded with anxious fish. The first to throw themselves on the beach are always males.

The function of these male scouts is to test the beach. If conditions are right, others follow. Veteran grunion fishermen never pick up these first males. To do so might postpone the entire run for a period of two weeks.

HOW DID A GRUNT GIVE THE GRUNION ITS NAME?

The name grunion is derived from the Spanish word, *gruñón,* which means, "one who grunts." As the female grunions spawn at high tide, they make a noise like a mouse, but lower in pitch. This sound brought about the name *grunion.*

HOW DOES A GRUNION USE ITS TAIL LIKE A DRILL?

As the female grunion swims out of a wave and onto the beach, it wiggles its tail into the soft sand and arches its body which is swollen with eggs. With continuous strong motions the tail goes deeper and deeper into the sand. Finally, when the grunion is buried up to its gills, it lays its eggs in the sand.

At that moment the males twist and flop sideways across the beach. As they bump into a buried female they saturate the sand with milt. This fertilizes the eggs.

WHY CAN A GRUNION QUICKLY RESPOND TO THE PROMPTING TO SPAWN ITS EGGS?

Grunions do not venture far out into the sea. They stay very close to the coastal beaches where they were born, spending most of their life within a mile of shore. They seldom swim in water more than forty feet deep.

HOW DO GRUNION EGGS RESEMBLE POPCORN?

After the grunion eggs are laid, they are warmed by the sun. Two weeks later they hatch. At this time they burst out of their shells like popcorn and go out with the tide.

HOW ARE HARDY GRUNIONS INDEBTED TO HOT SAND?

When grunion eggs are laid in the sand, they are less than one-fourteenth of an inch in diameter. These tiny orange eggs rest in clusters about four inches below the surface. A blanket of sand protects them while they develop. The hot sand also contributes to the incubation process by transmitting heat to the eggs.

HOW IS WATER FATAL TO GRUNION EGGS?

Experiments have shown that grunion eggs properly develop only when they are buried in sand. If the eggs are taken out of the sand and allowed to float freely in the ocean, they will die.

HOW DID GRUNIONS SPAWN THE TERM "SMALL FRY"?

The tiny grunion which develops within the yolk sac of the egg is called a *fry*. The contrast of its size with the seven- to eight-inch adult gives a vivid picture to the term "small fry."

WHAT KEEPS GRUNION EGGS FROM DRYING UP IN THE HOT SAND?

Grunion eggs are laid at just the right depth in the sand to provide a balance of warmth from the sun and coolness from the soil beneath. In addition to the blanket of sand that protects the grunion eggs, each embryo is surrounded by a clear membrane which keeps the egg from dehydrating.

HOW DO ONE THOUSAND EGGS LOOK LIKE TWO THOUSAND EYES IN ONE DAY?

Within twenty-four hours, two large, dark eyes become visible as the yolk sac begins to shrink. Soon blood can be seen circulating through the gray, threadlike body. Under ideal conditions the young fry will develop to maturity in nine days. However, it will remain coiled in the egg casing until the tide returns to release it on the fourteenth day.

HOW ARE YOUNG FRY LIKE YOUNG FLEAS?

Both grunions and fleas need to be shaken in order to hatch. The thud of a footstep by a man or animal is enough to shake a flea loose from its casing. The grunion is released by the pounding of the waves on the beach. The flea and the grunion can remain sealed in their casings for long periods of time until they are finally released by the necessary vibrations.

WHAT IS UNIQUE ABOUT THE TIMING OF THE GRUNION EGGS' HATCHING?

Just as the mother laid the eggs in the sand during an interval of less than three minutes, so the young fry hatch out of the eggs in less than three minutes.

Since the eggs are laid at the high tide point on the beach, it is essential that the young fry hatch quickly so that they can catch one of the few surfs that will sweep them back into the ocean.

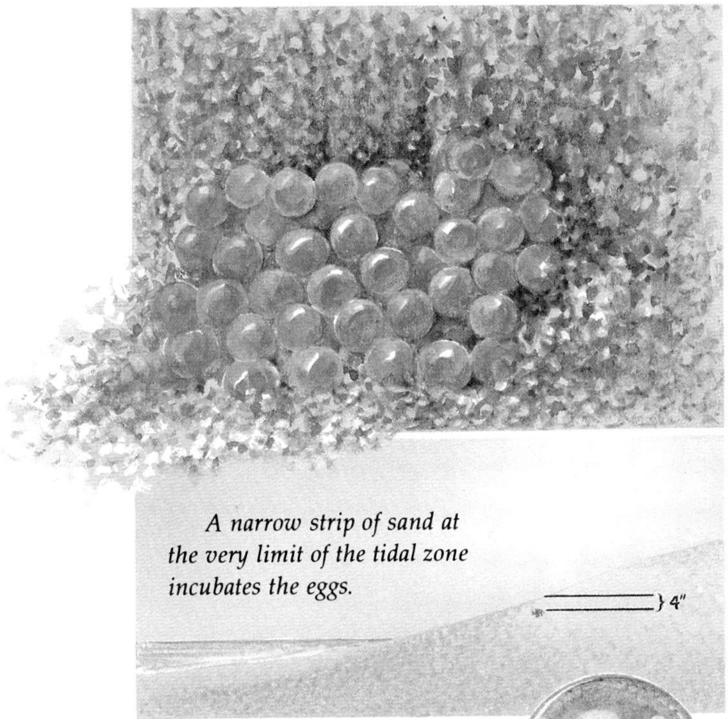

A narrow strip of sand at the very limit of the tidal zone incubates the eggs.

Grunion egg magnified fourteen times

Ten to fourteen days after the eggs are laid the tide returns to free the fully developed fry.

***Grunions are bluish green above** and silver below. Neither the male nor the female has teeth.*

Grunion fishermen do not need hooks. They use their bare hands.

Gull feeding on stranded grunion

HOW DO "BIRTH SCARS" TELL THE AGE OF A GRUNION?

As a grunion prepares to spawn, it stops growing. This creates a scar on each of its scales. By counting the number of scars with a microscope, its age can be determined. Grunions have relatively short life spans of only two to three years.

HOW COULD ONE GRUNION OVERRUN EIGHTY SQUARE MILES OF BEACH?

Females may spawn up to eight times in a season, laying 1,000 to 3,000 eggs each time, depending on their age. The young fry grow quickly, reaching adult size by the following spring. If unmolested by predators, a single female could theoretically produce over 64 billion offspring by the third year. That is enough grunions to cover almost eighty square miles of beach.

HOW DO SHOREBIRDS PROTECT BEACHES FROM BEING OVERRUN WITH GRUNIONS?

Compared to fish which spawn in water, the grunion has few enemies. The eggs, however, are eaten by shorebirds. These birds walk along the beach probing the sand with their long beaks. Upon finding a spawning area, a whole flock will gather and devour eggs by the thousands.

WHAT UNPLEASANT CONDITIONS DO "GRUNION RUNNERS" FACE?

Grunion fishermen are limited by law to the use of their bare hands. By running desperately after the writhing hordes of fish that cover the beach, grunion runners usually become drenched with salt water. Their hands and feet soon become covered with eggs, milt, and the smelly slime that coats the grunion's skin.

HOW DOES A GRUNION'S LIFE DEPEND UPON ITS PUNCTUALITY?

If the female grunion spends too much time in the sand laying its eggs, it will miss the receding surf and become stranded on the beach. If this happens it will soon become food for sea gulls.

How is the importance of the timing of a gift illustrated in Scripture?

When God prompts us to give a gift, He does so out of His infinite wisdom and foreknowledge. Our response will have far greater significance than the fulfillment of just one need. Who gave a gift that took on historic importance because it fulfilled the guidelines of punctuality?

(Pause for a response—see page 17.)

Two young men started out on a very important journey. Their objective was so important that it was later recorded in history. The similarities between these two men are remarkable.

Both men were sons of promise. The times and circumstances of their births were miraculously predicted by God. They were brought into the world by Godly mothers, who expected mighty accomplishments from them. Each mother was greatly praised in Scripture.

These young men lived in the same country and were trained by their fathers in a family business. Both were strong and courageous and greatly loved by their fathers.

Both sons began to prepare early in the morning for this special journey. As they walked, the way became more and more difficult.

The two men were accompanied by their fathers on this momentous journey. Although others followed along, only the two fathers and one of the sons recognized the true significance of the historic trip.

When these two young men neared their destination, they had to leave their companions behind. However, their companions were assured that they would return. Both returned after their journey.

The most amazing similarity of all can be seen in the things that took place when they reached their destination. These events should reveal the identity of the two men.

Both carried heavy wood up the mountainside. Both men allowed themselves to be bound and laid on the rough wood which they had carried. They were willing to give up their lives, for this was the purpose of their trip. At this agonizing moment both fathers turned their faces away from their sons.

God was well pleased with the faithfulness of each young man and they both left the mountain for another three-day journey.

Time and place are the basic differences between these two memorable journeys. Isaac carried a heavy bundle of sticks up the side of Mount Moriah, and Christ carried His cross up the side of nearby Golgotha.

Abraham's obedience to God's instructions and his willingness to give his only son provides a marvelous picture of God's gift of His Son.

If Abraham had not obeyed God in the timing of the gift of his son, he would have destroyed the analogy of God's gift of His Son two thousand years later.

From Genesis 22 and Matthew 27

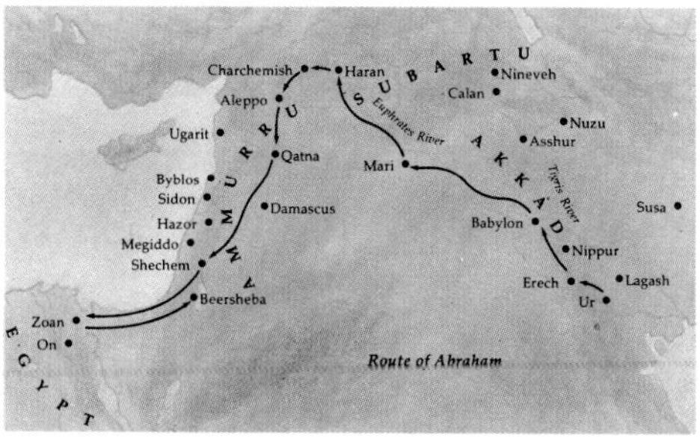

***Abraham's punctual response** to God's call took him over 1,000 miles from Ur to Haran and then more than 800 miles further until he arrived at Shechem.*

ABRAHAM, CALLED FROM HIS HOME TO FOLLOW GOD

Abraham was born in what is referred to as the "cradle of civilization." He lived in the city of Ur, prosperous focal point of the world's most important trade route. Excavations there have revealed a culture highly sophisticated in the arts and sciences. Ur's citizens enjoyed a level of comfort and culture which surpassed all other areas of the world, with the possible exception of Egypt. But Ur was also a center of gross idolatry and corrupt religions.

It was here that the Lord said to Abraham, *"... Get thee out of thy country, and from thy kindred, and from thy father's house, unto a land that I will shew thee: And I will make of thee a great nation, and I will bless thee ... and in thee shall all families of the earth be blessed" (Genesis 12:1–3).* (See Acts 7:2–3.) This command to leave Ur was the first of a series of tests in Abraham's life. Was his desire to know and obey God more important than his family, possessions, and ambition? It was, and Abraham passed these early tests. He left a land filled with worldly opportunity to enter a land of spiritual promise.

Ur of the Chaldees

Ur, the hometown of Abraham, was located about 140 miles southeast of Babylon. Clay tablets containing lessons in reading, writing, and several forms of mathematics have been found there by archeologists.

PROMISE OF A SON AND A GREAT NATION

In Canaan, the Lord continued to test His servant. Abraham occasionally failed a test but always learned from his failures. His faith in the Lord grew as he walked closely with Him. The ultimate test of faith dealt with Abraham's love for his son Isaac.

God had promised to make of Abraham a great nation, but he had no children. At first Abraham thought this promise would be fulfilled through his servant Eliezer, his appointed heir (see Genesis 15:1–4), but the Lord assured Abraham that the promise would be fulfilled through a natural son. Since his wife Sarah was old and barren, Abraham sought a child through Sarah's servant girl. (See Genesis 16:1–4.) Ishmael was born, and Abraham believed that the promise would be fulfilled through this son. Again the Lord corrected Abraham. The son of promise would be the natural son of his wife Sarah. (See Genesis 17:15–19.)

AN AWESOME TEST

Isaac was born according to the promise and grew to be a young man. Then God said, *"... Take now thy son, thine only son Isaac, whom thou lovest, and get thee into the land of Moriah; and offer him there for a burnt offering upon one of the mountains which I will tell thee of" (Genesis 22:2).* Abraham left for the designated place with his son. An altar was built and wood was placed on it. Without resistance, Isaac allowed his father to bind him and lay him upon the wood. Abraham had actually taken the knife in his hand to slay his son when *"... the angel of the Lord called unto him out of heaven, and said, Abraham, Abraham ..." (Genesis 22:11).*

Shechem, with Mount Gerizim

It was at Mount Gerizim that God promised Abraham that He would give the land of Palestine to Abraham's descendants. This established Israel as the Promised Land. It was near this mount that Jesus talked with the Samaritan woman and revealed to her that He was the Messiah. (See John 4.)

A SUBSTITUTE SACRIFICE

Abraham passed the most difficult test ever given any man. *"... For now I know that thou fearest God, seeing thou hast not withheld thy son, thine only son from me" (Genesis 22:12).* God provided a substitute ram, and Abraham *"... offered him up for a burnt offering in the stead of his son" (Genesis 22:13).* Abraham had already given up family, possessions, and ambition to know and obey God. Now he had demonstrated that he was also willing to give up his beloved son.

Abraham's great trust in God earned him the high commendation, *"... He was called the Friend of God" (James 2:23).* This dramatic episode taught all of his descendants an important aspect of the character of God. He is more concerned with the heart of the person than with the sacrifice itself. He is pleased with a heart of obedience, trust, and love. (See Isaiah 1:10–17.)

CHARACTER SKETCH OF ABRAHAM

WHY DID GOD ASK ABRAHAM TO SACRIFICE HIS BELOVED SON, ISAAC?

God had commanded against murder, *"Whoso sheddeth man's blood, by man shall his blood be shed: for in the image of God made he man" (Genesis 9:6)*. He later reiterated this command to the nation of Israel, *"Thou shalt not kill" (Exodus 20:13)*. In the Law, human sacrifice was regarded as the abomination of Molech worship. (See Leviticus 18:21; 20:1–5.)

When the Israelites and their kings burned their children in misguided worship, they were severely punished. It was an abomination which provoked the Lord to anger. The practitioners were considered slaves of evil. (See II Kings 16:3; 17:17; 21:6.) Why then would God subject Abraham to such a perplexing test?

The answer to this dilemma is that it was not Isaac whom God wanted, but Abraham; not the death of Isaac, but the death in Abraham of anything which would divide his affection toward God.

There is strong New Testament evidence that God explained to Abraham ahead of time what He was about to do. When Jesus called His disciples friends, He did so because *". . . all things that I have heard of my Father I have made known unto you" (John 15:15)*. Scripture affirms that Abraham was the friend of God. (See James 2:23.) Furthermore, his faith was based on the belief that God would raise up his son from the dead. (See Hebrews 11:19.) Thus, in either case he planned to return with Isaac.

WHY IS ABRAHAM CALLED THE FATHER OF FAITH?

It was Abraham who first pictured the nature of saving faith. (See Romans 4:16.) The New Testament declares, *". . . Believe on the Lord Jesus Christ, and thou shalt be saved . . ." (Acts 16:31)*. (See John 3:16.) But it is not mere intellectual assent that leads to salvation. The demons also believe true facts about God, but to no avail. (See James 2:19.)

Belief which leads to salvation is the type of belief demonstrated by Abraham. *"Even as Abraham believed God, and it was accounted to him for righteousness. Know ye therefore that they which are of faith, the same are the children of Abraham" (Galatians 3:6–7)*.

What did Abraham believe? He believed that the Messiah was coming as the descendant of Isaac to conquer sin and death. (See Genesis 12:3; 17:19; 22:17–18; John 8:56.) He so trusted in this promise that he believed that if he indeed killed Isaac, the Lord would raise him back to life in order to keep His Word. (See Genesis 22:5; Hebrews 11:17–19.)

Today our faith is to be the same as Abraham's, except we believe that Jesus, who was the descendant of Isaac through Mary, is that promised Messiah. We not only believe that God could raise one from the dead, we believe that He did, in fact, raise Jesus from the dead. (See I Corinthians 15:1–4.)

IS THERE ANY SIGNIFICANCE TO THE SITE OF ABRAHAM'S SACRIFICE?

God chose the site. Abraham was living in Beersheba when God said, *". . . Get thee into the land of Moriah; and offer him there for a burnt offering . . ." (Genesis 22:2)*. Jewish literature and Josephus specify that the Temple was built on Mount Moriah, the location of Abraham's sacrifice.

It was near this same place that Jesus was later crucified. The place called "Golgotha" was located "without the gate" of Jerusalem. (See Matthew 27:33; Hebrews 13:12.) But at this sacrifice, heaven remained silent. No substitute ram replaced the Son of God, for He was the Lamb of God. He was raised again on the third day to demonstrate the victory that has been won for all who believe.

Abraham's punctual giving *of his son provided an amazing parallel of Christ's future sacrifice. The mountain on which Abraham offered Isaac later became the site of Solomon's temple and the city of Jerusalem. To the side of this mountain was the place of Christ's crucifixion.*

ABRAHAM
ā-bre-ham

CHAPTER FOURTEEN

Punctuality

. . . Is honoring God's ways by the timing of a gift

". . . Behold, to obey is better than sacrifice, and to hearken than the fat of rams. For rebellion is as the sin of witchcraft, and stubbornness is as iniquity and idolatry. . . ."

I Samuel 15:22–23

Living Lessons on Punctuality . . .

FROM THE PAGES OF SCRIPTURE

When God exalts a man with honor and ability, it is very easy for that man to depend upon himself rather than upon the Lord in a time of desperate need. The results are always tragic.

God gives us a sobering illustration of a humble man who was singularly honored by the Lord. However, in a time of national distress, he violated the principles of punctuality by giving an inappropriate gift to the Lord.

Those who fail to understand the ways of God would conclude that God's judgment for his presumption was too harsh. However, his life emphasizes the truth that when God raises up a man, He does it to demonstrate His ways before others, especially in difficult circumstances.

ILLUSTRATED IN THE WORLD OF NATURE

ELK *Cervus canadensis*

The elk is a majestic wilderness animal standing five feet tall at the shoulders and weighing up to 1,100 pounds. The animal is beautifully proportioned and is the wildest of this continent's deer. The name "elk" originally belonged to the European moose.

Early English colonists gave the name to the animal the American Indian called *wapiti*. In the days of the Early West, elk inhabited the plains of Montana, Wyoming, and the Dakotas. Today they are found almost entirely in the high mountains of the West.

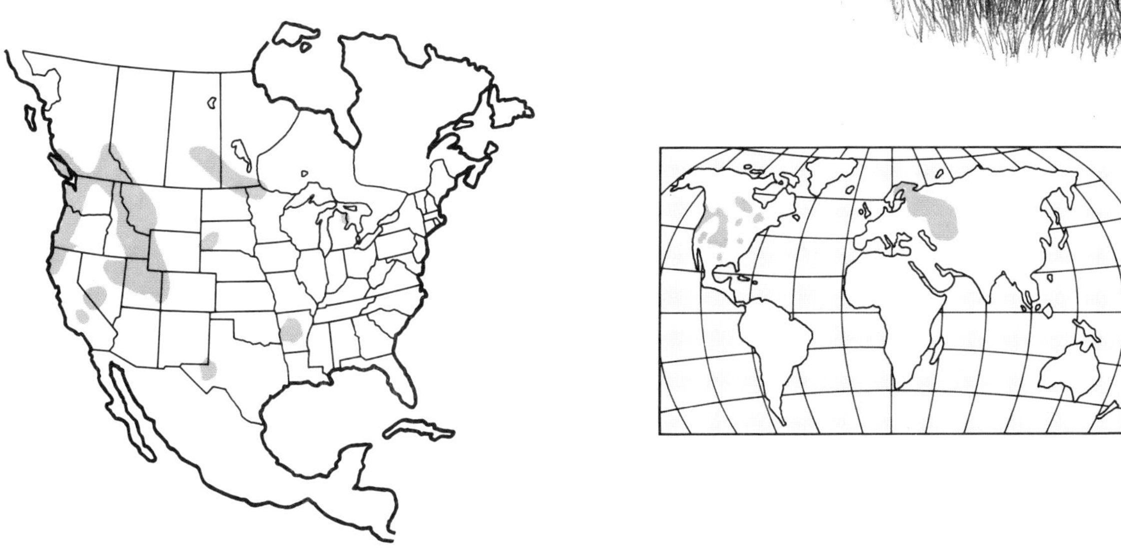

The range and habitat of the elk

How is the timing of a gift illustrated in the world of nature?

The young elk watched in awe as his majestic father reared up on powerful hind legs and aggressively charged a rival bull elk. The intruder was no match for his father's overpowering strength and menacing rack.

With one mighty blow he sent the unwelcome challenger reeling into the underbrush. Wounded from the encounter, the rival hastily retreated into the forest.

It was late autumn, snow was falling on the mountains, and the lush alfalfa pastures would soon be covered with a thick white blanket for the winter.

The young bull confidently trotted toward the nearby meadow. He cast an entreating glance in the direction of his father, but the older elk remained motionless, cautiously sniffing the air. Danger was present.

Without warning, two hungry wolves burst through the brush near the edge of the field. They paused for an instant.

With a twinge of fear, the young elk looked apprehensively to his father. Surely he would protect him from this impending danger. Then, with the wolves out of the way, he could graze to his heart's content in the pasture.

Surprisingly, the large bull stood still and silently beckoned to his son. With a whirl, he turned his massive frame and bolted toward the nearby mountainside.

The young elk followed close behind his father as other wolves broke through the thickets and joined the two scouts in pursuit.

The life-and-death sprint was an even race until the elk reached the rocky slopes of the mountain. Higher and higher they climbed. As the air grew colder, the hot breath of the elk formed clouds of steamy vapor.

The higher they climbed, the stronger the elk appeared to their weary pursuers. Finally, the wolves abandoned the chase. The young elk affectionately nuzzled his father, who had given him a valuable lesson.

There is a time to give protection and a time to flee. The experienced elk had given his son a better gift by teaching him to flee from dangers that would damage his life.

THE CHARACTERISTICS OF

THE ELK IN SCRIPTURE

The royal elk presents a vivid picture of the life and ministry of King David and of every Christian who desires fellowship with God and victory over sin.

In the spring the horns of the elk bud and grow rapidly into a majestic rack. God invited David to dwell with Him in Mount Zion and promised, *"There will I make the horn of David to bud . . ." (Psalm 132:17).*

God then told David how his horn would grow. *"He hath dispersed, he hath given to the poor; his righteousness endureth for ever; his horn shall be exalted with honour" (Psalm 112:9).*

God assured David that he would always have enemies, and that their purpose was to motivate him to honor the ways of God. *"The wicked shall see it, and be grieved; he shall gnash with his teeth, and melt away . . ." (Psalm 112:10).*

When David was pursued by Saul, he could have depended upon past abilities, honors, and popularity; instead, he fled to the mountains. There he borrowed more imagery from the life of the elk. *"He maketh my feet like hinds' feet: and setteth me upon my high places" (II Samuel 22:34).* (See also Psalm 18:33.)

David looked up to his mountain fortress and saw in it a symbol of God and His protection. *"And he said, The Lord is my rock, and my fortress, and my deliverer; The God of my rock; in him will I trust . . ." (II Samuel 22:2–3).*

CHARACTERISTICS AND PHYSICAL FEATURES OF THE ELK

The elk is a migratory animal and maintains a fixed yearly cycle. It has a winter feeding ground and a summer range. It must travel between the two in a punctual manner.

Elk that leave the summer range and reach the winter grazing lands too soon might use up the scarce supply of winter feed before the winter is over. Elk that linger too long in a summer range might not find enough food along the way to make it to the winter grounds.

HOW MUST ELK CHOOSE BETWEEN INSECTS AND ANTLERS?

In the spring the bull elk seek lush pasture for grazing, but there they encounter swarms of flies and mosquitoes. The bites of these insects on the head of the elk will cause the antlers to become deformed.

Bull elk that shy away from the insect-infested pastures soon run out of the food that is required to support the tremendous growth of their antlers.

HOW DOES AN ELK SHOVEL SNOW IN THE WINTERTIME?

If an elk cannot find an open slope where the wind has blown away the snow, it must dig through several feet of snow to find its favorite grasses.

When the snow is crusted over, the elk must use its sharp hoofs to break through the crust. To reach the grasses that are yet several feet beneath the surface, it uses its broad nose as a shovel. Sticking its head into the deep snow, it pushes forward and up, lifting the snow on its nose and dumping it to the side.

WHAT IS AN "ELK LINE"?

Elk eat the branches and bark of trees when other food is not available. They are particularly fond of aspen and will gouge out huge chunks of bark with their antlers. Occasionally whole areas of aspen may be damaged as high as the elk can reach. The damaged trees form a blackened scar called the "elk line" which may be as high as seven feet.

HOW DO ELK GAIN A DOUBLE BENEFIT FROM THE FOOD THEY EAT?

Elk are cud chewers, which simply means that they swallow their food twice. Feeding in the early morning just before dawn, elk eat quickly and swallow the grass without chewing it. The unchewed grass is called *fodder,* and it is stored in the first chamber of the elk's four chambered stomach. Here the fodder is softened and compressed into balls called *cud.* When elk have finished feeding, they lie down to rest and chew their cud. The cud is belched up into the mouth and ground into a pulp before being swallowed a second time and digested.

Elk shoveling snow

Trees damaged by elk

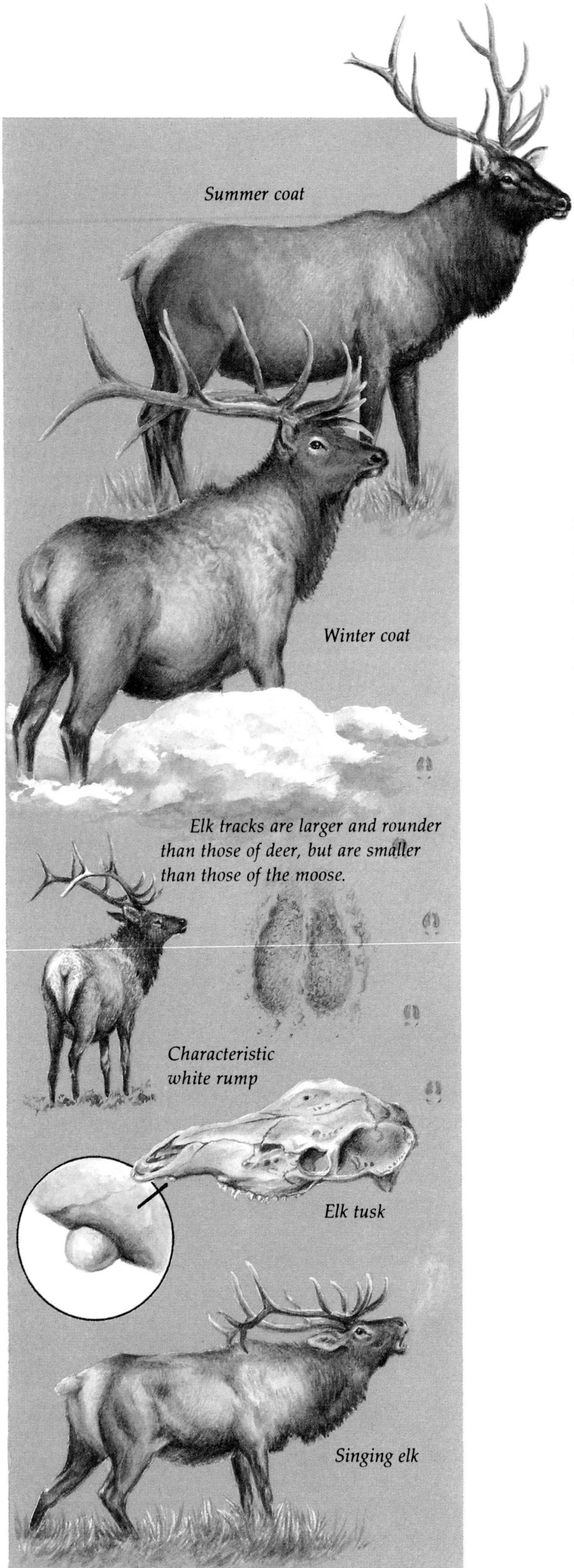
Summer coat
Winter coat
Elk tracks are larger and rounder than those of deer, but are smaller than those of the moose.
Characteristic white rump
Elk tusk
Singing elk

HOW DID THE ELK GET THE NAME WAPITI?

The name *wapiti* means "white rump." The elk was given that name by Algonquin and Shawnee Indians because of the light patch of hair surrounding the elk's tail.

During the summer, the elk's coat is short and sleek and lacks an underfur. It is tawny brown over the body and darker on the face, belly, neck, and legs. The winter coat has long guard hairs and a thick, crinkly underfur, which is less glossy and more faded than the summer coat. In May and June, when the animal sheds, the coat appears very matted and ragged.

HOW CAN AN ELK COVER MORE GROUND WITH A "SINGLE-FOOT"?

If the elk trots, it can travel at a speed of about nine miles per hour. If it runs at a full gallop, it can reach a speed of thirty-five to forty-five miles per hour, but it will soon tire. If the elk uses its single-foot gait, it can cover long distances at about twenty miles per hour without tiring.

The *single-foot* is a fast, smooth gait in which the elk lifts each foot and puts it down alone. Thus, at a speed of twenty miles per hour, each foot will hit the ground every twenty-four feet. An elk can far out distance a man since the best runners can reach speeds of only about fifteen miles per hour.

HOW DID AN IVORY TOOTH ALMOST CAUSE THE ELK TO BECOME EXTINCT?

Like several other species of deer, elk grow rudimentary upper teeth called *tusks.* These upper teeth are ivory but they are quite small. However, at one time, whole herds were killed solely for their ivory teeth which, when carved and polished, were very popular for jewelry.

In the Early West, elk meat fed explorers, settlers, and whole army camps. Elk hides also became valuable as leather. Shipments of as many as 33,000 hides at a time were carried down the Mississippi River in the late 1800s.

By the early 1900s, elk were almost extinct. Today, however, through wildlife conservation, elk herds are once again prospering.

WHAT IS THE TIMELY SIGNIFICANCE OF THE ELK'S BUGLE CALL?

For man the bugle is sounded for a time of war. For the elk it is sounded during the time of mating. In reality, this is wartime among bull elk.

The bugle call is a unique sound that fills the woods and echoes through the canyons during rutting season. It begins with a deep rasping note and rises in pitch as the elk stretches its neck. The note finally cracks and drops slowly, ending in a series of coughs and grunts.

Often two bulls will climb opposite ridges and begin calling defiantly to each other. This may continue for hours at a time.

WHEN MUST ELK BATTLE FOR LEADERSHIP?

When the first snows come to the high summer range in late September and early October, the bull elk begin to desire to lead small herds of cows. For six weeks this desire grows until it becomes the focus of his existence. This period is called *the rut.*

The whole summer has been spent in preparation for the rutting season. Each bull is at his peak. His coat is sleek, muscles are firm, and his antlers have been polished for battle. One bull after another begins his challenge for the leadership of small groups of cows.

HOW CAN LOCKING HORNS BE FATAL TO ELK?

Challenges are made by pawing, snorting, and thrashing at bushes with the antlers. When a fight breaks out, the confrontation can sometimes be heard a mile away. The two bulls may charge, locking antlers in a dramatic pushing and shoving contest. While the fight never purposely ends in death, it is always a possibility that one of the two bulls may die. The real danger develops as the two bulls rear up on their hind legs and begin stabbing with their forefeet. The sharp hoofs can easily slice open a chest or flank.

If, during a battle, the horns of the elk become inseparably locked together, it usually means that both elk will die. While the bull elk are battling for leadership the younger males, called "spikes," are free to mate.

WHEN DO ELK "PANT AFTER THE WATER BROOKS"?

During the rutting season, bulls drink large quantities of water, but they are so intent on protecting their cows that they forget to eat. Some bulls lose as much as one hundred pounds. By the end of the six-week season, they are exhausted and wander off to rest.

WHEN IS A BROKEN ANTLER A SERIOUS PROBLEM?

Antlers that break while in the velvet stage may cause a serious blood loss to the bull. Antlers that break after the velvet stage cause little damage except for a noticeable listing of the animal's head because of the weight difference.

Bulls fighting for control of a herd of cows
Itching antlers are polished against small saplings.
Names of tines:
Sur-royals
Royal
Tray
Bray
Brow
Antlers "bud" in the spring and grow to full length by early fall.

One-year-old bulls, called *yearlings*, grow spikes about a foot long. Royal stags may develop antlers up to six feet long and four feet wide. A trophy set of antlers is not measured by the number of points, but by the length of the beam, the width of the spread, and the length of the tines.

Stages of Antler Development

APRIL—Soft velvet-covered antlers begin to grow. They are filled with numerous blood vessels and grow quickly. During this time, the elk are said to be "in velvet."

AUGUST—The growth stops and the velvet is rubbed off against trees. The antler tissue is now dead and has become extremely hard.

MARCH—The heavy rack loosens and breaks off cleanly at the base.

Female elk baby-sitting

Coyotes attack elk that are weak or injured.

Thin ice may claim victims in late fall and early spring.

HOW IS A BABY ELK PROTECTED BY A BATH?

A calf weighs about thirty-five pounds when born in May or June. It is immediately washed by its mother to remove any odor that would attract predators. The newborn calf lies flat against the ground at the first sign of danger. It is born with its eyes open and can stand and nurse within an hour. The large white spots on its back are a perfect camouflage, resembling patches of sunlight.

HOW DO ELK REMOVE STRESS BY GIVING TO EACH OTHER?

Cows take turns guarding one another's calves. Sometimes a nursery of fifty calves may be watched over by only three or four females. There are additional ways that cows help one another. They band together to drive away enemies, look for a lost calf, or offer support to one another in times of stress.

WHY WON'T A RED FLAG BOTHER A BULL ELK?

Because elk are color-blind, they rely on the detection of movement rather than color to warn of danger. Since predominant colors change with the season, movement is a much more reliable warning than color. Hearing serves to confirm and identify danger more than to warn of its approach.

Without a doubt the elk's most acute sense is its sense of smell. Thus, elk will typically feed and rest downwind from potential danger areas.

HOW DOES THE ELK FIND GREATER SAFETY ON HIGHER GROUND?

The powerful legs of the elk and the design of its feet allow it to be especially agile in mountainous regions. While David was fleeing from his enemies, he had opportunity to identify with these features of the deer family, and he wrote of them in the following words.

"It is God that girdeth me with strength, and maketh my way perfect. He maketh my feet like hinds' feet, and setteth me upon my high places" (Psalm 18:32–33).

What is the Mixed Blessing of a Forest Fire to an Elk Herd?

Forest fires and logging operations at first decrease the amount of food available. But the overall effect is to greatly increase the amount of food after the first ten years. The fire and logging make it possible for a lush regrowth of weeds, grasses, and shrubs–the favorite diet of the elk. After twenty years, the regrowth of trees decreases the amount of vegetation available and the elk must seek new pastures.

HOW DOES A ROYAL ELK RENEW ITS STRENGTH AFTER A SEASON OF WARFARE?

The elk will find a dense clump of trees and brush in a very remote place. He will then enter this "pole thicket" and remain there for months. During that time he will find rest and solitude, nourishment through browsing, and refreshment from the snow. He will only leave his secluded haven when driven out by deep snows.

How are the consequences of a gift that dishonors the ways of God illustrated in Scripture?

One of the ways that God maintains humility in the life of a leader is by establishing a division of power. God gave the authority to govern His people to the kings of Israel. The kings were to be limited by the counsel and influence of the priests.

Who in Scripture tried to disrupt this delicate balance of power by accusing a priest of tardiness and offering a presumptuous gift?

(Pause for a response—see page 17.)

The leader of the nation's newly formed army was worried. The night before more of his soldiers had slipped into the darkness, hiding in nearby caves and escaping to neighboring countries.

In the distance the clamor of thirty thousand charioteers, six thousand horsemen, and a multitude of soldiers could be heard. The troubled leader looked nervously down the road awaiting the arrival of God's anointed priest.

The priest had promised that he would arrive in seven days. The seventh day had come. "Where was the priest?" the impatient leader began to reason within himself. "He may be anointed by the Lord, but so am I. God has called me to fight this battle. If I delay much longer, my entire army will desert me. If I go out to battle before the priest comes, I will not have to share the leadership with him."

The leader proudly remembered his last battle. Many had mocked him when he had been appointed. They claimed that he was weak and ineffective, but they had to take their words back when he was victorious. Surely God would give him the victory once again.

Before the battle could begin, a vital procedure had to be carried out. A sacrifice had to be offered. This was the priest's duty and responsibility, but he appeared to be tardy.

Finally, the orders were given. Several soldiers gathered large rocks and constructed an altar. Others collected wood and a sacrificial lamb. The leader ceremoniously slew the lamb and placed it on the altar. Six hundred men quietly watched as he solemnly ignited the wood. The flames slowly consumed the sacrifice.

The commander quickly ordered his troops to prepare for battle. Suddenly the priest entered the camp. He looked at the altar in disbelief and then focused his penetrating eyes on the leader.

"What have you done?" demanded the priest. "When I saw that my men were leaving and you had not yet come in the time that you specified and that the enemy was gathering for war, I feared that they would attack me before I made supplication to the Lord. So I forced myself to offer a burnt offering."

Sadness fell over the countenance of the Godly priest. Years earlier he had anointed this leader to be the first king of Israel. "You have acted foolishly and violated God's command. If you had followed my instructions, your kingdom would have been established forever. Now, because of your disobedience, God will search out a man after His own heart."

On that day the kingdom was taken from Saul and given to David, because the ways of God had been dishonored by an improper gift.

From I Samuel 13:5–14

SAUL, THE FIRST KING OF ISRAEL

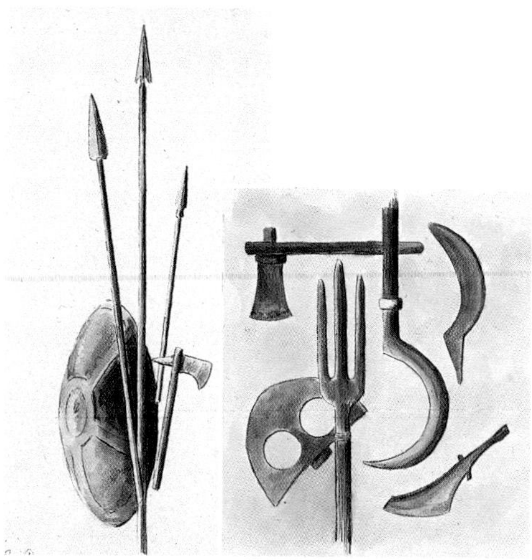

During the reign of King Saul, *the Philistines had disarmed Israel to such an extent that there were no iron workers in their country. The Israelites were forced to go to war using only their farm implements. (See I Samuel 13:19–23.)*

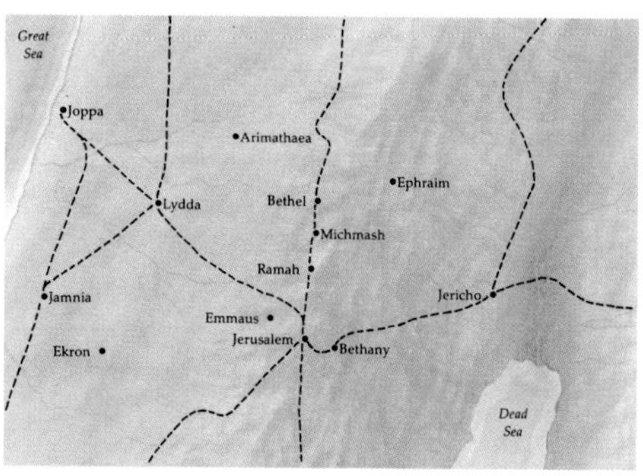

The Philistines gathered for war *against Israel at Michmash. It is located in a pass on the Shechem road seven miles north of Jerusalem.*

The Cliffs "Bozez" and "Seneh"

At one place in the pass three and one-half miles southeast of Michmash there are two great cliffs named "Bozez" and "Seneh." (See I Samuel 14:4.)

In 1918 an officer to the British General, Allenby, read the account of Jonathan's victory. By following the same strategy, they conquered the Turks.

Saul was a young man who began his career with great promise, but ended his life in defeat and disgrace. He grew up during a period of peace in the nation of Israel. Samuel, who had subdued the Philistines, was the Lord's spokesman and judged the people. But Samuel was an old man, and his two sons were corrupt. The Israelites wanted a king so they could rally around him like the other nations. The Ammonites threatened war from the east. The Philistines were threatening war from the west. The people felt vulnerable and wanted a warrior-king to lead them into battle. Samuel argued against their request but was told by the Lord to *"... hearken unto their voice, and make them a king ..." (I Samuel 8:22).*

CHOSEN BY THE PROPHET OF THE LORD

Through a series of God-ordained circumstances, Samuel recognized Saul as the Lord's choice. *"... There was not among the children of Israel a goodlier person than he: from his shoulders and upward he was higher than any of the people" (I Samuel 9:2).* Saul was a member of the tribe of Benjamin, a tribe which had almost been annihilated in civil war. The Benjamites lacked spiritual leadership and for a time spurned the Law of God. (See Judges 20–21.)

Saul appears to have been poorly trained in spiritual matters. He did not even know who Samuel was and was unaware that the Lord's prophets did not prophesy for money. (See I Samuel 9:6–10.) But in spite of this lack, Saul responded to Samuel's announcement with humility and obedience.

POLITICAL AND MILITARY SUCCESS FOLLOW

Saul soon demonstrated that he was capable of the strong leadership that the nation desired. The Ammonites besieged the city of Jabesh-gilead. When the city cried for help, Saul promptly and boldly responded. He threatened reprisal against any Israelite who refused to assist and routed the Ammonites. It was a great victory, and Saul was publicly confirmed as king at Gilgal. (See I Samuel 11.)

But the political and military success that God gave became a snare. Saul became impatient in having to share power and prestige with the aged Samuel. The kings of the surrounding nations had no limit to their authority; it was absolute. This, however, was not the Lord's program for His people. He allowed for a king, but only one who would submit to the Lord's rule through His spokesmen, the prophets. Instructing him before a battle against the Philistines, Samuel told Saul to *"... go down before me to Gilgal; and, behold, I will come down unto thee, to offer burnt offerings ... seven days shalt thou tarry, till I come to thee, and shew thee what thou shalt do" (I Samuel 10:8).*

A PROMISING START SPOILED BY PRESUMPTION

The command to wait was clear, but circumstances were different than Saul had anticipated. Jonathan had antagonized the Philistines with an embarrassing defeat at Geba. As a result, the entire Philistine army had been mustered. When Saul retreated to Gilgal, summoning the nation to war, the response was discouraging. Even his trained army of three thousand had dwindled to six hundred through desertions.

Saul refused to wait until the end of the seventh day as Samuel had instructed. He offered the burnt offering himself in preparation for an attack. Samuel arrived soon after and rebuked the impatient king. He announced that because of this disobedience, his throne would be given to another. (See I Samuel 13:13–14.) Saul continued to chafe against Samuel's counsel, leading to a complete separation between the two men. The blessing which could have been Saul's through an obedient walk with the Lord was forfeited. His throne was given to David.

CHARACTER SKETCH OF SAUL

WHY DID GOD CHOOSE SAUL TO BE THE NATION'S FIRST KING?

God gave the people what they desired. They wanted a king. When Samuel protested, they replied, *". . . Nay; but we will have a king over us; That we also may be like all the nations; and that our king may judge us, and go out before us, and fight our battles" (I Samuel 8:19–20).*

Saul possessed physical qualities which the people were looking for. He was young, handsome, strong, and he stood head and shoulders over the rest. In addition to these characteristics, he had qualities which could have made him a good king.

He was humble, willing to admit his unimportance as a Benjamite. He did not seek power or leadership; he even tried to evade it. (See I Samuel 9:21; 10:22.) He was attentive to Samuel in the beginning (see I Samuel 10:2–14) and demonstrated alertness to the prompting of God's Spirit during the crisis concerning the men of Jabesh-gilead. (See I Samuel 11:6.)

Even after the resounding victory, he evidenced no pride. On the contrary, he refused to allow his critics to be punished. (See I Samuel 10:27; 11:12–13.) Saul could have become a good king had he not rejected the Lord's counsel through Samuel.

HOW DID GOD PREPARE SAUL FOR HIS FIRST TEST?

Saul's first test was simply to wait for Samuel at Gilgal. In light of the circumstances we might excuse Saul for his impatience. But the seventh day was not yet over, and Samuel had promised to arrive on that day. Saul had no reason to disbelieve him. On the contrary, this command was the last of four given to Saul. The first three happened just as foretold. (See I Samuel 10:9.)

Furthermore, Saul had been chosen king through an amazing set of circumstances. The Lord was stretching Saul's faith. He had prepared him by confirming in many ways Samuel's prophetic office. But Saul failed the test. His faith shrank rather than grew. He acted impulsively because of the external circumstances rather than with faith on the basis of past evidence. He was unable to trust God and was thus unfit to lead God's people.

WHY WAS THE PUNISHMENT FOR SAUL'S DISOBEDIENCE SO SEVERE?

When Saul offered sacrifices without waiting for Samuel, he publicly declared to those six hundred soldiers that he was able to make war against the Philistines without the counsel of God. Samuel was coming not just to consecrate the men for battle but also to advise Saul on military strategy. His command was clear, *". . . seven days shalt thou tarry, till I come to thee, and shew thee what thou shalt do" (I Samuel 10:8).*

Saul's act, therefore, was one of rebellion against the true, heavenly commander, the "captain of the host of the Lord." (See Joshua 5:14.) How could God bless His people if their king disregarded His counsel?

In addition, Saul set a precedent with his rash action which could cause his sons and followers to stumble. If he could neglect the important commands of God's prophet, why could they not do the same? If Saul's disregard for God's spokesman was imitated, it would not be long before Samuel or any other prophet would be silenced. Then Israel would indeed be like the nations surrounding it.

Punctuality for Saul meant waiting. *Waiting upon God's timing requires greater faith than sacrificing for God's work. Saul's lack of faith permeated the hearts of his men who then fled to the rocks for their protection.*

CHAPTER FIFTEEN

Punctuality

. . . Is meeting basic needs when others are unable to do so

". . . Verily I say unto you, Inasmuch as ye have done it unto one of the least of these my brethren, ye have done it unto me."
Matthew 25:40

Living Lessons on Punctuality . . .

FROM THE PAGES OF SCRIPTURE

The ability to detect needs in the lives of others usually comes by experiencing these same needs in ourselves. Similarly, the most thoughtful and appreciated gifts are often those which the giver would like to receive himself.

When an embattled king fled to the wilderness, an alert man promptly brought him an abundance of practical provisions. The first item on the list is as significant as it is unusual. It suggests that the giver needed the same item in a similar emergency.

ILLUSTRATED IN THE WORLD OF NATURE

SKUNK CABBAGE *Symplocarpus foetidus*

Symplocarpus foetidus means, literally, "a foul smelling plant with a united fruit." Found in swamps of eastern and central North America, it grows a brownish purple and yellow hood that surrounds a large cluster of small yellow flowers.

The skunk cabbage looks so much like a tropical plant, that street vendors once gathered thousands from the swamps of New Jersey and sold them in New York as exotic lilies. As the first plant that appears in the spring, it often provided lifesaving food for early settlers and Indians whose winter provisions had run out.

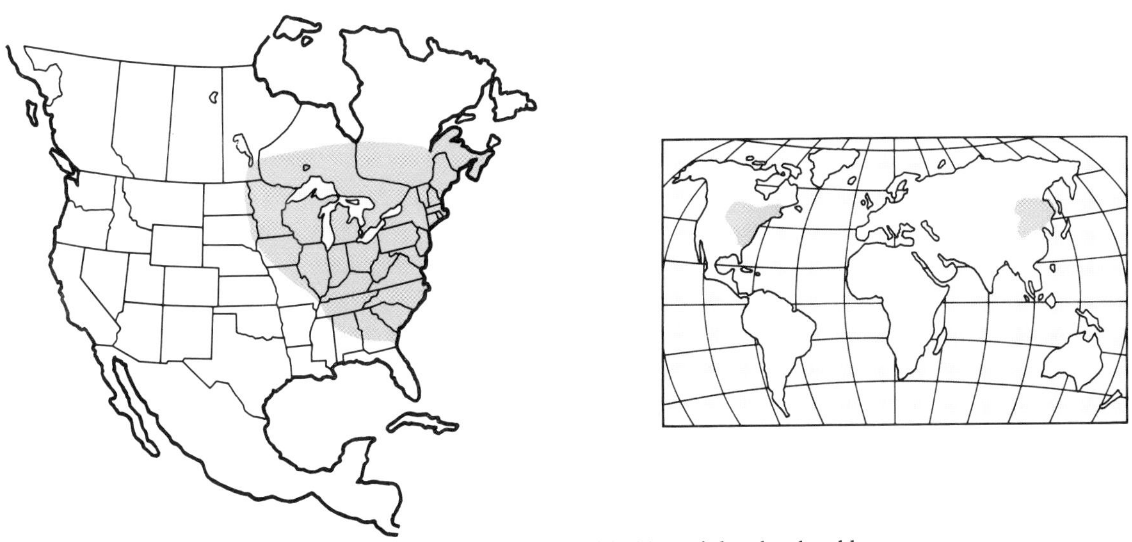

The range and habitat of the skunk cabbage

How is meeting needs when others are unable to do so illustrated in the world of nature?

A large black bear emerged from its winter den and lumbered into the forest. Its massive paws left a clear trail in the snow that still covered the ground. Because of the snowfall, the hungry bear was unable to locate any green plants or fresh berries.

Determined to find food, it approached a large beehive. With one swipe of its powerful paw, the bear knocked the hive to the ground. Breaking it open, the famished bear quickly began to devour the sticky honeycombs.

The startled bees tried in vain to defend their home and store of provisions, but the bear stomped on the fragments of the hive, killing many of the bees.

The dazed survivors fled the scene of destruction, but realized that it would only be a matter of seconds before they would perish. It was almost too cold for them to fly, and they possessed only enough energy to travel a very short distance. At this time of year there would be no flowers filled with nectar to replenish their strength.

Suddenly the bees sensed the sweet aroma of nectar. How could this be? It was only February, long before any forest flowers would appear. Throughout the swamp, little patches of snow had melted beside strange-looking hoods that had poked up through the ice and snow.

These unique plants had been prepared for such an emergency as this. The bees dropped down for a closer look. They saw a small cluster of yellow flowers within each protective hood.

The flowers had actually developed during the previous fall and were shielded from the harsh winter by their brownish purple hoods. Entering the hoods, the bees discovered another remarkable feature—an internal temperature of seventy-two degrees.

The excited bees flew from plant to plant gaining warmth and restoring their energy. After collecting an ample supply of nectar, they traveled the final distance to the safety of a new home. The bees survived because the skunk cabbage had met basic needs when other plants were unable to do so.

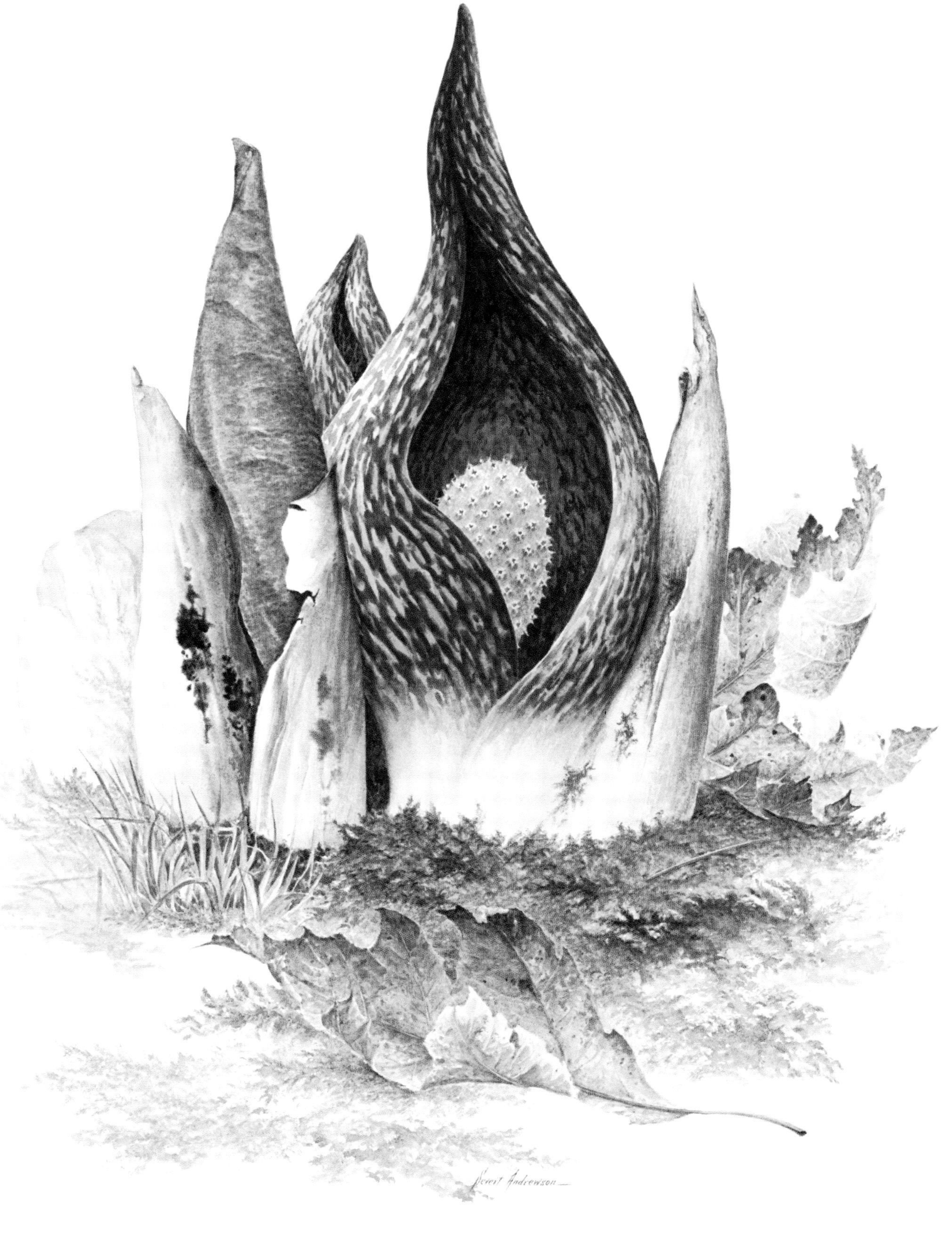

THE CHARACTERISTICS OF

THE SKUNK CABBAGE IN SCRIPTURE

The skunk cabbage is a flower. Its unique characteristics have clear parallels in Scripture.

Its ability to provide food and warmth while other plants are still dormant is a picture of God's command to believers to be ready at all times to share food and clothing with those who come to them with special needs. (See Isaiah 58:7.)

The skunk cabbage makes a spectacular appearance, but if winds are too cold, it will soon perish. God repeatedly affirms in Scripture that man's life is like a flower, and *"... as a flower of the field, so he flourisheth. For the wind passeth over it, and it is gone ..." (Psalm 103:15–16)*.

The skunk cabbage, like our lives, contains a mixture of the bitter and the sweet. God wants each of us, by meditating on His Word, to transform every experience into healthful spiritual food that we can share with others. The bee illustrates this by turning the nectar of the skunk cabbage into honey. (See Psalm 119:103.)

The amazing root system of the skunk cabbage allows it to overcome many adverse weather conditions. A Christian who has no roots in the Word will wither when pressures come, because he has no *"... root in himself, but dureth for a while: for when tribulation or persecution ariseth because of the word, by and by he is offended" (Matthew 13:21)*.

CHARACTERISTICS AND PHYSICAL FEATURES OF THE SKUNK CABBAGE

Although there may still be a layer of snow on the ground, the skunk cabbage sends up its hooded flower at the earliest possible moment.

If the weather turns too cold for the plant to keep its first growth warm, the flower dies; but the skunk cabbage prepares more flowers and repeats the process again and again.

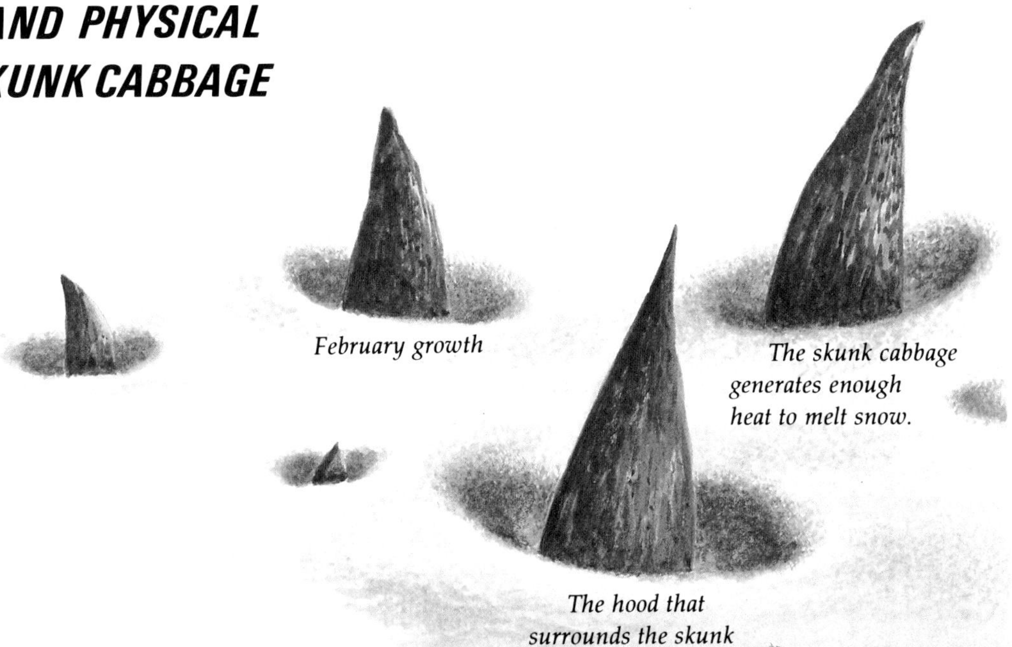

February growth
The skunk cabbage generates enough heat to melt snow.
The hood that surrounds the skunk cabbage flower is called a spathe.

HOW DOES THE SKUNK CABBAGE PRODUCE HEAT?

It produces heat in much the same way that animals produce heat. Oxygen is combined with food to produce carbon dioxide, water, and heat. This process is called *respiration.*

When the temperature drops, most plants slow down their rate of respiration; but the respiration rate of an animal increases in order for it to stay warm. The skunk cabbage, although a plant, also increases its rate of respiration to keep its hooded flower warm.

WHAT DO SKUNK CABBAGES AND HUMANS HAVE IN COMMON?

Both skunk cabbages and humans prefer a temperature in their homes of 72°F. Even if the outside temperature drops as low as 10°F, the skunk cabbage can generate enough heat to maintain an "indoor" temperature between 72° and 74°F. However, when extremely low temperatures remain for more than twenty-four hours, the hooded flower exhausts its heating ability and dies.

HOW IS A SKUNK CABBAGE LIKE A STYROFOAM CUP?

Styrofoam cups are made up of thousands of tiny bubbles that act as insulation. Each bubble contains a pocket of trapped air that does not conduct heat. The hood of the skunk cabbage is also made up of thousands of tiny air spaces that help the flower conserve its precious supply of heat.

WHAT KEEPS THE SKUNK CABBAGE FROM BECOMING TOO HOT?

The skunk cabbage has a thermostat similar in function to the thermostat on a furnace. If the flower becomes too cold, more heat is called for. If the flower becomes too warm, the heat is turned off. However, the skunk cabbage's thermostat does not work as fast as a house thermostat. It takes almost an hour for the plant to turn its "furnace" on or off.

The Maryland Yellow-throated Warbler nests in the warmth of the skunk cabbage.
March growth

Elk
Bear
The flowering stalk
is called a spadix.
Cross
section
of a spathe
Insects
often become
trapped in the
rainwater which collects in the spathe.

WHY WILL CATTLE STARVE BEFORE EATING SKUNK CABBAGE?

Skunk cabbages contain an acrid juice made up of crystals of calcium oxalate. These microscopic crystals are sharply pointed, feel like powdered glass, and taste extremely peppery. They sting the mouth so badly that cattle will starve to death before eating skunk cabbage leaves.

HOW DO ELK AND BEAR USE SKUNK CABBAGE TO ILLUSTRATE A PROVERB IN SCRIPTURE?

Even though cattle will not eat skunk cabbage, elk and bear will. After a long winter they are intensely hungry. They will look for almost anything that is green and eat it. They illustrate the truth in Proverbs 27:7, *"The full soul loatheth an honeycomb; but to the hungry soul every bitter thing is sweet."*

The skunk cabbage is the first plant to break through the snow in early spring. Therefore both the bear and elk consume it in large quantities. Bears dig up the roots of the skunk cabbage, while elk prefer the new leaves. Neither the elk nor the bear seems to be affected by the strong taste of the skunk cabbage.

HOW DOES THE SKUNK CABBAGE GIVE OUT A SWEET AROMA AND A FOUL SMELL AT THE SAME TIME?

Although the flower gives off a very sweet aroma that attracts bees, injured or bruised leaves give off a sulfurous odor that resembles the smell of rotten eggs. This odor masks the sweetness of the blossoms and draws a variety of insects that normally feed on decayed matter, such as scavenger beetles, carrion flies, and spiders.

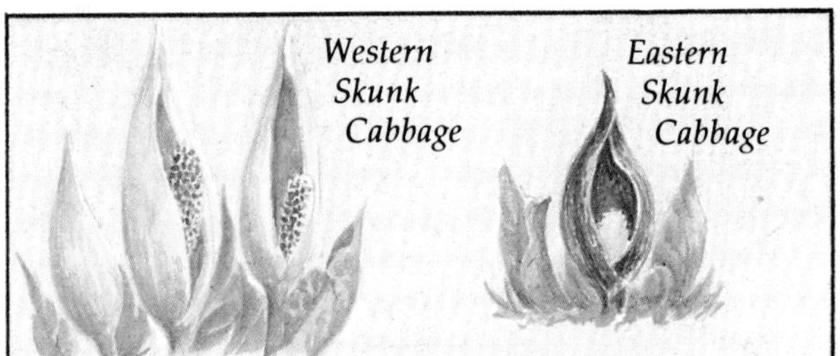
Western
Skunk
Cabbage
Eastern
Skunk
Cabbage

The western skunk cabbage is quite different from the eastern variety. The western skunk cabbage is smaller and has both yellow leaves and hood. The flower clusters of the western variety stand above the ground on a long stem.

HOW DOES THE SKUNK CABBAGE INCREASE THE FLYING SEASON OF THE HONEYBEE?

Normally, honeybees are unable to fly when the temperature is below 65°F. However, when skunk cabbages are in bloom, honeybees can fly about freely even though the air temperature may be as low as 45°F.

This is possible because of the heat in the skunk cabbage's hood. Inside the hood, honeybees warm up enough to travel to the next skunk cabbage. In cold weather the bees can travel from skunk cabbage to skunk cabbage as they make their way back to the hive.

WHY CAN THE SKUNK CABBAGE FLOWERS BLOOM MUCH FASTER THAN OTHER FLOWERS?

The flowers of the skunk cabbage begin forming underground in late autumn and rest there in their protective hoods until early spring. When the flower emerges through the snow, it is almost fully developed and can bloom within three days if the temperature stays above 45°F. Flowers of other plants may take weeks to develop and bloom.

HOW DOES A SKUNK CABBAGE LEAF RESEMBLE AN ELEPHANT EAR?

Actually they are about the same size. At first the leaves of the skunk cabbage look like long tubes, with each leaf rolled up tightly around its center vein. As the leaf unfurls, it may grow to a length of almost three feet and a width of two feet.

WHAT DOES THE LITTLE SKUNK CABBAGE AND THE GIANT SEQUOIA TREE HAVE IN COMMON?

Although a skunk cabbage is not nearly as impressive as a sequoia of California, it may be just as old. An individual plant may live indefinitely if its environment is not disturbed. It is not uncommon for skunk cabbage plants to be more than 1,500 years old.

WHY WILL YOU PROBABLY NOT BE ABLE TO DIG UP A SKUNK CABBAGE PLANT?

The skunk cabbage has a massive root system made up of a main tap root and hundreds of pencil-sized secondary roots that may occupy as much as twelve cubic feet of soil. The tap root may be several inches in diameter and over a foot in length. The foot-long secondary roots grow horizontally from the tap root and are so densely packed that it is almost impossible to dig up the skunk cabbage.

HOW DOES ROOT CONTRACTION INCREASE THE DEPTH OF SKUNK CABBAGE PLANTS?

As the plant grows, the wrinkled secondary roots anchor themselves firmly in the soil and then contract. As they contract, they pull the main root and upper stem down into the soil. Over many seasons, the end of this main root is rubbed smooth as it is pulled deeper and deeper into the ground.

HOW IS A SKUNK CABBAGE MORE LIKE A SKUNK THAN A CABBAGE?

The respiration rate of the skunk cabbage plant is equivalent to that of an animal its same size. This unique warming feature makes it more like a skunk than a cabbage plant.

Skunk cabbages are usually the oldest plants in a community.

Skunk cabbage bread
Iroquois Indian grinding leaves into flour
A compress of skunk cabbage leaves will stop bleeding.
Skunk cabbage leaves may "bite" the tongue that eats them. Chewing on a raw leaf may temporarily hinder one's speech.
Indian poke is a poisonous look-alike.

HOW CAN A PLANT THAT STINGS LIKE POWDERED GLASS RELIEVE PAIN?

The skunk cabbage plant has been used for a variety of medicinal purposes. The powdered root of the skunk cabbage was formerly used as styptic to stop the flow of blood. It was inhaled as a remedy for headaches, and it was recognized as a source of relief for a variety of chest complaints. A drug known as *dracontium* can be extracted from the skunk cabbage and used in the relief of pain.

HOW DID INDIANS USE THE SKUNK CABBAGE TO DETERMINE WHO WOULD BE THE NEXT CHIEF?

Indians used a number of plants, including the skunk cabbage, to test the courage of those who wanted to become chief. One test was to see which brave could keep a skunk cabbage leaf in his mouth and endure its fiery taste the longest.

WHY WAS THIS TEST OF COURAGE SOMETIMES FATAL?

When the Indians tested candidates for tribal leadership, they would sometimes accidentally use the poisonous Indian pokeberry. It was a plant that looked much like the skunk cabbage, but it could kill those being tested.

WHAT CAN BE DONE TO MAKE THE SKUNK PLANT MORE EDIBLE?

The root loses its peppery taste when it is ground and dried for a month or more. The leaves become edible when boiled in several changes of water. However, eating large amounts of skunk cabbage, even when boiled or dried, can cause dim eyesight or even temporary blindness.

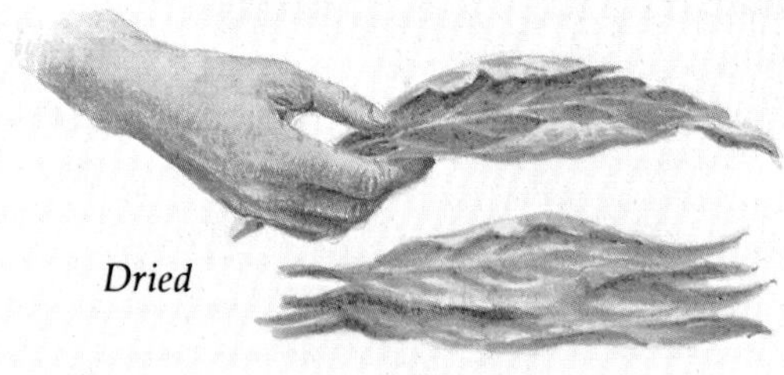

Recipes "for a starving explorer"

The young leaves of the skunk cabbage may be prepared like spinach or cabbage. The leaves must be washed and boiled at least three times in different changes of water containing baking soda. For greater nutrition, the leaves can be steamed in a pressure cooker for two minutes. The leaves can then be served with melted butter or vinegar. Cheese or sour cream can be served with them to absorb any of the remaining peppery oxalates.

How is giving to needs which others are not able to meet illustrated in Scripture?

Who gained recognition in Scripture because of his generosity to a king during a time of national crisis?

(Pause for a response—see page 17.)

He lived in the land of Gilead, east of the river Jordan. God called him "a very great man" for good reason. During his many years of life he experienced the joys of serving as a priest of the Lord. But in that capacity he also tasted hardships, sorrows, and disappointments.

The faithful priest became neither proud over success nor bitter over defeats. Instead, he developed a keen sensitivity to the needs of others and a generosity in meeting them.

One day he learned that a revolt was taking place in his nation and that his beloved king was being forced to flee for his very life. The king was even now seeking refuge in a large forest near this great man's home.

Quickly he met with two other friends and together they gathered a huge supply of vital provisions for the king and those who fled with him. As they did this, they must have realized that such an act would be considered treason by the rebel leader.

If the exiled king was unsuccessful in regaining the throne, this man and his friends would no doubt be killed. However, he lived up to the meaning of his name—iron hearted, and courageously brought the provisions to the king in his wilderness camp.

Included in his gift were wheat, barley, flour, corn, beans, honey, butter, sheep, cheese, and cattle. But first on the list was something both unique and significant. It revealed the ability of this great man to detect special needs. He brought beds for the use of the king and his men.

Refreshed and encouraged by all of these provisions, the king and his men went out to battle, and God gave them the victory. The rebel leader was killed and the king made preparations to return to his city.

Once again this great man gave the king assistance. The king was so moved by this kindness that he invited the man to return with him and eat at his royal table. This special invitation was humbly declined, as the great man explained that he was eighty years old and that he might become a burden to the king. However, he did offer to have his son take his place. The king welcomed the idea and brought Chimham back to the palace.

In the years that followed, this son not only served the king but many others as well. He founded an inn to care for travelers and strangers. This was very unusual in that day. So successful was this inn that it continued to be used for hundreds of years. In fact, it was mentioned by the prophet Jeremiah, 435 years later.

Another fact makes this inn and the history behind it even more significant. Many years later, a couple inquired at a very popular inn. It was already filled; however, the inn keeper graciously provided what accomodations he could.

The inn that Chimham established was by Bethlehem, the same city in which Christ was born. The beds which Barzillai gave to David in the wilderness established a tradition which his descendants continued. God may have honored this family by allowing one of its members to meet a need for Christ which others were unable to meet.

From II Samuel 17:27–29; 19:31–39
and Jeremiah 41:17

BARZILLAI, PREPARED TO BE AN ENCOURAGEMENT IN TIME OF NEED

Barzillai brought David and his men a wealth of practical supplies when they were forced to flee for their lives. Not only did these provisions bring physical strength, but they provided emotional support at a time when David needed it the most.

Although God often allows His servants to go through difficult and trying situations, it is characteristic of His nature to send a word or deed of encouragement just when it is most needed. For example, when Elijah was persecuted for his stand against Baal worship, he was fed by ravens and then by a poor widow. And at the lowest point in his life, when he wanted to die in depression, God provided food and drink for him through an angel. (See I Kings 17:6–15; 19:4–8.)

Elisha, always taking unpopular stands, was shown hospitality by a wealthy woman in Shunem. (See II Kings 4:8–10.) The Apostle Paul, persecuted for the sake of the Gospel, was shown kindness and friendship by many people such as Jason in Thessalonica and Aquila and Priscilla in Corinth. (See Acts 17:4–7; 18:1–3.)

CONSPIRACY TO OVERTHROW A KING

David had his share of difficulties as well. One of the most discouraging times of his life had to have been when his son Absalom stole the affection of the nation in an attempt to seize his throne. David had to flee for his life from the palace in Jerusalem. Then came news that Ahithophel, the most respected military strategist in the nation, had joined in the conspiracy against him. (See II Samuel 15:31.) Shimei, a relative of David's predecessor, added insult by cursing David, throwing stones at him, and kicking up dust all along David's way out of the city. (See II Samuel 16:5–13.)

TIMELY HELP IN DAVID'S DARKEST HOUR

When David and his loyal bodyguard reached the Jordan River, they were weary but could not take time to rest. By morning the entire company had crossed the river. They headed for the city of Mahanaim, their base of defense. It was at this time in David's life, when he was in desperate need of encourgement, that the Lord prompted three men—Shobi, Machir, and Barzillai—to help their friend.

"And it came to pass, when David was come to Mahanaim, that Shobi the son of Nahash of Rabbah of the children of Ammon, and Machir the son of Ammiel of Lodebar, and Barzillai the Gileadite of Rogelim, Brought beds, and basins, and earthen vessels, and wheat, and barley, and flour, and parched corn, and beans, and lentiles, and parched pulse, And honey, and butter, and sheep, and cheese of kine, for David, and for the people that were with him, to eat: for they said, The people is hungry, and weary, and thirsty, in the wilderness" (II Samuel 17:27–29). What an encouragement this must have been to David and his supporters.

THE BLESSING OF BARZILLAI

The rebellion was eventually crushed with the death of Absalom, and David started back to Jerusalem. At the Jordan River the king was thrust again into controversy and confusion. His own tribe of Judah was not enthusiastic about his return. Shimei met him and groveled for his life. Mephibosheth confronted David with intrigue involving his slanderous servant, Ziba.

As David faced all of these problems, the aged Barzillai appeared again. He requested no favor, and brought no word of intrigue. He merely wanted to say farewell and bestow a blessing from an eighty-year-old friend. When David asked to repay him for his generosity, Barzillai graciously refused. On the contrary, he dedicated his son Chimham to the service of David. The two men parted with affection. David would never forget the kindness shown to him by Barzillai.

CHARACTER SKETCH OF BARZILLAI

WHAT DANGER DID BARZILLAI RISK BY HELPING DAVID?

Barzillai and his family risked the sure vengeance of Absalom if he succeeded in his rebellion. At the time Barzillai first assisted David, Absalom clearly had the advantage. He enjoyed the outward support of the entire nation. The soldiers at his disposal were like *". . . the sand that is by the sea for multitude . . ." (II Samuel 17:11)*.

The city of Mahanaim was of little help in David's defense. *"Moreover, if he be gotten into a city, then shall all Israel bring ropes to that city, and we will draw it into the river, until there be not one small stone found there" (II Samuel 17:13)*.

Should Absalom succeed there was no hope that mercy would be shown to David's supporters. Absalom had murdered his brother and betrayed his father. David himself did not expect his son to show pity. *". . . Arise, and let us flee; for we shall not else escape from Absalom: make speed to depart, lest he overtake us suddenly . . ." (II Samuel 15:14)*. Barzillai committed himself to David's cause at the darkest hour because he would not be part of the wicked rebellion.

WHY DID BARZILLAI REFUSE DAVID'S OFFER TO COME TO JERUSALEM?

David was grateful to Barzillai for his courageous and generous support. He wanted to repay him for his kindness and would spare no expense or effort to make him comfortable in Jerusalem. But Barzillai's response gives another view of his exemplary character.

He was not interested in power, advantage, or palace pleasures. *". . . Can I discern between good and evil? can thy servant taste what I eat or what I drink? can I hear any more the voice of singing men and singing women? . . ." (II Samuel 19:35)*. He preferred to die near his beloved home in Gilead where he could continue his influence for good. Rather than be a burden to David in Jerusalem, he would be a beneficial ally in Gilead.

WHAT DOES BARZILLAI TEACH US ABOUT GIVING?

Barzillai demonstrates giving with a pure heart. His motive was simply stated, *". . . The people is hungry, and weary, and thirsty . . ." (II Samuel 17:29)*. What a contrast he provides to the impure motives of Mephibosheth's servant, Ziba. In similar circumstances he deceitfully gave his master's goods to David to gain his master's land. (See II Samuel 16:1–4.) What a contrast to the Pharisees who later would gather a crowd when they gave alms in order to win their applause. (See Matthew 6:2.) Barzillai was interested only in the Lord's approval.

He also demonstrated the importance of giving to those in need. God uses even the smallest acts of kindness in ways we cannot imagine. Barzillai knew that David was in need, but he could not have known how deeply discouraged and depressed he was. He had not seen the king leave Jerusalem when he *". . . wept as he went up, and had his head covered, and he went barefoot . . ." (II Samuel 15:30)*.

The Lord used Barzillai as His instrument to encourage David. Barzillai illustrates the principle, *"For I was an hungered, and ye gave me meat: I was thirsty, and ye gave me drink: I was a stranger, and ye took me in. . . . Verily I say unto you, Inasmuch as ye have done it unto one of the least of these my brethren, ye have done it unto me" (Matthew 25:35, 40)*.

Barzillai's son, Chimham, *returned with David as he crossed the River Jordan and regained his throne. Chimham continued his father's great example of generosity, especially in providing beds, by establishing an inn just outside of Bethlehem (See Jeremiah 41:17.) Could this have been the inn that Mary and Joseph visited?*

BARZILLAI
*bär-**zil**-la-i*

CHAPTER SIXTEEN

Punctuality

. . . Is remembering anniversaries that are important to others

"And this day shall be unto you for a memorial; and ye shall keep it a feast to the Lord throughout your generations. . . . Thou shalt therefore keep this ordinance in his season from year to year."
Exodus 12:14; 13:10

Living Lessons on Punctuality . . .

FROM THE PAGES OF SCRIPTURE

Anniversaries are memorials of the past and milestones for the future. They preserve the heritage of former generations and provide stability for future ones. The very nature of anniversaries requires the discipline of punctuality.

"In the fullness of time," God accomplished the most important event in history. During that period, there was tension between two world powers. When this is understood, it sheds significant light on why one of these powers attempted to destroy the most important anniversary in the world.

ILLUSTRATED IN THE WORLD OF NATURE

CLIFF SWALLOW *Petrochelidon pyrrhonota*

The cliff swallow, which is common to all parts of North America, is about six inches long with a whitish forehead, steel blue upper body, grayish underside, chestnut-colored head and throat, and reddish brown rump. The cliff swallow is one of more than eighty members of the swallow family.

Before North America was settled by the Indians, the cliff swallow nested on cliffs. Now, as the bird has adapted to civilization, it attaches its nest primarily to man-made structures. It prefers rural areas where stables and dung heaps provide a breeding ground for the flying insects it eats.

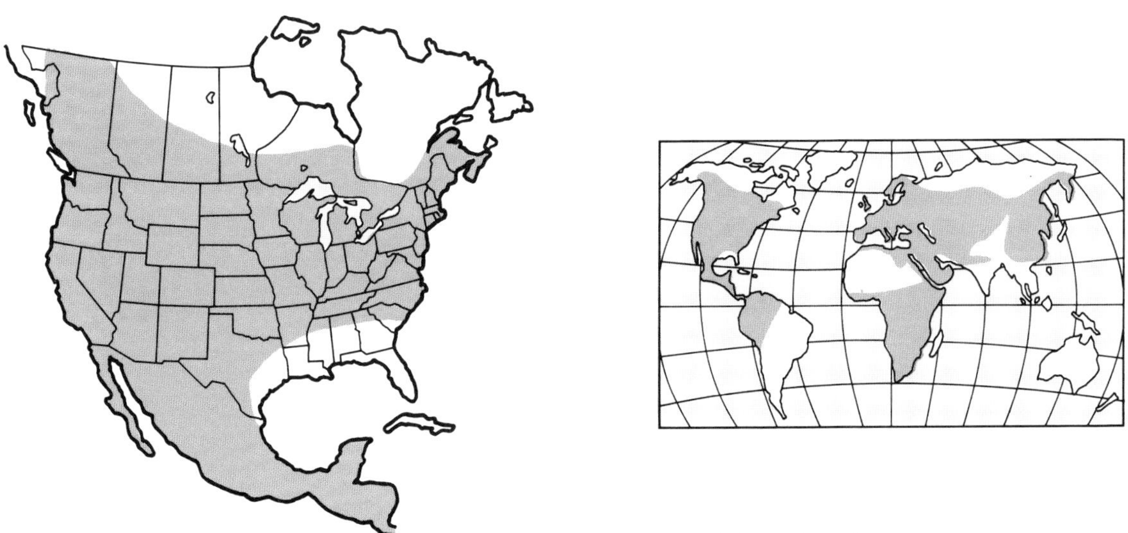

The range and habitat of the cliff swallow

How is the importance of anniversaries illustrated in the world of nature?

Two people in two widely separated parts of the country took a marker and carefully circled a special day on their calendars. They each circled the same date, but with two very different celebrations in mind.

One calendar hung in the kitchen of an attractive woman. She smiled with anticipation every time she glanced at the big red circle around March nineteenth. Whenever she visited a store, she thoughtfully wandered through the gift section searching for something that would best express the importance of that day.

As the special day approached, she purchased a gift and lovingly wrapped it. She also enclosed a beautiful card with a carefully written message.

The other calendar hung in a small town hall in southern California. Beaming with anticipation, the mayor leaned back in his chair and imagined the excitement that would fill his community with the arrival of March nineteenth.

The mayor called special meetings with local officials and established blue ribbon committees. Elaborate plans were worked out to make this the most memorable celebration the town had ever seen.

As March nineteenth drew near, banners were hung along the main streets, and streamers decorated storefronts. The citizens of the town would add to the occasion with festive outfits and colorful signs.

March nineteenth marked two very important arrivals. The young woman was confident that the one she was expecting would return from a trip and join her in celebrating the happiness of the occasion.

The residents of the western town could not be quite as confident. However, many years of punctuality had inspired an admiration for their notable arrival. In fact, that was what they were celebrating.

The day finally came. Thousands of enthusiastic tourists and townspeople crowded into the streets of that California town. Many carried binoculars to catch the first glimpse of their famous guests. Others bought souvenirs to commemorate the event they were about to witness.

Suddenly, a shout went up from several in the crowd. Heads turned and eyes strained. The distinguished guests had arrived on the very day that they were expected! Now the people could begin the celebration. The cliff swallows had not disappointed them!

March nineteenth also arrived for the loving wife. All day long she waited with excitement for her husband to call. This was their wedding anniversary. Friends and relatives who were aware of her preparations called to ask how her husband had surprised her.

That evening her husband came home. Glancing at the calendar that was hanging in the kitchen, he noticed the circled date. He realized that he had forgotten the anniversary that was so important to his wife and that should have been equally as important to him.

For this preoccupied husband, the punctuality of the cliff swallow has a vital message. Year after year these birds travel thousands of miles to return to San Juan Capistrano on March nineteenth. Their punctuality brings great joy to those who wait to celebrate their arrival, just as we can bring joy to others by remembering important anniversaries.

THE CHARACTERISTICS OF

THE CLIFF SWALLOW IN SCRIPTURE

The cliff swallow is a migratory bird. It is mentioned at least four times in Scripture. The tiny bird's most famous characteristic, returning at a predictable time, is referred to in Jeremiah 8:7. *". . . The swallow[s] observe the time of their coming; but my people know not the judgment of the Lord."*

Just as there are fixed times for the arrival of the swallow, there are fixed times for God's judgment. God reasons that if people can recognize when the swallow returns, they should be able to recognize the signs of His judgments and repent of their wickedness.

Isaiah gives a similar message but emphasizes the persistent sounds of the swallow to illustrate his continual warnings. *"Like a crane or a swallow, so did I chatter: I did mourn as a dove . . ." (Isaiah 38:14).*

The "chatter" of the swallow is not a loud, raucous sound, but a quiet cooing. Elijah learned on the mountain that God spoke most powerfully in a "still small voice." (See I Kings 19:12.)

Proverbs 26:2 reveals how an undeserved curse is as unpredictable as the flight of the swallow and returns to the one who spoke it without affecting the one who was cursed.

Psalm 84:3 has literal and figurative significance. Just as the swallow makes its nest and raises its young near the altar of the Lord, so the Christian and his family should desire to dwell in God's presence.

CHARACTERISTICS AND PHYSICAL FEATURES OF THE CLIFF SWALLOW

Because the cliff swallow is such a good insect catcher, those who provide surfaces for nests are thanked many times over by the swallow's characteristic return.

Migrating thousands of miles each spring, the swallow's return is usually predictable to within twenty-four to forty-eight hours. Even if a more suitable nesting place becomes available, as long as its present nest is not disturbed, the swallow returns year after year with punctuality.

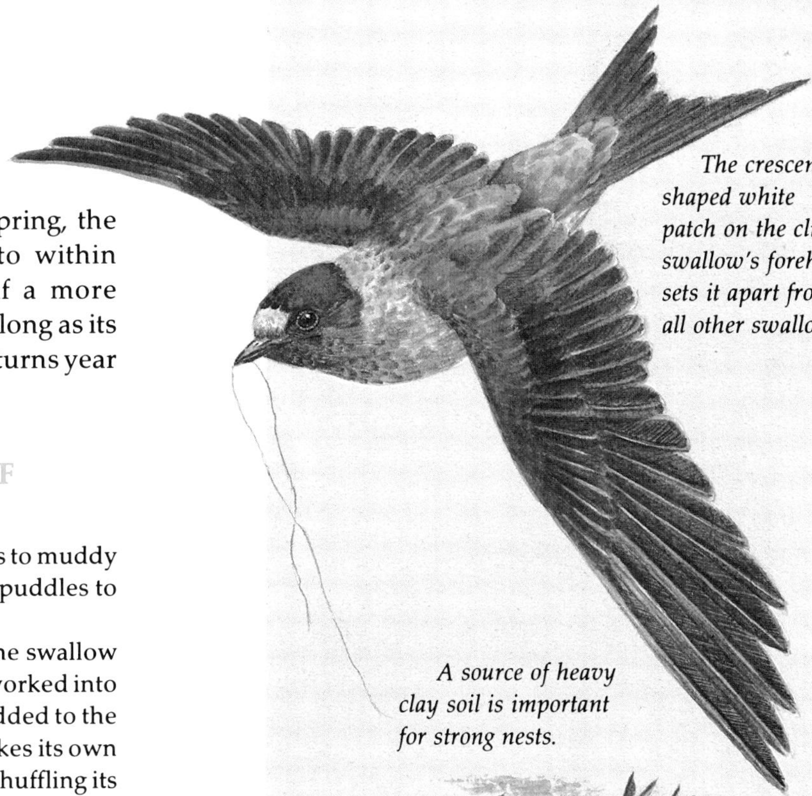

The crescent-shaped white patch on the cliff swallow's forehead sets it apart from all other swallows.

A source of heavy clay soil is important for strong nests.

Sandy soil causes nests to crumble during the heat of summer.

Cliff swallows mix dusty soil with moisture on their feet to make mud.

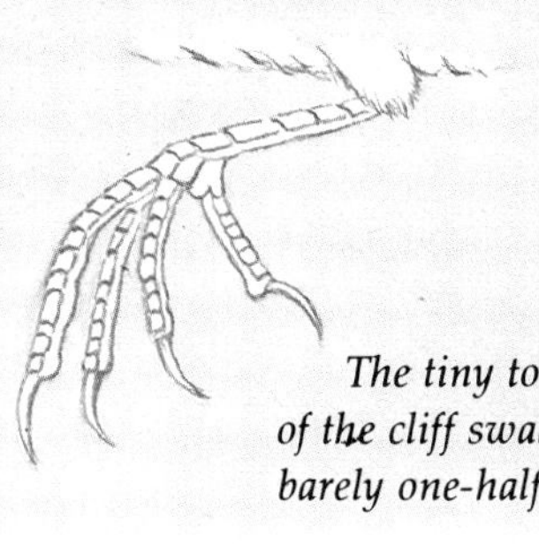

The tiny toes of the cliff swallow are barely one-half inch long.

WHY IS IT IMPORTANT FOR A CLIFF SWALLOW TO PLAY IN THE MUD?

During nest building, the cliff swallow goes to muddy banks of streams, ponds, rivers, and even small puddles to make mud pellets.

Fluttering its wings high above its head, the swallow scoops up mouthfuls of mud. Each mouthful is worked into a ball and carried to the nesting site where it is added to the nest. If mud is not available, the cliff swallow makes its own by first standing in water to wet its feet and then shuffling its feet in the dusty soil.

HOW CAN SEVEN DAYS AND A HUNDRED MILES BE NECESSARY FOR A CLIFF SWALLOW'S SURVIVAL?

The swallow's nest is usually located near the source of the mud. Occasionally, the nest-building process requires long trips to and from the mud supply. After a week's work, the cliff swallow may have traveled over one hundred miles to transport its mud bricks.

HOW CAN A CLIFF SWALLOW'S NEST TRAP ITS OWN BUILDER?

Horsehair is sometimes gathered and woven around and through the walls of the cliff swallow's nest just as steel rods are used to reinforce concrete. Unfortunately, the cliff swallow's tiny feet can become caught in these long hairs, and the little bird can become helplessly entangled.

HOW CAN CLIFF SWALLOWS PREDICT RAIN MORE ACCURATELY THAN MANY WEATHER FORECASTERS?

Although cliff swallows cannot predict all kinds of weather, they can predict rain. Old-timers claim that high-flying swallows mean fair weather and low-flying swallows mean rain. In this case, they are perfectly accurate.

Air that is saturated with moisture is denser than dry air and does not allow insects to fly very high. Dry air allows insects to fly higher. Hungry cliff swallows, feeding primarily on these flying insects, fly low to chase the insects on days before a rain, and fly high to catch them in dry, fair weather.

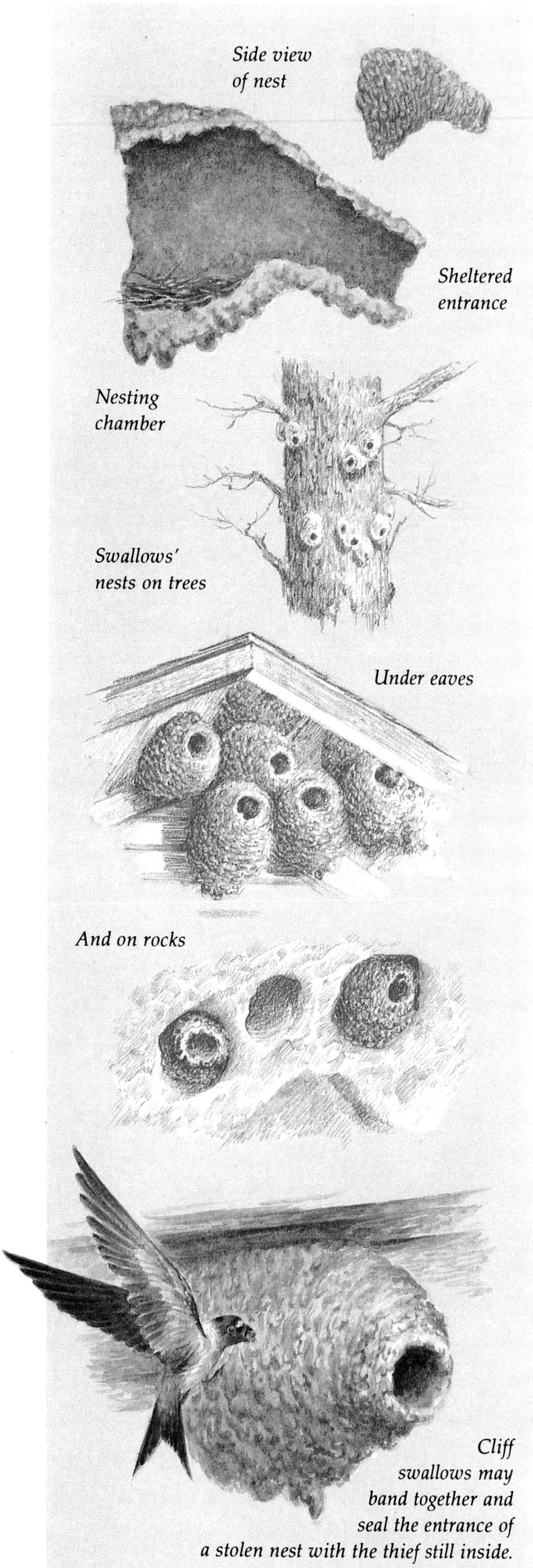

Cliff swallows may band together and seal the entrance of a stolen nest with the thief still inside.

WHAT WILL CAUSE A CLIFF SWALLOW TO LAY FIFTY EGGS IN ONE SMALL NEST?

A female cliff swallow lays one egg a day until there are from three to six eggs in the nest. If an egg is broken, the swallow will lay another to replace it. Swallows have been observed to lay as many as fifty eggs to get one full nest.

HOW DOES THE ENTRANCE OF THE CLIFF SWALLOW'S NEST REPEL RAIN?

The entrance to the cliff swallow's nest looks much like the neck of a bottle. It is four to eight inches long and is pitched slightly downward to keep out rain and intruders. The narrow neck prevents larger birds from entering. The cliff swallow's defense against small birds is the long narrow entrance that allows only one enemy to attack at a time.

HOW DOES A SINGLE MUD BALL CHANGE THE ACTIVITY OF AN ENTIRE FLOCK?

Nest building and feeding are group activities which may be initiated by an adult cliff swallow. As all of the adults are feeding the nestlings, one bird may appear with a pellet of mud. Within a minute, all of the birds will have switched from food gathering to mud packing. This continues for ten to twenty minutes until another adult appears with food. Again, within a minute, the mud-gathering activity is abandoned, and all of the birds are involved in feeding.

WHY IS IT IMPOSSIBLE FOR A SINGLE CLIFF SWALLOW TO BUILD A NEST?

During nest building, there is always one swallow inside the nest to shape the interior with its breast while the other swallow adds new pellets to the outside. Pressure from the inside is required to prevent the soft structure from caving in as the new pellets are pressed into place. With each new pellet, the birds switch roles.

WHY WOULD CLIFF SWALLOWS BUILD THEIR NESTS BY GOD'S ALTARS?

David observed, ". . . *The sparrow hath found an house, and the swallow a nest for herself . . . even thine altars . . .*" *(Psalm 84:3)*. Cliff swallows are extremely adaptable and easily adjust to a variety of nesting sites. However, nesting sites are chosen with extreme care. Often, with no apparent reason, nests are huddled together on a large cliff where space is plentiful; but when rains darken the cliff, it becomes obvious that the swallows selected the only dry spots.

If a cliff is not available, the swallows build their nests on the eaves of houses, barns, garages, and the underside of bridges. Almost any protected vertical surface will do.

ARE CLIFF SWALLOWS CONTENT WITH LAST YEAR'S MUD HOUSES?

Yes. In a maze of nests, with all of the entrances looking alike, cliff swallows distinguish their own nests from all the others, just as surely as if all the nests were numbered. Pairs returning in the spring fly directly to their old nests and begin remodeling for a new season.

*Normally, **two broods** of three to six young are raised each year. The first clutch of eggs is laid in early May and the second around the beginning of July. A third is sometimes started as late as September if weather conditions are favorable.*

While both the male and female incubate the eggs, the male lacks a functional brood patch and gives little warmth to the eggs. The young are ready for their first flight within three weeks, but they stay close to home and often help feed and care for the young of the next brood.

EIGHT STAGES OF NEST CONSTRUCTION

STAGE 1

Nest construction begins with a narrow, curved line of pellets located six to eight inches beneath a protective overhang. Each pellet is cemented into place with a twisting motion as the cliff swallow hangs precariously from the overhang.

STAGE 2

The crescent-shaped base becomes broad enough for the cliff swallow to stand on, and work proceeds more rapidly. The outline and size of the nest seem to be limited to how far the cliff swallow can reach from its homemade scaffold.

STAGE 3

By the second or third day the nest resembles a miniature baseball glove. Grass lining is added to the nest at this time, but it usually blows away before the eggs are laid.

STAGE 4

The walls are built up to secure the nest to the protective overhang above. The first clutch of eggs is typically laid at this time.

STAGE 5

The front of the nest is closed in preparation for the addition of the long, narrow entrance.

STAGE 6

A six- to ten-inch trough is extended from the mouth of the nest. It is approximately one and one-fourth inches in diameter and serves as the base for the entrance tunnel. Nesting material begins to accumulate in the nest and provides a soft, insulating lining for the eggs.

STAGE 7

The roof of the entrance tunnel is completed, and incubation of the eggs begins.

STAGE 8

Nest repairs continue throughout the summer, when dry weather causes the nest to crack or heavy rains loosen the nest from its foundation. Occasionally, extensive changes are made to make the nest more private if a neighbor becomes too noisy.

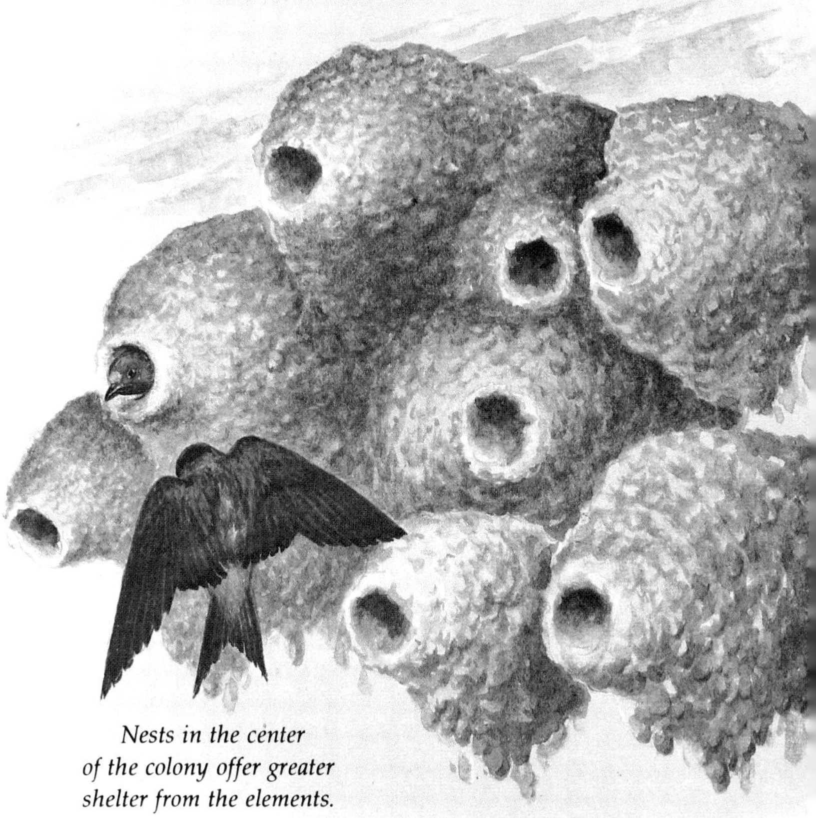

Nests in the center of the colony offer greater shelter from the elements.

HOW DO CLIFF SWALLOWS IMPROVE THE PRODUCTION OF OUR CLOTHING?

The cliff swallow eats a variety of harmful insects including mosquitoes, leafhoppers, squash bugs, and plant lice. Foremost in its diet is the boll weevil that attacks the cotton from which many clothes are made. A single cliff swallow will eat twenty or more boll weevils each day during the entire summer.

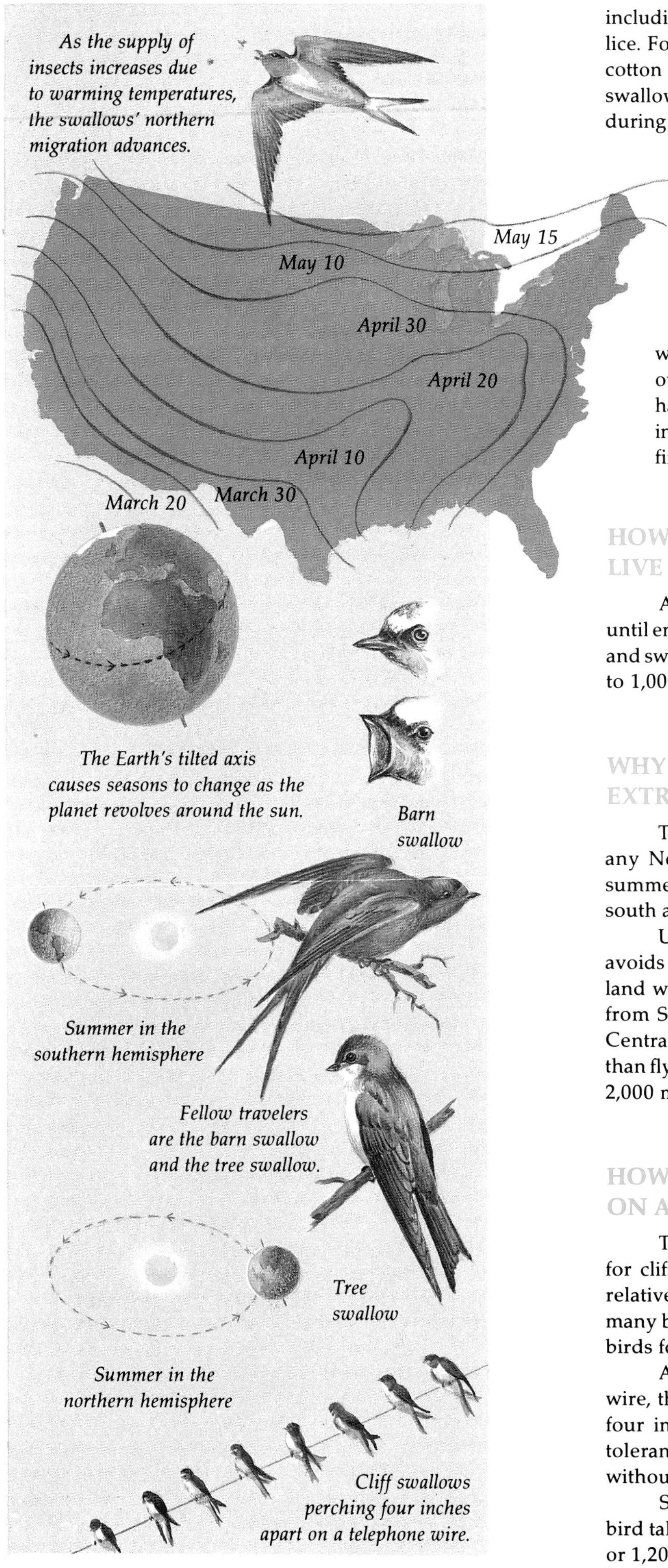

As the supply of insects increases due to warming temperatures, the swallows' northern migration advances.

The Earth's tilted axis causes seasons to change as the planet revolves around the sun.

Summer in the southern hemisphere

Fellow travelers are the barn swallow and the tree swallow.

Summer in the northern hemisphere

Cliff swallows perching four inches apart on a telephone wire.

WHY DO CLIFF SWALLOWS NOT STOP TO EAT OR DRINK?

They do both "on the fly." Since the cliff swallow spends most of its life in the air, it eats and drinks while flying. Skimming low over water, the swallow opens its mouth and, at a speed of over twenty miles per hour, gently touches the lower half of its beak to the water's surface. It also snatches insects from the air while flying at speeds in excess of fifty miles per hour.

HOW CAN A CLIFF SWALLOW KEEP LIVE MOSQUITOES IN ITS MOUTH?

A sticky saliva secures the insects to the bird's tongue until enough are accumulated to be rolled into a small lump and swallowed. It is estimated that the cliff swallow eats 900 to 1,000 insects a day.

WHY WILL A CLIFF SWALLOW FLY 2,000 EXTRA MILES TO AVOID OPEN WATER?

The cliff swallow makes the longest migratory trip of any North American bird. Some swallows spend their summers as far north as Alaska and their winters as far south as Brazil and Argentina.

Unlike other migratory birds, however, the cliff swallow avoids flying over long stretches of open water. It flies over land where insects are available. Thus, a swallow headed from South America to southern Florida will fly through Central America, Texas, and the southeastern states rather than fly across the Gulf of Mexico, a detour that adds at least 2,000 miles to the trip.

HOW MANY CLIFF SWALLOWS WILL PERCH ON A HUNDRED-FOOT TELEPHONE LINE?

Telephone wires afford a comfortable resting place for cliff swallows. Often there are hundreds perched on relatively short stretches of wire. However, no matter how many birds are in one flock, there are never more than 241 birds for each one hundred feet of wire.

As the birds constantly alight on and leave a span of wire, they continually adjust their spacing so that there is four inches between each bird. This space represents a tolerance zone—the distance that a cliff swallow can strike without moving its feet.

Since the swallow's body occupies one inch of wire, each bird takes up five inches. Thus, for each one hundred feet, or 1,200 inches of wire, only 241 birds can rest peacefully.

How is the importance of remembering anniversaries illustrated in Scripture?

Anniversaries are so important to God that He built the life of His nation and the Christian world around them.

Who might well hold the world's record for expending the most time, energy, and money to honor a very significant Christian anniversary?

(Pause for a response—see page 17.)

The Parthian kings of Persia advanced westward against the expanding Roman Empire in 53 B.C. The two major military powers met in battle approximately one hundred miles west of Antioch in Palestine.

The well-disciplined Roman army proved no match for the skillful Persian cavalry. Seven Roman legions, each consisting of over 5,000 fighting men, were destroyed. Ten thousand Roman soldiers were captured and the myth of Roman invincibility was shattered.

Thirteen years later the Roman senate appointed Herod as king of the Jews and dispatched him to the eastern fringes of their empire to guard against future Persian aggression.

Herod relished his new position and power. He answered only to the emperor in Rome. Internal affairs were left completely in his hands, and Roman legates did not require the "puppet ruler" to pay tribute money.

Despite his newly acquired benefits, Herod recognized the precarious position of his kingdom. Anyone suspected of disloyalty or subversion was swiftly eliminated. Although there were minor uprisings and rivalries, Persia remained Herod's greatest concern.

One day he became greatly alarmed when a Persian delegation entered his royal city. Their request to meet with the king caused further panic. Suspecting a plot, Herod increased the number of guards around the garrison and cautiously invited them into his presence.

The Persian representatives entered with impressive pomp and ceremony. These foreign officials were responsible to appoint the next king of the Persian Empire.

Herod's eyes brightened with ambition, but his vain thoughts were quickly dispelled when the dignitaries announced that they had come to honor the next king of the Jews.

The startled sovereign bitterly thought to himself, "I am the king of the Jews." He feigned interest in their mission and inquired as to the whereabouts of this new king. Finally, the delegation was dismissed with orders to report back to the palace.

A short time later, the Persian noblemen knelt in the presence of the one whom they had traveled so far to honor. They presented royal gifts to Christ. Then they returned to their Persian capital.

When Herod realized that the delegation had left without returning to him, he attempted in vain to destroy the "rival" king.

The spiritual kingdom of Christ ultimately conquered the pagan Roman Empire. The empire then established the birth of Christ as the focal point of history so that all men would honor its anniversary.

Today every time a date is written, it officially commemorates "the year of our Lord."

From Matthew 2:1–21

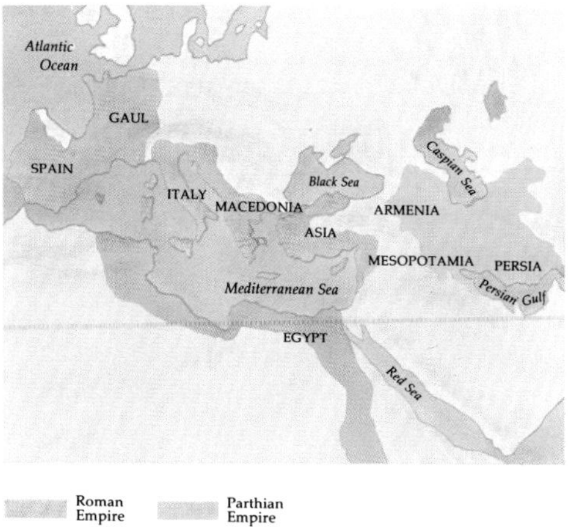

The Magi came from the Persian Empire. *In the time of Christ this empire and the Roman Empire were the two "superpowers" of the day.*

After a long journey the Magi arrived in Jerusalem *and went directly to Herod's palace. They may have entered the city through Herod's gate pictured above. Herod sponsored many ambitious building programs during his reign.*

By following the star of Christ, *the Magi demonstrated punctuality in giving valuable gifts of gold, frankincense, and myrrh.*

By following the instructions of God to flee from Herod, Joseph and Mary demonstrated punctuality in protecting the gift of God to the world.

THE MAGI, THEIR FIRST GIFTS BECAME AN EXAMPLE FOR MANY

The Magi were honored to be the first Gentiles to see, worship, and present gifts to Jesus. They have become such a part of our Christmas tradition that it is easy to confuse fact with fiction. Children around the world imagine these wealthy men traveling by camel from the east as they followed the star.

The men are thought of as three kings and have even been assigned names—Gaspar, Melchior, and Balthazar. Often they are pictured as men of different nationalities, representing three major population groups of the world. But the truth is that we know few specifics about these men. We do not, in fact, know how many there were or exactly what country they came from. What we do know about them is recorded only in the Gospel of Matthew. (See Matthew 2:1–21.)

THE MAGI

The word translated "wise men" is the Persian term *magi.* The Magi first appeared in history as a hereditary priesthood. They possessed great political power in the Median, Babylonian, Persian, and Parthian empires. Nergal-sharezer is mentioned as one of the principal officials in the Babylonian court of Nebuchadnezzar. He is referred to as *Rab-mag* which means "Chief of the Magi." (See Jeremiah 39:3, 13.) When Daniel interpreted Nebuchadnezzar's dream, he was appointed "Rab-mag," a position of both religious and political power. (See Daniel 2:48; 4:9; 5:11.)

At the time of the birth of Christ, the Magi were still very powerful in the Parthian Empire. They were not only priests but also comprised the upper house of the government. Their duties included the absolute choice and election of the king of the realm. Thus the Magi who came to worship the Lord were not kings, but rather king-makers.

HEROD, A TROUBLED KING OF A TROUBLED CITY

When the procession of the Magi reached Jerusalem, we are told that *". . . Herod the king . . . was troubled, and all Jerusalem with him" (Matthew 2:3).* This reaction is understandable in light of the political setting.

The Parthians were the only real threat to the current Roman rule. Herod's own father had reestablished Roman control in Palestine after a Parthian assault. Herod himself had retreated before another Parthian invasion in 40 B.C. In 37 B.C. after a five-month siege by Roman troops, Herod once again occupied the throne in Jerusalem. At the birth of Christ, the situation seemed ripe for another offensive. The appearance of the Magi, who probably traveled in force and with oriental pomp, was cause for great alarm in Jerusalem.

MISSION OF THE "KING-MAKERS"

But the Magi were not trying to provoke an incident in order to justify Parthian reprisal. Their purpose was far different. Their mission was to worship. How surprised they must have been to discover Jerusalem's lack of regard for their own Messiah. The religious leaders were indifferent and unbelieving. The baby was not in the capital, but in the poor village of Bethlehem, two hours away.

The Magi must have been amazed to find the babe in a cottage, surrounded by poverty, cared for by a homeless couple. And yet in spite of these obstacles to their faith, they *". . . fell down, and worshipped him: and when they had opened their treasures, they presented unto him gifts; gold, and frankincense, and myrrh" (Matthew 2:11).*

CHARACTER SKETCH OF THE MAGI

WHY DID THE MAGI ASSOCIATE A STAR WITH THE KING OF THE JEWS?

The unusual star was used to confirm, rather than initiate, the Magi's belief in the coming Messiah. Just as Jesus confirmed Himself to the fishermen through their knowledge of fish (see Luke 5:1–11), so the Lord drew the Magi to Himself through their knowledge of the heavens.

The Magi were undoubtedly familiar with the Messianic prophecies of the Old Testament, since the Scriptures had been known to them for centuries. Daniel, "Chief of the Magi" for a time, must have explained to them about the coming Messiah.

The prophecy of Balaam may have led some to expect a star as a sign. *"I shall see him, but not now: I shall behold him, but not nigh: there shall come a Star out of Jacob, and a Sceptre shall rise out of Israel . . ." (Numbers 24:17).* Isaiah's words may also have contributed to this expectation. *"And the Gentiles shall come to thy light, and kings to the brightness of thy rising" (Isaiah 60:3).*

Daniel himself predicted the coming of the Messiah and dated that coming near the time of the Magi's observation. (See Daniel 9:25.) Thus, an unusual astronomical phenomenon directed the Magi's thinking to the prophecies of the Messiah in Scripture. This in turn motivated them to pursue their search in the direction of the Jewish capital of Jerusalem.

WHY WAS HEROD SO DISTURBED BY THE VISIT OF THE MAGI?

Herod was aware of the fervid Messianism which had been gathering strength during the first century B.C. The Jews knew the promise that a descendant of David would be born in Bethlehem who would rule the nation in peace. (See Micah 5:2.) The previous outrages of the Maccabean age and the present harsh Roman rule greatly stimulated the expectation of a coming Messiah. Herod, not a Jew by birth, did not qualify as their deliverer.

The Jews' increasing displeasure with Herod and their anticipation of his replacement led to a climate of fear and suspicion. In fact, Herod had become so paranoid that two of his own sons were strangled under suspicion of treason.

Herod took great pride in the title "king" which had been given to him by the Roman Senate. When the Magi came to Jerusalem and inquired, *". . . Where is he that is born King of the Jews? . . .",* it is not surprising that such a man would be troubled. (See Matthew 2:2.)

WHAT WAS SIGNIFICANT ABOUT THE GIFTS OF THE MAGI?

The Magi presented gold, frankincense, and myrrh to Christ. Gold was the most precious of metals and represented anything of great value. (See Proverbs 3:14; 8:10, 19.) Gold was worthy of use in worship. (See Exodus 25.) Their gift of gold signified the Magi's belief that this babe was indeed born a king.

The other gifts, frankincense and myrrh, were also used in the worship of Jehovah. Frankincense, derived from the resin of special trees, produced a sweet, pleasant odor. It was used to make the holy incense for the tabernacle. (See Exodus 30:34–36.) Both frankincense and myrrh were found in the perfume worn by kings. (See Song of Solomon 3:6.) The Magi had brought gifts worthy of a king.

***The gifts which the magi brought to Christ** became the provision for Joseph and Mary to support themselves in Egypt during the two years that Herod sought to destroy Christ in Palestine. Their return was a happy reunion with friends and relatives.*

THE MAGI
***ma**-jī*

Resourcefulness

. . . Is the wise use of that which others would normally overlook or discard

"He that is faithful in that which is least is faithful also in much. . . ."

Luke 16:10

PART FIVE

RESOURCEFULNESS IN GIVING . . .

Resourcefulness is the foundation of generosity. When resourcefulness is neglected or stifled, people tend to reject God's principles of provision and fall prey to financial indebtedness or trust in riches which they can see. (See Psalm 52:7.)

CHAPTER SEVENTEEN

Resourcefulness

. . . Is seeing resources that are overlooked by those around me

"And God blessed them, and God said unto them, Be fruitful, and multiply, and replenish the earth, and subdue it: and have dominion over the fish of the sea, and over the fowl of the air, and over every living thing that moveth upon the earth."

Genesis 1:28

Living Lessons on Resourcefulness . . .

FROM THE PAGES OF SCRIPTURE

A life and death battle will always rage between the unresourceful, who depend upon human reasoning, and the resourceful, who depend upon Godly creativity to reveal unseen provisions.

Nowhere in Scripture is this eternal warfare more vividly portrayed than through the ministry of two men. They became a threat to the evil rulers of their day. They used resourcefulness to provide food for the hungry, strengthen the hands of those around them, and advance the work of God.

ILLUSTRATED IN THE WORLD OF NATURE

COMMON FLEA *Pulex irritans*

Fleas are curiously flat insects, usually less than one-sixteenth of an inch long. They feed on the blood of most mammals and birds and can also infest humans, at least temporarily.

Being a true insect, the flea goes through a complete metamorphosis of four stages. The flea was once a major health problem in American homes but it has now been virtually eliminated as a household pest.

There are at least 2,000 different types of fleas. Over half of these have been identified in the last thirty years. Each flea prefers its own type of host such as a cat, dog, rabbit, or human being.

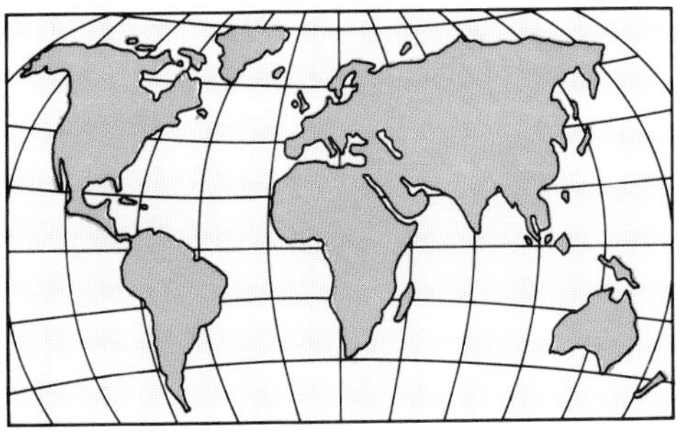

The range and habitat of the common flea

How is the warfare of resourcefulness illustrated in the world of nature?

A covered wagon slowly moved across the open prairie. Long, hard miles and unexpected challenges had already convinced the pioneer family that survival depended on their ability to be resourceful.

One of the more difficult problems they had encountered was a prolonged attack by mysterious intruders. The intruders had also shown resourcefulness as they cleverly concealed themselves and evaded detection. At first, they were tolerated in light of more pressing matters, but soon the combined efforts of each family member were needed to fight against them.

It was with great joy and much relief that the family finally arrived at the site of their new homestead. In a few weeks a cabin and a small chicken coop had been built.

Early one morning one of the children came running from the chicken coop shouting, "They're back again!" The entire family again battled for hours defending against the persistent intruders.

Several nights later the bloodthirsty creatures returned. Silently, one slipped out of his hiding place and approached his victim. With a spectacular leap his armor-plated body landed on the unsuspecting prey.

Without warning, he cut a small slit in the surface of the skin and began to extract blood. Some of it spilled onto the floor where it would later become useful. With amazing agility, he leaped to the floor below where he was joined by his partner. Together they concealed hundreds of tiny eggs in floor cracks near the blood.

A few days later, as the sun peeked over the prairie horizon, chicken eggs began to hatch. The small chicken coop was soon filled with the sound of chirping chicks. What could not be heard was the hatching of other eggs in the rough-hewn planks of the floor.

The lovable chicks were instantly adopted as an important part of the homestead. However, as the chicks grew, the new offspring of the intruders began to attack the helpless chicks.

Frustration turned to anger for the pioneer family. This anger became a spiritual defeat and only added to the frustration of their physical defeat. Finally, they realized that the only way they could win both battles was not by eradicating their enemies but by controlling them.

They could only achieve this by maintaining cleanliness of their hearts, lives, and everything they owned. Only then could they hope to overcome the resourcefulness of the little flea that had been a bothersome hitchhiker on one of the chickens they had brought to their new homestead.

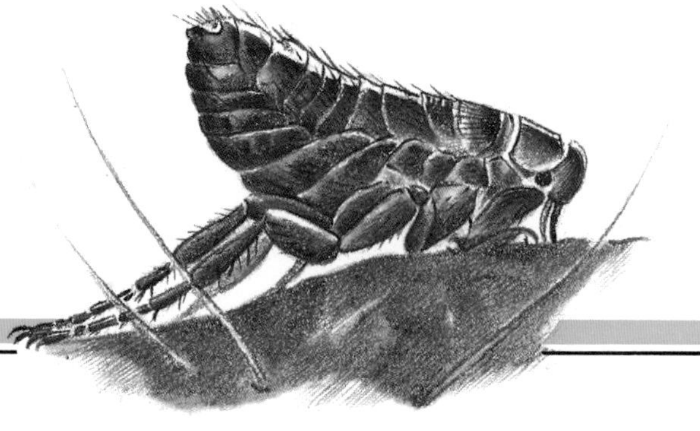

THE CHARACTERISTICS OF

THE FLEA IN SCRIPTURE

The flea is the most annoying insect in the East. It uses its resourcefulness to continually irritate its host and transmit devastating diseases to large numbers of people in short periods of time.

When Pharaoh refused to free Israel from slavery in Egypt, God sent different *". . . sorts of flies, and lice . . ." (Psalm 105:31)* upon the Egyptians. The Hebrew word for lice, *ken,* means a fastening or biting insect. These are characteristics of fleas as well as of lice and the word is used for both.

It is significant that the magicians of Egypt could not duplicate the flea as they could the first two plagues that came upon Egypt. In fact, it was the flea that caused the distressed magicians to observe, *". . . This is the finger of God . . ." (Exodus 8:19).*

Perhaps the thought of God's judgment was in the mind of David when he was fleeing from Saul. After cutting off Saul's robe, but sparing his life, David called out to Saul, *"After whom is the king of Israel come out? . . . After a flea" (I Samuel 24:14).*

No doubt David's primary purpose, however, was to convince the king of his harmlessness and his insignificance. David repeated the comparison in I Samuel 26:20.

CHARACTERISTICS AND PHYSICAL FEATURES OF THE FLEA

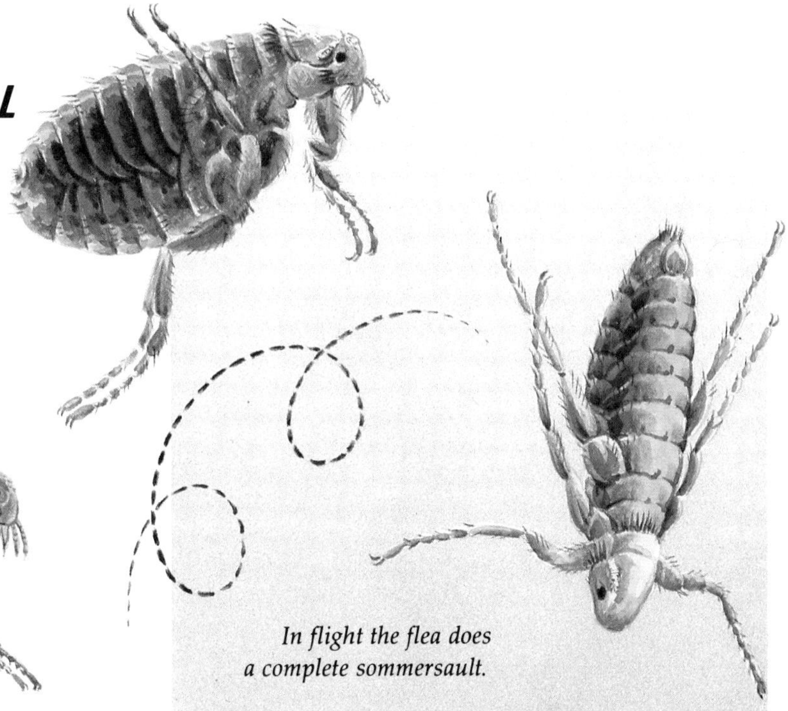

In flight the flea does a complete sommersault.

Outwardly the flea appears to be nothing more than a little pest. Yet, this "little pest" has a great deal of expertise at outsmarting those who would try to be rid of it. For each attempted extermination the flea has an escape. Through the creative use of all of its resources, it can survive cold, starvation, and the attacks of its host.

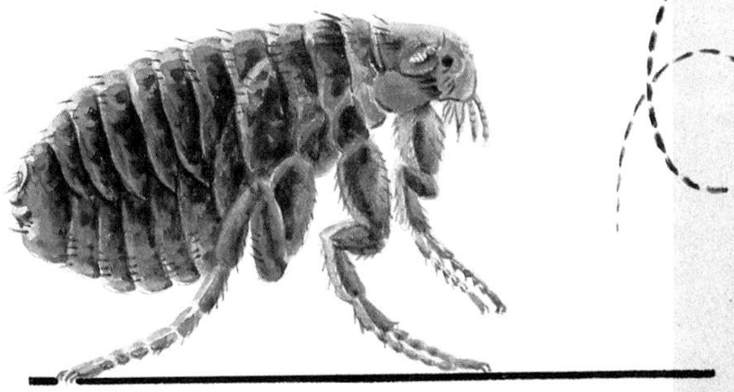

COULD A MAN LEAP OUT OF A STADIUM IF HE HAD THE JUMPING ABILITY OF A FLEA?

Fleas are the original supermen of the high jump and the long jump. They can easily jump 100 times their own height (eight inches) and 150 times their own length (thirteen inches). For a man six feet tall, that is equivalent to jumping over a fifty-story building or the length of two football fields. A man competing in a track meet with the ability of a flea could easily jump completely out of the stadium.

HOW DOES THE FLEA ACCELERATE ITSELF TWENTY TIMES FASTER THAN A MOON ROCKET?

A tiny pan of rubbery protein called *resilin* bulges at the top of each jumping leg. Strong muscles pull the flea's leg slowly up against the pad like the hammer of a gun being cocked.

A second muscle locks the leg in place. When the leg is released, the resilin snaps back into shape in less than 1/500 of a second. In that short time, the flea is accelerated at a rate twenty times greater than the acceleration of the Apollo moon rocket.

HOW DOES A HEAD HINGE DO THE WORK OF EYES FOR A FLEA?

Although some fleas have an eye on each side of the head, for all practical purposes fleas are blind. As the flea moves blindly about on its host, a hinge between the front and back of its head enables it to weave around the hairs into which it bumps.

WHY DID A FUGITIVE COMPARE HIMSELF TO A FLEA?

When being pursued by King Saul and his army, David attempted to discourage Saul by comparing himself to a flea. Just as it was beneath the dignity of a king to search for a trivial flea, so it was out of place for Saul to seek after him. (See I Samuel 26:20.)

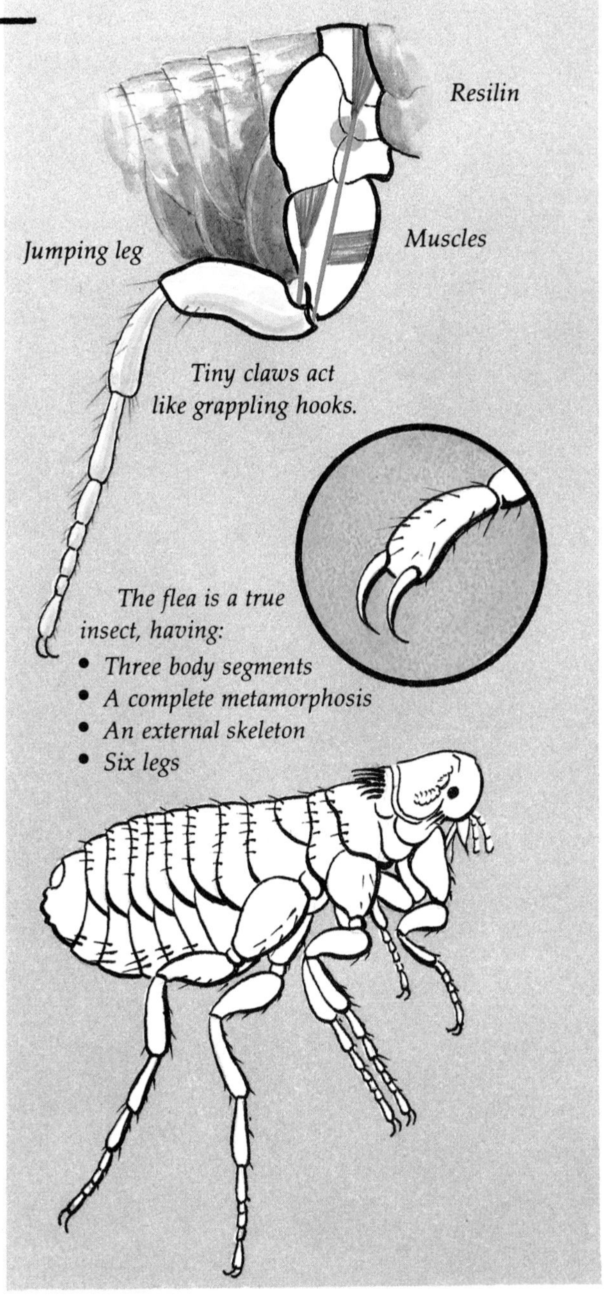

Resilin
Jumping leg
Muscles
Tiny claws act like grappling hooks.
The flea is a true insect, having:
• Three body segments
• A complete metamorphosis
• An external skeleton
• Six legs

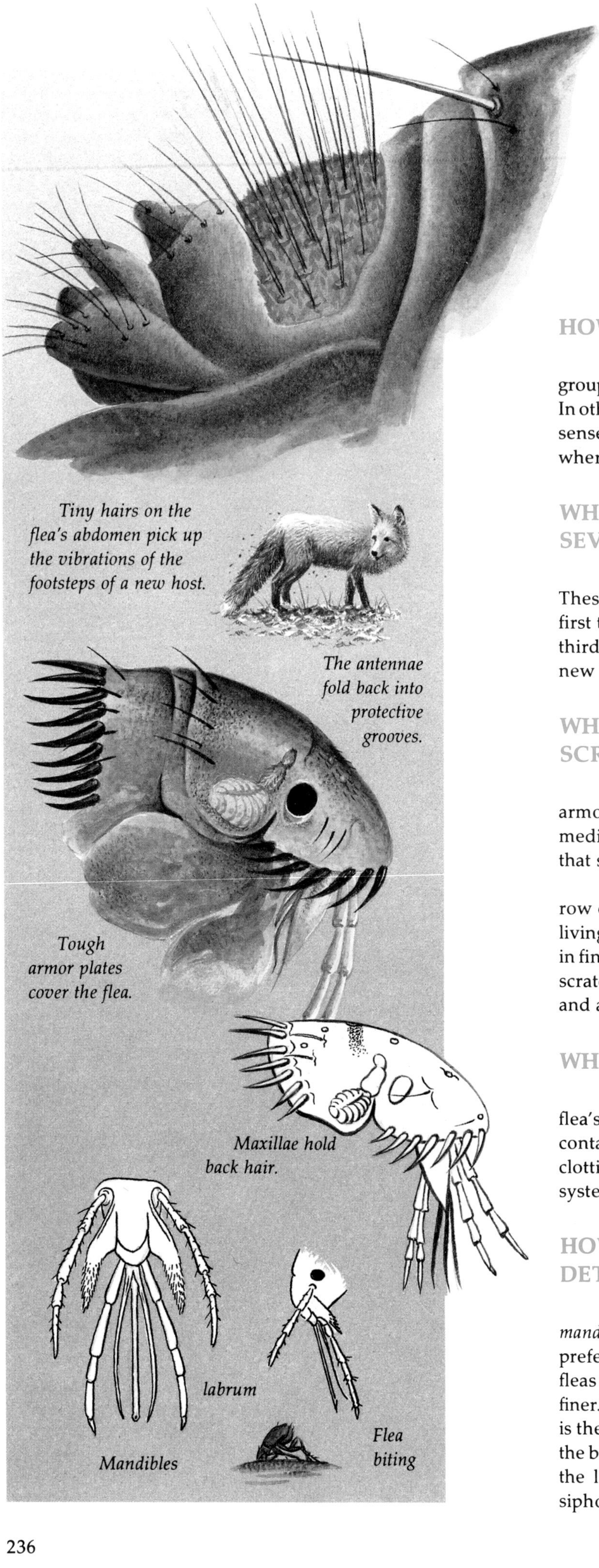

Tiny hairs on the flea's abdomen pick up the vibrations of the footsteps of a new host.

The antennae fold back into protective grooves.

Tough armor plates cover the flea.

Maxillae hold back hair.

HOW CAN A FLEA GO FOR 2,000 DAYS WITHOUT FOOD AND WATER?

The normal life span of a flea is about five hundred days under ideal conditions. However, if a flea is exposed to temperatures just below freezing, its life can be suspended for more than 2,000 days without food or water. When warmed it revives within minutes. Continued exposure to sunlight kills the flea in all stages of its development.

HOW DO FLEAS HEAR WITH THEIR HAIR?

Sound vibrations are picked up by the tiny hairs grouped together near the last segment of the flea's abdomen. In other words, fleas appear to hear with their tails. Fleas can sense heat and carbon dioxide and can accurately tell when, where, and how far to leap to get to a new host.

WHY DO FLEAS USUALLY BITE HUMANS SEVERAL TIMES IN A ROW?

Most fleas which bite humans are from dogs or cats. These fleas do not really like human blood and, after the first taste, will move to another spot and try again. After a third or fourth try, the flea will usually quit and search out a new host.

WHY CAN YOU NOT KILL A FLEA BY SCRATCHING IT?

Every segment of the flea's body is covered with armored plates which give the flea the appearance of a medieval knight dressed for combat. The armor is so tough that scratching cannot crush the flea.

Along the trailing edge of each section of armor is a row of spines spaced much like the teeth of a comb. Fleas living in coarse hair have widely spaced spines. Fleas living in fine hair have more narrowly spaced spines. As the flea is scratched, these spines become entangled in the host's hair and anchor the flea more tightly.

WHY DO FLEA BITES ITCH?

The itching sensation of a flea bite is caused by the flea's saliva which is injected into the wound. The saliva contains an anticoagulant which prevents the blood from clotting. If the blood were to clot in the flea's tiny digestive system, the system would become plugged.

HOW DO THE TEETH OF THE FLEA DETERMINE WHO ITS HOST WILL BE?

The actual biting is done by two tiny saws called *mandibles* that cut a small slit in the skin. Among fleas which prefer tough-skinned hosts, the saw teeth are coarse. Among fleas preferring thin-skinned hosts, the saw teeth are much finer. A sharp, hollow "hypodermic needle" called the *labrum* is then inserted into the hole and the saliva is injected into the bite. As the blood begins to flow, the two mandibles and the labrum fit together to form a triangular tube which siphons the blood into the mouth.

HOW IS A FLEA'S SURVIVAL DEPENDENT ON ITS ABILITY TO BE RESOURCEFUL?

The life cycle of the flea is completely dependent on its surrounding environment. If conditions are favorable, the cycle from egg to adult may take as little as two weeks. If conditions are not favorable, the cycle may take up to two years.

Eggs

LIFE CYCLE OF THE FLEA

The four stages of the complete metamorphosis of the flea are the egg, larva, pupa, and adult.

Egg stage

Several hundred round, white eggs are simply dropped by the adult female in clusters of four to eight among the hairs of the host animal. These eggs usually fall to the ground or to the bottom of the nest where they hatch in two to four days. While the eggs are smaller than grains of table salt, their size is comparable to that of a chicken laying eggs the size of grapefruit.

Larva

The eggs hatch into wormlike larvae that are studded with sensitive bristles. The larvae have no legs and no eyes. Their bodies are divided into thirteen segments, and they move about by twisting, jerking, and squirming.

Larvae eat anything organic, especially the droppings of excess blood passed from the adults. Occasionally the larvae are cannibalistic, forming a ring with each larva eating on the tail of the next. As the larvae grow, they shed their hard skins and double their size within two weeks.

Pupa

As the larva reaches maturity, it spins a sticky thread around itself. This protective capsule is soon covered with hair and dust and becomes lost in the debris of its surrounding nest, rug, or dirty floor.

Inside the cocoon, the adult flea begins to take shape. The jumping legs, antennae, and mouth parts all appear for the first time. This change is made in less than a week under warm, dry conditions. Once the adult is formed inside the cocoon, the pupa can remain in suspended animation until vibrated by the presence of a potential host.

Adult

Viewed from the front, adult fleas are paper thin, allowing them to pass easily among even the thickest hair. The female mates only once and may lay 400 to 500 eggs during the course of her life. Adult fleas may live as long as eighteen months under favorable conditions and even longer, when kept at temperatures just below freezing.

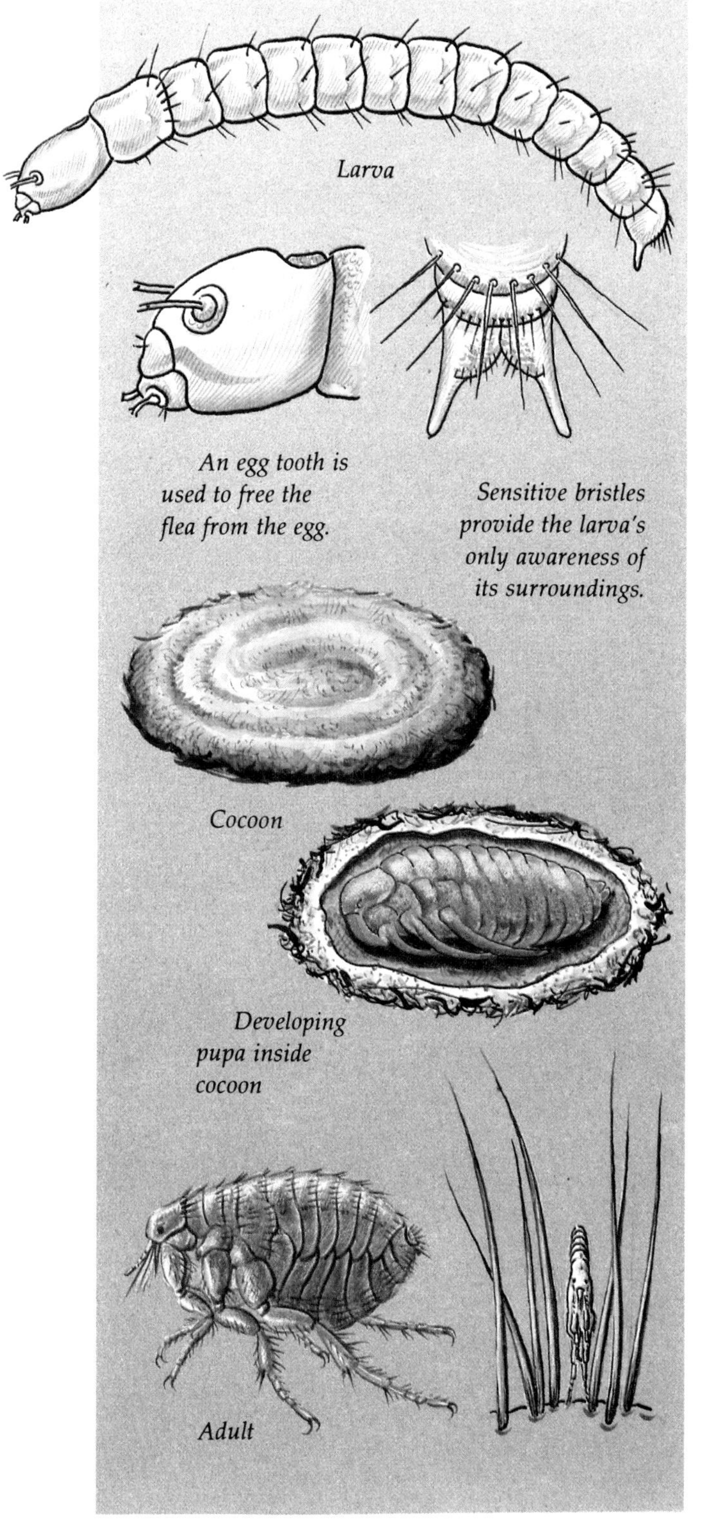
Larva
An egg tooth is used to free the flea from the egg.
Sensitive bristles provide the larva's only awareness of its surroundings.
Cocoon
Developing pupa inside cocoon
Adult

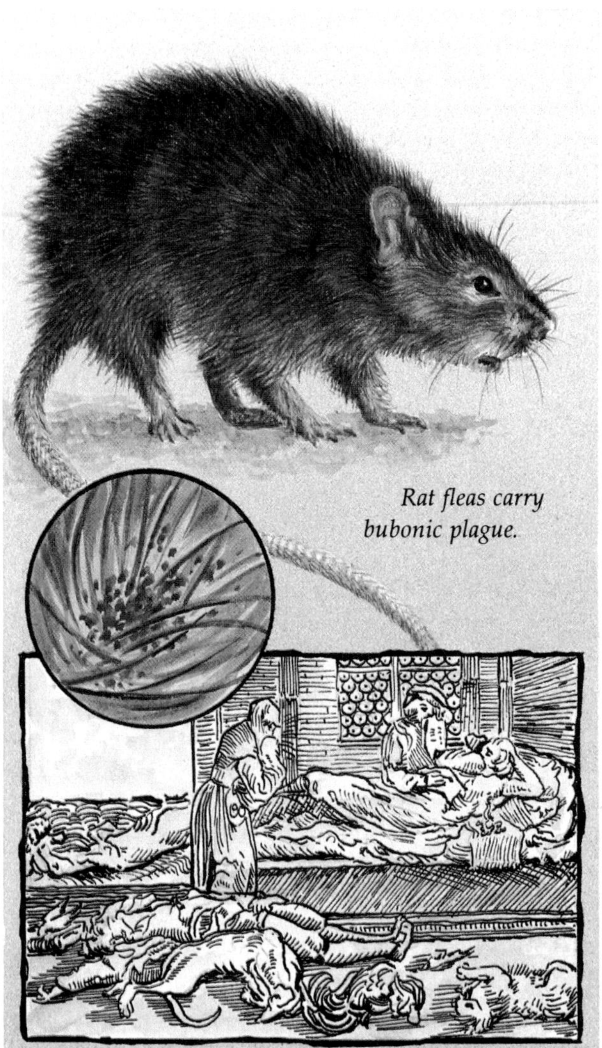

Rat fleas carry bubonic plague.

The plague killed 25,000,000 people in Europe between 1347 and 1350.

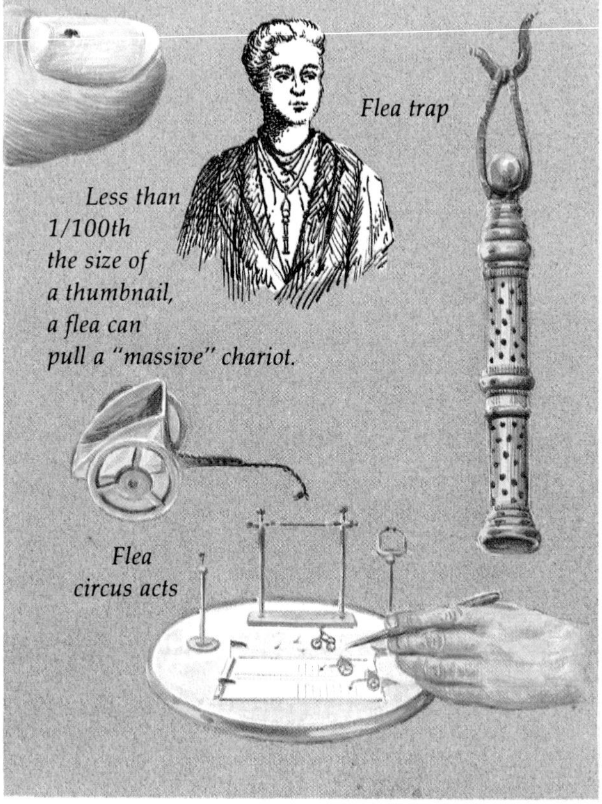

Flea trap

Less than 1/100th the size of a thumbnail, a flea can pull a "massive" chariot.

Flea circus acts

WHAT MODERN INVENTION IS CREDITED WITH REMOVING THE GREATEST NUMBER OF FLEAS?

The vacuum cleaner. Thousands upon thousands of eggs, larvae, and fleas have been sucked into vacuum cleaners. A broom over a wooden floor often swept over the fleas hidden away in cracks and crevices. However, the vacuum cleaner picks them up and removes them.

HOW HAVE FLEAS USED RESOURCEFULNESS IN THE WRONG WAY TO BRING ABOUT THE DEATHS OF OVER FIFTY MILLION PEOPLE?

The flea has killed over fifty million people through the spread of bubonic plague. In Rome around 262 A.D., as many as 5,000 people a day died from the plague. In London, between 1603 and 1665, over 150,000 people died.

The worst epidemic broke out in Europe between 1347 and 1350. During those three years the Black Death, as bubonic plague was called, killed twenty-five million people, one-fourth of the entire European population.

HOW DO RATS HELP FLEAS SPREAD DISEASE?

The plague is spread by infected rat fleas. As a diseased rat dies, the rat flea abandons the dead body, searches for a new host, and injects it with the now poisoned saliva.

HOW DOES THE PLAGUE AFFECT THE FLEA?

The plague affects the flea by plugging its digestive system. The diseased flea continues to bite but cannot swallow. It desperately goes from victim to victim, unable to satisfy its hunger, until it too dies.

WHY DO FLEAS PREFER WOMEN OVER MEN?

The life cycle of many fleas is dependent on the female hormones of its host. For this reason fleas are more likely to be attracted to women than they are to men.

HOW DID JEWELRY TRAP FLEAS?

To rid themselves of fleas, women wore hollow tubes around their necks. Fleas would crawl into the tube through the holes in the side. The trapped fleas were then simply discarded. Fashionable women wore elaborately decorated flea traps. Even today women continue to wear necklaces and pendants that are descendants of the flea traps.

Fur collars on coats also served the purpose of trapping fleas. Fur worn around the neck attracted fleas away from the body. The collars were then thrown away with the unwanted fleas.

HOW DO FLEA TRAINERS PAY FLEAS TO PERFORM?

Contrary to popular belief, fleas are not taught to do tricks. The trainer must harness the flea's incredible power in creative ways. The natural crawling movements of the flea have been used to race chariots, power tiny merry-go-rounds, ride tricycles, fire cannons, play musical instruments, and walk tightropes.

Traditionally, after a showing of a flea circus, the trainer rewards his performers by allowing them to feed from his own arm.

How is seeing overlooked resources illustrated in Scripture?

Resourcefulness is a requirement and also a result of fulfilling God's first command to "*. . . be fruitful and multiply*" *(Genesis 1:28)*. Lack of resourcefulness will encourage the lie that we must limit births because "we are running out of natural resources."

Who were two men who demonstrated unusual resourcefulness in order to provide food, but were condemned for it by jealous rulers who wanted to increase their own power?

(Pause for a response—see page 17.)

A group of men hurried down the trail. They were fleeing for their lives, having been falsely accused. Weary and hungry, they arrived at a temporary place of safety. The leader in charge looked at the men in surprise as they asked him for something to eat.

The Godly leader explained that no food was available. The men had only a few moments to spare and urged their kindly host to think of some way to help them.

Finally a creative way was worked out to meet their need. However, in the shadows an evil man watched what happened and later informed the king.

The news pleased the jealous king. It provided for him an excuse to destroy the kindly spiritual leader whom he looked upon as a troublesome rival. The vengeful king sent out messengers and had him arrested. Angrily the king accused the loyal leader of breaking the Law.

The leader assured the king that he had acted by the true spirit of the Law. The king coldly brushed him aside and called for his execution. The soldiers stood in astonishment at such an order. This leader was highly respected. They could not bring themselves to kill him.

The frustrated king then called for the evil man who had reported the event. This willing foreigner took the sword and carried out the bloody assignment.

The second resourceful man lived many years later. He too fed a hungry group of men, but in the process, evil men were watching His actions and later reported Him to jealous officials. They looked upon this spiritual leader as a threat to their authority.

Eventually they brought Him into court and accused Him of breaking the Law. He, too, received a sentence of death which was carried out by foreign executioners.

We recognize this second leader as the Lord Jesus Christ. He defended His disciples when they ate grain on the Sabbath day. It was then that He honored the first resourceful leader, Ahimelech, the high priest who gave the showbread to David and his men in the day of King Saul.

From I Samuel 21–22
and Matthew 12:1–4

AHIMELECH, A FAITHFUL PRIEST IN A TURBULENT TIME

Ahimelech lost his life doing what he thought was right—helping a person in need. Ahimelech was a descendant of Ithamar. He was the grandson of Phinehas, Eli's disobedient son who had been killed by the Philistines when the Ark of the Covenant was taken. (See I Samuel 4:11.)

Ahimelech served as priest during the reign of King Saul, a time of confusion among the priests of Israel. The Ark of the Covenant, the most important item in the formal worship of Jehovah, was cautiously stored in the house of Abinadab at Kirjath-jearim rather than residing in the Holy of Holies of the tabernacle. (See I Samuel 7:2.) The tabernacle was pitched in the city of Nob. There was confusion about who should serve as the high priest. Priests originally were descendants of Aaron's son Eleazar, but for a time the descendants of Aaron's younger son, Ithamar, superseded them.

It is a credit to Ahimelech's character that, in spite of the confusion of his day, he seems not only to have been thoroughly acquainted with the various laws given by God to the priests, but he also demonstrated an eagerness to keep them faithfully.

DAVID, FUGITIVE SOLDIER IN FLIGHT FOR HIS LIFE

David had been anointed by Samuel as the nation's future king. After he was warned by Jonathan that King Saul wanted to kill him, he sought refuge and assistance at Nob where Ahimelech served as chief priest. David knew that the Lord would protect him and provide for his needs. He must have felt that Ahimelech would be used by God to help, even though he was unaware that David was now a fugitive.

AN UNUSUAL REQUEST

Ahimelech was faithfully fulfilling the duties of his office when David arrived at Nob. The Law prescribed that every week on the Sabbath, twelve loaves of bread representing the twelve tribes were to be set on the table of showbread in the holy place of the tabernacle. (See Leviticus 24:8.)

The bread was made of fine flour and was the kind served to honored guests and the king. (See Genesis 18:6; Leviticus 24:5; I Kings 4:22.) When replaced by fresh loaves, the old loaves were still considered to be holy. Only the priests were allowed to eat them in the vicinity of the tabernacle. What remained was to be burned on the bronze altar. (See Leviticus 24:9.)

When David met Ahimelech, he asked for the loaves that were on hand. It is likely that these loaves had been left over and were about to be burned as an offering to the Lord. Ahimelech feared that it would be sacrilegious to give David, who was not a priest, the holy showbread if he or his men were not ceremonially clean. David assured the priest that they were not defiled. He received the bread for food and Goliath's sword for protection. (See I Samuel 21:3–9.)

A LEGACY OF INTEGRITY

Ahimelech had asked about David's mission when they first met. To protect Ahimelech from a charge of disloyalty, David claimed to be involved in a secret matter of the king. Therefore, to assist David would be the equivalent of helping Saul.

Ahimelech's life stands in sharp contrast to that of his grandfather, Phinehas. Phinehas had no regard for the Levitical Law. He despised the offering of the Lord, and grossly violated the clear commands of a priest. (See I Samuel 2:12–17, 22.) Ahimelech, on the other hand, showed respect for God's commands. He attempted to be faithful to the letter of the Law as well as its spirit. He had helped to restore the priesthood to the dignity and respect it deserved.

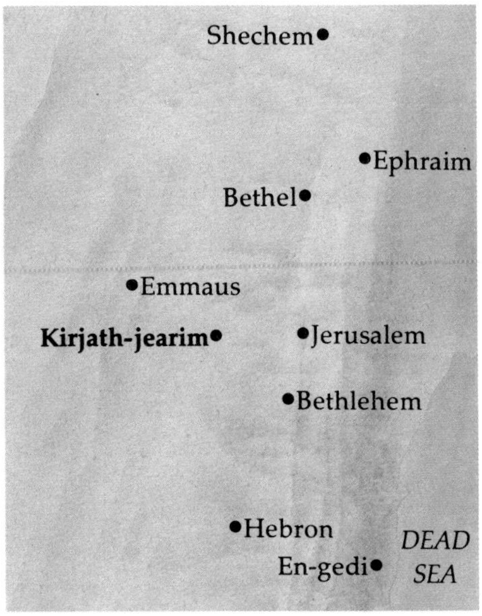

***Kirjath-jearim** was the city in which David received the showbread and sword of Goliath from the hand of Ahimelech.*

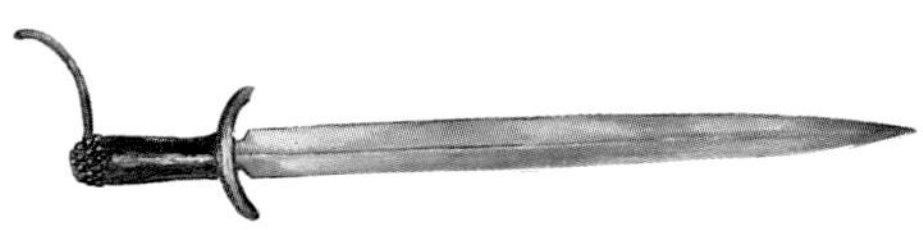

Sword of Goliath

Showbread

*"**And thou shalt take fine flour,** and bake twelve cakes thereof: two tenth deals shall be in one cake. And thou shalt set them in two rows, six on a row, upon the pure table before the Lord. . . . Every Sabbath he shall set it in order before the Lord . . . by an everlasting covenant. And it shall be Aaron's and his sons'; and they shall eat it in the holy place . . ." (Leviticus 24:5–6, 8–9).*

Table of Showbread

"Thou shalt also make a table of shittim wood: two cubits shall be the length thereof, and a cubit the breadth thereof, and a cubit and a half the height thereof. And thou shalt overlay it with pure gold. . . . And thou shalt set upon the table shewbread before me alway" (Exodus 25:23–24, 30).

CHARACTER SKETCH OF AHIMELECH

WHY DID DAVID NOT TELL AHIMELECH THE TRUTH?

He feared what the consequences would be for Ahimelech. When David arrived at Nob, he noticed a high-ranking member of Saul's court, *". . . Doeg, an Edomite, the chiefest of the herdmen . . ." (I Samuel 21:7)*. Doeg had been detained at the tabernacle for an unstated reason.

David knew Doeg would tell Saul everything that happened. (See I Samuel 22:22.) He did not want to give Doeg any reason to give a bad report about Ahimelech to Saul. Aiding a fugitive was an act of treason punishable by death.

Once Ahimelech's suspicions were aroused, David said, *". . . The king hath commanded me a business, and hath said unto me, Let no man know any thing of the business whereabout I send thee . . ." (I Samuel 21:2)*. David thought that his lie would protect Ahimelech, but he underestimated Doeg's wickedness.

When Doeg reported to Saul, he accused Ahimelech of aiding David and later carried out Saul's cruel order to kill the priest. In this tragic chapter of passion and politics, Ahimelech forfeited his life.

WAS AHIMELECH WRONG TO GIVE DAVID THE SHOWBREAD?

The Levitical Law declared that the showbread *". . . shall be Aaron's and his sons'; and they shall eat it in the holy place: for it is most holy unto him of the offerings of the Lord made by fire by a perpetual statute" (Leviticus 24:9)*. But there were other commands in the Law that compelled one to help a neighbor in need. (See Leviticus 19:18, 33–34.)

Ahimelech had to discern the spirit of the Law. The intent of the Law was a warning not to use things separated unto God in a profane or disrespectful manner. A person ceremonially unclean was specifically forbidden to eat of the holy thing. (See Leviticus 22:6, 10.) Ahimelech insisted that David and his men be clean. (See I Samuel 21:4.)

When Jesus referred to this event, He did not condemn Ahimelech. On the contrary, He used the incident to explain the picking of grain by Himself and His disciples on the Sabbath. (See Matthew 12:3–7; Mark 2:25–26; Luke 6:3–5.)

WHY DID SAUL REACT SO VIOLENTLY AGAINST AHIMELECH?

Saul's cruel reaction was a ruthless effort to consolidate his political power. Saul was becoming more and more jealous of sharing authority with the prophets and priests. When God permitted the nation of Israel to have a king, He established restrictions on the king's authority because God was still to be regarded as the nation's leader.

The office of prophet was established to reveal God's specific will. The function of the priests was to instruct the people and the king in God's general will as revealed in the Law. In a twofold act of disobedience to Samuel, Saul had rejected the office of prophet. (See I Samuel 13:13; 15:19.)

Now Saul had an opportunity to rid himself of the priests too. In spite of Ahimelech's plea of allegiance, Saul chose to believe the lies of Doeg. In an effort to destroy this important branch of power in Israel, Saul ordered Ahimelech and eighty-five other priests, their families, and their children to be killed. (See I Samuel 22:17–19.)

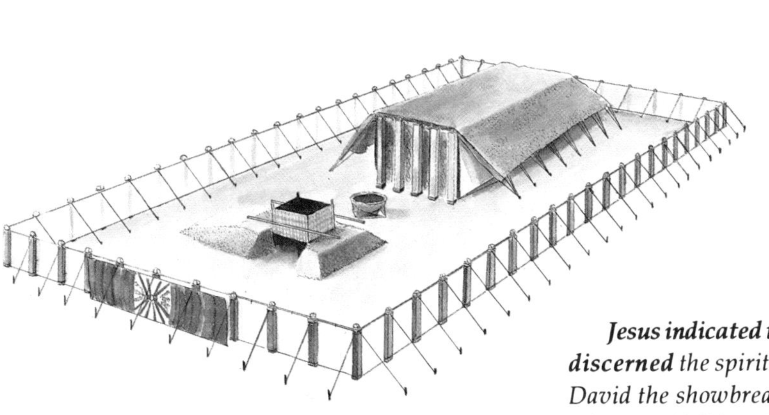

Jesus indicated that Ahimelech properly discerned *the spirit of the Law when he gave David the showbread. ". . . Have ye not read what David did . . . How he entered the house of God, and did eat the shewbread, which was not lawful for him to eat . . . but only for the priests?" (Matthew 12:3–4).*

AHIMELECH
*a-**hĭm**-əl-ek*

CHAPTER EIGHTEEN

Resourcefulness

. . . Is using my time, money, and possessions to extend the work of God

"Withhold not good from them to whom it is due, when it is in the power of thine hand to do it."

Proverbs 3:27

Living Lessons on Resourcefulness . . .

FROM THE PAGES OF SCRIPTURE

Among the valuable resources that we tend to overlook are strength, health, friendships, and time. Each day God gives every person twenty-four hours. The joy which we experience in life is directly related to the wisdom by which we invest this valuable resource to advance the kingdom of God.

What is true for time is also true for other resources, and what is true for individuals is true for kings. Two kings in Scripture provide a significant contrast in their use of the same natural resource. One invested it wisely and experienced God's blessing upon himself and upon his nation. The second invested it unwisely and brought total destruction to his nation.

ILLUSTRATED IN THE WORLD OF NATURE

AMERICAN EGRET *Casmerodius albus egretta*

The egret is perhaps the most elegant and graceful of all of the herons. Standing about three feet tall with a heavy yellow bill, black feet, and long white plumes, it nests throughout the marshes and wetlands of both North and South America. It is an excellent hunter, stalking its prey with slow, deliberate steps. The white plumes for which the egret is famous nearly led to its extinction in the late 1800s.

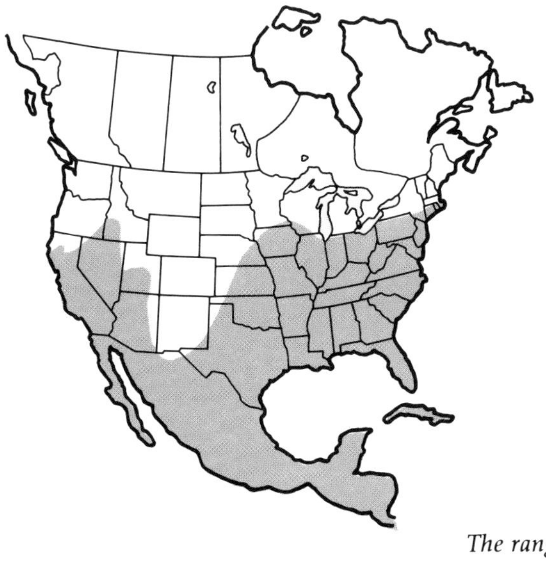

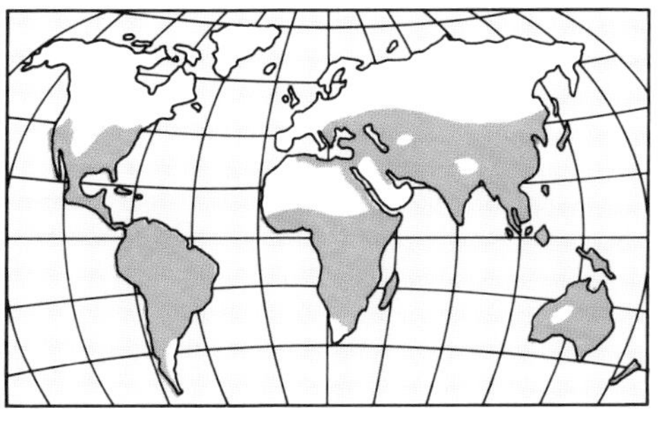

The range and habitat of the American egret

How is the potential of multiplying resources illustrated in the world of nature?

The beautiful white feather plumes on the back of the egret bounced rhythmically in the air as he picked up a twig and then bowed respectfully before his mate. The graceful ceremony was repeated several times. Then both egrets sprang into the air and seemed to defy gravity as their huge wings slowly lifted them higher and higher.

They had chosen their nesting site in the crotch of a tree one hundred twenty feet above the lonely marsh. Three eggs were laid in the nest, and the parents began the long vigil of incubation.

One night there was a violent storm. The tall tree swayed dangerously in the wind. The thinly lined nest was unable to prevent two eggs from slipping through the loose construction and falling on the rocks below.

The mother egret carefully guarded the remaining egg. Finally the day arrived for the little egret to break through the shell, totally dependent upon its parents for survival.

However, a new threat faced all three of them. Food had become unusually scarce. Each day it became harder to locate fish, frogs, snakes, or crayfish.

One day the egrets saw a visitor in a nearby meadow. They watched as he tossed a crust of bread into the brush. When he left, the male egret gracefully glided down, picked up the crust in its long, pointed bill, and flew back up to his hungry family.

His mate quickly broke off portions of the crust and gave them to her chick. While the chick was eating, its mother also devoured several pieces. In a very short time, only one piece of the crust remained. Rather than giving it to the chick or its mother, the male grabbed it and flew out of the nest.

He landed at the edge of an inlet in the marsh. Slowly he walked out into the water. Carefully he leaned over and placed the precious little piece of bread on the water. Then he waited.

A delicious-looking bass cautiously swam up to the bread and began nibbling on it. The egret slowly coiled his neck as the bass began to swim away. Then, in a flash of whiteness, the long neck struck out, piercing the water. He withdrew his beak, flipped the bass into the air, and caught it in his mouth. Then he returned to the nest.

Now he was able to share a nourishing fish with his hungry family because he had made the best use of a limited resource.

THE CHARACTERISTICS OF

THE AMERICAN EGRET IN SCRIPTURE

The egret belongs to the heron and bittern family. Both the heron and the bittern are identified in Scripture as unclean birds and therefore are not to be eaten by man. (See Leviticus 11:19.)

The most striking characteristics of the American egret are its beauty and its subtlety. It is significant that these are the same two qualities that were combined by Satan and the serpent when they beguiled Eve. (See Genesis 3:1.)

The witness of the egret and its flowing plumes during mating season can picture either Christ in His beauty or Satan in his deception, since he appears as an angel of light. (See II Corinthians 11:14.)

God describes the beauty that He gave to Satan in Ezekiel 28:12, *". . . Thou sealest up the sum, full of wisdom, and perfect in beauty."*

The long, snakelike neck of the egret and its barren appearance before maturity not only bear a striking resemblance to the cursed serpent, but serve as a reminder that if we allow Satan to use our resources for his purposes, the glory that God gave us will also be destroyed. *"When thou with rebukes dost correct man for iniquity, thou makest his beauty to consume away like a moth . . ." (Psalm 39:11).*

CHARACTERISTICS AND PHYSICAL FEATURES OF THE EGRET

The American or common egret is a skilled hunter. It combines its white plumage; graceful movements; long, slender neck; sharp, pointed bill; patient demeanor; and its cunning ways to catch fish, frogs, snakes, or crayfish. Because it is so resourceful, the egret expends far less energy in its hunt for food than do other birds of prey.

HOW DOES THE EGRET CATCH FISH BY SETTING OUT BAIT?

On numerous occasions egrets have been observed dropping bread crumbs or other picnic scraps into the water to lure fish. If crumbs are not available the egret will use its own resources to catch its prey.

WHAT DO THE EGRET AND THE SNAKE HAVE IN COMMON?

Wading slowly in the shallows, the egret uses its long yellow beak as a spear. Egrets hunt slowly—step by step—lifting each foot out of the water without a ripple. As a fish, frog, snake, or crayfish comes within striking distance, the egret slowly coils its long neck almost like a snake. Then in an instant it strikes out, piercing its victim with its sharp bill.

In the same movement, it tosses the prey into the air and swallows it whole. After this sudden burst of energy, the egret settles back, preens its ruffled feathers, and begins its hunt again.

WHY DOES THE EGRET ALWAYS SWALLOW FISH HEADFIRST?

Fish have sharp spines in their dorsal fins which point backward. When a fish is swallowed headfirst, the spines fold down easily. If a fish were swallowed tailfirst, the spines would be forced open, causing the fish to stick in the egret's throat.

WHY DOES THE EGRET BECOME A PASSING "CLOUD" TO ITS PREY?

Egrets use their five-foot wingspan to cut down the amount of glare on the water. By casting a shadow on the surface of the water, the egret can spot unsuspecting fish more easily. A fish looking up sees only that which resembles a large white cloud.

HOW IS THE NECK OF THE EGRET AN ASSET AND A HINDRANCE AT THE SAME TIME?

The long neck of the egret is an asset when used to send its sharp bill piercing into its prey. However, on windy days the neck creates problems in making headway through water. Since the neck is extended while hunting, the egret is often blown sideways. To compensate for this it may be forced to tack back and forth in the wind like a sailboat.

Flying low over the water or marsh grass, *the egret beats its wings more slowly and deliberately than other herons. The long wings give its delicate body a buoyancy that appears to defy gravity.*

WHAT HAPPENS TO THE LONG NECK OF THE EGRET DURING FLIGHT?

During takeoff the neck is extended for balance. But, as soon as the egret reaches its desired altitude, the neck is coiled into an S shape, with the head supported between the shoulders. This allows the neck muscles to relax and also makes the shape of the egret in flight more aerodynamic.

WHAT DO EGRETS DEPEND ON FOR A LIFT-OFF INTO THE AIR?

Egrets use their long legs to catapult themselves into the air. Their wings are so powerful and large that an egret can lift itself almost vertically into the air. As the bird begins to get underway, the legs hang horizontally. The neck contracts as the head settles down by successive jerks onto the shoulders, and the S-shaped position is attained.

IN WHAT WAY DO EGRETS "FLY" WITH THEIR LEGS?

Some birds tuck their legs beneath their bodies like retractable landing gear, but not the egret. Egrets stretch their long legs out behind them for balance and for use as rudders. Just like an airplane, egrets can turn to the left or right by merely twisting their feet. Only on short, low flights are the egret's legs allowed to dangle.

HOW DOES HEAT, RATHER THAN COLD, CAUSE THE EGRET TO MIGRATE?

Most birds migrate south during the winter months to get out of the cold. The egret does just the opposite. It flies north during the summer to get out of the heat. It may travel hundreds of miles, as far north as Canada.

HOW CAN THE EGRET WALK WITH ITS FEET NEVER TOUCHING THE GROUND?

The egret's lower leg appears to bend forward at the knee rather than backwards. This gives the egret and other wading birds a curious appearance as they walk. However, the joint halfway between the egret's toes and body is not the knee but the ankle. The portion below the joint is not the leg but rather the foot. The egret walks strictly on its toes, with its feet never touching the ground.

HOW DOES AN EGRET CLEAN ITS PREY AFTER EATING IT?

Because an egret swallows fish and other prey whole as soon as it catches them, there is no time to remove indigestible scales, bones, feathers, or fur. These gradually build up in the egret's stomach. Eventually they are compacted into pellets which the egret coughs up and spits out periodically.

WHY DO EGRETS BLUSH DURING THE MATING SEASON?

During the breeding season, hormonal changes occur in the egret, which cause its bill and the irises of its eyes to flush with blood. The yellow beak turns orange and the irises become bright circles of red.

As the mating season continues, these unique characteristics become even more noticeable. At the height of courtship they give the egret the appearance of blushing.

WHAT UNUSUAL ATTIRE DID GOD PROVIDE FOR THE EGRETS DURING THEIR COURTSHIP?

As the egrets enter into their mating season, both the male and the female develop long plumes called *aigrettes.* These finely feathered plumes drape from the shoulders, down over the back, and cover the tail of the egret. Each egret may have as many as fifty-four of these elegant feathers. Some are as long as twenty-four inches.

HOW DO EGRETS EXCHANGE THEIR GLORY FOR THEIR YOUNG?

The plumage of the mated egrets is quite impressive. However, as their young are raised, the plumes become damaged and deteriorate rapidly. The egret thus trades its beautiful plumes for the greater reward of its young egrets.

HOW DO EGRETS POWDER THEMSELVES?

Under the contour feathers are rows of downy feathers which flake into powder when brushed. Egrets rub their bills into this powder and then preen their feathers. The powder removes fish oil, dirt, and slime.

Originally called Great White Heron, *the egret adopted its name from the shortened form of the French word* aigrette, *meaning "plume."*

HOW DO EGRETS TIE A "LOVE KNOT" AFTER MATING?

After choosing a nesting site, a pair of egrets go through a period much like a honeymoon. The two birds will sit side by side for hours at a time. Occasionally they will stretch their long necks and then gently intertwine them, making a complete circle around each other.

HOW DO EGRETS TURN NEST BUILDING INTO AN ELEGANT CEREMONY?

As nest building begins, there is a ceremonious twig presentation. One egret picks up a twig and bows respectfully at the knees. As the knees bend deeply, the long filmy courtship plumes bounce rhythmically. Twigs may be presented many times before the ritual is ended and serious nest building begins.

Egrets prepare a flimsy, shallow nest on a tree platform. The nest is constructed of twigs and may be lined with leaves and moss. Three to four pale, greenish-blue eggs are laid. The nests are always close to marshes and waterways where the egrets feed during the day.

WHY IS IT BENEFICIAL FOR AN EGRET TO RAISE ITS LEVEL OF LIVING?

In order to reduce competition for nesting sites in a tree, egrets build nests on branches at different levels. Some build on the "first floor" only a few feet above the ground. Others nest on the "top floor" perhaps 130 feet above the ground. By nesting at different levels, many birds can share the same tree. Because of the amount of bird droppings and remains from the dead fish, frogs, crayfish, and other food, the lower level nests have a definite odor!

WHY IS IT IMPORTANT TO TREES THAT EGRETS KEEP MOVING?

Egret droppings and the leftover scraps of fish that fall to the base of nesting trees make good fertilizer. Initially this is good for the tree. As it accumulates over the years, however, the soil becomes too rich and the tree often dies.

WHY DOES THE EGRET TEND TO BE RARE?

The mortality rate for young egrets is surprisingly high. During their first year of life about seventy per cent of the young chicks die. Perhaps fewer than twenty per cent ever reach adulthood.

HOW DID THE BEAUTY OF THE EGRET ENDANGER ITS EXISTENCE?

Around the turn of the century, egret plumes were worth $32 an ounce, more than gold (then $25 an ounce). Because the latest Paris fashions demanded the use of flowing egret feathers, 200,000 birds were killed in one season.

Because the plumes grow on the egret only during courtship and mating, an estimated 300,000 nestlings also died, due to the death of the parents. The American Association of Audubon Societies was instrumental in enacting the Lacy Act of 1916, restricting the yearly slaughter that once took some fifty-five million birds for their skins and feathers.

How is the need to make wise use of resources illustrated in Scripture?

Two kings ruled the same nation at different times in history. Each king had the benefit of the same resources. One used them to promote freedom and the other to promote bondage. Who was the first king?

(Pause for a response—see page 17.)

A powerful army arrived and began taking up positions around three sides of the city. The soldiers were greeted with walls one hundred and fifty feet high. The invaders were prepared for a long and difficult siege.

Inside the city, the proud citizens remained confident. This was not the first time in their long history that invading armies had surrounded them.

They continued trading their silver coins which pictured an eagle with a palm branch and the inscription "Under divine guidance and impregnable." Up to this point that inscription was accurate—not because of them but because of the wisdom of a previous king.

Many years earlier, a wise king surveyed the magnificent cedar forests surrounding his kingdom. He decided to send lumber from them as a special gift to a neighboring king. This act of generosity established a significant relationship between the two nations and God.

This king and his nation became world famous as a trade center. Their power and prestige was remarkable since they were a small country.

But under a later king, their lust for gain caused their trading to expand to that which brought God's judgment. Godly prophets had warned, *"By the multitude of thy merchandise they have filled the midst of thee with violence."* The bills of lading included iron, tin, lead, slaves, emeralds, wheat, oil, wine, spices, gold, and rich apparel.

Among their slaves were the people of God whom they sold to other nations. These were the very people whom that earlier king had benefited.

God promised that those who blessed His people would be blessed and those who cursed His people would be cursed. The present siege was a fulfillment of God's judgment. After thirteen years, the great city of Tyre fell to the Babylonian army. The city and people were destroyed.

The king who was judged had used the cedars of Lebanon to build ships which carried the people of God into slavery. This was a striking contrast to King Hiram, who years earlier had used the same cedar tree forests to furnish lumber for the temple of God.

From II Samuel 5:11–12, I Kings 5:10–11, and Ezekiel 27–28:19

KING OF TYRE, A FRIEND TO ISRAEL WHO WAS BLESSED WITH PROSPERITY AND PEACE

***The cedar of Lebanon** grows to a height of 120 feet with a girth of 40 feet. Its wood repels insects, has a pleasing fragrance, a warm red color, and remarkable durability.*

This monarch of the evergreens is mentioned in seventy-one Scripture passages. It was Tyre's most valuable resource.

Hiram ruled Tyre and all of Phoenicia when David was king in Israel. His city of Tyre was ideally situated on the west end of the Mediterranean Sea. Part of the city was on an island, and part was on the mainland. The two harbors of the rocky island were connected by a canal; one harbor faced north and the other south. A barrier wall which reached 150 feet in height protected the side facing the shore.

If attacked, the mainland citizens sought refuge on the island where there was room for forty thousand people. Tyre had been given to the tribe of Asher as an inheritance by Joshua, and even at that time it was referred to as *"the strong city Tyre." (See Joshua 19:29.) "But the Asherites dwelt among the Canaanites, the inhabitants of the land: for they did not drive them out" (Judges 1:32).*

THE "GOLDEN AGE" OF HIRAM'S REIGN

Hiram reigned during the "Golden Age" of Tyrian affluence and power. Under his capable leadership Phoenicia became famous throughout the world as sea trade and exploration expanded rapidly. Hiram constructed a long breakwater at Tyre to improve its function as a seaport.

Because the country was small and unable to produce an adequate food supply, it imported many agricultural items. Commodities were needed to export in exchange, and the Phoenicians became experts in commerce. Their caravans by land and ships by sea combed the world for new areas of trade. As raw materials poured into the city, the people became skilled in the industrial arts, turning the materials into valuable articles of manufacture.

The prophet Ezekiel gave a lengthy list of their products and the countries with which they traded. He cataloged ship boards, masts, oars, benches of ivory, fine linen, blue and purple dye, silver, iron, tin, lead, slaves vessels of brass, horses, horsemen, mules, horns of ivory and ebony, emeralds, embroidered work, coral, agate, wheat, honey, oil, balm, wine, white wool, bright iron, cassia, calamus, precious clothes for chariots, lambs, rams, goats, spices, precious stones, gold, blue clothes, and chests of rich apparel. (See Ezekiel 27.)

Solomon's Temple

King Hiram used the cedars of Lebanon to establish a friendly relationship with Israel. This lumber was ideal for building the temple of God.

RECOGNITION FROM A RULER OF GREAT RESOURCES

In an official act of recognition and good will after David occupied Jerusalem, *". . . Hiram king of Tyre sent messengers to David, and cedar trees, and carpenters, and masons: and they built David an house" (II Samuel 5:11).* It was a most generous gift which David greatly appreciated.

The eastern part of Lebanon, which belonged to Israel, produced only fir, pine, and cypress trees. The northwestern area, where cedar flourished, belonged to Phoenicia. Because cedar is strong, durable, beautiful, and fragrant, it was used for the most expensive buildings. This wise gesture established a lifelong friendship between Hiram and David—one which proved to be mutually beneficial.

THE HIGHEST USE OF HIRAM'S ABUNDANCE

When David died and was succeeded by Solomon, Hiram wanted to maintain friendly relations with Israel. He supplied Solomon with lumber and skilled workers for the building of the temple. Solomon reciprocated with large quantities of wheat and oil. (See I Kings 5:10–11.) In addition, Hiram's servants, "shipmen that had knowledge of the sea," showed Solomon's sailors the route to Ophir where large quantities of gold were obtained and brought back. (See I Kings 9:27–28.)

Hiram is known as the friend of David and Solomon. He was the powerful and wealthy king of a pagan country, but he blessed the nation of Israel in many ways. His life is an example of the promise given to Abraham, *"And I will bless them that bless thee . . ." (Genesis 12:3).*

Phoenician Merchant Ship

A later king of Tyre used the cedars to build slave ships which carried God's people captive to other nations.

CHARACTER SKETCH OF HIRAM

HOW WAS HIRAM USED BY GOD TO ENCOURAGE DAVID?

When David was a young man, he received some staggering promises from the Lord. While just a shepherd, he was anointed to be king of Israel by the prophet Samuel. (See I Samuel 16:13.)

After Saul's death, David was proclaimed king by the tribe of Judah. He pursued peace with the rest of the nation and fought and defeated their enemies. Finally David was asked by the elders of Israel to be their king as well. (See II Samuel 5:1–3.) David conquered the Jebusite stronghold of Zion in Jerusalem and moved his headquarters there.

It was there that the Lord motivated Hiram of Tyre to encourage David by building him a beautiful palace in Jerusalem. *"And David perceived that the Lord had established him king over Israel, and that he had exalted his kingdom for his people Israel's sake" (II Samuel 5:12)*. David was in Jerusalem as the head of a unified nation, and now his most prosperous and influential neighbor had given official recognition to his kingdom. The great promises of God given in his youth were now a reality.

WHAT MOTIVATED HIRAM TO BE GENEROUS TOWARD DAVID AND SOLOMON?

Hiram was not generous simply to placate a strong neighbor. It is true that Israel's army had become powerful under David's leadership, but the Phoenician navy and the offshore island fortress of Tyre gave Hiram a measure of immunity against Israeli attack. Hiram was generous because he recognized David and later Solomon as men of great wisdom and leadership.

He was attracted to David as a person as well as a power. He had observed David's rise to leadership and knew that such a man would guide Israel to peace and prosperity for years to come.

When Solomon was appointed as David's successor, Hiram pledged continued support, *"... for Hiram was ever a lover of David" (I Kings 5:1)*. There is no doubt that Hiram was motivated by the best interests of his own country, but he was also motivated by personal respect and a deep friendship with these two kings of Israel.

WAS HIRAM A WISE RULER?

Yes, he was. Hiram knew his country's weaknesses and strengths and adapted his policies accordingly. He was renowned as a builder of magnificent edifices. He was considered brilliant in foreign and domestic policy.

The Jewish historian, Josephus, records Dius the Phoenician's account of an interesting game played by Hiram and Solomon. The men exchanged riddles and offered prizes for their solutions. It is said that although Solomon proved to be superior in wisdom, Hiram found a man of Tyre who finally invented a riddle that even Solomon could not solve (*Against Apion*, I, Section 17).

Hiram was what Jesus referred to as "worldly wise" in the parable of the dishonest steward. *"... For the children of this world are in their generation wiser than the children of light" (Luke 16:8)*.

There is no evidence to indicate that Hiram gave up his pagan beliefs. He did, however, have a certain amount of spiritual perception. *"And it came to pass, when Hiram heard the words of Solomon, that he rejoiced greatly, and said, Blessed be the Lord this day, which hath given unto David a wise son over this great people" (I Kings 5:7)*. It is unfortunate that Solomon became such a poor representative of Jehovah as he grew older.

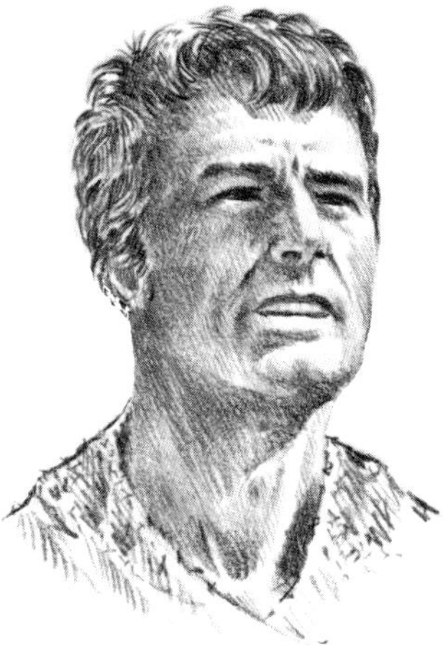

KING DAVID

KING SOLOMON

When King Solomon wrote, *"Thine own friend, and thy father's friend, forsake not..." (Proverbs 27:10), he could very well have had in mind the special friendship that his father had with King Hiram.*

HIRAM
hī-ram

CHAPTER NINETEEN

Resourcefulness

. . . Is recognizing that valuable resources come out of right relationships

"Honour thy father and mother . . . that it may be well with thee, and thou mayest live long on the earth."

Ephesians 6:2–3

"House and riches are the inheritance of fathers: and a prudent wife is from the Lord."

Proverbs 19:14

"Lo, children are an heritage of the Lord: and the fruit of the womb is his reward."

Psalm 127:3

Living Lessons on Resourcefulness . . .

FROM THE PAGES OF SCRIPTURE

Giving must be based on receiving. We came into the world with nothing, thus God asks, "*. . . What hast thou that thou didst not receive? . . .*" *(I Corinthians 4:7)*. Valuable resources are received by maintaining God-given relationships. God will enable a wise receiver of these resources to give to others.

Just as valuable resources can be gained by maintaining right relationships, tragic losses will occur when important relationships are broken for selfish purposes. God provides an awesome illustration of this principle in Scripture.

ILLUSTRATED IN THE WORLD OF NATURE

MUSK OX *Ovibos moschatus*

Musk oxen live in the Arctic where the summers are but one long day, and the winters are an endless night. They roam the treeless tundra in small herds of less than one hundred. Their compact bodies and short legs, which help conserve vital body heat, are covered by a thick outer layer of coarse, dark brown hair. The coat is so thick that it sheds both snow and rain. The inner coat of soft brown hair provides insulation against temperatures that approach -100°F.

Musk oxen do not migrate but seek exposed, windswept slopes where the snow is shallow and food is more easily accessible.

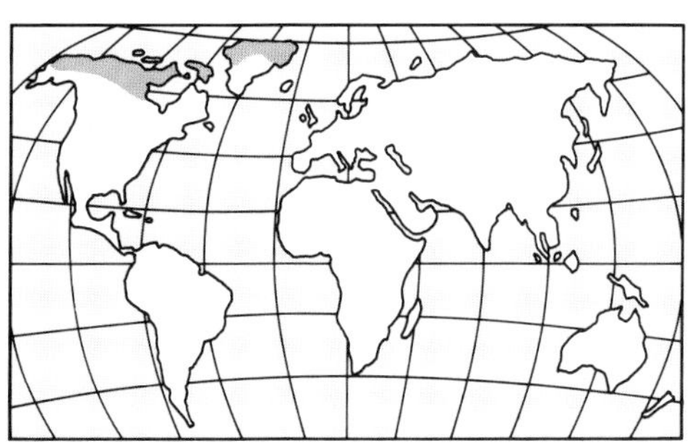

The range and habitat of the musk ox

How are the resources of right relationships illustrated in the world of nature?

Shortly after daybreak an arctic explorer stood at the base of an eight thousand foot mountain. The temperature was thirty degrees below zero. He studied the frigid environment approximately six hundred miles from the North Pole.

Suddenly, a strange feeling overcame him and he considered turning back. His uneasiness was heightened by an unusual pattern of tracks in the snow. He quickly recognized that most of the prints belonged to arctic wolves.

As he climbed the mountain, the wolf prints disappeared. However, he still sensed an eerie presence. Something was watching him. Pulling himself up to the next snowy rise, the explorer was stunned by a rush of fur that flashed by his face! Wolves!?

No. Musk oxen. The shaggy animals swiftly formed a defensive circle. With their long "guard hair" flowing in the arctic wind, they stood shoulder to shoulder facing forward with heads and horns lowered. The young calves huddled safely in the center of their impenetrable wall.

The awestruck explorer backed away, photographed the amazing sight, and hastily retreated down the mountainside. Along the way he again noticed the wolf prints. He tried to reassure himself as he frantically stumbled through the deep snow. "Wolves don't attack humans! Do they?"

After four hours of struggling through the snow, the exhausted explorer reached his snowmobile. Now he was safe—he thought. His base camp was still twenty-six miles away and he remembered that he had experienced trouble with his drive belt slipping on his way to the mountain.

In fear and apprehension he nervously turned the ignition key. He revved up the engine and started out over the white expanse of barren tundra and frozen lakes. A half mile from camp, out of the corner of his eye he spotted a bolt of white fur on the move.

His first thought was "polar bear," but a split second later he knew it was a wolf. He then spotted another wolf in the distance and realized that they were running full speed at him.

Under full throttle he sped toward his camp. Glancing back, he saw that the wolves were closing in on him. As he roared into the lonely camp, he hit the kill switch and dashed into his flimsy shelter.

He blocked the door and peered through the small window of his shack. Only five feet away stood the huge wolves. Their fearless expressions sent a wave of terror up and down his spine. He knew that it would have been no contest between himself and just one wolf.

His knees shook uncontrollably for an hour as the wolves encircled the cabin. During the four-day siege, he began to understand why the wolf tracks had stopped on the mountainside. The wolves were no match for the combined protection that the musk oxen gave to each other. But the wolves were fearless against one man who tried to make it on his own.

(A true story that took place in Canada's Northwest Territories in 1984 during preparations for a historic walk to the North Pole in 1985.)

THE CHARACTERISTICS OF

THE MUSK OX IN SCRIPTURE

The mutual defense that musk oxen provide is a significant illustration of the protection which Christians are to give to each other.

The musk ox knows that the wolf is out to destroy the weak and the young among its ranks, and the entire herd resolutely refuses to let this occur. Christ warned His disciples, *"Beware of false prophets, which come to you in sheep's clothing, but inwardly they are ravening wolves" (Matthew 7:15).*

Paul further warned, *"For I know this, that after my departing shall grievous wolves enter in among you, not sparing the flock" (Acts 20:29).*

Other herds and flocks flee from wolves, allowing them to destroy the weak and the young. The musk oxen unite, stand shoulder to shoulder, and face their enemy.

Similarly, Christians are to strengthen one another, *"Not forsaking the assembling of ourselves together, as the manner of some is . . ." (Hebrews 10:25).*

When it comes to standing and facing our enemy, we are commanded to *". . . stand against the wiles of the devil . . . and having done all, to stand" (Ephesians 6:11, 13).*

Outside enemies should only reinforce the awareness of our need for one another. (See I Corinthians 12:20–26.)

CHARACTERISTICS AND PHYSICAL FEATURES OF THE MUSK OX

Musk oxen rarely run from a fight. Instead they find strength in unity. When threatened, musk oxen form an impenetrable circle called a *phalanx*. The weak and the calves huddle in the center while the strong stand shoulder to shoulder with horns lowered. Together they can withstand the attack of any creature in the Arctic.

HOW DO MOTHERS PRESERVE THE LIVES OF THEIR YOUNG WITH A LICKING AND A MARKING?

When a calf is born, its immediate enemy is the cold. While it is still wet, ice may form on its fur, reducing its insulating value and allowing the calf to freeze. To prevent this, the mother licks her calf dry.

As she licks, she also places her own scent on the newborn so that she can distinguish it from other calves in the herd. A young calf will instinctively huddle under its mother whenever danger is present.

Calves are protected by a circle of horns.

A musk ox can throw a wolf so high that the fall alone may break its legs or ribs.

The rough, broad base of the horn, known as the boss, may be ten inches wide and several inches thick. The tips are worn smooth by rubbing.

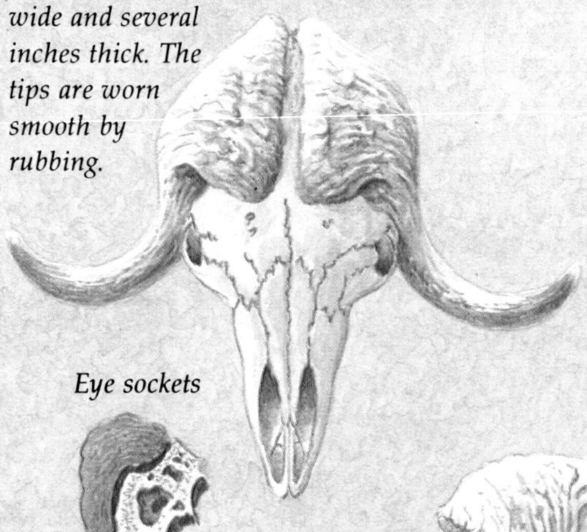

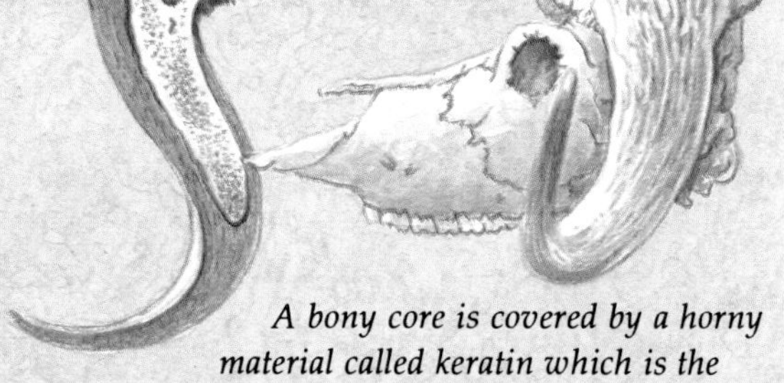

A bony core is covered by a horny material called keratin which is the same substance making up fingernails, beaks, claws, and even turtle shells.

HOW DOES A HERD OF MUSK OX DEFEAT A PACK OF WOLVES?

The chief enemy of the musk ox is the Great White Arctic Wolf. Even wolves, however, must band together in packs to have any chance against the solid defense of a phalanx of musk oxen. Individual wolves that come too close are charged by a single bull. As the bull leaves the circle, his vacant position vanishes as the others close together. The wolf and bull fight one on one.

A wolf caught on the horns of a bull may be thrown into the herd to be trampled. If a wolf is able to mount the back of a bull, the bull will buck and twist like a rodeo steer or may fall on one side, crushing the wolf between its massive shoulder and the ground.

When the bull tires, he backs up, and the phalanx formation opens to let him join the circle once more. As one bull leaves the battle, another will unexpectedly charge forth to take up the fight.

WHAT SOUND IS MORE THREATENING TO THE MUSK OX THAN THE HOWL OF A WOLF?

The buzz of a mosquito. As summer arrives on the tundra, so do mosquitoes and blackflies. While the outer coat of hair protects most of the musk ox from torment, its small ears and the edges of its eyelids are not protected. By the end of summer, both areas are very raw and swollen.

WHAT IS THE SURPRISING PHYSICAL FEATURE ABOUT THE IMPRESSIVE MUSK OX?

Its small stature. When fully grown a large bull will only stand four and a half to five feet at the shoulders and weigh between 500 to 600 pounds. Cows are even smaller, reaching a height of three and a half to four feet, and weighing 300 to 400 pounds. In captivity, however, bulls may weigh up to 1,400 pounds.

WHAT IS THE REAL SIGN OF A "BOSS" IN THE HERD?

By the second year after birth bulls are easily identified by a thick, broad plate called a "boss" which covers its head like a helmet. By the sixth year the boss on a bull's head becomes as hard as steel.

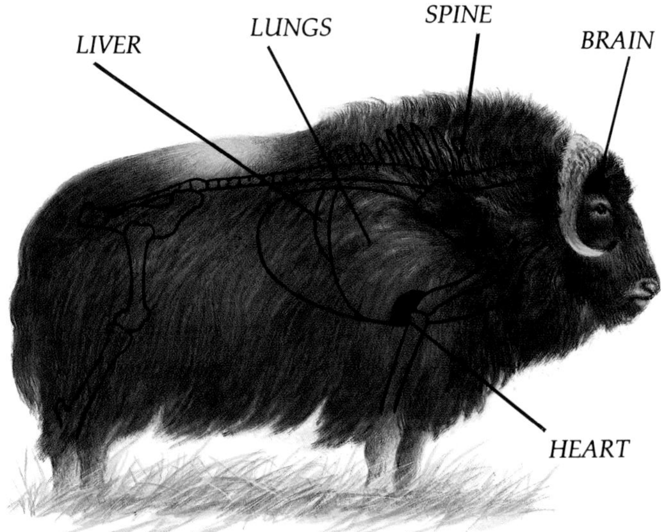

WHY IS IT IMPOSSIBLE TO CONCEAL CONFLICTS BETWEEN MUSK OXEN?

During the first two weeks of August the adult bulls begin to fight for the control of the herd. As one bull challenges another, they charge together with heads lowered. Their impact is greater than two cars hitting head-on at twenty miles an hour, and it can be heard over a mile away.

Somehow the crash is absorbed by the thick boss. The bulls continue charging each other until one bull finally staggers away, admitting defeat.

Bloodshot eyes, defiant snorts, and the strong smell of musk signal a musk ox's rage.

WHEN A GRIZZLY BEAR ATTACKS A MUSK OX, WHICH ONE WILL WIN?

The musk ox will be the winner in such a contest. Even the grizzly bear is no match for its powerful charge and hardened horns.

WHAT UNIQUE SIGNAL DOES A MUSK OX GIVE BEFORE IT CHARGES?

When an enraged bull is about to charge, it presses its nose against its front leg. This releases a liquid from a gland a few inches below its eye. This liquid has a strong musky odor which an attacker had better heed as a warning of the imminent charge. As the bull musk ox grows older, he becomes increasingly irritable, and it takes little to provoke a charge.

Running through snow

HOW DO MUSK OXEN DEMONSTRATE SKILL AND RESOURCEFULNESS IN WATER, SNOW, AND ON MOUNTAINS?

Musk oxen are really quite nimble and swift. They can maintain a speed of fifteen to twenty miles per hour for long distances without tiring. They are good swimmers, swimming with just the tops of their heads showing above the water. In the snow, they place their back feet in the same holes as the front to make running easier. They are even at home on rocky cliffs, often running across them at full speed with loose debris falling from beneath their hoofs.

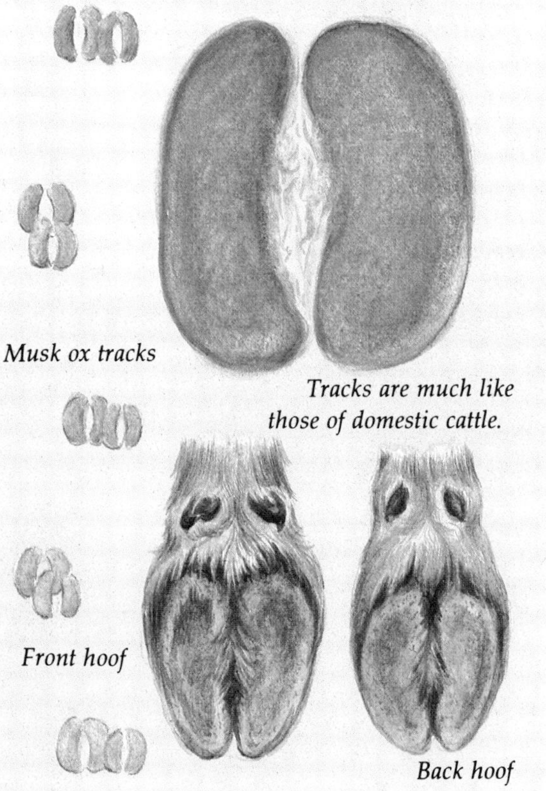

Musk ox tracks

Tracks are much like those of domestic cattle.

Front hoof

Back hoof

HOW DOES THE HAIR OF THE MUSK OX GIVE IT BETTER TRACTION IN THE SNOW?

Hair grows between the broad spreading hoofs, giving the musk ox greater traction on snow and ice. Because the hoofs spread, they act much like snow shoes, distributing the musk ox's weight over a greater area. The edges of the hoofs are quite sharp, enabling the musk ox to cut into and grip the surface of the frozen tundra.

Musk ox hoofs are peculiar because the front pair is larger than the rear pair. The larger front feet carry the weight of the massive head and shoulders. The smaller back feet follow in the same step carrying the much smaller hindquarter.

Long guard hairs cover a silky layer of underwool so dense that neither cold nor moisture can penetrate it.

Cowberry

Eskimo loom

The wool is woven for rich warm clothing because it does not shrink and is easily dyed.

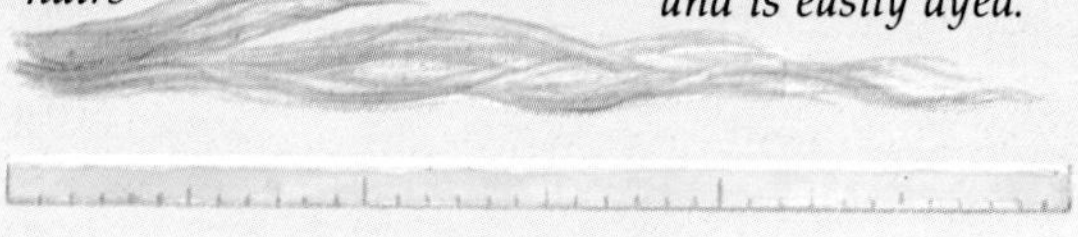

Guard hairs

Thirty-six inches

WHY ARE MUSK OXEN EIGHT TIMES WARMER THAN SHEEP?

Eskimos call the musk ox *oominomak,* meaning the "bearded one." This refers to long guard hairs which surround its body. Beneath this outer protection is a dense undercoat of silky hair which allows the musk ox to inhabit sub-zero polar regions.

The insulating underfur grows to lengths of four to eight inches. Its soft kinky fibers trap air, which provides the insulation, making the fur eight times warmer than sheep's wool.

HOW DOES THE MUSK OX DEMONSTRATE RESOURCEFULNESS DURING WINTER GRAZING?

In summer when vegetation is fresh and water is plentiful, musk oxen eat and drink heartily. When grazing is confined to wind-blown patches of grass, sedge, and low growing willows, the musk ox retains these high fiber and hard to digest foods longer in its digestive system. It thus extracts more nutrients from them, while having less water waste.

HOW MANY POUNDS OF MUSK OX WOOL WOULD IT TAKE TO MAKE A TWENTY-FIVE MILE LONG STRAND?

Just one pound. The wool of the musk ox is so light and thin that one pound of it can be spun into a forty-strand thread twenty-five miles long. The Eskimos call this wool *qiviut.* It is similar to cashmere which is produced by goats. However, goats usually produce less than three ounces of wool a year, while an adult musk ox can produce six pounds.

WHY WOULD IT BE DANGEROUS TO SHEAR A MUSK OX LIKE A SHEEP?

Hair must be gathered from the musk ox by combing it out in the early summer as the musk ox begins to shed, rather than by shearing it. If sheared like a sheep, the musk ox would not be able to survive the frigid winter.

How is the high cost of broken relationships illustrated in Scripture?

Who gained great resources by standing "shoulder to shoulder" with his father and with God but later "broke rank" for selfish reasons and passed a legacy of deception and division to many generations?

(Pause for a response—see page 17.)

In the year 1965 B.C. a caravan arrived at a distant city. The leader of the caravan nervously watched as several men approached.

The men responded exactly as he had feared. As they gave him a quick greeting, their eyes were attracted to his beautiful wife. Their attention deepened his alarm as he thought to himself, "They will kill me so they can marry her."

One of the men interrupted his thoughts, "Who, may I ask, is this beautiful woman?"

"She is my sister," he quickly responded. Immediately their attitudes changed toward him. They treated him like a long lost brother and offered their help in any way he could use it. He declined and finally the eager men left.

In the months that followed, his sensitive conscience forced him to justify the lie that he had told. "After all," he concluded, "I'm only following the example of my father. He was a Godly man, and he gave the same response. Nothing ever came of it. And besides, what good would I be to God if I were dead?"

For a long time he was careful to conceal his deception in public, and his family cooperated with his scheme. They cooperated too well.

Years later, the eyes of that man grew dim. He called in his firstborn son and said, "Go out into the field and kill a deer. Make me a venison dinner—the kind I love! Then I will give you a special blessing." The son left with eager anticipation.

Soon the father smelled the savory meat that he loved. But when the meal was brought to him, something seemed to be wrong. "How is it that you found the deer so quickly?" he asked.

"Because the Lord thy God brought it to me," responded his son. The answer increased the old man's apprehension.

"Come here, my son, so that I can be sure that you are my firstborn son." His son obeyed and satisfied the father's concerns. The father then ate the meal and gave the coveted blessing.

The son had no sooner left the room when a voice rang out to the father. "Let my father arise and eat of his son's venison and bless me."

Panic gripped the father's heart as he asked, "Who are you?" and heard the reply, "I am your firstborn son." At that moment, the old father began to tremble. Immediately the father realized what had happened. His second-born son had done to him what he had done to others—pretended to be a brother that he was not!

Isaac's lie continued a legacy of deception and division for generations to come.

From Genesis 20, 27

Abraham's well at Beer-sheba *is so named because of the agreement that Abraham made with Abimelech. It is "the well of the seven ewe lambs." (See Genesis 21:22–32.) Abraham and his family lived near this well for many years. (See Genesis 22:19.)*

ABRAHAM
SARAH
"And Abraham said of Sarah his wife, She is my sister . . ." (Genesis 20:2).
ISAAC
REBEKAH
"He said, she is my sister: for he feared to say, She is my wife . . ." (Genesis 26:7).
JACOB
ISAAC
LABAN
JACOB
LEAH
". . . I am thy son, thy firstborn son Esau . . ." (Genesis 27:32).
". . . Wherefore then hast thou beguiled me?" (Genesis 29:25).

When Abraham and Isaac *lied about their wives, they established a legacy of deception for generations to come.*

ISAAC, THE PATRIARCH WHO GAINED AND LOST GREAT RESOURCES THROUGH RELATIONSHIPS

In his youth Isaac demonstrated the qualities of a loyal and obedient son—even to the point of being willing to lay down his life at God's direction. (See Genesis 22.) Through his obedience, Isaac received a rich inheritance—not only in terms of money, but in rich relationships and in wise counsel on how to maintain them.

Because Isaac was in fellowship with his father, Abraham was able to provide God's choice of a wife for him. But he gave Isaac something equally as important: the method by which God provided the right wife.

THE HERITAGE THAT WAS OVERLOOKED

God lamented, *"Oh that my people had hearkened unto me, and Israel had walked in my ways!" (Psalm 81:13)*. Then God explained what He would have done, *"I should soon have subdued their enemies . . . but their time should have endured for ever" (Psalm 81:14–15)*. Based on this we are prompted to inquire, "What might God have done in Isaac's life if he would have followed with his sons the method which his father used to provide a wife for him?" If Isaac had sent a trusted servant back to his country and his kindred to secure a bride for his firstborn, Esau, he could have returned with Leah, Laban's firstborn daughter, since it was the custom for the oldest daughter to be married first. (See Genesis 29:26.)

It is easy then to also see what could have happened if Isaac had repeated this same procedure for his secondborn son. Jacob would have married Rachel, and he would have loved her just as his father had loved Rebekah. (See Genesis 24:67.)

Think of the conflicts that could have been avoided. Jacob's firstborn son would have been Joseph whom he favored! The constant marriage tensions between Leah and Rachel would not have taken place, nor the competition between Jacob and Laban. Thus there would have been no need for Rachel to steal her father's idol and die a premature death because of Jacob's curse upon whoever stole it. (See Genesis 31.)

Jacob could have also avoided the conflict with his brother Esau. Jacob could then have spent twenty years laboring for his own family rather than for someone else. And Rachel, with a longer life, could have given Jacob twelve sons, along with the heritage of harmony!

THE HIDDEN CAUSE OF FAILURE

Why did all this not take place? Scripture warns, *"Be not deceived; God is not mocked: for whatsoever a man soweth, that shall he also reap" (Galatians 6:7)*.

When Abraham was faced with the danger of being killed because of the attractiveness of his wife, he lied about her by saying, *"She is my sister." (See Genesis 20.)* Years later, when Isaac was faced with the same circumstances in the country of the Philistines, he also lied by saying that Rebekah was his sister. Abraham gave a "half lie"; Isaac gave a "full lie." (See Genesis 26:7–11.)

Isaac showed favoritism to his son Esau which caused rivalry between the brothers. Isaac's son Jacob showed favoritism to his son Joseph which caused deep resentment between Joseph and Jacob's other sons. In both Isaac's and Jacob's families anger turned into plans of murder.

CHARACTER SKETCH OF ISAAC

HOW DID ISAAC RECEIVE A "MIXED" HERITAGE?

Isaac received a full and rich inheritance from his father, since he was the son of promise. (See Genesis 25:5.) Also because of Isaac's submission to his father's direction for marriage, he received a beautiful wife whom he loved. (See Genesis 24:67.)

However, God explains that the sins of the fathers are also passed on to the children to the third and fourth generation. (See Exodus 20:5.) Abraham not only passed on to Isaac the general sin nature from Adam, but he also passed on his own special tendency to deception.

Isaac's father was a great man of faith. He was the friend of God. However, Scripture records his "half lie" about his wife to protect his own life. (See Genesis 20.)

WHY WAS ISAAC RESPONSIBLE FOR HIS OWN RESPONSES?

Isaac received God's empowering grace to overcome the sins of his forefathers—just as all of us do through faith in Christ's sacrificial work: *". . . Where sin abounded, grace did much more abound" (Romans 5:20).*

Isaac was therefore fully responsible for engaging in the same deception as his father. He too lied about his wife in order to save his own life, and by so doing he placed her in moral jeopardy. (See Genesis 26:6–11.)

His actions were directly contrary to God's design that a husband should lay down his life for his wife as Christ did for the Church. (See Ephesians 5:25.) God used a Philistine king to rebuke Isaac for his deception. (See Genesis 26:10.)

HOW DID ISAAC LOSE HIS MOST VALUABLE RESOURCES?

Isaac was of a sensitive spirit. When conflicts arose over the wells that his servants had dug, he refused to fight over them. Instead, he turned them over to the contending herdsmen. (See Genesis 26:19–22.)

The loss of two valuable wells to Abimelech could be considered restitution for the gifts Isaac received from him under false pretense. However, Isaac also diminished the potential of his own marriage and family to be a Godly influence.

His wife and son used deception on him to steal the blessing from his favorite son, Esau. Esau caused his father and mother grief by marrying a Hittite girl. (See Genesis 26:34.)

Isaac's greatest loss, however, was in the ranks of his grandchildren. They were his crown since *"children's children are the crown of old men . . ." (Proverbs 17:6).*

The deception multiplied in his grandchildren. The sons of Jacob sold Joseph into slavery and deceived their father into believing that Joseph was slain by a wild beast. That action resulted in God's discipline of the grandchildren and their descendents. For 430 years they served as slaves in Egypt—the high cost of broken relationships through deception!

The Arrival of Rebekah

The method by which Abraham secured a wife for Isaac was a valuable part of the heritage which he passed on to his son.

ISAAC
ī-zik

CHAPTER TWENTY

Resourcefulness

. . . Is extending my ability to give by avoiding entrapments

"A prudent man foreseeth the evil, and hideth himself: but the simple pass on, and are punished."

Proverbs 22:3

Living Lessons on Resourcefulness . . .

FROM THE PAGES OF SCRIPTURE

The more we give, the more dangers there are of entrapments which will cut off our ability to give. Thus, one of the most important ingredients of resourcefulness is a practical working knowledge of human nature. By it we recognize when and how to give a gift, as well as discern what kind of a gift to give to avoid entrapments.

A wise advisor to a king used the resource of understanding human nature to root out rebellion and restore the king. His resourcefulness has also greatly enriched our lives.

ILLUSTRATED IN THE WORLD OF NATURE

MUSKIE *Esox masquinongy*

The muskellunge, or muskie, is a predator fish with a body about five to six times as long as it is around. Like other members of the pike family, it has a head shaped like a duck's bill. Its fins are set much farther back on its body than fins on other fish, and its sides are typically marked with dark vertical bars.

A large muskie requires several acres of water to supply it with sufficient food. Growing from an egg one-tenth of an inch long, an average muskie reaches three to four feet in length. In its lifetime, it will have eaten over four tons of food.

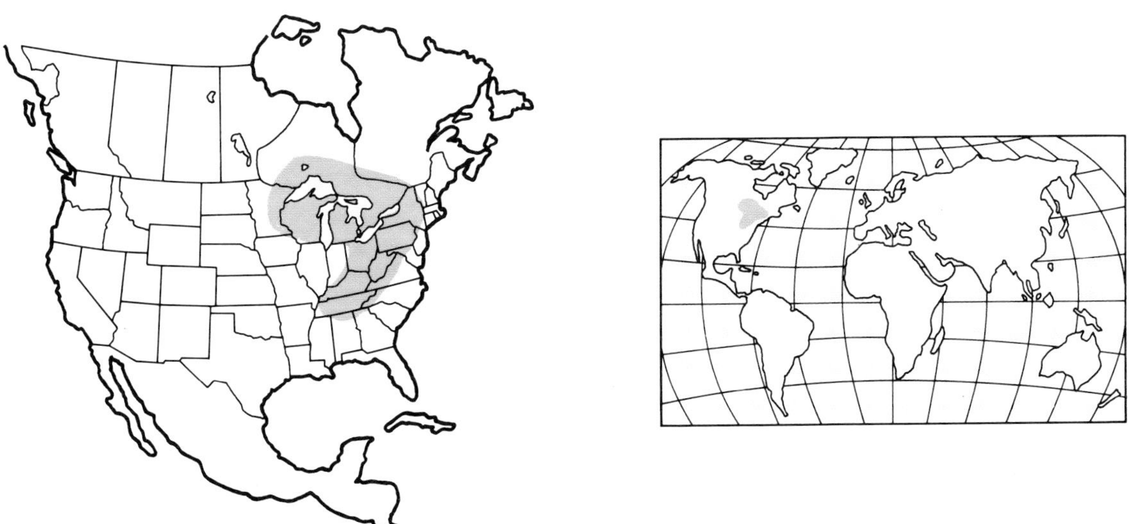

The range and habitat of the muskie

How is the God-given ability to escape entrapment illustrated in the world of nature?

A sleek, four and one-half foot muskie slowly weaved his way through the tall underwater weeds. The muskie's olive green back matched the dark lake bottom, and the rippled stripes on his sides blended with the water plants.

Suddenly, he spotted what looked like a meal moving through the lily pads up near the surface. In a burst of speed he headed for the object. His six inch wide mouth opened and then closed across his intended meal.

Too late, he realized that he had bitten onto a sharp-pronged fishing lure. Several times before he had struck lures; however, each time he had been able to spit them out. This time a quick strong jerk sank the sharp hooks deep into his mouth.

With a swift flick of his tail, he attempted to swim away. But now he was aware that he was no longer free. A taut line was connected to the lure that was hooked in his mouth. With great effort he tried to pull himself loose. Each time the taut line held him captive.

He then changed his approach. With a swift run he broke the surface of the water and made a spectacular leap into the air. As he danced on the tip of his tail, he threw his head back and forth trying to fling the lure out of his mouth. Unsuccessful, he toppled back into the water with a splash. As the water closed in around him he dove for the bottom. He lay there motionless for several moments.

Then, he began to rise and swim straight toward the ominous hull from which the line came. He circled it again and again instinctively sensing that a tangled line would produce slackness which would give greater opportunity to fling the lure from his mouth. However, the line was kept free, and he remained securely attached.

As his powerful body began to tire he found himself being pulled toward the boat. He dove again and again in fruitless attempts to gain his freedom. Finally, with strength dissipated, the muskie was pulled into a net and hauled up into the boat.

A cheer of delight echoed across the water as the hooks were removed from this trophy catch. Soon the motor on the boat was started, and the triumphant captor headed for the shore.

Deep within the muskie, the instinct for escape stirred. He summoned one final burst of energy and without warning unleashed a mighty series of flips in the boat. His tail flailed like a windmill. His sharp teeth were an awesome warning not to get near.

On his final leap he managed to throw himself over the side of the boat. The stunned fisherman helplessly watched as his prize disappeared below the surface of the water.

Once again the great muskie had prolonged his life by resourcefully using his God-given abilities to escape entrapment.

THE CHARACTERISTICS OF

THE MUSKIE IN SCRIPTURE

The unusual ability of the muskie to elude clever bait and even avoid capture when hooked is a characteristic that has rich spiritual application for every Christian.

The muskie does not jump at every lure, just as the Christian should suspect and reject temptations. *"But every man is tempted, when he is drawn away of his own lust . . ." (James 1:14).*

Even when snared, the muskie does not surrender in defeat, but gives his immediate and full attention to escape. God gives similar instruction to a man caught in a financial trap. *"Give not sleep to thine eyes, nor slumber to thine eyelids. Deliver thyself . . ." (Proverbs 6:4–5).*

When hooked, the muskie's first response is to flee. Often its strength and speed will break the line, and acids will cause the hook to eventually drop away. Scripture warns youths who are hooked by the allurements of immorality to *"flee also youthful lusts . . ." (II Timothy 2:22).*

If the muskie cannot break the line, it goes deep. *"Counsel in the heart of man is like deep water . . ." (Proverbs 20:5).*

The muskie's final lunge is an apt picture of our need to cry out to God when escape looks impossible. *". . . Call upon me in the day of trouble: I will deliver thee, and thou shalt glorify me" (Psalm 50:15).*

CHARACTERISTICS AND PHYSICAL FEATURES OF THE MUSKIE

Because of their elusive nature and spectacular fighting abilities, muskies are perhaps the most thrilling of all freshwater game fish to catch. Difficult to hook and even harder to land, the muskie has an uncanny set of skills that helps it avoid capture.

When hooked, it charges, leaps, rolls, thrashes, and dives. Even when lying in the boat, a muskie will use every possible resource to regain its freedom.

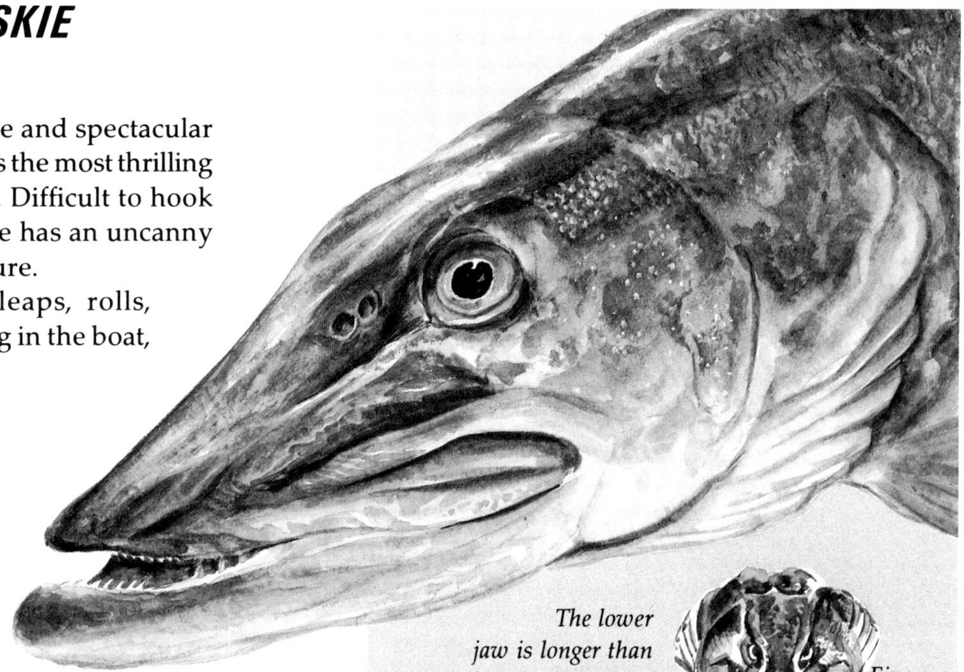

HOW DID THE MUSKIE GET ITS NAME?

The name *muskie* is short for *muskellunge* which may have come from the Ojibway Indian word *maskinonge*. The word *mas* means "ugly," and the word *kinonge* means "fish." *Maskinonge*, then, means "ugly fish." Another possible derivation may have come from French settlers who named the fish *maggue allongee* meaning "long face." Whatever the origin, the muskie is indeed an ugly fish with a long face.

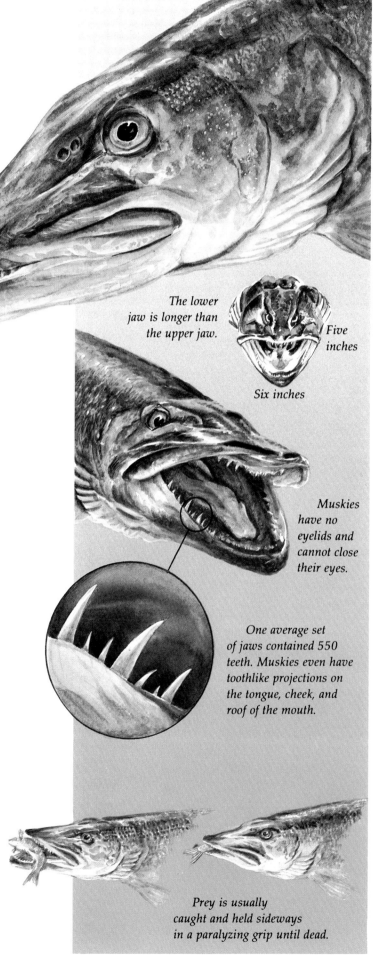

The lower jaw is longer than the upper jaw.

Five inches

Six inches

HOW CAN THE MUSKIE HEAR WITHOUT EARS?

Strictly speaking, muskies do not have ears, although they still have a keen sense of hearing. Muskies "hear" through a network of nerves that run along each side of the body. This network is called the *lateral line*. Scales that cover this line are dotted with holes to allow sound vibrations to enter the skin and stimulate the nerve endings. On a large muskie the lateral line, or "ears," may be almost as long as the fish itself.

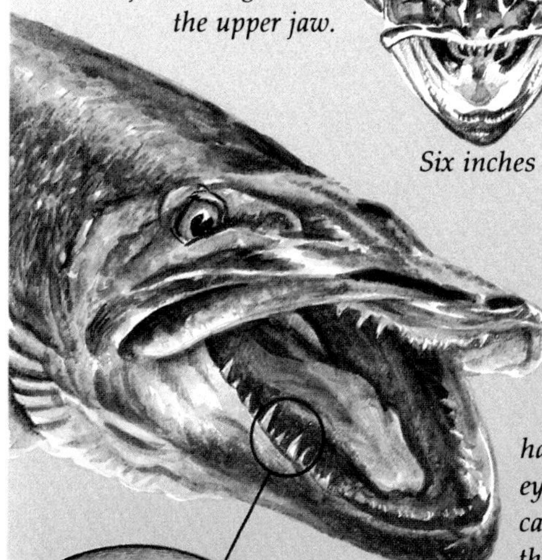

Muskies have no eyelids and cannot close their eyes.

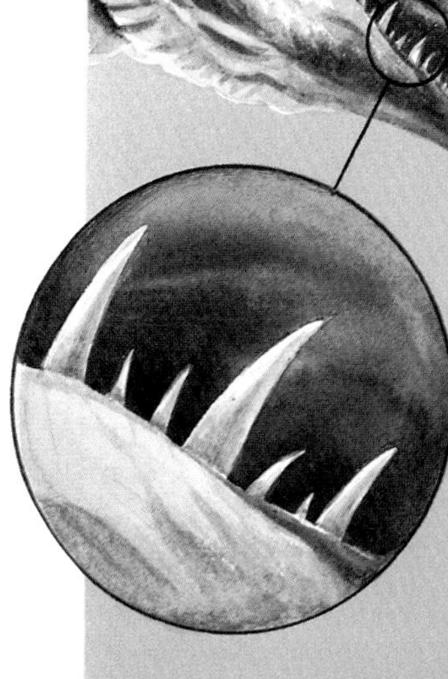

One average set of jaws contained 550 teeth. Muskies even have toothlike projections on the tongue, cheek, and roof of the mouth.

WHY DO MUSKIES HAVE 550 TEETH?

Unlike the shark, muskie do not grow new teeth as they lose old ones. However, they are born with an incredible number of teeth. The average muskie has about 550 of them.

The jaws are lined with a single row of razor-sharp teeth. In addition, they have toothlike projections on their tongue, cheek, and the roof of their mouth. The long wide jaws of an adult can open wide enough to swallow a twenty-inch fish. The muskie swallows the fish head first so that the spiny fins fold down as the fish slides down the muskie's throat.

WHEN WILL A MUSKIE ATTACK PEOPLE?

Muskies attack people only by accident. When the waters of a lake or river are murky, muskies cannot see well and have been known to occasionally mistake the foot or hand of a swimmer for a perch or bluegill. Reports of such attacks are very rare and often exaggerated. However, one fish management biologist required twenty-one stitches in his foot to close the gashes made by the single pass of a forty-inch muskie.

Prey is usually caught and held sideways in a paralyzing grip until dead.

Waiting patiently in ambush *rather than stalking their prey, muskies coil their long, slender bodies into an S shape and strike with lightning speed. After a crippling first strike, muskies usually examine their injured prey from a distance before moving in a second time to feed.*

Minnows often jump out of the water to escape from the jaws of a muskie.

"Invisible" muskies waiting in ambush

HOW MUCH FOOD CAN A MUSKIE CONSUME IN A SINGLE DAY?

If a muskie is hungry, it will eat almost anything that is smaller than itself. While over half of its diet is perch, bluegill, and suckers, a muskie also eats frogs, rats, squirrels, muskrats, and even water snakes. Adult muskies may consume twenty per cent of their body weight per day.

WHAT IS THE ONLY PREDICTABLE CHARACTERISTIC IN THE EATING HABITS OF A MUSKIE?

Generally, muskie eating habits are completely unpredictable. At times they fast for weeks, particularly in warm weather. At other times, they feed in such a frenzy that 105 were caught during a five-day period on a single lake in Wisconsin. The only predictable muskie behavior is that it will not eat anything that is motionless.

HOW DO MUSKIES CATCH BIRDS?

Muskies have been known to attack ducks and grebes as they paddle along the water's surface. They have struck at lures dangling a foot above the water and have leaped out of the water after birds resting on overhanging limbs.

HOW DO THE MARKINGS ON A MUSKIE REVEAL ITS AGE?

Age is measured by counting tiny growth rings on the scales of the fish. As the fish's growth slows each winter, a dark ring is left on each scale, similar to the growth ring on a tree. Each ring represents one year.

HOW DOES A MUSKIE BECOME INVISIBLE?

When seen from above, the muskie's olive green back blends in with the dark lake bottom. When seen from beneath, its light belly matches the light sky. The rippled stripes or bars on its sides imitate stems of underwater plants. Lying in wait among the weeds, the muskie is thus almost invisible.

WHY DO LARGE MUSKIES PREFER SHALLOW WATERS?

In spite of their tremendous size, muskies prefer the shallow water of small sheltered bays. In general, muskies seek clear water with plenty of submerged vegetation. Rarely does a muskie spend time in deep water. He can usually be found a few feet below the water's surface, lying motionless or swimming leisurely in a zigzag pattern, resting two to five minutes out of every ten.

River muskies are most likely to be found along sandbars and the inside bends of a river where there are fallen logs, rocks, or plant life.

HOW DID THE MUSKIE EARN THE TITLE OF THE FISH THAT REQUIRES ONE THOUSAND CASTS?

While there are stories of inexperienced fishermen landing big muskies on their first casts, the average time spent fishing to catch a muskie is considerable. Estimates are that it often takes 200 to 300 fishing hours to catch a muskie of legal size. In some areas it may take up to 1,000 hours. Because muskies are so unpredictable, experts who know the area are doing well if they catch a "keeper" every sixty hours of fishing.

HOW DO MUSKIES DEFEND THEIR RESOURCES?

Muskies are strictly solitary creatures that prefer to be the only fish within a certain area. Wherever he goes, a muskie "owns" the territory. Many fish wear scars that were received while doing battle over a prime piece of lake bottom.

WHY DO THE MUSKIE TERRITORIES VARY FROM YARDS TO MILES?

The size of a muskie's territory appears to change during the year. In the winter a muskie's home range may be less than a radius of twenty yards. In the spring this range expands to several miles but shrinks again to perhaps less than 500 yards during the summer.

In hot weather, some areas of the lake seem to be preferred over others. As the water cools in the fall, the muskie's range enlarges again to provide it with more food in preparation for the winter.

Muskies spawn in icy cold water *and are most active when the sun warms the water to 60°F. Above 70°F, however, muskies become sluggish and seek deeper and cooler water.*

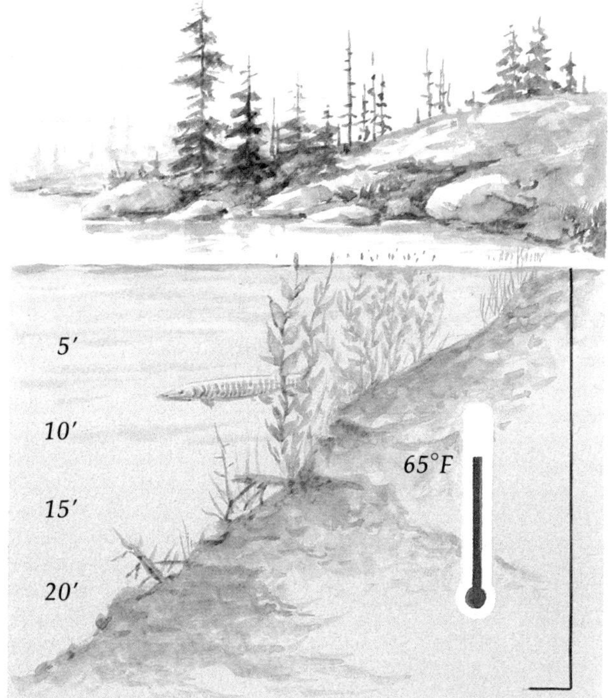

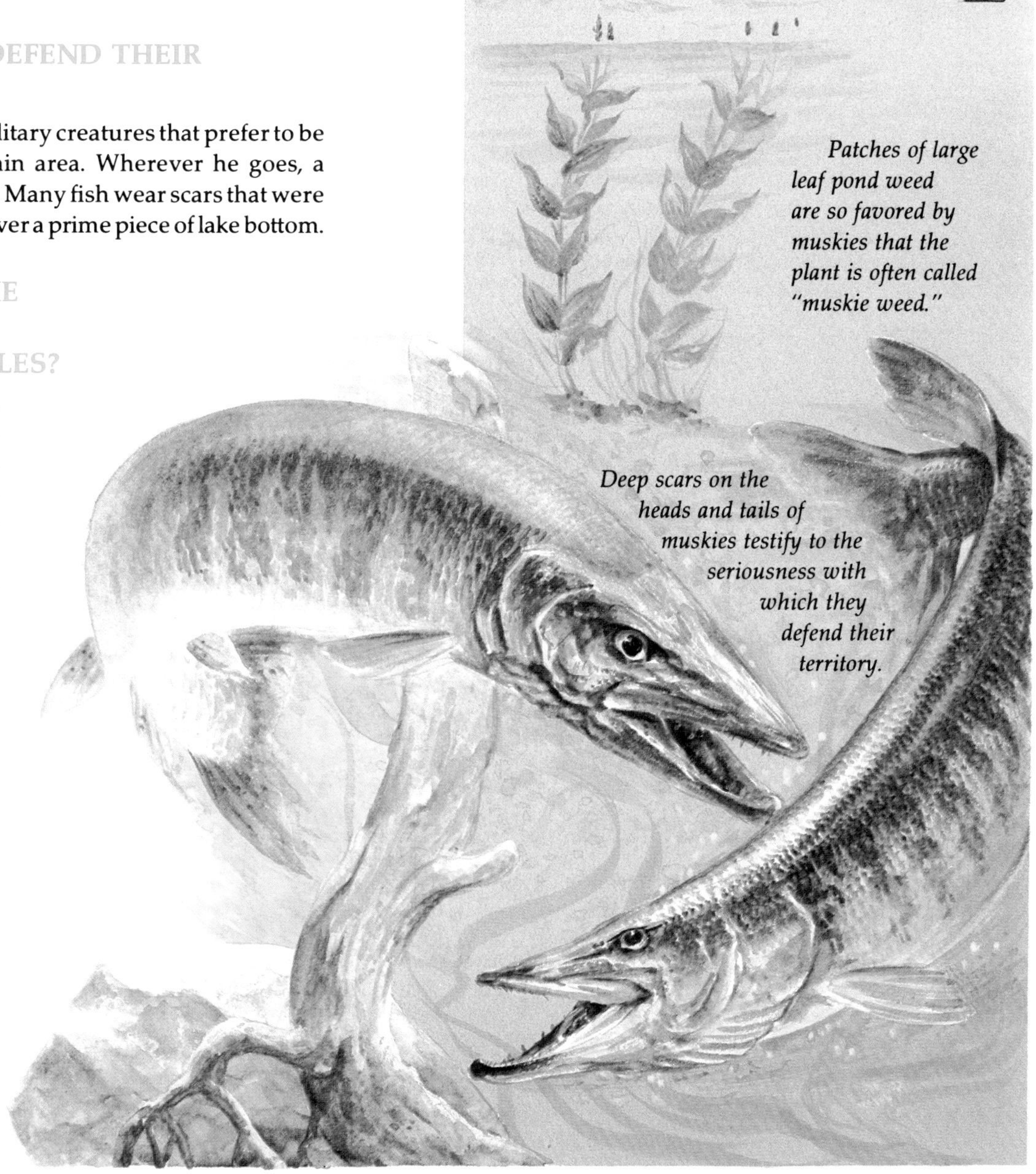

Patches of large leaf pond weed are so favored by muskies that the plant is often called "muskie weed."

Deep scars on the heads and tails of muskies testify to the seriousness with which they defend their territory.

Osprey

Adult muskies rule their underwater realm. Smaller muskies are easy prey for ospreys, great blue herons, northern pike, and even other muskies.

Northern

Muskie eating its own kind

HOW COULD ONE MUSKIE BECOME 300,000 IN ONE YEAR?

Cruising in water less than three feet deep, the female scatters her eggs over a mucky bottom. A large female may lay 100,000 to 300,000 eggs. The male follows close behind her and fertilizes the eggs.

The one-fourth to one-half inch young hatch in one to two weeks. They triple their size in the first sixteen days and are able to prey on whole fish in less than a week. By the end of the first year, surviving muskies will range from eight to twelve inches long.

WHAT FISH DESTROYS MOST OF THE YOUNG MUSKIE POPULATION EACH YEAR?

Surprisingly, the muskie's greatest enemy is the young northern pike only three to four inches long. Because the eggs of the northern hatch earlier than those of the muskie, northern fingerlings are substantially larger than muskie fingerlings, or fry.

This head start allows the young northerns to attack and eat the smaller muskie fry. The three-inch northern are so aggressive that they wipe out perhaps ninety-five per cent of the young muskie population within the first few weeks after hatching.

A second fish that a muskie must watch out for is another muskie! If food is not plentiful after hatching, muskie fry may turn cannibalistic and attack each other. In one hatchery pond, an attendant discovered five small muskies in a line, each larger fish trying to swallow the next smaller one.

Great Blue Heron

HOW CAN GOOD FOOD KILL A MUSKIE?

Normally, a large muskie may take several hours to completely swallow its food. If the fish being swallowed is so large that it blocks the flow of water through the mouth and over the gills, the muskie may drown.

It occasionally attacks fish that are too large to swallow. Once the swallowing process begins, a food fish cannot be easily coughed up. The fins which collapse as a fish is swallowed stand erect if the process is reversed.

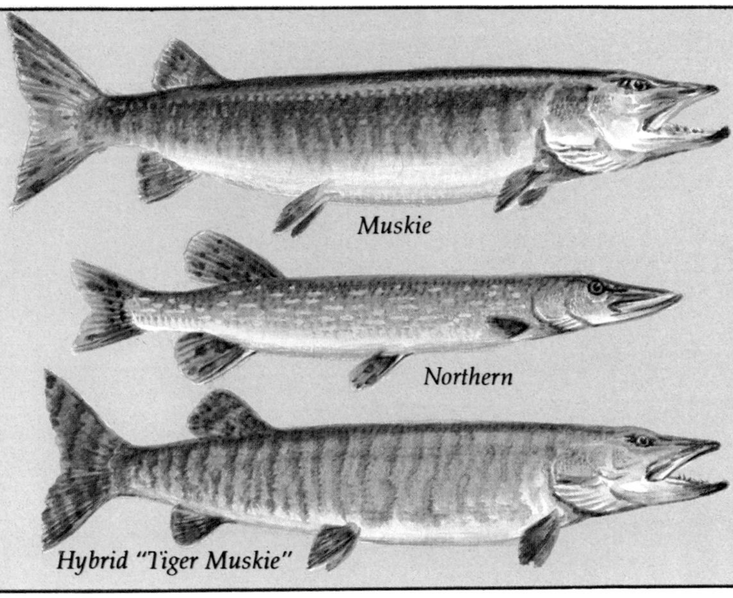

Muskie

Northern

Hybrid "Tiger Muskie"

How do Muskies and Northern Pike Differ?

Muskies and northern pike are easily distinguished by the scales around their cheeks. The northern's cheek is completely covered with scales but only the top half of the muskie's cheek has scales.

Crossbreeding between ripple barred muskies and spotted pike has resulted in a hybrid fish with a tiger stripe pattern known as the tiger muskie. Hundreds of thousands of these hybrids have been bred in captivity and released in lakes throughout the northern Midwest.

How is wisdom to escape entrapment illustrated in Scripture?

An advisor to a king was asked to give counsel. The lives of thousands of people and the future of the kingdom itself would be determined by what he said. Who was he?

(Pause for a response—see page 17.)

Fifty men ran down the street and called in unison, "Prepare the way for the prince." The royally dressed prince followed in his lavish chariot. He directed an entreating smile to bystanders who stared at this spectacle of pride and self-assertiveness. One bystander, however, was an advisor to the king. He carefully evaluated this scene.

During the months that followed a strange heaviness settled over the land. Something ominous was in the air. One day a breathless runner reached the palace. He gave the shocking news of a major conspiracy.

The king immediately sensed his danger and fled with his family and followers. On the way, he heard more foreboding news. His chief counselor had defected. When the king heard this, he cried out, "O Lord turn his counsel into foolishness."

As if in answer to this prayer, a faithful advisor arrived. The king welcomed him and quickly sent him back to the city to try to counteract the wise advice that his former chief counselor would give the rebel leader.

The faithful advisor returned to the capital and greeted the rebel leader when he triumphantly entered the city. He offered his counsel, and it was cautiously accepted.

Soon the proud new leader needed advice. How could he capture and kill the king? The king's former chief counselor told him what to do. "Attack quickly and kill only the king." The king's faithful advisor knew that this plan would be successful. How could he convince the rebel leader not to carry it out?

At that moment, the scene of this rebel leader in his chariot with the fifty men attending him became significant. The counselor wisely said, "I would advise you to gather the entire nation together, and you lead the army out to battle against the king." The idea appealed to the vain rebel, and he gave orders to carry it out.

When the chief counselor saw that his counsel was rejected, he went home and hanged himself. He knew that the rebel would be defeated and that he would be killed as a traitor.

Meanwhile, exiled King David was given the time that he needed to regroup his forces and prepare for the battle. When the armies met, his rebel son's forces were defeated. Absalom tried to escape, but his head caught in the branches of an oak tree, and he was killed by Joab. The king had escaped entrapment because of the resourcefulness of his faithful counselor, Hushai.

From II Samuel 15–18

Hushai counseled Absalom, saying, *". . . Thou knowest thy father and his men, that they be mighty men, and they be chafed in their minds, as a bear robbed of her whelps in the field. . . .*

"And he also that is valiant, whose heart is as the heart of a lion, shall utterly melt: for all Israel knoweth that thy father is a mighty man . . ." (II Samuel 17:8, 10).

"Therefore I counsel that all Israel *be generally gathered unto thee. . . . If he be gotten into a city, then shall all Israel bring ropes to that city, and we will draw it into the river, until there be not one small stone found there . . ." (II Samuel 17:11, 13).*

HUSHAI THE ARCHITE, THE KING'S COMPANION AND TRUSTED ADVISOR

When David's son, Absalom rebelled against him, David discovered who were his real friends and who were his real enemies. Some friends like Ziba were merely opportunistic. (See II Samuel 16:1–4; 19:24–30.) Some enemies like Shimei were merely a nuisance. (See II Samuel 16:5–14.) But, when David found out that Ahithophel had joined in Absalom's conspiracy against him, he recognized an enemy more threatening than any other.

AHITHOPHEL, A DANGEROUS DEFECTOR

Ahithophel had been a trusted member of David's select group of advisors. At one time the other members of the group were David's uncle Jonathan, Jehiel, and Hushai. (See I Chronicles 27:32–33.) It appears that Ahithophel had distinguished himself as the outstanding counselor of the court. *"And the counsel of Ahithophel, which he counselled in those days, was as if a man had inquired at the oracle of God . . ." (II Samuel 16:23)*. David's immediate response to Ahithophel's defection was prayer. *". . . O Lord, I pray thee, turn the counsel of Ahithophel into foolishness" (II Samuel 15:31)*.

HUSHAI IS SENT TO JERUSALEM

Soon after David made this petition, he was met by another trusted counselor—his good friend Hushai. Hushai had come to offer his support. David perceived Hushai to be the Lord's answer to his prayer. He sent him back to Jerusalem with the express purpose of defeating the counsel of Ahithophel. (See II Samuel 15:33–34.)

When Hushai entered Jerusalem, he convinced Absalom that he would provide him with the same good counsel that he had formerly given to David. Ahithophel, who was orchestrating the rebellion, was executing a carefully developed, brilliant plan.

His strategy was based on the tactics of surprise and stampede. The people must be quickly convinced that Absalom was the new king and that he was being unanimously received by all of the tribes. This news would cause a stampede effect throughout the nation which could only be sustained for a few days. Ahithophel knew that for the plan to work, David, and David alone, must be assassinated as soon as possible. Without a rival, the people would accept David's eldest son as king. But any delay would prove disastrous. David had his faults, but he was still respected by the vast majority of the people. (See II Samuel 19:9–10.)

HUSHAI'S COUNTERPROPOSAL—MATCHING WISDOM WITH INSIGHT INTO HUMAN NATURE

Hushai quickly grasped Ahithophel's clever plan. Ahithophel recommended that twelve thousand choice men pursue David immediately before he could organize support and while he was still in deep discouragement. He also advised killing only David so as not to alienate the survivors. Hushai countered by recommending an opposite tactic. He suggested that Absalom muster the entire reserve army and go after David in force. Such a plan would give David time to organize and would dull the stampede effect being generated during the early stages of the national crisis.

When Absalom rejected Ahithophel's plan and accepted Hushai's, Ahithophel knew that the Lord was working in behalf of David. Without even waiting for the outcome, he went home, put his affairs in order, and hanged himself. (See II Samuel 17:23.) The Lord had used Hushai to defeat David's enemy. *". . . For the Lord had appointed to defeat the good counsel of Ahithophel, to the intent that the Lord might bring evil upon Absalom" (II Samuel 17:14)*.

CHARACTER SKETCH OF HUSHAI

WHAT DOES HUSHAI TEACH US ABOUT FRIENDSHIP?

The fact that Hushai enjoyed an intimate friendship with David is indicated by repeated references to him as "David's friend." (See II Samuel 15:37; 16:16–17; I Chronicles 27:33.) One quality expected of a friend is constancy. Most people have friends in good times (see Proverbs 14:20; 19:4, 6–7), but Hushai was the kind of friend *". . . that sticketh closer than a brother" (Proverbs 18:24)* and *". . . loveth at all times . . ." (Proverbs 17:17).*

David had been wounded by the betrayal of his son, his tribe, and his most effective advisor. Hushai's love, however, endured through adversity. He remained loyal to his friend in need.

Another aspect of friendship is tact, being sensitive to the feelings and mood of another. (See Proverbs 25:17–20; 27:14.) Solomon expressed this idea. *"A time to weep, and a time to laugh; a time to mourn, and a time to dance" (Ecclesiastes 3:4).* Paul also spoke of it: *"Rejoice with them that do rejoice, and weep with them that weep" (Romans 12:15). "And it came to pass, that when David was come . . . behold, Hushai the Archite came to meet him with his coat rent, and earth upon his head" (II Samuel 15:32).*

WHAT DOES HUSHAI TEACH US ABOUT WISDOM?

Both Ahithophel and Hushai had applied their hearts unto wisdom and had sought for it diligently. They were two of the wisest men in the entire nation. They could both assimilate facts and immediately perceive the very heart of a matter. They knew what questions to ask and what answers to listen for. In fact, Ahithophel had a greater reputation for wisdom than Hushai. But, Ahithophel used his superior skills for a wicked cause, and as a result Hushai was able to defeat him.

Hushai teaches us that if we apply our skills in the work of the Lord, He will prosper our effort. Even if our abilities do not measure up to the abilities of others, He can effectively use what we consecrate to Him. Hushai teaches us that true wisdom comes from the Lord (see Proverbs 1:7; 9:10; 15:33), true wisdom may be asked of the Lord (see James 1:5), and true wisdom is able to "confound the wise." (See I Corinthians 1:27.)

When Hushai went to Jerusalem, he did not know what Ahithophel's strategy was. He had to assess the situation and quickly present an alternative. The Lord gave him the wisdom he needed at the moment he needed it. (See Mark 13:11.)

WHAT STRATEGY DID HUSHAI USE TO DEFEAT ABSALOM AND AHITHOPHEL?

Hushai appealed to major weaknesses in Absalom's character. Absalom was proud. He had become accustomed to flattery because of his handsome appearance and beautiful hair. (See II Samuel 14:25–26.) He was fond of pomp and *". . . prepared him chariots and horses, and fifty men to run before him" (II Samuel 15:1).* He sought the praise of men even at the expense of his father's reputation. (See II Samuel 15:2–6.)

Hushai capitalized on these weaknesses by encouraging Absalom to visualize himself leading the huge and powerful army of Israel in attack. He envisioned for Absalom a glorious campaign with sure victory. The strategy was not only personally safer than Ahithophel's surprise attack, but it was much more dramatic. The advice of Hushai was adopted, which gave David the time that he needed to turn the situation around.

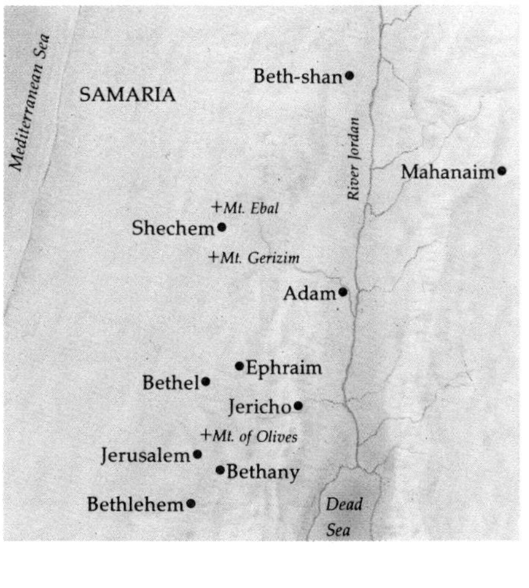

David's Trail of Despair

When David fled from Absalom, he went up the Mount of Olives. At the summit, David turned to his greatest resource—prayer. God answered that prayer by sending Hushai to David. After crossing the Jordan near Adam, David set up camp at Mahanaim. It was there that his army fought with Absalom's army.

HUSHAI
***hü**-shā-ī*

Thriftiness

. . . Is protecting myself and others from spending resources unnecessarily

"If therefore ye have not been faithful in the unrighteous mammon, who will commit to your trust the true riches?"
Luke 16:11

PART SIX

THRIFTINESS IN GIVING . . .

One of the most distinctive characteristics of a person with the spiritual gift of giving is personal frugality. The giver is able to be generous with others because of it. The ultimate expression of frugality is Christ, Who became poor so that we through His poverty might become rich. (See II Corinthians 8:9.)

21 *Making the most of limited resources*

Illustrated in the World of Nature . . . . Moss
From the Pages of Scripture . . . . The Boy with Loaves and Fish

22 *Preparing for known needs during times of plenty*

Illustrated in the World of Nature . . . . Acorn Woodpecker
From the Pages of Scripture . . . . Gaius

23 *Learning how to live with basic provisions*

Illustrated in the World of Nature . . . Alligator Snapping Turtle
From the Pages of Scripture . . . . The Rich Young Ruler

24 *Taking care of what I have to extend its usefulness*

Illustrated in the World of Nature . . . . Eastern Bluebird
From the Pages of Scripture . . . . Josiah

CHAPTER TWENTY-ONE

Thriftiness

. . . Is making the most of limited resources

"Moreover it is required in stewards, that a man be found faithful."

I Corinthians 4:2

"Redeeming the time, because the days are evil."

Ephesians 5:16

Living Lessons on Thriftiness . . .

FROM THE PAGES OF SCRIPTURE

The purpose of thriftiness is not to hoard more for ourselves, but to live on less so that we have more to give to others. God is the master of making a little go far. He kept the Israelites' shoes intact for forty years in the wilderness, and multiplied a cup of oil for a widow and her two sons. During a time of special need, Jesus demonstrated how He could make the best use of another's limited resource when it was first given to Him.

ILLUSTRATED IN THE WORLD OF NATURE

MOSS *Sphagnum sphagnum*

There are over 14,000 different kinds of mosses. Some varieties grow in hot deserts while others grow on the mountains of Antarctica. One species of moss grows 180 feet underwater. Most moss plants have a typical compact shape and grow in dense clusters close to the ground. One such moss, known as *sphagnum moss,* grows new generations on top of dead ones, forming thick layers of a substance called *peat.* In some countries peat is used for fuel and in the manufacture of paper and fabrics.

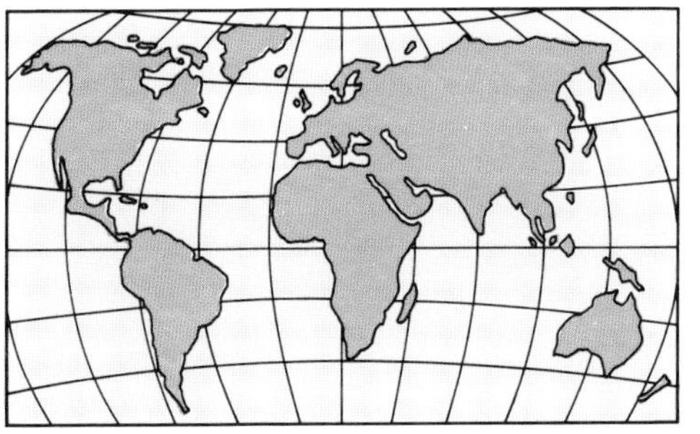

The range and habitat of moss

How is making the best use of limited resources illustrated in the world of nature?

History provides the amazing accounts of two field workers. One was more famous, or rather infamous, and the other was more common.

From outward appearances they both looked alike, but what a vast difference on the inside! And what a stark contrast resulted from their work.

One day the older and more mature field worker passed by a piece of land that no one wanted. It was filled with rocks. It was so barren and desolate that hardly a patch of grass could be seen anywhere on it. This was just the kind of challenge that he wanted. He went to work immediately exercising all the abilities which God had entrusted to him.

It was hard work, but finally he was able to get established. He had a major advantage over his look-alike, younger field worker. His way of life required less resources, and he made the best use of everything that he had. His basic motivation was to give rather than to get.

While he carried out this incredible work of reclaiming the soil, the younger field worker happened to wander by a lush potato field. It was here that he went to work.

He was also very diligent. His purpose, however, was to take from others and consume it himself. The potato fields provided an ideal place for this.

Unnoticed at first, he began to feed on the potatoes. Soon he claimed more and more for himself. When the owners of the field finally caught up with him, he had already put into motion a devastating plan that was impossible for them to stop.

Potato field after potato field came under his control, and whatever fell into his hand he destroyed. Soon the people in nearby villages were concerned, and those who lived in the cities became alarmed. They all depended upon the potato for their survival, both physically and financially. The potato was the staple crop of their country.

For two devastating years this destructive field worker carried out his deadly work. Soon, people began to die of starvation. They died by the thousands. By the time this field worker was finished, about 750,000 people had died. This destructive field worker was the spore, or seed, of a fungus. He was the cause of the 1847 potato famine in Ireland.

Meanwhile, his look-alike field worker continued to accomplish marvelous changes in the rocky land. It was becoming an area that would eventually sustain the lives of many cattle.

This worker was literally turning the surface of the rocks into soil, and the longer he worked, the more he increased its richness. This farm worker was the spore, or seed, of the moss, which continues to be a living demonstration of the potential of thriftiness.

Severt Andrewson

THE CHARACTERISTICS OF

THE MOSS IN SCRIPTURE

The moss plant can do in the natural world what God tells us to do in the spiritual world—cling to the rock and grow.

In Scripture a rock is a symbol of Christ. *". . . That Rock was Christ" (I Corinthians 10:4).* Christians are to build their lives on the Rock. *". . . A wise man . . . built his house upon a rock" (Matthew 7:24).* Christ established His Church upon the Rock. *". . . Upon this rock I will build my church . . ." (Matthew 16:18).*

Moss is able to cling to a rock and grow because it requires so little for survival. Thus Christians are instructed, *". . . Having food and raiment let us be therewith content" (I Timothy 6:8).*

Moss also retains water in itself, and thus its roots have the primary purpose of anchoring the moss plant to the rock. The high moisture retention allows the moss to grow during times of drought.

Jesus compares those who receive His Word and then fall away from it, to seed that falls in stony places. They "dry up" because they have no root in themselves. (See Matthew 13:20–21.) In contrast to this, the seed (or spores) of moss do remain because they have water within themselves.

As moss clings to the rock, it turns the rock into soil for its own future growth as well as that of other plants. As Christians, we are to edify the lives of others as we grow in Christ.

CHARACTERISTICS AND PHYSICAL FEATURES OF MOSS

Moss plants are soil builders. By being able to survive on very little, their thriftiness provides resources that are used by other plants that require more. Without the action of moss plants on rocks, there would be a much slower production of soil.

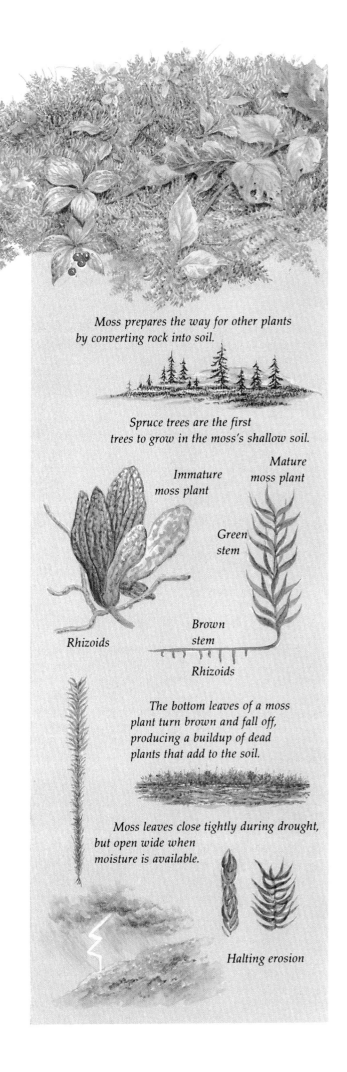

Moss prepares the way for other plants by converting rock into soil.

Spruce trees are the first trees to grow in the moss's shallow soil.

HOW CAN TINY MOSS TURN HARD ROCKS INTO SOIL?

Moss plants cling to bare rocks with small rootlike structures called *rhizoids*. Rhizoids do not soak up water and minerals like normal roots. Instead, their purpose is to anchor the moss plant. Once in place, rhizoids grip so tightly that they actually break off pieces of rock. Over long periods of time they can grind rocks into a fine powder. This powder forms the first layer of fresh soil needed for new plant growth.

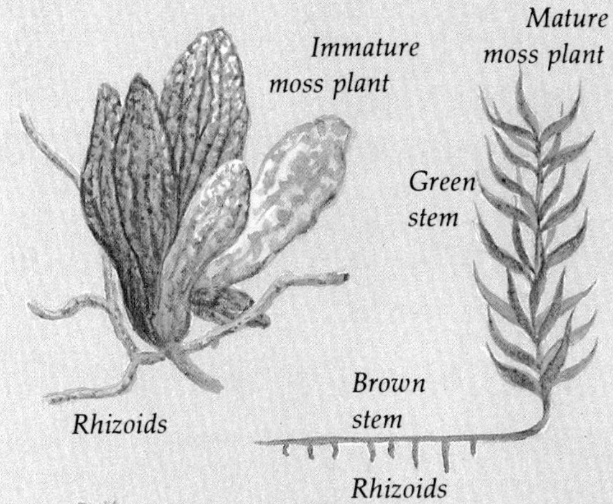

HOW CAN SOME MOSS PRODUCE LIGHT IN "THE VALLEY OF THE SHADOW"?

Most types of moss like to grow in moist, shady areas. However, because moss contains green chlorophyll and produces its own food, it must have some sunlight. One particular type of moss that grows in dark recesses of woods requires less than 1/500 the light used by plants that grow in full sunlight. Another, called *goblin gold*, is luminescent. It also requires light, but acts as if it were trying to produce its own.

HOW DOES MOSS RESPOND WHEN FROZEN?

A moss plant can be frozen solid. When thawed, it will continue to grow. Living mosses have been found in Antarctica, where the winter temperatures reach -75°F. Each spring the plant resumes its growth at the point that it left off the previous fall.

The bottom leaves of a moss plant turn brown and fall off, producing a buildup of dead plants that add to the soil.

HOW IS MOSS SUPERIOR TO A CAMEL IN RETAINING WATER FOR DRY TIMES?

Sphagnum moss is able to absorb over twenty times its weight in water. While a camel can drink as much as thirty gallons of water at a time, this is only one-tenth of its body weight. If compared by their body weights, a sphagnum moss can hold 200 times as much water as a camel.

Moss leaves close tightly during drought, but open wide when moisture is available.

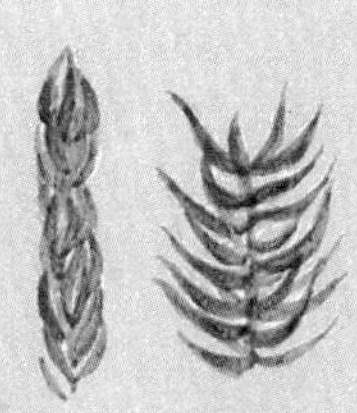

IN WHAT FOUR WAYS DOES MOSS CONTROL SOIL EROSION?

First, moss leaves cushion the fall of rain droplets that would otherwise wear away the soil. Second, moss forms a ground cover that slows the evaporation of water. This prevents soil from turning to dust that could be easily eroded in a storm. Third, the stems of moss plants act like tiny dams to prevent run-off from carrying away the soil. Fourth, the rhizoids form webs that hold the soil in place.

Halting erosion

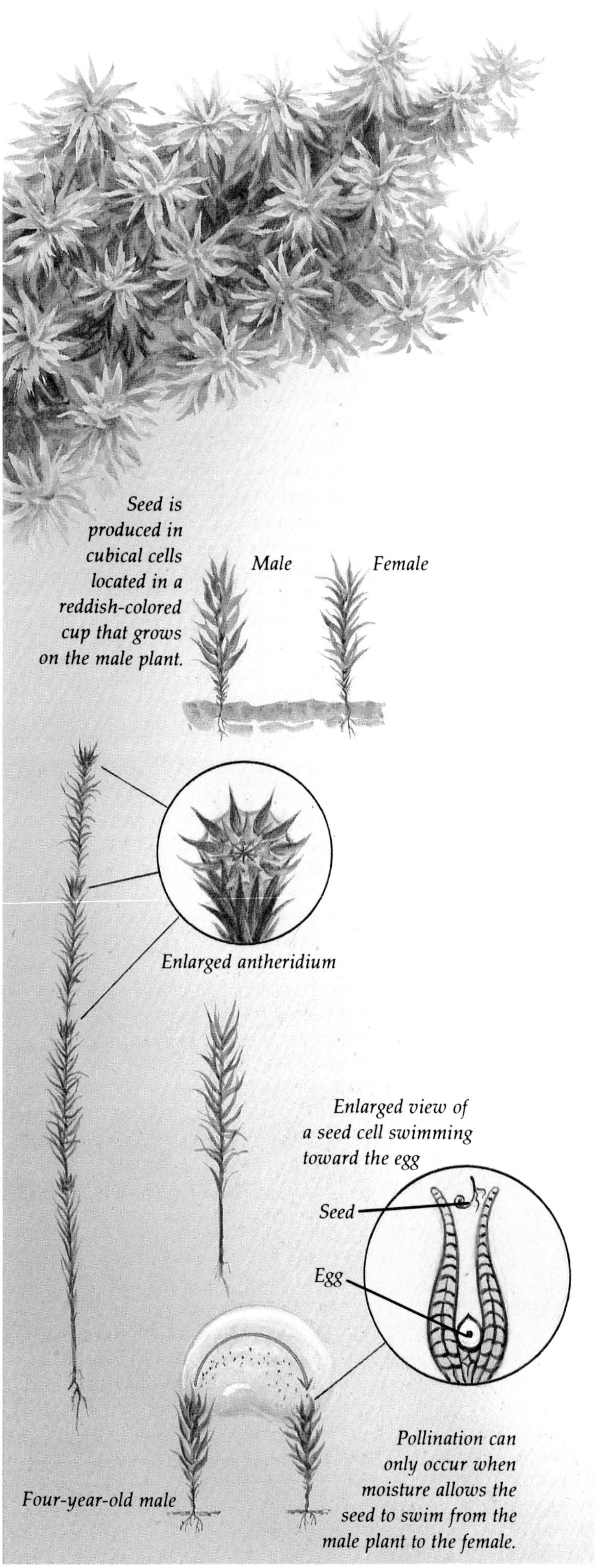
Seed is produced in cubical cells located in a reddish-colored cup that grows on the male plant.
Male
Female
Enlarged antheridium
Enlarged view of a seed cell swimming toward the egg
Seed
Egg
Four-year-old male
Pollination can only occur when moisture allows the seed to swim from the male plant to the female.

HOW DO MOSS PLANTS ILLUSTRATE THE POTENTIAL OF MARRIAGE?

Moss plants go through two stages in their life cycle. The first is called the "gametophyte stage." The word *gametophyte* is a combination of two Greek words, *gameo* and *phyte. Gameo* means "to marry or to wed." It is used in Matthew 22:2 for the king *". . . which made a marriage for his son,"* in John 2:1 for the marriage in Cana, and in Revelation 19:7–9 for the marriage supper of the Lamb. The Greek word *phyte* simply means "plant." A gametophyte is literally the marriage of two plants.

After moss plants "marry," they continue to cling to the rock and retain life-giving water for times of dryness. Together they produce a new plant for the purpose of multiplying their work in other places. The success of their work means the laying down of their own lives.

HOW DOES THE LIFE-GIVING WORK OF MOSS MEAN DEATH TO ITSELF?

Moss provides a home for hundreds of animals and other plants. Salamanders, snails, worms, and insects, as well as various forms of bacteria, fungi, and algae, live in the dense miniature forest created by a small patch of moss.

However, as moss plants convert barren rocks into soil, ferns and other large plants begin to grow alongside the moss. As these new plants flourish, they grow taller than the tiny moss plant and shade out precious sunlight. The new life that the moss made possible signals that its purposes are fulfilled in that area. The seed that it produces is now able to carry on its work in new areas.

WHAT DOES MOSS HAVE IN COMMON WITH JOHN THE BAPTIST?

John the Baptist lived a very frugal life in the barren wilderness and prepared the way for Christ in the same way moss prepares the way for other plant life.

When the popularity of Christ overshadowed John, he said: *"He must increase, but I must decrease" (John 3:30).* Jesus honored this attitude by saying, *". . . Among those that are born of women there is not a greater prophet than John the Baptist . . ." (Luke 7:28).*

HOW IS MOSS REPRODUCTION UNIQUE?

The two different stages of a moss's life cycle are called *alternation of generations.* The pollinated seed does not produce another moss plant. Instead, it produces a second, different plant that in turn produces a spore. It is the spore that finally forms a new moss plant.

GAMETOPHYTE STAGE

The pollen-producing plant, called the *antheridium,* has a cuplike rosette at the top of a stalk. Pollen cells mature and are stored inside the rosette. They are released only when the plant is covered with water.

The seed-producing plant, called the *archegonium,* is usually larger than the pollen-producing plant. A single seed is embedded at the tip of the plant and is surrounded by a jacket of cells called a *calyptra* that protects it from drying out.

When it rains, the mature antheridium absorbs water and swells until it bursts. This releases the pollen which is able to navigate through the rain water by means of two tiny propellerlike whips. Pollen cells find their way to the seed by searching for the sugar that the archegonium produces.

SPOROPHYTE STAGE

The biological term *sporophyte* is also a combination of two Greek words, *sporo* and *phyte*. *Sporo* means "seed." A sporophyte is literally a seed plant. It is used in the parable of the seeds as recorded in Luke 8:4–15, the mustard seed in Luke 13:19, and the corruptible seed in I Peter 1:23.

The pollinated seed (embryo) grows until it becomes too large for its protective casing. Instead of producing another moss plant, the embryo grows into a spear-shaped plant without leaves. This is the sporophyte. It neither looks nor acts like a moss.

Maturation of spores

The sporophyte is composed of a foot, stem, and capsule. The foot remains attached to the female parent and continues to receive nourishment throughout its lifetime. The stem supports a capsule that contains ripening spores. These spores are the seeds that will eventually produce new moss plants.

Dispersal of spores

The capsule that contains the spores is airtight. On hot days the air inside it expands. This builds up pressure until the lid pops off, shooting spores into the air like a cannon.

Under the lid is a ring of sixty-four teeth which act like tiny catapults to disperse the remaining seeds. When the air is moist, the teeth swell and drop down. When the air is dry, the teeth straighten up with a snap. As the teeth flex back and forth, they fling the spores into the air so that they can be carried away by the wind.

Germination

Spores usually germinate within a few days. Under laboratory conditions, some spores have germinated after having been kept for as long as fourteen years. When wet, the spores divide and form long threads called *protonema*. At certain spots along these threads the buds of new male and female moss plants finally begin to grow.

After the new buds of male and female moss begin to grow, the green connecting strands of protonema gradually die and decay, leaving separate moss plants growing side by side.

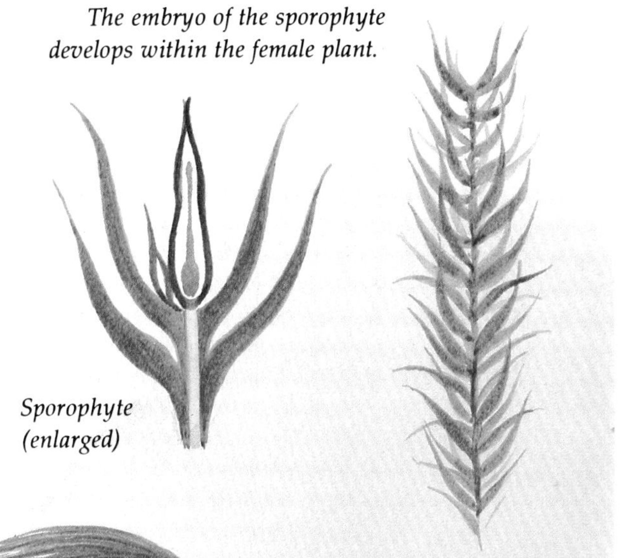

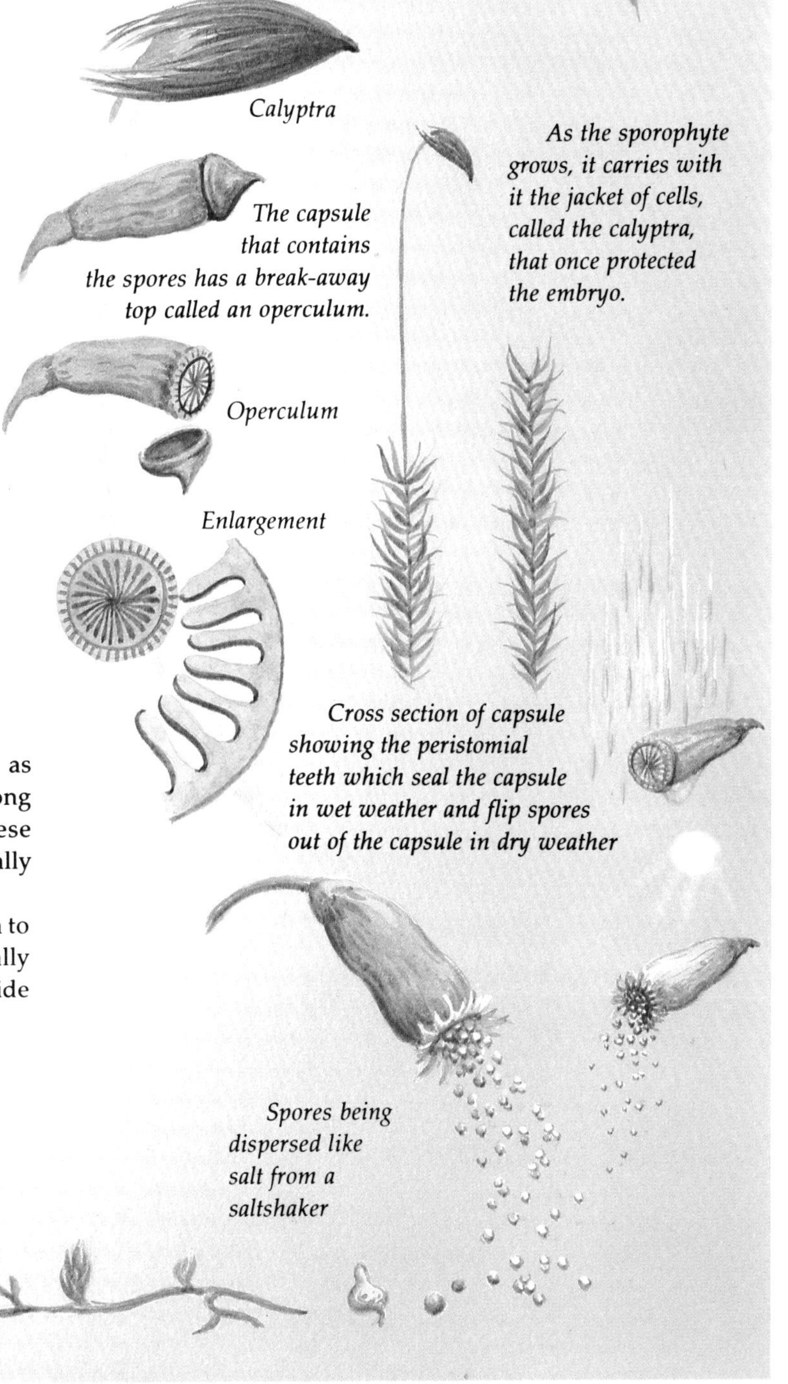

Calyptra
As the sporophyte grows, it carries with it the jacket of cells, called the calyptra, that once protected the embryo.
The capsule that contains the spores has a break-away top called an operculum.
Operculum
Enlargement
Cross section of capsule showing the peristomial teeth which seal the capsule in wet weather and flip spores out of the capsule in dry weather
Spores being dispersed like salt from a saltshaker

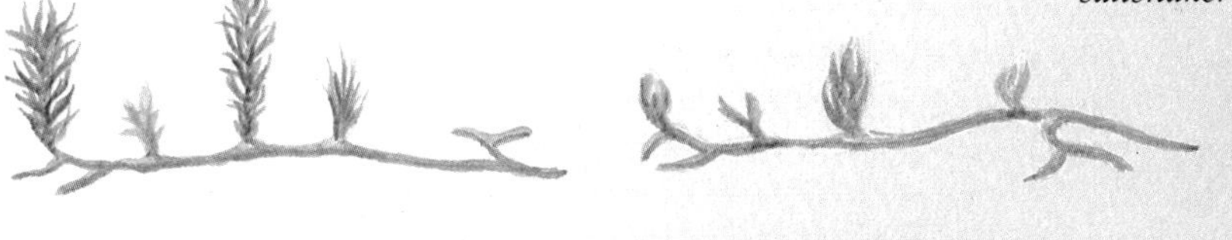

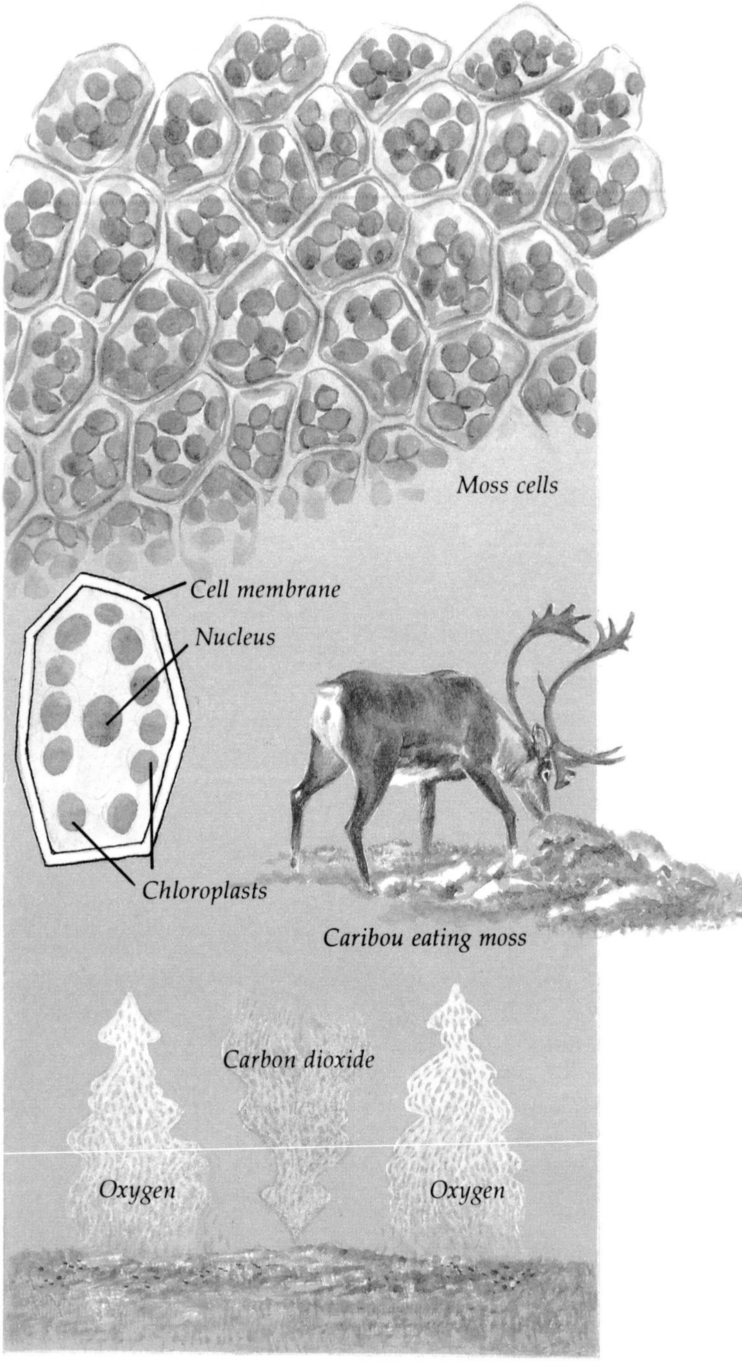

WHAT LESSON DOES A MOSS CELL HAVE FOR A DRIED-UP CHRISTIAN?

Every cell within a moss plant must be directly responsible for its own supply of water. Just as every Christian must be responsible for his own cleansing and nourishment from the water of God's Word.

The moss plant has no root or vascular system that will automatically provide its daily water needs. The function of the roots is to anchor the plant to the rock. A cell therefore, must either absorb water from the outside, or tap water from large storage cells within the plant itself.

HOW DOES THE CENTER OF THE MOSS PLANT PROVIDE LIFE-GIVING NOURISHMENT AFTER ITS DEATH?

In the broad stem, some cells are buried deep in the center of the plant and have no contact with the surface. They soon shrivel and die without water. However, their long hollow shells remain. These serve as storage tanks which fill with water when it is available and then slowly release it to the surrounding cells when it is needed. As a result moss plants can survive droughts which other plants cannot.

HOW DO CARIBOU DEPEND UPON THE MOSS PLANT?

Moss is a staple food for the caribou, especially during the winter. The moss not only provides direct nourishment to caribou, but it also protects the environment so that other food plants can grow.

HOW DOES MOSS HELP TO PRODUCE BETTER AIR?

Moss plants cover hundreds of thousands of square miles of land and are one of the major suppliers of oxygen to the atmosphere. Moss converts carbon dioxide into oxygen faster than do trees and most other green plants. However, because of its rapid respiration, it is also very sensitive to the quality of air it breathes and can be easily injured.

Sphagnum moss

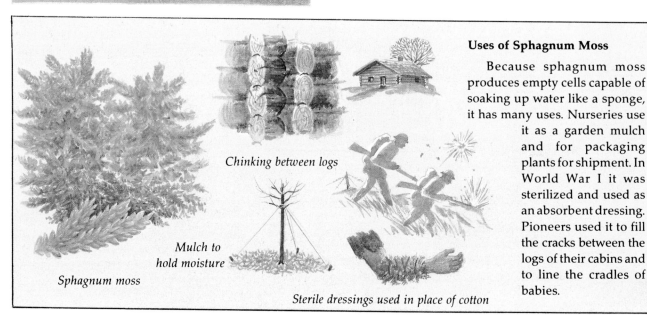

Chinking between logs

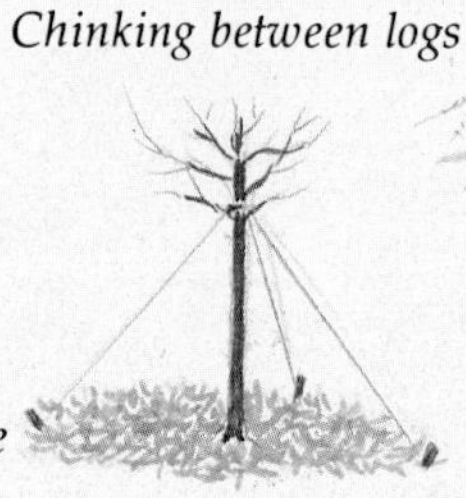

Mulch to hold moisture

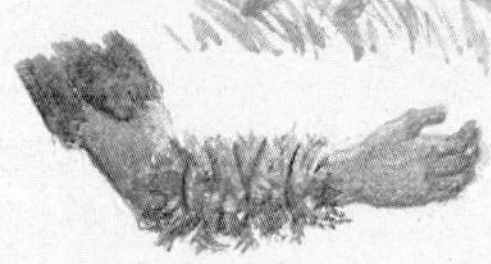

Sterile dressings used in place of cotton

Uses of Sphagnum Moss

Because sphagnum moss produces empty cells capable of soaking up water like a sponge, it has many uses. Nurseries use it as a garden mulch and for packaging plants for shipment. In World War I it was sterilized and used as an absorbent dressing. Pioneers used it to fill the cracks between the logs of their cabins and to line the cradles of babies.

How is the need to make the best use of limited resources illustrated in Scripture?

This is the story of two young boys. Although living at different times in history, each one saw the miraculous provision of God for his family in response to his faith and obedience.

The first boy was the older son of a widow during Elisha's day. Who was the second boy?

(Pause for a response—see page 17.)

The quiet weeping of a mother could be heard by her son. He understood; he, too, shared in her sorrow. His father had died. They were a close family, and the father was greatly missed by him, his mother, and his little brother.

But the loss of the father was now to be deepened by further tragedy. The creditors were coming to take the boy and his younger brother away from their sorrowing mother. They would have to work to pay off the debts which their father had accumulated.

With no food in the house except a pot of oil, the grieving mother had nowhere to turn but to the Lord, Who began to work in a very unique and marvelous way.

God directed the prophet Elisha to tell the mother to get empty pots and pans from her neighbors. "Get as many as you can," he said. The boy and his brother worked with their mother, and soon they had a house full of empty pots. Then they shut the door.

The older son began bringing the pots to his mother. She poured her oil into each one according to the instructions of the prophet. Miraculously the oil was never used up. It filled every container! The jubilant widow sold this oil, paid the creditors, and lived on the rest.

The account of this widow and her sons was passed on years later to another young boy. He also had a mother in need. Their provisions for food were sparse. Rather than having rich wheat, they survived on barley, the grain of the poor.

Like the widow's son of earlier years, this boy purposed to help his mother. One day he listened to the excitement of villagers going out into the countryside to hear a wise teacher. That gave him an idea. He went home, got what he needed, and hurried out to join them.

That day the boy listened to the rich and refreshing truths of Christ. The boy's faith was stirred as he heard and understood.

He decided to put the teachings on giving into action and made his way up to the front of the crowd. He told a disciple by the name of Andrew that he wanted to give something to Christ. Andrew agreed to tell Jesus about his offer.

A few minutes later Andrew returned and received from the boy a basket of five barley loaves and two fish. Christ blessed them, broke them, and then gave them to His disciples to feed over 5,000 people! Not only did Christ satisfy the hungry multitude, but He had His disciples gather up twelve baskets of food that was left over. With these baskets Christ was able to demonstrate to this boy and his mother the potential of multiplied returns when limited resources are first given to Him.

From II Kings 4:1–7 and John 6:5–14

Barley

Barley, corn, oats, rice, and wheat all belong to the same family of plants. Farmers often plant one and two-thirds bushels of seed per acre and harvest about fifty-four bushels per acre. For this reason, barley is a good illustration of making the most of limited resources.

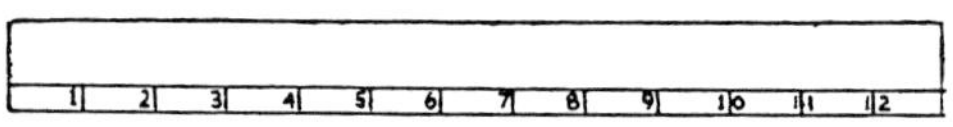

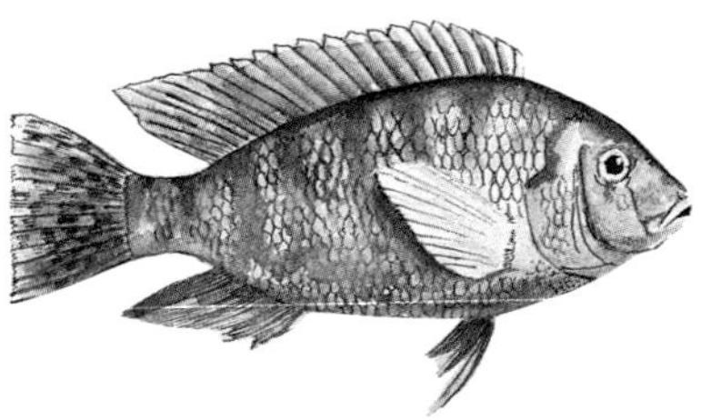

St. Peter's Fish

The fish that the thrifty boy made available to the Lord could well have been the excellent eating tilapia species known as "St. Peter's fish."

Twelve baskets *were used by the disciples to gather up the fragments that remained after feeding the 5,000.*

A BOY WITH LIMITED RESOURCES WHO ALLOWED CHRIST TO DEMONSTRATE HIS POWER

Herod Antipas, who had ordered John the Baptist beheaded, had learned of Jesus' ministry and growing popularity among the common people. To escape the pressures of Antipas, Jesus withdrew from the tetrarch's dominion of Galilee and took His disciples by boat to a wilderness spot belonging to the city of Bethsaida. This area was governed by the more moderately tempered Herod Philip.

Jesus and His disciples were in need of rest. They had been so busy in their ministry of teaching and healing that there had not even been time to eat. (See Mark 6:31.) The disciples had just returned from their first preaching tour in Galilee without Jesus. They had many things to discuss with Him about their journey and many questions to ask. But to be assured of the quiet they needed, it was necessary for them to cross over to the eastern shore of the Sea of Galilee.

INESCAPABLE CROWDS

It must have been disappointing to the disciples to find crowds waiting when they reached the other shore, but the Lord's response was compassionate. The religious leaders, whose duty it was to teach these people, had themselves rejected the truth. Jesus likened the people to sheep without a shepherd. (See Mark 6:34.) His plan for rest and for time with the disciples had to be postponed. He spent the day teaching about the kingdom of God and healing those in need. (See Luke 9:11.)

AN OVERWHELMING NEED

Then an unexpected situation enabled the Lord to teach His disciples, and the crowds as well, an important truth about the nature of the kingdom of God. In their enthusiasm to meet Jesus, the people had not anticipated or adequately prepared for their need of food. The hour had grown late, and they were hungry.

Jesus asked His disciple Philip, *". . . Whence shall we buy bread, that these may eat?" (John 6:5)*. Philip quickly calculated that even two hundred denarii would not satisfy the need. And where were they to get the money? Where could they buy that much food? The other disciples suggested the people be dismissed to purchase their own food in neighboring towns. They could not imagine how to provide for the crowds. Andrew evidenced the most faith. He had found a boy with five barley loaves and two small fish. But he admitted, *". . . What are they among so many?" (John 6:9)*.

MIRACULOUS PROVISION

Jesus, knowing all along what He would do, told His disciples to bring the food to Him and organize the crowd for a meal. After thanking His Father for the bread and fish, Jesus distributed them to His disciples who in turn gave them to the people. To the amazement of all present, approximately five thousand hungry men ate bread and fish until they were fully satisfied. After the meal, there were twelve baskets of food left over.

Jesus had shown the people that He could satisfy their physical needs through supernatural means. Now He was able to teach them that He could abundantly satisfy their spiritual needs through supernatural means as well. He had revealed another truth to His disciples, taking inadequate resources and making them adequate for the occasion. Their ordinary lives and abilities could be supernaturally used if they were brought to the Lord, broken by Him, and used for His service.

CHARACTER SKETCH OF THE BOY WITH THE LOAVES AND FISH

WHY WAS THE BOY THE ONLY ONE WITH FOOD?

The fact that the boy had five loaves of bread suggests that the food was intended for sale rather than for his own use. It was just too much for one person to eat. There was a food supply in Jerusalem designated for the poor. A daily ration was the equivalent of one loaf of bread. The loaves were usually flat, about seven inches across and one inch thick. Thus, five loaves would have met the daily needs of five men.

The boy was probably a bread vendor working in the market places. When the people left the city in the morning, he followed them. From the word in John's account which is used to describe the fish, we know that they were cooked or roasted and intended to be used as a relish for the bread.

The fact that the loaves were made of barley is significant. Barley bread was a staple in the diet of poor people. The growing season for barley was shorter than that for wheat, and the grain thrived in less fertile soil. As a result, the price of barley grain was about half that of wheat. (See II Kings 7:1.) The boy may have been trying to help support a very poor family by selling barley bread to other poor people.

WHAT DID THE BOY GAIN BY GIVING JESUS ALL OF HIS FOOD?

First, he gained a good meal. His job was to sell his food, not to eat it. By giving the bread and fish to Jesus, the boy was able to eat as much as he wanted along with everyone else in the crowd. Second, he gained a valuable lesson in business. Solomon had advised the businessmen of his day, *"Cast thy bread [literally, barley loaves] upon the waters: for thou shalt find it after many days" (Ecclesiastes 11:1).* The boy could have exploited the situation by selling the loaves to the highest bidders. But when Andrew asked for the food, he gave it up recognizing a wiser investment.

The boy benefited in another way by entrusting all of his resources to the Lord. After the meal was over, the disciples were asked to *". . . gather up the fragments that remain, that nothing be lost" (John 6:12).* It is likely that the twelve baskets of food which remained were given back to the boy. Finally, he gained a full and personal impact of the miracle. It was his food that the Lord used to feed the crowd. This was no mere man. This was truly the Son of God.

WHY DO ALL FOUR GOSPELS RECORD THIS PARTICULAR MIRACLE?

The miracle has profound meaning as to the Lord's nature. Jesus explained its significance the following day in Capernaum. The crowds wanted to make Him their king. He had satisfied their hunger with barley bread and fish, and now they desired more miracles of a similar kind. But the Lord rebuked them for missing the point.

". . . Ye seek me, not because ye saw the miracles, but because ye did eat of the loaves, and were filled. Labour not for the meat which perisheth, but for that meat which endureth unto everlasting life, which the Son of man shall give unto you: for him hath God the Father sealed" (John 6:26–27).

The poor wanted a Messiah to deliver them from the oppression of the rich. Jesus declared that they were just as needy spiritually and should hunger instead for spiritual food. He claimed to be the Bread which alone could satisfy their needs. *"I am the living bread which came down from heaven: if any man eat of this bread, he shall live for ever: and the bread that I will give is my flesh, which I will give for the life of the world" (John 6:51).*

Christ's use of the boy's loaves and fish *provides an important encouragement to all young boys: learn early in life how God will multiply what you give to Him so that you can be a wise provider when you have a family.*

BOY WITH LOAVES AND FISH

CHAPTER TWENTY-TWO

Thriftiness

. . . Is preparing for known needs during times of plenty

"And God is able to make all grace abound toward you; that ye, always having all sufficiency in all things, may abound to every good work."

II Corinthians 9:8

Living Lessons on Thriftiness . . .

FROM THE PAGES OF SCRIPTURE

Wise saving during times of plenty avoids self-indulgence and makes it possible to distribute to the needs of the saints. (See Romans 12:13.)

When saving is practiced out of fear of an unknown future, it tends to produce hoarding and greed. The result is the heaping up of treasures, which God condemns. (See Psalm 39:6.)

When saving is carried out for the purpose of meeting needs as God reveals them, it produces faith and unity among Christians. God illustrated the potential of such giving through the dedicated work of a leader in the church at Corinth.

ILLUSTRATED IN THE WORLD OF NATURE

ACORN WOODPECKER *Melanerpes formicivorus*

Acorn woodpeckers stand about nine inches tall. They live in groups of two to twelve members, with four to eight being the most common. Half of the bird's diet is made up of acorns, which it not only eats in the fall but also stores in tree granaries to eat in the winter.

All the members of the group share in the work of harvesting and storing acorns. No individual bird has its own storage tree. Acorn woodpeckers also defend their territory, raise their young, and maintain their storage site as a group.

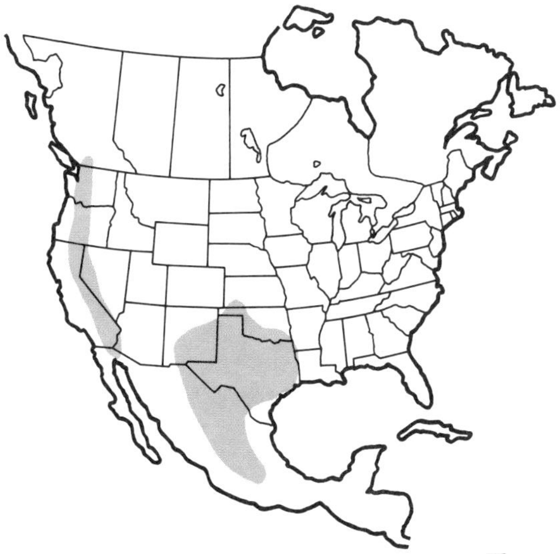

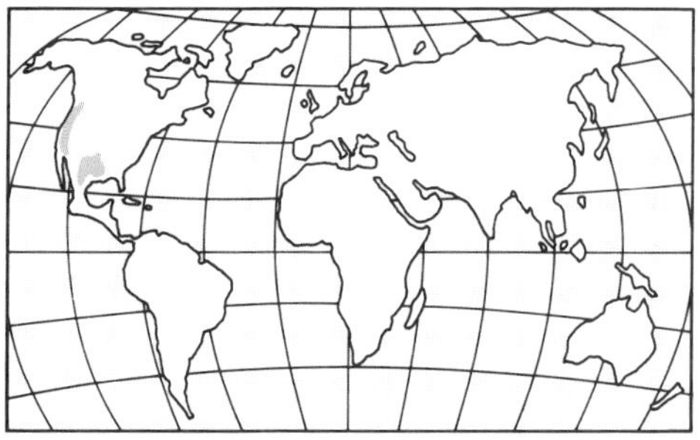

The range and habitat of the acorn woodpecker

How is saving during times of plenty illustrated in the world of nature?

One of the most important lessons about life can be learned from the labors of two different kinds of workers in the country fields.

Both of these workers toiled long hours during the springtime and summer. Both enjoyed an abundant harvest and both gathered in all the provisions they could.

Yet, each worker had an entirely different motive for working, and therein lies the valuable lesson that must be learned.

The wise worker started early in the morning and labored until evening. His diligence was amazing, as well as his ability not to be distracted from his primary goal of a fruitful harvest.

Each item that he harvested was carefully stored. He used his head in a unique way to make sure that his crop was securely protected, often moving each item at least two or three times. During his lifetime, he gathered tons of food, and many in his community benefited from his labors.

The foolish worker also labored long hours during the day and into the night. He used all the farming knowledge he had to raise a crop. His efforts were rewarded with a bumper harvest far greater, in fact, than he could even store in his barns.

It was at this point that his goal for working became clear. He said to himself, "I now have an abundant supply for many years. I will store it in bigger barns and retire to a life of ease."

He saved during times of plenty so that he would not be dependent upon God for his daily food. He thought that he could now depend only upon himself and thus live the way he wanted. He would "eat, drink, and be merry."

God said to this worker, "You fool. This night your soul will be required of you. Then who shall own those things which you have provided?"

On the other hand, God praised the wise worker and all his fellow creatures by telling us to think about them and learn from their ways. Their purpose in working is not to heap up provisions for a future life of ease, but to provide for their needs in daily dependence upon God.

The acorn woodpecker, who stores his harvest in trees and posts, has no thought of a retirement to ease. He works to store provisions during times of plenty for the needs of his family, his fellow workers, and others in his community who depend upon his skillful labors.

THE CHARACTERISTICS OF

THE ACORN WOODPECKER IN SCRIPTURE

The acorn woodpecker is unique to the realm of birds in that during times of plenty it "reaps and gathers into barns."

In Matthew 6:26 God instructs us to consider the fowls of the air which do not sow or reap or gather into barns, *". . . yet your heavenly Father feedeth them. . . ."*

Thus, God uses the labor of the acorn woodpecker to help carry out His commitment to provide food for other birds. In the same way, God allows some Christians to provide for others who have special needs.

". . . That now at this time your abundance may be a supply for their want, that their abundance also may be a supply for your want . . ." (II Corinthians 8:14).

The amazing diligence of the acorn woodpecker is a sharp rebuke to the slothful man described in Proverbs 20:4. *". . . Therefore shall he beg in harvest, and have nothing."*

As the acorn woodpecker secures thousands of acorns in its storehouses, it illustrates the condition of the righteous man in Psalm 112:3. *"Wealth and riches shall be in his house. . . ."*

Just as the acorn woodpecker does not gather only for himself, the righteous man is one who *". . . hath dispersed, he hath given to the poor; his righteousness endureth for ever . . ." (Psalm 112:9).*

CHARACTERISTICS AND PHYSICAL FEATURES OF THE ACORN WOODPECKER

Times of plenty often lead to overindulgence, carelessness, or laziness. However, the acorn woodpecker makes the most of abundant times by consuming only what it needs and storing the rest.

By storing extra nuts for the lean winter to come, the acorn woodpecker is assured of enough food for itself. This also helps to provide food for squirrels, titmice, jays, and deer.

Storage trees attract nuthatches, titmice, jays, squirrels, and even deer.

HOW DOES THE ACORN WOODPECKER TURN FENCE POSTS INTO BARNS?

Acorn woodpeckers prefer to store acorns in softwood trees such as the Douglas fir or white pine. If these trees are not available, they store their acorns in oak, sycamore, and eucalyptus trees. Acorns have also been found stored in fence posts, under loosened shingles, and in the cracks of fallen logs and the walls of buildings.

HOW MANY ACORNS HAVE BEEN STORED IN A SINGLE TREE?

Acorn woodpeckers store about 1,000 acorns for each member of the group. Since all the group's acorns are stored together, a single tree may hold 10,000 acorns. As many as sixty acorns can be stored in a space five inches wide and twenty-four inches long.

In one tree 50,000 acorns were found tucked away in a neat pattern. In most trees, the storage pattern resembles a Chinese checkerboard. In deeply furrowed sycamore bark, however, acorns are stored in lines that follow the thick ridges of the bark.

Douglas fir

HOW WILL A KNOTHOLE INCREASE THE PERSISTENCE OF AN ACORN WOODPECKER?

Usually acorn woodpeckers are very careful not to penetrate the wood that grows beneath the bark of a tree. But in one old hollow pine, acorn after acorn was accidentally pushed through a hole in the bark and into the tree's hollow center. The woodpeckers continued pushing acorns through the hole until the eight inch by twenty foot cavity was filled!

In another incident, acorn woodpeckers tried repeatedly to plug a knothole on the outside of an old building only to have the acorns land on the floor inside.

WHY DOES AN ACORN WOODPECKER NOT FLY IN A STRAIGHT LINE?

Like the flight of an airplane with a sputtering engine, the acorn woodpecker's flight is one of ups and downs. When the acorn woodpecker beats its wings, it rises. As it pauses and folds its wings to its side, it falls. This alternating pattern of wing beats and pauses prevents the acorn woodpecker from flying in a straight horizontal line.

Thousands of acorns may be stored in a single telephone pole.

Old siding may also be perforated with storage holes.

Harvesting, storing, and re-storing acorns occupies the entire fall season. If the harvest is plentiful, every available crack and hole within a fifteen acre area is filled with an acorn.

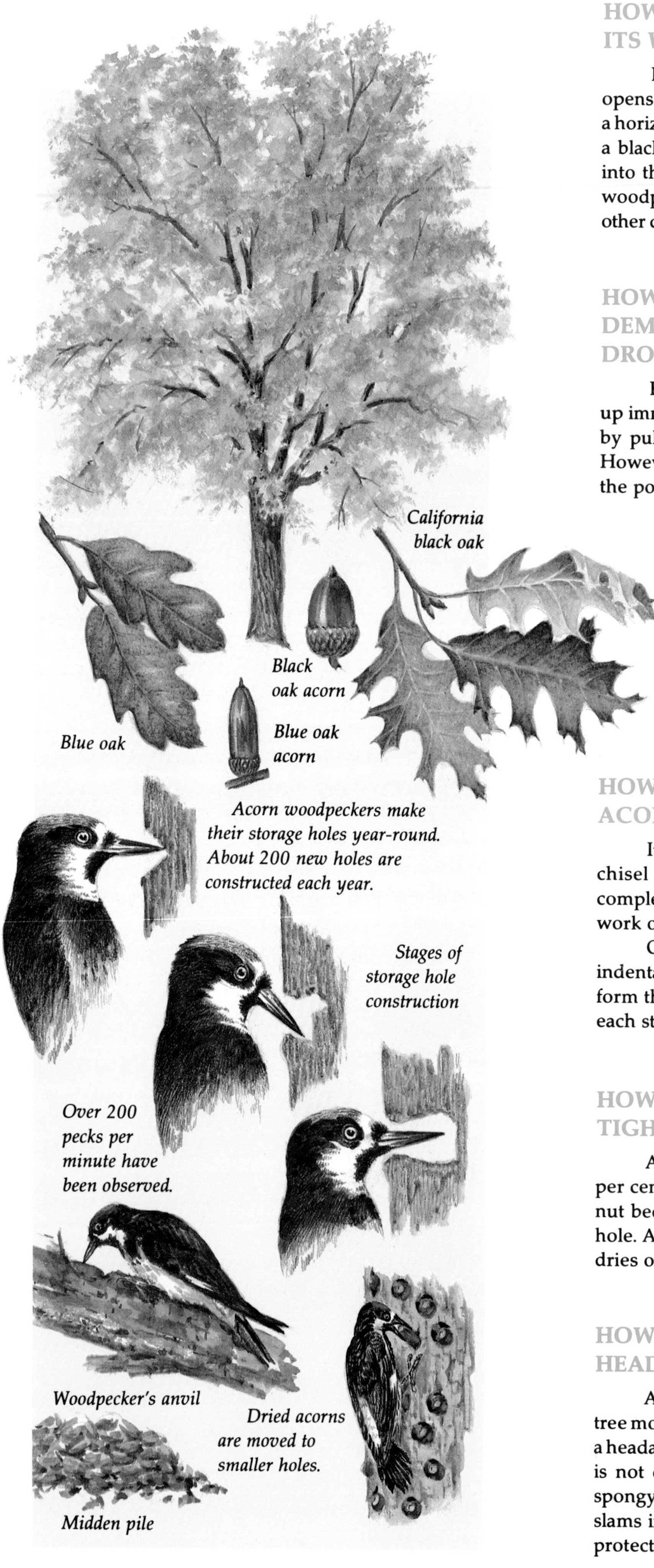
California
black oak
Black
oak acorn
Blue oak
Blue oak
acorn
Acorn woodpeckers make
their storage holes year-round.
About 200 new holes are
constructed each year.
Stages of
storage hole
construction
Over 200
pecks per
minute have
been observed.
Woodpecker's anvil
Dried acorns
are moved to
smaller holes.
Midden pile

HOW DOES AN ACORN WOODPECKER KEEP ITS WORK AREA ORGANIZED?

Each acorn woodpecker has a favorite place where it opens acorns. This is usually a crack on the upper surface of a horizontal limb. The crack is used much the same way that a blacksmith uses an anvil. An acorn is wedged securely into the crack and then decapped and split open for the woodpecker to eat. A large pile of acorn caps, shells, and other debris, called a *midden,* builds up under the "anvil" site.

HOW DOES AN ACORN WOODPECKER DEMONSTRATE THRIFTINESS WHEN IT DROPS AN ACORN?

Every acorn is important. If one is dropped, it is picked up immediately. A woodpecker picks an acorn from a tree by pulling on the pointed end of the nut with its beak. However, to store the nut, it must be turned around so that the pointed end goes into the tree first. The bird reverses the nut's position by laying the nut down and turning it around at the "anvil" site.

Since it uses only its beak to make the switch, the woodpecker sometimes drops the nut. To catch it, the woodpecker forms a pocket with its wings and traps the acorn before it falls off the anvil. If the woodpecker drops the nut in flight, it is usually quick enough to swoop down and catch it before it hits the ground.

HOW LONG DOES IT TAKE TO MAKE AN ACORN STORAGE HOLE?

It takes about thirty minutes of actual working time to chisel out a storage hole. However, the task is rarely completed during a single work session and is seldom the work of just one bird.

One acorn woodpecker may make a cone-shaped indentation in the bark. Then others enlarge the cone to form the pocket that holds the acorn. The narrow neck of each storage hole keeps the acorns from slipping out.

HOW IS A SHRINKING ACORN KEPT TIGHT IN A STORAGE HOLE?

As ripe acorns dry out, they shrink by as much as six per cent and become loose in their storage holes. When a nut becomes loose, it is removed and stored in a smaller hole. A nut may have to be moved up to six times before it dries out completely.

HOW DO WOODPECKERS AVOID GETTING HEADACHES FROM PECKING ALL DAY?

Acorn woodpeckers can slam their heads against a tree more than one hundred times a minute without getting a headache. This is possible because the woodpecker's beak is not directly connected to its skull. Instead, a layer of spongy material separates the two. Each time the beak slams into a tree, the spongy layer absorbs the shock and protects the woodpecker's brain from damage.

WHAT DO ACORN WOODPECKERS EAT BESIDES ACORNS?

Acorn woodpeckers also eat fruit, insects, and sap. Throughout the year acorn woodpeckers feed on whatever is most abundant. In the spring when their supply of stored acorns is low, they tap the rising flow of sap in oak trees. In the summer they sit in trees that overlook grassy areas to hunt for insects. The woodpecker swoops down from its perch and catches the unsuspecting insect from below. In the fall they feed on ripening apples and pears. However, each of these foods is only a supplement to their major diet of acorns.

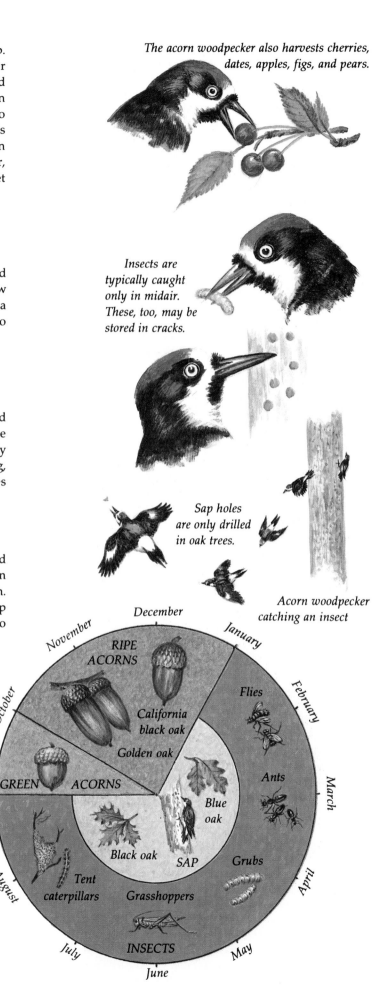

The acorn woodpecker also harvests cherries, dates, apples, figs, and pears.

HOW DO ACORN WOODPECKERS SHOW THRIFTINESS WHEN EATING AN APPLE?

Acorn woodpeckers peck a hole in a pear or apple and eat the fruit from the inside out. Also, instead of taking a few bites out of many different fruits, they concentrate on only a few, eating one piece of fruit entirely before starting to eat another.

Insects are typically caught only in midair. These, too, may be stored in cracks.

HOW ARE ACORN WOODPECKER TERRITORIES LIKE CITIES?

Each group of acorn woodpeckers claims its own land and defends its own borders. Each territory includes all the essentials of a well-organized city—a stand of oaks to supply acorns, grasslands for hunting insects, and trees for nesting, roosting, and storage. Usually neighboring communities coexist peacefully.

Sap holes are only drilled in oak trees.

Acorn woodpecker catching an insect

WHAT CAUSES WOODPECKER WARS?

Because of the tremendous investment of time involved in the construction of thousands of new storage holes, acorn woodpeckers seldom start a new territory from scratch. Instead, the group will attempt to drive a neighboring group from its land, and "wars" may break out between the two communities.

A group which has been driven from its homeland often turns against a third neighbor. Peace returns only after all the groups have found new territories.

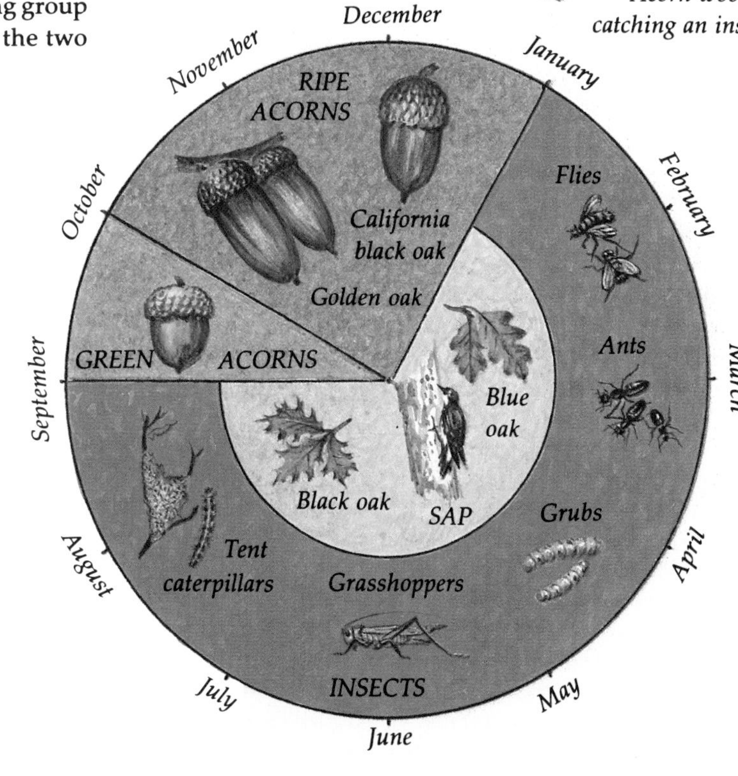

HOW DOES A WOODPECKER USE ROCKS FOR ITS TEETH?

The stomach of an acorn woodpecker will usually contain rocks. Since acorn woodpeckers have no teeth, rocks are needed to grind their food. At any given time, approximately half of the acorn woodpecker's stomach is filled with rocks.

WHAT EXTRA EQUIPMENT COMES WITH A WOODPECKER'S TONGUE?

The acorn woodpecker's tongue is two to three times longer than its beak and is equipped with a brush at the tip. The brush is used for sweeping bits of leftover acorn crumbs from old storage holes.

Strong tail feathers brace the acorn woodpecker when pecking.

Acorn woodpeckers never live alone. The average group size is six.

Acorn woodpeckers lay four to six white eggs in a hollowed-out cavity of a tree.

HOW DO ACORN WOODPECKERS ILLUSTRATE PROVERBS?

The unusual diligence of the acorn woodpecker illustrates Proverbs 10:4, *"He becometh poor that dealeth with a slack hand: but the hand of the diligent maketh rich."* Its manner of work demonstrates Proverbs 10:5, *"He that gathereth in summer is a wise son. . . ."* The acorn woodpecker gathers in summer and in harvest.

HOW DOES THE "DRESS" OF FEMALE WOODPECKERS SHOW THEIR MATURITY?

The plumage of all young acorn woodpeckers matches that of the adult male. It is almost impossible to identify a female until it is a year old and has developed the characteristic black band that separates her white forehead from her red cap.

HOW CAN AN ACORN WOODPECKER WORK WHILE UPSIDE DOWN?

Acorn woodpeckers cling sideways and upside down to the trunks of trees by using the four sharp claws of each foot. Two claws point forward and two backwards to hold the bird securely to the tree.

For balance, the woodpecker leans against its tail. The middle two tail feathers are particularly strong. During the molt, these two feathers do not fall out until all the other tail feathers have been replaced. By using its two legs and tail as a base, the acorn woodpecker can use its head to hammer away at a tree.

HOW DO ACORN WOODPECKERS "TURN IN" AT NIGHT?

All the birds of a group averaging six or less in number roost together in a single tree. A cylindrical cavity is hollowed out of a tree trunk or limb. Although the roost may be vertical or horizontal, the entrance never faces up.

The hole is usually large enough for the entire group to sleep together. If the number of birds is too large for one nest, several cavities may be hollowed out of the same limb. This often weakens the tree and the woodpeckers soon have to look for another roosting site.

HOW DO THE FAMILIES OF ACORN WOODPECKERS DEMONSTRATE TOGETHERNESS?

An entire group of acorn woodpeckers will lay only one clutch of eggs a season. There is probably only one set of parents, although it is difficult to tell which two birds they are.

All the members of the group help to incubate the eggs, but only the dominant male sits on the nest at night. In the morning, all the birds take two-hour turns incubating the eggs. When the young hatch, they are cared for by the entire group and are fed as often as every thirty seconds. Sometimes a group of eight or ten acorn woodpeckers produce only one or two young in a breeding season.

How is preparing for known needs during times of plenty illustrated in Scripture?

In 52 A.D. the Roman deputy of Corinth almost heard Paul speak. This deputy, Gallio, was the older brother of the famous Seneca, whose philosophies he believed. When these were later discredited by Nero, Seneca and Gallio both committed suicide. In contrast, what respected citizen of Corinth heard the Gospel and believed?

(Pause for a response—see page 17.)

An angry mob shoved a wealthy and respected citizen of Corinth aside and moved in to seize his courageous houseguest. The assortment of confused religious leaders, misguided worshipers, and town rabble then moved down the main thoroughfare to the Roman judgment hall.

The newly appointed Roman deputy came out to the rostrum and listened to the frenzied demands for punishment and banishment. Gallio, the deputy, looked at the accused and recalled the bitter cup of public scorn that his family had recently endured, and would probably endure again.

With sympathetic understanding he decided to protect the accused and his followers—whatever their views may be.

Just then the condemned guest attempted to speak, but Gallio interrupted him and said to the threatening crowd, "If it were a matter of wrong or wicked lewdness, I would listen to you. But since it is a question of your own religious laws, I will not be a judge of such matters." He then drove them all out of the judgment hall.

The God-fearing host was greatly relieved. Now he and other believers would be free to prosper in their work and witness.

His guest had risked his life to bring the Gospel to them. How could they show their gratefulness? The answer soon came when he learned of a special need. A serious famine in Jerusalem was causing many Christians to suffer hunger.

How fitting that such a need would be met by citizens of Corinth. This very city was restored by Julius Caesar as a Roman colony to help poor people improve their living conditions.

It was now the wealthiest seaport in the world. In these times of plenty the Corinthian believers and Gaius, host of the Apostle Paul, demonstrated thriftiness by setting aside funds for the famine-stricken Christians at Jerusalem.

From Acts 18:1–18 and II Corinthians 8

Ruins of Corinth

Corinth's location made it ideal for trade by both land and sea. The city maintained economic supremacy for about 1,300 years. The Romans destroyed the city in 146 B.C. However, after it was rebuilt, the area once again became prosperous.

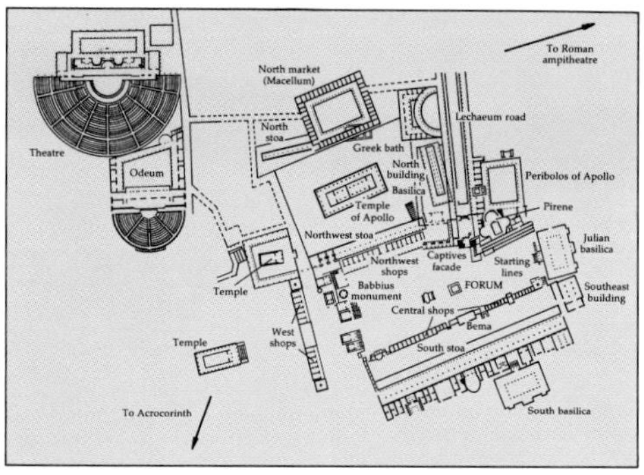

Map of the "City Center" of Corinth

The Apostle Paul was tried in the forum in the city of Corinth. Paul's letters to the Corinthians show how the church was affected by the current problems of society such as immorality, idol worship, and mystery religions.

Temple of Apollo

Doric columns were once part of the Temple of Apollo. (See the center of the map of Corinth.) Each column is a single stone twenty-three and one-half feet high and over seventeen feet around at the base. The Apostle Paul saw people go into this building to worship heathen gods.

GAIUS OF CORINTH, AN UNCOMMON BELIEVER WITH AN ORDINARY NAME

The name *Gaius* is the Greek form for one of the most common of all Roman names. In fact, Roman lawyers used Gaius in the same way that American lawyers use the name "John Doe." There are actually four different men of this name mentioned in the New Testament. But despite his ordinary name, Gaius of Corinth was no ordinary person. He was an outstanding individual who showed great generosity and hospitality to the Apostle Paul and the church of Corinth.

AN UNLIKELY PLACE OF MINISTRY

Gaius was a citizen of the prosperous city of Corinth. Corinth was located on a narrow strip of land, six miles wide, which separated the long Gulf of Corinth on the west from the shorter Saronic Gulf to the east. The city was served by ports in each gulf and became wealthy through extensive commerce. Corinth had been destroyed once but was later rebuilt by Julius Caesar. He resettled the city with discharged Roman soldiers in 46 B.C. Because of its location, merchants flocked back after the city's restoration. Among those returning were Jews of the Dispersion. The new Corinth quickly regained its former reputation as a center for organized and commercialized vice.

This was the Corinth that Paul entered without companions after a somewhat disappointing ministry in Athens. As was his custom, Paul preached to Jews and Jewish converts in the synagogue. He persuaded some that Jesus was the Messiah, but was opposed and scorned by the majority. No longer welcome in the synagogue, he based his ministry in a home which adjoined it. The house was owned by Justus, "*. . . one that worshipped God . . .*" *(Acts 18:7)*.

GAIUS'S HOME BECOMES THE CENTER FOR THE CHURCH AND FOR PAUL'S TEACHING AMONG THE CORINTHIANS

It is almost certain that Justus and Gaius are one and the same person. A Roman name consisted of three parts. For example, the full name of the Roman statesman Cicero was "Marcus Tullius Cicero." By comparing various references in the original New Testament manuscripts, it appears that Gaius's full name was "Gaius Titius Justus." This Gaius, along with Crispus, the chief ruler of the synagogue, were among the first believers in Corinth. Gaius was one of the few converts personally baptized by Paul. (See I Corinthians 1:14.)

Paul did not originally intend to stay in the city. He had a strong desire to resume his work in Thessalonica. (See I Thessalonians 2:17.) Because of the intense hostility of the Jews in Corinth, he was afraid to speak there for fear of harm. But the Lord encouraged Paul in the night through a vision. "*. . . Be not afraid, but speak, and hold not thy peace: For I am with thee, and no man shall set on thee to hurt thee: for I have much people in this city*" *(Acts 18:9–10)*. With the support of Gaius, who hosted the new church, Paul maintained an unexpectedly successful ministry there for a year and a half.

A LASTING AND FRUITFUL ASSOCIATION

When Paul did leave, Gaius would naturally have assumed a leadership role in Corinth. During the Apostle's absence, the church experienced both decline and then revival. The carnality of the city kept creeping in. When Paul returned, he spent three months in the general area (see Acts 20:2–3), and Gaius remained a faithful supporter. Indeed, Paul wrote his letter to the Romans while staying at Gaius' home. (See Romans 16:23.)

CHARACTER SKETCH OF GAIUS

IN WHAT WAY DID PAUL COMMEND GAIUS TO THE ROMAN CHRISTIANS?

At the conclusion of his letter to the Romans, Paul sent greetings from the Corinthian Christians and from Gaius. He used the occasion to commend Gaius by identifying him as *"... mine host, and of the whole church ..." (Romans 16:23)*. Paul characterized him as a man of generous and extensive Christian hospitality.

It is not certain precisely what Paul meant by the second phrase "and the whole church." It is likely that the church continued to meet in Gaius's home. (See Acts 18:7.) The phrase may indicate that he provided lodging to many who flocked to his house while Paul was present. It may also mean that Gaius had a reputation for hospitality toward believers traveling through Corinth. In any case, Gaius met Paul's requirement that leaders of the church be "given to hospitality" and "a lover of hospitality." (See I Timothy 3:2; Titus 1:8.)

HOW DID PAUL BOAST ABOUT THE CORINTHIAN BELIEVERS?

One of Paul's great desires was to help the very poor and persecuted Christians of Jerusalem. He wanted to unify the Body of Christ and remove tension between Jewish and Gentile believers. The church at Corinth was more able than most to contribute to this cause. The Corinthians had been spared the severe persecution which had affected many other Gentile churches.

In Paul's first letter to the Corinthians, he exhorted them to systematically set aside a portion of their income in order to be prepared when he came. Although other problems and divisions in that church caused Paul concern, he was almost apologetic when reminding them of the collection. *"For as touching the ministering to the saints, it is superfluous for me to write to you: For I know the forwardness of your mind, for which I boast of you to them of Macedonia ..." (II Corinthians 9:1–2).*

The Corinthians, who constituted the main church of Achaia, had been ready with their gifts for over a year. It is most likely that the generous and hospitable Gaius was a leading force and example in this ministry.

WHY WERE THE CORINTHIANS ABLE TO HELP SUPPLY THE NEEDS OF OTHERS?

God used the political influence of the Roman ruler Gallio to protect the Corinthian Christians. Many times Paul's preaching resulted in intense persecution. The initiators were often Jews who accused Paul of being a heretic. In fact, Paul's recent ministry in Thessalonica had been shortened because of Jews "moved with envy." (See Acts 17:5.) Jason, Paul's host there, had also suffered.

In Ephesus, idol-making silversmiths led the persecution effort. As a result of such harassment, Christians often lost their jobs, were reduced to poverty, and had little to share with others. Those in Jerusalem were particularly in need.

But such was not the case in Corinth. When a Jewish mob dragged Paul before the Roman proconsul Gallio, he refused to be intimidated by the influential Jews and declined to take sides. Gallio judged Paul innocent under Roman law and afforded him the protection of that law. As a result, the Corinthian Christians were protected from the persecution experienced in other cities. Now Paul expected them to use their surplus to help others. (See II Corinthians 8:13–15.)

Stater c. 350 B.C.

__In the days of Gaius,__ Corinth was the wealthiest seaport in the world. In their times of plenty the Corinthian believers and Gaius, host of the Apostle Paul, could demonstrate thriftiness by setting aside funds for the famine-stricken Christians at Jerusalem.

Dracma c. 400–388 B.C.
Corinthian Coins

GAIUS
gā-yəs

CHAPTER TWENTY-THREE

Thriftiness

. . . Is learning how to live with basic provisions

"Remove far from me vanity and lies: give me neither poverty nor riches; feed me with food convenient for me: Lest I be full, and deny thee, and say, Who is the Lord? or lest I be poor, and steal, and take the name of my God in vain."

Proverbs 30:8–9

Living Lessons on Thriftiness . . .

FROM THE PAGES OF SCRIPTURE

Thriftiness involves learning to live on less. This does not mean just reducing a high standard of living. It means learning to be content with food and clothing. (See I Timothy 6:8.)

Once, a man was offered great treasures if he would learn how to be content with basics. The man, however, was unable to even attempt it. He possessed riches which to him seemed greater than the ones he would receive. He went away with great sorrow.

ILLUSTRATED IN THE WORLD OF NATURE

ALLIGATOR
SNAPPING TURTLE *Macrochelys temminckii*

The alligator snapping turtle is the largest freshwater turtle found in North America. It often reaches weights of 150 to 200 pounds and lengths of more than four feet. Since these turtles do not stop growing, fifty-year-old "monster" snappers have been found that have weighed over 400 pounds.

Alligator snapping turtles are not as aggressive as common snapping turtles. When disturbed in the water, they are more likely to sit passively with their mouths open. If disturbed out of water, they strike only at objects that come very close to them. When picked up, their most common defense is to eject large amounts of liquid.

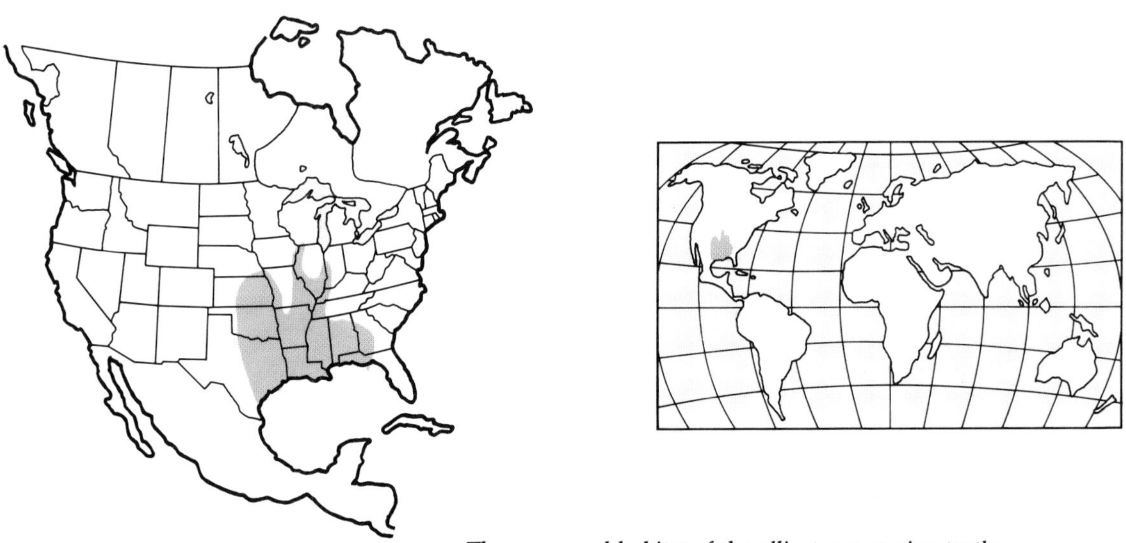

The range and habitat of the alligator snapping turtle

How is the potential of living with less illustrated in the world of nature?

An eighty-pound creature pushed his way through the tall grass like a massive armored tank. When he reached the edge of a small, secluded lake, he slowly stretched out his leathery neck and raised it like a large turret with two active periscopes.

With no further introduction he plunged into the water and slid beneath its surface. His new world revealed a wide variety of potential meals: schools of fish, frogs, mussels, snails, and vegetation.

Instead of immediately grabbing up a meal, the new monarch of the lake swam to the bottom and settled half-buried in the soft mud and underwater growth. He looked like a large rock.

There he remained throughout the day except for brief trips to the surface to breathe. Soon a blue gill was attracted to something and swam straight for the camouflaged creature. A moment later it vanished.

Two days later another small pan fish was curiously drawn to the rocklike form—it, too, disappeared.

As the days grew shorter and the water colder, the submerged creature rarely needed to surface for air. He remained on the bottom of the lake.

Over the next few weeks, his meals were spaced further and further apart. Rather than building up a store of food as other hibernating animals do, he ate less and less. He was in the process of cleansing his digestive system.

Finally, he ate nothing at all. When his system was empty of all food, the great creature covered its entire body with mud and began a fast which would last the entire winter.

His discipline in not eating is extraordinary considering the amazing ability he has to easily catch food. The fish that were strangely attracted to his mouth were drawn there by a very effective lure.

Whenever this creature was hungry, he simply opened his mouth. Suddenly, something that looked like a pink worm appeared. Slowly the worm wiggled back and forth. Its motion would catch the attention of a hungry fish. It would swim toward the lure and then—snap! The water would swirl and the fish would disappear.

The "worm" was actually a growth attached to the middle of the giant snapping turtle's tongue. By pulling down on one side of the tongue and then the other side, he could cause his built-in worm to wiggle. The action was so lifelike that it lured unsuspecting fish right into his open mouth.

With this feeding ability, the alligator snapping turtle becomes an outstanding demonstration of the discipline of living with less.

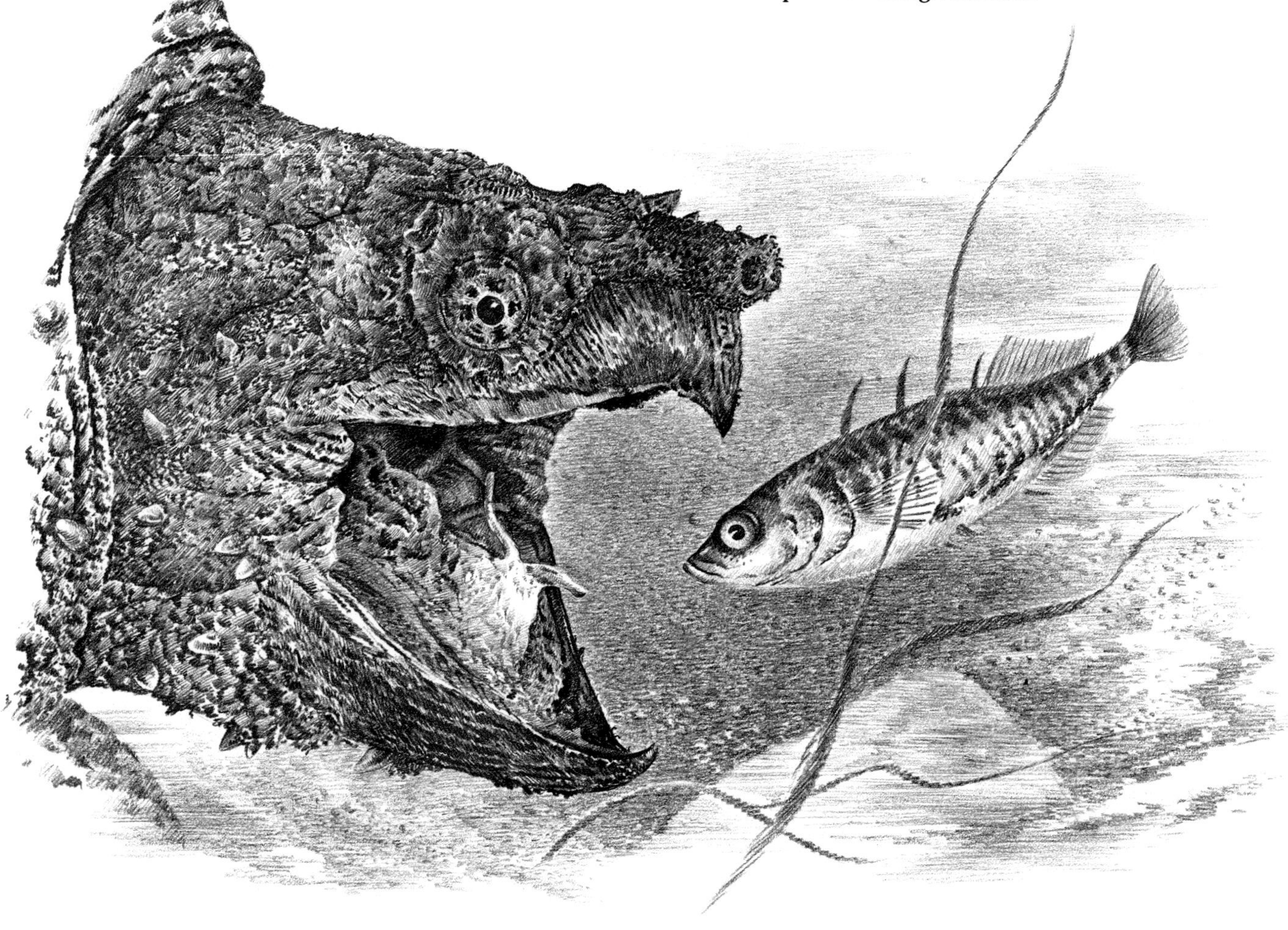

Severt Andrewson

THE CHARACTERISTICS OF

THE ALLIGATOR SNAPPING TURTLE IN SCRIPTURE

The alligator snapping turtle illustrates one of the essential disciplines that must be learned by every Christian who desires the spiritual rewards of living within basic provisions. The discipline is fasting.

The alligator snapping turtle finds seclusion to engage in its fasting. Jesus promises that if we fast secretly, He will reward us openly. (See Matthew 6:18.)

Esther and all her companions fasted for three days and God rewarded them with deliverance from their enemies. (See Esther 4:16.)

Nehemiah fasted for several days and God rewarded him with direction and provision for accomplishing a great work. (See Nehemiah 1–2.)

Extended fasting for the alligator snapping turtle marks a new season for its life. The same was true for Moses, Daniel, Christ, Paul, and others.

The alligator snapping turtle also illustrates the trap that food can be to Christians who do not conquer uncontrolled appetites. Just as the alligator snapping turtle ensnares unsuspecting victims with the bait of its dangling tongue, so Adam and Eve fell victim to their appetite. (See Genesis 3:6.)

The mixed multitude in the wilderness learned the same hard lesson. *"And he gave them their request; but sent leanness into their soul" (Psalm 106:15).*

CHARACTERISTICS AND PHYSICAL FEATURES OF THE ALLIGATOR SNAPPING TURTLE

Most animals prepare for winter by storing up food, stuffing themselves to add layers of fat to their bodies, or by migrating to places where food is available all winter.

Many fish simply adapt to the temperature of the surrounding water and continue to feed in spite of the colder weather. However, the alligator snapping turtle does none of these things. Instead, each fall it gradually decreases the amount of food it eats until it eats nothing at all.

HOW DOES THE ALLIGATOR SNAPPING TURTLE MAINTAIN ITS WELCOME?

A fifty-pound turtle could easily devour everything in sight within a few months, leaving nothing for others to eat in the creek or pond in which it lives. However, by learning to exist on less food, the alligator snapping turtle makes it possible for other pond fish and creatures to survive.

HOW DOES AN ALLIGATOR SNAPPING TURTLE SEE WITH ITS EYES SHUT?

The eyes of the alligator snapping turtle are on each side of the head and cannot be seen directly from above. Each eye has three lids that protect it. A short, thick upper lid closes from the top down. It meets a much thinner and longer lower lid that closes from the bottom up. Both are opaque.

The third eyelid is transparent and lets the alligator snapping turtle see even when it is closed. When not in use, it folds into the eye's front corner. He can see well even in muddy water because of the special construction of the retina.

WHY IS AN ALLIGATOR SNAPPING TURTLE CONSIDERED DEAF?

The turtle has no external ears. Its only sense of hearing comes from a thin piece of skin, called a *tympanic membrane,* located on each side of the head just behind the angle of the jaw. Although the alligator snapping turtle is considered deaf, it will come to the surface and lift its head above water in response to loud noises.

HOW DOES THE ALLIGATOR SNAPPING TURTLE ACQUIRE "LIVING COLOR"?

The natural color of the turtle's shell is grayish brown. Within a month after birth, algae begin to grow on the shell and turn it green. Because the alligator snapping turtle lives almost motionless underwater much of its life, the algae continue to grow and do not dry out. By the time the turtle is several years old, the shell looks like a rock covered with long green hair. The algae camouflage the turtle so well that it is almost undetectable in the muddy water.

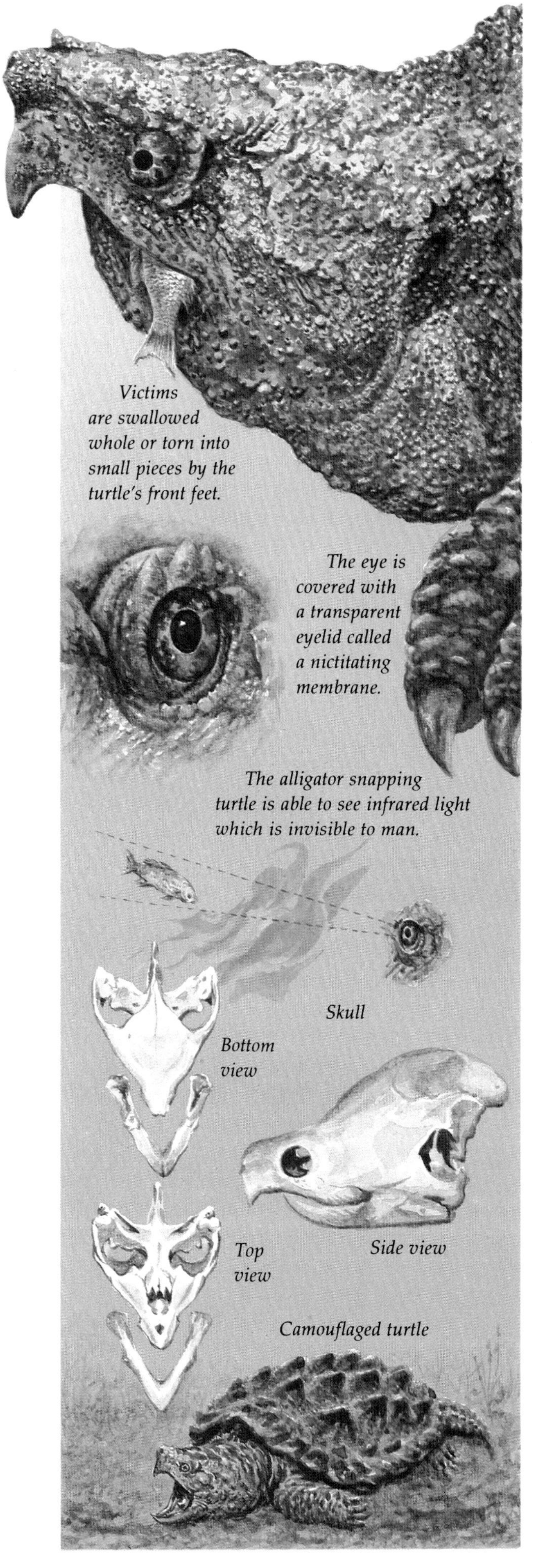

Victims are swallowed whole or torn into small pieces by the turtle's front feet.
The eye is covered with a transparent eyelid called a nictitating membrane.
The alligator snapping turtle is able to see infrared light which is invisible to man.
Skull
Bottom view
Side view
Top view
Camouflaged turtle

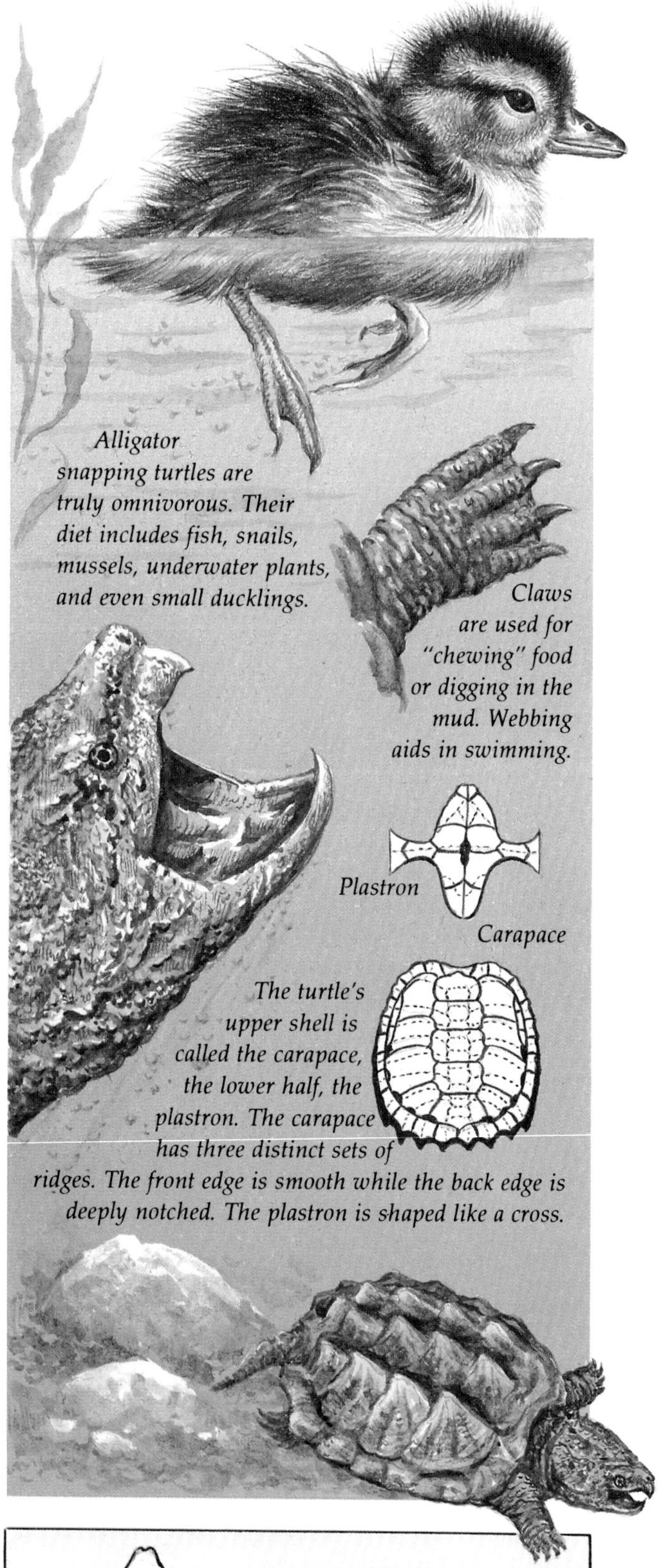

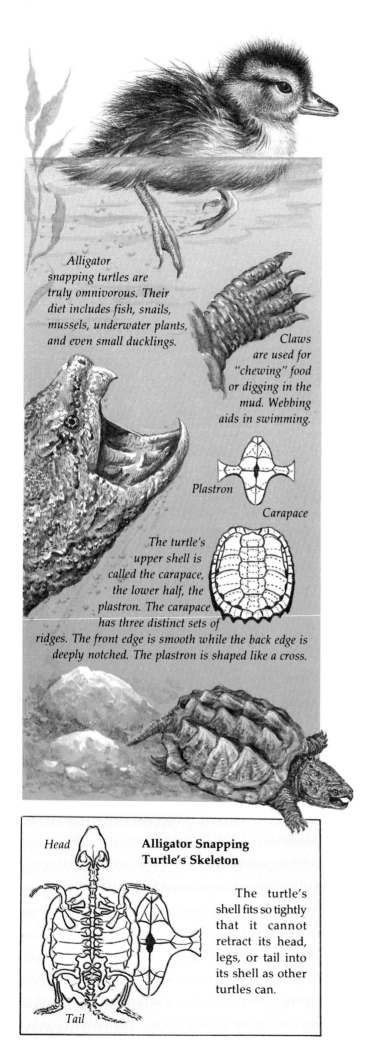

Alligator snapping turtles are truly omnivorous. Their diet includes fish, snails, mussels, underwater plants, and even small ducklings.

Claws are used for "chewing" food or digging in the mud. Webbing aids in swimming.

The turtle's upper shell is called the carapace, the lower half, the plastron. The carapace has three distinct sets of ridges. The front edge is smooth while the back edge is deeply notched. The plastron is shaped like a cross.

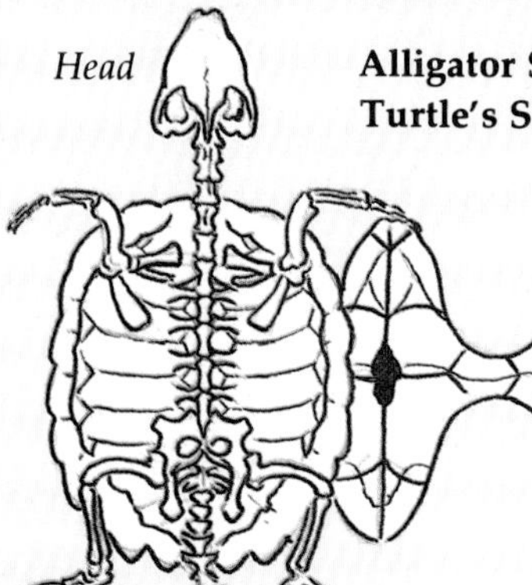

Alligator Snapping Turtle's Skeleton

The turtle's shell fits so tightly that it cannot retract its head, legs, or tail into its shell as other turtles can.

HOW DOES THE ALLIGATOR SNAPPING TURTLE CHEW WITH ITS FEET?

The alligator snapping turtle has no teeth. Its sharp jaws can rip food into pieces but cannot chew them, so the alligator snapping turtle chews its food with its front feet. Each foot has five toes tipped with strong claws. Chunks of food too large to swallow are held in the mouth and shredded by the front feet. The bits are then swallowed individually. The turtle also eats rocks. As they pass through the intestinal tract, they help to grind up the food.

HOW DO THE LUNGS OF AN ALLIGATOR SNAPPING TURTLE WORK THE OPPOSITE OF HUMAN LUNGS?

Because of its rigid shell, the alligator snapping turtle cannot expand its ribs to breathe the way most mammals do. Instead it has a special pair of lung muscles that squeeze air out of the lungs as they contract. When the muscles relax, outside air pressure forces air into the turtle's lungs. Human lungs are empty when they are relaxed.

HOW DOES TWENTY DEGREES TURN FIFTY MINUTES UNDERWATER INTO A MONTH FOR THE ALLIGATOR SNAPPING TURTLE?

An alligator snapping turtle can stay underwater for only twenty minutes when the water temperature is above 75°F. But as water cools down to 70°F, the turtle can remain submerged for up to fifty minutes. When the water temperature drops below 50°F, the alligator snapping turtle can stay underwater for more than a month.

IF THE NOSE AND MOUTH OF AN ALLIGATOR SNAPPING TURTLE WERE SEALED SHUT, WOULD IT SUFFOCATE?

No, it will simply take in oxygen from the other end. If trapped underwater, the alligator snapping turtle "breathes" by taking in water through a special chamber called the *cloaca.* It is lined with blood vessels that absorb oxygen directly from the water. Old water is "exhaled" and fresh water is "inhaled" every few minutes.

WHY DOES THE ALLIGATOR SNAPPING TURTLE BREATHE EASIER IN WATER?

The turtle has the most difficulty breathing when it is completely out of the water. The buoyancy of the water lifts the turtle's body and makes it easy for the turtle to breathe. But out of the water, a turtle will have as much as fifteen times greater pressure.

HOW DOES THE ALLIGATOR SNAPPING TURTLE USE ITS NECK AND LEGS TO BREATHE?

When on land, the turtle often uses its neck and legs as pumps to help force air in and out of its lungs. By pulling its neck in like a plunger, the turtle can force air out of its lungs. By stretching its neck and legs, the turtle can help draw air back into its lungs.

HOW IS WATER THE GREATEST DANGER TO NEWBORN ALLIGATOR SNAPPING TURTLES?

Drowning is the greatest danger to young alligator snapping turtles. They do not swim well until they are four to five months old and may drown in as little as six inches of water. They must stand on underwater vegetation, sticks, or rocks in order to lift their heads above water to breathe. They wrap their long tails around the stems of plants to keep from being swept into deep water by the current.

Fewer than thirty per cent of alligator snapping turtle eggs ever hatch. Many eggs are dug up by skunks and raccoons soon after they are laid. Those that do hatch may fall victim to herons, bitterns, gulls, muskrats, mink, and even larger turtles.

WHY IS IT HARD TO BREAK AN ALLIGATOR SNAPPING TURTLE EGG?

Alligator snapping turtle eggs are not covered with a brittle shell like that of birds. Instead, the shell is slightly rubbery and elastic. The female digs a hole in a sunny spot near the water. When the hole is completed, she actually drops her eggs into it. Although she slows the fall of her eggs slightly with her hind feet, the eggs still slide into the hole on top of each other. If the shells were brittle, all the eggs would break as soon as they were laid.

WHEN MUST NEWLY HATCHED SNAPPING TURTLES WORK TOGETHER TO SEE THE LIGHT OF DAY?

Eggs are laid close to water in a clearing where there is direct exposure to the sun. Turtles do not incubate their own eggs. They rely on the heat of the sun to keep the eggs warm. The incubation period requires 70 to 120 days, depending on the amount of sunlight available.

Young turtles hatch underground. If the soil is hard and dry, several young turtles must work together to dig their way through the soil to the surface. Occasionally a clutch of newly hatched turtles may remain buried for days waiting for a rain to soften the ground.

Young turtles have enormous heads in comparison to the rest of their bodies. An adult head may exceed seven inches in width.

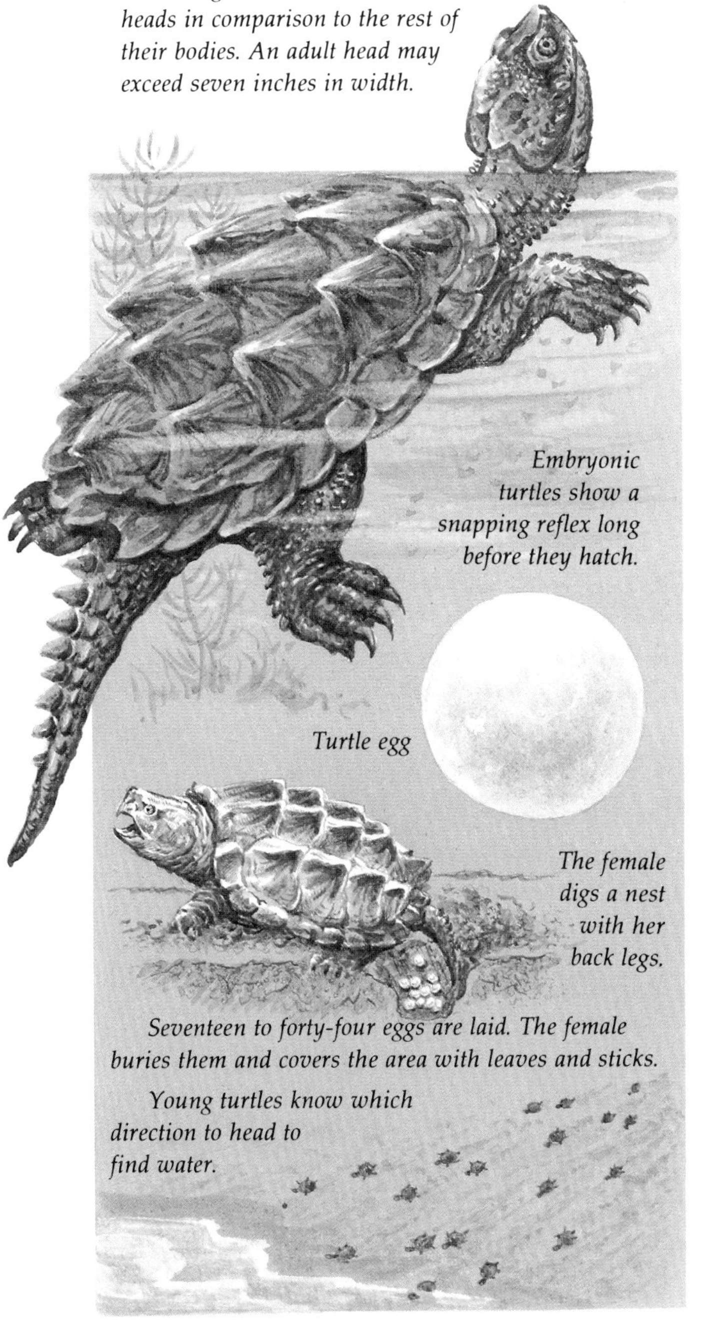

Embryonic turtles show a snapping reflex long before they hatch.

Turtle egg

The female digs a nest with her back legs.

Seventeen to forty-four eggs are laid. The female buries them and covers the area with leaves and sticks.

Young turtles know which direction to head to find water.

Comparison Between the Alligator Snapping Turtle and the Common Snapping Turtle

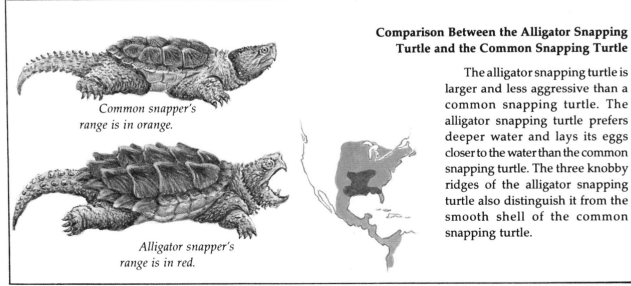

Common snapper's range is in orange.

Alligator snapper's range is in red.

The alligator snapping turtle is larger and less aggressive than a common snapping turtle. The alligator snapping turtle prefers deeper water and lays its eggs closer to the water than the common snapping turtle. The three knobby ridges of the alligator snapping turtle also distinguish it from the smooth shell of the common snapping turtle.

Leeches, or bloodsuckers as they are commonly called, *often attach themselves to the exposed parts of a turtle. Three small white teeth, located in the center of the leech's sucking disc, cut a hole in the turtle's skin. The blood flows directly into the leech's mouth.*

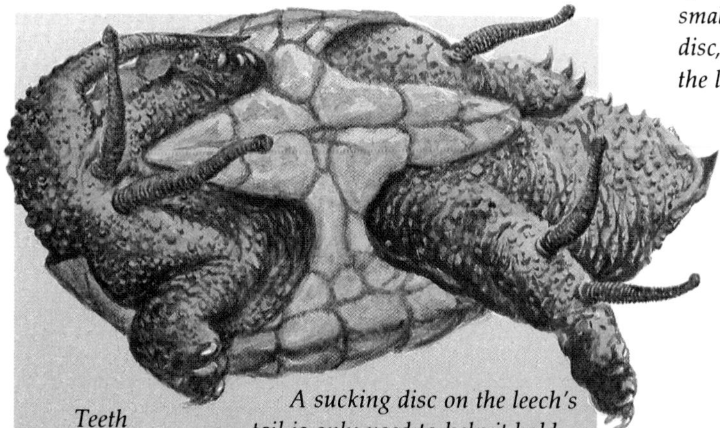

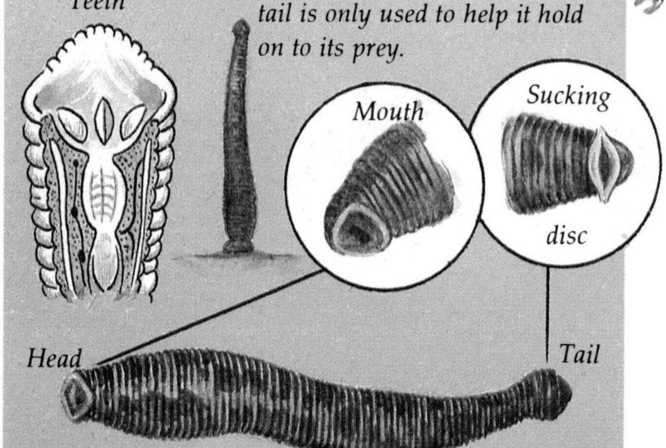

A sucking disc on the leech's tail is only used to help it hold on to its prey.

In the water, young alligator snapping turtles fall easy prey to alligators.

A Florida snapping turtle breaking a stick

HOW DOES THE ALLIGATOR SNAPPING TURTLE RESEMBLE A SKUNK?

Both use a chemical defense to warn intruders to stay away. While the skunk is able to spray its infamous "smell" up to sixteen feet, the turtle is limited to the use of a thick yellow substance that sticks to its own body. When threatened, the alligator snapping turtle spreads the foul-smelling liquid over its neck and legs for protection.

CAN AN ALLIGATOR SNAPPING TURTLE SNAP AN OAR WITH ITS MOUTH?

Although the alligator snapping turtle can bite, the power of its "snap" is overrated. Stories of alligator snapping turtles' biting oars and broomsticks in two may or may not be true. One forty-pound snapper was unable to break a pencil. However, when an alligator snapping turtle does strike, it is quick and has a surprising reach. The momentum of its massive head is often great enough to pull its whole body off the ground. Although it is toothless, its jaws are capable of inflicting severe wounds to a human hand.

HOW DOES AN ALLIGATOR SNAPPING TURTLE USE ITS TONGUE TO LURE ITS PREY?

An alligator snapping turtle will eat anything it can capture and swallow. Although it eats vegetation, it prefers to eat meat. It hunts most actively at night, when it goes after snails, mussels, and larger prey such as ducklings and even other turtles. During the day it lies motionless on the bottom and fishes with its "lure." The turtle can wiggle this lure, which is attached to its tongue, to make it look like a worm. Fish attracted to the lure fall easy prey and are trapped in the turtle's mouth.

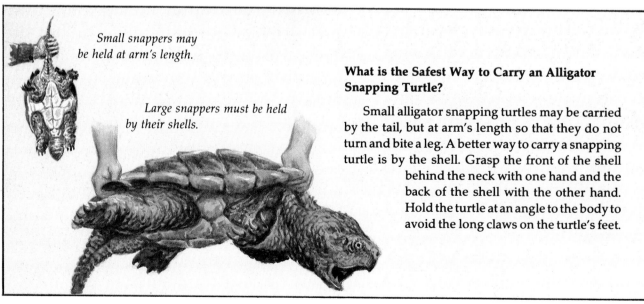

Small snappers may be held at arm's length.

Large snappers must be held by their shells.

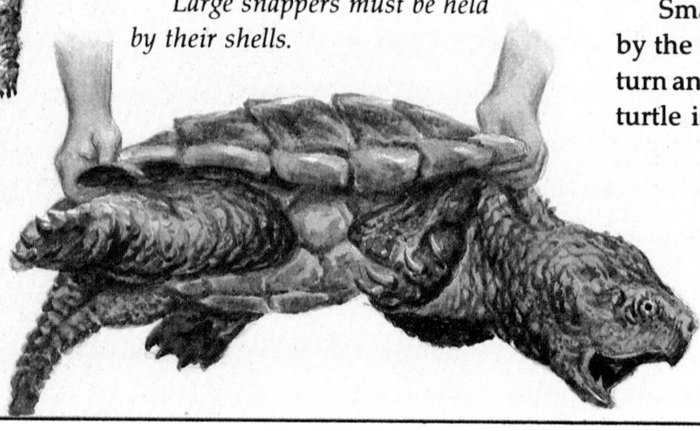

What is the Safest Way to Carry an Alligator Snapping Turtle?

Small alligator snapping turtles may be carried by the tail, but at arm's length so that they do not turn and bite a leg. A better way to carry a snapping turtle is by the shell. Grasp the front of the shell behind the neck with one hand and the back of the shell with the other hand. Hold the turtle at an angle to the body to avoid the long claws on the turtle's feet.

How is the importance of learning to live with basics illustrated in Scripture?

Who was the man that was unable to receive great treasures because he was absorbed in personal treasures which would soon be lost?

(Pause for a response—see page 17.)

One day two rulers met together. The fact that their meeting was recorded in history is an indication of its importance. It turned out to have far-reaching implications.

Both rulers were young, came from wealthy backgrounds, and were aware of all the riches which were available to them. Both rulers had been trained in the Law of God and both had purposed to keep His commandments. Each one was aware of the importance of life after death, and uppermost in each of their minds at that moment was eternal life.

There were also differences between these two rulers. One was older and more mature. The older ruler possessed far greater riches than the younger even imagined.

The more mature ruler had a far greater grasp of God's Law and its true meaning. However, he was deeply impressed by the young ruler and desired to greatly increase his riches.

In order to prepare the young ruler for the treasures that he would receive, he quoted several commandments. The younger ruler quickly responded, "All of these commandments I have kept from my youth up."

These commandments, however, are summed up in the following words, "Thou shalt love the Lord thy God will all thy heart... and thou shalt love thy neighbor as thyself." Based on this, the older ruler gave him a perceptive test.

Failing the test would reveal that he did not understand the basic principles upon which the Law or life were built. If he passed the test, he would immediately receive vast treasures which would make his present possessions seem insignificant by comparison.

The test Jesus gave him was to sell his possessions and give the money to the poor, whom he had just implied he loved as himself. It is not hard to keep money for oneself.

The rich young ruler understood the test and slowly walked away sorrowing. He had never learned the valuable secret of thriftiness which would allow him to be secure with basic provisions.

From Matthew 19:16–22

THE RICH IN CHRIST'S DAY, UNINTERESTED IN THE KINGDOM OF GOD

Needle Gate in Jerusalem Wall

Many assume that Christ's statements about a rich man and the eye of a needle refer to the Needle Gate in the wall of Jerusalem. A camel would have to be unloaded and made to crawl through on its knees.

This offers valid lessons. However, the words which Christ used actually meant the eye of a household needle. His statement emphasized the impossibility of entering heaven by dependence upon riches or good works.

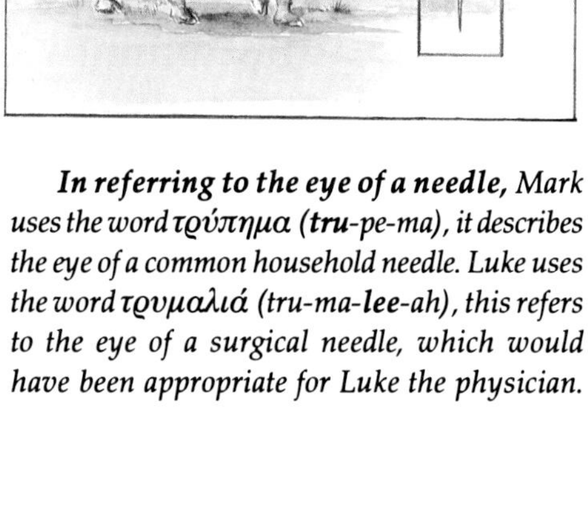

***In referring to the eye of a needle,** Mark uses the word τρύπημα (**tru**-pe-ma), it describes the eye of a common household needle. Luke uses the word τρυμαλιά (tru-ma-**lee**-ah), this refers to the eye of a surgical needle, which would have been appropriate for Luke the physician.*

During the time of Christ, the nation of Israel was composed of the wealthy class, the middle class, and the poor. Members of the wealthy class were wholesale merchants, landowners, tax farmers, bankers, ranking politicians, and the priestly aristocracy. The middle class consisted of retail merchants and craftsmen—those who were self-employed and did not have to hire themselves out for daily wages. Slaves, day laborers, and beggars were the poor of the land.

With a few notable exceptions such as Nicodemus, Joseph of Arimathea, Zacchaeus, and Joanna the politician's wife, the rich had little to do with Jesus. They were so involved with their interests in the kingdom of Herod and the kingdom of Caesar that they had no interest in the kingdom of God. Like the religious leaders who stumbled over the Lord's lack of formal training, the wealthy stumbled over His humble economic status. Jesus clashed with their preconceived ideas on the nature of the expected Messiah.

A RULER WHO ASKED LIFE'S MOST IMPORTANT QUESTION

It was an unusual event when one day, toward the end of His ministry, a young and influential member of the wealthy class ran to Jesus, knelt down, and asked, *". . . Good Master, what shall I do that I may inherit eternal life?" (Mark 10:17)*. From his question Jesus discerned a basic error in the young man's thinking. He did not yet believe that Jesus was the Son of God, yet he addressed Him as a "good" man. The rabbis refused to call a man good because it ascribed to him an attribute possessed only by God. The young man believed that goodness was a result of good works.

"WHO IS GOOD?"

In an effort to expose man's lack of goodness, Jesus asked, *". . . Why callest thou me good? there is none good but one, that is, God" (Mark 10:18)*. Jesus wanted the ruler to compare himself with the perfect character of God rather than fellow sinners. Then He reminded him of God's perfect standards. A good man could not commit adultery, murder, steal, commit perjury, or cheat. On the positive side, a good man must respect his parents and love his neighbor as much as himself.

The young man was familiar with these commandments. He was also familiar with the casuistic teaching of the scribes which had stripped the commands of their original meaning. (See Matthew 5:21–48.) As a result, he sincerely believed he had obeyed the commands throughout his entire life.

THE CHOICE: TREASURE IN HEAVEN OR RICHES ON EARTH

Rather than argue, Jesus tried a third time to convince the man of his sinful nature and need of grace. *". . . One thing thou lackest: go thy way, sell whatsoever thou hast, and give to the poor, and thou shalt have treasure in heaven: and come, take up the cross, and follow me" (Mark 10:21)*. The young man was looking for a challenge, but he did not anticipate anything like this.

Jesus was confronting him with indisputable evidence of his violation of the Tenth Commandment, the one concerning covetousness and greed. Why was this member of the wealthy class able to enjoy his extravagance and feel no pain for the suffering of the poor? The rich young ruler was covetous of possessions and greedy for gain because he was not good. He was a sinner who needed God's grace and forgiveness. *"And he was sad at that saying, and went away grieved: for he had great possessions" (Mark 10:22)*.

CHARACTER SKETCH OF THE RICH YOUNG RULER

WHAT WAS THE RICH YOUNG RULER'S REAL PURPOSE IN COMING TO JESUS?

When the young man knelt before Jesus and asked, *". . . What shall I do that I may inherit eternal life?" (Mark 10:17)*, he was not acknowledging a need for salvation from sin. To him eternal life merely meant a life which experienced the full blessings of salvation. He was taught that the way to blessing was to please God by performing good works such as giving alms to the poor, reciting daily prayers, and fasting twice a week—three methods taught by the religious leaders. (See Matthew 6:1–18.)

The young man believed he was already in good standing with God because of his strict adherence to the letter of the Law as weakened by the rabbis. But he was not at peace. He wanted a special task which he could perform, possibly using his influence and resources, in order to receive special blessing and standing before God.

When the Philippian jailer fell down before Paul and Silas and asked, *". . . Sirs, what must I do to be saved?"* he had clearly recognized his need for salvation. Paul and Silas could immediately reply, *". . . Believe on the Lord Jesus Christ, and thou shalt be saved . . ." (Acts 16:30–31)*. But the rich young man had not yet recognized his great need and could not trust in Jesus while still trusting in his wealth. (See Matthew 6:24.)

WHY DID CHRIST ASK THE RULER TO GIVE EVERYTHING TO THE POOR?

The Lord gave the young man a very challenging assignment—to give everything he owned to the poor. It was not uncommon for pious Jews to give away one-fifth of their income to the poor. The rich man would probably have given more than that to purchase the peace he lacked. But to give everything away would remove him from the wealthy class altogether. He would no longer have his luxuries, his servants, his friends, his security, or his power.

Jesus knew that possessions owned this man and not the man his possessions. He was chained to the world system by his love of money, and the Lord knew the young man would struggle with money as long as he owned it. He needed to learn to trust in God alone.

WHY WERE THE DISCIPLES "ASTONISHED OUT OF MEASURE" AT CHRIST'S RESPONSE?

After the young man sadly departed, Jesus told the disciples, *". . . How hardly shall they that have riches enter into the kingdom of God!"* He went on, *"It is easier for a camel to go through the eye of a needle, than for a rich man to enter into the kingdom of God" (Mark 10:23, 25)*.

The disciples thought the young man was an ideal candidate for the kingdom. Although they themselves had left all to follow Jesus, they still clung to the common opinion that the wealthy were looked upon more favorably by God. Were not the rich more blessed? Were they not able to give more alms and perform greater acts to earn God's favor? But Jesus said without ambiguity that it is impossible for a man to earn favor with God through his wealth.

Man cannot earn salvation. But God can reach out in grace and provide a way for him. The only requirement is a recognition of this fact and the humble reception of it. These things are especially hard for the rich who are not accustomed to admitting need or receiving help. But God can even change the heart of the rich.

JOB

__The rich young ruler and Job__ were both wealthy men, yet their responses to riches were entirely different. Job looked at riches as a trust from God and was therefore able to bless God when he lost all of them. The young ruler looked at his wealth as belonging to himself and was therefore not able to exchange it for greater riches.

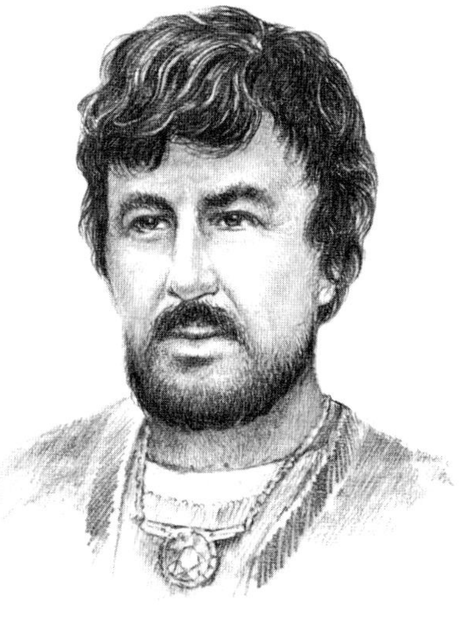

RICH YOUNG RULER

CHAPTER TWENTY-FOUR

Thriftiness

. . . Is taking care of what I have to extend its usefulness

"The slothful man roasteth not that which he took in hunting: but the substance of a diligent man is precious."

Proverbs 12:27

Living Lessons on Thriftiness . . .

FROM THE PAGES OF SCRIPTURE

In order to properly care for our possessions, we must first recognize that what we have has been entrusted to us by the Lord. Only then can we view ourselves as stewards and have the excitement in life that comes by using our resources to advance God's kingdom.

Cleanliness is a vital part of thriftiness. Cleanliness is not "next to Godliness," it is "part of Godliness." One of the most successful kings of Judah demonstrated through his life and work how cleansing and care of God's possessions must begin within the heart and life of God's people.

ILLUSTRATED IN THE WORLD OF NATURE

EASTERN BLUEBIRD *Sialia sialis*

Once called the "blue robin," the bluebird wears the colors found in the flag of the United States of America. It has a brilliant blue back, red chest, and white underside. Bluebirds are extremely beneficial. They eat harmful insects by the thousands. A single bird may eat as many as 50,000 cutworms in a season. In the winter bluebirds eat wild berries, including those of the mistletoe and poison ivy. The young weigh only three grams when they hatch but multiply their weight nine times in their first two weeks.

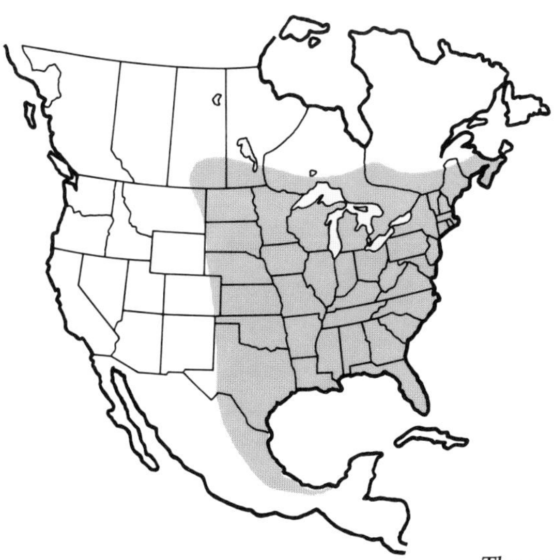

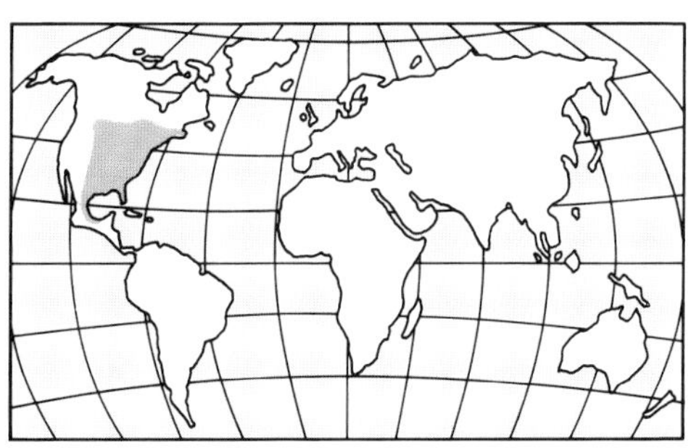

The range and habitat of the eastern bluebird

How is the need to take care of resources illustrated in the world of nature?

While the Second World War was causing the British people to live in daily dread of German attacks, another war was taking place in the fields of America. Longtime residents feared a threat from the sky just as real as the German rockets in Britain.

The eerie sound of sirens in Britain caused the inhabitants to run to the safety of their bomb shelters. The shrieking sound of the terror in American skies caused country residents to flee to the safety of their homes. After the raids, the dead were strewn about in both Britain and America.

Parents in both countries would train their young how to detect the enemy flying overhead and give stern warnings not to wander far from safety.

After air attacks, mothers were kept busy cleaning their homes and removing debris. While the mothers were taking care of their infants, the fathers were teaching their youth and preparing them to assist with family responsibilities.

One day in a peaceful countryside in America the dreaded alarm was given–the aggressive attackers were coming. Quickly, the residents fled to their homes. Mothers huddled with their young while fathers sat nervously waiting.

Moments later, thousands of invaders descended from the sky. Some landed in the open field, others in trees.

As soon as the invaders surveyed the territory, they entered the homes. Brazenly they burst in and forced the occupants out. If there were infants in the home, they threw them out in the dirt. Many of them perished.

The cruel invaders then treated the homes as their own, confiscating the contents for their own use. No longer was the sound of happy singing to be heard in this region. Instead, there would be the strange sound of the new arrivals.

Once they were established in their stolen homes, they advanced into new territories, plundering the crops of berries, cherries, apples, and pears. When news of this reached the cities of America, it caused alarm and concern, but little could be done.

The intruders were so well equipped to survive in America that they had multiplied into millions. Those whom they displaced dwindled in number.

The invaders from the sky who descended upon American fields were starlings. The longtime residents which they displaced and scattered were the red, white, and blue eastern bluebirds.

During the Second World War the starlings multiplied into millions and reduced the bluebird population by ninety per cent. Ironically, starlings were introduced to America when about one hundred of them were imported from Great Britain in 1890–1891.

The bluebirds that have remained have done so because of their thriftiness in finding and maintaining homes which the starlings could not enter.

THE CHARACTERISTICS OF

THE BLUEBIRD IN SCRIPTURE

The importance of the nest to the survival of the bluebird provides significant parallels to the importance of the home for the continuing health and well-being of the family.

The danger of a bluebird being forced to aimlessly wander from its nest is compared to the danger of a parent or child wandering from his home. *"As a bird that wandereth from her nest, so is a man that wandereth from his place" (Proverbs 27:8).* (See also Isaiah 16:2.)

The affection and care of the male bluebird for his partner speaks of the self-sacrifice which the husband is to provide for his wife. (See Ephesians 5:25.)

As the male bluebird teaches its young, so fathers are to bring up their children in the nurture and admonition of the Lord. (See Ephesians 6:4.)

The large number of offspring that the bluebirds have coincides with God's command to parents, *". . . Be fruitful, and multiply . . ." (Genesis 1:28).*

The teaching of older chicks to help with the rearing of the young illustrates the admonition of I Timothy 5:4 to learn first to show piety at home. The mother bluebird's amazing care of the nest is a beautiful example of being a keeper at home. (See Titus 2:5.)

CHARACTERISTICS AND PHYSICAL FEATURES OF THE EASTERN BLUEBIRD

A family of bluebirds will increase the usefulness of an old nest by using it a second time. By caring for the nest, keeping it clean, and making repairs as they are needed, the pair is able to refurbish the nest and successfully raise their young.

Bluebirds nest in the holes made by woodpeckers.

WHY DO BLUEBIRDS NOT LIVE IN FORESTS?

Bluebirds stay away from deep forests. They prefer open country, roadside trees, and orchards. The open fields provide a greater abundance of grasshoppers and other insects, which make up the greater part of a bluebird's diet.

During the breeding and nesting seasons, bluebirds live in the holes of trees, wooden fences, and man-made bird houses. Their favorite places are the holes in old stumps and limbs in orchards.

HOW DOES THE THRIFTINESS OF A BLUEBIRD RELATE TO A MAILBOX?

Nesting holes are in such great demand among bluebirds, that they will choose unusual sites in which to build a nest. They have even been known to nest in the back of mailboxes. By maintaining and reusing the same nesting site, bluebirds are able to invest more of their time and energy in the care of their young.

WHY HAVE FEW PEOPLE SEEN A WILD BLUEBIRD?

Since 1940 the bluebird population has dropped as much as ninety per cent. Today, few people have ever seen a wild bluebird. The primary reason for their decline has been a decrease in the number of suitable nesting sites. Wooden fences have been replaced with metal ones. Unsightly tree limbs and stumps have been cleared out with chain saws. With the introduction of the English sparrow and the starling, which also nest in tree holes, the bluebird has been evicted from its former nests.

The English sparrow and the starling are native to the British Isles.

HOW DID A SHAKESPEAREAN PLAY ENDANGER THE SURVIVAL OF BLUEBIRDS IN THE U.S.?

On March 6, 1890, a group called the Acclimatization Society released about sixty imported starlings in New York's Central Park. The following year another forty were released. The purpose of the group was to introduce to the park every species of bird mentioned in Shakespeare's plays.

The group did not realize that the starling would adapt so well to city and country life that it would become a nuisance over the entire continent and drive the bluebirds out of most of their available nesting sites. Forty years earlier sparrows were also introduced in Central Park. The entire population of house sparrows and starlings in the United States are descendants of these original birds.

Starlings are too large to fit through a 1½″ hole.

English sparrows prefer nests that are ten or more feet off the ground.

Wrens prefer nests with a perch just outside the entrance.

HOW HAS A 2,000 MILE BLUEBIRD TRAIL BEEN CONSTRUCTED?

Eighty-five bluebird boxes, located just seven miles from Washington, D.C., have produced over 1,000 bluebird chicks a year. A trail of 7,000 boxes extends 2,000 miles across Canada. Many of these boxes, however, have been taken over by tree swallows, sparrows, and wrens. These boxes have been responsible for the successful hatching of 8,000 bluebirds annually.

IN WHAT WAYS IS A MALE BLUEBIRD AN IDEAL MATE?

A male bluebird is often seen sitting with his mate. He demonstrates his affection by singing to his partner and bringing bright little gifts to her. He protects her by driving off any intruder or rival.

The male bluebird and his partner, and later their young, work together as a team. While the female is preparing for a second brood, the male helps to care for the young by teaching them and feeding them.

HOW CAN A BLUEBIRD BE TRAINED TO COME WHEN ITS NAME IS CALLED?

Bluebirds are extremely friendly to people. When orphaned, a two- to three-day-old bluebird will take food from a human hand. A young bluebird will also curl up under its human protector's chin or crawl up his shirt sleeve. Their gregarious nature allows them to quickly learn to come for food when called. They even appear to learn names given to them.

WHY IS MIGRATION MORE DANGEROUS FOR BLUEBIRDS?

In winter, bluebirds move only as far south as the cold weather forces them. The rest of the year they range as far north as Canada, always staying east of the Rocky Mountains. They are often the last birds to leave in the fall and the first to return in the spring.

Because of this, they sometimes encounter early winter or late spring snowstorms that wipe out entire flocks. One year during a late March snowstorm, an observer found thirteen bluebirds huddled together in a 4″ x 4″ x 9″ nesting box. They had suffocated in the bottom of the box as they tried to stay warm.

WHAT THREE FEATURES ARE IMPORTANT FOR A BLUEBIRD HOUSE?

The three design features which will make the nest less attractive to wrens, sparrows, and starlings, and more attractive to bluebirds are:

1. An entrance hole cut exactly 1½″ in diameter. This will keep out the larger starlings.
2. An absence of any outside perch. This discourages wrens from using the box.
3. A location less than four feet from the ground. This makes the nest unattractive to sparrows.

HOW TO CONSTRUCT A BLUEBIRD HOUSE

A bluebird house can be made from a three-foot-long piece of 1″ x 6″ lumber, a two-foot piece of 1″ x 8″ lumber, and a 7½″ x ½″ dowel rod. The pieces can be screwed together or simply glued and nailed.

The 1″ x 6″ piece makes the front, sides, and floor of the box and the 1″ x 8″ makes the back and top. The dowel rod serves as a hinge so that the top can be opened for cleaning the nest.

Front: Cut the front of the box 9⅛″ long and center a 1½″ hole 7″ from the bottom.

Sides: The top of each side must be angled so that the roof slopes. The front edge should be 9″ and the back edge 11″.

Floor: Cut the floor 4″ wide and then trim a diagonal off each corner so that the nest will drain. The floor should be recessed above the bottom edge at least ¼″ for added protection.

Back: Center the box on a 16″ x 8″ back. Leave enough room above and below the box so that it can be attached easily to a post or tree.

Roof: An 8″ roof will give enough of an overhang to prevent rain from dripping into the nest. Do not attach the roof to the box.

Cleat: Tack a ¾″ x 4″ cleat to the underside of the roof, 1 and 11/16″ back from the front edge. This will keep the roof from sliding off.

Hinge: Set the roof in place and hold the dowel rod firmly against the roof. Nail or screw the rod to the back of the box. The roof should fit snugly against the frame so that it will not slip out. There will be a gap between the roof and the sides to allow for ventilation.

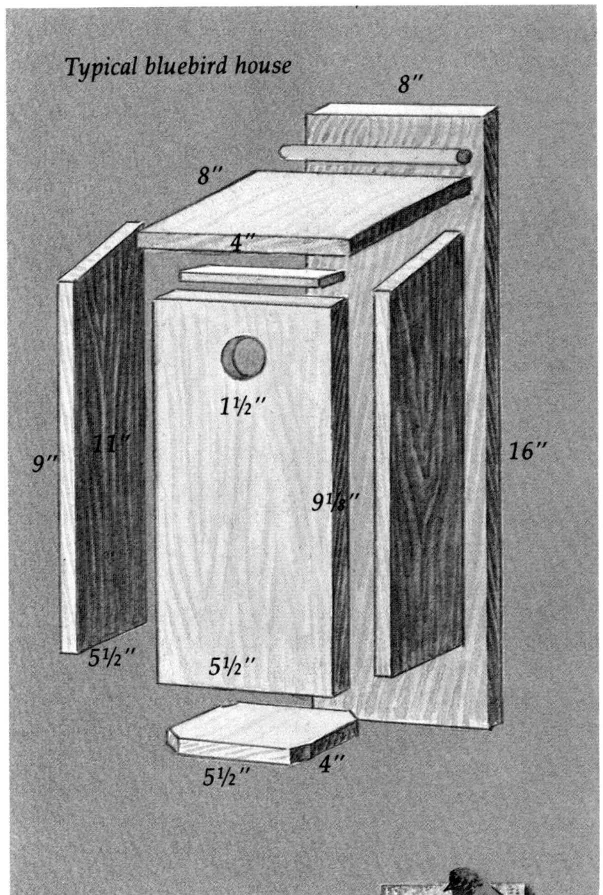

Spoiler feathers allow the bluebird to land more accurately by breaking up the flow of air over the wings.

WHAT DO BLUEBIRD CHICKS USE THAT ARE BETTER THAN DIAPERS?

Bluebirds have a better way of keeping their nests clean than using diapers. Excreta from young bluebirds comes wrapped neatly in tough little sacs. These are carried from the nest and disposed of without ever soiling the nest.

Sharp claws and a strong tail help the bluebird to cling to surfaces.

Bluebird eggs are generally pale blue.

WHEN IS IT LEGAL TO CAGE A BLUEBIRD?

It is illegal to keep bluebirds in captivity without a proper license. Local authorities should be notified if an orphaned nestling is to be raised in a cage.

Nesting boxes should be placed 100 yards apart.

Bluebirds drive other birds away from their nests and feeding grounds.

Male carrying a fecal sac from the nest

Bluebird parents feed their young every six to ten minutes.

Bluebird eggs hatch in twelve to fourteen days. The young grow quickly and make their first flights in two to three weeks.

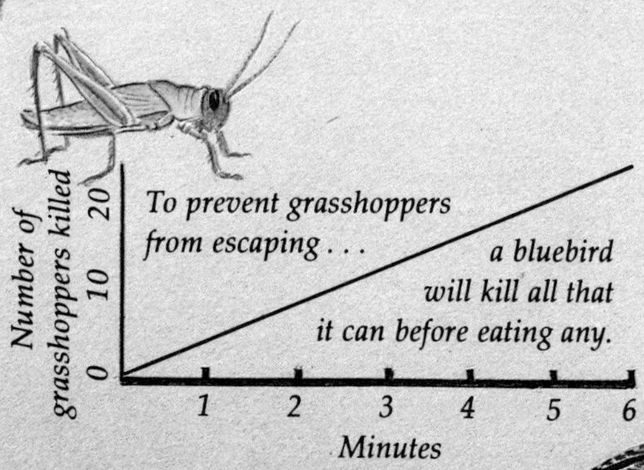

Like the robin, the juvenile has a spotted breast.

Six-week-old bluebirds help to feed the next brood of young.

HOW DO BLUEBIRD FAMILIES DEMONSTRATE TEAMWORK IN AND AROUND THEIR HOMES?

The companionship and teamwork which the parents demonstrate before nesting is carried over in the raising of their young. The female lays four to six eggs and incubates them for about twelve days. The nestlings are fed by the mother until they are ready to fly.

Then, the father takes over the care of the young while the female repairs the nest and prepares for the second brood. After the second brood hatches the young birds from the earlier hatches will help care for them.

WHY DO BLUEBIRDS USUALLY NOT SING IN APRIL?

The bluebird's song is a series of short single notes that are sung quickly like a warble. The sound is beautiful but does not carry far. The sounds of the song, *ta, te, to, tay, taloo, totlay,* and *ee,* are slurred together.

Bluebirds sing more often during the month of March, the month when the males serenade their mates. After incubation begins, the bluebird usually does not sing again until the young have left the nest.

HOW DOES A MOTHER BLUEBIRD DEMONSTRATE HER CLEANLINESS?

During the two to three weeks that the young are in the nest, a mother bluebird continuously cleans house and feeds her babies. Watching one bluebird nest closely for two hours revealed the following.

The mother cleaned the nest six times and brought her five youngsters twenty grasshoppers, four katydids, two crickets, several small worms, and as many small grubs. She averaged feeding her babies once every six minutes.

HOW OFTEN MUST YOU FEED ORPHANED BLUEBIRD CHICKS TO KEEP THEM ALIVE?

They must be fed at least every thirty minutes until they are a week old. Then meals can be separated by no more than an hour. By 7:30 in the evening, the chicks huddle together and sleep until the next morning.

Orphaned bluebirds will eat grasshoppers, crickets, peanut butter, pokeberries, banana bits, chopped raisins, water-soaked bread, and cornmeal mixed with water.

SINCE A BLUEBIRD'S FEATHERS ARE NOT BLUE, WHY IS IT CALLED A BLUEBIRD?

The color pigments in bird feathers are black, brown, red, yellow, and green. Blue comes from the feather's structure, not from a pigment. A thin, colorless, and transparent layer of cells separates light like a prism and reflects only blue light. When a bluebird is wet, or perched between an observer and the sun, it looks brown instead of blue.

How is the need to take care of possessions illustrated in Scripture?

God promises that if judgment begins at the house of God, He will deal with the heathen. (See I Peter 4:17.) Who was the king that began a spiritual cleansing and by it marked the end of a cruel heathen empire?

(Pause for a response—see page 17.)

The year was 632 B.C. An Assyrian emperor educated by the priests of his day looked from his huge palace in Nineveh to the amazing architectural achievements of his city. There was the famous library with priceless historical records. Then there was the magnificent aqueduct with huge archways over the valley brook. It was constructed with millions of large, cut limestone blocks.

Also under his leadership was a well-trained army, which had maintained control of conquered territories through ruthless and brutal tactics.

In that same year, a sixteen-year-old king, who lived within the domain of that emperor, began to seek after the Lord God that made heaven and earth.

His seeking after God was in contrast to the wicked rule of his father. However, his grandfather had repented of his wicked ways at the end of his reign and had begun to tear down the false worship centers in the land.

As the youthful king began to seek the Lord, the grip of that powerful emperor suddenly weakened to the point that he had to flee from Nineveh and rule the empire from a new western location.

Four years later, that young, God-fearing king began to cleanse his kingdom from the perversion and immorality accepted through the false philosophies which permeated the music, art, and sculptures of the day.

He and those with him broke down carved and molten images, ground them into dust, and threw the dust upon the graves of those who had worshiped them. It is significant that after this was accomplished, God heralded the end of the Assyrian empire with the death of its brilliant ruler—Ashurbanipal.

Josiah, the Godly king of Judah, at the age of twenty-six, began the monumental task of repairing the house of the Lord. Large, hewn stones were pulled to the site to rebuild sections that were broken down, and timber was brought in for floors and couplings.

As the work progressed, God crowned their efforts with a valuable discovery—a book of the Law of the Lord, given by Moses. It had been lost for many years. In caring for the things entrusted to him, King Josiah gained valuable direction for his life and his leadership.

From II Chronicles 34

JOSIAH, THE KING WHO RESTORED A NATION BY REBUILDING THE TEMPLE

The cuneiform tablet *pictured above describes the plundering of the Jewish temple. The temple was plundered by the Syrians. It was stripped by the Assyrians. Finally, it was desecrated by the apostate Jews. For this reason, during the reign of Josiah (640 B.C., three centuries after its construction), the temple was in need of major repair.*

The once magnificent temple built by Solomon was in a condition of disgrace. Its intended function as the center for worship of Jehovah was all but forgotten. Duties of its priests to picture the character and nature of God through various ceremonies had been abandoned. The written Law of God, a copy of which was to be kept in the Ark of the Covenant, was lost.

The condition of the temple revealed more than a case of spiritual neglect. Prescribed worship had been replaced by abhorrent pagan practices. Altars for worship of the sun, moon, and stars had been erected in the very courts of the temple. Carved images of Asherah, wife of the pagan god Baal, had been placed within. Hebrew children were sacrificed to the Ammonite god, Molech. Male prostitutes associated with the temple participated in perverse rituals of twisted religious practices. Such gross blasphemy could not be tolerated.

HOPE FOR A NEW BEGINNING

But the Lord, in keeping with His great mercy and long-suffering, raised up a new, young king to spare the nation from His predicted wrath for three more decades. *"Josiah was eight years old when he began to reign, and he reigned in Jerusalem one and thirty years" (II Chronicles 34:1).*

From a human perspective, Josiah was an unlikely candidate to lead a reformation movement. His grandfather, Manasseh, was the most wicked of all the former kings of Judah. His evil father, Amon, was assassinated by his own servants. The general populace, thoroughly disillusioned with the confusion in Jerusalem, had the assassins executed and made young Josiah their new king.

As Josiah grew older, he grew in wisdom; and when he was sixteen, *". . . he began to seek after the God of David . . ." (II Chronicles 34:3).* At twenty, he applied the knowledge of the Lord which he had learned from the true prophets and faithful priests who had endured the previous era of apostasy. The king destroyed the centers of pagan worship throughout Judea and even went into the region of Israel to the north. (See II Chronicles 34:3–7.)

The reward of Josiah's restoration of the temple *was the discovery of the Law of Moses. The Law shed new light on the reforms which needed to come in order to renew the nation. The discovery illustrates the axiom: "light received brings more light, but light rejected brings darkness."*

THE LAW WAS REVEALED AND RESTORATION BEGAN

When Josiah was twenty-six, the single most significant aspect of the reform began. He saw the pathetic physical condition of the temple and was motivated to restore it. An offering was collected throughout the land to pay for the construction. In the process of paying the workers, Hilkiah the priest found a copy of the book of the Law. (See II Chronicles 34:14.) The book was immediately brought and read to Josiah.

When the king realized how far the nation had strayed from God's Law, he tore his clothes as a symbol of grief and repentance. He sent for someone who could instruct him further concerning the serious consequences of their disobedience. Huldah the prophetess confirmed that the curses of the book were immutable, but the evil would come after Josiah's death. (See II Chronicles 34:22–28.)

Josiah did not let this announcement discourage him. In fact, he was motivated to intensify the reform to reach into the very hearts of the people. The king committed himself to obey the words of God revealed in the newly discovered Law and encouraged the officials, priests, and people to do the same. The Passover and Feast of Unleavened Bread were commanded to be kept in strict accordance with the words of the Law. The temple would again function as originally intended.

CHARACTER SKETCH OF JOSIAH

HOW WAS JOSIAH INFLUENCED TO SEEK THE LORD?

Although Josiah grew up in the court of two of the most disobedient kings of Judah, it is likely that he received Godly instruction when young. He was born six years before the death of his grandfather, Manasseh, in a time of brief reform. King Manasseh had been captured by the Assyrians and thoroughly humiliated by them. After his release, he was allowed to regain his throne in Jerusalem.

Because of this experience, his heart was softened, and he *". . . commanded Judah to serve the Lord God of Israel" (II Chronicles 33:16)*. Josiah's very name hints to the climate of the time. His name resumed the custom of compounding royal names with that of Jehovah. Josiah means "may the Lord support or heal."

The new freedom and encouragement for followers of the Lord, which resulted from Manasseh's change of heart, provided the Godly remnant among the priests an opportunity to train the royal prince. These same tutors were probably allowed to continue their teaching duties through the rule of King Amon and during the early years of Josiah's reign.

HOW DID JOSIAH ENCOURAGE THE PEOPLE TO FOLLOW THE LORD?

First, he set a good example. *"And he did that which was right in the sight of the Lord, and walked in all the way of David his father. . ." (II Kings 22:2)*. Second, Josiah destroyed the centers of pagan worship and the idolatrous priests who were leading the people astray. Third, he began reconstruction of the temple in order to reinstate proper worship of Jehovah. Fourth, when confronted with the Law, he acknowledged the sins of his fathers and the people and fully repented. He then gathered all the people, great and small, *". . . and he read in their ears all the words of the book of the covenant. . ." (II Chronicles 34:30)*.

Josiah committed himself to obey the Law and urged the people to do the same. He destroyed the centers of false worship, removing the temptation to resume activities after the initial stages of reform. He reinstituted the Passover and generously provided sacrificial animals from his own herds. *"And there was no passover like to that kept in Israel from the days of Samuel the prophet; neither did all the kings of Israel keep such a passover as Josiah kept. . ." (II Chronicles 35:18)*.

WERE JOSIAH'S REFORMS POLITICALLY MOTIVATED?

The king might be accused of merely being an astute politician by instituting religious reform. Refurbishing the temple and destroying competing religious centers could be viewed as an attempt to centralize the kingdom in Jerusalem and reunite the remnant remaining in the north.

Destroying Assyrian idols could be considered a bold, calculated insult to the weakened northern empire, a declaration of complete independence. But there is evidence to believe that Josiah's reforms were motivated primarily out of a pure love for the Lord. When he heard the Law, *". . . he rent his clothes" (II Chronicles 34:19)*.

Huldah the prophetess declared Josiah's heart to be pure. *"Because thine heart was tender, and thou didst humble thyself before God . . . and didst rend thy clothes, and weep before me; I have even heard thee also, saith the Lord" (II Chronicles 34:27)*. Jeremiah, in the prophet's lament, declared Josiah to be a just, unselfish judge who had compassion on the poor. (See Jeremiah 22:11–16.)

HILKIAH

Many important items were in short supply *during the ministry of Hilkiah. These included knowledge of God's Word, righteous leadership, spiritual worship, and God's blessing on the nation. By taking care of Josiah during his early years, Hilkiah blessed the nation with an abundance of all these vital qualities.*

JOSIAH
jo-sī-ə

Kindness

. . . Is seeing needs in the lives of others as opportunities to demonstrate my love for Christ

". . . Verily I say unto you, Inasmuch as ye have done it unto one of the least of these my brethren, ye have done it unto me."
Matthew 25:40

PART SEVEN

KINDNESS IN GIVING . . .

The purpose of all giving must be to demonstrate our love for Christ. For *"though I bestow all my goods to feed the poor, and though I give my body to be burned, and have not charity [love], it profiteth me nothing" (I Corinthians 13:3).*

When someone with the gift of giving sees Christ as the real recipient of his gifts, he or she is motivated to meet needs which others overlook.

CHAPTER TWENTY-FIVE

Kindness

. . . Is using a gift to show the worth of a person

"But God commendeth his love toward us, in that, while we were yet sinners, Christ died for us."

Romans 5:8

Living Lessons on Kindness . . .

FROM THE PAGES OF SCRIPTURE

A warm, loving smile is a precious gift to a lonely person, and precise words, properly spoken, are often more appreciated than silver or gold. *"A word fitly spoken is like apples of gold in pictures of silver" (Proverbs 25:11).*

Such kindnesses are usually learned during times of personal suffering. In those times God gives comfort and counsel which can then be passed on to others in their times of trouble. One who received and gave comfort during a time of deep sorrow illustrates for us the importance of using these gifts to show the worth of a person.

ILLUSTRATED IN THE WORLD OF NATURE

COMMON REDPOLL *Acanthis flammea*

The redpoll looks like a small brown sparrow. It is about five and one-half inches long, with a bright red cap and black chin. It lives in the low arctic tundra in areas where the tree growth has been stunted. When winters in the Arctic are severe, the redpoll migrates to Canada and the northern United States. In summer it feeds on insects, while in winter it eats only seeds. It is against the law to keep a redpoll in captivity.

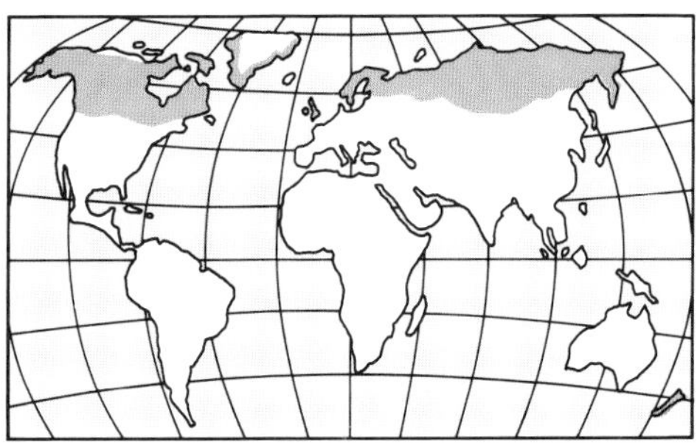

The range and habitat of the redpoll

How is the secret of longsuffering illustrated in the world of nature?

An arctic explorer struggled onward against bitter cold temperatures. It was fifty degrees below zero. His strength was drained after battling unexpected storms. His food supply would barely sustain him back to the base camp.

Icy winds cut through his clothes, and finally the exhausted man slumped to the frozen tundra. He cried out to God for help, although he did not know what God would do in this desolate wilderness. Even the wildlife had left for warmer climates.

Suddenly, he heard an unusual sound. He listened more closely. The sound was getting louder. It was bright and cheery. He turned around, and there to his surprise was another arctic traveler. This one had gained far more experience than he had in traveling throughout the polar regions. During a two-month period, this veteran traveler had covered thousands of miles of arctic territory.

The weary explorer had heard about this famous traveler, and he recalled what he knew about him. He listened to him and watched him demonstrate the secret that kept him going while others gave up.

First, he went over to a nearby bush and shook a branch until many of its seeds fell on the snow-crusted tundra. Then, he quickly picked up all the seeds and went over to a sheltered place, sat down, and one by one cracked open the seeds which he had gathered. He gained nourishment from each one.

As long as he had a supply of seeds and slowly ate them, he had amazing strength and unusual ability to withstand arctic conditions.

As the explorer watched, he understood the life-giving message that he had just received. He had learned many Scripture verses as a young boy, but had failed to gain strength by meditating on them day and night.

He had been depending on his own strength, and that had been exhausted. He remembered the words of Isaiah 40:31 which this arctic traveler had just demonstrated. "*. . . They that wait upon the Lord shall renew their strength; they shall mount up with wings . . . they shall run, and not be weary; and they shall walk, and not faint.*"

With that verse strengthening his heart and mind, the revived explorer stood up and walked on. God had answered his prayer for help by demonstrating the importance of meditating on Scripture.

The more experienced arctic traveler was the common redpoll. This arctic bird gave a valuable gift of kindness to the explorer by giving this secret of longsuffering.

THE CHARACTERISTICS OF

THE REDPOLL IN SCRIPTURE

The common redpoll's characteristic of storing seeds in an esophageal pouch and bringing them up again for nourishment is a clear picture of the process of Scriptural meditation.

Scripture is compared to seeds, *". . . The seed is the word of God" (Luke 8:11).* The redpoll searches for seeds daily. The early Christians *". . . received the word with all readiness of mind, and searched the scriptures daily . . ." (Acts 17:11).* We are to do the same.

Once found, Scripture must be taken and stored in the heart, as emphasized in the following verses. *"Thy words were found, and I did eat them; and thy word was unto me the joy and rejoicing of mine heart . . ." (Jeremiah 15:16). "Thy word have I hid in mine heart, that I might not sin against thee" (Psalm 119:11).*

The redpoll's ability to bring the seeds up again day and night is parallel to the command of God to meditate upon His Word day and night. *". . . Thou shalt meditate therein day and night, that thou mayest observe to do according to all that is written therein: for then thou shalt make thy way prosperous, and then thou shalt have good success" (Joshua 1:8).*

As the redpoll cracks open the seeds, it reingests them. We are to "crack open" the words of truth in order to gain the rich application and meaning of each one. (See II Timothy 2:15.)

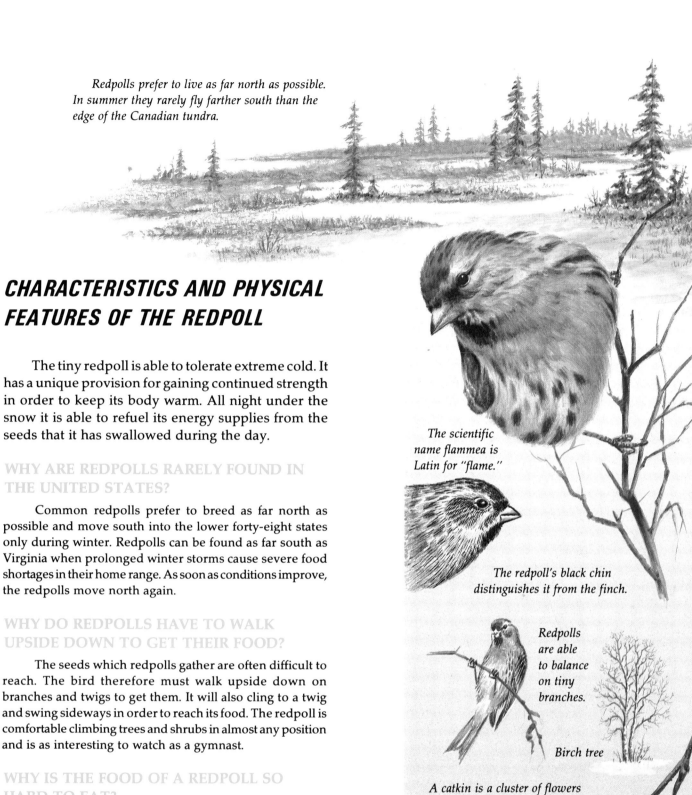

Redpolls prefer to live as far north as possible. In summer they rarely fly farther south than the edge of the Canadian tundra.

CHARACTERISTICS AND PHYSICAL FEATURES OF THE REDPOLL

The tiny redpoll is able to tolerate extreme cold. It has a unique provision for gaining continued strength in order to keep its body warm. All night under the snow it is able to refuel its energy supplies from the seeds that it has swallowed during the day.

WHY ARE REDPOLLS RARELY FOUND IN THE UNITED STATES?

Common redpolls prefer to breed as far north as possible and move south into the lower forty-eight states only during winter. Redpolls can be found as far south as Virginia when prolonged winter storms cause severe food shortages in their home range. As soon as conditions improve, the redpolls move north again.

WHY DO REDPOLLS HAVE TO WALK UPSIDE DOWN TO GET THEIR FOOD?

The seeds which redpolls gather are often difficult to reach. The bird therefore must walk upside down on branches and twigs to get them. It will also cling to a twig and swing sideways in order to reach its food. The redpoll is comfortable climbing trees and shrubs in almost any position and is as interesting to watch as a gymnast.

WHY IS THE FOOD OF A REDPOLL SO HARD TO EAT?

The seeds which the redpoll prefers come from black birch, alders, linseed, flax, and hemp. Many of these seeds are very hard; so hard, in fact, that the redpoll does not attempt to crack them open at first but simply swallows them. In addition to these, the redpoll also eats seeds from small plants and enjoys insects such as ants, aphids, and flies.

HOW DOES THE REDPOLL EAT IN THREE STAGES?

The redpoll begins by hopping from branch to branch or from shrub to shrub shaking seeds to the ground. After covering the ground with seeds, the redpoll drops down and collects them as quickly as it can. The seeds are then eaten rapidly without removing the hulls. In the third stage, the redpoll brings up the seeds, shells them, and then swallows them a second time.

The scientific name flammea is Latin for "flame."

The redpoll's black chin distinguishes it from the finch.

Redpolls are able to balance on tiny branches.

Birch tree

A catkin is a cluster of flowers that grows at the tips of the branches.

Birch catkin containing seeds

Only the bird below is eating. The other is scattering seeds to be picked up later.

Redpolls hiding in a sheltering tree.

The esophageal pouch is used to store seeds.
Dissection

Red crossbill

Crossbills have crossed beaks which are great for opening pinecones.

Redpolls often feed seeds to one another.

Redpolls are easily attracted to feeders.

HOW DOES THE REDPOLL CONSERVE ENERGY BY EATING IN STAGES?

To live in a climate where temperatures may reach -100°F, it is necessary to conserve energy in every way. Therefore, redpolls do not try to eat seeds while they are hanging upside down and exposed to the wind. Instead, they quickly shake the seeds to the ground where there is more shelter.

Feeding on the ground also requires less movement of the bird's insulating feathers and keeps the cold air away from the little bird's body. The redpoll can stand in one place and collect all the seeds it can reach by bending only its neck.

HOW DOES A NECK POUCH MAKE THE REDPOLL BEHAVE LIKE A COW?

When the seeds are first swallowed by the redpoll, they are stored in an enlarged throat cavity called the *esophageal diverticulum*. The cavity is located along the side of the neck so that when it is full, it does not interfere with the movement of the head.

Just as the cow lies down in the pasture and brings up its cud, the redpoll goes off to a secluded area and brings up its seeds. When the seeds are brought up from its pouch, they are much easier to break open because the hulls have already been softened by moisture in the diverticulum.

HOW LONG CAN A REDPOLL CONTINUE TO GET STRENGTH BY RE-EATING SEEDS?

The esophageal pouch of the redpoll is large enough to carry up to twelve hours' worth of food. This store of food is especially important during bitter cold nights when the redpoll is in an underground snow tunnel.

WHY DO REDPOLLS PATIENTLY WAIT FOR THE ARRIVAL OF CROSSBILLS?

Redpolls are too little to open large pinecones. Instead, they wait for a stronger bird, the crossbill, to tear apart the woody scales that protect the seeds. After waiting patiently for the seeds to fall to the ground, they clean up what the crossbills leave behind.

HOW DO REDPOLLS STAY WARM AND FLY FARTHER BY SUBSTITUTING FOOD FOR FAT?

Redpolls do not have a fatty layer of insulation to keep them warm during the Arctic's long, cold winter. Instead, they depend upon the constant availability of food to provide them with energy.

Their lean and muscular frames allow them to fly long distances. One redpoll was banded in upper Michigan. Two months later its band was removed in Siberia—4,000 miles away.

WHY DOES THE REDPOLL HAVE TWO TYPES OF BURROWS?

In order to gain protection from the cold, the redpoll digs tunnels in the snow. Some burrows are used only between feeding times. Others are strictly for overnight use.

Redpoll tunnels may be almost three feet long.

WHY IS SNOW A GREATER THREAT TO A REDPOLL THAN TEMPERATURES OF -100°F?

With its diverticulum full of food to snack on, a redpoll can withstand temperatures of -81°F. When this cavity is empty, a redpoll can handle only -22°F. When sheltered in its snow tunnel with plenty to eat, a redpoll can withstand surface temperatures colder than -100°F. A redpoll's only real threat is from heavy snowfalls that may trap it in its snow tunnel.

WHY DOES IT TAKE LONGER FOR A REDPOLL TO REPLACE ITS FEATHERS THAN MANY OTHER BIRDS?

All birds regularly change or replace their feathers in a process called *molting*. Redpolls molt once a year after each breeding season. It takes fifty days for the redpoll to lose every feather and replace it with a new one. Some kinds of birds molt much faster than the redpoll. Those that migrate long distances change theirs in less than thirty-five days, while those that do not migrate usually take over eighty days.

Fluffing its
feathers to trap more
warm air next to its body

HOW DO REDPOLLS ACHIEVE PRECISION IN LANDING AND TAKING OFF TOGETHER?

Redpolls use simple "call notes" to keep in touch with each other. Although a flock of redpolls may contain several hundred birds, by communicating "ready, set, go" to each other, all of the birds take off and land at the same time.

When in flight, a group of redpolls will make a *chit, chit, chit* sound. The combined noise makes the flock sound like it is rattling in the air.

Other birds that often travel with the redpoll include goldfinches, siskins, and crossbills. They seem to understand the redpoll's language and also respond to these calls.

WHAT IS THE DIFFERENCE BETWEEN NIDIFUGOUS YOUNG AND NIDICOLOUS YOUNG?

Nidifugous (ni-**dif**-ye-ges) young are simply young birds that leave the nest when they hatch. Nidifugous young usually take much longer to develop. Nidicolous (ni-**dik**-e-les) young are hatchlings that remain in the nest and are fed by their parents. Redpolls raise nidicolous young. By staying in the nest the young grow much faster and are able to fly in only twelve to fifteen days. While in the nest, the young are able to consume a huge amount of food because the parents, aided by nearly twenty-four hours of daylight, feed them all day long.

Immature
Female
Male
The song of the redpoll sounds like: "Twsweet, Twsweet."
The discarded feathers of the rock ptarmigans are used to line the redpoll's nest.
Rock ptarmigan
Eggs are lightly specked.
It is illegal in most states to cage redpolls.

Male redpolls can be distinguished from females *by the red on their front and rear. The females are white underneath. Immature males and females have no red markings.*

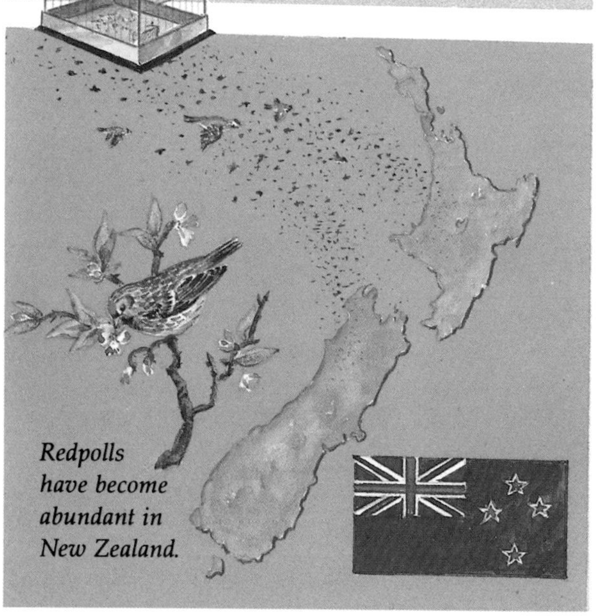

Redpolls have become abundant in New Zealand.

HOW MANY DAYS DOES IT TAKE REDPOLLS TO RAISE A FAMILY?

Redpolls can raise a complete brood of young in just over one month. If weather permits, they will raise two broods in one summer.

The female builds her nest of twigs, down, and feathers either on the ground or in the lower branches of a bush. She lays three to six green eggs which she incubates for eleven to thirteen days. During this time, the male supplies all her food.

After the young hatch, they are fed predigested food for their first two weeks. Seeds are collected by the male and then brought up for the female to eat. She then brings them up a second time for the young.

HOW CAN GATHERING FOOD BE DANGEROUS FOR A REDPOLL?

Redpolls can be easily captured without any danger to either man or bird. They readily adapt to captivity and make beautiful, caged birds. Because redpolls are not afraid of man, they can be captured by hand at a window feeder, in their winter snow tunnels, or even on the ground as they pick up their seeds. Unfortunately, their lack of fear also makes them easy prey for domestic cats.

WHY ARE REDPOLLS CONSIDERED PESTS IN NEW ZEALAND?

When first introduced to New Zealand in the late 1800s, the redpoll was thought to be strictly beneficial. Although the climate of New Zealand is much milder than that of the Arctic, the redpoll has multiplied until it is now one of the ten most common birds in the country. Because of its fondness for fruit tree buds and blossoms, the redpoll population threatens to destroy hundreds of acres of young fruit trees each year.

WHY DO REDPOLLS SEEM TO APPEAR OUT OF THIN AIR?

Redpolls fly extremely high; so high, in fact, that the human eye is not able to detect them. If the redpolls decide to land in a field, they give the right call note and suddenly three or four hundred redpolls appear and settle on the ground.

How is strengthening the heart of a discouraged person illustrated in Scripture?

An act of kindness is far more than meeting a physical need. It is emphasizing the worth of a person. It is honoring God's design for a life. Who was one that gave such honor to Christ when He needed it most?

(Pause for a response—see page 17.)

After His arrest in the middle of the night, Jesus was brought before the Sanhedrin, the Jewish supreme court. During questioning by the high priest, a soldier struck Jesus across the face. The palace guards then blindfolded Him and taunted Him to identify them as each one passed by, spitting on Him and striking Him in the face.

Early the next morning, Jesus was battered, bruised, dehydrated, and exhausted from a sleepless night. He was taken to the Roman fortress and brought before an angry mob. They shouted, "Crucify Him!"

Pilate had Him beaten. The heavy thongs of the whip cut through the skin of His back and soon turned it into a mass of torn, bleeding tissue.

The Roman soldiers compounded His torment by throwing a cloak over his lacerated back and by mocking Him. Sharp thorns were pressed into His scalp, producing copious bleeding. The cloak was then ripped off, reopening His wounds, and the heavy beam of the cross was placed on His bleeding shoulder. The grim procession slowly proceeded toward the execution site.

At Golgotha, large, wrought iron nails were driven through His wrists and deep into the beam. While hanging on the cross, the searing agony of the nails tore through the nerves of the skin. Great waves of cramps swept over His muscles, knotting them in deep, relentless, throbbing pain. For hours, this limitless torture continued.

Soon another agony began, a crushing pain deep within His chest. His compressed heart struggled to pump thick, sluggish blood through His veins. His tortured lungs made frantic efforts to gasp in small gulps of air. His dehydrated body sent its message screaming to His brain, and He cried out, "I thirst!"

He looked down from the cross, and in that dreadful hour He received something more refreshing than a drink of water—a look of reassurance from one who believed in Him and who was committed to Him regardless of what others thought of Him.

This friend who had been delivered from the bondage of tormenting spirits honored Him as a person by identifying with Him while others mocked Him and railed upon Him. She honored the great work which He came to perform by assisting with His burial and was the last to leave the tomb.

The kindness of Mary Magdalene was singularly rewarded by Christ. She became the first one to whom He appeared after His resurrection. He returned her kindness by strengthening her heart with the truth of His resurrection.

From John 18:12–20:18

The Village of Magdala

Often the source of a person's name is the place were they live. This is the case with Mary Magdalene. Her name literally means "Mary of Magdala." Magdala is located on the western shore of the Sea of Galilee. This is the area to which Jesus crossed over after feeding the 5,000 men.

MARY MAGDALENE, AN EFFECTIVE EYEWITNESS BECAUSE SHE SOUGHT THE LORD

In the city of Magdala, on the coast of the Sea of Galilee, lived a demon-possessed woman named Mary. We do not know how the demons tormented her, but from other New Testament accounts of demon possession we know that Mary's life was most miserable.

A Canaanite's daughter, for example, was grievously vexed with a devil. (See Matthew 15:22.) The Gadarene demoniac could neither be bound nor tamed. *"And always, night and day, he was in the mountains, and in the tombs, crying, and cutting himself with stones" (Mark 5:5)*. Another man's son was described as a *"... lunatic, and sore vexed: for ofttimes he falleth into the fire, and oft into the water" (Matthew 17:15)*. This boy was afflicted with only one demon. Mary, however, was tormented by seven. (See Luke 8:2.)

But one day, while preaching in Galilee, Jesus and His disciples met Mary of Magdala and cast out the seven demons. Mary was so grateful to the Master that she ministered to Him as well as to the disciples.

MARY STOOD AT THE CROSS TO WITNESS THE LORD'S CRUCIFIXION

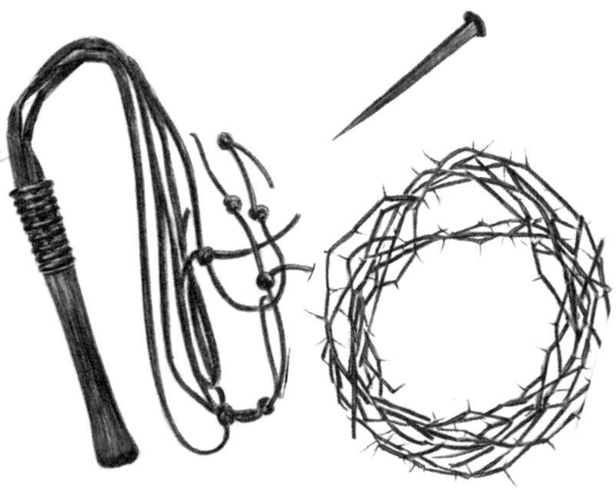

Crucifixion *was unanimously considered the most cruel form of death. There was great degradation, pain, and humiliation with the cross.*

Mary had come to love Jesus not only for what He had removed from her life, but also for what He placed into it. She experienced daily His peace, encouragement, and teaching. She witnessed His compassion to others who were sick and demon-possessed. Helplessly and mournfully she watched as the One who had done so much good was being cruelly put to death under the false charge of blasphemy.

MARY SAT BY THE GRAVE TO WITNESS THE LORD'S BURIAL

After the Lord's death, Mary did not leave for her home in Galilee. She wanted to make sure that Jesus was properly prepared for burial. She was grateful that Joseph and Nicodemus took the body, laid it in a nearby tomb, and began to make preparations for its burial. (See John 19:38–40; Mark 15:47.) The Sabbath was about to begin. Nothing more could be done, so Mary reluctantly left the gravesite at last to observe the day of rest.

MARY WAS THE FIRST PERSON TO WITNESS THE RESURRECTION

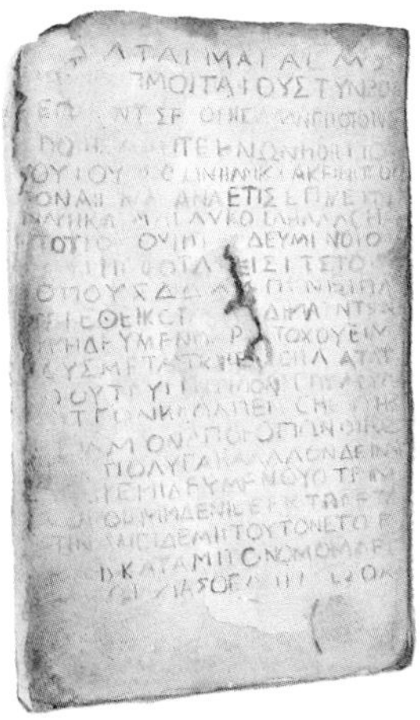

The fear of severe punishment *and the tight security of the Roman guard around the tomb of Christ ruled out the Pharisees' claim that Christ's body was stolen.*

Death Notice to Grave Robbers

Mary was one of the last to leave the grave on Friday evening and one of the first to return Sunday. (See John 20:1.) She wanted to finish preparing the Lord's body for burial—the task which had been interrupted because of the Sabbath. She wondered how she could get the stone rolled away from the tomb.

But when she arrived, the stone had already been moved. Mary immediately feared that robbers had broken in and removed the body in order to recover the expensive spices which Nicodemus had used. She ran to tell Peter and John what she had seen. (See John 20:2.)

After the two men left, Mary remained at the tomb, weeping. She wept because her beloved Lord had been murdered, and now she feared that even His dead body was being desecrated by disrespectful thieves. It was to this woman in her deep sorrow that the Lord first revealed Himself in His resurrected body. When Mary recognized Jesus, she clung to her Master, not willing to part with Him again. The Lord told her that it was necessary for Him to leave. *"... Go to my brethren, and say unto them, I ascend unto my Father..." (John 20:17)*. He left her to share her excitement and joy with those who were still mourning.

CHARACTER SKETCH OF MARY MAGDALENE

WHY DID JESUS FIRST APPEAR TO MARY MAGDALENE?

The resurrection appearances of Christ can teach us much. We learn that the risen Lord is just as tender, compassionate, and loving as He was while living among men.

On that first Easter morning, Mary Magdalene missed her Lord greatly. The disciples, of course, felt great loss, but they were preoccupied with their fear of the Jews and remained in hiding behind locked doors. (See John 20:19.) It was Mary who had maintained a vigil at the tomb and stood there, weeping.

In an act of love, the Lord appeared to her and gave her hope. Later that day He appeared to the disciples, who had refused to believe her report. (See John 20:19–20.) But Thomas was not present then; and in order to stimulate Thomas's weak faith, the Lord made another appearance eight days later. (See John 20:26–27.)

The risen Lord chose not to overpersuade men into His kingdom. Jesus appeared only to believers. Although He was crucified publicly and was subjected to the insults of His enemies, He did not show Himself to unbelievers in His resurrected body.

How easy it would have been for Him to have appeared before the members of the Sanhedrin who had tried Him for blasphemy. But salvation is by faith. He gives men the evidence of His Word. *". . . Blessed are they that have not seen, and yet have believed" (John 20:29).*

WHY DID THE LORD ASK MARY NOT TO TOUCH HIM?

When Mary recognized the voice of Jesus, she tried to cling to her Master and keep Him in her presence. But the Lord said to Mary, *". . . Touch me not; for I am not yet ascended to my Father . . ." (John 20:17).*

Nothing could prevent Him from completing His ascent and entering into His rightful inheritance. The very thing Mary desired, His comfort and companionship, would be frustrated if she held on to Him. The Lord would send the Holy Spirit to comfort, teach, and abide with Mary at all times. (See John 14:26–28.)

WHY DID THE DISCIPLES DISBELIEVE MARY'S TESTIMONY?

When Mary told Peter and John that the stone had been removed and that the Lord's body had been taken, they believed her without any doubt and ran to the tomb to investigate. (See John 20:1–4.) But when Mary testified that she had seen the risen Lord, the disciples dismissed her claim. *"And they, when they had heard that he was alive, and had been seen of her, believed not" (Mark 16:11).*

Later, when the Lord appeared to them, He *". . . upbraided them with their unbelief and hardness of heart, because they believed not them which had seen him after he was risen" (Mark 16:14).*

The same is true for us today. We have not seen the risen Lord with our own eyes, but we have credible witnesses like Mary and many others who did. He expects us to believe His Word and to act in faith on the basis of it.

The loyalty and kindness of Mary *at Christ's crucifixion and by the tomb have won for her an honored place in the Gospel record.*

MARY MAGDALENE
me(ə)r-ē măg-*də-lēn*

CHAPTER TWENTY-SIX

Kindness

. . . Is bringing joy out of sorrow

"I have not hid thy righteousness within my heart; I have declared thy faithfulness and thy salvation: I have not concealed thy lovingkindness and thy truth from the great congregation."

Psalm 40:10

Living Lessons on Kindness . . .

FROM THE PAGES OF SCRIPTURE

The loss of a loved one or the depletion of financial resources can produce bitterness. These same circumstances can also open up a life to the amazing potential of daily dependence upon our heavenly Father. One believer who had suffered the loss of a partner and financial provisions responded correctly and experienced unusual freedom and security. The outward evidence of trust in God's lovingkindness was so unusual that it brought public acclaim and inspired untold numbers of other believers to depend upon God's faithfulness.

ILLUSTRATED IN THE WORLD OF NATURE

MONARCH BUTTERFLY *Danaus plexippus*

The life cycle of the monarch butterfly has four distinct stages: egg, caterpillar, pupa, and adult. Each stage is a separate and distinct living creature. But it is during the pupa stage that the caterpillar undergoes a radical metamorphosis, which changes it into a butterfly.

Although scientists understood much about this complex metamorphosis, for many years they did not know what happened to the monarch during the winter months. It was not until the mid-1970s that the monarchs were tracked to their wintering grounds in central Mexico. They had flown distances in excess of 2,500 miles during their short lifetimes.

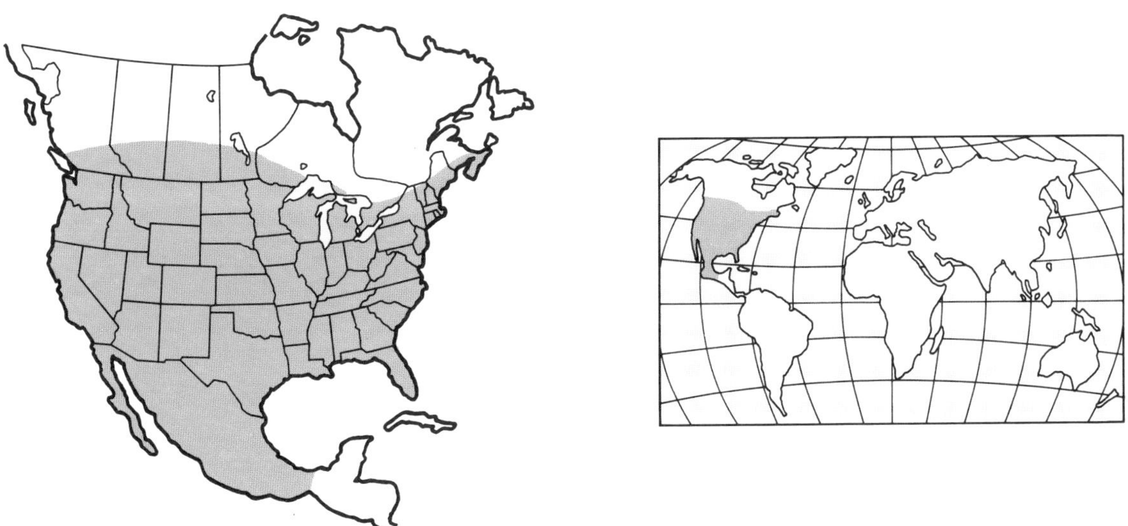

The range and habitat of the monarch butterfly

How is the benefit of bitter experiences illustrated in the world of nature?

A beautifully colored monarch butterfly felt itself being jerked from the sky by a hungry predator which seemed to come from nowhere.

Its blue-crested captor flew up to its nest. The stunned monarch was then released a few inches from three hungry mouths that were open wide, demanding to be fed. Just then the mate of the blue jay arrived and dropped a large juicy grasshopper at the feet of its young.

Immediately, the blue jay tore apart the grasshopper and poked the bits and pieces into each eager mouth. Then it looked around for additional food.

The jay that had brought in the monarch watched in total surprise as its more mature mate stepped over to the monarch, picked him up, and dropped him out of the nest. The uninjured monarch flew away to the fragrant flowers of the field below.

This unexpected freedom was the result of what the monarch experienced when he was young. During his caterpillar stage, the bitter leaves of a poisonous plant was the only food available to him. Amazingly, he was not damaged by the toxins in the plant. However, they would remain in his system for the rest of his life.

It was this very diet that had now saved him from the hungry mouths of the blue jays. When the blue jay saw the monarch, the jay was immediately reminded of the first and last monarch that it had ever caught.

Hoping to satisfy its hunger, the blue jay had swallowed a monarch in midair. Within a few minutes the blue jay became sick; its stomach seemed to be twisting and turning inside out.

The pain and discomfort became worse and worse until the jay was finally gripped with convulsions. It vomited out the remains of the butterfly along with the rest of the day's catch.

Once the butterfly was out of its stomach, the blue jay had instant relief. It had never experienced anything like this before and would never choose to do so again.

Thereafter, in its search for food, the blue jay avoided anything that looked like a monarch. Not only could monarchs fly by this blue jay without harm, but viceroy butterflies could also carry on their work in safety.

The viceroy butterflies had never eaten the poisonous leaves of the milkweed plant. However, they had orange and black markings similar to a monarch butterfly.

Thus, the bitter diet of the monarch's early days not only saved its own life but kindly benefited the lives of other butterflies.

THE CHARACTERISTICS OF

THE MONARCH BUTTERFLY IN SCRIPTURE

The unique ability of the monarch butterfly to tolerate the toxins of the milkweed plant provides a picture of the need for Christians to endure the bitterness of discipline, trial, and persecution.

The monarch butterfly absorbs bitter toxins during its early development, which protects its life when it matures. Similarly, God allows harsh experiences in our youth. *"It is good for a man that he bear the yoke in his youth. . . . He giveth his cheek to him that smiteth him . . . For the Lord will not cast off for ever" (Lamentations 3:27, 30–31).*

"But the God of all grace, who hath called us unto his eternal glory by Christ Jesus, after that ye have suffered a while, make you perfect, stablish, strengthen, settle you" (I Peter 5:10).

More importantly, bitter experiences help to conform us to the image of Christ. *"And we know that all things work together for good to them that love God, to them who are the called according to his purpose. For whom he did foreknow, he also did predestinate to be conformed to the image of his Son . . ." (Romans 8:28–29).*

Perhaps the most spectacular characteristic of the butterfly that illustrates conformity to Christ is its transformation from caterpillar to butterfly. In going through its metamorphosis, it not only illustrates the truth of Christ's resurrection, but also the principle of the birth, death, and fulfillment of a vision.

"It is sown in dishonour; it is raised in glory . . ." (I Corinthians 15:43).

CHARACTERISTICS AND PHYSICAL FEATURES OF THE MONARCH BUTTERFLY

While still a caterpillar, the monarch eats the bitter leaves of the milkweed plant without any harm to itself. The caterpillar not only tolerates the toxins, it even thrives on them. The toxins remain present in the body of the adult butterfly. It takes only one lesson for a bird to learn that monarchs are to be avoided and not eaten.

The monarch weighs no more than a down feather.

HOW CAN A MONARCH BUTTERFLY "OUTRUN" A HORSE?

Monarchs fly an average of ten to twenty-five miles per hour during their migratory flights. The fastest pacers and trotters of harness racing can usually run thirty miles per hour. However, the monarch may fly eighty miles in one day while the horse seldom races more than one mile in a week.

In an endurance test, the monarch butterfly would be the clear winner. It has been observed to fly over 650 miles without landing. With a tail wind it can fly even farther. By comparison, a Pony Express horse was ridden nonstop only ten to fifteen miles at a time.

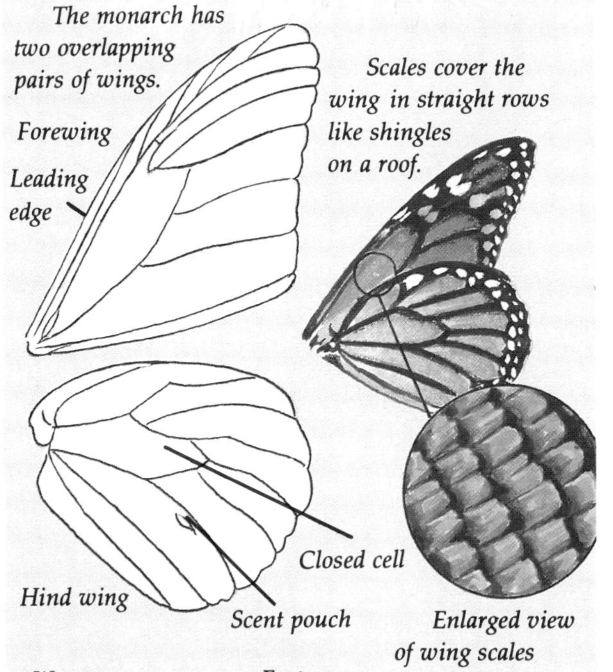

WHY IS MIGRATION ALWAYS A NEW EXPERIENCE FOR EVERY MONARCH?

Although monarchs are one of the few insects that migrate, not every monarch is part of the migration. Only those that hatch late in the summer make the long trip south.

These young butterflies are several generations removed from those that flew north the past spring. They have never before seen their destination and yet they fly straight to the wintering grounds of their great grandparents.

WHEN IS 32°F REQUIRED FOR THE SURVIVAL OF THE MONARCH BUTTERFLY?

Monarchs choose the same wintering areas generation after generation. They are most often located in the foothills of large mountain ranges. The area selected must be protected from strong winds and maintain a constant temperature of about 32°F all winter long. If the area is too cold, the monarch will freeze. If it is too warm, the monarch will become too active and exhaust all of the energy that it has stored for the return trip in the spring.

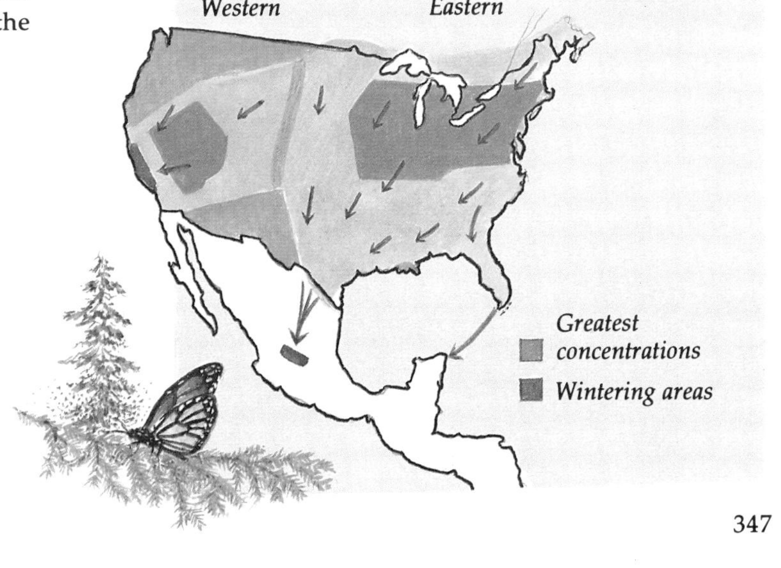

WHERE DO MILLIONS OF MONARCHS SPEND THEIR WINTER?

Eastern monarchs head for Mexico where they gather by the millions in several small areas of less than twenty acres each. Some migrate by way of Florida and cross the Gulf of Mexico in a single nonstop flight. Western monarchs fly to groves of pine and eucalyptus trees in southern California. These predetermined spots are close enough to the ocean to avoid winter frosts, but far enough away to gain protection from winter ocean storms.

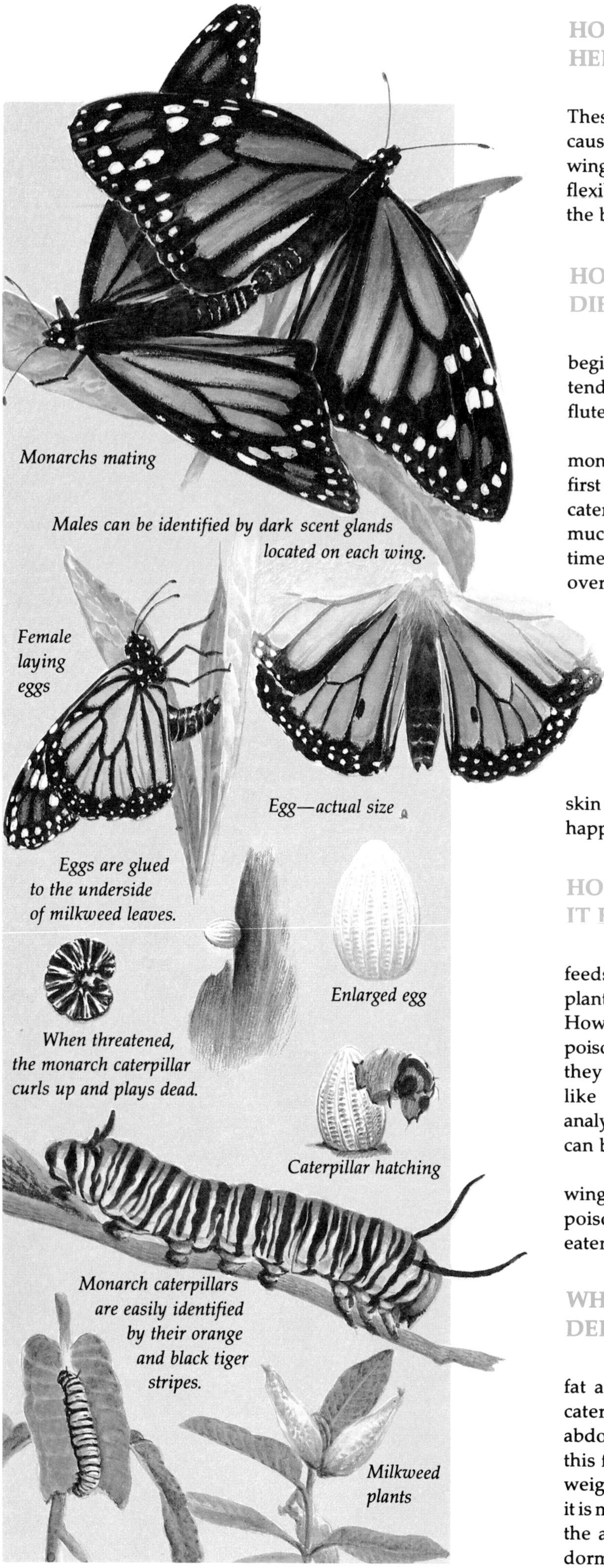

Monarchs mating
Males can be identified by dark scent glands located on each wing.
Female laying eggs
Egg—actual size
Eggs are glued to the underside of milkweed leaves.
Enlarged egg
When threatened, the monarch caterpillar curls up and plays dead.
Caterpillar hatching
Monarch caterpillars are easily identified by their orange and black tiger stripes.
Milkweed plants

HOW DO VEINS IN A BUTTERFLY'S WINGS HELP IT TO FLY?

Veins form the framework of the butterfly's wings. These veins are closer together near the edges of the wings, causing them to be thicker and stiffer. The middle of the wings have fewer veins, making them thinner and more flexible. As the wings bend, air passes over them and gives the butterfly lift.

HOW DOES THE MONARCH'S BITTER DIET INCREASE ITS SIZE 2,700 TIMES?

The development of a mature monarch butterfly begins with an egg glued securely to the underside of tender, young shoots of the milkweed plant. The delicately fluted eggs are no larger than the head of a pin.

Tiny orange and white caterpillars hatch from the monarch's eggs several days after they are laid. A caterpillar's first food is its own egg shell. When the shell is gone the caterpillar turns to the nearest leaf, the milkweed. It eats so much that within two weeks it has increased its size 2,700 times. That is equivalent to a six-pound infant growing to over eight tons.

HOW DOES A CATERPILLAR AVOID ENTRAPMENT IN ITS OWN SKIN?

Monarch caterpillars grow so fast that their skin cannot keep up. As often as every three days, a caterpillar becomes trapped in its own skin and must free itself or die. To do this, the skin splits along the back and the caterpillar crawls out. This happens five times during the life of each caterpillar.

HOW DOES A MONARCH'S DIET PROTECT IT FROM PREDATORS?

During the caterpillar stage the monarch butterfly feeds exclusively on the poisonous leaves of milkweed plants. This poison remains in the body of the adult butterfly. However, milkweeds vary greatly in the strength of their poison. Since monarchs may feed on several different plants, they each have a unique combination of toxins which act like a "fingerprint" to identify different individuals. By analyzing the poison found in the adult butterfly, the poison can be matched to a specific type of milkweed plant.

Birds can also "fingerprint" monarchs. By sampling a wing, some birds have learned to tell the strength of the poison the butterfly contains. If it is weak, the butterfly is eaten. If the poison is strong, the butterfly is cast aside.

WHY DOES THE LIFE OF THE MONARCH DEPEND UPON ITS BEING FAT?

It is very important for a monarch caterpillar to be as fat as possible. Almost eighty per cent of the food the caterpillar eats is converted to fat which is stored in a large abdominal organ called the *fat body*. In migrating monarchs, this fat body makes up almost one-third of their total dry weight. Because the adult butterfly does not eat much while it is migrating, the energy contained in the fat body must last the adult butterfly through the fall migration and winter dormancy, a period of many months.

HOW DOES THE MONARCH BUTTERFLY ILLUSTRATE CREATIVE TRANSFORMATION RATHER THAN NATURAL ADAPTATION?

The metamorphosis that changes a caterpillar to a butterfly is not merely a rearrangement of parts but a complete transformation. Internal organs of the caterpillar liquefy and are recycled into new tissue. Jaws disappear and a specialized tongue appears. Old stubby legs are absorbed and new wings develop.

WHAT SPECTACULAR ESCAPE TRICK CAN A MONARCH BUTTERFLY PERFORM?

When a caterpillar matures, it stops eating and seeks out a sheltered spot where it can hang upside down for a period of two to three weeks. This is called the *pupa stage.* The caterpillar first weaves a silk mat on the underside of a twig and attaches itself firmly with a cluster of hooks called a *cremaster.* Then, while still holding onto the twig with its cremaster, the caterpillar carefully sheds its skin for the fifth time.

HOW CAN THE TRANSFORMATION OF A CATERPILLAR BE STOPPED FROM WITHIN?

During these two to three weeks, the pupa's only defense is its unpleasant taste. It has no way of escaping mice or birds that do not know about its poison. There exists an even bigger threat from parasites that are not affected by the poison. If eggs from these parasites are laid on the caterpillar and hatch during the pupa stage, the larvae feed on the helpless pupa and leave behind only the empty shell.

HOW DID GOD MAKE IT POSSIBLE FOR US TO ACTUALLY VIEW THE TRANSFORMATION TAKING PLACE WITHIN THE BUTTERFLY?

The gold-studded turquoise skin, or *chrysalis,* of the monarch pupa becomes transparent after two weeks, making it possible to actually watch the last stages of the metamorphosis. Wings, legs, eyes, and antennae are all visible. During the last few days, cracks spread in the chrysalis wall and allow the butterfly to break free.

WHY IS THE FIRST HALF HOUR THE MOST CRITICAL IN A BUTTERFLY'S LIFE?

The butterfly's wings have been folded inside the cramped chrysalis and contain hundreds of creases. At first, the wings are soft and limp. But as fluid is pumped through the veins, the wings unfold and become rigid. If all of the creases have not been worked out within the first half hour, the butterfly may be crippled for life.

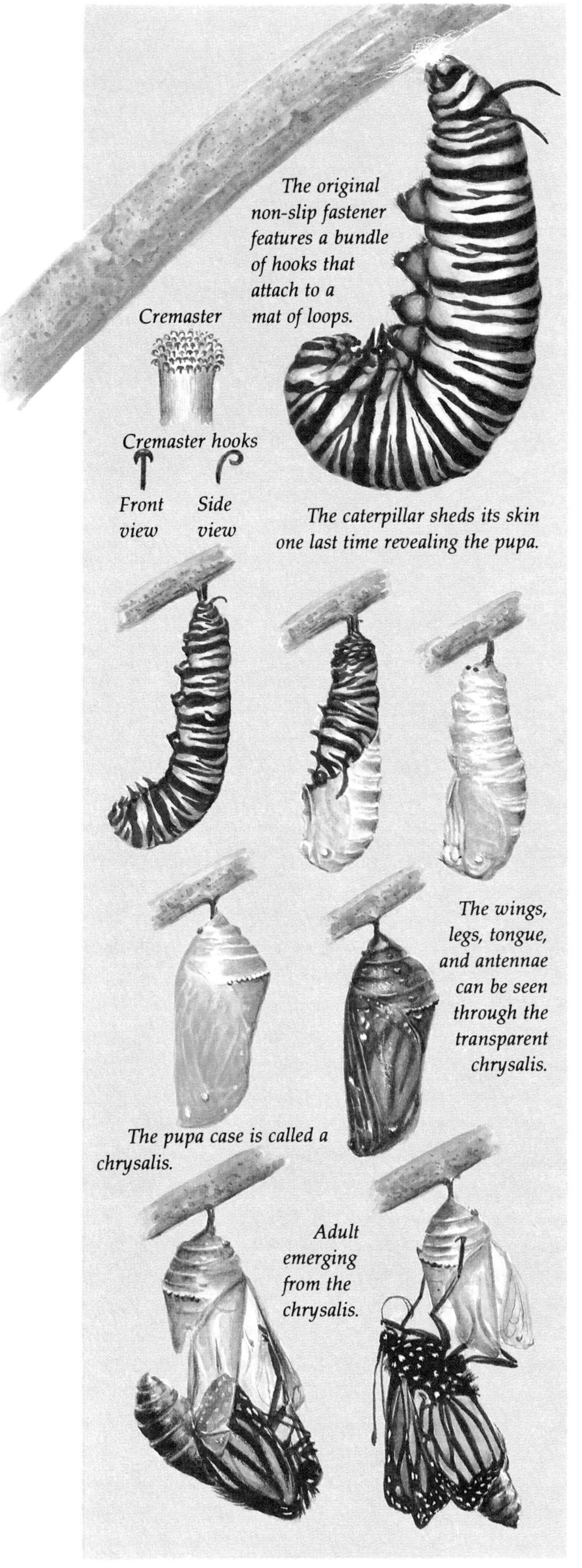

The original non-slip fastener features a bundle of hooks that attach to a mat of loops.
Cremaster
Cremaster hooks
Front view
Side view
The caterpillar sheds its skin one last time revealing the pupa.
The wings, legs, tongue, and antennae can be seen through the transparent chrysalis.
The pupa case is called a chrysalis.
Adult emerging from the chrysalis.

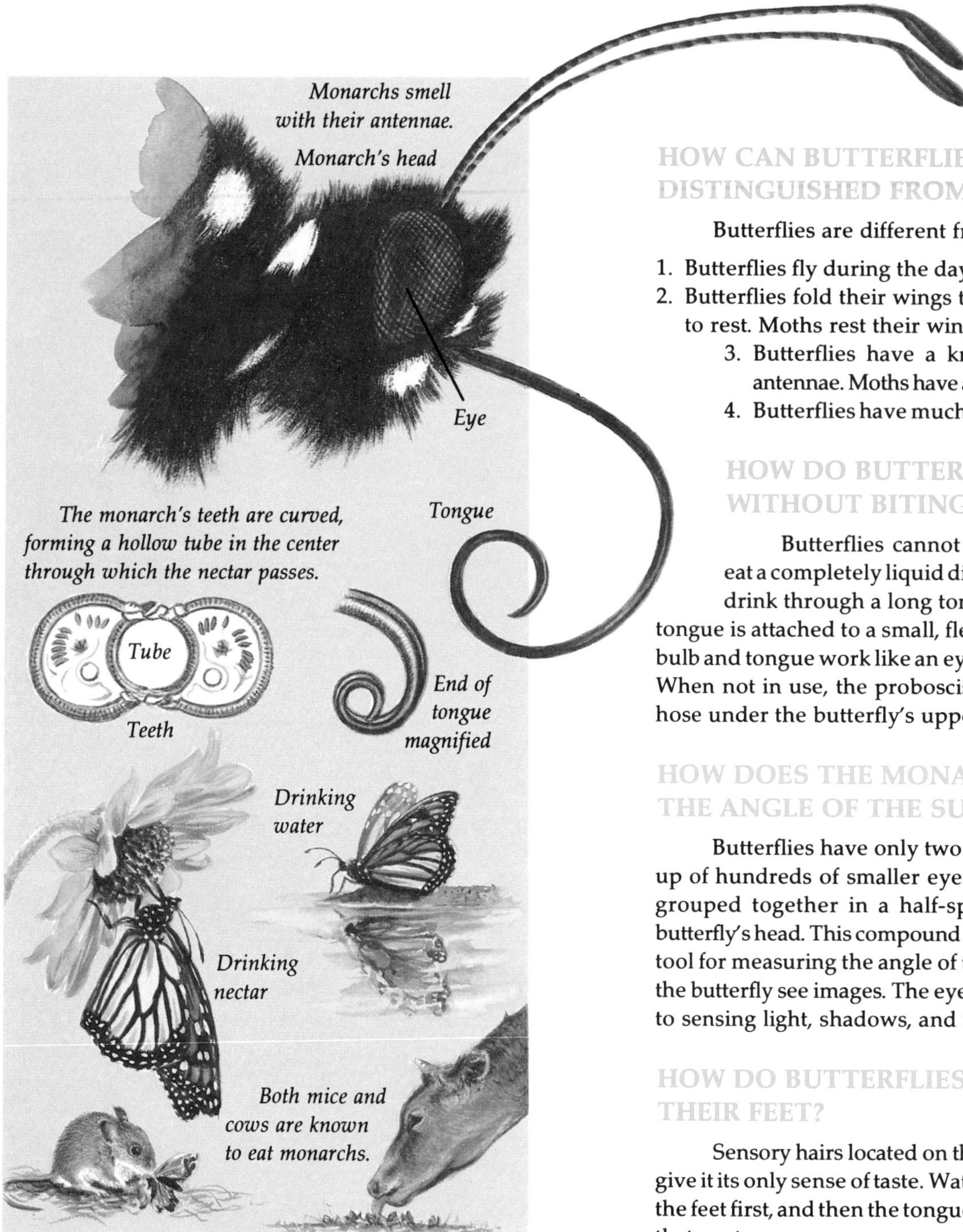
Monarchs smell
with their antennae.
Monarch's head
Eye
The monarch's teeth are curved, forming a hollow tube in the center through which the nectar passes.
Tongue
Tube
Teeth
End of tongue magnified
Drinking water
Drinking nectar
Both mice and cows are known to eat monarchs.

HOW CAN BUTTERFLIES BE DISTINGUISHED FROM MOTHS?

Butterflies are different from moths in four ways.

1. Butterflies fly during the day. Moths fly mostly at night.
2. Butterflies fold their wings together above their bodies to rest. Moths rest their wings flat.
3. Butterflies have a knob at the end of smooth antennae. Moths have antennae that are often fuzzy.
4. Butterflies have much thinner bodies than moths.

HOW DO BUTTERFLIES EAT WITHOUT BITING?

Butterflies cannot bite. Therefore, they must eat a completely liquid diet of nectar and water. They drink through a long tongue called a *proboscis*. This tongue is attached to a small, flexible bulb in the head. The bulb and tongue work like an eyedropper to suck up nectar. When not in use, the proboscis is coiled up like a garden hose under the butterfly's upper lip.

HOW DOES THE MONARCH MEASURE THE ANGLE OF THE SUN?

Butterflies have only two eyes, but each one is made up of hundreds of smaller eyes. Tiny six-sided lenses are grouped together in a half-sphere on each side of the butterfly's head. This compound eye is probably an important tool for measuring the angle of the sun, but it does not help the butterfly see images. The eyesight of a butterfly is limited to sensing light, shadows, and movement.

HOW DO BUTTERFLIES TASTE WITH THEIR FEET?

Sensory hairs located on the legs and feet of a butterfly give it its only sense of taste. Water and nectar are located by the feet first, and then the tongue is uncoiled and directed to that spot.

Monarch
Viceroy

The Viceroy Butterfly

The viceroy butterfly closely resembles the monarch. Even though it is not poisonous, the viceroy benefits from the poisonous reputation of its look-alike. Any bird that refuses to eat a monarch will also refuse to eat a viceroy.

Viceroy caterpillars lack orange and black stripes and feed on willows and poplar trees instead of milkweeds. They do not migrate, but hibernate wherever they are over the winter. Adult viceroys have shorter and chunkier bodies than monarchs and have only a single row of white spots along the edges of their wings. Monarchs have a double row of spots.

How is bringing joy out of sorrow illustrated in Scripture?

Who demonstrated the principle that kindness in giving is not measured by how much is given?

(Pause for a response—see page 17.)

A spirit of celebration filled the city as thousands of men and their sons converged upon the temple area from all parts of the land. They were there to take part in the week-long feast of unleavened bread.

Happy reunions took place among friends who had not seen each other for several months. Music echoed over the hillsides as worshipers ascended to the city. The baaing of sheep and lowing of cattle being led to the temple added to the special sounds of the day.

While all this was taking place, one person stood alone, watching as the people passed. She noticed the items which the men and their sons had brought for the presentation of sacrificial gifts. This was one of the highlights of the feast.

As she observed the jubilant crowds, she realized that she had neither father, son, husband, nor gift. Since the death of her husband, times had been difficult for her. She barely had enough money for food. The sum total of all her money could buy only an eighth of a loaf of bread!

She followed the crowds at the temple, giving a warm smile to all who met her eyes. As she walked, there was much to think about. The God whom she worshiped was the same God whom Elisha served. God worked through Elisha to take care of a widow and her son for many months when she gave her last bit of food to him.

Then there was the example of Anna, who had gone throughout the city thirty-three years earlier proclaiming that the Messiah had been born and that she had seen him with her own eyes.

Anna was also a widow. For eighty-five years she had trusted the Lord for her provisions through fasting and prayer. What a beautiful example she was!

Suddenly this woman knew what she would do. She increased her step and headed for the east side of the temple area. As she entered the court of the women, the crowds were especially large. She walked over and stood in one of the lines. The line slowly moved toward a box with a trumpet-shaped mouth. Those in front of her contributed valuable silver and bronze coins. Some gave bags of money.

As she neared the box, she reached out her hand and threw in the money that was in it—two little coins. They were all she had. As she turned to walk away, she noticed a man who had been watching those giving. He seemed encouraged by her gift. He called together his disciples, and in a rich, clear voice she heard Him say, "Truly I say to you, this poor widow has given more than all who have given to the treasury. For they gave out of their abundance, but she out of her want gave all that she had!"

Out of her sorrow and poverty this poor widow brought joy to the heart of Jesus by illustrating the true meaning of sacrificial giving.

From Mark 12:41–44 and Luke 2:36–38

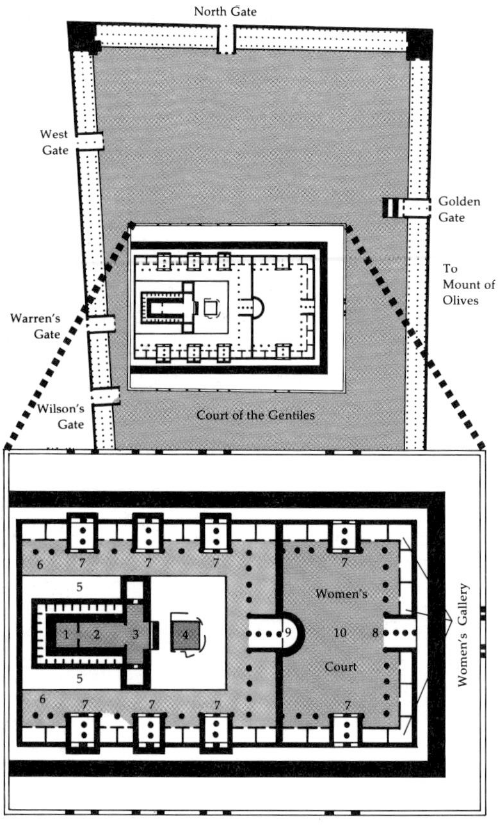

The Temple in Jesus' Day

1. Holy of Holies 2. Holy Place 3. Porch 4. Altar 5. Court of the Priests 6. Court of the Men 7. Sanctuary Gates 8. Gate Beautiful 9. Where the Levites stood to sing 10. Court of the Women and area where the collection boxes were located.

The location of the treasury is not certain; however, the free will offerings were accessible to women. Jesus sat near the treasury which had to be located in the Court of the Women. This court was just inside the Eastern Gate of the temple, called Gate Beautiful. Outside of this gate beggars would sit and ask for mercy as people brought their money into the temple. (See Acts 3:2.)

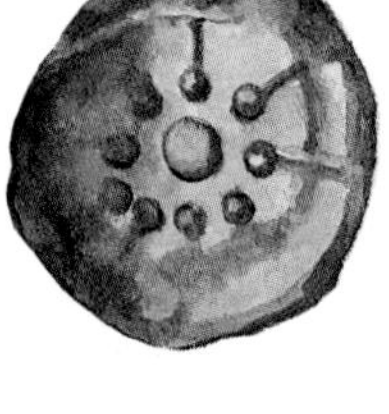

The "Widow's Mite"

Penny

***The front of a mite** had a picture of the sun on it with eight rays. This was to represent the Sun of Righteousness. (See Malachi 4:2.) The back side pictured a ship's anchor which was to be a reminder of God's promises. Smaller than a penny, the buying power of a mite was equal to a nickel today.*

THE POOR WIDOW, AN EXAMPLE OF SACRIFICIAL GIVING DURING THE FEAST OF UNLEAVENED BREAD

Jesus was in Jerusalem during Passover week. Jews from all over the world had converged upon the city to celebrate the Feast of Unleavened Bread. One event in which many had participated was the presentation of sacrificial gifts. *"Three times in a year shall all thy males appear before the Lord thy God in the place which he shall choose; in the feast of unleavened bread, and in the feast of weeks, and in the feast of tabernacles: and they shall not appear before the Lord empty: Every man shall give as he is able, according to the blessing of the Lord thy God which he hath given thee" (Deuteronomy 16:16–17).*

As a result, there was a steady stream of people filing in and out of the temple. Gifts of money were deposited in one of thirteen collection boxes with trumpet-shaped mouths. The boxes were located in the Court of the Women.

A SCATHING REBUKE FOR THE RELIGIOUS ESTABLISHMENT

Jesus had been teaching the large crowds that gathered in the temple. He knew that the time of His death was near. In fact, this would be the last day He would ever enter Herod's temple.

One of the themes He spoke of was the twisted teaching and hypocrisy of the scribes and the Pharisees. His warnings against these men had never been stronger. He called them "hypocrites," "fools," "blind guides," "full of extortion and excess," "full of hypocrisy and iniquity," "whited sepulchres full of dead men's bones," "serpents," and "vipers." (See Matthew 23.)

He accused the scribes, recognized teachers of God's Law, of devouring widows' houses. (See Mark 12:40; Luke 20:47.) Jesus was clear in His warnings against these men because they had led the people astray with teaching contrary to the truth about the kingdom of God. However, His final words in the temple were words of praise.

A GIFT SMALL IN MEASURE BUT GREAT IN SIGNIFICANCE

A poor widow inconspicuously made her way to one of the collection boxes in the Court of the Women and cast in two copper coins. To the rich who had been putting large sums of money into the boxes, this contribution seemed practically worthless. The effort to sort, count, and store her two mites was probably more costly than their worth. The Lord's disciples, who had just been so enamored with the rich young ruler, took no notice.

A WORD OF PRAISE FOR A GENUINE GIVER

But the Lord praised her, *". . . Verily I say unto you, That this poor widow hath cast more in, than all they which have cast into the treasury: For all they did cast in of their abundance; but she of her want did cast in all that she had, even all her living" (Mark 12:43–44).*

The Lord was explaining what kind of gift really pleases God. He is not concerned with the actual offering as much as the heart condition of the giver. The widow did not give to gain the praise of men. She gave because of her genuine love for God, His work, and His temple. Her attitude was expressed not by what she gave, but by what remained afterward.

Although this woman had no husband to support her, she must have felt blessed. She acknowledged that God was her comfort and support by giving back to Him everything she had. Her heavenly Father would provide for her through His infinite resources.

CHARACTER SKETCH OF THE POOR WIDOW

HOW DID THE SCRIBES "DEVOUR WIDOWS' HOUSES"?

The scribes, responsible for the teaching of God's Word, were themselves living contrary to the Law's demands. When Jesus accused them of devouring the houses of widows, He referred to their destructive teaching and possibly to their actions as well.

The Law of God was sensitive to the greater needs of widows. As God's representatives, the leaders of Israel were to protect the legal rights of widows and to make sure that they were fed and clothed. (See Deuteronomy 10:17–18.) Grapes, grain, and olives were to be available for them to glean. (See Deuteronomy 24:19–21.) Widows were also to be included in the third year tithe. (See Deuteronomy 14:28–29.)

But the teaching of the scribes provided ways for hard-hearted people to evade these merciful commands. For instance, the scribes taught that a son could vow to devote to God everything he would otherwise have used to support his mother. The son gained the praise of men while his mother lived in poverty. (See Matthew 15:3–9.)

The famous rabbi, Hillel, devised a "legal" way to evade the Law's command to cancel debts during the Sabbatical year. One tragic result of this scheme was to deprive widows who were in debt of the ownership of their houses.

The Lord may also have been referring to the scribes' habit of taking advantage of the hospitality of people of limited means. Since it was technically forbidden to accept remuneration for their teaching, the scribes themselves were often poor. Yet, they were not reluctant to accept contributions from those who were least able to give.

WHAT WAS THE VALUE OF THE POOR WIDOW'S OFFERING?

In the eyes of men, her offering was practically worthless. We know that *". . . she threw in two mites, which make a farthing" (Mark 12:42)*. Jerusalem's fund of food for transients set the daily ration at no less than the equivalent of one loaf of bread. At that time a loaf was worth a twelfth of a denarius, or about sixteen mites.

Thus, the entire wealth of the poor widow was one-eighth of a loaf of bread, one-eighth the daily ration of a beggar. But her offering was of inestimable worth in the eyes of God. The Lord saw in her heart genuine love and total trust in her faithful Provider. He measured her offering not by what she gave, but by what she kept for herself.

FOR WHAT PURPOSE WAS THE WIDOW'S OFFERING USED?

Her offering provided for the physical functioning of the temple. Four of the thirteen collection boxes were for freewill offerings. The others were for tribute money. The widow's two mites fell far short of the required half-shekel tribute amount. Thus, we can assume she was presenting the customary freewill offering given in association with the Feast of Unleavened Bread.

The proceeds from the four freewill boxes were designated for wood, incense, temple decorations, and burnt offerings. These represented the major expenses for the temple. It is significant that even though the chief priests and temple leaders were corrupt at that time, the Lord still praised the widow for contributing to the temple's support. Although some had turned the temple into a den of thieves, it was still considered by the Lord to be the house of prayer. (See Luke 19:46.)

ANNA

***The first time Jesus entered the temple,** Anna "gave thanks" and spoke of him to all who were looking for redemption. (See Luke 2:38.)*

The last time Jesus entered the temple, the poor widow gave all she had to the Lord. (See Mark 12:44.)

Both had experienced the sorrow of widowhood, and both brought joy to the heart of Jesus by their kindness.

THE POOR WIDOW

CHAPTER TWENTY-SEVEN

Kindness

. . . Is giving honor to whom honor is due

"Honour thy father and thy mother. . . ."

Deuteronomy 5:16

"Be kindly affectioned one to another with brotherly love; in honour preferring one another."

Romans 12:10

". . . [If] one member be honoured, all the members rejoice with it."

I Corinthians 12:26

Living Lessons on Kindness . . .

FROM THE PAGES OF SCRIPTURE

The world says, "The good that men do is soon forgotten, the evil lives on forever." God says, *"The memory of the just is blessed: but the name of the wicked shall rot" (Proverbs 10:7)*. By honoring the memory of those who benefited our lives, we are performing a kindness that fulfills an important purpose of the Lord.

Only after the death of a righteous person did another person fully appreciate the benefits that had been received. It was then that the memory of that righteous person was properly honored.

ILLUSTRATED IN THE WORLD OF NATURE

ARCTIC LEMMING *Dicrostonyx torquatus*

There are two kinds of lemmings—the *common* and the *collared.* Only collared lemmings turn white in the winter. The arctic lemming of North America is one of several collared varieties. It is clearly distinguished from the common lemming by a golden collar that contrasts with its chestnut pelt.

Lemmings are plump little animals related to the mouse. They are from four to five inches long including their stubby tails. They eat tremendous amounts of food and carry out emigrations every three to four years.

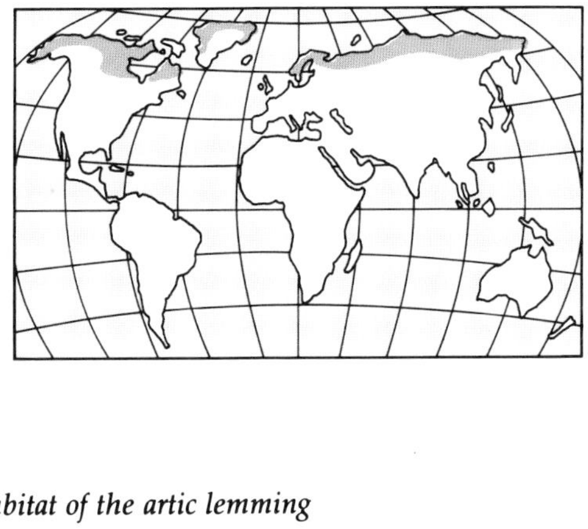

The range and habitat of the artic lemming

How are the consequences of unkindness illustrated in the world of nature?

Shrill hissing and sharp, snapping teeth served as a warning to either move or get bitten.

These ominous sounds did not come from some attacking predator. They came from a neighbor—one of his own kind. This fellow lemming could have had plenty to eat if he would just move to a different level on the mountainous terrain. But the intruder wanted what he saw at that moment and was willing to fight for it.

Another hiss was given and then sharp teeth flashed in the cold arctic air—the defender was bitten. The wounded lemming was forced to leave the safety of his nest and feeding ground and retreat to unfamiliar territory. There he encountered more hissing and snapping from other lemmings who had also been forced to abandon their nests. After receiving several more wounds, he fled down the mountainside.

Soon many others followed him and forced him to move again. This continued until one day he found himself at the edge of a high cliff overlooking a mountain river.

His attempt to retrace his steps was prevented by fellow lemmings. Panic gripped him as he found himself being pushed over the precipice. Down he went, rolling, bouncing, and tumbling into the swirling water below! He surfaced and swam frantically to the bank.

As he crawled up on the shore, hundreds more followed him. Soon their ranks were swelled with converging migrations of other lemmings. Hissing and biting continued among them as new destruction came upon them. Caribou used their sharp hoofs to trample many, while they bit and swallowed others whole.

The crowded conditions produced new hazards to their survival as an epidemic of "lemming fever" broke out among them, decimating their ranks. Then hungry bears, attracted to the hordes, devoured as many lemmings as they could.

One destruction after another came as the contentious throng continued slowly down the mountainside. The more they traveled together, the more aggressive they became. Noisy fights broke out among them.

Suddenly, the lemming halted. Before him was a large body of water; he was a good swimmer, but the choppy waves signaled danger. Forced by the press of the crowd, he plunged in—there was no turning back.

Squabbles ended as each one swam desperately forward. Some were able to swim farther than others, but none reached the other shore. This destruction is a vivid illustration of the consequences of unkindness.

THE CHARACTERISTICS OF

THE ARCTIC LEMMING IN SCRIPTURE

The voracious appetite and irritable nature of the lemming provide a vivid illustration of what happens among people who sacrifice kindness for personal gain.

"From whence come wars and fightings among you? come they not hence, even of your lusts that war in your members?" (James 4:1).

Lemmings fight each other to feed themselves. Scripture warns against such behavior among Christians. *"But if ye bite and devour one another, take heed that ye be not consumed one of another" (Galatians 5:15).*

In the beginning, mankind tended to become like lemmings by congregating in cities rather than scattering throughout the world. *"So the Lord scattered them abroad from thence upon the face of all the earth: and they left off to build the city" (Genesis 11:8).*

The dangers of the herd instinct among the lemmings is a precise illustration of the dangers of joining a demonstration against authority. (See Exodus 23:2.)

The amazing march of the lemmings to destruction is a tragic illustration of crowd pressure among unbelievers. *"Enter ye in at the strait gate: for wide is the gate, and broad is the way, that leadeth to destruction, and many there be which go in thereat" (Matthew 7:13).*

CHARACTERISTICS AND PHYSICAL FEATURES OF THE ARCTIC LEMMING

Every three or four years lemmings can no longer live together peacefully. The tensions become so great that many of them leave; but in leaving, they expose themselves to destruction through disease, predators, exhaustion, or drowning.

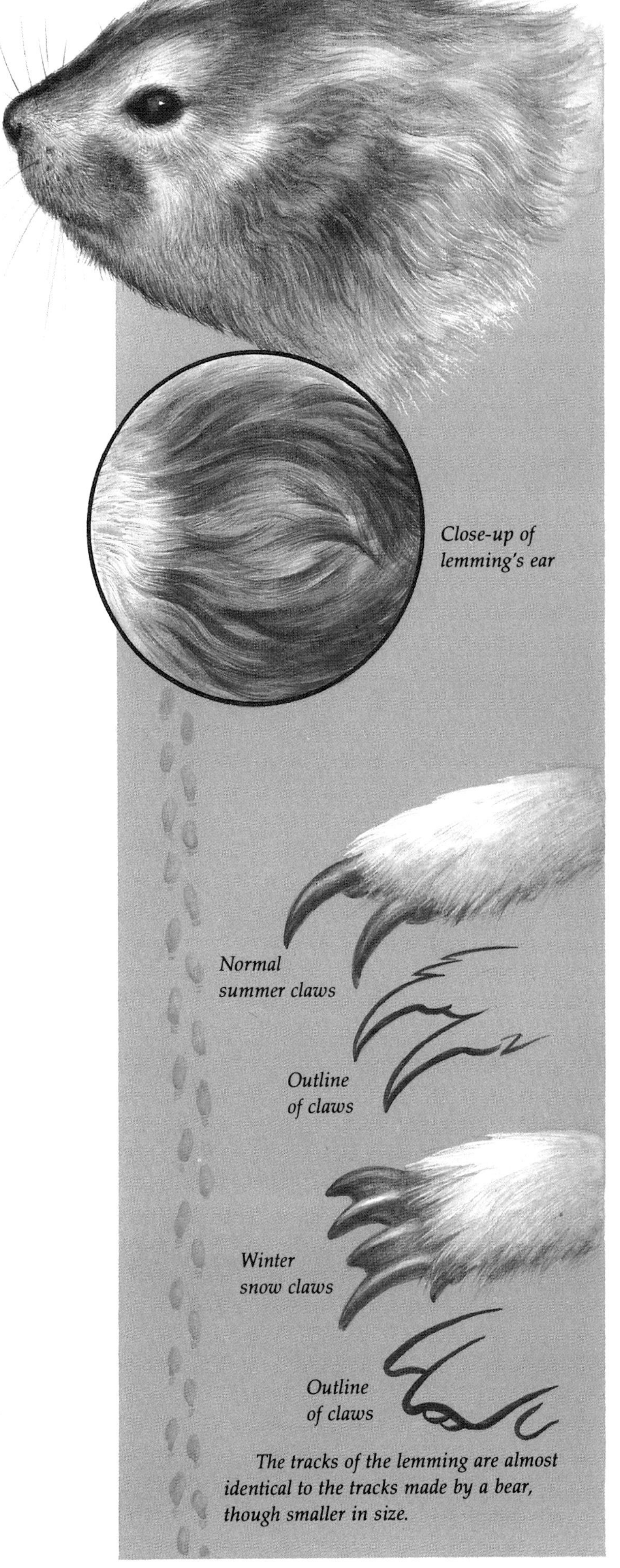

The tracks of the lemming are almost identical to the tracks made by a bear, though smaller in size.

WHY DO LEMMINGS NEED BUILT-IN EARMUFFS?

Because the lemmings of the Arctic do not hibernate, they need maximum protection against the cold. Their small ears, which are little more than rims, help to prevent excessive heat loss. The ears are also hidden by stiff hairs that are controlled by muscles in front of the ear. These hairs can cover or uncover ears in order to protect the inner parts from frostbite.

WHY IS THE LEMMING NOT BOTHERED IN THE SUMMER BY INSECTS?

The irritation with insects which other animals have during the summertime does not appear to be as much a problem to the lemming. Its small ears and stubby tail are both covered, thus eliminating exposed skin for the flies to bite.

HOW DO THE CLAWS OF THE LEMMING INDICATE THAT WINTER IS ARRIVING?

As the snow begins to fall in September, the arctic lemming develops snow claws on the third and forth toes of each front foot. These snow claws grow directly below the normal claws. The two are separated by a groove with a deep notch at the tip. These snow claws are so effective that lemmings have been known to dig through the walls of igloos.

HOW DO SNOW CLAWS INDICATE THE ARRIVAL OF SPRING?

When the snow begins to melt in the spring, the snow claws stop growing. As the lemming continues to use the snow claws, they are simply worn away. Even though the common lemming does more digging, only the collared varieties grow these special claws.

HOW DO LEMMINGS GET FROZEN OUT OF THEIR HOME IN THE WINTER?

During the summer, lemmings hide their nests of grass in shallow burrows underground. They may also build them under large rocks. In the winter, however, the arctic tundra freezes too solidly for the lemming to dig through it. Therefore, the arctic lemming builds its winter nest above the ground in hard-packed snow and ice.

Snow tunnels
A lemming, apparently chewing on a rock, is actually eating lichens.
Lichens are a combination of two plants, algae and fungi, which grow together to form one plant.
Snow
Lemmings prefer to live along the lichen belt.
Lichen belt
Willow belt
Birch forest
Coniferous forest

HOW DO LEMMINGS ELUDE PREDATORS DURING THE WINTER?

Lemmings do not hibernate, but continue their living activities under the snow. The arctic lemming builds tunnels up to sixty feet long. This underground shelter not only keeps them safe from predators, but also provides a more plentiful supply of food. The snow around the tunnel entrance becomes hard-packed and is often the last to thaw in the spring.

WHY IS SNOW COVER NECESSARY FOR LEMMINGS TO SURVIVE?

Lemmings typically dig their burrows so that the snowdrifts will bury their homes even deeper. A three- to four-foot snowdrift will act as insulation against the intense cold of the arctic air above. With this snow cover, the nest will be more than forty degrees warmer than the surface temperature. If, however, the wind shifts and the snow cover is blown away, the nest will be exposed and the severe cold will endanger the lemming's life.

HOW DOES THE FUR OF THE LEMMING ALLOW IT TO TURN AROUND IN A TUNNEL NO WIDER THAN ITS OWN BODY?

The tunnels of the lemming's winter nest are usually no bigger than two to three inches in diameter, just large enough for the lemming to pass through. Yet, the lemming never gets stuck when it turns around because it has very loose skin that lets it turn completely around in a space no wider than its own body. This loose skin also provides it with valuable insulation against the cold.

HOW IS THE LEMMING A CLEAN AND AN UNCLEAN ANIMAL AT THE SAME TIME?

Since the lemming is a part of the mouse family, it is listed in Scripture as an unclean animal. Thus, it is not to be eaten for food. (See Leviticus 11:29.) In regard to nest maintenance, however, the lemming is extremely clean. Its droppings are all placed in one heap.

HOW DOES A LEMMING'S APPETITE CHANGE A LANDSCAPE?

The appetite of a lemming is enormous. A single pair of lemmings and their young can eat every living plant in a twenty-five yard enclosure in just eight weeks. Lemmings are particularly fond of grasses, lichens, mosses, and sedges. In the winter they feed on roots, eating the same plants from the bottom up.

HOW COULD A WARM SUMMER DAY BE FATAL TO A LEMMING?

If temperatures become as mild as 77°F, lemmings can die of heat prostration. Because of this, lemmings prefer marshy mountain meadows above the tree line.

__During a peak year there may__ be forty to seventy lemmings per acre. The following year there may be less than one lemming per acre.

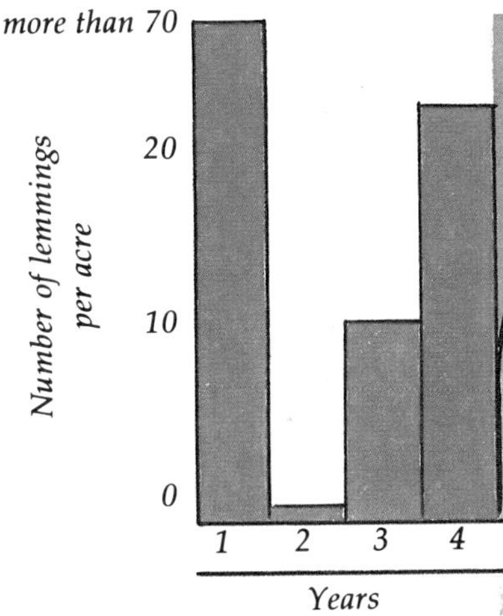

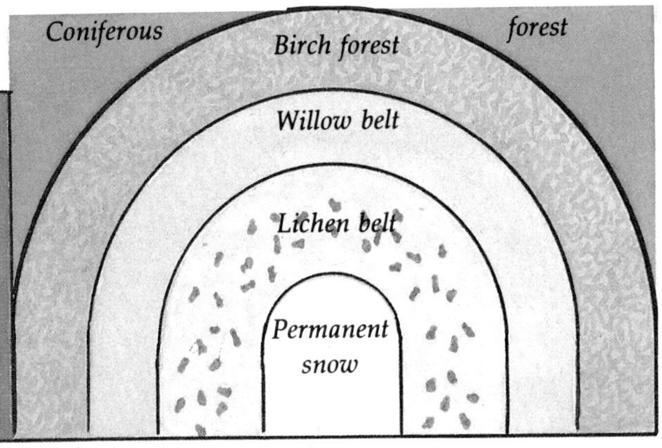

HOW CAN A SINGLE PAIR OF LEMMINGS PRODUCE A THOUSAND OFFSPRING IN ONE YEAR?

The growth and reproduction of lemmings is phenomenal. At birth, the pink and hairless lemmings weigh only four grams. By the fourth day they cut their first teeth. By the twenty-fifth day they molt into their adult fur, and by the thirtieth day the female can reproduce.

Theoretically, lemmings could have a new litter every fifty-one days and with litters of four to eight young, the population increase can be enormous. Every three or four years their population peaks and then abruptly declines due to predators, starvation, disease, or mass emigration.

HOW DO WE KNOW THAT FOOD SHORTAGE IS NOT THE CAUSE OF LEMMING STRIFE?

Although small numbers of lemmings can get along together, there is a point at which the addition of just one or two more lemmings creates a marked increase in hostile behavior. Experiments have shown that even with plenty of available food, pushing, shoving, biting, and fighting become commonplace. A hostile lemming will bounce up and down chattering its teeth, hissing, and spitting at other lemmings.

WHAT CAUSES THOUSANDS OF LEMMINGS TO SWIM TO THEIR DEATHS?

This unusual phenomenon is probably the result of stampede conditions. Many lemming emigrations go unnoticed, but when natural obstacles such as rivers and mountain ranges funnel smaller, separate migrations together, the numbers become spectacular. Occasionally the swarms have become so concentrated that observers have counted almost one lemming a second as they passed. In areas where the valleys lead to the sea, such as in Norway and Sweden, lemmings may rush headlong off cliffs or into the ocean, dying by the thousands.

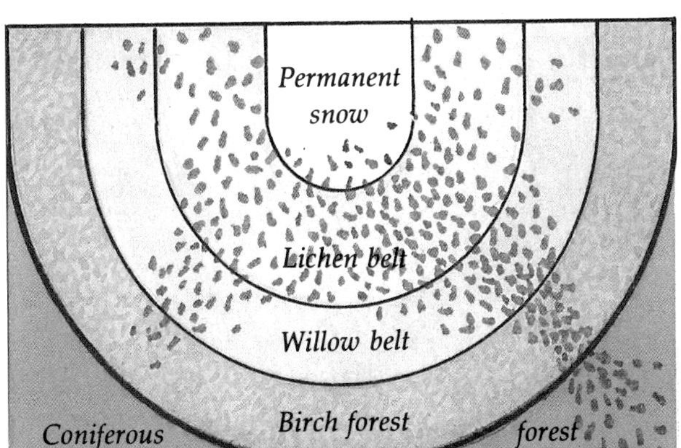

__In a normal year (top) lemmings limit their__ wanderings to the lichen belt. But in an emigration year (bottom) they move into unfamiliar habitats. Normally lush fields are stripped bare (center).

WHY DOES A TRAPPER COUNT LEMMINGS BEFORE SETTING OUT HIS TRAPS?

The snowy owl and the arctic fox depend on the lemming for food. In years when the lemming population declines, these animals also decline. Trappers who hunt arctic foxes for their valuable pelts, count lemmings to predict successful trapping seasons.

WHEN DO LEMMINGS INCREASE THE LIFE EXPECTANCY OF CARIBOU?

The caribou of the arctic tundra are normally hunted by wolves. During "lemming years," when lemmings are overpopulated, wolves feed almost exclusively on the little animals and leave the caribou alone.

WHEN IS A LEMMING IN DANGER OF DROWNING?

Lemmings are good swimmers and can swim the smooth waters of small lakes and rivers without difficulty. In fact, some lemmings have actually swum from the coast of Norway to Lofoten Island about thirty miles away. However, waves of only a few inches can cause a lemming to drown. Lemmings may also drown from stress induced by exhaustion and hypothermia.

WHY IS IT SAFER TO BE BITTEN BY A FAST LEMMING THAN BY A SLOW LEMMING?

Normally lemmings are very quick. However, when they are infected by parasites, they become diseased, and this causes them to run slowly. If a man is bitten by a slow-moving lemming, he has probably been infected by the disease called *lemming fever* (tularemia). Transmission of tularemia leads to pneumonia in humans.

WHEN DOES A LEMMING FIGHT AND WHEN DOES A LEMMING RUN?

The lemming stubbornly holds its ground when cornered, even though it is not able to defend itself. The lemming will hiss, brace itself against the rock and die. When not cornered, the lemming will run from danger.

WHY IS THE FUR OF THE LEMMING BETTER FOR PROTECTION THAN FOR CLOTHING?

The attractive fur of the lemming has little commercial use because the hide is too thin and not very durable. Its only common use is in the making of doll clothing for Eskimo children.

Because arctic lemmings do not hibernate and thus eat constantly throughout the winter, they must spend some of their time above ground. Their white winter coat serves as a camouflage protection against the white snow. Without such protection, the lemmings would be easy prey for the hawk, owl, weasel, and fox.

How is giving honor to whom honor is due illustrated in Scripture?

Who was the man who did not fully understand or appreciate what he had received until after the giver was dead? It was then that he properly honored his memory.

(Pause for a response—see page 17.)

The shocking event that caused other men to flee in fear caused him to advance in boldness. What brought discouragement to others brought confidence and reassurance to him.

He was a ruler. It was his job to know what was taking place among his people, so when he began to hear alarming reports of a countermovement in his country, he decided to investigate.

From behind the scenes, he gathered all the information he could. The more he learned, the more baffled and confused he became. Facts just did not add up in his mind. He concluded that his next step must be a private meeting with the movement's leader.

But how could he get to him? During the day the leader was constantly surrounded by hostile critics and zealous followers. He concluded that the best time would be at night.

Arrangements were made, and when the night arrived, he was present with carefully thought out questions. No sooner had the conversation begun than the one whom he was questioning made an unusual statement and an even more unusual analogy.

The analogy related to an event which had taken place in their nation's history many years earlier. Thousands of poisonous snakes had come in and bitten the people. When the victims cried out to God, He commanded Moses to make a brass snake and nail it on a pole. Then all those who believed the Word of God were to go outside the camp and look at that snake. Those who obeyed were healed.

The baffled ruler slipped out into the darkness of that night still pondering what he had heard. He continued to listen and watch and think.

Then one day it all became clear. The one who gave him that analogy was nailed to a wooden cross just as the serpent was nailed to the pole. Now it was his opportunity to fulfill that analogy. He got up, walked outside the city, and looked upon Jesus, fully believing the Word of God. Then, Nicodemus honored Christ by providing one hundred pounds of myrrh and aloes for His burial.

From John 3:1–21; 19:16–40

Nicodemus was the brother of Josephus, the famous historian during the time of Christ.

Myrrh Branches

Resin "tears" from this bush are processed to make an oil which is used for perfume, medicine, and embalming. Myrrh was given to Jesus at His birth (see Matthew 2:11), and Nicodemus gave one hundred pounds of myrrh for His burial.

***This medical symbol** has its roots in the serpent on the pole which Moses lifted up for healing in the wilderness. Jesus used this Old Testament account while reasoning with Nicodemus.*

NICODEMUS, THE PHARISEE WHO WAS "RIGHTEOUS" IN WORKS

The account of Nicodemus is a beautiful illustration of the miraculous work of God's Spirit in the heart of a man. Nicodemus was one of the prominent religious leaders of Israel, yet he was spiritually blind. He had the great responsibility of leading the people in the ways of God, but he had not grasped even the most rudimentary truths concerning the nature of God's kingdom. Nicodemus fully embraced the teaching of the religious establishment of his day. He belonged to the Pharisees, a group of men committed to the scrupulous observance of the traditional rules and regulations of the scribes, who were the official teachers of the Law.

MEMBERSHIP IN THE KINGDOM OF GOD

Although the Pharisees spent hours debating obscure details of their many observances, they were in agreement as to how a man entered and stayed in the kingdom of God. The easiest way to enter was to be born an Israelite, a physical descendant of Abraham, Isaac, and Israel. A Gentile could enter the kingdom only by becoming a convert to Judaism through circumcision and submission to the ceremonial Law.

The way to prominence as a member of God's kingdom was through works of righteousness. Almsgiving was first in the catalog of good works. To give alms was to gain merit in the sight of God and even to win atonement for sin. One Jewish authority claimed, "It is better to give alms than to lay up gold; almsgiving doth deliver from death, and it purges away all sin" (Tobit 12:8). Another meritorious act was prayer. The pious Jew was required to recite two sets of prayers each day—the "Shema" and "The Eighteen." The third great pillar in the religious life of a Jew was fasting. There was only one compulsory fast, the Day of Atonement, but zealous Pharisees fasted every Monday and Thursday.

A LIFE-CHANGING INTERVIEW

When Nicodemus met with Jesus by night, he did not understand His words, *". . . Verily, verily, I say unto thee, Except a man be born again, he cannot see the kingdom of God" (John 3:3)*. Now if Jesus had said, "Except a Gentile be born again, he cannot see the kingdom of God," Nicodemus would have agreed. In fact, Jews viewed Gentile conversion to Judaism as a sort of rebirth. But why would Nicodemus need to be born again? He was a Jew by birth and believed that the kingdom of God was his rightful due.

But Jesus declared that any man, Jew or Gentile, must be born from above. A person does not enter the kingdom because of his parentage or good works. A person enters the kindom through belief in the Son of God. *"For God so loved the world, that he gave his only begotten Son, that whosoever believeth in him should not perish, but have everlasting life" (John 3:16)*.

Nicodemus's immediate response to these words is not recorded. But it becomes clear that they penetrated his heart and that his doubts were replaced by a dynamic faith in Jesus as the Messiah. At the Feast of Tabernacles, when some members of the Sanhedrin rebuked their officers for refusing to arrest Jesus, Nicodemus defended Him on a point of Jewish law. *"Nicodemus saith unto them, (he that came to Jesus by night, being one of them,) Doth our law judge any man, before it hear him, and know what he doeth?" (John 7:50–51)*.

After the Lord's crucifixion, he publicly declared himself a disciple by providing one hundred pounds of myrrh and aloes to prepare His body for burial. The Spirit of God had visited Nicodemus and given him new birth and a new life. He resisted the pressure of hostile peers and stood strong with the few.

CHARACTER SKETCH OF NICODEMUS

WHY DID NICODEMUS COME TO JESUS AT NIGHT?

The Pharisee's decision to visit Jesus during the evening may have been motivated simply by caution and convenience. Nicodemus was an influential leader. People looked to him for advice and counsel in religious matters. He wanted to know what Jesus was teaching to compare it to the traditional teaching of the scribes. He felt that this could best be accomplished by means of a private interview, away from the atmosphere of hostile critics and zealous followers.

Furthermore, it was almost impossible to find time to meet with the Lord during the day. Because of His ministry of healing, Jesus was besieged by crowds. A quiet, uninterrupted discussion during the evening hours, possibly in the home of one of the disciples, would have been ideal for Nicodemus's purpose.

WHO DID NICODEMUS THINK JESUS WAS AT FIRST?

Nicodemus thought Jesus was a prophet like Moses, Joshua, Elijah, and Elisha. *". . . Rabbi, we know that thou art a teacher come from God: for no man can do these miracles that thou doest, except God be with him"* (John 3:2).

Nicodemus knew that miracles in his nation's history were relatively rare. Most had occurred during two periods—the first during Israel's deliverance from Egypt and their occupation of Canaan, the second during a time of great apostasy under the reign of Ahab. Throughout both eras, God used miracles to warn the wicked and to encourage the faithful.

Now Jesus performed signs and wonders of the same nature as these former men of God, and Nicodemus was perceptive enough to recognize this. It is significant that he was open to the truth and had not hardened his heart like some of his fellow Pharisees who had attributed Jesus' works to Beelzebub, the prince of the devils. (See Matthew 12:22–24.) To Nicodemus, Jesus was a man from God, but He was still only a man.

WHY DID NICODEMUS BECOME SO BOLD AFTER THE LORD'S DEATH?

It is interesting that the same event which caused the Lord's disciples to desert and deny Him, to become discouraged and to cower in fear behind closed doors, had just the opposite effect on Nicodemus. Why did he take no thought for his reputation, position, or wealth to assist in the burial of Jesus? The disciples viewed the crucifixion as a catastrophe, ending their cause and future hopes. Nicodemus was stirred to action by the same event.

Nicodemus had believed that Jesus was a prophet sent by God. Jesus had told him, *"And as Moses lifted up the serpent in the wilderness, even so must the Son of man be lifted up: That whosoever believeth in him should not perish, but have eternal life"* (John 3:14–15).

When Nicodemus saw Jesus lifted up on the cross, he remembered those words. This story which Nicodemus knew so well took on new meaning. Jesus was not just a prophet, He was the Suffering Servant predicted by Isaiah. He was more than a prophet, He was his Redeemer.

Nicodemus Ben Gorion *was counted one of the three richest men of Jerusalem. He was a member of the Sanhedrin which Herod brought under his control as soon as he became king.*

NICODEMUS
nik-ō-dē-məs

CHAPTER TWENTY-EIGHT

Kindness

. . . Is returning good for evil

"Therefore if thine enemy hunger, feed him; if he thirst, give him drink: for in so doing thou shalt heap coals of fire on his head. Be not overcome of evil, but overcome evil with good."

Romans 12:20–21

Living Lessons on Kindness . . .

FROM THE PAGES OF SCRIPTURE

The kindness of returning good for evil is totally opposite to our natural inclinations. Therefore, this type of kindness can only be carried out by an act of faith in God's Word. Unexpected rewards are waiting for the person who practices it.

Such was the case when a rival used every opportunity to belittle and ridicule one who was envied. The anguish and personal distress that this continual attack produced forced the victim to make an amazing vow that brought great benefit to many people, including the rival.

ILLUSTRATED IN THE WORLD OF NATURE

PELICAN *Pelecanus occidentalis*

Pelicans are among the largest birds in the world. Their body length, including the bill, may extend four to six feet. Their wing spread can be from five to ten feet, and an individual bird can weigh from six to twenty-five pounds. There are seven species of pelicans, the most widely known being the brown pelican of the Atlantic, Gulf, and Pacific coasts.

The only food that the brown pelican eats is fish. After World War I, Gulf fishermen complained that pelicans were eating too many fish and reducing the size of their catch. Studies have shown that the pelican eats fish that have little, if any, commerical value.

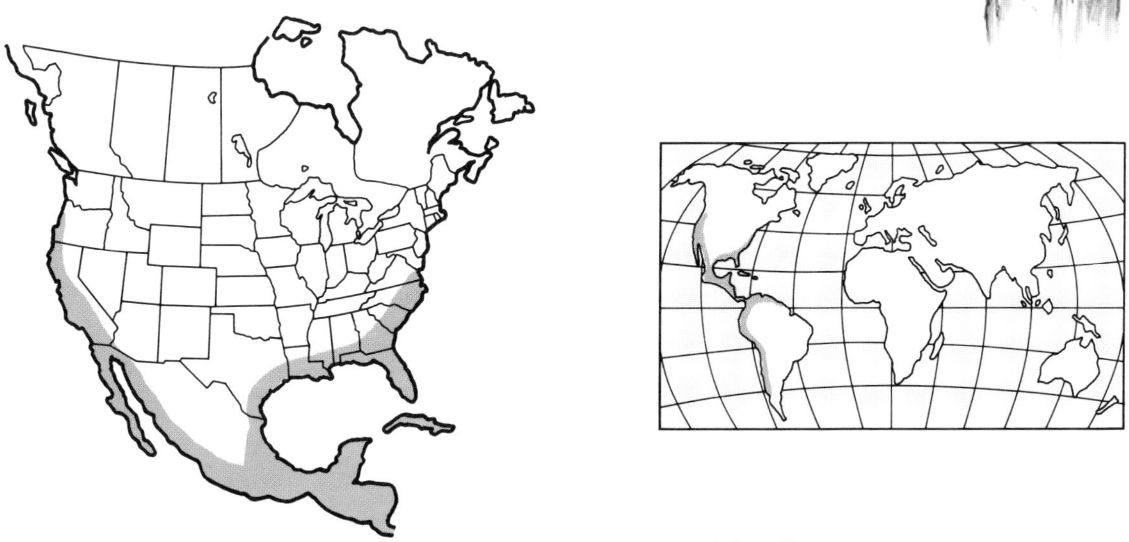

The range and habitat of the pelican

How is returning good for evil illustrated in the world of nature?

In a desolate marshy inlet, a three-day watch was coming to an end. Both feet of a huge waterfowl were cupped around two eggs which he had been keeping warm.

When his mate arrived, he stepped off the nest, stretched out his seven-foot wings, and climbed into the morning breeze. For three days he had not eaten; now he was able to take care of his hunger by using his God-given equipment to catch fish.

He flew to an altitude of seventy feet; there he spotted a fish just below the surface of the water. The giant bird wheeled in flight and began to dive. With wings and legs outstretched, he looked very awkward as he descended. The awkwardness was intensified as he twisted his body; yet he always kept his eyes fixed on the target.

Then, less than a foot above the water, he quickly folded back his wings, stretched his feet beneath his tail, thrust his neck forward, and parted the waters with a mighty splash.

Beneath the surface he opened his long bill, and his pouch quickly filled with two and a half gallons of water, plus his fish. The skin of his pouch was stretched so tightly that the blood vessels could be seen.

He bobbed to the surface and began to drain water from his pouch, being careful to contain the fish. Just then a screaming gull flew down and landed on the head of this huge bird. The gull looked small by comparison.

The crafty gull had been waiting for just this moment. It hopped back and forth to keep its balance and slowly worked its way onto the long bill while his host finished draining the salt water from his pouch.

Then, in one quick, bold move the thieving sea gull grabbed the fish out of the pouch, and with a quick toss of its head flipped it into the air and swallowed it. Then it turned, stepped in the face of its provider, and flew into the air.

With four quick wing beats the great bird lifted himself off of the water and followed the thief. As he reached the altitude of the gull, he again wheeled and dove. The gull screamed and darted aside, but the great bird's target was not the gull; he had spotted a school of fish.

His second dive produced more fish. Once again the sea gull picked off one for itself. The patient provider swallowed the rest and flew back to his nest.

By returning good for evil, the pelican was rewarded in at least two ways. First, he increased his fish-catching skills. Second, he was prepared for the gentle and generous care of his own young. When they hatched, they would be picking fish out of his pouch for three months!

THE CHARACTERISTICS OF

THE PELICAN IN SCRIPTURE

The pelican provides ample illustrations of Christ's relationship to the church and our work as a Christian.

Just as the male pelican selects the nesting site and then allows for a long courtship, so Christ is making preparations for the Church. *". . . I go to prepare a place for you" (John 14:2).*

The tender care the pelican gives its young is a picture not only of Christ's care of the Church, but of the nurture which parents must give to their children. (See Ephesians 6:4.)

Just as the pelican could not have successful hatches without regular fasting, so Christ emphasized the importance of fasting for the success of Christians. *". . . When ye fast . . . thy Father, which seeth in secret, shall reward thee openly" (Matthew 6:16, 18).*

The unusual abilities of the pelican to catch fish attracts birds that rob him. His response to them is an illustration of the patient kindness which Christians should have toward those who wrong them. *"Not rendering evil for evil . . . but contrariwise blessing . . ." (I Peter 3:9).*

The silent loneliness of the pelican in wilderness marshes was referred to by David in Psalm 102:6. *"I am like a pelican of the wilderness. . . ."*

The bowing of pelican mates to each other at their nesting site is a picture of the honor that should exist between husband and wife. (See Ephesians 5:22–25.)

CHARACTERISTICS AND PHYSICAL FEATURES OF THE PELICAN

The pelican is remarkably equipped to catch fish; however, this ability attracts other fish-eating fowl which become predators to the fish it catches. The patient demeanor of the pelican is a significant demonstration of kindness in returning good for evil.

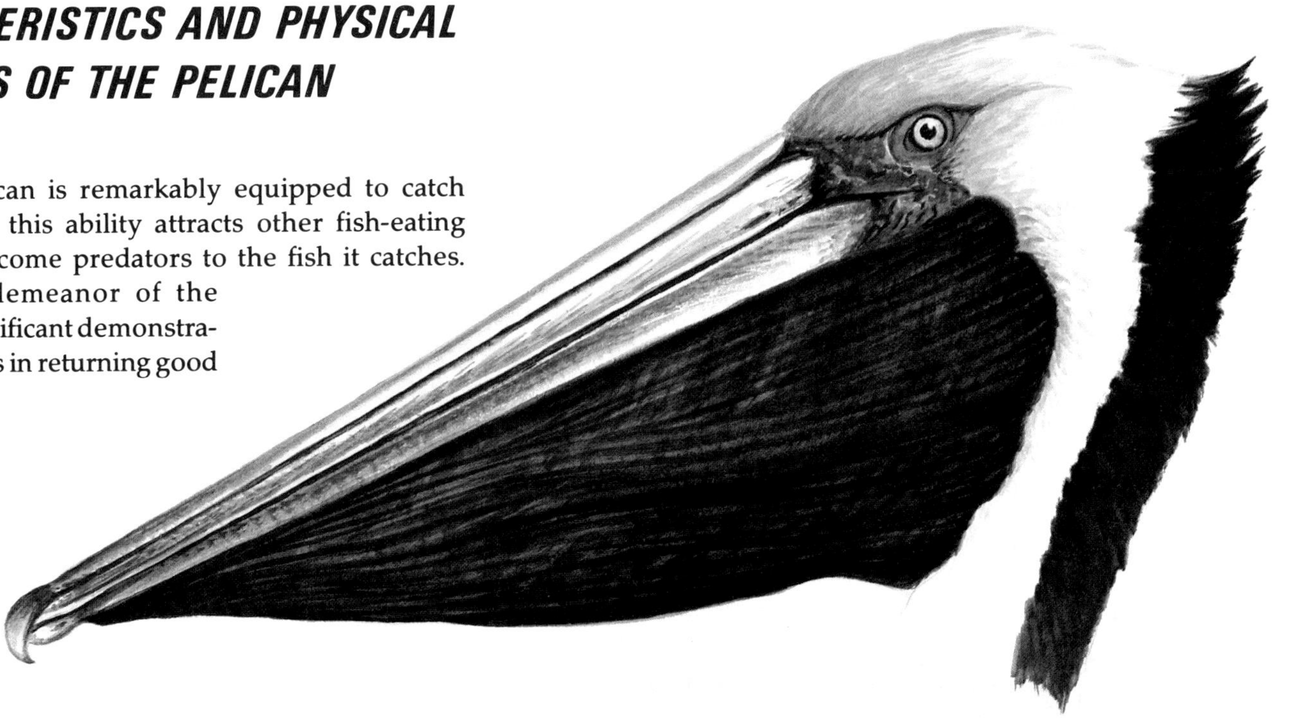

WHY DO ALL PELICANS FACE THE SAME DIRECTION FOR SEVERAL HOURS EACH DAY?

Most of the day a pelican faces any direction. However, from two to six in the afternoon, the hottest hours of the day, the pelican faces away from the sun. Since its pouch is not covered with feathers, it must be protected from the direct rays of the sun to prevent it from drying out and cracking. By facing away from the sun, the pelican can use its own shadow to shelter its sensitive pouch.

HOW DOES A NESTING PELICAN EXPRESS HONOR TO A MATE WHEN IT RETURNS TO THE NEST?

An unusual practice of bowing takes place between a pair of pelicans while they are mating and nesting. Both male and female pelicans bow to each other but not at the same time. The bird who is on the nest, whether it be male or female, is the first to bow. It stands up in the nest, arches the neck, spreads its wings, and greets the returning mate with a deep sweep of the head.

HOW DO PELICANS COMMUNICATE WITHOUT UTTERING A SOUND?

Adult pelicans are voiceless, communicating with each other by means of a highly developed body language. The height at which the head is held above the shoulders indicates a bird's alertness. A snap of the beak signals attack. Swaying of the head in a figure eight is part of courtship. A wing spreading routine must be performed by the male before he is allowed to enter the nesting site with building material.

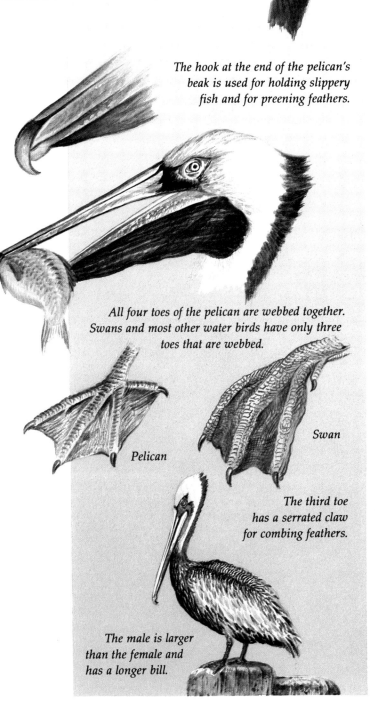

The hook at the end of the pelican's beak is used for holding slippery fish and for preening feathers.

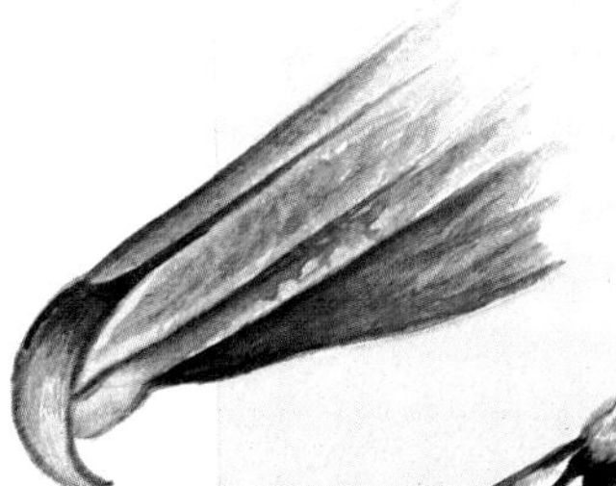

All four toes of the pelican are webbed together. Swans and most other water birds have only three toes that are webbed.

The third toe has a serrated claw for combing feathers.

The male is larger than the female and has a longer bill.

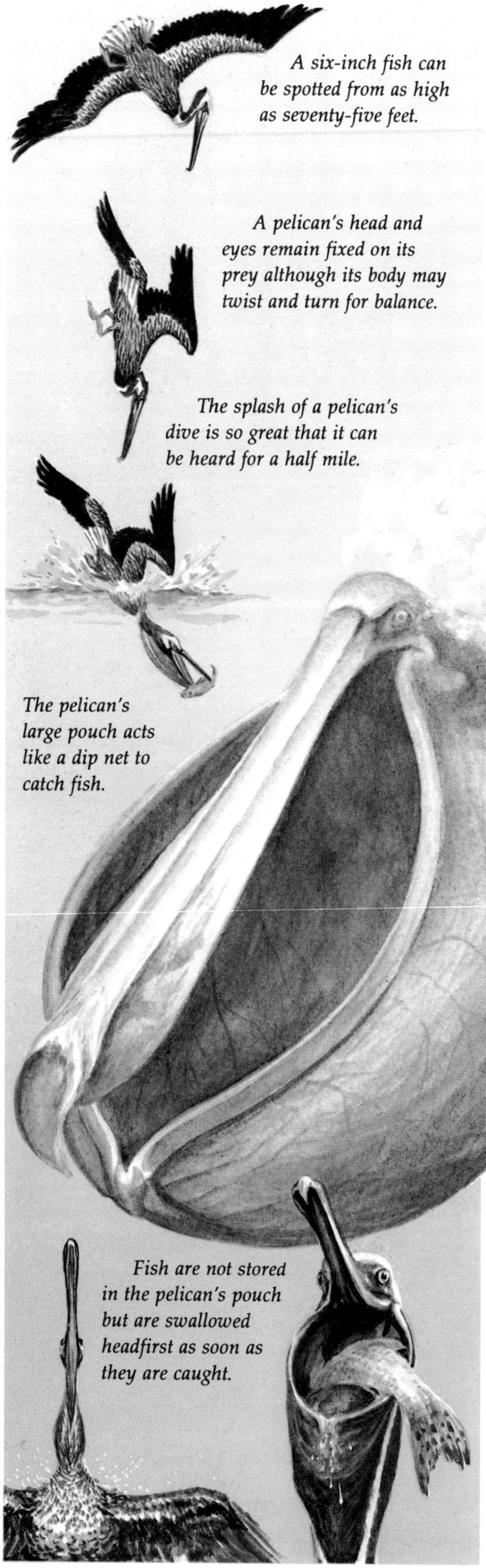

A six-inch fish can be spotted from as high as seventy-five feet.

A pelican's head and eyes remain fixed on its prey although its body may twist and turn for balance.

The splash of a pelican's dive is so great that it can be heard for a half mile.

The pelican's large pouch acts like a dip net to catch fish.

Fish are not stored in the pelican's pouch but are swallowed headfirst as soon as they are caught.

HOW DO FISH CAUSE A PELICAN TO MEASURE THE HEIGHT OF ITS DIVE?

Pelicans searching for food cruise at heights from thirty to seventy feet. The height of the pelican's dive is carefully calculated for a plunge to the exact depth at which its prey is swimming. Deep fish may require heights of up to one hundred feet.

IN WHAT WAY IS A PELICAN EQUIPPED WITH A "LIFE JACKET"?

Air sacs located under the pelican's skin work like a life jacket to keep the pelican afloat. These inflatable air sacs run from the lungs along the pelican's neck all the way to its head. The sacs also serve to cushion the pelican against the impact of a dive and cause the pelican to bob back to the surface like a cork.

WHY MUST A PAIR OF PELICANS CATCH A HALF TON OF FISH IN THREE MONTHS?

Young pelicans remain in the nest for about three months and depend on their parents for food until they learn how to fly. During these three months each young pelican eats approximately 150 pounds of fish.

With as many as three chicks in the nest, the adults must supply 450 pounds of fish to raise a family. Since the parents themselves may consume another 600 pounds of fish, the total catch for a family of five may be over 1000 pounds, or a half ton of fish.

HOW DO PELICANS KNOW WHEN TO FACE THE SHORE OR THE SEA WHEN DIVING?

Pelicans always dive with the wind. They do a somersault under the water and come up facing into the wind ready for takeoff. During the morning, when sea breezes blow inland, pelicans face the shore as they dive. In the evening when the breezes blow out to sea, pelicans dive facing away from the shore.

HOW MUCH OF THE SEA DOES A PELICAN CATCH WITH THE FISH?

Each time the pelican dives under water, its pouch takes in two and one-half gallons of water. This water must be drained before the fish can be swallowed.

HOW DID INDIANS USE PELICANS TO CATCH FISH?

The Seri Indians of the California Bay area used pelicans instead of fishing poles or nets to catch fish. A live pelican was tied securely to a stake and left on an open stretch of beach. Other pelicans would feed the captive by dropping fish to it. The Indians simply waited and took the fish.

CAN A PELICAN QUENCH ITS THIRST BY DRINKING SALT WATER?

Yes. The pelican is one of the few birds equipped to drink salt water from the ocean. To do this it must be able to rid its body of salt in concentrations higher than that of the salt water it drinks.

A special salt gland located near the eye of the pelican allows the body to rid itself of salt concentrations. After collecting and concentrating the salt, this gland expels it in the form of a thick liquid through a hole in the pelican's beak.

WHY DO PELICANS FOLLOW THE LEADER IN FLIGHT?

Pelicans rarely fly alone. Instead, they fly in either a single file or a V-shaped formation. Each bird follows the one in front of it. If the leader glides, all glide. If the leader flaps its wings, the other birds do likewise.

Flying in formation helps the pelicans conserve energy. Each bird is able to take advantage of a cushion of turbulent air that rises from the wake of the bird in front of it. Of the two flight patterns, the straight line is the most efficient because both wings are assisted. Only the inside wing is aided in the V formation.

HOW DO PELICANS INDICATE WIND DIRECTION BY THE HEIGHT OF THEIR FLIGHT?

Some pelicans fly low across the water almost skimming the tops of the waves. Others fly much higher. The difference is the direction of the wind. Pelicans flying into the wind always fly as close to the surface of the water as they can. Pelicans flying with the wind take advantage of it by flying high.

HOW DOES THE MALE PELICAN ILLUSTRATE THE WORK OF JESUS CHRIST AS THE BRIDEGROOM?

Just as Christ has gone to prepare a place for His Bride, so the male pelican chooses a nesting site before the mating begins. Only after a lengthy courtship does the male pelican allow the female to enter the nesting site. When this happens, a bond is formed that lasts throughout the nesting cycle.

WHY DOES THE COLOR OF THE PELICAN CHANGE DURING BREEDING SEASON?

The spectacular color changes of adult pelicans during breeding season help attract prospective mates. During courtship the head is bright yellow, the brown neck becomes white, the eyes turn yellow, the pouch darkens, and the bill shifts to varying shades of orange. The colors fade as the bird molts during nest building.

Pelican skull
Lacrymal gland
Salt gland
Eye
Harderian gland
A pelican shakes its head to flip salt off its beak.
From land a pelican becomes airborne with a single wing beat. From water it never takes more than four.
Pelicans flying in formation
Wings are folded high on the pelican's back to keep them from becoming waterlogged.
Spring plumage
Winter plumage
A pelican may live for more than thirty years.

WHY IS IT DANGEROUS FOR PELICANS TO LEAVE THEIR NEST?

The pelican's commitment to its own young will prompt it to take nesting material from nearby nests. A female trying to incubate chicks during this time may have the nest ripped apart and the young killed by trespassing males. This aggression ceases when the nests are completed and the birds settle down to incubate the eggs.

Males gather nesting materials.
A pelican stands on its eggs for thirty days.
Parents shelter the young with their wings.
Pelican chicks are born blind and without feathers. They may become sunburned in minutes if left unattended.
As droppings evaporate, the skin cools.
Chicks climb down their parent's throat to search for food.
A pelican vibrates its pouch to keep cool.

WHAT SACRIFICES DO PELICANS MAKE TO INCUBATE THEIR YOUNG?

Both male and female incubate the eggs. They switch every seventy-two hours and each bird fasts while it is in charge of the eggs. As hatching time approaches, parents switch more often until they are fasting only twenty-four hours at a time.

WHY DO CHICKS WEIGH TWENTY PER CENT MORE THAN THEIR PARENTS BEFORE THEY LEAVE THE NEST?

For the first week to ten days the young are fed hourly. Partially digested food is brought up for the young. By the tenth day the chicks are strong enough to take food directly from the parent's pouch. Within five to six weeks the chicks are very aggressive. They scream, squawk, and poke their bills down the throat of the adults, forcing them to throw up the entire contents of their stomachs. By the time the youngsters are ready for their flight at eleven to twelve weeks, they outweigh their parents by twenty per cent.

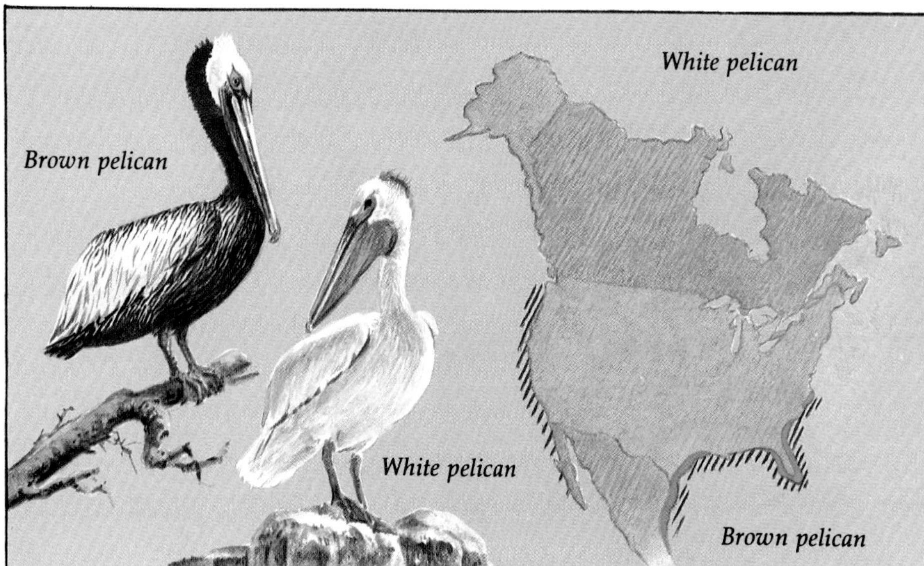

How do brown pelicans and white pelicans differ?

White pelicans are much larger than brown pelicans, having a wing span that occasionally exceeds ten feet. Whites do not dive for fish from the air. Instead, they band together and drive schools of fish into shallow water where they can be easily scooped up. White pelicans are at home in fresh water or in salt water.

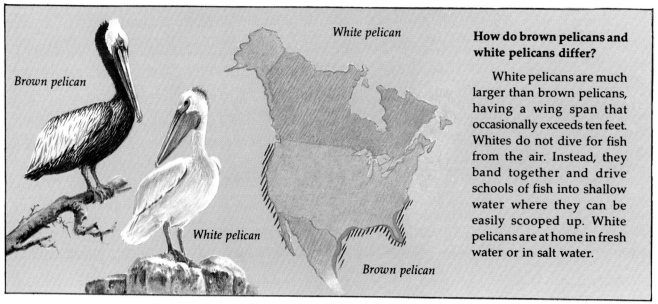

How is returning good for evil illustrated in Scripture?

The most painful enemies are usually those who were closest to us. Their unexpected attacks are often allowed by God to bring us to the place of crying out to Him. Who greatly benefited God's people by using a difficult family conflict as motivation to make a significant covenant with the Lord?

(Pause for a response—see page 17.)

The contrasting lives of two people are woven together into one of the most unique and significant accounts in Scripture. Both of them knew the Lord and wanted to please Him. Both of them had painful relationships within their own families. Each was being mocked and tormented day after day and year after year.

In each family God desired to do a special work through the children. But that would require both of these individuals to cry out to God and give to Him that which they cherished the most. At this point the responses and results in the lives of these two individuals became remarkably different.

One day the younger of the two traveled to the city of the older. Both of them met for the first time in the house of the Lord.

It was here that the younger set the example that the older should have followed. With deep agony of soul this young victim of continual reviling silently cried out to the Lord and then entered into a vow that was to have great significance in the days to come.

The sincerity of this act of worship was misunderstood by the older individual and further abuse came in the form of a false accusation. However, the younger gave a kind response and gained the assurance that God had heard that prayer. Several years later, the younger was able to return good for the older's insulting remark.

The younger brought a very special gift to the older. That gift became a continual encouragement to him, but also a constant reminder that he should follow the younger's example. He refused to do so.

As a result, the nation under his spiritual leadership suffered a disastrous military defeat, and the enemy captured the ark of God's glory. Through that battle the sons whom he should have consecrated to God were killed, and he fell to his death.

The example he had refused to follow was that of Hannah, a young wife who, after years of torment from a jealous and competing wife, cried out to the Lord for a son.

The son that God gave became her gift back to the Lord. Her son, Samuel, served Eli, the high priest who had falsely accused her of being drunk when she prayed in anguish for a son.

Samuel also became a great gift to the nation of Israel. He restored the spiritual strength of the people and led the armies to victory. He was his mother's means of returning good for evil, and God crowned his ministry by returning to the nation the treasured ark of His glory.

From I Samuel 1–6

***Hannah not only fulfilled her vow** of dedicating her son to God's service, but she also gave three bullocks, one ephah of flour, and a bottle of wine. (See I Samuel 1:24.)*

***As soon as Samuel was weaned,** Hannah "Lent him to the Lord . . . and the child did minister unto the Lord before Eli the priest" (I Samuel 1:28; 2:11).*

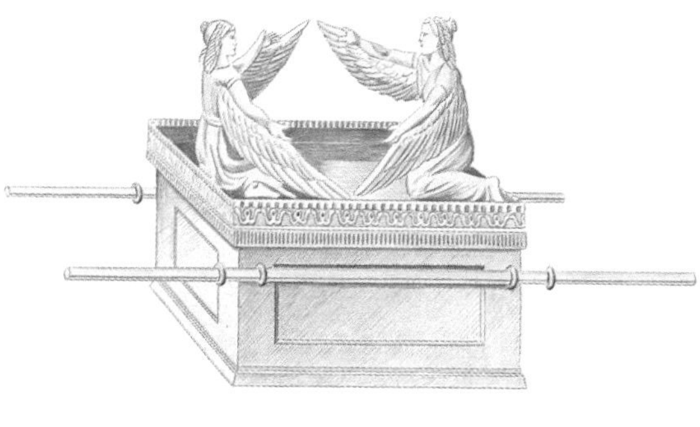

***The ark of the covenant,** carried into battle by Eli's wicked sons, was captured by the Philistines. The loss of the ark shocked and grieved the nation more than the loss of the battle.*

HANNAH, A GODLY WOMAN IN AN EVIL DAY

The nation of Israel was in spiritual decline. Eli, the high priest, was ineffectual in his old age. His sons Hophni and Phinehas had brought the priesthood into such disrepute that the people did not even want to bring their offerings to the tabernacle in Shiloh. (See I Samuel 2:12–17.) God needed someone totally committed to Him to guide the nation out of this dark era. He chose a God-fearing woman named Hannah to give birth to the man for this task.

Hannah was the wife of a Levite named Elkanah. Elkanah had married twice. Hannah was loved by her husband, but she was not content. She had no children, but her jealous rival, Peninnah, had both sons and daughters. Peninnah envied Elkanah's favor toward Hannah and resorted to petty mocking to hurt her. She ridiculed Hannah for her inability to bear Elkanah any sons.

A TEARFUL PETITION AND A PROMISE

One year, when Elkanah took his family to Shiloh to worship and to offer sacrifices, Hannah became very distressed. Peninnah had again reminded her of her barrenness. Hannah was too upset to participate in the sacrificial meal, normally an occasion of great joy and celebration. Even Elkanah was unable to console her. *"And she was in bitterness of soul, and prayed unto the Lord, and wept sore. And she vowed a vow, and said, O Lord of hosts, if thou wilt indeed look on the affliction of thine handmaid, and remember me, and . . . give unto thine handmaid a man child, then I will give him unto the Lord all the days of his life . . ." (I Samuel 1:10–11).*

This was a sacred moment for Hannah as well as for the nation of Israel. But the aged high priest was insensitive to the spiritual communion which was taking place. Eli insulted the already distraught Hannah by accusing her of being drunk. She defended herself respectfully, explaining that she was pouring out her soul to the Lord. After hearing her explanation, Eli encouraged her in her request, and there was an immediate lifting of her heavy burden. *". . . So the woman went her way, and did eat, and her countenance was no more sad" (I Samuel 1:18).*

A SON FOR HANNAH AND A PROPHET FOR THE NATION

The Lord remembered Hannah. She bore to Elkanah a son and named him *Samuel* which means "asked of God." Hannah delighted in her child. She loved him, played with him, prayed for him, and began to train him. But true to her promise, she brought Samuel to the tabernacle at Shiloh after he was weaned. Under the supervision of Eli, Samuel was reared in the presence of the Lord. (See I Samuel 1:19–28.)

Hannah's prayer, after bringing her beloved son to the tabernacle, is one of the most beautiful in the Bible. She was not possessive of Samuel or regretful that she had made such a serious vow. Instead, she was full of praise. *". . . My heart rejoiceth in the Lord, mine horn is exalted in the Lord: my mouth is enlarged over mine enemies; because I rejoice in thy salvation. There is none holy as the Lord: for there is none beside thee: neither is there any rock like our God" (I Samuel 2:1–2).*

The Lord blessed Hannah with three more sons and two daughters. (See I Samuel 2:21.) But her greatest joy must have been in seeing Samuel grow before the Lord and become a man used to reform the nation. *"And the child Samuel grew on, and was in favour both with the Lord, and also with men" (I Samuel 2:26).*

CHARACTER SKETCH OF HANNAH

WHAT WAS THE FULL SIGNIFICANCE OF HANNAH'S VOW?

Hannah desperately desired a son. She knew that the "Lord of hosts" Who controlled the heavenly powers could also take away her barrenness. She asked that He look on her, remember her, and give her a son. If God granted her request, Hannah promised two things in return. *". . . I will give him unto the Lord all the days of his life, and there shall no razor come upon his head" (I Samuel 1:11).*

As a Levite, Hannah's son would be required to serve periodically at the tabernacle. But Hannah was committing her son to serve for his entire life. The second part of her promise was the Nazarite vow. This commitment included totally abstaining from wine and all intoxicating drink, letting his hair grow, and avoiding defilement by corpses. (See Numbers 6.)

The positive nature of these prohibitions lies in the special devotion and consecration to the Lord which they signify. Abstinence from intoxicating drink maintained clearness of mind and avoided the danger of sensual indulgences which hinder communion with God. Long hair identified the Nazarite as one peculiarly set apart from the affairs of life and separated to the work of God.

Avoiding contact with the dead symbolized purity from moral defilement and complete dedication to the living God. Such devotion and commitment would be required from Hannah's son, who was to perform such an important function in the nation.

WHY WAS ELI SO QUICK TO ACCUSE HANNAH?

The high priest was probably trying to prevent improper or disrespectful activity in the vicinity of the tabernacle. When he observed Hannah moving her lips without speaking aloud, he assumed the worst and accused her of drunkenness. It is probable that Eli had seen drunken people in the tabernacle area, especially during the annual feasts.

What had been intended as a time of worship, celebration, and joy had degenerated into occasions for overindulgence and sensuality. Eli's own sons, Hophni and Phinehas, were guilty in this area. (See I Samuel 2:13–16, 22.) Eli acknowledged his mistake, however, when Hannah explained her situation. *"Then Eli answered and said, Go in peace: and the God of Israel grant thee thy petition that thou hast asked of him" (I Samuel 1:17).*

WHAT WAS HANNAH'S REAL NEED?

Hannah was anxious, grieved, and bitter in spirit. Elkanah believed that Hannah needed to know how much he loved and appreciated her. (See I Samuel 1:8.) Peninnah felt that her rival was loved too much and needed to be humbled. (See I Samuel 1:4–6.) Eli thought that she had had too much to drink. (See I Samuel 1:14.) Hannah believed that the solution was a son. (See I Samuel 1:11.)

What proved to be the most joyful and satisfying event in her life, however, was not receiving the gift of a son, but giving him back to the Lord. It was on the occasion of bringing Samuel back to the tabernacle that Hannah's heart was bursting with praise and adoration. She was as full of joy as she had been of grief. (See I Samuel 2:1–10.) Hannah's true need was for something of worth to give to God. Her real joy came not from receiving but from giving.

ELI

Hannah saw beyond the high priest's *lack of personal discipline and his false accusation to God's ability to hear and answer prayer. Because she refused to become bitter toward God, He rewarded her faith with six children.*

HANNAH
han-*nə*

INDEX

Listing of names, places, animals, and selected words

M

N

O

P

Q

R

INDEX OF SCRIPTURE REFERENCES

Genesis

Exodus